Current Law

STATUTES

1997

VOLUME THREE

AUSTRALIA
LBC Information Services
Sydney

CANADA AND USA
Carswell
Toronto

NEW ZEALAND
Brooker's
Auckland

SINGAPORE AND MALAYSIA
Thomson Information (S.E. Asia)
Singapore

Current Law

STATUTES

1997

VOLUME THREE

SWEET & MAXWELL EDITORIAL TEAM

SHIRLEY ARCHER SALLY DREVER
FIONA CLEAVELEY RACHAEL LOCKLEY
CHERRY DEXTER LISA MOORE
PENNY DICKMAN JANICE SAYER

W. GREEN EDITORIAL TEAM

STEPHEN HARVEY PETER NICHOLSON

LONDON

SWEET & MAXWELL
LEGAL INFORMATION RESOURCES

EDINBURGH

W. GREEN

1998

Published by
SWEET & MAXWELL LIMITED
of 100 Avenue Road, London
and Legal Information Resources
of The Hatchery, Hall Bank Lane, Mytholmroyd
and W. GREEN LIMITED
of Alva Street, Edinburgh,
Typeset by MFK Information Services Limited, Hitchin, Herts.
and printed in Great Britain
by The Bath Press,
Bath, Avon.

ISBN This Volume only : 0 421 62880 4
As a set   : 0 421 62890 1

CONTENTS

CHRONOLOGICAL TABLE

VOLUME THREE

Public General Acts

*c.*64.   Firearms (Amendment) (No. 2) Act 1997
    65.   Local Government (Contracts) Act 1997
    66.   Plant Varieties Act 1997
    67.   Consolidated Fund (No. 2) Act 1997
    68.   Special Immigration Appeals Commission Act 1997
    69.   Supreme Court (Offices) Act 1997

Private Acts

*c.*i.   Southampton International Boat Show Act 1997
   ii.   Imperial College Act 1997
   iii. King's College London Act 1997
   iv.   Scottish Agricultural College Order Confirmation Act 1997

Pensions Measure

    1.   Pensions Measure 1997

Commencement Orders

    1.   Commencement Diary 1997
    2.   Commencement Orders 1997 C.1–116 (C.7 and C.48 were never issued)

Numerical Table of Statutory Instruments

Listing of all Instruments released for 1997

Alphabetical Table of Statutes

Listing of all Public Acts passed, 1700–1997

Index 1997

CHRONOLOGICAL TABLE

VOLUMES 1–3

VOLUME 3

Private Acts

*c.*i.   Southampton International Boat Show Act 1997
ii.   Imperial College Act 1997
iii.   King's College London Act 1997
iv.   Scottish Agricultural College Order Confirmation Act 1997

Pensions Measure

1.   Pensions Measure 1997

Commencement Orders

1.   Commencement Diary 1997
2.   Commencement Orders 1997 C.1–116 (C.7 and C.48 were never issued)

Numerical Table of Statutory Instruments

Listing of all Instruments released for 1997

Alphabetical Table of Statutes

Listing of all Public Acts passed, 1700–1997

Index 1997

ALPHABETICAL INDEX OF SHORT TITLES

PUBLIC GENERAL ACTS 1997

(References are to chapter numbers of 1997)

ALPHABETICAL INDEX OF SHORT TITLES

PRIVATE ACTS 1997

(References are to chapter numbers of 1997)

FIREARMS AMENDMENT (No. 2) ACT 1997*

(1997 c. 64)

An Act to extend the class of prohibited weapons under the Firearms Act 1968 to include small-calibre pistols. [27th November 1997]

PARLIAMENTARY DEBATES

Hansard, H.C. Vol. 294, col. 851, Vol. 295, col. 1160, Vol. 296, cols. 22, 89, 349, Vol. 300, col. 30. H.L. Vol. 580, col. 1347, Vol. 581, cols. 9, 921, Vol. 582, cols. 568, 936, Vol. 583, col. 91.

INTRODUCTION AND GENERAL NOTE

The Firearms (Amendment) Act 1997 (c. 5) had been passed in the last days of the Conservative Government, and made major changes to the circumstances when handguns could be held. The then Labour Opposition stated that there should have been a free vote on whether handguns should be banned altogether. This belief was elevated into the status of a manifesto commitment. Early in the new Parliament, the new Home Secretary, Mr Jack Straw, introduced into the House of Commons the Bill which has become the Firearms (Amendent) (No. 2) Act. The House of Lords attempted to make considerable changes to the legislation, in particular allowing disabled shooters and shooters training for disciplines approved by the International Committee to possess weapons that would otherwise be outlawed. The Commons refused to accept these amendments and the Lords gave way.

In essence, the Act makes it an offence to possess any handgun, unless the holder has a special exemption to possess such a weapon.

COMMENCEMENT

The changes introduced by the Act are to come into effect on such day as the Secretary of State may by statutory instrument appoint (s.3(3)). Different days may be appointed for different purposes and different areas. (ibid.). Transitional provisions and savings may be included: s.3(4). Under s.2(6) the provisions of s.51 of the FASA 1997 shall have effect; under these provisions the Secretary of State has the power to make transitional and consequential provisions. This power must be exercised by statutory instrument subject to the negative resolution procedure and may modify anything in the FAA 1997 or in any other Act.

EXTENT

The Act does not apply to Northern Ireland: s.53(5).

ABBREVIATIONS

FA 1968	: Firearms Act 1968.
FAA 1988	: Firearms (Amendment) Act 1988.
FAA 1997	: Firearms (Amendment) Act 1997.
FAA (No. 2) 1997	: Firearms (Amendment) (No. 2) Act 1997.

Prohibition of small-calibre pistols

1. In paragraph (aba) of section 5(1) of the Firearms Act 1968 (which describes a category of prohibited weapons consisting of all firearms less than 30 cm in barrel length or 60 cm in overall length, other than specified kinds of firearm) the words "small-calibre pistol" shall cease to have effect.

DEFINITIONS

"firearm": FA 1968, s.57(1) applied to FAA 1997 by FAA 1997, s.50(2).

"small-calibre pistol": FA 1968, s.57(A) as added by FAA 1997, s.1(9). This definition is now repealed: FAA (No. 2) 1997, s.2(7) and Schedule.

GENERAL NOTE

This is the principal section in the Act. FA 1968, s.5(1)(aba) was added by FAA 1997, s.1. It had the effect of making handguns other than small calibre pistols (and certain other categories of weapon) prohibited weapons. (Under FA 1968, s.57(1A) [added by FAA 1997, s.1(9)] the term "small-calibre pistol" was defined, in essence, as a pistol chambered for .22 or smaller rim-fire cartridges, or certain air weapons designed to fire .22 or smaller diameter ammunition. The authority of the Secretary of State was required for their possession, purchase, acquisition or manufacture, sale or transfer. The amendment to FA 1968, s.5(1)(aba) removes

*Annotations by Peter J. Clarke, B.C.L., M.A., Barrister, Fellow and Tutor in Law, Jesus College, Oxford.

the phrase "small-calibre pistol"; this has the effect of making all handguns prohibited weapons, unless they are air weapons, a muzzle loading gun, or signalling apparatus. It was confirmed by Lord Williams of Mostyn, the Parliamentary Under-Secretary of State, Home Office, in the Third Reading in the House of Lords (*Hansard*, Vol. 582, col. 936) that self-loading air pistols are "rifled guns" within the meaning of the legislation, and are thus prohibited weapons, despite the understanding of both the Home Office and the Association of Chief Police Officers that the legislation had not intended to ban such pistols. (Lord Monson, *ibid.*) See, generally, the Note to FAA 1997, s.1. The special exemptions provided by FAA 1997, s.2 (slaughtering instruments), s.3 (firearms used for humane killing of animals), s.4 (shot pistols used for shooting vermin), s.5 (firearms used for starting races at athletic meetings), s.6 (trophies of war), s.7 (firearms of historic interest), and s.8 (weapons and ammunition used for treating animals) continue to have effect. Thus, whatever the calibre of the weapons covered by those sections, the sections still continue to operate.

Consequential amendments and repeals

2.—(1) The Firearms (Amendment) Act 1997 shall have effect subject to the following amendments.

(2) In section 15 (arrangements for the surrender of firearms prohibited by virtue of section 1 of that Act), after subsection (2) there shall be inserted—

"(3) This section applies in relation to small-calibre pistols with the substitution for the reference in subsection (1) above to section 1 above of a reference to section 1 of the Firearms (Amendment) (No. 2) Act 1997 (prohibition of small-calibre pistols)."

(3) In section 16 (payments in respect of prohibited weapons), after subsection (3) there shall be inserted—

"(4) This section applies in relation to small-calibre pistols surrendered at designated police stations in accordance with the arrangements made under section 15 above with the substitution—
    (a) for the reference in paragraph (a) of subsection (2) above to October 16, 1996 of a reference to May 14, 1997; and
    (b) for the reference in that subsection to section 1(2) above of a reference to section 1 of the Firearms (Amendment) (No. 2) Act 1997 (prohibition of small-calibre pistols)."

(4) In section 17 (payments in respect of ancillary equipment), after subsection (6) there shall be inserted—

"(7) This section applies in relation to equipment designed or adapted for use in connection with small-calibre pistols with the substitution—
    (a) for the reference in subsection (2)(a) above to firearms prohibited by virtue of section 1(2) above of a reference to small-calibre pistols; and
    (b) for the reference in subsection (3)(a) above to October 16, 1996 of a reference to May 14, 1997."

(5) In section 18 (Parliamentary control of compensation schemes), for subsection (3) there shall be substituted—

"(3) Subsections (1) and (2) above apply to an alteration to a compensation scheme as they apply to a compensation scheme."

(6) Section 51 (power to make transitional and consequential provisions, etc) shall apply in relation to the provisions of this Act as it applies to the provisions of that Act.

(7) The enactments mentioned in the Schedule to this Act are repealed to the extent specified in the third column.

DEFINITIONS
    "ancillary equipment": FAA 1997, s.17(2).
    "compensation scheme": FAA 1997, s.18(4).
    "firearm": FAA 1968, s.57(1) applied to FAA 1997 by FAA 1997, s.50(2).
    "small-calibre pistol": FAA 1968, s.57(A) as added by FAA 1997, s.1(9). This definition is now repealed: FAA (No. 2) 1997, s.2(7) and Schedule.

GENERAL NOTE
This section contains certain consequential amendments.

Subs. (2)

FAA 1997, s.15 authorised the Secretary of State to make arrangements for the surrender of weapons and ammunition the possession for which had become unlawful by virtue of FAA 1997, s.1 or s.9 [which dealt with expanding ammunition]. FAA (No. 2) Act 1997, s.2(1) gives the Secretary of State similar powers in respect of compensation for small-calibre pistols. The sub-section is a classic example of legislation by reference; introducing the Bill to the House of Lords, Lord Williams of Mostyn, Under Secretary of State at the Home Office, stated that the scheme would cover small-calibre pistols and "ancillary equipment": *Hansard*, H.L. Vol. 581, col. 11. The original FAA 1997, s.15 did not include payment of compensation for ammunition; this was added in the House of Lords at the Third Reading stage. There is no specific reference in the new subsection to ammunition; and the wording of the subsection seems to exclude it. More-over, the reference by Lord Williams of Mostyn to "ancillary equipment" does not seem appo-site to cover ammunition; ancillary equipment is specifically covered by subs. (4) below.

Subs. (3)

This applies the provisions of FAA 1997, s.16 (which relate to payments for the surrender of prohibited small firearms and ammunition) to small-calibre pistols. Only such pistols lawfully held on May 14, 1997 (the date of the announcement of the proposed legislation) qualify for compensation. The comments made in respect of ammunition in connection with subs. (2) above apply here with equal force.

Subs. (4)

The scheme established by FAA 1997, s.17 for payments of ancillary equipment is applied to ancillary equipment for small calibre-pistols. See FAA 1997, s.7 and the Note thereto.

Subs. (5)

FAA 1997, s.18 provided for the approval of the compensation scheme set up under that Act. Such schemes have to be laid before Parliament in draft, and the draft approved by a resolution of each House. The original Bill included a provision that an order making a compensation scheme for surrender of prohibited small firearms and ammunition should be subject to laying before Parliament after it had been made. This provision was removed by government con-cession in the Report Stage in the House of Lords (*Hansard*, H.L. Vol. 582, cols. 579 to 582.).

Subs. (6)

See General Note, and the Note to FAA 1997, s.51.

Subs. (7)

See Note to Schedule.

Citation, commencement and extent

3.—(1) This Act may be cited as the Firearms (Amendment) (No. 2) Act 1997.

(2) This Act shall be included in the Acts which may be cited as the Fire-arms Acts 1968 to 1997.

(3) This Act shall come into force on such day as the Secretary of State may by order made by statutory instrument appoint; and different days may be appointed for different purposes and different areas.

(4) An order under subsection (3) may contain such transitional provision and savings (whether or not involving the modification of any statutory pro-vision) as appear to the Secretary of State to be necessary or expedient in connection with any provisions brought into force.

(5) This Act does not extend to Northern Ireland.

       SCHEDULE

REPEALS

Chapter	Short Title	Extent of repeal
1968 c. 27.	Firearms Act 1968.	In section 5(1)(aba), the words "a small-calibre pistol". Section 32(2B). Section 57(1A).
1988 c. 45.	Firearms (Amendment) Act 1988.	Section 15A.
1997 c. 5.	Firearms (Amendment) Act 1997.	Section 1(9). Sections 11 to 14. Sections 19 to 31. Section 45(2). Section 46. Section 49(2). In section 50(1), the definition of "licence", "licensed pistol club" and "licensed premises". Schedule 1. In Schedule 2, paragraph 13.

The repealed sections all relate to the controls of small-calibre pistols and the position of licensed pistol clubs, both contained in FAA 1997 (though sometimes incorporated in earlier legislation), and matters consequential thereto.

INDEX

References are to sections

LOCAL GOVERNMENT (CONTRACTS) ACT 1997*

(1997 c. 65)

An Act to make provision about the powers of local authorities (including probation committees and the Receiver for the Metropolitan Police District) to enter into contracts; to enable expenditure of local authorities making administrative arrangements for magistrates' courts to be treated for some purposes as not being capital expenditure; and for connected purposes.   [27th November 1997]

Parliamentary Debates
    Hansard, H.C. Vol. 295, col. 1298; Vol. 296, col. 623, 624; Vol. 297, col. 825; Vol. 300, col. 810. H.L. Vol. 581, col. 629; Vol. 582, cols. 124, 616, 982, 1324.
    The Bill was considered by House of Commons Standing Committee B on July 1, 1997.

Introduction and General Note
    The purpose of this Act is simple to state. It is to facilitate the policy of encouraging the Private Finance Initiative (P.F.I.), partnerships, and other contractual relationships between local authorities and the private sector by removing concerns about legal powers which have grown up over recent years as a result of litigation. While the purpose is simple to state, the nature of the problem and the proposed solution is rather more complicated. In order to understand this problem and assess the utility of the Act, it is necessary to comment briefly on the policy impera-tive and the nature of the problem.

The general policy
    While moving away from compulsion in relation to tendering and the use of the private sector in the delivery of services, the Government nevertheless wishes to encourage public-private partnerships. It was stated that such partnerships offer the possibility for increased value for money by, *inter alia*, contracting facilities management to the private sector; resolving the ten-sion between short term financial constraints and long term cost effectiveness; preventing under-investment; and maximising the scope for outside revenues by the use of surplus capacity. Support for partnership as one approved form of service delivery, and for joint venture projects, was included in the manifesto of the Labour Party for the 1997 election. In addition, P.F.I. was

---

*   Annotations by Colin Crawford, Barrister, Northern Circuit, and Senior Lecturer, Faculty of Law, Univer-sity of Birmingham.

inherited from the previous Government, although in local government and the National Health Service it had not been progressing as fast as desired, partly because of legal uncertainty and partly because of the capital finance controls.

This general approach was seen in a 12 point business manifesto of the Labour Party, one point of which was to clarify the position and provide the full legal power for such partnerships. Soon after the election in May 1997, the Government established a review of the then current P.F.I. and partnership arrangements, under the chairmanship of Malcolm Bates. This review was completed in early June 1997. One recommendation was speedy action to reduce legal uncertainty and thus the Bill had its second reading in the House of Commons on June 23, 1997. A similar aim resulted in a separate Bill for the National Health Service.

The legal problem
The legal 'problem' operates at two levels. First, the perception resulting from recent judicial decisions. Secondly, the underlying legal framework.

The relationship between local government and financial institutions had been the subject of a number of well publicised cases, including *Hazell v. Hammersmith L.B.C.* [1992] 2 A.C. 1, *Credit Suisse v. Allerdale B.C.* [1997] Q.B. 302, and *Credit Suisse v. Waltham Forest B.C.* [1997] Q.B. 362. For a description of these cases see the *Encyclopedia*, para. 1–12. Whether or not these high profile cases did as a matter of strict law inhibit P.F.I. and other partnership contracts is not directly to the point. What is important is that it was generally considered that the legal uncertainty surrounding such issues inhibited the financial institutions from entering commercial relationships with local authorities because of the risk that the contract would be found subsequently to be unlawful and void, and they would be left to recover their investment through uncertain restitutionary remedies. It was therefore considered essential that reassurance be given, as evidenced by a report from the Financial Law Panel, established by institutions in the City to investigate the problem of legal uncertainty in local government contracts.

The real problem is the underlying legal framework. The *ultra vires* doctrine, originally imported from company law, where it was subsequently reformed, has been a general problem in local government law. Despite being enacted in statutory form in s.111 of the Local Government Act 1972 (c.70) (s.69 of the Local Government (Scotland) Act 1973) (c.73) it remained essentially a flexible and uncertain doctrine. Again perception is as important as the reality and cases since the 1980s had resulted in the doctrine being considered more restrictive than previously thought. This, together with the report from the Financial Law Panel, has given added momentum to the debate over possible reform of the doctrine, such as the introduction of a power of general competence.

The general effect of the Act
The Act is an ingenious short term solution to a specific problem. It provides a safe harbour for particular types of contracts by means of two stages. First, by establishing a strong presumption that where the contract has been self-certified by means of a specified process then it is lawful and, in order not simply to shift the problem of *vires*, by a presumption that the certificate is also lawful. The presumption may be rebutted but the Act provides that the contract may be challenged only on public law challenge, by an application for judicial review or by audit review. Thus, the contract cannot be challenged in private law. The second stage deals with the eventuality of the courts nevertheless finding the contract to be unlawful, despite the presumption and an explicitly stated discretion to allow an unlawful contract to continue. This eventuality is met by provision for special discharge terms, either agreed or imposed, which will operate to compensate the contractor or those providing the finance for the contractor, even where the main contract is deemed unlawful. The former Master of the Rolls Lord Donaldson considered that these discharge terms "survive everything, judicially engineered or not. They are the sheet anchor of the contractor's protection" [*Hansard*, H.L., Vol. 582, col. 629].

The Bill met with general political acceptance. Indeed the Conservatives have stated that they would probably have introduced similar provisions if re-elected. Like many Acts, the importance of the regulation making power must be noted. The main controls and powers established by the Act can all be changed by regulation by the Secretary of State, although the most important element of the contracts included within the provisions of the Act can be changed only by affirmative resolution of both Houses. The annotations provided here include reference to the substance of the first set of regulations issued.

The structure of the Act
Clarification of the basic power of a local authority to enter contracts for specified purposes is provided by s.1. This section is not intended to change the law, merely to make the power explicit. The section also makes clear that the authority may make direct arrangements with the financier of the project or contract. The presumption of legality of self-certified contracts is

established by s.2. Ss.3 and 4 define the contracts which can be certified, regulate the certification process, and establish a presumption of legality of these certificates. By giving this protection, it could be claimed that this is subverting the principle that the courts should be able to declare such contracts to be unlawful. However, the Act preserves, but modifies, the right to challenge the contract in court. The presumption established by s.2 may be rebutted but s.5 provides that the contract may be challenged only on public law challenge, by an application for judicial review or by audit review. That section also makes explicit the discretion of the court to allow an unlawful contract to continue so that public services are not disrupted or additional costs placed on the authority. The eventuality of the contract being found to be unlawful and not allowed to continue is dealt with by s.6 and s.7. The sections provide for the special discharge terms which will ensure that the contractor or financier is compensated. Section 8 defines audit review for the purposes of this Act and makes clear that, in England and Wales a prohibition notice will not affect the contract until after the possible appeals have been exhausted. Section 9 permits the contracting out period under the Deregulation and Contracting Out Act 1994 (c.40), normally limited to 10 years, to be extended to the period for which the contract is to run, subject to a maximum of 40 years, so that longer term investments can be made. Section 10 amends s.57 of the Justices of the Peace Act 1997 (c.25) to enable partnership contracts in respect of magistrates' courts to be more easily promoted. Sections 11 and 12 deal with the regulation making power and commencement provisions.

What the Act does not do
    The Act may best be termed 'sticking plaster' legislation in that it deals with an existing legal framework which is far from perfect and is causing problems. The Act does not deal with the cause of the problem or of itself provide a final cure, as seen in the disarmingly frank admission by the Minister that "None of us is certain that what we want from the Bill is what we will end up with" [*Hansard*, H.C. Vol. 297, col. 831]. It does not remove the uncertainty of the *ultra vires* doctrine as a whole. It patches up the legislative framework to allow a desired activity to continue. Any attempt to establish a power of general competence through this Act was rejected and the wider debate about powers of local authorities will be the subject of a consultation paper in 1998.
    While the Act creates a presumption of legality for the contract, the certification process and the special discharge terms, it does not, and arguably could not, remove the ability of the courts to find that these aspects are *ultra vires*. It would be possible for a court, on a similar basis to *Anisminic v. Foreign Compensation Commission* [1969] 2 A.C. 147, to find that a purported contract, certificate, or term was so erroneous as to void *ab initio* and thus not capable of being protected by the provisions of this Act. While this may be possible in regard to sympathetic facts, judicial restraint is likely in most instances to follow the statutory intention. While this extreme outcome is unlikely, provision is made in any event by s.7(3) for this situation. That subsection makes clear that the default provision for discharge terms in s.7 will apply, even where a court declares that the discharge terms which are incorporated into an unlawful contract, or are themselves unlawful, shall have no legal effect. It is no criticism of the drafting of the Act, but merely a reflection of the uncertainties of judicial review that it is impossible to legislate for more certainty in the response of the courts. This is clearly seen from the comments of Lord Donaldson, a former Master of the Rolls, who in discussing whether agreed discharge terms could be found to be *ultra vires* stated:
    "I just do not know whether a court could set aside discharge terms. I say 'I do not know' because I venture to think that no one knows. I had considerable experience as Master of the Rolls in dealing with judicial review cases and at no time regarded myself in that field as bound by precedent. I and my colleagues looked at the situation as it was developing in a public law context and decided on the right course to take."
    [*Hansard*, H.L., Vol. 582, col. 629]
    The Act, while giving the Secretary of State wide regulation making power, does not give to the Secretary of State the power to approve each contract as has been done in the equivalent legislation for the Health Service, the National Health Service (Private Finance) Act 1997 (c.56). This would have been simply unworkable given the number of contracts involved.

Position of officers
    One matter which caused concern was the position of officers who signed certificates which were later found to be *ultra vires*. The general perception of the case of *Burgoine v. Waltham Forest L.B.C.* (1997) 95 L.G.R. 520 in the local government world was that officers had been held personally liable when the council had acted *ultra vires*. This perception resulted in an amendment being proposed which would have made it clear that officers could not be sued when they sign certificates because they did so under a duty to the authority. In response to this the Minister stated:

". . . some authorities have expressed concern that officers would be reluctant to sign certificates if they felt that they might owe a duty in negligence to a contractor should it turn out that there were no powers to enter the contract.

The generally held position is that an officer may be liable in damages to a third party where the officer is not only responsible for an ultra vires act, but has acted in bad faith or with knowledge of the ultra vires nature of the action. Since the purpose of certification is to ensure that the authority carries out a degree of due diligence concerning its powers, that seems unlikely to arise. There is no suggestion from case law that officers acting properly and in the ordinary course of their duties need have any concerns about potential liability to contractors if they certify a contract."

[*Standing Committee B*, July 1, 1997]

When the matter was pursued at later stage, a clear statement of intent resulted, the Minister stating:

"Local council officers who carry out their normal duties in good faith are not liable to third parties for the acts of a local authority, even where those acts turn out to be ultra vires. The Bill does nothing to add further burdens. Officers will be no more liable in signing a certificate than in putting their name to the contract to which it relates. I am sure that they will exercise the same care in signing certificates as they do at present in binding the authority under any contract or other transaction."

[*Hansard*, H.C., Vol. 297, col. 829]

and in relation to the *Burgoine* case it was correctly pointed out that

"The problems in that case were of a very different nature and flowed from the authority's lack of capacity to set up a particular company and appoint its officers as company directors. It was not concerned with the day-to-day activities of an officer, of which certification would naturally form a part. The officers in that case were acting not as local authority officers but as company directors, and that difference created the problem."

[*Hansard*, H.C., Vol. 297, col. 829]

In the light of this response, the member who had sought the amendment, Mr Paul Burstow, noted that "in the unlikely event that the courts look into this matter, the fact that it is set out in *Hansard* will undoubtedly be of great benefit to judges in deciding what we legislators were attempting to achieve through the Bill".

While this does not solve the problem in *Burgoine*, of indemnities for officers who are required to be company directors by their authority, it is clear that the certification process will not lead to liability provided that officers have taken proper professional care, do not act negligently, and do not act in bad faith. In reality this probably means that counsel's opinion will be taken on most matters.

Accountability

There is a fundamental tension underlying this Act. The doctrine of *ultra vires* is justified as ensuring that public authorities act within their powers and that public money is spent on law activities. Yet it is the operation of that doctrine which caused the practical problems addressed by his Act. The Act tries to make clear that certain contracts will be *prima facie* lawful but, as explained above, that will not mean it is impossible for the contract to be struck down. The solution in this Act is to restrict the routes for challenging the contract, to limit the power of the auditor, and to ensure that even if it is unlawful the contract will in effect be fulfilled in relation to the sums to be paid to the contractor. While this maintains the constitutional right to have access to the courts, albeit restricted to certain procedures only, it does not ensure that unfair burdens are not placed on the taxpayer. It does, however, provide various procedural safeguards to minimise the possibility.

One proposed solution was to have the auditor involved at an earlier stage, and to require the signature of the auditor to the certificate, thus not making the process one of self-certification. This was rejected because the Audit Commission considered that

"auditors should remain independent and not get involved in decision making or in a management capacity in an authority. Auditors should not act in a way that might fetter their discretion in the exercise of their powers. The auditor is not a financial accounting or legal adviser to the authority and no views are to be expressed in that capacity."

[*Standing Committee B*, July 1, 1997]

COMMENCEMENT

Sections 1 and 10 to 12 came into force on the passing of the Act on November 27, 1997.

The regulation making power of the Secretary of State contained in subs. (2)(e) and (f) and (3) of s.3 came into force for England and Wales on December 1, 1997, and for Scotland on December 2, 1997. The remaining sections of the Act, namely ss.2, 4 to 9, and the rest of s.3, came into force for England and Wales on December 30, 1997, and for Scotland on January 1, 1998. (See the Local Government (Contracts) Act 1997 (Commencement No. 1) Order 1997 (S.I. 1997 No. 2843) for England and Wales and the Local Government (Contracts) Act 1997 (Commencement No. 2) Order 1997 (S.I. 1997 No. 2878) for Scotland.

(See also the annotations to s.12.)

ABBREVIATIONS

"*Encyclopedia*": *Encyclopedia of Local Government Law*, (Sweet & Maxwell).

"P.F.I.": Private Finance Initiative.

"the 1972 Act": the Local Government Act 1972.

"the 1973 Act": the Local Government (Scotland) Act 1973.

"the 1982 Act": the Local Government Finance Act 1982.

"the 1989 Act": the Local Government and Housing Act 1989.

"the 1994 Act": the Deregulation and Contracting Out Act 1994.

Contracts for provision of assets or services

Functions to include power to enter into contracts

1.—(1) Every statutory provision conferring or imposing a function on a local authority confers power on the local authority to enter into a contract with another person for the provision or making available of assets or services, or both, (whether or not together with goods) for the purposes of, or in connection with, the discharge of the function by the local authority.

(2) Where—

(a) a local authority enters into a contract such as is mentioned in subsection (1) ("the provision contract") under any statutory provision, and

(b) in connection with the provision contract, a person ("the financier") makes a loan to, or provides any other form of finance for, a party to the provision contract other than the local authority,

the statutory provision also confers power on the local authority to enter into a contract with the financier, or any insurer of or trustee for the financier, in connection with the provision contract.

(3) The following are local authorities for the purposes of this Act—

(a) any authority with respect to the finances of which Part IV of the Local Government and Housing Act 1989 has effect at the time in question,

(b) any probation committee,

(c) the Receiver for the Metropolitan Police District, and

(d) any local authority or joint board as defined in section 235(1) of the Local Government (Scotland) Act 1973.

(4) In this Act "assets" means assets of any description (whether tangible or intangible), including (in particular) land, buildings, roads, works, plant, machinery, vehicles, vessels, apparatus, equipment and computer software.

(5) Regulations may be made amending subsection (4).

DEFINITIONS

"assets": subs. (4).

"financier": subs. (2)(b).

"local authority": subs. (3).

"provision contract": subss. (1) and (2).

GENERAL NOTE

The intention behind this section is to clarify, but not extend, the law by confirming the power of specified local authorities to enter into a wide range of contracts for the provision of assets or services, wherever the discharge of its functions involves such assets or services. Although this is designed to facilitate P.F.I. initiatives, the formulation of this power is not restricted to these. Instead, a wider power is provided in relation to any contract for assets and services, and a very wide definition is given to the term "assets". The section also makes clear that protection can be given to those providing finance to the contractor, by allowing the local authority to enter a separate contract with the financier, or the insurer to or trustee for the financier of the contract. This basic intention met with general acceptance in Parliament, but some amendments to the general approach were based on two criticisms.

First, reflecting the fact, as discussed in the Introduction and General Note, that the Act is a 'sticking plaster' approach to the problems of *vires*, amendments were proposed which would have widened this power to all activities which could be undertaken by authorities, not simply for "the purposes of, or in connection with, the discharge of functions" conferred by statute. Thus, for example, one amendment attempted to widen this to all functions whether or not conferred by statute, and to all reasonable purposes. This was rejected on the basis that it would involve a much wider and more contentious debate over whether there were non-statutory functions.

Another proposed amendment sought to import the wording drawn from s.111 of the 1972 Act (s.69 of the 1973 Act) and expand the meaning of "functions" in this section to include activities which are conducive or incidental to the functions as defined in s.111 (s.69). Such an approach was rejected by the Minister on the basis that

> "The amendment would enable authorities to enter into contracts for assets or services when relying on subsidiary powers under section 111, instead of primary powers. . . . The amendment would therefore seem to widen the effect of the Bill, which is not our intention. The Bill does not add to local authorities' powers."
> [*Hansard*, H.C. Vol. 297, col. 827]

To translate that into more specific legal terms, this means that such a contract cannot be an 'incidental to an incidental', see *R. v. Richmond Upon Thames London Borough Council, ex p. McCarthy & Stone (Developments) Ltd* [1990] 2 W.L.R. 1294.

Secondly, there was concern expressed, by the Local Government Association and the Association of Council Secretaries and Solicitors, that the effect of subs. (1) was actually to narrow down the discretion which already existed under s.111 of the 1972 Act (s.69 of the 1973 Act) which is expressed more widely and is taken as general authority to enter all contracts. An assurance that this was not the case was sought which received the response by the Minister that

> "That section will still be available and will still have effect. However, local authorities will not need to rely on it for the purpose of entering into contracts for the provision of assets and services. The section will remain, but we need the Bill to ensure that we meet the overall objectives that I have already outlined."
> [*Standing Committee B*, July 1, 1997]

Similarly, when asked whether any contracts that are reliant on s.137 could still be entered into an assurance was given.

However, the general lack of clarity in this area of law is seen in the fact that, in regard to another amendment, the Minister stated that

> "There were doubts in some quarters whether the main statutory function, or section 111, empowered an authority to enter into contracts in all cases. The Bill removes that uncertainty. It does so by confirming, in clause 1, that the statutory provisions that confer functions also confers power to enter contracts for assets or services in connection with the discharge of those functions. The Bill makes this implicit power explicit."
> [*Hansard*, H.C. Vol. 297, col. 827]

In this regard it is interesting to note that the regulations made under the Act have accepted that an authority may nevertheless continue to try to rely on s.111 (s.69) as the power to enter the contract. Under s.3(2)(d), the authority is required, in relation to a certified contract, to specify in the certificate the legal power under which it enters the contract. Where it specifies s.111 of the 1972 Act (or s.69 of the 1973 Act) as the statutory provision, or one of the Act provisions, for the power to enter the contract, then it is by regulation additionally required to "specify in the certificate each statutory provision conferring a relevant function, or, where there are two or more relevant functions, the statutory provisions conferring the main relevant functions" (Reg. 6 of the Local Authorities (Contracts) Regulations 1997 (S.I. 1997 No. 2862), and Reg. 5 of the Local Authorities (Contracts) (Scotland) Regulations 1997 (S.I. 1997 No. 2879)). The regulations also specify that for the purpose of that regulation "a function is a relevant function if the contract is calculated to facilitate, or is conducive or incidental to, the discharge of the function".

Subs. (1)

This subsection is not intended to change the law but simply to confirm the power of those local authorities specified by subs. (3) to enter into contracts, under which assets or services, or both, are made available, but only in relation to the discharge of the functions of the authority. Thus, it is not limited to P.F.I. or other partnership contracts but includes all procurement arrangements including leases and service agreements.

On the meaning of "functions", as it has been interpreted in relation to s.111 of the 1972 Act, see the *Encyclopedia of Local Government Law* para. 2–250. In relation to this Act, it was stated by the Minister that "the word 'functions' in the Bill covers both duties and discretions" [*Standing Committee B*, July 1, 1997].

Subs. (2)

Once a contract within the meaning of subs. (1) has been entered into, the authority may also enter a separate contract, associated with the main contract, with the financier of the contractor, or the financier's insurer, or a trustee for the financier. The purpose of this is, where a third party finances the contractor to allow that party to step into the shoes of the contractor in the event of the original contractor producing an unacceptably poor performance, becoming insolvent, or otherwise being unable to honour the contract.

In subs. (2)(b), the original drafting in the Bill defined "the financier" as the person providing the assistance to the person with whom the authority entered the contract under subs. (1). This was subsequently amended, in Committee in the House of Commons, to "a party to the provision contract other than the local authority" because

> "we want to make it clear that an authority's ability to enter into a contract with a financier in connection with a provision contract . . . includes a power to contract with a financier of a contractor who replaces the original contractor under the provision contract. . . . For the same reason, we also want to make it clear that a contract can have the protection of certification under the Bill if it is a contract with a person providing finance for any provider who takes over as a contractor under a certifiable provision contract."
>
> [*Standing Committee B*, July 1, 1997]

In addition, the range of persons with whom the authority may enter the associated contract was amended during the legislative process. As originally drafted, the Bill limited this to "the financier", but further consultation on the Bill resulted in the Government being informed that in such contracts parties other than the financier may be given step-in rights by the local authority. These could be insurers who by stepping-in can forestall a claim by the financier, or a trustee appointed by a group of loan stockholders or other persons providing finance, where the trustee is given the step-in rights rather than to the financiers directly.

One important question is whether these contracts would constitute guarantees. If they were, the concession relating to public/private partnerships under the capital finance regulations would not operate. The Minister stated that "I doubt whether contracts for step-in rights would constitute such a guarantee" [*Standing Committee B*, July 1, 1997]. Certainly, if this is not correct, it would undermine the intention of the Act and the encouragement of P.F.I. projects.

Subs. (3)

This subsection ensures that the major local authorities are covered by the provisions of this Act. By defining these by reference to other legislation, this ensures that the definition changes automatically in the event of reorganisation or alteration of type of authorities. For English and Welsh authorities the close relationship of this Act with the capital control regime is seen from the authorities being defined by Part IV of the 1989 Act. At the time this Act was passed, the authorities covered in England and Wales were those specified in s.39(1) of the 1989 Act (c.42), as amended, namely a county or county borough council; a district council; a London borough council; the Common Council of the City of London; the Council of the Isles of Scilly; a waste disposal authority; a joint authority for fire services, civil defence and transport; a joint planning board constituted for an area in Wales outside a National Park; the Broads Authority; a National Park authority; a fire authority constituted by a combination scheme; a police authority; the Service Authority for the National Crime Squad, when appointed; and any other body prescribed by regulations under s.39(3), on which see the *Encyclopedia* para. 3–999/140. The authorities included for Scotland are those specified by s.235 of the 1973 Act, as amended, namely any council constituted under s.2 of the Local Government etc (Scotland) Act 1994 (c.39), which is the unitary authority for a local government area.

Subs. (4)

The term "assets" is defined very widely by this subsection. Indeed, the Government accepted that the intention was intended to be as inclusive as possible. In relation to a proposed amendment to delete subs. (5), which authorises regulations to be made altering the definition of "asset", the Minister stated that, while it might be true that such flexibility may never be needed, it was nevertheless desirable to retain the flexibility to amend the definition to change or extend the scope of protection, and to respond to new products. The example of computer software was cited as an asset, expressly included in definition, over which there may have been a debate in the past. Without making this explicit, the general tenor of the Government's statement was that the definition would only be expanded not restricted. [*Standing Committee B*, July 1, 1997]

Subs. (5)

Regulations made under this subsection are subject to the negative resolution procedure, see s.11.

Certified contracts

Certified contracts to be intra vires

2.—(1) Where a local authority has entered into a contract, the contract shall, if it is a certified contract, have effect (and be deemed always to have had effect) as if the local authority had had power to enter into it (and had exercised that power properly in entering into it).

(2) For the purposes of this Act a contract entered into by a local authority is a certified contract if (and, subject to subsections (3) and (4), only if) the certification requirements have been satisfied by the local authority with respect to the contract and they were so satisfied before the end of the certification period.

(3) A contract entered into by a local authority shall be treated as a certified contract during the certification period if the contract provides that the certification requirements are intended to be satisfied by the local authority with respect to the contract before the end of that period.

(4) Where a local authority has entered into a contract which is a certified contract ("the existing contract") and the existing contract is replaced by a contract entered into by it with a person or persons not identical with the person or persons with whom it entered into the existing contract, the replacement contract is also a certified contract if—

    (a) the period for which it operates or is intended to operate ends at the same time as the period for which the existing contract was to operate, and

    (b) apart from that, its provisions are the same as those of the existing contract.

(5) In this Act "the certification period", in relation to a contract entered into by a local authority, means the period of six weeks beginning with the day on which the local authority entered into the contract.

(6) Subsection (1) is subject to section 5 (special provisions about judicial reviews and audit reviews).

(7) The application of subsection (1) in relation to a contract entered into by a local authority does not affect any claim for damages made by a person who is not (and has never been) a party to the contract in respect of a breach by the local authority of any duty to do, or not to do, something before entering into the contract (including, in particular, any such duty imposed by a statutory provision for giving effect to any Community obligation relating to public procurement or by section 17(1) of the Local Government Act 1988).

DEFINITIONS

    "certified contract": subs. (2).
    "certification period": subs. (5) and s.12(3) of this Act.
    "certification requirements": s.3(1) of this Act.
    "existing contract": subs. (4).
    "local authority": s.1(3) of this Act.

GENERAL NOTE

    This section provides the first stage in providing the 'safe harbour' for contracts. It does this by introducing a presumption that a certified contract is legal for private law purposes. Even if the authority had no power at all to enter such a contract, or abused a power it did have, the contract is presumed to be legal until it is successfully challenged by means of a public law review under s.5. The second stage in providing the 'safe harbour' is provided by s.6 and s.7 in relation to the discharge terms which will apply in the event of a court in a public law challenge finding that a certified contract unlawful and that it should not continue. This presumption applies not to all contracts but only to a certified contract. A contract is a certified contract if there has been compliance with the provisions of s.3 and s.4. Thus, by s.4(3), the contract must be one operating for at least five years for the provision or making available of services, whether or not with assets, in connection with the discharge of the functions of the authority. It is also deemed to be certified during the period for such compliance, the "certification period", if the contract states that it is intended to be a certified contract. Where a certified contract is replaced by a 'step-in' contract then the protection of the certification applies also to the replacement contract. The presumption of legality in private law does not affect the right to damages by a party to the contract in respect of any breach of duty at the stage before entering the contract, such as a breach of competition and procurement requirements.

Subs. (1)

This subsection establishes that where a contract under s.1(1) is a certified contract, as defined by subss. (2), (3) and (4), it is assumed that the contract is *intra vires*. This applies to both the narrow *vires* to enter such a contract at all, and the wider issue of abusing the *prima facie* power to enter a contract to such an extent that it is deemed to be *ultra vires*. Under subs. (6), this presumption may be displaced by a public law challenge. By subs. (7), the presumption does not apply to the breach of any duty applicable to stages before entering a contract, for which damages will remain available.

Subs. (2)

This provides the first situation under which a contract will constitute a certified contract. It will be a certified contract if the certification requirements, under s.3, have been complied with before the end of the certification period, as defined by subs. (5) and s.12(3). This means that the local authority must have issued a certificate, dealing with the matters specified in s.3(2), obtained the consent to issue the certificate from each person with whom the authority is entering the contract, and secured that the certificate is signed by any person required to do so by regulation. While this can be done before or after the signing of the contract, it must be done before the expiry of a period of six weeks from the date of the authority entering the contract. Under s.12(3), for contracts entered into between June 12, 1997 (the date of the introduction of the Bill) and November 27, 1997 (the date of the passing of the Act), the certification period of six weeks runs from the latter date. Once issued, by s.4(1) there is a presumption that the certificate is lawful, and it is not invalidated by its contents being inaccurate or untrue or the procedural steps have not been carried out.

Subs. (3)

This provides the second situation under which a contract will constitute a certified contract. It will be treated as a certified contract from the date of entering the contract until the certification requirements are met, subject to a maximum of six weeks, provided that the contract states that it is intended to be a certified contract. Presumably, if a contract is not so certified within that period it loses the protection conferred by subs. (1).

Subs. (4)

This provides the third situation under which a contract will constitute a certified contract. It will be a certified contract if it is a replacement contract in a 'step-in' situation where another party steps into the shoes of the original contractor in the event of the original contractor producing an unacceptably poor performance, becoming insolvent, or otherwise unable to honour the contract. However, the replacement contract must differ only in terms of the party to the contract and the commencement date. The finishing date of the replacement contract, and all other provisions, must be the same as the original contract.

Subs. (5)

The certification period within which the certification requirements under s.3 must be complied with is six weeks from the date of entering the contract. Under s.12(3), for contracts entered into between June 12, 1997 (the date of the introduction of the Bill) and November 27, 1997 (the date of the passing of the Act), the certification period of six weeks runs from the latter date, not the date of entering the contract.

Subs. (6)

This preserves the constitutionally important right of the courts to review the legality of the contract in public law proceedings. While subs. (1) raises the presumption that a certified contract is lawful, this subsection makes clear that the presumption is subject to review under s.5, which makes clear that a certified contract may nevertheless be questioned in an application for judicial review or in audit proceedings, as defined by s.8. In such public law review under s.5, the court is given express discretion to decide that an unlawful contract may nevertheless continue. Even if the court decides that it may not continue, the contractor will be entitled to damages under the discharge terms as specified in s.6 and s.7.

Subs. (7)

This subsection was introduced at the Committee stage for the purposes of clarification. While the original drafting would not have removed such rights, this makes clear that the presumption of legality raised by subs. (1) does not take away the right of any party to the contract to damages in relation to a breach by the authority of any duty placed upon it in matters before entering the contract. This, damages for breach of competition requirements, or of procurement regulations will remain.

The certification requirements

3.—(1) In this Act "the certification requirements", in relation to a contract entered into by a local authority, means the requirements specified in subsections (2) to (4).

(2) The requirement specified in this subsection is that the local authority must have issued a certificate (whether before or after the contract is entered into)—

(a) including details of the period for which the contract operates or is to operate,

(b) describing the purpose of the contract,

(c) containing a statement that the contract is or is to be a contract falling within section 4(3) or (4),

(d) stating that the local authority had or has power to enter into the contract and specifying the statutory provision, or each of the statutory provisions, conferring the power,

(e) stating that a copy of the certificate has been or is to be given to each person to whom a copy is required to be given by regulations,

(f) dealing in a manner prescribed by regulations with any matters required by regulations to be dealt with in certificates under this section, and

(g) confirming that the local authority has complied with or is to comply with any requirement imposed by regulations with respect to the issue of certificates under this section.

(3) The requirement specified in this subsection is that the local authority must have secured that the certificate is signed by any person who is required by regulations to sign it.

(4) The requirement specified in this subsection is that the local authority must have obtained consent to the issue of a certificate under this section from each of the persons with whom the local authority has entered, or is to enter, into the contract.

DEFINITIONS
"certification requirements": subs. (1).
"local authority": s.1(3) of this Act.

GENERAL NOTE
Together with s.4, this section regulates the certification process. The requirements for the certification process are provided by this section. It requires a certificate to be issued, and by s.4(1) a certificate so issued is not invalidated because anything stated in the certificate is untrue or inaccurate or the procedural steps have not been carried out. By s.4(3), for a contract to be certifiable at all the contract must be one operating for at least five years for the provision or making available of services, whether or not with assets, in connection with the discharge of the functions of the authority. This basic requirement is subject to the ability of the Secretary of State, under s.4(5), to amend these requirements by regulation.

In regard to such contracts, the requirements of the process of certification are that, by subs. (4), the contractor must agree to the issue of a certificate, but not its contents, and that the certificate must contain the information specified in subs. (2) and be signed by any person specified by regulation under subs. (3). The requirements of the regulations are included in the annotations to the appropriate subsection.

The Government resisted a proposed amendment to require consent to the content as well as the issue of the certificate, on the basis that this

"would mean that the contractor would have to be assured that his concerns had been properly assessed in the certificate. He would have to spend time and money ensuring that the content was satisfactory. . . . It would place more burdens on the contractor and would detract from the protection that the Bill will provide for the private sector, thus adversely affecting its willingness to enter into partnerships."
[*Standing Committee B*, July 1, 1997]

Instead it was pointed out that the purpose of certificate

> "is not to form an agreement between the parties, but to ensure that local authorities have done everything possible to satisfy themselves that the contract is in an area within which it can legally operate.
>
> The certificate will therefore constitute a proper holding of local authorities to account so that they investigate and ensure, on behalf of their electors, that the contract is legal. Contractors may not be in a position to do that; again, it will cost them a great deal of money to employ lawyers who understand that area of law so as to assure themselves that they have understood the statutory powers under which a local authority may enter into the contract. Local authorities have responsibility to assure themselves and their electors that they have done everything possible to investigate the legality of a contract. Only at that point would they issue a certificate."

[*Standing Committee B*, July 1, 1997]

The Parliamentary debates reflected the widespread concern in the local government world about the possible liability of officers for the issue of defective certificates. This is discussed above in the Introduction and General Note to the Act.

Subs. (1)

Under s.2(2), a contract can be a certified contract only if the certification requirements have been satisfied. This subsection defines the certification requirements as being those specified in the rest of this section and any regulations made thereunder.

Subs. (2)

Either before or after the contract is entered into, the authority must issue a certificate. The certificate must comply with the provisions of this subsection but, by s.4(1) a certificate so issued is not invalidated because anything stated in the certificate is untrue or inaccurate. The provisions of this subsection fall into two categories. First, the provisions specified only by this subsection and, secondly, those which depend on regulation for further specification.

In the former category are four requirements. The certificate must state that it is a contract which can be certified under s.4(3), namely one operating for at least five years for the provision or making available of services, whether or not with assets, in connection with the discharge of the functions of the authority (subs. (2)(c)); the purpose of the contract (subs. (2)(b)); the period for which it is to operate (subs. (2)(a)); and the statutory provision under which the contract is entered which shows that the authority has or had power to enter the contract (subs. (2)(d)). In the latter category are three matters dependent on regulation.

First, the certificate must deal in any specified way with any further matters to be specified by regulation (subs. (2)(f)). Under the first set of regulations, only one further matter has been specified. That is in relation to where, under subs. (2)(d), the authority specifies s.111 of the 1972 (or s.69 of the 1973 Act) as the statutory provision, or one of the provisions, for the legal authority to enter the contract. Where this is so, then the authority is by regulation additionally required to "specify in the certificate each statutory provision conferring a relevant function, or, where there are two or more relevant functions, the statutory provisions conferring the main relevant functions" (Reg. 6 of the Local Authorities (Contracts) Regulations 1997 (S.I. 1997 No. 2862), and Reg. 5 of the Local Authorities (Contracts) (Scotland) Regulations 1997 (S.I. 1997 No. 2879)). The regulations also specify that for the purpose of that regulation "a function is a relevant function if the contract is calculated to facilitate, or is conducive or incidental to, the discharge of the function. This is of interest given the legal uncertainty over whether s.111 (s.69) does provide authority for entering a contract, on which see the annotations to s.1.

Secondly, the certificate must confirm that a copy has been given to all those specified by regulation (subs. (2)(e)).

For England and Wales, the parties are specified by Regs. 3–5 of the Local Authorities (Contracts) Regulations 1997 (S.I. 1997 No. 2862). Under Reg. 3, all authorities must give a copy to each of the persons with whom the authority has entered, or is to enter, the contract to which the certificate relates. Under Reg. 4, those authorities with a monitoring officer, appointed under s.5(1) of the 1989 Act, must give a copy to that officer and also to the auditor. Under Reg. 5, provision is made for a copy to be given to the auditor of the following authorities: the Broads Authority; the London Pensions Fund Authority; the South Yorkshire Pensions Fund Authority; the Lee Valley Regional Park Authority; the Residuary Body for Wales; and a probation committee other than the inner London probation committee. For the inner London probation committee the copy must go to the Receiver for the Metropolitan Police and the Comptroller and Auditor General, and where the Receiver for the Metropolitan Police issues a certificate he must give a copy to the Comptroller and Auditor General.

For Scotland, the parties are specified by Reg. 3 of the Local Authorities (Contracts) (Scotland) Regulations 1997 (S.I. 1997 No. 2879) to be the auditor and the monitoring officer of the authority, and each of the persons with whom the authority has entered, or is to enter, the contract to which the certificate relates.

Thirdly, the certificate must confirm that any other requirement imposed by regulation has been, or will be complied with in respect to the issue of the certificate (subs. (2)(g)). No further requirements were imposed by the 1997 regulations.

One proposal was to have the auditor involved at an earlier stage, and to require the signature of the auditor to the certificate, thus not making the process one of self-certification. This was rejected because the Audit Commission considered that

> "auditors should remain independent and not get involved in decision making or in a management capacity in an authority. Auditors should not act in a way that might fetter their discretion in the exercise of their powers. The auditor is not a financial accountant or legal adviser to the authority and no views are to be expressed in that capacity."
> [*Standing Committee B*, July 1, 1997]

Subs. (3)

The authority is placed under a duty to ensure that the certificate is signed by those persons specified by regulation. Under the regulations, this is defined differently for England and Wales from Scotland.

For Scotland, Reg. 4 of the Local Authorities (Contracts) (Scotland) Regulations 1997 (S.I. 1997 No. 2879) provides that it must be signed by the "proper officer". This is defined by the regulations as having the same meaning as s.235(3) of the 1973 Act, which in turn defines the proper officer as "an officer appointed for that purpose by that body or for that area, as the case may be".

For England and Wales, this is specified by Regs. 7 and 8 of the Local Authorities (Contracts) Regulations 1997 (S.I. 1997 No. 2862) dealing with two separate groups of authorities. Regulation 7 provides for the larger group, namely those authorities with a chief finance officer who has responsibility for the administration of the authority's financial affairs. This in fact covers all authorities other than the ones specifically mentioned in Reg. 8, namely the Broads Authority; the Lee Valley Regional Park Authority; the Residuary Body for Wales; a probation committee, including the inner London probation committee; and the Receiver for the Metropolitan Police.

Under Reg. 7, the main group is itself split into two, based on whether or not the authority is required by s.4(1) of the 1989 Act to designate one of its officers as the head of its paid service. For those not so required, by Reg. 7(3) the certificate must be signed by the chief finance officer or a person who, as respects most or all of the duties of his post, is required to report directly, or is directly accountable, to the chief finance officer. For those with a head of paid service, the certificate must be signed by either a statutory chief officer, or a non-statutory chief officer, or a deputy chief officer, within the meaning of s.2 of the 1989 Act.

Under Reg. 8, a certificate issued by the Broads Authority must be signed by the chairman, vice-chairman or chief officer. For the Lee Valley Regional Park Authority the certificate must be signed by the chairman or vice-chairman, while the Residuary Body for Wales must have the certificate signed by the chairman. For a probation committee, other than the inner London probation committee, it must be signed by the secretary to the committee, the treasurer to the committee, or the Chief Probation Officer appointed by the committee. The inner London probation committee must ensure that it is signed by the secretary to the committee, by the Receiver for the Metropolitan Police or someone who, as respects most or all of the duties of his post, is required to report to him, or by the Chief Probation Officer appointed by him. The Receiver for the Metropolitan Police must ensure that the certificate is signed by him or someone who, as respects most or all of the duties of his post, is required to report to him. The drafting of Reg. 8 raises an ambiguity as to whether one or more signatures are required in some instances. While not technically part of the Regulation, the explanatory note states clearly that a certificate "must be signed by one of the persons prescribed in relation to the authority concerned". This would seem to be the clear intention of the legislation, as evidenced by Reg. 7 and the Scottish regulation.

Subs. (4)

This provides that the authority must have obtained the consent of the other parties to the contract before issuing it. The consent, however, goes only to the issuing of a certificate, not to the precise content. The Government resisted a proposal amendment to require consent to the content, on which see the General Note to this section.

Certified contracts: supplementary

4.—(1) Where the certification requirements have been satisfied in relation to a contract by a local authority, the certificate which has been issued shall have effect (and be deemed always to have had effect) as if the local authority had had power to issue it (and had exercised that power properly in issuing it); and a certificate which has been so issued is not invalidated by reason that anything in the certificate is inaccurate or untrue.

(2) Where the certification requirements have been satisfied in relation to a contract by a local authority within section 1(3)(a) or (d), the local authority shall secure that throughout the period for which the contract operates—

    (a) a copy of the certificate which has been issued is open to inspection by members of the public at all reasonable times without payment, and

    (b) members of the public are afforded facilities for obtaining copies of that certificate on payment of a reasonable fee.

(3) A contract entered into by a local authority falls within this subsection if—

    (a) it is entered into with another person for the provision or making available of services (whether or not together with assets or goods) for the purposes of, or in connection with, the discharge by the local authority of any of its functions, and

    (b) it operates, or is intended to operate, for a period of at least five years.

(4) A contract entered into by a local authority falls within this subsection if it is entered into, in connection with a contract falling within subsection (3), with—

    (a) a person who, in connection with that contract, makes a loan to, or provides any other form of finance for, a party to that contract other than the local authority, or

    (b) any insurer of or trustee for such a person.

(5) Regulations may be made amending subsection (3) or (4).

DEFINITIONS
"asset": s.1(4) of this Act.
"certification requirements": s.3(1) of this Act.
"local authority": s.1(3) of this Act.

GENERAL NOTE
While s.3 specifies the requirements of the certification process itself, this section both defines the range of contracts which may be certified and also attempts to balance the conflicting aims of providing accountability for the public while protecting the contracting parties. The range of contracts which may be certified is defined by subss. (3) and (4), subject to the power of the Secretary of State to make regulations under subs. (5). The aim of providing protection to the contracting parties is achieved by subs. (1) which, similarly to s.2(1), introduces a presumption that the certificate is lawful. This ensures that the problem of *vires* is not simply moved one stage from the contract itself to the certification process. While this clearly tilts the balance in favour of protecting the contracting parties from unlawful action by the local authority, subs. (2) attempts to maintain some accountability to the public by ensuring that adequate publicity is given.

Subs. (1)
Given that the protection for the contractor from the *ultra vires* doctrine depends on the contract being a certified contract, and that a certified contract depends on the certification requirements, an important issue is whether a court may find that the certificate is *ultra vires* because the requirements have not been met. Provided that the certificate is issued under s.3 and the associated regulations, this subsection makes it clear that the certificate cannot be invalidated because the content of the certificate in any way inaccurate or untrue. Thus, a certificate which did not purport to meet the requirements of s.3 at all, for example by failing to state the purpose of the contract or by not meeting the requirement to have it signed, could be struck down and so this protection for the public is maintained. Where, however, the certificate purports to meet these requirements, but it states all or some of these erroneously, this subsection changes that balance and attempts to give protection to the contractor.

As is explained above in the Introduction and General Note to the Act, it is possible, for a court to find that an error of law is so grave that the certificate is deemed to be void *ab initio* and so the attempted protection provided by this subsection could not be triggered at all. However, this extreme outcome is unlikely given that the requirements of the certificate are laid down by the same Act which provides that a defect is not fundamental. In any event s.6 and s.7 provide for special terms of the contract, whether the main or associated contract, which come into play in the event that a court finds the contract to be unlawful and that it should be set aside. The aim is that these terms will remain even if the contract itself is set aside.

Subs. (2)

This subsection was an addition to the Bill in order to help ensure adequate accountability to the public. Concern had been expressed that the self-certification process was not sufficiently open to promote accountability, but the Government initially rejected the suggestion on the ground that existing rules required authorities to give the necessary information before meetings so adequate accountability had been provided. Nevertheless, the Government undertook to examine the matter further and it was then accepted that the amendment should be included. Presumably this was because the current provisions regarding access to information would have permitted details of such contracts to remain confidential as being exempt information under Sched. 12A of the 1972 Act, as inserted by the Local Government (Access to Information) Act 1985 (c.43).

This subsection therefore requires the authority to make available to the public a copy of any certificate where the certification requirements have been satisfied. The certificate must be available for inspection at all reasonable times throughout the period for which the contract is operative, and facilities provided for the public to obtain copies. No charge may be made for inspection, but a reasonable charge may be made for copies taken. This does not apply to the receiver for the Metropolitan Police district or a probation committee because these bodies are not subject to the other open government provisions applicable to local government. Instead, these bodies are accountable to Parliament.

Subs. (3)

Under s.3(2), one of the matters to which the authority must certify before a contract can be a certified contract, and thus the contractor protected, is that the contract is of a type qualifying for protection. These contracts may be the main contract or the associated contract with the financier or the insurer or trustee of such a person. The main contract is defined by this subsection and the associated contract by subs. (4). The main contract follows the definition of a permitted contract in s.1(1) and it must satisfy three tests. First, it must be for the provision or making available of services (whether or not together with assets or goods). Secondly, the services must be for the purposes of, or in connection with, the discharge of any of the functions of the authority. Thirdly, the contract must operate, or at least be intended to operate, for a minimum of five years.

The Bill as introduced limited the contracts qualifying for protection to those for the provision of both assets and services. It was amended at the Committee stage in the House of Commons to cover contracts which were simply for services, so as to include, for example, contracts for the provision of a school meals service or for care and services in residential homes.

Amendments were also proposed in relation to the time limit and in relation to establishing a *de minimis* threshold. First, it was proposed to limit the length of such contracts to 25 years, on the basis that any longer would provide a burden on the citizens of the future. This was rejected as being unduly restrictive because it was considered that to achieve value for money some contracts required a contract period of 30 years or more.

Secondly, there was an attempt to limit the Act to contracts in excess of £1m. The Government did not reject this but stated that "We believe that regulation-making powers are the right way to proceed on that *de minimis* figure."

Subs. (4)

The subsection defines the associated contract, in connection with the main contract as defined in subs. (3). The definition of the associated contract follows that of s.1(2) which permits the authority, in connection with the original main contract, also to enter a separate associated contract with the financier of the contractor, or the financier's insurer, or a trustee for the financier. The purpose of this is, where a third party finances the contractor, to allow that party to step into the shoes of the contractor in the event of the original contractor producing an unacceptably poor performance, becoming insolvent, or otherwise unable to honour the contract.

Subs. (5)

By s.11(2), regulations made under this subsection, to alter the type of contracts able to be certified under subs. (3) and subs. (4), are subject to an affirmative resolution by both Houses of Parliament.

Special provision for judicial reviews and audit reviews

5.—(1) Section 2(1) does not apply for the purposes of determining any question arising on—

(a) an application for judicial review, or

(b) an audit review,

as to whether a local authority had power to enter into a contract (or exercised any power properly in entering into a contract).

(2) Section 2(1) has effect subject to any determination or order made in relation to a certified contract on—

(a) an application for judicial review, or

(b) an audit review.

(3) Where, on an application for judicial review or an audit review relating to a certified contract entered into by a local authority, a court—

(a) is of the opinion that the local authority did not have power to enter into the contract (or exercised any power improperly in entering into it), but

(b) (having regard in particular to the likely consequences for the financial provision of the local authority, and for the provision of services to the public, of a decision that the contract should not have effect) considers that the contract should have effect,

the court may determine that the contract has (and always has had) effect as if the local authority had had power to enter into it (and had exercised that power properly in entering into it).

(4) In this section and sections 6 and 7 references to an application for judicial review include any appeal (or further appeal) against a determination or order made on such an application.

Definitions

"application for judicial review": subs. (4).

"audit review": s.8(1) of this Act.

"certified contract": s.2(2) of this Act.

"local authority": s.1(3) of this Act.

General Note

One method of achieving the intention of the Act to remove the legal uncertainty surrounding such contracts would have been to remove the right to challenge the lawfulness of any contract defined in the Act. However, this would have met with constitutional objections. Instead, the certification process under s.2 was introduced, which raises the presumption of the contract being lawful. However, the right to challenge the lawfulness of any contract was preserved but restricted to public law challenge by means of either judicial review or the audit process as defined by s.8 of this Act.

Thus, although for private law purposes the presumption is that the certified contract is lawful, the spectre of a contract being declared unlawful remains and, in the absence of the associated provisions, the danger would be that the private sector would continue to be deterred from entering P.F.I. or other partnership contracts. Thus, there are three main elements in the Act to remove that danger while preserving the constitutional niceties. First, s.8 contains a provision which, where a prohibition notice is served by the auditor, allows the contract to continue in operation until the authority accepts the order or the matter is determined on appeal, or the time limit for appeal has expired. Secondly, subs. (3) makes explicit the courts' discretion in public law to give effect to a contract which is unlawful. Thirdly, ss.6 and 7 provide for discharge terms to be included in contracts which will continue to have effect even if the court determines that the main contract is unlawful and void.

By these means, the Act attempts to achieve the impossible, namely to protect the contractor from the effect of the contract being declared unlawful while preserving the right of local taxpayers or the auditor to challenge the contract. What it does achieve is to preserve the right of the citizen to challenge procedurally but not the right to be protected financially from unlawful action by the authority since, even if the contract is unlawful, it will either be allowed to continue or the authority will be required to pay damages to the contractor.

Subs. (1)

The presumption established by s.2(1) of this Act, that any certified contract is *intra vires*, does not extend to an application for judicial review or review by audit proceedings. Thus, the basic jurisdiction of the courts to determine the legality of a contract in public law remains.

Subs. (2)

Although subs. (1) retains the ability of the court to determine in public law whether the contract is unlawful, this subsection confirms the presumption established by s.2(1), that the contract is for private law purposes *intra vires*. However, it is also made clear that the presumption is subject to any determination or order of the court in the public law challenge and can in principle thus be displaced. However, as emphasised by subs. (3), a successful public law challenge will not result in the contract automatically being declared void. Instead, the court has the discretion to allow the contract to continue.

Subs. (3)

This subsection makes clear that even if, on a public law challenge, the court determines that the contract is unlawful, then it may nevertheless decide that the contract can continue. While the court may take into account a wide range of factors in determining whether to allow the contract to continue, subs. (3)(b) requires that particular regard must be had to the financial position of the authority, and on the public, in determining that the contract shall not have effect. This means that the court will be required to have regard to the cost of discharging a certified contract, under s.6 and s.7.

As originally drafted, subs. (3) simply gave to the courts in an audit review the same power as possessed in relation to an application for judicial review to allow the contract to continue. The Government took the view that in both actions the court would therefore be able to decide that the public interest lies in not terminating the contract, and that this discretion would have to be exercised in the light of all the circumstances, including the contractor's right to compensation in the event of the setting-aside of the contract. The view was expressed in Committee in the House of Commons that "in many cases the court would find the balance of interest to lie in allowing the contract to continue despite a finding of unlawfulness".

The subsection was, however, amended in response to representations by the Local Government Association. The Association was of the view that it should be made as clear as it could be that the cost of the discharge provisions has to be taken into account by the court. This was initially resisted in the House of Commons on the grounds that the authority would have satisfied itself of the legality of the contract before certifying it, and that to specify one factor in relation to the discretion

"will have the opposite effect and raise doubts about what the court should consider in the contract. . . . The amendment could make matters more difficult rather than ease the path." [*Hansard*, H.C. Vol. 297, col. 830]

However, by the time of the Committee stage in the House of Lords, the Government had reconsidered and introduced an amendment to make explicit this discretion in both judicial review and audit review.

"The court would have to consider the likely consequences of a decision to set the contract aside, first, for the authority's financial position and second, for the provision of services to the public.

It is important that these matters, in particular, should be looked at by a court in deciding the outcome of a judicial review or audit review. A certified contract is likely to operate for a long period of time and to involve heavy investment by the parties to the contract. Furthermore, an order setting such a contract aside would be likely to disrupt the provision of public services and generally be against the wider interests, financial and otherwise, of the local community. The objective is to ensure that the court is clearly empowered to decide that a certified contract found to be *ultra vires* shall nevertheless continue to have effect and to require the court, in deciding on this, to give full weight to these factors." [*Hansard*, H.L. Vol. 582, col. 621]

Subs. (4)

This makes it clear that any reference in the Act to an application for judicial review means the whole process, including all appeals and not simply the initial action.

Relevant discharge terms

6.—(1) No determination or order made in relation to a certified contract on—

    (a) an application for judicial review, or

    (b) an audit review,

shall affect the enforceability of any relevant discharge terms relating to the contract.

(2) In this section and section 7 "relevant discharge terms", in relation to a contract entered into by a local authority, means terms—
  (a) which have been agreed by the local authority and any person with whom the local authority entered into the contract,
  (b) which either form part of the contract or constitute or form part of another agreement entered into by them not later than the day on which the contract was entered into, and
  (c) which provide for a consequence mentioned in subsection (3) to ensue in the event of the making of a determination or order in relation to the contract on an application for judicial review or an audit review.
(3) Those consequences are—
  (a) the payment of compensatory damages (measured by reference to loss incurred or loss of profits or to any other circumstances) by one of the parties to the other,
  (b) the adjustment between the parties of rights and liabilities relating to any assets or goods provided or made available under the contract, or
  (c) both of those things.
(4) Where a local authority has agreed relevant discharge terms with any person with whom it has entered into a contract and the contract is a certified contract, the relevant discharge terms shall have effect (and be deemed always to have had effect) as if the local authority had had power to agree them (and had exercised that power properly in agreeing them).

DEFINITIONS
  "application for judicial review": s.5(4) of this Act.
  "asset". s.1(4) of this Act.
  "audit review": s.8(1) of this Act.
  "certified contract": s.2(2) of this Act.
  "local authority": s.1(3) of this Act.
  "relevant discharge term": subs. (2).

GENERAL NOTE
  Given the uncertainty over how the doctrine of *ultra vires* would apply to contracts under this Act, even with the introduction of the clear statutory presumption that the contract is lawful, it was considered necessary to provide further protection for the parties to a certified contract with the local authority. Thus, this is the first of two sections which provide for special terms of the contract, whether the main or associated contract, which come into play in the event that a court finds the contract to be unlawful and that it should be set aside. The aim is that these terms will remain even if the contract itself is set aside. This section therefore makes clear the power of the authority to agree discharge terms and provides for the safeguarding of any discharge terms incorporated into the contract. Section 7 provides for the situation where no discharge terms are incorporated or those incorporated are held to be of no legal effect.
  In constructing these discharge provisions the Government examined whether to adopt provisions similar to those relating to the "safe harbour" in the Companies Act 1985 (c.6) or those in the Local Government and Housing Act 1989. This was rejected on the basis that those provisions, applying to a loan agreement, were too simple to deal with the more complicated matters which are likely to be found in partnership contracts.
  An important statement of the intention behind the legislation, and the relationship of s.6 to s.7, was made by Lord Donaldson, the former Master of the Rolls.
    "Let me say one general word about the special discharge terms. The secretariat of the Financial Law Panel and I have looked carefully at that matter. For what it may be worth, our view is that neither local authorities nor contractors should spend much time on special terms. Local authorities can hardly be heard to say that the basis of repudiation is unreasonable and dangerous since they may well have had no power to enter into the contract. Nor can the contractor say, 'I want something better than the standard fall-back repudiation', which provides full compensation for any loss that he suffered.
    It may well make more sense economically therefore, certainly in terms of managerial time, to forget about special terms and either simply provide in the contract that the discharge terms shall be on the statutory basis . . . or leave it with no discharge terms, in which case the statutory discharge terms will apply. They survive everything, judicially engineered or not. They are the sheet anchor of the contractor's protection."
  [*Hansard*, H.L. Vol. 582, col. 630]

Subs. (1)

In order to protect the parties to a certified contract with a local authority, the special terms relating to discharge of an unlawful certified contract, as defined by subs. (2), will remain valid even if the contract itself is set aside. Given that, by s.5, the only procedures available for questioning the *vires* of a certified contract are by an application for judicial review or an audit review, the wording of this subsection means that no challenge to a certified contract an affect the enforceability of the relevant discharge terms. Of course, as discussed above in the Introduction and General Note to the Act, the effect of the whole contractual relationship being declared void *ab initio* would mean that these terms and sections could not be triggered at all. While this extreme outcome is unlikely, in any event provision is made by s.7(3) for this situation. That subsection makes clear that the default provisions in s.7 will apply even where a court declares that the discharge terms, which are incorporated into an unlawful contract or are themselves unlawful, shall have no legal effect.

Subs. (2)

This subsection defines the term "relevant discharge terms" for the purposes of this section and s.7. The definition involves three stages. First, it must be an agreement between these parties. The power of the local authority to agree such terms is made clear by subs. (4). Secondly, it can be part of the main contract, but need not be provided that the terms are incorporated into another agreement between the relevant parties entered into not later than the same day they enter the main contract. Thirdly, the terms must provide for the consequence of an order made on an application for judicial review or audit review. The consequence must be one of those specified in subs. (3), namely compensatory damages, division of assets or goods provided or made available under the contract, or both.

Subs. (3)

A "relevant discharge term", as defined by subs. (2), must provide for the consequence of an order made on an application for judicial review or audit review. This subsection specifies the possible consequences, namely compensatory damages, division of assets or goods provided or made available under the contract, or both. In relation to damages, the measure of damages may be restricted to loss, but may also include loss of profits or be measured in relation to any other circumstance. These are basically contractual damages. The payment of compensation is not restricted, to payments from the authority to another party. Thus, it could provide for payment from a party other than the authority to another party or, less likely, payment to the authority from another party. In relation to assets or goods provided under the contract, the discharge term could, for example, provide that an asset be transferred to, or made available for use by, the authority. This is similar to the approach taken in regard to frustrated contracts, see the Law Reform (Frustrated Contracts) Act 1943 (c.40).

Subs. (4)

This subsection makes clear that the local authority may agree terms with any person with whom the local authority entered a contract. It also provides that where discharge terms have been agreed in relation to a certified contract then, even if the local authority abused the power to agree such terms, they are to be treated as if the power had been used lawfully. Again, as explained above in the Introduction and General Note to the Act, it would be possible for a court to find that the error of law was so grave as to deem the discharge terms to be void *ab initio* and so this subsection could not be triggered at all. While this extreme outcome is unlikely, in any event provision is made by s.7(3) for this situation. That subsection makes clear that the default provisions in s.7 will apply even where a court declares that the discharge terms, which are incorporated into an unlawful contract or are themselves unlawful, shall have no legal effect.

An attempt was made in the House of Lords to specify the circumstances in which the courts should conclude that this subsection did not apply and the terms should be struck down. The Government rejected this, stating that

> "Only in exceptional circumstances would a court decide to set aside the discharge terms.
> . . .
> The Government do not feel it right or appropriate to prescribe or limit the circumstances under which a court could conclude that clause 6(4) did not apply. The circumstances would be so individual and specific that it is a matter of law and discretion best left to the courts."

[*Hansard*, H.L. Vol. 582, col. 630]

Instead, the point was made that it was more important for the contractors and banks to have protection under s.7.

Absence of relevant discharge terms

7.—(1) Subsection (2) applies where—

(a) the result of a determination or order made by a court on an application for judicial review or an audit review is that a certified contract does not have effect, and

(b) there are no relevant discharge terms having effect between the local authority and a person who is a party to the contract.

(2) That person shall be entitled to be paid by the local authority such sums (if any) as he would have been entitled to be paid by the local authority if the contract—

(a) had had effect until the time when the determination or order was made, but

(b) had been terminated at that time by acceptance by him of a repudiatory breach by the local authority.

(3) For the purposes of this section the circumstances in which there are no relevant discharge terms having effect between the local authority and a person who is a party to the contract include (as well as circumstances in which no such terms have been agreed) circumstances in which the result of a determination or order of a court, made (despite section 6(4)) on an application for judicial review or an audit review, is that such terms do not have effect.

DEFINITIONS

"application for judicial review": s.5(4) of this Act.
"audit review": s.8(1) of this Act.
"certified contract": s.2(2) of this Act.
"local authority": s.1(3) of this Act.
"relevant discharge term": s.6(2) of this Act.

GENERAL NOTE

This is the second of the two sections which provide for special terms of the contract, whether the main or associated contract, which come into play in the event that a court finds the contract to be unlawful and that it should be set aside. While s.6 provides for terms to be agreed between the parties for this eventuality, this section provides for the situation where no discharge terms have been agreed or where, despite the provision in s.6(4), the court finds that such terms are themselves unenforceable.

Subs. (1)

This section, the substance of which is contained in subs. (2), applies where two conditions are satisfied. First, a certified contract is found to be of no legal effect. This can be done only by means of an application for judicial review or by an audit review. Secondly, there are no relevant discharge terms, as defined by s.6(2), having effect between the authority and a party to the contract. There will be no relevant discharge terms where none were agreed in accordance with s.6(2) or, as is made clear by subs. (3), where such purported terms are found to have no legal effect.

Subs. (2)

Where a certified contract is found to be unlawful and there are no effective relevant discharge terms between the authority and a party to the contract then protection is given to that party. The protection amounts to the payment of the sums by the authority as if there was a repudiatory breach of the contract by the authority. These terms were described by Lord Donaldson as "They survive everything, judicially engineered or not. They are the sheet anchor of the contractor's protection" [*Hansard*, H.L. Vol. 582, col. 630]. On the relationship of these terms to those which can be agreed under s.6, see the General Note to s.6.

Subs. (3)

This subsection makes clear that there are no relevant discharge terms where it is held that purported relevant discharge terms are void, despite the provision of s.6(4) that purported terms should have effect even if the authority had not exercised its power properly. While this extreme finding is unlikely, this subsection which makes clear that the default provisions in subs. (2) will apply. By s.5, these purported terms can be found to have no legal effect only by means of an application for judicial review or by an audit review.

Audit reviews

8.—(1) In this Act "an audit review" means—

(a) an application or appeal under section 19 of the Local Government Finance Act 1982 (application by auditor, or appeal by person objecting to accounts, for declaration as to unlawful item of account),

(b) consideration by an auditor of whether to give a certificate under section 20 of that Act (certificate about sum not accounted for or loss or deficiency caused by wilful misconduct) or an appeal under that section,

(c) consideration by an auditor of whether to issue a prohibition order under section 25A of that Act (unlawful expenditure etc.) or an appeal under section 25B of that Act (appeals against a prohibition order),

(d) consideration by the Controller of Audit of whether to make a special report to the Accounts Commission for Scotland under section 102(3) of the Local Government (Scotland) Act 1973 (reports to Commission by Controller of Audit),

(e) consideration by the Accounts Commission for Scotland of whether to send a special report to the Secretary of State under section 103(3) of that Act (action by Commission on reports by Controller of Audit), or

(f) consideration by the Court of Session of a case stated under section 103(2)(c) of that Act (Commission may state case on a question of law for opinion of Court of Session),

or any appeal (or further appeal) against a decision made on an application referred to in paragraph (a) or on an appeal referred to in any of paragraphs (a) to (c).

(2) A prohibition order issued under section 25A of the Local Government Finance Act 1982 shall not make it unlawful to—

(a) make or implement any decision,

(b) take or continue to take any course of action, or

(c) enter any item of account,

relating to a certified contract before the determination or withdrawal of any appeal against the order under section 25B(3) of that Act or, if no appeal is brought during the period within which it is permitted to bring any such appeal, before the end of that period.

<small>DEFINITIONS</small>
"Accounts Commission": s.97(1) of the 1973 Act.
"audit review": subs. (1).
"auditor": s.36(1) of the 1982 Act, and s.97(6) of the 1973 Act.
"Controller of Audit": s.97(4) of the 1973 Act.

<small>GENERAL NOTE</small>
This section provides the definition of "audit review" for the purposes of preserving, under s.5, public law review of contracts subject to this Act. It also includes, for most authorities in England and Wales, a provision to ensure that prohibition orders issued by the auditor will not prevent a certified contract from continuing until the authority accepts the order or the matter is determined on appeal, or the time limit for appeal has expired.

Unlike applications for judicial review, audit review is not limited to a three month period from the date of the contract and in principle contracts could be challenged many months later. However, the fact that the authority is required, by regulation made under s.3, to notify the auditor under the certification requirements means that prompt action by means of a prohibition notice is possible in England and Wales. See the Local Authorities (Contracts) Regulations 1997 (S.I. 1997 No. 2862) and the Local Authorities (Contracts) (Scotland) Regulations 1997 (S.I. 1997 No. 2879).

Contracting out of functions in connection with certified contracts

9.—(1) An authorisation given by virtue of an order under section 70 of the Deregulation and Contracting Out Act 1994 (authorisation by local authority of exercise by another person of functions of authority for period not exceeding ten years) may specify that it is to be for a period exceeding ten years if it is given in connection with a certified contract.

(2) But an authorisation given in connection with a certified contract may not by virtue of subsection (1) specify that it is to be for a period exceeding the shorter of—

(a) the period for which the contract is to operate, and

(b) forty years.

(3) For the purposes of this section an authorisation is given in connection with a certified contract if—

(a) the authority by which it is given is a local authority for the purposes of this Act,

(b) the authority and the authorised person are parties to the contract, and

(c) the authorisation is given to enable the authorised person to perform or better perform his obligations under the contract.

DEFINITIONS
"certified contract": s.2(2) of this Act.
"local authority": s.1(3) of this Act.

GENERAL NOTE
This section was introduced at the Committee stage in the House of Lords.

Under the Deregulation and Contracting Out Act 1994, the Secretary of State may make an order authorising a local authority to contract out the exercise of the functions specified in the order. Such schemes of delegation are limited to 10 years. The Government anticipated that many contracts certified under the present Act would be public-private partnerships where functions of the authority would need to be delegated to the contractor.

Following representations, the Goverment accepted that the 10 year period under the 1994 Act may be too short for certain projects. Because of commercial reasons, the period over which the investment would be recovered may be 20 years or more. The Government considered that the projects most likely to face this constraint are for the construction and maintenance of highways, but that the same difficulty would be faced in relation to other cases "where the success of the partnership depends on the contractor being authorised to exercise a function without continual instructions from the authority."

This section therefore permits the contracting out period under the 1994 Act to be extended to the period for which the contract is to run, subject to a maximum of 40 years. By subs. (3)(c), the extended period for contracting out will only apply where a function is delegated so that a contractor can "perform or better perform his obligations" under a certified contract. Thus, the extension of time is not limited to creating the conditions for the contract to be made at all. It may also be invoked where, although a shorter period is still possible, the longer period will enable the contractor to better perform his obligations. No criteria are laid down in the Act as to what can be taken into account in assessing this. Presumably the criteria can be determined only in relation to the aims of a particular contract.

Given this extensive delegation of public power, it is worth noting the statement of the Government that:

"It is also important to understand that a local authority which delegates a function to a contractor retains full responsibility for the exercise of the function concerned. So, for example, if a member of the public is adversely affected by a decision made by a contractor in the exercise of a local authority function, he will complain to the local authority—and be able to take any proceedings against it—as if the authority itself had made the decision."
[*Hansard*, H.L. Vol. 582, col. 633]

Grants relating to expenditure in respect of magistrates' courts

Power to treat expenditure as not being capital expenditure

10. In section 57 of the Justices of the Peace Act 1997 (grants by the Lord Chancellor towards the capital and other expenditure of authorities responsible for providing accommodation etc. for magistrates' courts), after subsection (4) insert—

"(4A) The Lord Chancellor, with the concurrence of the Treasury, may by statutory instrument make regulations providing that any expenditure of responsible authorities in pursuance of their functions under this Part of this Act which is of a description specified in the regulations shall be taken not to be capital expenditure for the purposes of section 55(3) or (7) above or this section.

(4B) A statutory instrument containing (whether alone or with other provisions) regulations made by virtue of subsection (4A) above shall be subject to annulment in pursuance of a resolution of either House of Parliament."

GENERAL NOTE

This amends s.57 of the Justices of the Peace Act 1997. That section provides for payments of grants to local authorities in relation to expenditure incurred on magistrates' courts. Under the strict capital finance rules such payments were treated as capital expenditure, thus reducing the amount available to the authority. The amendment introduced by this section permits the making of regulations by the Lord Chancellor to allow such grants to be treated as revenue expenditure. This will enable partnership contracts in respect of magistrates' courts to be more easily promoted. It was stated that the Government hoped to encourage public/private projects for information technology and new court-houses.

As originally drafted, the Bill envisaged that all such partnership would be entered into by the paying authority. However, by an amendment to the clause, which introduced the reference to s.55(3) of the Justices of the Peace Act 1997, enables regulations to be made to treat expenditure under certain partnership contracts as revenue for the purposes of allowing magistrates' courts committees to procure direct. As was stated by the Government,

"The effect of this will be to allow magistrates' courts committees to enter into specified contracts direct with suppliers. . . . The intention is to make regulations which will allow magistrates courts' committees to enter into partnership contracts for the provision of IT services. It is not intended that this be extended to contracts for the provision of serviced accommodation, which will remain the responsibility of the paying authority."
[*Hansard*, H.L. Vol. 582, col. 634]

Supplementary

Regulations

11.—(1) Any power to make regulations under this Act is exercisable by the Secretary of State by statutory instrument and may be exercised so as to make different provision for different purposes or for different cases (including different provision for different areas).

(2) No regulations shall be made under section 4(5) unless a draft of the statutory instrument containing them has been laid before and approved by a resolution of each House of Parliament.

(3) Subject to that, a statutory instrument containing regulations under this Act shall be subject to annulment in pursuance of a resolution of either House of Parliament.

GENERAL NOTE

The power of the Secretary of State to make regulations under the various provisions of this Act is subject to the negative resolution procedure, except for s.4(5), which provides for the Secretary of State to be able to amend the types of contracts and the relevant persons protected by this Act, which is subject to the affirmative resolution procedure.

Short title, commencement and extent

12.—(1) This Act may be cited as the Local Government (Contracts) Act 1997.

(2) Sections 2 to 9 shall not come into force until a day appointed by the Secretary of State by order made by statutory instrument; and different days may be appointed for different provisions or purposes.

(3) Sections 1 to 9 apply to any contract which a local authority enters into after 12th June 1997; but in relation to a contract entered into before the day on which section 2 comes into force "the certification period" means the period of six weeks beginning with that day.

(4) Section 10 does not extend to Scotland.

(5) This Act does not extend to Northern Ireland.

DEFINITIONS

"certification period": s.2(5) of this Act and subs. (3).

"local authority": s.1(3) of this Act.

GENERAL NOTE

Sections 1 and 10 to 12 came into force on the passing of the Act on November 27, 1997.

The regulation making power of the Secretary of State contained in subsections (2)(e) and (f) and (3) of s.3 (prescribing to whom a copy of the certificate required under s.3 is to be given, the matters to be dealt with in the certificate, and by whom the certificate must be signed), came into force on a different date for England and Wales from Scotland. For England and Wales this was December 1, 1997; see the Local Government (Contracts) Act 1997 (Commencement No. 1) Order 1997 (S.I. 1997 No. 2843). For Scotland this was December 2, 1997; see the Local Government (Contracts) Act 1997 (Commencement No. 2) Order 1997 (S.I. 1997 No. 2878).

The remaining sections of the Act, namely ss.2, 4 to 9, and the rest of s.3, also came into force on a different date for England and Wales from Scotland. For England and Wales this was December 30, 1997; see the Local Government (Contracts) Act 1997 (Commencement No. 1) Order 1997 (S.I. 1997 No. 2843). For Scotland this was January 1, 1998; see the Local Government (Contracts) Act 1997 (Commencement No. 2) Order 1997 (S.I. 1997 No. 2878).

Section 1 applies to any contract before or after the passing of the Act, in so far as it simply confirmed the existing law. The certification process introduced by ss.1 to 9, being a change to the law, could not apply retrospectively without express authority. Subs. (3) permits the process to apply to any contract entered into, on or after the date of the introduction of the Bill to the House of Commons, namely June 12, 1997, and the date on which section came into force, namely December 30, 1997 for England and Wales, and January 1, 1998 for Scotland. This is achieved by enacting that for contracts entered into with those periods the certification period of six weeks, which normally runs from the day on which the contract was entered into, would run from the date of the passing of the Act, namely November 27, 1997.

INDEX

References are to sections

PLANT VARIETIES ACT 1997*

(1997 c. 66)

<small>ARRANGEMENT OF SECTIONS</small>

<small>PART I</small>

<small>PLANT VARIETIES</small>

Preliminary

---

* Annotations by Hume Hargreave, Partner at Dickinson Dees, Newcastle upon Tyne.

An Act to make provision about rights in relation to plant varieties; to make provision about the Plant Varieties and Seeds Tribunal; to extend the time limit for institution of proceedings for contravention of seeds regulations; and for connected purposes. [27th November 1997]

PARLIAMENTARY DEBATES
Hansard, H.C. Vol. 295, col. 1298, Vol. 296, col. 690, Vol. 301, col. 1042. H.L. Vol. 580, col. 1636, Vol. 581, col. 1121, Vol. 582, cols. 555, 825, 1325, Vol. 583, col. 90.

The Act implements the 1991 revisions to the International Convention for the Protection of New Varieties of Plants—or the UPOV Convention as it is commonly known, the Union for the Protection of Varieties. At the same time, it aligns the standards of protection offered by the U.K. national system of plant breeders' rights with those already available under the parallel, but separate, European Community plant breeders' rights regime established in September 1994.

Plant breeders' rights are a form of intellectual property, similar to patents, which enable plant breeders to obtain protection for new varieties and an income, through royalties, on their commercial exploitation. They are underpinned at international level by the UPOV Convention. The U.K. played a major role in the development of the first UPOV Convention, signed in 1961, and was a founder member of the union which it established.

The plant breeders' rights regime established by the Plant Varieties and Seeds Act 1964 (c. 14) implemented the first UPOV convention.

As well as enabling the U.K. to ratify the 1991 Convention, the Act brings the national system of protection into line with that provided by the Community regime (Reg. EC 2100/94—see subs. (38(1))). Plant breeders have a choice between national systems of protection and the Community system which offers a right valid in all 15 member states. The Act puts an end to the confusion which can arise when two systems which are different, but each of which have the same users (plant breeders, nurserymen, farmers and seed processors), operate side by side.

The Act is concerned only with plant breeder's rights. It does not have any implications for the regulation of releases of genetically modified plant varieties.

The statutory controls on releases, which include releases of genetically modified plant varieties, are quite separate from the Act. Their effect is that a consent must be issued by the Secretary of State for the Environment, if the release is in England, or the Secretaries of State for Scotland or Wales as appropriate, each acting jointly with the Minister of Agriculture in matters of joint interest, before any genetically modified organism can be released into the environment. No consent can be issued without the agreement of the Health and Safety Executive.

The independent expert members of the statutory Advisory Committee on Releases into the Environment—ACRE—consider applications to release and market genetically modified organisms. ACRE advises Ministers whether a consent should be granted and which conditions should be attached to any consent. The Plant Variety Rights Office cannot undertake the tests necessary to establish whether a variety meets the criteria for plant breeders' rights unless and until the necessary clearance has been obtained. Nothing in the Act alters or affects that position.

The Act sets out a new framework for plant breeders' rights in the United Kingdom and makes provision about the Plant Varieties and Seeds Tribunal. It also extends the time limit for institution of proceedings for contravention of seed regulations.

The Act repeals and re-enacts with amendment Part I of the Plant Varieties and Seeds Act 1964 (as amended). The new regime conforms to the UPOV Convention as last revised on March 19, 1991, thus enabling the United Kingdom to ratify it. It will be ratified when the following secondary legislation has come into force:

The Plant Breeders' Rights Regulations 1998
The Plant Breeders' Rights (Fees) Regulations 1998
The Plant Breeders' Rights (Farm Saved Seed) (Specification) Order 1998
The Plant Breeders' Rights (Farm Saved Seed) (Specified Information) Regulations 1998
The Plant Breeders' Rights (Information Notices) Regulations 1998

PART I

PLANT VARIETIES

Preliminary

Plant breeders' rights

1.—(1) Rights, to be known as plant breeders' rights, may be granted in accordance with this Part of this Act.

(2) Plant breeders' rights may subsist in varieties of all plant genera and species.

(3) For the purposes of this Act, "variety" means a plant grouping within a single botanical taxon of the lowest known rank, which grouping, irrespective of whether the conditions for the grant of plant breeders' rights (which are laid down in section 4 below) are met, can be—

    (a) defined by the expression of the characteristics resulting from a given genotype or combination of genotypes,

(b) distinguished from any other plant grouping by the expression of at least one of those characteristics, and

(c) considered as a unit with regard to its suitability for being propagated unchanged.

GENERAL NOTE

This section provides that plant breeders' rights may subsist in any variety of a plant genus or species, and defines "variety" for the purposes of the Act.

The Plant Variety Rights Office

2.—(1) The office known as the Plant Variety Rights Office shall continue in being for the purposes of this Part of this Act under the immediate control of an officer appointed by the Ministers and known as the Controller of Plant Variety Rights ("the Controller").

(2) Schedule 1 to this Act (which makes further provision about the Plant Variety Rights Office) shall have effect.

GENERAL NOTE

This section provides for the continued existence of the Plant Variety Rights Office, headed by the Controller and introduces Schedule 1 which makes further provision about the staffing of the Office and the authority of its officers.

Grant of plant breeders' rights

Grant on application

3.—(1) Subject to this Part of this Act, plant breeders' rights shall be granted to an applicant by the Controller on being satisfied that the conditions laid down in section 4 below are met.

(2) The Controller may by notice require an applicant for the grant of plant breeders' rights to provide him, within such time as may be specified in the notice, with such information, documents, plant or other material, facilities or test or trial results relevant to the carrying out of his function under subsection (1) above as may be so specified.

(3) If an applicant fails to comply with a notice under subsection (2) above within the period specified in the notice, the Controller may refuse the application.

GENERAL NOTE

This section requires the Controller to grant plant breeders' rights to an applicant if he is satisfied that the conditions in s.4 and Schedule 2 are met. It enables the Controller to require an applicant to submit certain information or material.

Conditions for the grant of rights

4.—(1) The conditions which must be met in relation to an application for the grant of plant breeders' rights are—

(a) that the variety to which the application relates is a qualifying variety, and

(b) that the person by whom the application is made is the person entitled to the grant of plant breeders' rights in respect of the variety to which it relates.

(2) For the purposes of subsection (1) above, a variety is a qualifying variety if it is—

(a) distinct,
(b) uniform,
(c) stable, and
(d) new;

and Part I of Schedule 2 to this Act has effect for the purpose of determining whether these criteria are met.

(3) Subject to subsections (4) and (5) below, the person entitled to the grant of plant breeders' rights in respect of a variety is the person who breeds it, or discovers and develops it, or his successor in title.

(4) If a person breeds a variety, or discovers and develops it, in the course of his employment, then, subject to agreement to the contrary, his employer, or his employer's successor in title, is the person entitled to the grant of plant breeders' rights in respect of it.

(5) Part II of Schedule 2 to this Act shall have effect as respects priorities between two or more persons who have independently bred, or discovered and developed, a variety.

(6) In this section and Schedule 2 to this Act, references to the discovery of a variety are to the discovery of a variety, whether growing in the wild or occurring as a genetic variant, whether artificially induced or not.

GENERAL NOTE

This section and Schedule 2 define the conditions for a grant of rights, and provide that the person applying for rights must be the person entitled to them in respect of the variety. The conditions are that the variety must be distinct, stable, uniform and new, and Schedule 2, Part I states how it is determined whether these criteria are met. The person entitled to a grant of rights in a variety is the person who breeds it, or discovers and develops it, or an employer where the variety is bred, or discovered and developed, by an employee in the course of his employment. Schedule 2, Part II explains how priority is established where two or more people have independently bred, or discovered and developed, the same variety.

Rights in relation to application period

5.—(1) If an application for plant breeders' rights is granted, the holder of the rights shall be entitled to reasonable compensation for anything done during the application period which, if done after the grant of the rights, would constitute an infringement of them.

(2) In subsection (1) above, "application period", in relation to a grant of plant breeders' rights, means the period—

    (a) beginning with the day on which details of the application for the grant of the rights are published in the gazette, and

    (b) ending with the grant of the rights.

GENERAL NOTE

This section provides for provisional protection of a variety in the period between submission of an application for a grant of rights and the grant.

Scope of plant breeders' rights

Protected variety

6.—(1) Plant breeders' rights shall have effect to entitle the holder to prevent anyone doing any of the following acts as respects the propagating material of the protected variety without his authority, namely—

    (a) production or reproduction (multiplication),

    (b) conditioning for the purpose of propagation,

    (c) offering for sale,

    (d) selling or other marketing,

    (e) exporting,

    (f) importing,

    (g) stocking for any of the purposes mentioned in paragraphs (a) to (f) above, and

    (h) any other act prescribed for the purposes of this provision.

(2) The holder of plant breeders' rights may give authority for the purposes of subsection (1) above with or without conditions or limitations.

(3) The rights conferred on the holder of plant breeders' rights by subsections (1) and (2) above shall also apply as respects harvested material obtained through the unauthorised use of propagating material of the protected variety, unless he has had a reasonable opportunity before the harvested material is obtained to exercise his rights in relation to the unauthorised use of the propagating material.

(4) In the case of a variety of a prescribed description, the rights conferred on the holder of plant breeders' rights by subsections (1) and (2) above shall also apply as respects any product which—

    (a) is made directly from harvested material in relation to which sub-section (3) above applies, and

    (b) is of a prescribed description,

unless subsection (5) below applies.

(5) This subsection applies if, before the product was made, any act mentioned in subsection (1) above was done as respects the harvested material from which the product was made and either—

    (a) the act was done with the authority of the holder of the plant breeders' rights, or

    (b) the holder of those rights had a reasonable opportunity to exercise them in relation to the doing of the act.

(6) In this section—

    (a) "prescribed" means prescribed by regulations made by the Ministers, and

    (b) references to harvested material include entire plants and parts of plants.

GENERAL NOTE

The fundamental changes made by the Act to the previous legislation are in ss.6 to 10 which are about the scope of plant breeders' rights. The basic right in the Plant Varieties and Seeds Act 1964 is the exclusive right to sell propagating material of a protected variety, or produce propagating material for sale. The key change in s.6 is the much wider scope of things which a breeder can prevent others from doing with propagating material of a protected variety, without his authority. This includes, for example, any production or reproduction of propagating material, conditioning—which means preparing for planting—import, export and so on. Taken together, provisions in s.6(1) give the breeder control over all the things necessary to exploit a variety.

The International Convention for the Protection of New Varieties of Plants (the UPOV Convention)—see Introduction and General Note—found it impossible to define "propagating material". The nature of plant material, and the technology, is such that a variety may be propagated from a much wider range of material than seeds or cuttings. Plant material which is commonly disposed of as the final product may be used as propagating material. For example, tissue culture techniques mean that a plant of a vegetatively propagated variety may be obtained from a cut flower. A whole plant or bush, which is sold to the public, may alternatively be used as propagating material to produce more plants. The Act, like the 1991 Convention, does not include a definition of propagating materal—any material which is actually used as propagating material is propagating material for the purposes of s.6(1).

The breeder can authorise others to undertake any of the acts in s.6(1), and may make his authority subject to conditions. This is the basis for plant breeders' rights licences, which are the means whereby the breeder gives permission to others to exploit the variety, subject to payment of a royalty, while at the same time retaining overall control of it.

The control which the breeder has over his variety is—as with other forms of intellectual property—wide ranging, but it is not unlimited. Acts done for private, non-commercial purposes or to breed another variety, for example, do not come within the breeder's control; see s.8. The breeder must act reasonably in taking commercial decisions on whether to issue licences and on what terms. If he does not do so, the controller has powers to issue a compulsory licence and to set the terms, provided that it is in the public interest; see s.6(2) and s.17.

In normal circumstances, under s.10, the breeder's right is exhausted once propagating material is disposed of with his consent to produce a commercial crop. However, if material sold with the breeder's authority for a purpose which results in exhaustion of rights, is used for another purpose, then the breeder's right may not be exhausted. For example, if a finished pot plant is used as source material for vegetative propagation of further plants, then the breeder's right is not exhausted.

Subs. (1)

This sub-section defines the scope of the breeder's rights. Specific acts which the holder of rights can prevent anyone doing as respects propagating material are listed. Ministers may by regulations prescribe additional acts. The holder of rights may authorise a person to do these acts, with or without conditions.

Subs. (3)

Where harvested material is obtained through the unauthorised use of propagating material, and the holder of rights has not had reasonable opportunity to exercise those rights in respect of the propagating material, he may exercise them in respect of the harvested material.

Subs. (4)

Ministers may also prescribe by regulations products in respect of which the holder may exercise rights, where these products are obtained through the unauthorised use of harvested material and the holder has not had reasonable opportunity to exercise his rights in respect of the propagating or harvested material.

Dependent varieties

7.—(1) The holder of plant breeders' rights shall have, in relation to any variety which is dependent on the protected variety, the same rights as he has under section 6 above in relation to the protected variety.

(2) For the purposes of this section, one variety is dependent on another if—

(a) its nature is such that repeated production of the variety is not possible without repeated use of the other variety, or

(b) it is essentially derived from the other variety and the other variety is not itself essentially derived from a third variety.

(3) For the purposes of subsection (2) above, a variety shall be deemed to be essentially derived from another variety ("the initial variety") if—

(a) it is predominantly derived from—

(i) the initial variety, or

(ii) a variety that is itself predominantly derived from the initial variety,

while retaining the expression of the essential characteristics resulting from the genotype or combination of genotypes of the initial variety,

(b) it is clearly distinguishable from the initial variety by one or more characteristics which are capable of a precise description, and

(c) except for the differences which result from the act of derivation, it conforms to the initial variety in the expression of the essential characteristics that result from the genotype or combination of genotypes of the initial variety.

(4) For the purposes of subsection (3) above, derivation may, for example, be by—

(a) the selection of—

(i) a natural or induced mutant,

(ii) a somaclonal variant, or

(iii) a variant individual from plants of the initial variety,

(b) backcrossing, or

(c) transformation by genetic engineering.

(5) Subsection (1) above shall not apply where the existence of the dependent variety was common knowledge immediately before the coming into force of this Act.

GENERAL NOTE

This section extends the breeder's right in a protected variety to encompass a second variety dependent on it. The Plant Varieties and Seeds Act 1964 recognised that there is a form of dependency in production of hybrids, which can only be obtained through repeated use of parent lines. The concept of essential derivation is introduced to address developments in plant breeding technology.

It can take many years and a heavy financial investment to develop a commercially successful new variety using traditional breeding techniques. Newer techniques in plant breeding, or natural mutations, may result in very small changes to a protected variety in a relatively short time. The change may be only one characteristic of no commercial significance, but it may be freely commercialised in competition with the initial variety, without any acknowledgement of the contribution made by the latter. See also General Note to s.6.

Subs. (1)
  This sub-section extends the umbrella of protection in the initial variety to cover the essentially derived variety. In consequence, the breeder of the initial variety has the right to prevent anyone doing any of the acts in s.6 in respect of the essentially derived variety. In other words he can prevent its commercial exploitation.

Subs. (3)
  This sub-section provides that where the resultant change is sufficient to make the second variety distinct, but in all other respects the second variety expresses the same characteristics as the initial protected variety, then it may be essentially derived from the initial variety.

Exceptions

General exceptions

  8. Plant breeders' rights shall not extend to any act done—
  (a) for private and non-commercial purposes,
  (b) for experimental purposes, or
  (c) for the purpose of breeding another variety.

GENERAL NOTE
  This section enables the use of protected varieties for private or other non-commercial purposes, or for experiments or in a breeding programme. These are compulsory exceptions in the 1991 Convention; see Introduction and General Note. See also General Note to s.6.

Farm saved seed

  9.—(1) Subject to subsection (2) below, plant breeders' rights shall not extend to the use by a farmer for propagating purposes in the field, on his own holding, of the product of the harvest which he has obtained by planting on his own holding propagating material of—
  (a) the protected variety, or
  (b) a variety which is essentially derived from the protected variety.
  (2) Subsection (1) above only applies if the material is of a variety which is of a species or group specified for the purposes of this subsection by order made by the Ministers.
  (3) If a farmer's use of material is excepted from plant breeders' rights by subsection (1) above, he shall, at the time of the use, become liable to pay the holder of the rights equitable remuneration, which shall be sensibly lower than the amount charged for the production of propagating material of the same variety in the same area with the holder's authority.
  (4) Subsection (3) above shall not apply to a farmer who is considered to be a small farmer for the purposes of Article 14(3) third indent of the Council Regulation.
  (5) Subsection (3) above shall not apply if—
  (a) before the day on which this Part of this Act comes into force, the farmer has, in relation to the variety concerned, engaged in use of the kind to which subsection (1) above applies, and
  (b) no remuneration was payable in respect of that use.
  (6) The Ministers may by order provide that, on such date after 30th June 2001 as may be specified in the order, subsection (5) above shall cease to have effect in relation to a variety so specified, or varieties of a species or group so specified.
  (7) The Ministers may by regulations—
  (a) make provision enabling—
          (i) holders of plant breeders' rights to require farmers or seed processors, and
          (ii) farmers or seed processors to require holders of plant breeders' rights,

to supply such information as may be specified in the regulations, being information the supply of which the Ministers consider necessary for the purposes of this section,

(b) make provision restricting the circumstances in which the product of a harvest of a variety which is subject to plant breeders' rights may be moved, for the purpose of being processed for planting, from the holding on which it was obtained, and

(c) make provision for the purpose of enabling the Ministers to monitor the operation of any provision of this section or regulations under this section.

(8) Regulations under subsection (7)(a) above may include provision imposing obligations of confidence in relation to information supplied by virtue of the regulations.

(9) Subsections (3) and (4) of section 7 above shall apply for the purposes of subsection (1)(b) above as they apply for the purposes of subsection (2) of that section.

(10) For the purposes of subsection (3) above, remuneration shall be taken to be sensibly lower if it would be taken to be sensibly lower within the meaning of Article 14(3) fourth indent of the Council Regulation.

(11) In this section, references to a farmer's own holding are to any land which he actually exploits for plant growing, whether as his property or otherwise managed under his own responsibility and on his own account.

(12) The Ministers may by order amend this section as they think fit for the purpose of securing that it corresponds with the provisions for the time being of the law relating to Community plant variety rights about farm saved seed.

GENERAL NOTE

This section exempts from the breeder's right a farmer's use as seed, on his own holding, of harvested material obtained from the holding (i.e. the use of farm saved seed). This exemption is limited to species or groups prescribed by Ministers by order. Farmers who use farm saved seed of a protected variety are liable to pay the holder of rights equitable remuneration which is "sensibly lower" than the royalty payable on certified seed in the same area. Small farmers are exempt from this requirement.

Farmers who have saved seed of a particular variety before this Act comes into force may continue to do so, free of charge, until Ministers discontinue this exemption by Order. This clause also gives Ministers powers to make regulations providing for other matters relating to farm saved seed. A similar "prior use" exemption is in the Community regime. This expires on June 30, 2001, though the Council Regulation (Reg. E.C. 2100/94—see s.38(1)) makes it clear that this date is subject to review in the light of a report which the Commission is required to make before then, and may be extended on a variety, group or species basis, depending on the findings in the report.

Subs. (4)

In the case of arable crops, "a small farmer" is one who does not "grow plants on an area bigger than the area which would be needed to produce 92 tonnes of cereals". For the calculation of area, see Article 8(2) of Reg. E.C. 1765/92. In the case of other crops, "comparable appropriate criteria" apply.

Subs. (6)

It is the Government's intention to discontinue the prior use exemption at the same time as the corresponding provision in the Community regime is discontinued. This will not be before June 30, 2001, which means that the majority of farmers who have saved seed of older U.K. protected varieties before this Act comes into force may continue to do so free of charge until June 30, 2001.

Exhaustion of rights

10.—(1) Plant breeders' rights shall not extend to any act concerning material of a variety if the material—

(a) has been sold or otherwise marketed in the United Kingdom by, or with the consent of, the holder of the rights, or

(b) is derived from material which has been so sold or otherwise marketed.

(2) Subsection (1) above shall not apply where the act involves—

(a) further propagation of the variety, or

(b) the export of material which enables propagation of the variety to a non-qualifying country, otherwise than for the purposes of final consumption.

(3) For the purposes of subsection (2)(b) above, a non-qualifying country is one which does not provide for the protection of varieties of the genus or species to which the variety belongs.

(4) In this section, "material", in relation to a variety, means—

(a) any kind of propagating material of the variety,

(b) harvested material of the variety, including entire plants and parts of plants, and

(c) any product made directly from material falling within paragraph (b) above.

GENERAL NOTE

This section describes the circumstances in which plant breeders' rights are exhausted. See also General Note to s.6.

Duration and transmission of plant breeders' rights

Duration

11.—(1) A grant of plant breeders' rights shall have effect—

(a) in the case of potatoes, trees and vines, for 30 years from the date of the grant, and

(b) in other cases, for 25 years from that date.

(2) The Ministers may by regulations provide that, in relation to varieties of a species or group specified in the regulations, subsection (1) above shall have effect with the substitution in paragraph (a) or (b), as the case may be, of such longer period, not exceeding—

(a) in the case of paragraph (a), 35 years, and

(b) in the case of paragraph (b), 30 years,

as may be so specified.

(3) The period for which a grant of plant breeders' rights has effect shall not be affected by the fact it becomes impossible to invoke the rights—

(a) because of Article 92(2) of the Council Regulation (effect of subsequent grant of Community plant variety right), or

(b) because of suspension under section 23 below.

GENERAL NOTE

This section prescribes the duration of plant breeders' rights as 25 years, except for trees, vines and potatoes where rights are granted for 30 years. Ministers may by regulations extend the duration of rights for species or groups for up to five years.

Transmission

12. Plant breeders' rights shall be assignable like other kinds of proprietary rights, but in any case rights under section 6 above and rights under section 7 above may not be assigned separately.

GENERAL NOTE

This section provides for plant breeders' rights to be assignable like other proprietary rights.

Remedies for infringement

Remedies for infringement

13.—(1) Plant breeders' rights shall be actionable at the suit of the holder of the rights.

(2) In any proceedings for the infringement of plant breeders' rights, all such relief by way of damages, injunction, interdict, account or otherwise shall be available as is available in any corresponding proceedings in respect of infringements of other proprietary rights.

This section provides remedies for infringement.

Presumptions in proceedings relating to harvested material

14.—(1) This section applies to any proceedings for the infringement of plant breeders' rights as respects harvested material.

(2) If, in any proceedings to which this section applies, the holder of the plant breeders' rights proves, in relation to any of the material to which the proceedings relate—

    (a) that it has been the subject of an information notice given to the defendant by or on behalf of the holder, and

    (b) that the defendant has not, within the prescribed time after the service of the notice, supplied the holder with the information about it requested in the notice,

then, as regards the material in relation to which the holder proves that to be the case, the presumptions mentioned in subsection (3) below shall apply, unless the contrary is proved or the defendant shows that he had a reasonable excuse for not supplying the information.

(3) The presumptions are—

    (a) that the material was obtained through unauthorised use of propagating material, and

    (b) that the holder did not have a reasonable opportunity before the material was obtained to exercise his rights in relation to the unauthorised use of the propagating material.

(4) The reference in subsection (2) above to an information notice is to a notice which—

    (a) is in the prescribed form,

    (b) specifies the material to which it relates,

    (c) contains, in relation to that material, a request for the supply of the prescribed, but no other, information, and

    (d) contains such other particulars as may be prescribed.

(5) In this section, "prescribed" means prescribed by regulations made by the Ministers.

Presumptions in proceedings relating to products made from harvested material

15.—(1) This section applies to any proceedings for the infringement of plant breeders' rights as respects any product made directly from harvested material.

(2) If, in any proceedings to which this section applies, the holder of the plant breeders' rights proves, in relation to any product to which the proceedings relate—

    (a) that it has been the subject of an information notice given to the defendant by or on behalf of the holder, and

    (b) that the defendant has not, within the prescribed time after the service of the notice, supplied the holder with the information about it requested in the notice,

then, as regards the product in relation to which the holder proves that to be the case, the presumptions mentioned in subsection (3) below shall apply, unless the contrary is proved or the defendant shows that he had a reasonable excuse for not supplying the information.

(3) The presumptions are—

    (a) that the harvested material from which the product was made was obtained through unauthorised use of propagating material,

    (b) that the holder did not have a reasonable opportunity before the harvested material was obtained to exercise his rights in relation to the unauthorised use of the propagating material, and

(c) that no relevant act was done, before the product was made, as respects the harvested material from which it was made.

(4) An act is relevant for the purposes of subsection (3)(c) above if it is mentioned in section 6(1) above and is—

(a) done with the authority of the holder, or

(b) one in relation to the doing of which he has a reasonable opportunity to exercise his rights.

(5) The reference in subsection (2) above to an information notice is to a notice which—

(a) is in the prescribed form,

(b) specifies the product to which it relates,

(c) contains, in relation to that product, a request for the supply of the prescribed, but no other, information, and

(d) contains such other particulars as may be prescribed.

(6) In this section, "prescribed" means prescribed by regulations made by the Ministers.

Duties of holder of plant breeders' rights

Maintenance of protected variety

16.—(1) The holder of any plant breeders' rights shall ensure that, throughout the period for which the grant of the rights has effect, he is in a position to produce to the Controller propagating material which is capable of producing the protected variety.

(2) The holder of any plant breeders' rights shall give to the Controller, within such time as he may specify, all such information and facilities as he may request for the purpose of satisfying himself that the holder is fulfilling his duty under subsection (1) above.

(3) The facilities to be given under subsection (2) above include facilities for the inspection by or on behalf of the Controller of the measures taken for the preservation of the protected variety.

GENERAL NOTE

This section sets out the duty of a holder of plant breeders' rights to maintain the existence of a protected variety.

Compulsory licences

17.—(1) Subject to subsections (2) and (3) below, if the Controller is satisfied on application that the holder of any plant breeders' rights—

(a) has unreasonably refused to grant a licence to the applicant, or

(b) has imposed or put forward unreasonable terms in granting, or offering to grant, a licence to the applicant,

he may grant to the applicant in the form of a licence under this section any such rights as might have been granted by the holder.

(2) The Controller shall not grant an application for a licence under this section unless he is satisfied—

(a) that it is necessary to do so for the purpose of securing that the variety to which the application relates—

(i) is available to the public at reasonable prices,

(ii) is widely distributed, or

(iii) is maintained in quality,

(b) that the applicant is financially and otherwise in a position to exploit in a competent and businesslike manner the rights to be conferred on him, and

(c) that the applicant intends so to exploit those rights.

(3) A licence under this section shall not be an exclusive licence.

(4) A licence under this section shall be on such terms as the Controller thinks fit and, in particular, may include—

(a) terms as to the remuneration payable to the holder of the plant breeders' rights, and

(b) terms obliging the holder of the plant breeders' rights to make propagating material available to the holder of the licence.

(5) In deciding on what terms to grant an application for a licence under this section, the Controller shall have regard to the desirability of securing—

(a) that the variety to which the application relates—

(i) is available to the public at reasonable prices,

(ii) is widely distributed, and

(iii) is maintained in quality, and

(b) that there is reasonable remuneration for the holder of the plant breeders' rights to which the application relates.

(6) An application for a licence under this section may be granted whether or not the holder of the plant breeders' rights to which the application relates has granted licences to the applicant or any other person.

(7) If and so far as any agreement purports to bind any person not to apply for a licence under this section, it shall be void.

(8) If—

(a) a licence under this section is granted as respects a variety of a species or group in relation to which a period is specified for the purposes of this provision by regulations made by the Ministers, and

(b) the grant takes place before a period of that length has passed since the date of grant of the plant breeders' rights to which the licence relates, the licence shall not have effect until a period of that length has passed since that date.

(9) The Controller may, at any time, on the application of any person, extend, limit or in any other respect vary a licence under this section, or revoke it.

GENERAL NOTE

This section enables the Controller to issue a compulsory licence where he is satisfied that the holder of rights has unreasonably refused to grant a licence to an applicant, or has put forward or imposed unreasonable terms in offering or granting a licence. The Controller must be satisfied that it is in the public interest to issue a compulsory licence and that the applicant intends and is able to exploit the rights in the licence. The Controller sets the terms of a compulsory licence, taking account of the need both to make the variety available and to provide a reasonable return for the holder of the rights.

Naming of protected varieties

Selection and registration of names

18.—(1) The Ministers may by regulations—

(a) make provision for the selection of names for varieties which are the subject of applications for the grant of plant breeders' rights,

(b) make provision about change of name in relation to varieties in respect of which plant breeders' rights have been granted, and

(c) make provision for the keeping of a register of the names of varieties in respect of which plant breeders' rights have been granted.

(2) Regulations under subsection (1) above may, in particular—

(a) make provision enabling the Controller to require an applicant for the grant of plant breeders' rights to select a name for the variety to which the application relates,

(b) make provision enabling the Controller to require the holder of plant breeders' rights to select a different name for the protected variety,

(c) prescribe classes of variety for the purposes of the regulations,

(d) prescribe grounds on which the registration of a proposed name may be refused,

(e) prescribe the circumstances in which representations may be made regarding any decision as to the name to be registered in respect of any variety,

(f) make provision enabling the Controller—

(i) to refuse an application for the grant of plant breeders' rights, or

(ii) to terminate the period for which a grant of plant breeders' rights has effect,

if the applicant or holder fails to comply with a requirement imposed under the regulations,

(g) make provision for the publication or service of notices of decisions which the Controller proposes to take, and

(h) prescribe the times at which, and the circumstances in which, the register may be inspected by members of the public.

(3) The Controller shall publish notice of all entries made in the register, including alterations, corrections and erasures—

(a) in the gazette, and

(b) in such other manner as appears to the Controller to be convenient for the publication of these to all concerned.

(4) For the purposes of subsection (1) above, the variety in respect of which plant breeders' rights are granted is the protected variety.

GENERAL NOTE

This section provides for Ministers to make regulations laying down detailed requirements relating to the naming of varieties. It also provides for the publication of names and proposed names.

Duty to use registered name

19.—(1) Where a name is registered under section 18 above in respect of a variety, a person may not use any other name in selling, offering for sale or otherwise marketing propagating material of the variety.

(2) Subsection (1) above shall have effect in relation to any variety from the date on which plant breeders' rights in respect of that variety are granted, and shall continue to apply after the period for which the grant of those rights has effect.

(3) Subsection (1) above shall not preclude the use of any trade mark or trade name (whether registered under the Trade Marks Act 1994 or not) if—

(a) that mark or name and the registered name are juxtaposed, and

(b) the registered name is easily recognisable.

(4) A person who contravenes subsection (1) above shall be liable on summary conviction to a fine not exceeding level 3 on the standard scale.

(5) In any proceedings for an offence under subsection (4) above, it shall be a defence to prove that the accused took all reasonable precautions against committing the offence and had not at the time of the offence any reason to suspect that he was committing an offence.

GENERAL NOTE

This section imposes a duty to use the registered name in selling, offering for sale or otherwise marketing propagating material of a protected variety. Contravention is a criminal offence, for which a fine of up to £1,000 (on the scales in force at November 27, 1997) may be imposed.

Improper use of registered name

20.—(1) If any person uses the registered name of a protected variety in offering for sale, selling or otherwise marketing material of a different variety within the same class, the use of the name shall be a wrong actionable in proceedings by the holder of the rights.

(2) Subsection (1) above shall also apply to the use of a name so nearly resembling the registered name as to be likely to deceive or cause confusion.

(3) In any proceedings under this section, it shall be a defence to a claim for damages to prove that the defendant took all reasonable precautions against committing the wrong and had not, when using the name, any reason to suspect that it was wrongful.

(4) In this section—

"class" means a class prescribed for the purposes of regulations under section 18(1) above,

"registered name", in relation to a protected variety, means the name registered in respect of it under section 18 above.

GENERAL NOTE

This section makes it an infringement of plant breeders' rights to use the registered name of a protected variety in selling, offering for sale or otherwise marketing any material of another variety within the same, or a closely related, class or group as a protected variety.

Termination and suspension of plant breeders' rights

Nullity

21.—(1) The Controller shall declare the grant of plant breeders' rights null and void if it is established—

  (a) that when the rights were granted the protected variety did not meet the criterion specified in paragraph (a) or (d) of section 4(2) above,

  (b) where the grant of the rights was essentially based upon information and documents furnished by the applicant, that when the rights were granted the protected variety did not meet the criterion specified in paragraph (b) or (c) of that provision, or

  (c) that the person to whom the rights were granted was not the person entitled to the grant of the rights and the rights have not subsequently been transferred to him, or his successor in title.

(2) If, because of paragraph 6 of Schedule 2 to this Act, priority is established for an application for the grant of plant breeders' rights after such rights have been granted in pursuance of an application against which priority is established, subsection (1)(c) above shall only apply to the grant if the Controller decides that the application for which priority is established should be granted.

(3) Where the grant of plant breeders' rights is declared null and void under this section, it shall be deemed never to have had effect.

GENERAL NOTE

This section requires the Controller to declare a plant breeder's right null and void if it is subsequently established that the variety was not distinct or new at the time rights were granted, or that rights were granted to a person not entitled to them. The Controller must also declare rights null and void where uniformity or stability were established from information provided by the applicant which is subsequently shown to have been incorrect.

Cancellation

22.—(1) The Controller may terminate the period for which a grant of plant breeders' rights has effect if—

  (a) he is satisfied that the protected variety no longer meets the criterion specified in paragraph (b) or (c) of section 4(2) above,

  (b) it appears to him that the holder of the rights is no longer in a position to provide him with the propagating material mentioned in section 16(1) above,

  (c) he is satisfied that the holder of the rights has failed to comply with a request under section 16(2) above, or

  (d) on application by the holder of the rights, he is satisfied that the rights may properly be surrendered.

(2) Before determining an application under subsection (1)(d) above, the Controller shall—

(a) give notice of the application in the manner prescribed by regulations made by the Ministers, and

(b) follow the procedure so prescribed for hearing any person on whom the right to object is conferred by such regulations.

(3) If the Controller is satisfied, not only that the protected variety no longer meets the criterion specified in paragraph (b) or (c) of section 4(2) above, but also that it ceased to do so at some earlier date, he may make the termination retrospective to that date.

GENERAL NOTE

This section enables the Controller to terminate rights where the variety is no longer uniform or stable, or where the holder of rights is not able to comply with his duty to maintain the variety. The Controller may also terminate rights on application by the holder.

Suspension

23.—(1) The Controller may suspend the exercise of any plant breeders' rights if, on application by the holder of a licence under section 17 above, he is satisfied that the holder of the rights is in breach of any obligation imposed on him by the licence.

(2) The Controller shall terminate a suspension under subsection (1) above if, on application by the holder of the plant breeders' rights concerned, he is satisfied that the holder is no longer in breach of the obligation whose breach led to the suspension.

(3) Subsection (1) above is without prejudice to the remedies available to the holder of a licence under section 17 above by the taking of proceedings in any court.

GENERAL NOTE

This section enables the Controller to suspend plant breeders' rights where the holder of rights fails to comply with the terms of a compulsory licence.

Proceedings before the Controller

Right to be heard: general

24. The Ministers shall by regulations make provision for any decision of the Controller against which an appeal lies to the Tribunal to be made only after an opportunity of making representations to him, and of being heard by him or by a person appointed by him for the purpose, has been afforded—

(a) to the person entitled to appeal to the Tribunal against that decision, and

(b) to persons of such other descriptions as may be prescribed by the regulations.

GENERAL NOTE

This section enables Ministers to make regulations providing for rights to make representations to the Controller, or a person appointed by him, in the case of decisions where an appeal lies to the Plant Varieties and Seeds Tribunal.

Right to be heard: applications for compulsory licences

25.—(1) This section applies to an application for the grant of a licence under section 17 above if the holder of the plant breeders' rights to which the application relates is, or includes, or is represented by, a society or other organisation falling within subsection (2) below.

(2) A society or other organisation falls within this subsection if it has as its main object, or one of its main objects, the negotiation or granting of licences to exercise plant breeders' rights, either as the holder of the rights or as agent for holders.

(3) If—

(a) any organisation or person applies to the Controller for an opportunity of making representations concerning an application to which this section applies, and

(b) the Controller is satisfied that the conditions mentioned in subsection (4) below are met,

he shall afford to the organisation or person by whom the application under this subsection is made an opportunity of making representations to him and of being heard by him or by a person appointed by him for the purpose.

(4) The conditions referred to in subsection (3) above are—

(a) that the organisation or person has a substantial interest in the application for a licence under section 17 above,

(b) that that application involves issues which may affect other applications for licences under that section, and

(c) where the application under subsection (3) above is made by an organisation, that the organisation is reasonably representative of the class of persons which it claims to represent.

(5) The rights conferred by this section are in addition to any rights which may be conferred under section 24 above.

GENERAL NOTE

This section enables the Controller to hear representations on compulsory licence applications from interested parties other than the applicant where the holder of rights is, or is represented by, a trade or similar organisation.

Appeals to the Tribunal

26.—(1) An appeal shall lie to the Tribunal against the following decisions of the Controller—

(a) a decision to allow or refuse an application for the grant of plant breeders' rights,

(b) any decision preliminary to the determination of such an application as to the conditions laid down in section 4 above,

(c) a decision to allow or refuse an application under section 17(1) or (9) above,

(d) any decision under section 21 or 22(1)(a), (b) or (c) above,

(e) a decision to refuse an application under section 22(1)(d) above, and

(f) a decision to allow or refuse an application under section 23(1) or (2) above.

(2) The Ministers may by regulations confer a right of appeal to the Tribunal against—

(a) a decision of the Controller to refuse an application under section 25(3)(a) above, or

(b) any decision of the Controller under regulations made under section 18 above or section 28 or 29 below.

GENERAL NOTE

This section defines which decisions taken by the Controller can be appealed to the Plant Varieties and Seeds Tribunal. It also enables Ministers to make regulations prescribing other matters on which appeals may be made to the Tribunal.

Discharge of the Controller's functions

Ministerial guidance

27. The Controller shall, in exercising his functions, act under the general direction of the Ministers, except in relation to the taking of a decision from which an appeal lies to the Tribunal.

GENERAL NOTE

This section provides that the Controller is to act under the general direction of Ministers, except when taking decisions which can be appealed to the Tribunal.

Regulations

28.—(1) The Ministers may by regulations make such provision as they think fit as respects the manner in which the Controller is to discharge his functions under this Part of this Act, in particular as respects applications for the grant of plant breeders' rights and other applications to the Controller under this Part of this Act.

(2) Regulations under subsection (1) above may, in particular—

(a) make provision for restricting the making of repeated applications on the same subject,

(b) prescribe the circumstances in which representations may be made regarding any decision on an application or in connection with the charging of fees,

(c) make provision as to the keeping of registers and records by the Controller and their rectification, and prescribe the circumstances in which they may be inspected by members of the public,

(d) make provision for the publication or service of notice of applications and of the Controller's decisions,

(e) prescribe the manner of dealing with objections to applications.

GENERAL NOTE

This section provides for Ministers to make regulations concerning the way in which the Controller is to discharge his functions under this part of the Act.

Fees

29.—(1) The Ministers may make regulations as respects the charging of fees by the Controller, including periodical fees payable by persons holding plant breeders' rights.

(2) Regulations under subsection (1) above may authorise the Controller—

(a) in the case of a failure to pay any fees payable in connection with any application to him under this Part of this Act, to refuse the application, and

(b) in the case of a failure by a holder of plant breeders' rights to pay any fees payable in connection with those rights, to terminate the period for which the grant of those rights has effect;

and may provide for the restoration of the application or the rights if the failure to pay fees is made good.

GENERAL NOTE

This section enables Ministers by regulations to prescribe fees in respect of plant breeders' rights and authorise the Controller to refuse applications or terminate rights for non-payment of fees.

Use of outsiders

30. The Controller may use the services of persons who are not appointed as officers or servants of the Plant Variety Rights Office—

(a) in carrying out the tests and trials which he considers expedient for the purposes of this Part of this Act, and

(b) in assessing the results of any tests and trials (whether carried out by him or not) which he considers relevant for those purposes.

GENERAL NOTE

This section allows the Controller to use the services of people not employed by the Plant Variety Rights Office to do tests and trials on plant varieties.

False information and representations as to rights

False information

31.—(1) If any information to which this section applies is false in a material particular and the person giving the information knows that it is false or gives it recklessly, he shall be guilty of an offence and liable on summary conviction to a fine not exceeding level 3 on the standard scale.

(2) The information to which this section applies is—

(a) information given in an application to the Controller for a decision against which an appeal lies to the Tribunal,

(b) information given by or on behalf of the applicant in connection with such an application, and

(c) information given in pursuance of a request under section 16(2) above.

GENERAL NOTE

This section makes it an offence punishable by a fine of up to £1,000 (on the scales in force at November 27, 1997) to give false information in applications to the Controller for decisions against which an appeal may be submitted to the Plant Varieties and Seeds Tribunal. It is also an offence to give false information about whether a protected variety is being properly maintained in accordance with the requirements of s.16.

False representations as to rights

32.—(1) If, in relation to any variety, a person falsely represents that he is entitled to exercise plant breeders' rights, or any rights derived from such rights, and he knows that the representation is false, or makes it recklessly, he shall be guilty of an offence and liable on summary conviction to a fine not exceeding level 3 on the standard scale.

(2) It is immaterial for the purposes of subsection (1) above whether or not the variety to which the representation relates is the subject of plant breeders' rights.

GENERAL NOTE

This section makes it an offence punishable by a fine of up to £1,000 (on the scales in force at November 27, 1997) for a person to make a false claim that he is entitled to exercise plant breeders' rights.

Miscellaneous

Exclusion from Restrictive Trade Practices Act 1976

33. The Restrictive Trade Practices Act 1976 shall not apply—

(a) to any licence granted by the holder of plant breeders' rights or by any other person authorised to grant a licence in respect of such rights,

(b) to any assignment of plant breeders' rights or of the title to apply for the grant of such rights, or

(c) to any agreement for such a licence or assignment,

being a licence, assignment or agreement under which no such restrictions as are described in section 6(1) of that Act are accepted, except in respect of goods which are plants or parts of plants of a variety to which the plant breeders' rights relate, or a variety to which those rights will relate if they are granted.

GENERAL NOTE

This section exempts plant breeders' rights, licences and assignments from the provisions of the Restrictive Trade Practices Act 1976.

Disclosure of information obtained under section 14 or 15

34.—(1) If the holder of plant breeders' rights obtains information pursuant to a notice given for the purposes of section 14 or 15 above, he shall owe an obligation of confidence in respect of the information to the person who supplied it.

(2) Subsection (1) above shall not have effect to restrict disclosure of information—

(a) for the purposes of, or in connection with, establishing whether plant breeders' rights have been infringed, or

(b) for the purposes of, or in connection with, any proceedings for the infringement of plant breeders' rights.

Reference collections of plant material

35.—(1) The Controller may establish and maintain reference collections of plant material.

(2) The Controller may by means of grants of such amounts as he may determine defray or contribute towards the expenses incurred by any other person in maintaining any reference collection of plant material.

GENERAL NOTE

This section allows the Controller to establish and maintain reference collections of plant material and to contribute to the expenses of other persons who maintain reference collections.

General

Offences by bodies corporate, etc.

36.—(1) Where an offence under this Part of this Act committed by a body corporate is proved to have been committed with the consent or connivance of, or to be attributable to any neglect on the part of, any director, manager, secretary or other similar officer of the body corporate, or any person who was purporting to act in any such capacity, he, as well as the body corporate, shall be guilty of the offence and liable to be proceeded against and punished accordingly.

(2) Where an offence under this Part of this Act committed by a Scottish partnership is proved to have been committed with the consent or connivance of, or to be attributable to any neglect on the part of, a partner, he, as well as the partnership, shall be guilty of the offence and liable to be proceeded against and punished accordingly.

GENERAL NOTE

This section provides that where an offence is committed by a corporate body with the consent of a director, secretary or similar officer, or can be attributed to negligence by that person, the individual as well as the corporate body is guilty of the offence and can be punished accordingly.

Jurisdiction in relation to offences

37.—(1) Proceedings for an offence under this Part of this Act may be taken against a person before the appropriate court in the United Kingdom having jurisdiction in the place where that person is for the time being.

(2) Subsection (1) above is without prejudice to any jurisdiction exercisable apart from that subsection.

GENERAL NOTE

This section allows proceedings to be brought in whichever part of the United Kingdom the accused person is.

Interpretation of Part I

38.—(1) In this Part of this Act—

"the Council Regulation" means Council Regulation (EC) No 2100/94 of 27th July 1994 on Community plant variety rights, and references to particular provisions of the Council Regulation shall be construed as references to those provisions, or provisions of any Community instrument replacing them, as amended from time to time;

"gazette" means the gazette published under section 34 of the Plant Varieties and Seeds Act 1964;

"name" includes any designation;

"protected variety", in relation to any plant breeders' rights, means the variety which was the basis of the application for the grant of the rights;

"variety" has the meaning given by section 1(3) above.

(2) In this Part of this Act references to an applicant for the grant of plant breeders' rights, or to the holder of plant breeders' rights, include, where the context allows, references to his predecessors in title or his successors in title.

(3) For the purposes of this Part of this Act, the existence of a variety shall be taken to be a matter of common knowledge if—

(a) it is, or has been, the subject of a plant variety right under any jurisdiction,

(b) it is, or has been, entered in an official register of plant varieties under any jurisdiction, or

(c) it is the subject of an application which subsequently leads to its falling within paragraph (a) or (b) above.

(4) Otherwise, common knowledge may be established for those purposes by reference, for example, to—

(a) plant varieties already in cultivation or exploited for commercial purposes,

(b) plant varieties included in a recognised commercial or botanical reference collection, or

(c) plant varieties of which there are precise descriptions in any publication.

Application of Part I to the Crown

39.—(1) If—

(a) any servant or agent of the Crown infringes any plant breeders' rights or makes himself liable to civil proceedings under section 20 above, and

(b) the infringement or wrong is committed with the authority of the Crown,

civil proceedings in respect of the infringement or wrong shall lie against the Crown.

(2) Except as provided by subsection (1) above, no proceedings shall lie against the Crown by virtue of the Crown Proceedings Act 1947 in respect of the infringement of plant breeders' rights or any wrong under section 20 above.

(3) This section shall have effect as if contained in Part I of the Crown Proceedings Act 1947.

GENERAL NOTE

This section defines the extent to which the Act applies to the Crown.

Application of Part I to existing rights

40.—(1) Subject to the following provisions of this section, this Part of this Act applies in relation to existing rights as it applies in relation to plant breeders' rights granted under this Part of this Act.

(2) Section 5 above shall not apply in relation to existing rights.

(3) Section 11 above shall only apply to existing rights if the effect is to extend the period for which the rights are exercisable.

(4) In this section, "existing rights" means plant breeders' rights granted under Part I of the Plant Varieties and Seeds Act 1964 which are exercisable on the coming into force of this Part of this Act.

This section applies the Act to plant breeders' rights granted under the Plant Varieties and Seeds Act 1964.

Transition

Varieties of recent creation

41.—(1) This section applies where, before the end of the period of 12 months beginning with the day on which this Part of this Act comes into force, an application for the grant of plant breeders' rights is made in respect of a variety—

(a) which was in existence on the coming into force of this Part of this Act,

(b) which is of a species or group which was not, immediately before the coming into force of this Part of this Act, prescribed by a scheme under Part I of the Plant Varieties and Seeds Act 1964 (grant of plant breeders' rights), and

(c) to which paragraph 4(2) of Schedule 2 to this Act does not apply.

(2) The variety to which the application relates shall, for the purposes of section 4(2) above, be deemed to be new if no sale or other disposal of propagating or harvested material of the variety for the purposes of exploiting the variety has, with the consent of the applicant, taken place earlier than 4 years, or, in the case of trees or vines, 6 years, before the day on which this Part of this Act comes into force.

(3) Paragraph 4(4) and (10) of Schedule 2 to this Act shall also apply for the purposes of subsection (2) above.

(4) If plant breeders' rights are granted by virtue of this section, the period for which the grant of those rights has effect shall be reduced by the period before the application since the first date on which a sale or other disposal of propagating or harvested material of the variety for the purposes of exploiting the variety took place in the United Kingdom with the consent of the applicant, less one year.

GENERAL NOTE
This section enables applications for a grant of rights to be considered for varieties of recent creation. These are varieties which have been exploited for up to 4 years (6 years for trees and vines) in the United Kingdom and which would otherwise not meet the requirement in s.4 that they must be new. In order to qualify, a variety must be of a species or group which was not offered protection under the Plant Varieties and Seeds Act 1964 and the application for rights must be submitted within a year of Part I of the Act coming into force.

PART II

THE PLANT VARIETIES AND SEEDS TRIBUNAL

The Tribunal

42.—(1) There shall continue to be a tribunal known as the Plant Varieties and Seeds Tribunal ("the Tribunal").

(2) Schedule 3 to this Act (which makes provision about the Tribunal) shall have effect.

GENERAL NOTE
Ss.42–46 provide for the continued existence of the Plant Varieties and Seeds Tribunal and define its jurisdiction. Ministers are given powers to make regulations about appeals. Matters of detail are laid down in Schedule 3 which prescribes such matters as the constitution and membership of the Tribunal, where it may sit and how it makes decisions and awards costs. Schedule 3

also provides for the Lord Chancellor to make rules of procedure in connection with proceedings before the Tribunal.

Jurisdiction under arbitration agreements

43.—(1) The Tribunal shall hear and determine any matters agreed to be referred to the Tribunal by any arbitration agreement relating to the infringement of plant breeders' rights, or to matters which include the infringement of plant breeders' rights.

(2) The fees payable to the Tribunal for acting under any arbitration agreement shall be such as the Tribunal may determine.

(3) Nothing in section 4 of the Arbitration (Scotland) Act 1894 (power to name oversman) shall be taken as applying to the Tribunal.

(4) In the application of this section to England and Wales or Northern Ireland, "arbitration agreement" has the same meaning as in Part I of the Arbitration Act 1996.

GENERAL NOTE
See General Note to s.42.

Statutory jurisdiction: regulations

44. The Ministers may, as respects appeals to the Tribunal under their statutory jurisdiction, by regulations—
  (a) make provision for determining in which part of the United Kingdom an appeal is to be heard,
  (b) make provision authorising persons other than the person by whom an appeal is made and the authority whose decision is appealed against to appear and be heard as parties to the appeal,
  (c) make provision for suspending, or authorising or requiring the suspension of, the operation of a decision pending final determination of an appeal against it, or
  (d) make provision for the publication of notices or the taking of other steps for securing that the persons affected by the suspension of the operation of a decision appealed against will be informed of its supension.

GENERAL NOTE
See General Note to s.42.

Appeals from the Tribunal

45.—(1) In relation to any decision of the Tribunal on an appeal under their statutory jurisdiction, section 11 of the Tribunals and Inquiries Act 1992 (appeal on point of law) shall apply as if the Tribunal were included among the tribunals mentioned in subsection (1) of that section.

(2) Subject to any right of appeal by virtue of subsection (1) above, any decision of the Tribunal on an appeal under their statutory jurisdiction shall be final and conclusive.

GENERAL NOTE
See General Note to s.42.

Interpretation of Part II

46. In this Part of this Act, references to the statutory jurisdiction of the Tribunal are to any jurisdiction of the Tribunal under Part I of this Act, Part

II of the Plant Varieties and Seeds Act 1964 or the Seeds Act (Northern Ireland) 1965.

GENERAL NOTE
See General Note to s.42.

PART III

MISCELLANEOUS AND GENERAL

Miscellaneous

Extension of time limit for institution of proceedings for contravention of seeds regulations

47. In section 28 of the Plant Varieties and Seeds Act 1964 (institution of criminal proceedings), after subsection (2) there shall be inserted—

"(2A) Notwithstanding anything in section 127(1) of the Magistrates' Courts Act 1980 or section 136 of the Criminal Procedure (Scotland) Act 1995, proceedings for contravening a provision contained in seeds regulations may be brought at any time not more than one year from the time when the contravention occurred."

GENERAL NOTE
This section amends the Plant Varieties and Seeds Act 1964 to extend the time limit for bringing proceedings for contravention of seeds regulations from 6 to 12 months. The section does not apply to Northern Ireland.

General

Regulations and orders

48.—(1) Any regulations or order under this Act made by the Ministers—
(a) may make different provision for different cases or circumstances, and
(b) may contain such supplemental, incidental and transitional provisions as appear to the Ministers to be expedient.

(2) Any regulations or order under this Act made by the Ministers shall be made by statutory instrument.

(3) A statutory instrument containing any regulations or order under this Act made by the Ministers, other than an order under section 9(12) above, shall be subject to annulment in pursuance of a resolution of either House of Parliament.

(4) No order shall be made under section 9(12) above unless a draft of the order has been laid before and approved by resolution of each House of Parliament.

(5) Before making any regulations or order under this Act, the Ministers shall consult such organisations as appear to them to be representative of persons likely to be substantially affected by the regulations or order.

(6) Nothing in this section applies to an order under section 54(3) below.

General interpretation

49.—(1) In this Act—
"the Controller" has the meaning given by section 2(1) above;
"the Ministers" means the Minister of Agriculture, Fisheries and Food, the Secretary of State for Scotland, the Secretary of State for Wales and the Secretary of State for Northern Ireland acting jointly; and

"the Tribunal" has the meaning given by section 42 above.

(2) In this Act, references to plant breeders' rights include rights under section 7 above.

Receipts

50. Any fees received by virtue of this Act by the Controller or the Tribunal shall be paid into the Consolidated Fund.

Consequential amendments

51.—(1) In section 34 of the Plant Varieties and Seeds Act 1964—

(a) in subsection (1), at the end there shall be inserted "or Part I of the Plant Varieties Act 1997", and

(b) in subsection (2), for "section 5 of this Act" there shall be substituted "section 18 of the Plant Varieties Act 1997".

(2) In section 38 of that Act, for the definition of the expression "the Tribunal" there shall be substituted—

""the Tribunal" means the Plant Varieties and Seeds Tribunal;".

(3) In Schedule 4 to the Parliamentary Commissioner Act 1967, in the entry relating to the Plant Varieties and Seeds Tribunal, for the words after "Tribunal" there shall be substituted "(referred to in section 42 of the Plant Varieties Act 1997)".

(4) In section 2(4) of the Trade Descriptions Act 1968, after paragraph (g) there shall be inserted—

"(h) the Plant Varieties Act 1997;".

(5) In Schedule 1 to the Tribunals and Inquiries Act 1992, in paragraph 36—

(a) in sub-paragraph (a), for "section 11(5) of the Plant Varieties and Seeds Act 1964 (c. 14)" there shall be substituted "paragraph 3 of Schedule 1 to the Plant Varieties Act 1997", and

(b) in sub-paragraph (b), for "established by section 10 of that Act" there shall be substituted "(referred to in section 42 of that Act)".

Repeals

52. The enactments mentioned in Schedule 4 to this Act are hereby repealed to the extent specified in the third column of that Schedule.

Extent

53.—(1) This Act, except section 47 above, extends to Northern Ireland.

(2) Her Majesty may by Order in Council direct that any of the provisions of this Act shall, subject to such modifications as appear to Her Majesty to be appropriate, extend to any of the Channel Islands or the Isle of Man.

(3) An Order in Council under subsection (2) above may contain such transitional and consequential provisions as appear to Her Majesty to be expedient.

Short title and commencement

54.—(1) This Act may be cited as the Plant Varieties Act 1997.

(2) This section and sections 49 and 53 above shall come into force on the day on which this Act is passed.

(3) The remaining provisions of this Act shall come into force on such day as the Ministers may by order made by statutory instrument appoint; and different days may be so appointed for different purposes.

(4) An order under subsection (3) above may contain such transitional provisions and savings as appear to the Ministers to be expedient.

Subs. (2)
The Act received Royal Assent in November 1997.

SCHEDULES

Section 2   SCHEDULE 1

THE PLANT VARIETY RIGHTS OFFICE

Staff

1. The Ministers may appoint a deputy controller and such other officers and servants to act in the Plant Variety Rights Office as the Ministers may determine.

Remuneration

2. There shall be paid to the Controller and any other officers or servants appointed under paragraph 1 above such remuneration and allowances as the Ministers may with the consent of the Minister for the Civil Service determine.

Authority of officers

3. Any act or thing directed to be done by or to the Controller may be done by or to any officer authorised by the Ministers.

Proof of documents

4. Prima facie evidence, or in Scotland sufficient evidence, of any document issued by the Controller may be given in all legal proceedings by the production of a copy or extract certified to be a true copy or extract by an officer appointed under paragraph 1 above and authorised to give a certificate under this paragraph.

5. Any document purporting to be certified in accordance with paragraph 4 above shall, unless the contrary is proved, be deemed to have been duly certified without proof of the official character or handwriting of the person appearing to have certified the document.

Section 4   SCHEDULE 2

CONDITIONS FOR THE GRANT OF PLANT BREEDERS' RIGHTS

PART I

CRITERIA FOR GRANT OF RIGHTS

Distinctness

1. The variety shall be deemed to be distinct if it is clearly distinguishable by one or more characteristics which are capable of a precise description from any other variety whose existence is a matter of common knowledge at the time of the application.

Uniformity

2. The variety shall be deemed to be uniform if, subject to the variation that may be expected from the particular features of its propagation, it is sufficiently uniform in those characteristics which are included in the examination for distinctness.

Stability

3. The variety shall be deemed to be stable if those characteristics which are included in the examination for distinctness, as well as any others used for the variety description, remain unchanged after repeated propagation or, in the case of a particular cycle of propagation, at the end of each such cycle.

Novelty

4.—(1) The variety shall be deemed to be new if sub-paragraphs (2) and (3) below apply.
(2) This sub-paragraph applies if no sale or other disposal of propagating or harvested

material of the variety for the purposes of exploiting the variety has, with the consent of the applicant, taken place in the United Kingdom earlier than one year before the date of the application.

(3) This sub-paragraph applies if no sale or other disposal of propagating or harvested material of the variety for the purposes of exploiting the variety has, with the consent of the applicant, taken place elsewhere than in the United Kingdom earlier than 4 years, or, in the case of trees or vines, 6 years, before the date of the application.

(4) For the purposes of sub-paragraphs (2) and (3) above, there shall be disregarded any sale or other disposal to which sub-paragraph (5), (6), (8) or (9) below applies.

(5) This sub-paragraph applies to any sale or other disposal of a stock of material of the variety to a person who at the time of the sale or other disposal is, or who subsequently becomes, the person entitled to the grant of plant breeders' rights in respect of the variety.

(6) This sub-paragraph applies to—
(a) any sale or other disposal of propagating material of the variety to a person as part of qualifying arrangements, and
(b) any sale or other disposal to the applicant, by a person who uses propagating material of the variety under any such arrangements, of the material produced directly or indirectly from the use.

(7) For the purposes of sub-paragraph (6) above, qualifying arrangements are arrangements under which—
(a) a person uses propagating material of the variety under the applicant's control for the purpose of increasing the applicant's stock, or of carrying out tests or trials, and
(b) the whole of the material produced, directly or indirectly, from the material becomes or remains the property of the applicant.

(8) This sub-paragraph applies to any sale or other disposal of material of the variety, other than propagating material, produced in the course of—
(a) the breeding of the variety,
(b) increasing the applicant's stock of material of the variety, or
(c) carrying out tests or trials of the variety,
which does not involve identifying the variety from which the material is produced.

(9) This sub-paragraph applies to any disposal of material of the variety, otherwise than by way of sale, at an exhibition or for the purposes of display at an exhibition.

(10) For the purposes of sub-paragraphs (2) and (3) above, any sale or other disposal of propagating or harvested material of a variety for the purposes of exploiting the variety shall, if the variety is related to another variety, be treated as being also a sale or other disposal of propagating or harvested material of the other variety for the purposes of exploiting that variety.

(11) For the purposes of sub-paragraph (10) above, a variety is related to another if its nature is such that repeated production of the variety is not possible without repealed use of the other variety.

PART II

PRIORITIES BETWEEN APPLICANTS FOR RIGHTS

5.—(1) If a variety is bred, or discovered and developed, by two or more persons independently, the first of those persons, and any successors in title of theirs, to apply for the grant of plant breeders' rights in respect of it shall be the person entitled to the grant.

(2) As between persons making applications for the grant of plant breeders' rights in respect of the same variety on the same date, the one who was first in a position to make an application for the grant of plant breeders' rights in respect of that variety, or who would have been first in that position if this Part of this Act had always been in force, shall be the person entitled to the grant.

6.—(1) If the following conditions are met, an application for the grant of plant breeders' rights shall be treated for the purposes of paragraphs 1, 4 and 5 above as made, not on the date on which it is in fact made, but on the earlier date mentioned in sub-paragraph (7) below.

(2) The first condition is that, in the 12 months immediately preceding the application under this Part of this Act, the applicant has duly made a parallel application under the law of—
(a) the European Community,
(b) any other intergovernmental organisation, or any State, which is, and was at the time of the application, a member of the Union as defined by Article 1(xi) of the Convention, or
(c) any country or territory which is, and was at the time of the application, designated for the purposes of this provision by order made by the Ministers.

(3) The second condition is that the applicant has not duly made such a parallel application earlier than 12 months before the application under this Part of this Act.

(4) The third condition is that the application under this Part of this Act includes a claim to priority under this paragraph by reference to the parallel application.

(5) The fourth condition is that the application by reference to which priority is claimed has not been withdrawn or refused when the application under this Part of this Act is made.

(6) The fifth condition is that, within 3 months from the date of the application under this Part of this Act, the applicant submits to the Controller a copy of the documents constituting the parallel application, certified as a true copy by the authority to whom it is made.

(7) The earlier date referred to in sub-paragraph (1) above is the date of the parallel application mentioned in sub-paragraph (2) above.

(8) If more than one parallel application has been duly made as mentioned in sub-paragraph (2) above, the references in sub-paragraphs (4) to (7) above to the parallel application shall be construed as references to the earlier, or earliest, of the applications.

(9) In this paragraph—

(a) "the Convention" means the International Convention for the Protection of New Varieties of Plants done on 2nd December 1961 and revised at Geneva on 10th November 1972, 23rd October 1978 and 19th March 1991, and

(b) references to a parallel application, in relation to an application for the grant of plant breeders' rights, are to an application for the grant of plant variety rights in respect of the variety to which the application under this Part of this Act relates.

7.—(1) Any priority which an application for the grant of plant breeders' rights enjoys by virtue of paragraph 6 above shall be forfeited if the applicant does not, before the end of the relevant period, satisfy all the requirements which are to be satisfied by an applicant before plant breeders' rights can be granted to him.

(2) For the purposes of sub-paragraph (1) above, the relevant period is the period of 2 years beginning with the day after the last day on which the applicant could have claimed priority under paragraph 6 above for his application.

(3) Where—

(a) an application for the grant of plant breeders' rights enjoys priority by virtue of paragraph 6 above, and

(b) the application by reference to which it enjoys priority is withdrawn or refused before the applicant has satisfied all the requirements which are to be satisfied by an applicant before plant breeders' rights can be granted to him,

sub-paragraph (1) above shall have effect with the substitution for "the relevant period" of "such period as the Controller may specify".

Section 42   SCHEDULE 3

THE PLANT VARIETIES AND SEEDS TRIBUNAL

Constitution of the Tribunal

1. In any case, the jurisdiction of the Tribunal shall be exercised by—

(a) the relevant chairman,

(b) a member of the panel constituted under paragraph 7(1)(a) below, and

(c) a member of the panel constituted under paragraph 7(1)(b) below;

and references to the Tribunal in this Act or the Plant Varieties and Seeds Act 1964 shall be construed accordingly.

Chairman

2.—(1) The Lord Chancellor shall appoint a person to be chairman of the Tribunal for the purpose of proceedings brought before them in England and Wales.

(2) A person may only be appointed under this paragraph if he has a seven year general qualification, within the meaning of section 71 of the Courts and Legal Services Act 1990.

3.—(1) The Lord President of the Court of Session shall appoint a person to be chairman of the Tribunal for the purpose of proceedings brought before them in Scotland.

(2) A person may only be appointed under this paragraph if he is an advocate or solicitor in Scotland of at least 7 years' standing.

4.—(1) The Lord Chief Justice of Northern Ireland shall appoint a person to be chairman of the Tribunal for the purpose of proceedings brought before them in Northern Ireland.

(2) A person may only be appointed under this paragraph if he is a member of the Bar of Northern Ireland or solicitor of the Supreme Court of Northern Ireland of at least 7 years' standing.

5.—(1) Subject to sub-paragraph (2) below, a person's appointment under paragraph 2, 3 or 4 above shall be for such term as the appointing authority may determine before the person's appointment.

(2) No appointment of a person under paragraph 2, 3 or 4 above shall be such as to extend beyond the day on which he attains the age of 70.

(3) A person who ceases to hold office under paragraph 2, 3 or 4 above shall be eligible for re-appointment.

(4) A person may resign his appointment under paragraph 2, 3 or 4 above by notice in writing to the appointing authority.

(5) The appointing authority may revoke a person's appointment under paragraph 2, 3 or 4 above if satisfied that the person is unfit to continue in office or incapable of discharging his duties.

(6) Sub-paragraph (2) above is subject to section 26(4) to (6) of the Judicial Pensions and Retirement Act 1993 (power to authorise continuance in office up to the age of 75).

6.—(1) In the case of the temporary absence or inability to act of a person appointed under paragraph 2, 3 or 4 above, the appointing authority may appoint another person to act as deputy for that person.

(2) A person may only be appointed to act as deputy for a person appointed under paragraph 2, 3 or 4 above if he has the qualification required for appointment under that paragraph.

(3) A person appointed under sub-paragraph (1) above shall, when acting as deputy for a person appointed under paragraph 2, 3 or 4 above, have all the functions of that person.

The two panels

7.—(1) The Ministers shall draw up and from time to time revise—

(a) a panel of persons who have wide general knowledge in the field of agriculture, of horti-culture or of forestry, and

(b) a panel of persons who have specialised knowledge of particular species or groups of plants or of the seeds industry.

(2) The power to revise the panels drawn up under this paragraph shall include power to terminate a person's membership of either of them, and shall accordingly to that extent be sub-ject to section 7 of the Tribunals and Inquiries Act 1992 (which makes it necessary to obtain the concurrence of the Lord Chancellor and of certain judicial officers in Scotland and Northern Ireland to dismissals in certain cases).

Selection from the panels

8.—(1) The members of the panels who are to deal with any case shall be selected as follows—

(a) the Ministers may select a member or members to deal with that particular case or class or group of cases, or

(b) the Ministers may select for a class or group of cases members from amongst whom mem-bers to deal with any particular case shall be selected, and the selection from amongst those members of a member or members to deal with the particular case shall then be made either by the Ministers, or, if they so direct, by the relevant chairman.

(2) The member from the panel constituted under paragraph 7(1)(b) above shall be selected for his knowledge of the subject matter of a particular case or class or group of cases.

Sittings of the Tribunal

9. The Tribunal may, for the purpose of hearing proceedings brought before them in any part of the United Kingdom, sit anywhere in the United Kingdom.

Decisions of the Tribunal

10.—(1) Any decision of the Tribunal in exercise of their jurisdiction shall be taken, in the event of a difference between members dealing with the case, by the votes of the majority.

(2) If, after the commencement of the hearing of any proceedings before the Tribunal, one of the three members of the Tribunal becomes incapable of continuing to hear the proceedings on account of sickness or for any other reason, the proceedings may, with the consent of all parties to the proceedings, be continued before the remaining two members of the Tribunal and heard and determined accordingly.

(3) If, in the case of proceedings continued under sub-paragraph (2) above, the two members differ in opinion, the case shall, on the application of any party to the proceedings, be re-argued and determined by the Tribunal as ordinarily constituted.

(4) A decision of the Tribunal shall not be questioned on the ground that a member was not validly appointed or selected.

Costs

11.—(1) In any proceedings brought before the Tribunal in England and Wales or Northern Ireland under their statutory jurisdiction, the Tribunal may order any party to the proceedings to pay to any other party to the proceedings—
  (a) a specified sum in respect of the costs incurred in the proceedings by the second-mentioned party, or
  (b) the taxed amount of those costs.

(2) In the case of an order under sub-paragraph (1) above relating to proceedings brought in England and Wales, any costs required by the order to be taxed may be taxed in the county court according to such of the scales prescribed by the county court rules for proceedings in the county court as may be directed by the order or, if the order gives no direction, by the county court.

(3) In the case of any order under sub-paragraph (1) above relating to proceedings brought in Northern Ireland, any costs required by the order to be taxed may be taxed by the taxing master of the Supreme Court of Judicature of Northern Ireland according to such of the scales provided for equity suits or proceedings in the county courts under the County Courts (Northern Ireland) Order 1980 as may be directed by the order or, if the order gives no direction, by the taxing master.

12. In any proceedings brought before the Tribunal in Scotland under their statutory jurisdiction, the Tribunal may order any party to the proceedings to pay to any other party to the proceedings any expenses incurred in the proceedings by the second-mentioned party and may tax or settle the amount of any expenses to be paid under any such order or direct in what manner they are to be taxed.

Rules

13.—(1) The Lord Chancellor may make rules as to the procedure in connection with proceedings brought before the Tribunal in exercise of their statutory jurisdiction and as to the fees chargeable in respect of those proceedings, and the rules may in particular make provision—
  (a) as to the circumstances in which the Tribunal need not sit, or are not to sit, in public,
  (b) as to the form of any decision of the Tribunal,
  (c) as to the time within which any proceedings are to be instituted,
  (d) as to the evidence which may be required or admitted in any proceedings,
  (e) as to the examination of the parties, and of witnesses, on oath or affirmation in any proceedings,
  (f) as to the procedure for securing the attendance of witnesses and the production of documents in any proceedings.

(2) Rules under sub-paragraph (1) above shall be made by statutory instrument which shall be subject to annulment in pursuance of a resolution of either House of Parliament.

Remuneration of Tribunal members

14. The Ministers may pay to members of the Tribunal such remuneration and allowances as the Ministers may determine.

Officers and servants

15.—(1) The Ministers may appoint such officers and servants of the Tribunal as the Ministers may determine.

(2) There shall be paid to the officers and servants appointed under this paragraph such remuneration and allowances as the Ministers may determine.

Interpretation

16. In this Schedule—
  "appointing authority" means—
      (a) in relation to an appointment under paragraph 2 above, the Lord Chancellor,
      (b) in relation to an appointment under paragraph 3 above, the Lord President of the Court of Session, and
      (c) in relation to an appointment under paragraph 4 above, the Lord Chief Justice of Northern Ireland; and
  "relevant chairman" means—
      (a) in relation to proceedings brought before the Tribunal in England and Wales, the person appointed under paragraph 2 above,

(b) in relation to proceedings brought before the Tribunal in Scotland, the person appointed under paragraph 3 above, and

(c) in relation to proceedings brought before the Tribunal in Northern Ireland, the person appointed under paragraph 4 above.

Section 52   SCHEDULE 4

REPEALS

Chapter	Short Title	Extent of repeal
1964 c. 14.	The Plant Varieties and Seeds Act 1964.	Part I. In section 37, in subsection (1), paragraphs (a) to (c), and, in subsection (2), the words "or the Controller or the Tribunal". In section 38(1), the definitions of the expressions "the Controller", "plant variety" and "variety". In section 39, in subsection (2), paragraph (a) and the word "and" immediately following it, and subsection (3)(b). Schedules 1 to 4.
1968 c. 34.	The Agriculture (Miscellaneous Provisions) Act 1968.	Section 43. Schedule 7.
1972 c. 68.	The European Communities Act 1972.	In Schedule 4, paragraph 5(5).
1976 c. 34.	The Restrictive Trade Practices Act 1976.	In Schedule 5, the third paragraph.
1976 c. 53.	The Resale Prices Act 1976.	In section 10(4)(b), the words from "or" to the end.
1983 c. 17.	The Plant Varieties Act 1983.	The whole Act.
1990 c. 41.	The Courts and Legal Services Act 1990.	In Schedule 10, paragraph 21.
1992 c. 53.	The Tribunals and Inquiries Act 1992.	In Schedule 3, paragraph 2.
1993 c. 8.	The Judicial Pensions and Retirement Act 1993.	In Schedule 6, paragraph 54.
1994 c. 26.	The Trade Marks Act 1994.	In Schedule 4, in the table in paragraph 1(2), the entry relating to the Plant Varieties and Seeds Act 1964.
1996 c. 23.	The Arbitration Act 1996.	In Schedule 3, paragraph 18.

INDEX

References are to sections and Schedules

CONSOLIDATED FUND (NO. 2) ACT 1997

(1997 c. 67)

An Act to apply certain sums out of the Consolidated Fund to the service of the years ending on 31st March 1998 and 1999.   [17th December 1997]

PARLIAMENTARY DEBATES
Hansard, H.C. Vol. 302, col. 907 (2R, 3R). H.L. Vol. 584, cols. 151 (1R), 503 (2R, rem.).

INTRODUCTION
   This Act makes provision for the application of £634,729,000 from the Consolidated Fund for the service of the year ending on March 31, 1998 and for the application of £97,354,245,000 for the service of the year ending on March 31, 1999.

Most Gracious Sovereign,

   We, Your Majesty's most dutiful and loyal subjects, the Commons of the United Kingdom in Parliament assembled, towards making good the supply which we have cheerfully granted to Your Majesty in this Session of Parliament, have resolved to grant unto Your Majesty the sums hereinafter mentioned; and do therefore most humbly beseech Your Majesty that it may be enacted, and be it enacted by the Queen's most Excellent Majesty, by and with the advice and consent of the Lords Spiritual and Temporal, and Commons, in this present Parliament assembled, and by the authority of the same, as follows:—

Issue out of the Consolidated Fund for the year ending 31st March 1998

   1. The Treasury may issue out of the Consolidated Fund of the United Kingdom and apply towards making good the supply granted to Her Majesty for the service of the year ending on 31st March 1998 the sum of £634,729,000.

Issue out of the Consolidated Fund for the year ending 31st March 1999

   2. The Treasury may issue out of the Consolidated Fund of the United Kingdom and apply towards making good the supply granted to Her Majesty for the service of the year ending on 31st March 1999 the sum of £97,354,245,000.

Short title

   3. This Act may be cited as the Consolidated Fund (No. 2) Act 1997.

INDEX

References are to sections

SPECIAL IMMIGRATION APPEALS COMMISSION ACT 1997*

(1997 c. 68)

ARRANGEMENT OF SECTIONS

An Act to establish the Special Immigration Appeals Commission; to make provision with respect to its jurisdiction; and for connected purposes.

[17th December 1997]

Parliamentary Debates
    Hansard, H.L. Vol. 580, cols 262 (1R), 733 (2R), 1430 (Comm.), Vol. 581, cols 481 (Rep.), 912 (3R), Vol. 583, col. 1246 (CA). H.C. Vol. 299, col. 1053 (2R), Vol. 301, col. 1032 (3R).

Introduction and General Note
    There is nothing novel in the proposition that the interests of national security can override normally applicable immigration rules. Indeed, such interests will override even the requirements of natural justice (see *R. v. Secretary of State for the Home Department, ex parte Hosenball* [1977] 1 W.L.R. 766 (CA)). Thus for example a person could not appeal against a decision to make a deportation order against him if the ground of the decision was that his deportation is conducive to the public good as being *inter alia* "in the interests of national security" (Immigration Act 1971 s.15(3)). Such cases were subject to a "non statutory advisory procedure" (see immigration rules, paragraph 374 of HC 395) whereby deportees are informed "so far as possible, of the nature of the allegations against them and will be given the opportunity to appear before the advisors, and to make representations to them, before they tender advice to the Secretary of State".
    Such procedure was first introduced when the then Labour government responded to the 1967 report of the Wilson Committee by the enactment of the Immigration Appeals Act 1969. In fact the procedure did not remotely reflect the Wilson Committee's recommendation:

        After discussion with the Home Office we are satisfied that there is no need to exclude a case from the appeal system merely because the decision was taken on security grounds. It will, however, probably be necessary to make special arrangements for the disposal of such cases . . . the hearing would presumably have to be heard in camera, but there would be no question of withholding from the applicant particulars of what is alleged against him.

The procedure was described by one commentator as a "Star Chamber in the Strand" and had long been widely regarded as entirely unsatisfactory (see *Macdonald's Immigration Law and Practice*, Fourth Edition by Macdonald and Blake at 15.52–15.56). Even where refugees were concerned the same panel was used and it is a trite observation that the courts have required only minimal evidence of the nature of the allegation in national security cases to be satisfied that there are reasonable grounds for regarding a refugee as a danger to national security (see *NSH v. Secretary of State for the Home Department* [1988] Imm.A.R. 389 (CA); *CCSU v. Minister for the Civil Service* [1985] A.C. 374 and *R. v. Secretary of State for the Home Department, Ex p. Chahal* [1994] Imm.A.R. 107).
    But to what extent does such procedure and approach measure up to the United Kingdom's obligations under the European Convention on Human Rights 1950, in particular in cases where it is asserted that expulsion would expose an applicant to a real risk of torture or inhuman or degrading treatment or punishment in breach of ECHR 1950 Art. 3? Such obligation after all is

---

* Annotations by Rick Scannell, barrister at law, 2 Garden Court, Temple, EC4Y 9BL.

absolute and applies (even) in a terrorist case irrespective of conduct (indeed, protection is wider than under the 1951 Refugee Convention). These and other questions were considered by the European Court of Human Rights in the landmark case of *Chahal v. United Kingdom* (1997) 23 E.H.R.R. 413. It was argued on Mr Chahal's behalf before the European Court of Human Rights *inter alia* that the national security advisory panel was not a "court" within the meaning of ECHR 1950 Art. 5(4), nor that judicial review was an "effective remedy" within the meaning of Article 13. The Court delivered its judgment on November 16, 1996. Although the procedure before the panel provided some degree of control,

> "bearing in mind that Mr Chahal was not entitled to legal representation before the panel, that he was only given an outline of the grounds for the notice of intention to deport, that the panel had no power of decision and that its advice to the Home Secretary was not binding and was not disclosed"

the Court concluded that "the panel could not be considered a 'Court' within the meaning of article 5.4" (paragraph 130 refers). The Court's judgment continues:

> "The Court recognises that the use of confidential material may be unavoidable where national security is at stake. This does not mean, however, that the national authorities can be free from effective control by the domestic courts whenever they choose to assert that national security and terrorism are involved. The Court attaches significance to the fact that . . . in Canada a more effective form of judicial control has been developed in cases of this type. This example illustrates that there are techniques which can be employed which both accommodate legitimate security concerns about the nature and sources of intelligence information and yet accord the individual a substantial measure of protection. . . ."

Thus the Court unanimously found violation of article 5.4—and indeed article 13—in respect of *inter alia* both the advisory panel procedure and judicial review.

The Canadian model had been drawn to the Court's attention by Amnesty International, Liberty, the AIRE centre and the JCWI (see paragraph 144). It is perhaps ironic that had the Wilson Committee's original recommendation been followed Mr Chahal's complaint under Article 5.4 might not have arisen, let alone be upheld. The Special Immigration Appeals Commission Act 1997 represents the Labour government's response to the *Chahal* judgment. The main intention of the legislation was expressed by Lord Williams to be "in providing appeal rights . . . to ensure that there is no risk of a breach of ECHR 1950 Art. 3 in cases where there is presently no right of appeal on national security grounds" (*Hansard*, HL Vol. 581, col. 481).

Indeed, that the Act is aimed at bringing the United Kingdom into line with its obligations under (*inter alia*) the European Convention could not be clearer from reading the debates—and not only in relation to Article 3. The Government introduced an amendment at report stage in the Lords so as to give rights of appeal where otherwise there would be none because of the 1971 Act s.13(5) (Secretary of State personally certifies exclusion "conducive to public good") in cases where the Applicant seeks entry clearance in the exercise of the right to family life under ECHR 1950 Art. 8 (see s.2(2)(b) of the 1997 Act and commentary below).

Seen against this background it is perhaps surprising that the Act makes no mention at all of the European Convention on Human Rights itself. The scope of the appeal jurisdiction is wide and reflects s.19 of the 1971 Act (s.4 1997 Act refers). Thus an appeal shall be allowed if the decision was "not in accordance with the law or with any (applicable) immigration rules" or if "discretion should have been exercised differently". In this respect the scope of the appeal is on its face wider than in asylum cases where appeal under Asylum and Immigration Appeals Act 1993 s.8 is limited to arguing that removal would breach the United Kingdom's obligations under the 1951 Refugee Convention. One option would have been to expressly refer to the European Convention in s.4 of the 1997 Act. Assuming that the Human Rights Bill is enacted the Convention will be part of "the law" and European Convention issues will be plainly "justiciable" within the meaning of s.4. But until incorporation the 1997 Act will be ineffective precisely because it is not part of "the law" within the meaning of section 4.

The Bill was ordered to be printed on May 20, 1997; it was enacted less than 7 months later on December 17, 1997. It began its passage through Parliament in the Lords, passing through Parliament unopposed at all stages. Such spirit of co-operation is in stark contrast to the stormy passage of the two previous immigration acts (Asylum and Immigration Appeals Act 1993 and Asylum and Immigration Act 1996). Responding for the Government at the conclusion of the second reading debate Mike O'Brien stated that "the commission will try to strike a balance between the rights of those engaged in due process and the need to protect national security. We are creating a mechanism that will fulfill our obligations in the light of the European Court of Human Rights judgment in the Chahal case" (*Hansard*, HC Vol. 299, col. 1069). It is estimated that the number of cases heard by the commission will be approximately five a year (*ibid.* at col. 1073).

Establishment of the Commission

1.—(1) There shall be a commission, known as the Special Immigration Appeals Commission, for the purpose of exercising the jurisdiction conferred by this Act.

(2) Schedule 1 to this Act shall have effect in relation to the Commission.

GENERAL NOTE

This section establishes the body known as the Special Immigration Appeals Commission. The character of such body is spelt out by Schedule 1. Members of the Commission are appointed by the Lord Chancellor—with one member appointed as Chairman by the Lord Chancellor (Schedule 1, para. 1 refers). At third reading on November 26, 1997, the Government Minister Mike O'Brien MP informed the House that the Lord Chancellor had decided to appoint Mr Justice Potts as chairman of the Commission when it is established (*Hansard*, HC Vol. 301, col. 1033). The Commission will be "duly constituted" if it consists of three members of whom at least one holds or has held high judicial office (*vis* a High Court judge—Potts, J.) and at least one "is or has been" chief adjudicator or a legally qualified member of the Immigration Appeal Tribunal (Schedule 1, para. 5 refers). The Act is silent as to the qualifications of the third member. During second reading Mr O'Brien stated (*Hansard*, HC Vol. 299, col. 1055) "it is intended that the person will have some experience of national security matters and will be familiar with the evidence that is likely to be presented to the commission"—an observation justified by reference to the fact that "the Lord Chancellor takes the view that those arrangements will best represent a proper balance of knowledge and experience for the commission" (*ibid.*). At third reading Mr O'Brien elaborated further: "the third member will be someone who has experience of dealing with security matters, not necessarily someone who is a member of the Security Service".

Jurisdiction: appeals

2.—(1) A person may appeal to the Special Immigration Appeals Commission against—

(a) any matter in relation to which he would be entitled to appeal under subsection (1) of section 13 of the Immigration Act 1971 (appeal to an adjudicator against refusal of leave to enter), but for subsection (5) of that section (exclusion conducive to public good),

(b) any matter in relation to which he would be entitled to appeal under subsection (1) of section 14 of that Act (appeal to an adjudicator against variation of limited leave or any refusal to vary it), but for subsection (3) of that section (departure conducive to public good),

(c) any matter in relation to which he would be entitled to appeal under subsection (1)(a) of section 15 of that Act (appeal to an adjudicator or the Appeal Tribunal against a decision to make a deportation order), but for subsection (3) of that section (deportation conducive to public good),

(d) any matter in relation to which he would be entitled to appeal under Article 15(1) of the Immigration (European Economic Area) Order 1994 (appeal against refusal of admission), but for Article 20(2)(b) of that Order (exclusion conducive to public good),

(e) any matter in relation to which he would be entitled to appeal under Article 15(2) of that Order (appeal against decision to remove), but for Article 20(2)(d) of that Order (removal conducive to public good),

(f) any matter in relation to which he would be entitled to appeal under Article 18 of that Order (appeal against refusal or withdrawal of residence permit or residence document), but for Article 20(2)(c) of that Order (departure conducive to public good), and

(g) any matter in relation to which he would be entitled to appeal under section 8(1), (2) or (3) of the Asylum and Immigration Appeals Act 1993 (appeal to special adjudicator in cases involving claim to asylum), but for paragraph 6 of Schedule 2 to that Act (exclusion, departure or deportation in the interests of national security).

(2) A person may appeal to the Special Immigration Appeals Commission against the refusal of an entry clearance if he would be entitled to appeal against the refusal under subsection (2) of section 13 of the Immigration Act 1971, but for subsection (5) of that section (exclusion conducive to public good), and—

(a) he seeks to rely on an enforceable Community right or any provision made under section 2(2) of the European Communities Act 1972, or

(b) he seeks to enter the United Kingdom under immigration rules making provision about entry—

(i) to exercise rights of access to a child resident there,

(ii) as the spouse or fiance of a person present and settled there, or

(iii) as the parent, grandparent or other dependent relative of a person present and settled there.

(3) Schedule 2 to this Act (which makes supplementary provision relating to appeals under this section) shall have effect.

(4) In this section, "immigration rules" has the same meaning as in the Immigration Act 1971.

GENERAL NOTE

Section 2 identifies the categories of cases in which a person may appeal to the Special Immigration Appeals Commission. The categories are largely reflective of the provisions of the Immigration Act 1971 where persons are not entitled to appeal, in broad terms, on the grounds that the decision is based on conducive to public good grounds in national security and/or political cases (Immigration Act 1971, ss. 13(5), 14(3) and 15(3) refer). Subsection (1)(a) to (c) refers. The provision of the right of appeal to the Special Immigration Appeals Commission in the various categories of case otherwise excluded by the *Immigration (European Economic Area) Order 1994* Art. 20 (SI 1994 1895) (subs. (1)(d) to (f) refers) was prompted by the decision of the European Court of Justice in *R. v. Secretary of State for the Home Department Ex p. Shingara* [1997] All E.R. (E.C.) 577 which made it clear that there must be a merits review, including proportionality, to satisfy the requirements of Community law. And subs. (1)(g) covers asylum cases where persons are otherwise prevented from appealing by virtue of the Asylum and Immigration Appeals Act 1993, Sch. 2, para. 6.

Despite the breadth of these provisions there are certain lacunae. There is no appeal where there has been a refusal to revoke a deportation order (s.15(4) *ibid.*), nor in a refusal of entry clearance case (s.13(5) *ibid.*) unless the person seeks to rely on an enforceable Community right or seeks entry in circumstances relating to the exercise of ECHR Art. 8 rights (Special Immigration Appeals Commission Act 1997 s. 2(2) refers). Such lacunae were sought to be justified by Lord Williams (*Hansard*, HL Vol. 581, col. 481) on the basis that the Government "wish to ensure that there is a proper review in those cases where detention is in issue (which) for the most part . . . means that a right of appeal is required in those cases where there is an in-country right of appeal which is precluded only by the existing provisions restricting rights of appeal in national security cases". The *general* absence of appeal rights in entry clearance cases is thereby justified on the basis that "there is no question of detention or an Article 3 risk".

The Art. 8 limb of s.2 (subs. (2)(b)(i) to (iii) refers) was a Government amendment introduced at report stage in the House of Lords. Lord Williams (*ibid.* at cols 481–2) stated as follows:

"Article 8 allows that national security considerations can justify interference with this right, but there is nevertheles a need to provide for an effective review of any decision to ensure that any interference is in accordance with the law and is necessary.

For the ECHR rights arising from Article 8 considerations to be properly dealt with, the national security case underlying the refusal of entry clearance would need to be examined. If we do not provide a right of appeal to the new commission there would be a strong likelihood, following incorporation of the convention at least, that a court of judicial review would insist on seeing the national security details . . . We believe . . . That it would be preferable for any consideration of the national security case to be dealt with by a commission which has been set up especially to deal with any such issue."

Such reasoning would apply *mutatis mutandis* in "family" revocation cases and there would seem little justification for such omission. Indeed, if such a person is not entitled to appeal against a refusal to revoke a deportation order s/he will in practice not be in position to apply for an entry clearance, let alone rely on the s.2(2) right of appeal.

Subsection (3) gives effect to Sch. 2 which contains various supplementary provisions applying Immigration Act 1971 "caveats" and "stays" to s.2 appeals (suspension of variation of limited leave and not being required to leave pending appeal; deportation order not to be made while appeal pending; stay of removal directions pending appeal and bail; construction of references to pending appeal, *etc.*).

Particular mention should be made of Sch. 2, para. 5. This provides that asylum appeals before the Special Immigration Appeals Commission (*i.e.* where a person would be entitled to appeal under the Asylum and Immigration Appeals Act 1993, s.8 but for the "national security" element—s.2, subs. (1)(g) of the Act refers) "shall in the same proceedings" deal with any other Immigration Act 1971 or Immigration (European Economic Area) Order 1994 appeal. One obvious *disadvantage* of such "mixed" appeal will be that in respect of any other such appeal right there would be no further right of appeal to the Immigration Appeal Tribunal. At report stage an amendment moved by Baroness Anelay had sought to prevent the commission considering such "mixed" appeals by requiring the appeal (if allowed) to be remitted to an adjudicator or special adjudicator as appropriate "to determine the remaining issues". Such approach might have had much to commend it—although in the view of Lord Morris and others this would have resulted in "fractured jurisdiction" which was said not to be "an efficient use of resources or an efficient way of coming to these difficult decisions" (*Hansard*, HL Vol. 581, cols 483–489). Such amendment was ultimately withdrawn. Given the loss of appeal rights to the Tribunal identified and the limited numbers of cases an argument based on "resources" hardly bears close scrutiny.

Jurisdiction: bail

3.—(1) In the case of a person to whom subsection (2) below applies, the provisions of Schedule 2 to the Immigration Act 1971 specified in Schedule 3 to this Act shall have effect with the modifications set out there.

(2) This subsection applies to a person who is detained under the Immigration Act 1971 if—

  (a) the Secretary of State certifies that his detention is necessary in the interests of national security,

  (b) he is detained following a decision to refuse him leave to enter the United Kingdom on the ground that his exclusion is in the interests of national security, or

  (c) he is detained following a decision to make a deportation order against him on the ground that his deportation is in the interests of national security.

GENERAL NOTE

Section 3 provides a bail jurisdiction in respect of the persons detained in any of the three situations described in subs. (2). The jurisdiction is spelt out in Sch. 2 to the 1971 Act—with the Special Immigration Appeals Commission Act 1997, Sch. 3 making the necessary modifications to the Immigration Act 1971 in this respect.

Determination of appeals

4.—(1) The Special Immigration Appeals Commission on an appeal to it under this Act—

  (a) shall allow the appeal if it considers—

      (i) that the decision or action against which the appeal is brought was not in accordance with the law or with any immigration rules applicable to the case, or

      (ii) where the decision or action involved the exercise of a discretion by the Secretary of State or an officer, that the discretion should have been exercised differently, and

  (b) in any other case, shall dismiss the appeal.

(2) Where an appeal is allowed, the Commission shall give such directions for giving effect to the determination as it thinks requisite, and may also make recommendations with respect to any other action which it considers should be taken in the case under the Immigration Act 1971; and it shall be the duty of the Secretary of State and of any officer to whom directions are given under this subsection to comply with them.

(3) In this section, "immigration rules" has the same meaning as in the Immigration Act 1971.

GENERAL NOTE

This crucial provision is reflective of the jurisdiction of the immigration appellate authorities under Immigration Act 1971, s.19(1). The bill as originally drafted entirely omitted *any* provision dealing with determination of appeals by the commission, albeit that Lord Williams was unequivocal at second reading that "the intention of the Government is that the commission should have the same jurisdiction as the existing appeal bodies, which means a full appeal on the merits" [*Hansard*, HL Vol. 580, col. 752). The "not in accordance with the law" jurisdiction is wide and covers principles of administrative law (see *DS Abdi v. Secretary of State for the Home Department* [1996] Imm.A.R. 148), although not at present ECHR 1950 (see comments in introduction above and further below). The section was introduced by the Government at committee stage in the Lords (*Hansard*, HL Vol. 580, col. 1431) with Lord Williams accepting the suggestion made during second reading that "it was not clear on the face of the Bill whether or not the commission would be in a position to make decisions which would be binding on the Home Secretary". The parliamentary intention that decisions are binding has plainly been achieved. Where an appeal is allowed the commission "shall give directions for giving effect to the determination as it thinks requisite" with which the Secretary of State is obliged to comply (*cf.* Immigration Act 1971, s.19(3)).

At the same time Lord Williams also stated expressly that "those who believe that their rights under Article 3 have been or would be violated will be able to rely on Article 3 in domestic proceedings once incorporation has been achieved". However, although at time of writing the Act has yet to be brought into force (see s.9(2) below) there may well be a hiatus until the Human Rights Bill comes into force and if there were to be cases heard by the commission prior to incorporation appellants might find themselves having to raise arguments based on "legitimate expectation" in order to be able to rely on the provisions of the EHCR at all!

Procedure in relation to jurisdiction under sections 2 and 3

5.—(1) The Lord Chancellor may make rules—

(a) for regulating the exercise of the rights of appeal conferred by section 2 above,

(b) for prescribing the practice and procedure to be followed on or in connection with appeals under that section, including the mode and burden of proof and admissibility of evidence on such appeals, and

(c) for other matters preliminary or incidental to or arising out of such appeals, including proof of the decisions of the Special Immigration Appeals Commission.

(2) Rules under this section shall provide that an appellant has the right to be legally represented in any proceedings before the Commission on an appeal under section 2 above, subject to any power conferred on the Commission by such rules.

(3) Rules under this section may, in particular—

(a) make provision enabling proceedings before the Commission to take place without the appellant being given full particulars of the reasons for the decision which is the subject of the appeal,

(b) make provision enabling the Commission to hold proceedings in the absence of any person, including the appellant and any legal representative appointed by him,

(c) make provision about the functions in proceedings before the Commission of persons appointed under section 6 below, and

(d) make provision enabling the Commission to give the appellant a summary of any evidence taken in his absence.

(4) Rules under this section may also include provision—

(a) enabling any functions of the Commission which relate to matters preliminary or incidental to an appeal, or which are conferred by Part II of Schedule 2 to the Immigration Act 1971, to be performed by a single member of the Commission, or

(b) conferring on the Commission such ancillary powers as the Lord Chancellor thinks necessary for the purposes of the exercise of its functions.

(5) The power to make rules under this section shall include power to make rules with respect to applications to the Commission under paragraphs

22 to 24 of Schedule 2 to the Immigration Act 1971 and matters arising out of such applications.

(6) In making rules under this section, the Lord Chancellor shall have regard, in particular, to—

(a) the need to secure that decisions which are the subject of appeals are properly reviewed, and

(b) the need to secure that information is not disclosed contrary to the public interest.

(7) Section 9(1) of the Interception of Communications Act 1985 (exclusion of evidence) shall not apply to proceedings before the Commission.

(8) The power to make rules under this section shall be exercisable by statutory instrument.

(9) No rules shall be made under this section unless a draft of them has been laid before and approved by resolution of each House of Parliament.

GENERAL NOTE

This section which empowers the Lord Chancellor to make rules for appeals under the 1997 Act reflects the starting point for the procedures of the commission. The right to legal representation guaranteed by subsection (2) taken together with the binding nature of the commission's decisions (s.4(2) refers) begins to meet the concerns of the European Court of Human Rights in *Chahal*. However, such rules may also enable proceedings to take place without full particulars being given to the appellant (subs. 3(a)), enable proceedings to be held in the absence of any person (subs. (3)(b)) and enable the commission "to give the appellant a summary of any evidence taken in his absence" (subs. (3)(d)). In making rules the Lord Chancellor is obliged to have regard to "the need to secure that decisions which are the subject of appeals are properly reviewed" and "the need to secure that information is not disclosed contrary to the public interest". Some may feel that these powers tilt the "balance" against the appellant—although such concerns are perhaps met to some extent by the use of the security vetted "special advocate"— who despite the power in subs. (3)(b) to exclude "any person" was expressly stated by Lord Williams to be someone who would probably need to be present throughout (see commentary on s.6 below).

"Draft" rules were available to and considered by the House of Lords at Committee stage. At the time of writing it is believed that a final version of the rules will be published sometime in March 1997. It should be noted that the rules must be approved "by resolution of each House of Parliament" (subs. (9) refers). A draft dated June 18, 1997 (believed to be the draft considered by the House of Lords in Committee on June 23, 1997) is available to the writer. Lord Lester said this of the draft:

"I have gone carefully through the draft rules. They seem to me to be an extremely well designed set of rules that seek to be fair without incorporating the full panoply of natural justice as though it were a criminal trial . . .

I believe that where a national security is at stake, one needs to do the best one can for the individual appellant without sacrificing the overriding interests of national security. One of the reasons that I am so complimentary to Ministers and officials is that they looked carefully at the Canadian immigration law and practice which was commended by the European Court of Human Rights. I do not go into much detail, but they have produced a solution which improves upon the Canadian position. It would not satisfy a purist. It would not satisfy someone who believed that nothing less than a full trial with full natural justice would suffice.

However, I believe that the amendment is a fair compromise."

Hansard, HL Vol. 580, cols 1437–1438.

In *summary*, the June 18, 1997 draft included the following. Notice of appeal within 7, 14 or 42 days (asylum claims, "others" and out of country appeals), to "set out the grounds of appeal", be signed by the appellant or his representative and with power to accept late notices if the Secretary of State is of the opinion that it is "just to do so" (rule 4 refers). Secretary of State 'no later than 42 days after receiving notice of appeal' to provide commission with a statement summarising the facts of the grounds on which the appeal is opposed and providing a "schedule of any evidence which he wishes to adduce in the absence of the appellant . . . and the reasons for so wishing". A statement of facts must be provided in a form which can be shown to the appellant. The commission is to decide "with the assistance of any special advocate who has been appointed" whether the schedule of evidence should be shown to the appellant and his representative and whether the statement of facts is sufficient (rule 5). Proceedings may be held "in private" and in the absence of any person "including the appellant and his representative". The commission has power to give similar directions to those contained in the Asylum Appeals (Procedure) Rules 1996 r.23 (rule 9 of the draft Rules 1997) "A special advocate shall be appointed whenever any proceedings before the commission are to be held in the absence of the appellant or his representative". The special advocate "shall do whatever is necessary to enable him to perform his function"—including assisting a decision to be reached under rule 5, cross examining witnesses, making submissions or representations, assisting and advising the commission (rule 10). Evidence may be given orally or in writing and except where proceedings are held in his absence the appellant or his representative is entitled to cross examine witnesses. Where proceedings are held in the absence of the appellant or his representative the commission is required to provide a summary of evidence taken in his absence—such summary to be provided by the commission with the assistance of the special advocate (rule 11). Provision is made also for the inspection of documentary evidence (rule 12), the summoning of witnesses (rule 13), the "mode of giving evidence" (rule 14), bail (rule 15), the giving of "notices, etc." (rule 16) and the promulgation of decision and reasons (rule 17).

However, the foregoing is perhaps of only historic interest. It must be stressed that a final draft has yet to be completed, let alone approved by resolution of each House of Parliament.

Appointment of person to represent the appellant's interests

6.—(1) The relevant law officer may appoint a person to represent the interests of an appellant in any proceedings before the Special Immigration Appeals Commission from which the appellant and any legal representative of his are excluded.

(2) For the purposes of subsection (1) above, the relevant law officer is—

(a) in relation to proceedings before the Commission in England and Wales, the Attorney General,

(b) in relation to proceedings before the Commission in Scotland, the Lord Advocate, and

(c) in relation to proceedings before the Commission in Northern Ireland, the Attorney General for Northern Ireland.

(3) A person appointed under subsection (1) above—

(a) if appointed for the purposes of proceedings in England and Wales, shall have a general qualification for the purposes of section 71 of the Courts and Legal Services Act 1990,

(b) if appointed for the purposes of proceedings in Scotland, shall be—

(i) an advocate, or

(ii) a solicitor who has by virtue of section 25A of the Solicitors (Scotland) Act 1980 rights of audience in the Court of Session and the High Court of Justiciary, and

(c) if appointed for the purposes of proceedings in Northern Ireland, shall be a member of the Bar of Northern Ireland.

(4) A person appointed under subsection (1) above shall not be responsible to the person whose interests he is appointed to represent.

GENERAL NOTE

The provision for the appointment of a "special advocate" was moved as a Government amendment at committee stage in the Lords by Lord Williams—although the intention to amend the Bill was mentioned at second reading on June 5, 1997. Lord Williams then described such person as "security vetted counsel to the commission who will be able to act as though for the appellant" albeit that they would not disclose material *to* the appellant (*Hansard*, HL Vol. 580, cols 755–6). More detail was provided in committee. Lord Williams explained that "the role of the special advocate should be to represent the interest of the appellant in those parts of the proceedings from which he and his legal representative are excluded. That will probably mean that he or she will need to be present throughout the whole proceedings. . . . (I)t would be the same sort of vetted person as one who prosecutes for the Treasury in important, delicate, sensitive national security matters" (*Hansard*, HL Vol. 580, col. 1437).

Mr O'Brien on second reading described the relationship of the special advocate and appellant as "like a person who is appointed by a court to represent a minor—a child—or someone with a psychiatric or mental problem. That person does not take instructions from the client and he is not obliged to do what the client says. A special advocate is not obliged to disclose information that he may become privy to. He does not have the lawyer-client relationship that one commonly expects, so the special advocate will not take any instructions from the appellant" (*Hansard*, HC Vol. 299, col. 1071). Such "special advocate" system operates in Canada (see *Chahal* judgment at para. 144) and as Mr O'Brien states was a relationship "commended" by the European Court of Justice.*

Appeals from the Commission

7.—(1) Where the Special Immigration Appeals Commission has made a final determination of an appeal, any party to the appeal may bring a further appeal to the appropriate appeal court on any question of law material to that determination.

(2) An appeal under this section may be brought only with the leave of the Commission or, if such leave is refused, with the leave of the appropriate appeal court.

(3) In this section "the appropriate appeal court" means—

(a) in relation to a determination made by the Commission in England and Wales, the Court of Appeal,

(b) in relation to a determination made by the Commission in Scotland, the Court of Session, and

(c) in relation to a determination made by the Commission in Northern Ireland, the Court of Appeal in Northern Ireland.

(4) In section 33(4) of the Immigration Act 1971, after "1993" there shall be inserted "or section 7 of the Special Immigration Appeals Commission Act 1997".

GENERAL NOTE

The provision of a right of appeal to the Court of Appeal on a question of law was introduced at committee stage in the Commons—although Mr O'Brien gave notice of such intention during second reading (Standing Committee D, Tuesday November 11, 1997, col. 11). This provision reflects that in the Asylum and Immigration Appeals Act 1993, s.9(4) and is a consequential amendment of the Immigration Act 1971, s.33(4) defining when an appeal is "pending".

Procedure on applications to the Commission for leave to appeal

8.—(1) The Lord Chancellor may make rules regulating, and prescribing the procedure to be followed on, applications to the Special Immigration Appeals Commission for leave to appeal under section 7 above.

(2) Rules under this section may include provision enabling an application for leave to appeal to be heard by a single member of the Commission.

(3) The power to make rules under this section shall be exercisable by statutory instrument.

(4) No rules shall be made under this section unless a draft of them has been laid before and approved by resolution of each House of Parliament.

GENERAL NOTE

This section enables the Lord Chancellor to make rules regulating the procedure to be followed on applications for leave to appeal under s.7 above. Again, such rules must be "approved by resolution of each House of Parliament" (subs. (4)). No such rules (or draft rules) are available at time of writing.

Short title, commencement and extent

9.—(1) This Act may be cited as the Special Immigration Appeals Commission Act 1997.

(2) This Act, except for this section, shall come into force on such day as the Secretary of State may by order made by statutory instrument appoint; and different days may be so appointed for different purposes.

---

* For further details of the likely role of the special advocate, see commentary at s.5 above.

(3) Her Majesty may by Order in Council direct that any of the provisions of this Act shall extend, with such modifications as appear to Her Majesty to be appropriate, to any of the Channel Islands or the Isle of Man.

(4) This Act extends to Northern Ireland.

GENERAL NOTE

At time of writing no statutory instrument has been published to bring the Act into force. It is believed to be intended that the Act will come into force in March 1998.

SCHEDULES

Section 1   SCHEDULE 1

THE COMMISSION

Members

1.—(1) The Special Immigration Appeals Commission shall consist of such number of members appointed by the Lord Chancellor as he may determine.

(2) A member of the Commission shall hold and vacate office in accordance with the terms of his appointment and shall, on ceasing to hold office, be eligible for re-appointment.

(3) A member of the Commission may resign his office at any time by notice in writing to the Lord Chancellor.

Chairman

2. The Lord Chancellor shall appoint one of the members of the Commission to be its chairman.

Payments to members

3.—(1) The Lord Chancellor may pay to the members of the Commission such remuneration and allowances as he may determine.

(2) The Lord Chancellor may, if he thinks fit in the case of any member of the Commission pay such pension, allowance or gratuity to or in respect of the member, or such sums towards the provision of such pension, allowance or gratuity, as he may determine.

(3) If a person ceases to be a member of the Commission and it appears to the Lord Chancellor that there are special circumstances which make it right that the person should receive compensation, he may pay to that person a sum of such amount as he may determine.

Proceedings

4. The Commission shall sit at such times and in such places as the Lord Chancellor may direct and may sit in two or more divisions.

5. The Commission shall be deemed to be duly constituted if it consists of three members of whom—

(a) at least one holds or has held high judicial office (within the meaning of the Appellate Jurisdiction Act 1876), and

(b) at least one is or has been—

(i) appointed as chief adjudicator under paragraph 1 of Schedule 5 to the Immigration Act 1971, or

(ii) a member of the Immigration Appeal Tribunal qualified as mentioned in paragraph 7 of that Schedule.

6. The chairman or, in his absence, such other member of the Commission as he may nominate, shall preside at sittings of the Commission and report its decisions.

Staff

7. The Lord Chancellor may appoint such officers and servants for the Commission as he thinks fit.

Expenses

8. The Lord Chancellor shall defray the remuneration of persons appointed under paragraph 7 above and such expenses of the Commission as he thinks fit.

See general note to section 1 above.

Section 2   SCHEDULE 2

APPEALS: SUPPLEMENTARY

Suspension of variation of limited leave pending appeal

1. The limitation on the taking effect of a variation and on a requirement to leave the United Kingdom contained in section 14(1) of the Immigration Act 1971 shall have effect as if appeals under any of the following provisions of section 2(1) above were appeals under section 14(1) of the 1971 Act—

(a) paragraph (b),

(b) paragraph (f), and

(c) paragraph (g), so far as relating to section 8(2) of the Asylum and Immigration Appeals Act 1993.

Deportation order not to be made while appeal pending

2. In section 15(2) of the Immigration Act 1971 references to an appeal against a decision to make a deportation order shall include references to an appeal against such a decision under any of the following provisions of section 2(1) above—

(a) paragraph (c),

(b) paragraph (e), and

(c) paragraph (g), so far as relating to section 8(3)(a) of the Asylum and Immigration Appeals Act 1993.

Stay of removal directions pending appeal and bail

3.—(1) Part II of Schedule 2 to the Immigration Act 1971 shall have effect as if the references to appeals under section 13(1) of that Act included appeals under any of the following provisions of section 2(1) above—

(a) paragraph (a),

(b) paragraph (d), and

(c) paragraph (g), so far as relating to section 8(1) of the Asylum and Immigration Appeals Act 1993,

and as if sub-paragraph (5) of paragraph 28 of Schedule 2 were omitted.

(2) Paragraph 3 of Schedule 3 to the Immigration Act 1971 shall have effect as if the reference to appeals under section 15(1)(a) of the 1971 Act included appeals under any of the following provisions of section 2(1) above—

(a) paragraph (c),

(b) paragraph (e), and

(c) paragraph (g), so far as relating to section 8(3)(a) of the Asylum and Immigration Appeals Act 1993.

Construction of references to pending appeal

4. For the purposes of the Immigration Act 1971 as applied by paragraphs 1 to 3 above, an appeal under section 2 above shall be treated as pending during the period beginning when notice of appeal is duly given and ending when the appeal is finally determined or withdrawn; and an appeal shall not be treated as finally determined so long as a further appeal can be brought by virtue of section 7 above, nor, if such an appeal is duly brought, until it is determined or withdrawn.

Appeals involving asylum

5. Where a person brings an appeal under section 2(1)(g) above, the Special Immigration Appeals Commission shall in the same proceedings deal with—

(a) any appeal against the refusal, variation or decision (as the case may be) which the person is entitled to bring under—

(i) Part II of the Immigration Act 1971, or

(ii) the Immigration (European Economic Area) Order 1994,

on any other ground on which he seeks to rely, and

(b) any appeal brought by the person under that Part of that Act or that Order against any other decision or action.

Notice of appealable decisions and statement of appeal rights etc.

6. Section 18 of the Immigration Act 1971 shall have effect as if section 2 above were contained in Part II of that Act.

Financial support for organisations helping persons with rights of appeal

7. Section 23 of the Immigration Act 1971 shall have effect as if section 2 above were contained in Part II of that Act.

See general note to section 2 above.

Section 3   SCHEDULE 3

BAIL: MODIFICATIONS OF SCHEDULE 2 TO THE IMMIGRATION ACT 1971

1.—(1) Paragraph 22 shall be amended as follows.

(2) In sub-paragraph (1A), for the words from the beginning to "adjudicator" there shall be substituted "The Special Immigration Appeals Commission".

(3) In sub-paragraph (2)—

(a) for the words "immigration officer or adjudicator" there shall be substituted "Special Immigration Appeals Commission", and

(b) for the words "officer or adjudicator" there shall be substituted "Commission".

(4) In sub-paragraph (3)—

(a) for "an immigration officer or adjudicator" there shall be substituted "the Special Immigration Appeals Commission", and

(b) for "officer or adjudicator", in both places, there shall be substituted "Commission".

2.—(1) Paragraph 23 shall be amended as follows.

(2) In sub-paragraph (1)—

(a) for "an adjudicator" there shall be substituted "the Special Immigration Appeals Commission", and

(b) for "the adjudicator", in each place, there shall be substituted "the Commission".

(3) In sub-paragraph (2)—

(a) for "an adjudicator" there shall be substituted "the Special Immigration Appeals Commission", and

(b) for "the adjudicator" there shall be substituted "the Commission".

3.—(1) Paragraph 24 shall be amended as follows.

(2) For sub-paragraph (2), there shall be substituted—

"(2) A person arrested under this paragraph shall be brought before the Special Immigration Appeals Commission within twenty-four hours."

(3) In sub-paragraph (3), for the words from the beginning to "above" there shall be substituted "Where a person is brought before the Special Immigration Appeals Commission by virtue of sub-paragraph (2) above, the Commission—".

4.—(1) Paragraph 29 shall be amended as follows.

(2) For sub-paragraphs (2) to (4) there shall be substituted—

"(2) The Special Immigration Appeals Commission may release an appellant on his entering into a recognizance or, in Scotland, bail bond conditioned for his appearance before the Commission at a time and place named in the recognizance or bail bond."

(3) For sub-paragraph (6) there shall be substituted—

"(6) In any case in which the Special Immigration Appeals Commission has power to release an appellant on bail, the Commission may, instead of taking the bail, fix the amount and conditions of the bail (including the amount in which any sureties are to be bound) with a view to its being taken subsequently by any such person as may be specified by the Commission; and on the recognizance or bail bond being so taken the appellant shall be released."

5. Paragraph 30(2) shall be omitted.

6.—(1) Paragraph 31 shall be amended as follows.

(2) In sub-paragraph (1)—

(a) for "an adjudicator or the Tribunal" there shall be substituted "the Special Immigration Appeals Commission",

(b) for "the adjudicator or the Tribunal, as the case may be," there shall be substituted "the Commission", and

(c) for "the adjudicator or Tribunal", in both places, there shall be substituted "the Commission".

(3) In sub-paragraph (3)—

(a) for "an adjudicator or the Tribunal" there shall be substituted "the Special Immigration Appeals Commission", and

(b) for "the adjudicator or Tribunal" there shall be substituted "it".

7. Paragraph 32 shall be amended as follows—

(a) for "an adjudicator or the Tribunal" there shall be substituted "the Special Immigration Appeals Commission",

(b) for "the adjudicator or Tribunal" there shall be substituted "the Commission", and

(c) for "the adjudicator or the Tribunal" there shall be substituted "the Commission".

8.—(1) Paragraph 33 shall be amended as follows.

(2) For sub-paragraph (2), there shall be substituted—

"(2) A person arrested under this paragraph shall be brought before the Special Immigration Appeals Commission within twenty-four hours."

(3) In sub-paragraph (3), for the words from the beginning to "above" there shall be substituted "Where a person is brought before the Special Immigration Appeals Commission by virtue of sub-paragraph (2) above, the Commission—".

See general note to section 3 above.

INDEX

References are to sections and Schedules

SUPREME COURT (OFFICES) ACT 1997

(1997 c. 69)

An Act to make provision with respect to the qualification for appointment as, and tenure of office of, Permanent Secretary to the Lord Chancellor and Clerk of the Crown in Chancery. [17th December 1997]

PARLIAMENTARY DEBATES
Hansard, H.C. Vol. 299, col. 914 (1R), Vol. 300, col. 407 (2R, rem.). H.L. Vol. 583, cols. 11 (1R), 932 (2R), Vol. 584, col. 503 (3R).

INTRODUCTION
This Act repeals the Supreme Court Act 1981, Sch. 2, Part 1, which sets out requirements for the appointment of certain officers of the Supreme Court.

Qualification for, and tenure of, office

1.—(1) In Part I of Schedule 2 to the Supreme Court Act 1981 (which sets out the qualifications required for appointment of certain officers of the Supreme Court and, by virtue of section 92 of that Act, provides for the age at which any such officer must retire), the entry relating to the Permanent Secretary to the Lord Chancellor and the Clerk of the Crown in Chancery is repealed.

(2) The repeal made by subsection (1) does not apply to the person who, on the date on which this Act comes into force, holds the offices.

Short title

2. This Act may be cited as the Supreme Court (Offices) Act 1997.

INDEX

References are to sections

SOUTHAMPTON INTERNATIONAL BOAT SHOW ACT 1997

(1997 c. i)

An Act to amend section 60 of the Hampshire Act 1983 to permit closure of Mayflower Park in Southampton or the restriction of public access to it for 10 rather than 9 consecutive days each year for the purposes of the Southampton International Boat Show; and for connected purposes.

[15th July 1997]

PARLIAMENTARY PROGRESS

The Bill's progress through Parliament was as follows:

House of Commons: First Reading, January 22, 1997; Second Reading, January 29, 1997; Bill committed, January 29, 1997; Bill committed to an unopposed Committee, February 27, 1997; Third Reading, March 6, 1997.

House of Lords: First Reading, March 6, 1997; Second Reading, March 20, 1997; Bill committed, March 20, 1997; Motion to revive the Bill from previous Session, June 16, 1997; Bill committed to an unopposed Committee, June 26, 1997; Third Reading, July 3, 1997.

Royal Assent: July 15, 1997.

INTRODUCTION

This Act allows public access to Mayflower Park to be restricted for 10 rather than nine consecutive days in order for the Southampton International Boat Show to take place. The Show makes a significant contribution to the economic prosperity and commercial reputation of the city, and this increase is highly desirable in order to fully exploit its potential. The maximum number of days permitted for the establishment and removal of the Show is reduced from 25 to 24 days so as to maintain the current maximum period of disruption allowed.

Whereas—

(1) Mayflower Park is a park on the waterfront in the city of Southampton and has been used as the site of the annual Southampton International Boat Show ("the Show") since the Show's inception in 1969:

(2) The use of public parks for such purposes is generally subject to a constraint, contained in section 44 of the Public Health Acts Amendment Act 1890 as amended, whereby such parks cannot be closed for more than six days consecutively:

(3) By section 60 of the Hampshire Act 1983, provision was made to enable Mayflower Park to be closed to the public or for public access to be restricted for the purposes of the Show for nine consecutive days each year:

(4) That provision has enabled the Show to encompass two whole weekends or to run from one Friday to the Saturday of the following week but does not enable the show to open on a Friday and then continue over two whole weekends:

(5) It is now highly desirable if the potential of the Show is to be fully exploited and its international reputation sustained that the Show should be able to open for 10 consecutive days. This would allow in particular the Show to open and then continue over two weekends as happens with many international shows:

(6) An increase by one day in the maximum length of the Show can be matched by an equivalent decrease in the maximum number of days permitted for the establishment and removal of the Show so as to maintain the maximum period of disruption currently permitted of 34 consecutive days:

(7) The show makes a significant contribution to the economic prosperity and commercial reputation of the city of Southampton and is an important event for the recreational boat trade:

(8) It is expedient to amend the provisions of the Hampshire Act 1983 applicable to Mayflower Park as provided by this Act:

(9) The purposes of this Act cannot be effected without the authority of Parliament:

(10) The requirements of section 239 of the Local Government Act 1972 have been observed by Southampton City Council in the promotion of this Bill:

May it therefore please Your Majesty that it may be enacted, and be it enacted, by the Queen's most Excellent Majesty, by and with the advice and consent of the Lords Spiritual and Temporal, and Commons, in this present Parliament assembled, and by the authority of the same, as follows:—

Short title

1. This Act may be cited as the Southampton International Boat Show Act 1997.

Amendment of section 60 of the Hampshire Act 1983

2.—(1) Section 60 of the Hampshire Act 1983 (Use of Mayflower Park for Boat Show) shall be amended as follows.

(2) In subsection (2)(a) and in subsection (2)(b)(i) and (ii), for the number "9" there shall be substituted the number "10".

(3) In subsection 2(b)(i) and (ii), for the number "25" there shall be substituted the number "24".

INDEX

IMPERIAL COLLEGE ACT 1997

(1997 c. ii)

An Act to unite the Charing Cross and Westminster Medical School and the Royal Postgraduate Medical School with the Imperial College of Science, Technology and Medicine; to transfer all rights, properties, assets and liabilities from those medical schools to the said College; to make provision with respect to the merger of the National Heart and Lung Institute with the said College; and for connected purposes.   [15th July 1997]

PARLIAMENTARY PROGRESS

The Bill's progress through Parliament was as follows:

House of Commons: First Reading, January 22, 1997; Second Reading, January 28, 1997; Bill committed, January 28, 1997; Bill committed to an unopposed Committee, February 27–March 3, 1997; Third Reading, March 19, 1997.

House of Lords: First Reading, March 19, 1997; Motion to revive the Bill from previous session, June 16, 1997; Second Reading, July 1, 1997; Bill committed to an unopposed Committee, July 9, 1997; Third Reading, July 14, 1997.

Royal Assent: July 15, 1997.

INTRODUCTION

This Act enables the union of the Charing Cross and Westminster Medical School and the Royal Postgraduate Medical School with the Imperial College of Science, Technology and Medicine ("the University") and to provide for the merger of the National Heart and Lung Institute with the University. The linking of London Medical Schools to multi-faculty colleges is consistent with the policy of the University that the academic strength and financial viability of those medical schools should be enhanced by the merger.

Whereas—

(1) The Imperial College of Science and Technology was established by Royal Charter in 1907, combining the Royal College of Science, the Royal School of Mines and the City and Guilds College, for the purpose of giving the highest specialised instruction, and providing the fullest equipment for the most advanced training and research in various branches of science, especially in its application to industry:

(2) The Imperial College of Science and Technology became a school of the University of London ("the University") in 1908:

(3) On 22nd June 1988, the Royal Charter of the Imperial College of Science and Technology was amended by Order in Council to change the name of the body to the Imperial College of Science, Technology and Medicine ("Imperial College") with the purpose, inter alia, of carrying on the work of St. Mary's Hospital Medical School:

(4) By the Imperial College Act 1988, which came into effect on 1st August 1988, St. Mary's Hospital Medical School became united with Imperial College:

(5) Under schemes made pursuant to section 15 of the National Health Service Act 1946, both the Charing Cross Hospital Medical School and the Westminster Medical School ("the Medical Schools") were, on 23rd June 1948, constituted bodies corporate and in accordance with those schemes were administered as schools of the University with the main objects of providing for the education of students in medicine and allied subjects, promoting research work for the advancement of medical sciences and engaging in ancillary activities:

(6) In pursuance of the policy of the University that the academic strength and financial viability of the Medical Schools of the University should be enhanced by the merger of some of those schools, the Medical Schools were dissolved, and a new body corporate constituted, on 1st August 1984 by the Charing Cross and Westminster Medical School Act 1984, which also pro-

vided for the new body corporate to be known as the Charing Cross and Westminster Medical School and for the schemes made pursuant to section 15 of the National Health Service Act 1946 to be revoked:

(7) The Royal Postgraduate Medical School was originally incorporated by Royal Charter dated 10th July 1931 and by Royal Charter dated 25th February 1974 it was reconstituted as a University medical school, having the objects of the teaching and practice of and research into the science and art of medicine and such allied subjects as may be decided upon from time to time by the Council of the Royal Postgraduate Medical School:

(8) The National Heart and Lung Institute ("the Institute") was originally incorporated in 1973 under the name "the Cardiothoracic Institute" as a company limited by guarantee with the main objects of promoting the study of disease and particularly diseases of the heart, circulation and chest and generally improving the standard of knowledge of the means of prevention, diagnosis and methods of treatment and cure of such diseases:

(9) The Report of the Inquiry into London's Health Service, Medical Education and Research under the chairmanship of Sir Bernard Tomlinson, published in October 1992, recommended the linking of London Medical Schools to multi-faculty colleges and it is consistent with the policy of the University that the academic strength and financial viability of the medical schools of the University should be enhanced by the merger of some of those schools with certain multi-faculty institutions of the University:

(10) On 1st August 1995 the Institute transferred its assets and rights to Imperial College:

(11) Imperial College, the Charing Cross and Westminster Medical School and the Royal Postgraduate Medical School have agreed that it is expedient that they should be united as one college in accordance with the provisions of this Act and that the Charter of Imperial College should be amended so as to make suitable provision in consequence thereof:

(12) It is expedient that provision should be made in consequence of the transfer referred to in recital (10) above and for the company incorporating the Institute to be dissolved:

(13) It is expedient that the other provisions contained in this Act should be enacted:

(14) The objects of this Act cannot be attained without the authority of Parliament:

May it therefore please Your Majesty that it may be enacted, and be it enacted, by the Queen's most Excellent Majesty, by and with the advice and consent of the Lords Spiritual and Temporal, and Commons, in this present Parliament assembled, and by the authority of the same, as follows:—

Citation

1. This Act may be cited as the Imperial College Act 1997.

Interpretation

2. In this Act, except where the context otherwise requires, the following expressions have the following meanings:—

"the appointed day", in reference to an existing body, means such day as may be agreed by Imperial College and that body under section 3 (Appointed day) of this Act and, in reference to the Institute, means the date on which this Act is passed;

"the charter" means the charter reconstituting the Royal Postgraduate Medical School, granted by Her Majesty on 25th February 1974;

"existing body" means the Charing Cross and Westminster Medical School or the Royal Postgraduate Medical School;

"the Governing Body" means the Governing Body of Imperial College;

"Imperial College" means the Imperial College of Science, Technology and Medicine;

"the Institute" means the National Heart and Lung Institute.

Appointed day

3.—(1) Imperial College and an existing body may agree a day to be the appointed day for the purposes of this Act in its application to that body.

(2) Not less than 14 days before any such day as may be agreed under subsection (1) above, Imperial College shall—

(a) give notice to the Council of the University of London of the day so agreed; and

(b) publish in the London Gazette a notice stating the day so agreed.

Dissolution of existing bodies and Institute

4.—(1) On the appointed day—

(a) the Charing Cross and Westminster Medical School shall be dissolved and the Charing Cross and Westminster Medical School Act 1984 shall be repealed;

(b) the Royal Postgraduate Medical School shall be dissolved and the charter shall be revoked; and

(c) the company incorporating the Institute shall be dissolved.

(2) Imperial College shall notify the registrar of the effect of subsection (1)(c) above and of section 10 (Restriction on use of certain names) of this Act within 14 days beginning with the date on which this Act is passed; and the registrar shall record the dissolution of the company referred to in that subsection.

(3) In subsection (2) above, "the registrar" has the meaning given in section 744 of the Companies Act 1985.

Transfer of property, etc.

5. All property, real and personal, of every description (including things in action) and all rights and privileges of an existing body or of the Institute which immediately before the appointed day belonged to or were vested in or exercisable by that body shall on the appointed day, without any conveyance, transfer, assignment or other instrument, be transferred to and vested in, or be exercisable by, Imperial College for all the estate and interest therein of that body.

Transfer of obligations, etc.

6. All debts and obligations of an existing body or of the Institute existing immediately before the appointed day shall, on the appointed day, be transferred and attached to Imperial College and shall thereafter be discharged and satisfied by Imperial College.

Saving for agreements, deeds, actions, etc.

7. All agreements, appointments, awards, contracts, deeds and other instruments, and all actions and proceedings and causes of action which immediately before the appointed day were existing or pending in favour of, or against, an existing body or the Institute shall on and after the appointed day continue and may be carried into effect, enforced and prosecuted by, or in favour of, or against, Imperial College to the same extent and in like manner as if Imperial College instead of the existing body or the Institute, as the case may be, had been a party to, or interested in, the same respectively.

Construction of bequests, etc. and powers of trustees

8.—(1) Subject to subsection (2) below, any scheme, will, deed or other instrument, whether made or executed before, on or after the appointed day which contains any bequest, gift, trust or other benefit in favour of or connected with an existing body or the Institute shall, on and after the appointed day, be read and have effect as if Imperial College were named therein instead of that body.

(2) Imperial College shall administer any bequest, gift, trust or other benefit referred to in subsection (1) above as nearly as may be for the purposes intended in the original scheme, will, deed or other instrument conferring such a benefit.

(3) Without prejudice to subsection (1) above, any trustees who, immediately before the appointed day, had power, for all or any purposes relating to hospital services (including research) or to any other part of the health service associated with hospitals, to assist, support or otherwise benefit an existing body or the Institute, shall, on and from that day, have power to assist, support or otherwise benefit Imperial College as if it were a hospital for which those trustees were appointed.

(4) In this section "the health service" and "hospital" have the same meaning as in the National Health Service Act 1977.

Transfer of powers to appoint or nominate

9. Any power or right of an existing body or of any officer or employee of an existing body to appoint or nominate a member of any education authority, or of the governing body of any educational, charitable or other institution, shall on the appointed day be transferred to, and may be exercised by, Imperial College or the officer or employee of Imperial College who in the opinion of the Governing Body most nearly performs the functions formerly performed by the former officer or employee in question.

Restriction on use of certain names

10.—(1) No person other than Imperial College shall, within a period of 25 years beginning with the date on which this Act is passed, use any of the names mentioned in subsection (2) below without the consent of Imperial College.

(2) The names referred to in subsection (1) above are—
(a) National Heart and Lung Institute;
(b) Charing Cross and Westminster Medical School; and
(c) Royal Postgraduate Medical School.

INDEX

KING'S COLLEGE LONDON ACT 1997

(1997 c. iii)

ARRANGEMENT OF SECTIONS

An Act to unite the United Medical and Dental Schools of Guy's and St. Thomas's Hospitals and King's College London; to transfer all rights, properties and liabilities from the Schools to the College; and for connected and other purposes.   [31st July 1997]

PARLIAMENTARY DEBATES

The Bill's progress through Parliament was as follows:

House of Lords: First Reading, January 11, 1995; Second Reading, February 16, 1995; Bill committed, February 16, 1995; Bill committed to an unopposed Committee, July 6, 1995; Motion to suspend the Bill to subsequent Sessions, October 26, 1995; Third Reading, May 9, 1996.

House of Commons: First Reading, May 9, 1996; Second Reading, June 24, 1996; Bill committed, June 24, 1996; Bill committed to an unopposed Committee, April 7, 1996; Motion to suspend the Bill to subsequent Sessions, October 15, 1996; Motion to revive the Bill from previous Sessions debated on the date given, December 19, 1997; Motion to revive the Bill from previous Sessions debated on the date given, June 19, 1997; Third Reading, July 29, 1997.

Royal Assent: July 31, 1997.

INTRODUCTION

This Act provides for the union of the United Medical and Dental Schools of Guy's and St. Thomas's Hospitals and King's College London. The union follows recommendations contained in the Report of the Inquiry into London's Health Service, Medical Education and Research under the chairmanship of Sir Bernard Tomlinson dated October 1992 ("the Tomlinson Report"). In particular, the Report recommended that the London Medical Schools should merge with King's College School of Medicine and Dentistry within the College, and that this merger should be pursued and implemented with all speed. The Department of Health endorsed the broad conclusions of the Tomlinson Report and the Secretary of State for Education asked the Higher Education Funding Council for England to take these conclusions forward.

Whereas—

(1) King's College London (hereinafter referred to as "the College") was founded by Royal Charter granted on 14th August 1829 by His late Majesty

King George the Fourth and, notwithstanding the annulment of that Charter by the King's College London Act 1882, remained incorporated by virtue of that Act and subsequently by virtue of the King's College London (Transfer) Act 1908 and, since 1st April 1980, by virtue of the King's College London Act 1978 and a Royal Charter granted by Her Majesty on 1st April 1980:

(2) From its foundation the College included medical subjects in its curriculum and soon thereafter established a school of medicine and dentistry (hereinafter referred to as "the College's School of Medicine and Dentistry"):

(3) In 1839 the College acquired certain premises and there established King's College Hospital as a teaching hospital:

(4) Under the King's College Hospital Act 1851 the College's School of Medicine and Dentistry was established as a separate body corporate and King's College Hospital was transferred thereto:

(5) Under the said Act of 1908 further functions and property of the College were transferred to the College's School of Medicine and Dentistry which, under that Act, became a school of medicine and dentistry of the University of London (hereinafter referred to as "the University") and was thereafter administered as one entity with King's College Hospital:

(6) Under a scheme made pursuant to section 15 of the National Health Service Act 1946 the College's School of Medicine and Dentistry was constituted as a body corporate under the name of "King's College Hospital Medical School (University of London)" and, in accordance with that scheme, was thereafter separately administered from King's College Hospital as an independent school of the University;

(7) By virtue of the King's College London Act 1983 King's College Hospital Medical School (University of London) was reunited with the College and in accordance with that Act the College now maintains a school of medicine and dentistry known as King's College School of Medicine and Dentistry:

(8) Under the said Act of 1983 there was constituted a Committee of the Council of the College known as the Delegacy of King's College School of Medicine and Dentistry to advise that Council on, and to superintend, the work carried on by King's College School of Medicine and Dentistry:

(9) Guy's Hospital was established in 1724 and Guy's Hospital Medical School was founded in 1769. Lectures in dental surgery commenced there in 1799 and a dental school was established as part of Guy's Hospital Medical School in 1889. Guy's Hospital Medical School was admitted as a School of the University in 1900 and remained a constituent part of Guy's Hospital until 5th July 1948 when, pursuant to a scheme made under the said section 15, the School was reconstituted:

(10) St. Thomas's Hospital was established in 1173 and St. Thomas's Hospital Medical School was founded in about 1550, St. Thomas's Hospital Medical School was admitted as a School of the University in 1900 and remained a constituent part of St. Thomas's Hospital until 5th July 1948 when, pursuant to a scheme made under the said section 15, the School was reconstituted:

(11) On 1st August 1982 Guy's Hospital Medical School was reconstituted pursuant to a scheme under the said section 15 as the United Medical Schools of Guy's and St. Thomas's Hospitals (hereinafter referred to as "the United Medical Schools") and on the same day St. Thomas's Hospital Medical School was reconstituted as the Administration Council of the United Medical Schools of Guy's and St. Thomas's Hospitals (hereinafter referred to as "the Administration Council"):

(12) The Royal Dental Hospital of London was established in 1858 and the Royal Dental Hospital of London School of Dental Surgery (hereinafter referred to as "the Dental School") was founded in 1859. The Dental School was admitted as a School of the University in 1911 and remained a constitu-

ent part of the Royal Dental Hospital of London until 1948 when, pursuant to a scheme made under the said section 15, the Dental School was reconstituted.

(13) On 1st August 1983 the United Medical Schools were reconstituted pursuant to a scheme made under the said section 15 as the United Medical and Dental Schools of Guy's and St. Thomas's Hospitals (hereinafter referred to as "the Schools"), the Administration Council was also reconstituted pursuant to a scheme made under the said section 15 as the First Administration Council of the United Medical and Dental Schools of Guy's and St. Thomas's Hospitals (hereinafter referred to as "the First Administration Council") and the Dental School was reconstituted as the Second Administration Council of the United Medical and Dental Schools of Guy's and St. Thomas's Hospitals (hereinafter referred to as "the Second Administration Council"):

(14) On 1st August 1985 the Institute of Dermatology (hereinafter referred to as "the Institute") which had been incorporated in 1950 as a company limited by guarantee, transferred its assets and rights to the Schools which were reconstituted on that day pursuant to a scheme made under the said section 15 and on the same day the First Administration Council and the Second Administration Council were also reconstituted pursuant to schemes made under the said section 15:

(15) The Institute was dissolved in May 1988:

(16) By virtue of the United Medical and Dental Schools Act 1990 the First Administration Council and the Second Administration Council were dissolved and a centralised management was created for the Schools pursuant to a scheme made under the said section 15:

(17) The Report of the Inquiry into London's Health Service, Medical Education and Research under the chairmanship of Sir Bernard Tomlinson dated October 1992 (hereinafter referred to as "the Tomlinson Report") recommended the linking of London Medical Schools to multi-faculty colleges and in particular that the Schools should merge with King's College School of Medicine and Dentistry within the College and that this merger should be pursued and implemented with all speed. The Tomlinson Report also recognised that co-location of medical schools and multi-faculty institutions and rationalisation of facilities would need to be contingent on suitable financial arrangements being made and more particularly on the release of funds to finance it:

(18) The Department of Health has endorsed the broad conclusions of the Tomlinson Report, including the recommended merger of the College and the Schools, and the Secretary of State for Education has asked the Higher Education Funding Council for England to take them forward:

(19) The College and the Schools have agreed that it is expedient that provision should be made for the Schools and the College to be united in accordance with this Act:

(20) It is expedient that the other provisions contained in this Act should be enacted:

(21) The objects of this Act cannot be attained without the authority of Parliament:

May it therefore please Your Majesty that it may be enacted, and be it enacted, by the Queen's most Excellent Majesty, by and with the advice and consent of the Lords Spiritual and Temporal, and Commons, in this present Parliament assembled, and by the authority of the same, as follows:

Short title

1. This Act may be cited as the King's College London Act 1997.

Interpretation

2. In this Act, unless the subject or context otherwise requires, the following expressions shall have the following meanings:—

"the appointed day" means such day as may be agreed by the Council of the College, the Delegacy and the Council of Governors under section 3 (Appointed day) of this Act;

"the Charter" means the Royal Charter granted by Her Majesty on 1st April 1980 to the College;

"the College" means King's College London;

"the College Statutes" means the Statutes referred to in article 14 of the Charter;

"the Continuing Trustees" means the Continuing Trustees of the United Medical and Dental Schools of Guy's and St. Thomas's Hospitals constituted under section 6 (Constitution of Continuing Trustees of Schools) of this Act;

"the Council of Governors" means the Council of Governors of the Schools;

"the Council of the College" means the Council of King's College London;

"the Delegacy" means the Delegacy of King's College School of Medicine and Dentistry;

"the Former Establishments" means the United Medical Schools of Guy's and St. Thomas's Hospitals, the First Administration Council of the United Medical and Dental Schools of Guy's and St. Thomas's Hospitals, the Second Administration Council of the United Medical and Dental Schools of Guy's and St. Thomas's Hospitals and the Institute of Dermatology;

"the Principal" means the Principal for the time being of the College;

"the relevant property" has the meaning assigned to it by the said section 6;

"the Schools" means the United Medical and Dental Schools of Guy's and St. Thomas's Hospitals and, except in section 4 (Dissolution of Schools) of this Act, references to the Schools shall be construed as including reference to the Council of Governors;

"the University" means the University of London.

Appointed day

3.—(1) The Council of the College, the Delegacy and the Council of Governors may agree a day to be the appointed day for the purposes of this Act.

(2) Not less than 14 days before such day as may be agreed under subsection (1) above the Council of the College shall—

(a) give notice to the Council of the University of the day so agreed; and

(b) publish in the London Gazette a notice stating the day so agreed.

Dissolution of Schools

4. On the appointed day the Schools and the Council of Governors shall hereby be dissolved and the scheme made pursuant to section 15 of the National Health Service Act 1946 constituting the Council of Governors and defining the duties and powers of that Council and the Schools and providing for the management and control of the Schools shall hereby be revoked.

Transfer of property, etc.

5.—(1) All property, real and personal, of every description (including things in action) and all rights and privileges of the Schools which immediately before the appointed day belonged to or were vested in or exercisable by the Schools shall on the appointed day, subject to the provisions of this Act, without any conveyance, transfer, assignment or other instrument, be transferred to and vested in, or be exercisable by, the College for all the estate and interest therein of the Schools.

(2) Any property which by any scheme, deed, will or other instrument or otherwise is held upon trust for any specific foundation or object of the Schools or of King's College School of Medicine and Dentistry shall, on and after the appointed day, be held upon trust for and applied, so far as is possible, to the same foundation or object of the College:

Provided that—

(a) any such foundation or object may from time to time be varied or added to by deed under the common seal of the College which shall have been approved by a special resolution (as defined in article 1 of the Charter) of the Council of the College but so that the funds and investments or share in an investment pool for the time being allocated to that specific foundation or object shall remain allocated for that specific object or foundation; and

(b) any such deed shall not be of any validity until the same shall have been submitted to and approved by the Privy Council and a certificate of their approval thereof signed by the Clerk of the Privy Council, or by any other person authorised by the Privy Council, in that behalf, shall be endorsed on the deed.

(3) Subject to the provisions of subsection (2) above, any property held by the Schools upon or subject to any trust or trusts shall be held by the College upon or subject to the trust or trusts upon or subject to which that property was held by the Schools previously to the appointed day.

(4) Without prejudice to the general effect of subsection (1) above, the property of the Schools transferred to the College by that subsection shall include such interests as the Schools may have in the freehold or leasehold properties and other interests in property specified in Part I of Schedule 1 to this Act and the trust funds specified in Part II of that Schedule.

Constitution of Continuing Trustees of Schools

6.—(1) On the appointed day there shall be constituted a body to be known as the Continuing Trustees of the United Medical and Dental Schools of Guy's and St. Thomas's Hospitals which shall exist for a period of 10 years from that day and which shall on the expiry of that period hereby be dissolved and cease to exist.

(2) Prior to the appointed day the Council of Governors shall appoint four persons, and the Delegacy shall appoint one person, and the persons so appointed together with the Principal shall be the members of the Continuing Trustees.

(3)(a) A member of the Continuing Trustees, other than the Principal, may, by notice in writing to the other members, resign his membership; and if a member other than the Principal becomes, in the opinion of the other members, unfit to discharge his duties as a member, the other members may, by notice in writing to him, terminate his membership.

(b) Where a member of the Continuing Trustees, other than the Principal, dies or resigns or has his membership terminated, the surviving or continuing members may by writing appoint another person to be a member in his place.

(4) The Continuing Trustees shall—

(a) consider for the purposes of section 7 (Restriction on use of certain property) of this Act, any proposals by the Council of the College to use or permit the use of any of the relevant property otherwise than for the purposes of educating, or providing facilities for, students of medicine or dentistry or of promoting and advancing the teaching of, or research into, medicine and dentistry, or subjects allied thereto, within the College; and

(b) consider any other proposals or matters which may be referred to it by the Council of the College including any proposals for changes to the composition and functions of the Board of Management constituted under Statute 8A of the College Statutes.

(5) The Continuing Trustees shall determine its own quorum and procedure.

(6) For the purposes of this section and section 7 (Restriction on use of certain property) of this Act "the relevant property" means such interests in the properties specified in Schedule 2 to this Act as are transferred to the College under section 5 (Transfer of property, etc.) of this Act and such other property as may be designated by the Council of Governors before the appointed day, or by the Council of the College from time to time during the existence of the Continuing Trustees, as subject to the provisions of the said section 7.

Restriction on use of certain property

7. The College shall not during the existence of the Continuing Trustees use or permit the use of any of the relevant property otherwise than for the purposes referred to in subsection (4) of section 6 (Constitution of Continuing Trustees of Schools) of this Act without the prior consent in writing of a majority of the members of the Continuing Trustees.

Transfer of liabilities, etc.

8. All debts and obligations of the Schools shall on the appointed day be transferred and attached to the College and shall thereafter be discharged and satisfied by the College.

Savings for agreements, deeds, actions, etc.

9. All agreements, appointments, awards, contracts, deeds and other instruments, and all actions and proceedings and causes of action, which immediately before the appointed day were existing or pending in favour of, or against, the Schools shall on and after the appointed day continue and may be carried into effect, enforced and prosecuted by, or in favour of, or against, the College to the same extent and in like manner as if the College instead of the Schools had been party to, or interested in, the same respectively.

Construction of bequests, etc.

10. Any scheme, will, deed or other instrument, whether made or executed before, on or after the appointed day, which contains any bequest, gift or trust or other benefit in favour of or connected with the Schools shall, on and after the appointed day, be read and have effect as if the College were referred to therein instead of the Schools.

Transfer of powers to appoint or nominate

11. Any power or right of the Schools or of any of the Former Establishments or of any of their officers or employees to appoint or nominate a member of any health or educational authority, or of the governing body of any health, educational, charitable or other institution, shall on the appointed day be transferred to, and may be exercised by the College or by the officer or employee of the College who, in the opinion of the Council of the College, most nearly performs the functions formerly performed by the former officer or employee in question.

Name of College school of medicine and dentistry

12. On and after the appointed day, the medical and dental school of the College shall be known as Guy's, King's College and St. Thomas' Hospitals' Medical and Dental School.

Dissolution of Delegacy

13. On the appointed day the Delegacy shall hereby be dissolved and shall cease to exist.

Repeals and amendments

14. On the appointed day, the provisions of the King's College London Act 1983, the King's College London Act 1985 and the United Medical and Dental Schools Act 1990 specified in Part I of Schedule 3 to this Act (which include provisions that are spent) shall be hereby repealed to the extent specified in that Part and section 7 (Construction of bequests, etc.) of the United Medical and Dental Schools Act 1990 shall be amended as provided by Part II of that Schedule.

Amendments to College Statutes

15. On the appointed day, the College Statutes shall have effect as if they were amended as follows:—

(1) In Statute 1 (Membership of the Council)—

(a) for paragraph (1) there shall be substituted the following paragraph:—

"(1) The Council shall consist of the following persons:

    (A) Ex-officio Members:—

        (i) The Principal.

        (ii) The Vice-Principals.

        (iii) The Dean or Deans of the Guy's, King's College and St. Thomas' Hospitals' Medical and Dental School.

    (B) Appointed Members:—

        (i) one person after consultation with the Visitor.

        (ii) one person after consultation with the King's College London Association.

        (iii) eighteen other persons who are neither employees nor students of the College.

    (C) Elected Members:—

        (i) eight persons elected from among their number by the academic staff of the College.

        (ii) three persons elected from among their number by the students of the College.

        (iii) two persons elected from among their number by the staff of the College who are not members of the academic staff;

    such persons to be elected in the manner prescribed by Regulations.";

(b) in paragraph (3) for the words "categories (i), (ii) and (iv) of paragraph (1)(D)" there shall be substituted "categories (i) and (iii) of paragraph (1)(C)";

(c) in paragraph (4) for the words "category (iii) of paragraph (1)(D)" there shall be substituted "category (ii) of paragraph (1)(C)";

(d) the words "Life and" shall be deleted from paragraph (7).

(2) For Statute 4 (Membership of the Academic Board) there shall be substituted the following Statute:—

"MEMBERSHIP OF THE ACADEMIC BOARD

4. The Academic Board shall consist of—
    (1) *Ex-officio Members*—
        The Principal.
        The Vice-Principals.
        The Reverend The Dean.
        The Heads of Schools, Faculties, Divisions, Departments
           and Subject Groups recognised for this purpose in
           Regulations.
        The heads of academic services recognised for this purpose
           in Regulations.
        The President of the Students' Union;
    (2) one student member from each School, Faculty or other constituency defined for this purpose in Regulations elected by the undergraduate and postgraduate students registered in that constituency;
    (3) other members in number not less than the number of the ex-officio members to be appointed or elected in the manner prescribed in Regulations: Provided that a majority of the members of the Academic Board shall be Professors, Readers or Senior Lecturers.".

(3) After Statute 8 there shall be inserted an additional Statute:—
    "8A. There shall be a Board of Management constituted in accordance with Regulations which shall advise the Council on the discharge of its responsibilities in matters relating to medicine and dentistry under the Medical Act 1983 and the Dentists Act 1984, or any Act repealing and replacing either of those Acts, and any other legislation relevant to the subjects within the purview of the Board of Management and on such other matters as may from time to time be prescribed in Regulations.".

(4) For Statute 11 there shall be substituted the following Statutes:—

"VICE-PRINCIPALS

11. The Council shall, on the recommendation of the Principal, appoint from among the staff of the College one or more Vice-Principals who shall, subject to these Statutes, assist the Principal in such matters as the Principal may from time to time delegate to them. In the event of two or more Vice-Principals being so appointed, one of their number shall be appointed to act for the Principal during a vacancy in that office or during the absence or disability of the Principal.

DEANS OF THE GUY'S, KING'S COLLEGE AND ST. THOMAS'
HOSPITALS' MEDICAL AND DENTAL SCHOOL

11A. The Council shall, on the recommendation of the Principal, appoint one or more Deans of the Guy's, King's College and St. Thomas' Hospitals' Medical and Dental School who, in each case, shall hold office for such period and with such responsibilities as the Council may determine and who shall be or become a member of the academic staff of the College in the relevant discipline. The Principal shall recommend the appointment of one such Dean as a Vice-Principal of the College.".

Transitional amendments to College Statutes

16. On the passing of this Act, the College Statutes shall have effect as if, for Statute 20, there were substituted the following Statute:—

"20.—(1) The foregoing Statutes shall have effect subject to the following transitional provisions:—

(A) Prior to the Appointed Day there shall be nominated by the Council of Governors six persons to be appointed to be members of the Council ("the Additional Appointed Members") in category (iii) of paragraph (1)(B) of Statute 1 of the revised statutes.

(B) On the Appointed Day the persons appointed as Appointed Members in categories (iii), (iv) and (v) of paragraph (1)(C) of Statute 1 of the existing statutes shall be deemed to be Appointed Members in category (iii) of paragraph (1)(B) of Statute 1 of the revised statutes.

(C) On the Appointed Day paragraph (1)(B)(iii) of Statute 1 of the revised statutes shall have effect for a period of three years as if for the word "eighteen" there were substituted "twenty-four" and the Council shall appoint the Additional Appointed Members as members of the Council for that period.

(D) Prior to the Appointed Day there shall be elected by the academic staff of the Schools four of their number to be members of the Council ("the Additional Academic Staff Members") in category (i) of paragraph (1)(C) of Statute 1 of the revised statutes.

(E) On the Appointed Day the persons elected as Elected Members in categories (i) and (ii) of paragraph (1)(D) of Statute 1 of the existing statutes shall be deemed to be Elected Members in category (i) of paragraph (1)(C) of Statute 1 of the revised statutes.

(F) On the Appointed Day paragraph (1)(C)(i) of Statute 1 of the revised statutes shall have effect for a period of four years as if for the word "eight" there were substituted "twelve" and the Additional Academic Staff Members shall be members of the Council for that period.

(G) Prior to the Appointed Day there shall be elected by the students of the Schools one of their number to be a member of the Council ("the Additional Student Member") in category (ii) of paragraph (1)(C) of Statute 1 of the revised statutes.

(H) On the Appointed Day paragraph (1)(C)(ii) of Statute 1 of the revised statutes shall have effect for a period of one year as if for the word "three" there were substituted "four" and the Additional Student Member shall be a member of the Council for that period.

(I) Prior to the Appointed Day there shall be elected by the staff of the Schools who are not members of the academic staff one of their number to be a member of the Council ("the Additional Non-Academic Staff Member") in category (iii) of paragraph (1)(C) of Statute 1 of the revised statutes.

(J) On the Appointed Day paragraph (1)(C)(iii) of Statute 1 of the revised statutes shall have effect for a period of four years as if for the word "two" there were substituted "three" and the Additional Non-Academic Staff Member shall be a member of the Council for that period.

(K) On and after the Appointed Day the persons who were Fellows of King's College Hospital Medical School (University of London) or of Chelsea College (University of London) or Fellows or Associates of the Principal and Governors of Queen Elizabeth College immediately prior to the respective dates on which those bodies were dissolved and the Fellows of the Schools shall be Fellows of the College.

(2) In this Statute—
   "the Appointed Day" means the day which is the appointed day for the purposes of the King's College London Act 1997;
   "the Council of Governors" means the Council of Governors of the Schools;
   "the existing statutes" means these Statutes as they have effect immediately prior to the Appointed Day;
   "the revised statutes" means these Statutes as they have effect on the Appointed Day;
   "the Schools" means the United Medical and Dental Schools of Guy's and St. Thomas's Hospitals.".

SCHEDULES

Section 5   SCHEDULE 1

SPECIFIED FREEHOLD OR LEASEHOLD PROPERTIES AND OTHER INTERESTS IN
PROPERTY AND TRUST FUNDS TRANSFERRED TO THE COLLEGE

PART I—SPECIFIED FREEHOLD OR LEASEHOLD PROPERTIES AND OTHER
INTERESTS IN PROPERTY

*A—Properties on or adjacent to the site of Guy's Hospital in
the London Borough of Southwark*

(1) The freehold property known as the Medical School Building (subject to a perpetual rent-charge of £707.70) and numbers 127, 129 and 131 Borough High Street registered in her Majesty's Land Registry under title number SGL 33774.

(2) The freehold property numbers 133 and 135 Borough High Street registered in Her Majesty's Land Registry under title number SGL 272912.

(3) The freehold property numbers 137, 139, 141 and 143 Borough High Street registered in Her Majesty's Land Registry under title number 174863.

(4) The freehold property numbers 1/3 Newcomen Street registered in Her Majesty's Land Registry under title numbers SGL 101683 and LN 181121.

(5) The freehold property numbers 4/8 Newcomen Street registered in Her Majesty's Land Registry under title number LN 181121.

(6) The freehold property 9 Newcomen Street known as Mollison House registered in Her Majesty's Land Registry under title number SGL 43635.

(7) The freehold property the sites of 10/13a Newcomen Street registered in Her Majesty's Land Registry under title number LN 91142.

(8) The freehold property numbers 14/17 Newcomen Street registered in Her Majesty's Land Registry under title number SGL 291470.

(9) The freehold property known as St. Christopher's House situated at 208 Long Lane and 1/7 Castle Buildings, currently in use as a student hostel with out-buildings and registered in Her Majesty's Land Registry under title numbers 152766 and 443201.

(10) Those parts of Guy's Tower, on floors 3, 7, 8, 12, 17, 18 and 20 to 32 (inclusive) occupied by the Schools as tenant or licensee of the National Health Service and/or the Guy's and St. Thomas's NHS Trust.

(11) The leasehold property comprising the 2nd Floor of New Guy's House, together with the NMR Building.

(12) The leasehold property comprising the 4th Floor of Hunts House.

(13) The leasehold property comprising part of Boland House, being a majority of the basement, ground and 1st floors including the area leased to McDonald's.

(14) The leasehold property at Wolfson House comprising those parts used as a student hostel.

(15) An interest in Phase 3 of Guy's Hospital Redevelopment.

*B—Properties on or adjacent to the site of St. Thomas' Hospital in
the London Borough of Lambeth*

(1) The freehold property situated at the southern end of the site known as the Medical School Building (Block 9) and including the Dudgeon Building attached thereto.

(2) The freehold property situated to the north of Block 9 known as the Prideaux Building.

(3) The freehold property known as St. Thomas' House being a student hostel with attached sports and social facilities including the property registered in Her Majesty's Land Registry under title numbers LN 120876 and LN 128780.

(4) The freehold property The Rectory, 214 Lambeth Road, SE1 7JY.

(5) The leasehold property Brian Creamer House, Lambeth Road, SE1 7JY including the Lodge.

(6) Those parts of St. Thomas's Hospital in the North Wing, the East Wing and the South Wing occupied by the Schools as tenant or licensee of the National Health Service and/or the Guy's and St. Thomas's NHS Trust.

(7) Premises at St. Thomas's Hospital registered in Her Majesty's Land Registry under title number LN 120874.

(8) The leasehold property known as the first floor of the former Lambeth Baths in Lambeth Walk being part of the property registered in Her Majesty's Land Registry under title number TGL 84665.

C—Other properties

(1) The freehold properties numbers 24 and 26 Ferndale Road, Brixton, London, SW4 7SF registered in Her Majesty's Land Registry under title number SGL 181272.

(2) The freehold property number 28 Ferndale Road, Brixton, London, SW4 7SF.

(3) The freehold property 46 Riverview Grove, Chiswick, London, W4 3QP registered in Her Majesty's Land Registry under title number NGL 4512.

(4) Freehold property in Lewisham SE23 known as Honor Oak Park Athletic Ground, extending to approximately 3.6 hectares.

(5) Freehold property in Lewisham SE23 adjacent to Honor Oak Park Athletic Ground registered in Her Majesty's Land Registry under title number 444196.

(6) Freehold property in Lewisham SE23 adjacent to Honor Oak Park Athletic Ground registered in Her Majesty's Land Registry under title number 448520.

(7) The freehold property 50 Stillness Road, Honor Oak Park, SE23 forming part of the above-mentioned athletic ground registered in her Majestey's Land Registry under title number LN 15854.

(8) The freehold property 52 Stillness Road, Honor Oak Park, SE23 forming part of the above-mentioned athletic ground registered in Her Majesty's Land Registry under title number LN 32546.

(9) The freehold property 54 Stillness Road, Honor Oak Park, SE23 forming part of the above-mentioned athletic ground registered in Her Majesty's Land Registry under title number LN 16978.

(10) Freehold property in Stillness Road, Honor Oak Park, SE23 forming part of the above-mentioned athletic ground registered in Her Majesty's Land Registry under title number SGL 5494.

(11) The freehold property 138 Brockley Rise, Honor Oak Park, SE23 registered in Her Majesty's Land Registry under title number LN 85097.

(12) The freehold property 140 Brockley Rise, Honor Oak Park SE23 registered in Her Majesty's Land Registry under title number LN 79482.

(13) The freehold property at Stoke Road, Stoke d'Abernon, Cobham, Surrey known as the sportsground part of which was previously known as the Polo Ground extending to approximately 9.84 hectares and including Pavilion and staff bungalow.

(14) The freehold property in the Borough of Colwyn, Wales known as Ty'n Lidiart Chapel, Pentrefoelas currently used as a mountaineering hut and registered in Her Majesty's Land Registry under title number K 3732334.

(15) The licensed use of facilities at Lewisham Hospital in connection with the provision of teaching facilities at that Hospital.

(16) The leasehold property 71 Rainham Road, Gillingham, Kent registered in Her Majesty's Land Registry under title number K 405679.

(17) The leasehold property Vine Cottage, 1A Longfellow Road, Gillingham, Kent registered in Her Majesty's Land Registry under title number K 610643.

(18) The leasehold property 96 Windmill Road, Gillingham, Kent registered in Her Majesty's Land Registry under title number K 90492.

(19) The leasehold property 285 Marlborough Road, Gillingham, Kent registered in Her Majesty's Land Registry under title number K 91819.

(20) The leasehold property 287 Marlborough Road, Gillingham, Kent registered in Her Majesty's Land Registry under title number K 50500.

(21) The leasehold property 289 Marlborough Road, Gillingham, Kent registered in Her Majesty's Land Registry under title number K 54320.

(22) The leasehold property Broomhill House, David Salomons' Estate, Broomhill Road, Tunbridge Wells, Kent.

(23) Use of Tideway Scullers School Boat House, Dukes Meadow, Hounslow under licence from that School.

PART II—SPECIFIED TRUST FUNDS

Specific endowments—academic appointments

The Wolfson Foundation Fund
The Doubleday Research Fellowship Fund
The Martin Rushton Research Fellowship
The Dunhill Dermatology Research Fellowship Fund
The Mary Dunhill Chair of Cutaneous Medicine Fund
The Dounglas Research Trust Fund
The Dudgeon Memorial Fund
Royal College of Surgeons Ophthalmology Research Fund
The Readership in Neuropathology Fund
The Arthritis and Rheumatism Council Chair of Rheumatology Fund
The Imperial Cancer Research Fund Chair of Clinical Oncology Fund
The Paediatric Research Unit Lectureship Fund
The Joseph Levy Chair of Paediatric Cardiology Fund
Children's Nationwide Research Lectureship in Paediatric Nephrology
Children's Nationwide Medical Research Chair of Paediatric Nephrology
The Prince Philip Chair of Paediatric Research
The Paediatric Research Unit Appeal Fund
The Ferdinand James de Rothschild Chair of Paediatrics Fund
The Children's National Medical Research Fund
Lectureship in Paediatric Biochemistry Fund
The Paediatric Nephrology Lectureship Fund
The Philip Harris Chair of Radiological Sciences Fund
The Gordon Lectureship Fund
The Sir William Dunn Lectureship Fund
The Nettleship Legacy Fund

Specific endowments—other academic purposes

The Herbert and Emily Stroyan Fund
The Marston Research Fund
The Grainger Testimonial Endowment Fund
The Gordon Thomas Fund
The Agnes Shore Memorial Fund
The Anstie Library Bequest Fund
The Warwick James Research Fund
J G Turner Research Fund
Guy's Centenary Fund
The RDS Centenary Fund
The Newland Pedley General Fund
The Newland Pedley Building Fund
The Newland Pedley Scholarship in Dental Research
Richard Dickinson (General) Trust
The Richard Dickinson (USA) Trust
The Haematology Research Fund
The Montague Travelling Fellowship
The Featherstonehaugh Legacy Fund
R Forrest Memorial Fund
Mrs Lucy Wood Legacy Fund
E J Hopkins Fund
The Lilian Hilton Fund
The Desvignes Fund
The Adrian Stokes Memorial Fund
The Wyatt Fund
The Hyman Frankenburg Fund
The Anderson Trust Fund
The Dimbleby Endowment Fund

The Elsie Wall Cancer Research Fund
The Sackler Research Fellowship in Palliative Medicine
The William Dunn Fund
The Starling Memorial Fund
The M I Osmund Fellowship Fund
The Sir Arthur Fripp Memorial Fellowship Fund
The Sydney Ernest Banks Fund
The Mollison Memorial Library Fund
Bunty Orchard Lisle Research Fund
Mrs Gill's Charitable Settlement Fund
William Henry Dickinson Trust
The Robert Boyle Legacy Fund
The Gertrude Brownjohn Legacy Fund
The Louis Jenner Research Scholarship
The Michael and Sidney Herbert Fund
The Griffiths Fund
The Medical School Research Fund
The L R de M Thompson Subscriptions Fund
The Hilda and Ronald Poulton Fellowship Fund
The Targett Pathological Trust Fund
The H A Brown Fund
Mote Bequest
The Davies Colley Memorial Fund
The Usherwood Library Bequest Fund
The Stobie Memorial Fund
Harvey Bequest

Specific endowments—lectures

The J H Badcock Legacy Fund
The Berry Lecture Fund
The Conybeare Fund
The Guymer Memorial Lecture Fund
The H E Herbert Memorial Lecture Fund
Mortyn Jones Memorial Fund
Amalie and Edward Kass Lecture Fund
The Sarah Stolz Memorial Fund

Specific endowments—prizes for students

The James Rink Memorial Fund
The Mrs Doris Victoria Hopkins Legacy Fund
The Woolmer Fund
The Davies Prize Fund
The Roger Warwick Prize Fund
The McSwinney Scholarship Fund
The Tewfik Prize in Anatomy and Physiology Fund
The Hilton Prize Fund
The Michael Harris Prize Fund
The Gowland Hopkins Prize Fund
The Plimmer Scholarship Fund
The Prunty Prize Fund
The Leonard Lubbock Prize Fund
The Henry Levitt Memorial Prize Fund
The John Simon Prize Fund
The Stephen D Hey Prize Fund
The Hugh Dornhurst Prize Fund
The Professor Walther Prize Fund
The Emslie Prize in Periodontology and Preventive Dentistry Fund
The Gain Prize
The Harry Radin Prize
The David Frank Sturdee Prize Fund
The J A Smith Scholarship Fund
The Newland Pedley Prize Fund
The Jack Wheatley Memorial Prize Fund

The Malleson Prize for Student Dental Research Fund
The Dolamore Prize Fund
The F R Moser Prize Fund
The Parris Prize Fund
The Iain Benson Prize Fund
The Alfred Woodhouse Scholarship Fund
The Robert Woodhoue Prize Fund
The Arthur Cohen Prize Fund
The Saunders Scholarship
The Sidney James Kaye Prize Fund
The Rowe Prize in Conservative Dental Surgery
The Peter Lunt Scholarship/Prize Fund
The Baldwin Scholarship Fund
The Lonnon Bursary Fund
The Dermatology Prize Fund
The Leslie Hillman Prize in Haematology
The Pinniger Prize Fund
The Gilbert Prize Fund
The Mortyn Jones Prize Fund
The Sir Charles Symonds Prize Fund
R Warwick Prize in Oto-Rhino Laryngology
C Warwick Prize in Thoracic Medicine
The Wrigley Prize Fund
The Sutton Sams Memorial Prize Fund
The Rickford Prize Fund
The Rickford Prize in Gynaecology
The Bhatia Medal Fund
The Paediatric Prize Fund
The Pharmacology Prize Fund
The Bayer Prize Fund
ICI Prize in Clinical Pharmacology
The Wooldridge Memorial Prize Fund
The John Mellanby Scholarship Fund
The Pembrey Prize Fund
The Pearce Prize in Child Psychiatry
The Planck Bequest Fund
Tewfik Prize for Surgery Fund
The Treasurers' Prize for Clinical Surgery Fund
The Solly Memorial Prize Fund
The Beaney Scholarship Fund
The Stewart Rouquette Award Fund
The Lady Thatcher Prize in Surgery
The Evan Jones Prize Fund
The Charles Forster Prize Fund
The Irvine Prize Fund
The Charles Oldham Prize Fund
The Surgeon Rear Admiral Clark Exhibition Fund
The Laidlaw Prize Fund
The Beaney Fund for Prizes in Histopathology and Immunology
The Nevin Prize Fund
The Frederick George Larkin Prize Fund
The Box Scholarship Fund
The Treasurer's Prize for Clinical Medicine 1st Prize Fund
The Treasurer's Prize for Clinical Medicine 2nd Prize Fund
The Baldwin Clinical Prize Fund
The Clutton Memorial Medal Fund
The Wainwright Prize Fund
The Preliminary Clinical Prize Fund
The Ridley Bequest Fund
The Seymour Graves Toller Prize Fund
The Edgcumbe Prize Fund
The Bristow Medal Fund
The Upjohn Clinical Prize Fund

The Cheselden Medal Fund
The Hadden Memorial Prize Fund
The Woolrich Legacy Fund
The Guy Ramsey Prize Fund
The Jean Hall Morton Prize Fund
The Hutt Prize Fund
The T J Evans Prize Fund
The William Tite Scholarship Fund
The Carleton Hunter Memorial Prize Fund
The Perkins Bequest Fund
The Ian Howat Memorial Prize Fund
The Golding Bird Prize Fund
The Mead Medal Fund
The Foord Caiger Exhibition Fund
The Beddard Prize Fund
The Louis Meyer Harris Prize Fund
The General Scholarship Fund
The Anderson Scholarship Fund
The Sands Cox Scholarship Fund
The Musgrove and Peacock Scholarship Fund
A M Clover Prize

Specific endowments—scholarships and bursaries for students

The Dental Postgraduate Travelling Scholarship Fund
The Joel Winter Bursary
The Storer-Bennett Research Scholarship
Wetherley-Mein Bursary
The Graeme Wilkinson Research Fund
The Greville Studentship Fund
The Henry Myers Exhibition Fund
National Backpain Association
The Carolyn Warwick Studentship in Pathology Fund
The Guy's Hospital War Memorial Fund
J H Keesey Bursary
The Mr and Mrs Leung Woon Keung Fund
The Beaney Scholarship in Materia Medica Fund
The Lambrinudi Memorial Scholarship Fund
The Rowley Bristowe Memorial Fund
The Dr James Leighton Hopkins Travelling Scholarship Fund
The Arthur Durham Travelling Studentship Fund
The Hector MacKenzie Exhibition Fund
The Murray Falconer Fellowship Fund
Astley Cooper Studentship
Medical Sickness Society Travel Scholarship (Dental)
Medical Sickness Society Travel Scholarships (Medical)
City of London/Merchant Taylors Scholarship
RTZ Bursary
The John Henry Wignell Legacy Fund

Specific endowments—staff and student welfare

The Pavy Gymnasium Fund
The Weller Memorial Fund
The James Hawker Memorial Fund
The L D Dinnes Memorial Fund
Guy's Gazette

Specific endowments—to support mature students

The Laura Ashley Student Bursaries Fund
The Cochrane Prize Fund

The Marjory Murray Scholarship Fund
The Beryl Mitchell Fund

Specific endowments—to support intercalated BSc students

The Lord Riddell Scholarship (Medical) Fund
The Gull Studentship
The Lord Riddell Scholarship (Surgical) Fund
The Francis Lett Scholarship Fund
The Payling Wright Research Studentship Fund
The Borland Scholarship Fund
The Clothworkers' Awards Fund
The Schofield Scholarship
The V Urmson Smith Fund
The Clutton Trust Fund
The Box Legacy Fund
Haberdasher's Company Bursary
Mercer's Company Scholarship
Smith & Nephew Bursaries
The Roger Warwick Dental Scholarship
The Hudson Bequest
Wolfson Foundation Intercalated Awards
Goldberg-Schachmann Memorial Fund
The Bernard Sunley Charitable Foundation
The Jean Shanks Research Foundation

Specific endowments—student financial hardship funds

The Dr David Owen Fountaine Students' Exhibition Fund
The Jane Ortzen Abbott Fund
The Mrs Emily Davison Legacy Fund
The Dr George W Matthews Memorial Fund
The H P Mabe Bursary Fund
The Lewin Payne Discretionary Fund
The Students' Exhibition Fund
The Hampson Discretionary Fund
The Principal's Fund
    The J E Adams Memorial Bursary (1928)
    The Ian McGow Memorial Bursary (1936)
    The Sannyer Atkins Memorial Fund (1947)
    The Special Grant from Mrs F Wrey (1947)
The Richard Newitt Fund
Sidney Smith Sanderson Fund

Specific endowments—student electives

The John Willis Memorial Elective Fund
The Wakeford Elective Award Fund
The National Westminster Bank Elective
The Dorothy Arnold Elective Award Fund
The Alfred Rycroft Memorial Scholarship in Dental Surgery Fund
The Alex Boulger Memorial Fund
The Sachedina Elective
The Joseph Maitland Fund
Hisako Ikeda Fund

Other

The Abbott Laboratory Award Fund
The Gladstone, Stansfield, Stewart Memorial Prize Fund
The Dennis Deuchar Memorial Prize Fund
Dr George Michael Morris Electives
The Riker Elective Award Fund
The Howard Rogers Memorial Prize Fund
The Gatsby Charitable Foundation
Rayne Foundation Electives

Specific endowments—student clubs and societies

The Cartwright Benefaction Fund
The Kenneth McKenzie Biggs Fund
The C C de Birch Legacy Fund
United Clubs Boathouse Fund
The Woodward Legacy Fund
The Dr R H Hayes Legacy Fund
The St. Thomas's Hospital Amalgamated Clubs Fund

General endowments

The Abbott Legacy Fund
The L A Dunn Trust Fund
The Grant Massie Legacy Fund
The Milward Trust Fund
The Memorial Research Fund
The Platt Orme Legacy Fund
The School Endowment Fund
The St. Thomas's Hospital Medical School Fund
The Martin John Turner Fund
The Thompson Bequest
The Williams Legacy Fund

Earmarked funds

The Cardiovascular Research Fund
The Public Health Medicine Fund
The Commercial Development Fund
The Dental School Fund
The Dermatology Fund
The Microbiology Fund

Sections 6 and 7   SCHEDULE 2

SPECIFIED PROPERTIES SUBJECT TO RESTRICTIONS

*A—Properties on or adjacent to the site of Guy's Hospital in
the London Borough of Southwark*

(1) The freehold property numbers 133 and 135 Borough High Street registered in Her Majesty's Land Registry under title number SGL 272912.

(2) The freehold property numbers 1/3 Newcomen Street registered in Her Majesty's Land Registry under title numbers SGL 101683 and LN 181121.

(3) The freehold property numbers 4/8 Newcomen Street registered in Her Majesty's Land Registry under title number LN 181121.

(4) The freehold property 9 Newcomen Street known as Mollison House registered in Her Majesty's Land Registry under title number SGL 43635.

(5) The freehold property the sites of 10/13a Newcomen Street registered in Her Majesty's Land Registry under title number LN 91142.

(6) The freehold property known as St. Christopher's House situated at 208 Long Lane and 1/7 Castle Buildings, currently in use as a student hostel with out-buildings and registered in Her Majesty's Land Registry under title numbers 152766 and 443201.

(7) The leasehold property at Wolfson House comprising those parts used as a student hostel.

*B—Properties on or adjacent to the site of St. Thomas' Hospital in
the London Borough of Lambeth*

(1) The freehold property known as St. Thomas' House being a student hostel with attached sports and social facilities including the property registered in Her Majesty's Land Registry under title numbers LN 120876 and LN 128780.

(2) The freehold property The Rectory, 214 Lambeth Road, SE1 7JY.

(3) The leasehold property Brian Creamer House, Lambeth Road, SE1 7JY including the Lodge.

(4) The leasehold property known as the first floor of the former Lambeth Baths in Lambeth Walk being part of the property registered in Her Majesty's Land Registry under title number TGL 84665.

C—*Other properties*

(1) The freehold properties numbers 24 and 26 Ferndale Road, Brixton, London, SW4 registered in Her Majesty's Land Registry under title number SGL 181272.

(2) The freehold property number 28 Ferndale Road, Brixton, London, SW4 7SF.

(3) The freehold property 46 Riverview Grove, Chiswick, London, W4 3QP regisetered in Her Majesty's Land Registry under title number NGL 4512.

(4) Freehold property in Lewisham, SE23 known as Honor Oak Park Athletic Ground extending to approximately 3.6 hectares.

(5) Freehold property in Lewisham, SE23 adjacent to Honor Oak Park Athletic Ground registered in Her Majesty's Land Registry under title number 444196.

(6) Freehold property in Lewisham, SE23 adjacent to Honor Oak Park Athletic Ground registered in Her Majesty's Land Registry under title number 448520.

(7) The freehold property 50 Stillness Road, Honor Oak Park, SE23 forming part of the above-mentioned athletic ground registered in Her Majesty's Land Registry under title number LN 15854.

(8) The freehold property 52 Stillness Road, Honor Oak Park, SE23 forming part of the above-mentioned athletic ground registered in Her Majesty's Land Registry under title number LN 32546.

(9) The freehold property 54 Stillness Road, Honor Oak Park, SE23 forming part of the above-mentioned athletic ground registered in Her Majesty's Land Registry under title number LN 16978.

(10) Freehold property in Stillness Road, Honor Oak Park, SE23 forming part of the above-mentioned athletic ground registered in Her Majesty's Land Registry under title number SGL 5494.

(11) The freehold property 138 Brockley Rise, Honor Oak Park, SE23 registered in Her Majesty's Land Registry under title number LN 85097.

(12) The freehold property 140 Brockley Rise, Honor Oak Park, SE23 registered in Her Majesty's Land Registry under title number LN 79482.

(13) The freehold property at Stoke Road, Stoke d'Abernon, Cobham, Surrey known as the sports ground part of which was previously known as the Polo Ground extending to approximately 9.84 hectares and including Pavilion and staff bungalow.

(14) The freehold property in the Borough of Colwyn, Wales known as Ty'n Lidiart Chapel, Pentrefoelas currently used as a mountaineering hut and registered in Her Majestey's Land Registry under title number K 3732334.

(15) The leasehold property 71 Rainham Road, Gillingham, Kent registered in Her Majesty's Land Registry under title number K 405679.

(16) The leasehold property Vine Cottage, 1A Longfellow Road, Gillingham, Kent registered in Her Majesty's Land Registry under title number K 610643.

(17) The leasehold property 96 Windmill Road, Gillingham, Kent registered in Her Majesty's Land Registry under title number K 90492.

(18) The leasehold property 285 Marlborough Road, Gillingham, Kent registered in Her Majestey's Land Registry under title number K 91819.

(19) The leasehold property 287 Marlborough Road, Gillingham, Kent registered in Her Majesty's Land Registry under title number K 50500.

(20) The leasehold property 289 Marlborough Road, Gillingham, Kent registered in Her Majesty's Land Registry under title number K 54320.

(21) The leasehold property Broomhill House, David Salomons' Estate, Broomhill Road, Tunbridge Wells, Kent.

Section 14

SCHEDULE 3

PART I

PROVISIONS REPEALED

Chapter	Short title	Provision and extent of repeal
1983 c. xii	King's College London Act 1983	Sections 3 to 5 Sections 8 and 9
1985 c. xvi	King's College London Act 1985	Section 3 Section 4(1) and (4) Section 5
1990 c. vi	United Medical and Dental Schools Act 1990	Sections 3 to 5 Sections 8 to 15

PART II

PROVISIONS AMENDED

Chapter	Short title	Provision	Amendment
1990 c. vi	United Medical and Dental Schools Act 1990	Section 7 (Construction of bequests, etc.)	For the words "appointed day" where they secondly occur there shall be substituted "day which is the appointed day for the purposes of the King's College London Act 1997". For the words "the Schools" there shall be substituted "King's College London".

INDEX

References are to sections and Schedule

SCOTTISH AGRICULTURAL COLLEGE ORDER CONFIRMATION ACT 1997

(1997 c. iv)

An Act to confirm a Provisional Order under the Private Legislation Procedure (Scotland) Act 1936, relating to Scottish Agricultural College.

[17th December 1997]

PARLIAMENTARY DEBATES

The Bill's progress through Parliament was as follows:

House of Commons: First Reading, December 3, 1997; Bill considered by Commons, December 9, 1997; Third Reading, December 10, 1997.

House of Lords: First Reading, December 10, 1997; Bill considered by Lords, December 15, 1997; Third Reading, December 16, 1997.

Royal Assent: December 17, 1997.

INTRODUCTION

This Act, made under the Private Legislation Procedure (Scotland) Act 1936 (c. 52), transfers the assets, functions and responsibilities of The East of Scotland College of Agriculture, The West of Scotland College of Agriculture and The North of Scotland College of Agriculture to The Scottish Agricultural College.

Whereas the Provisional Order set forth in the Schedule hereunto annexed has been made by the Secretary of State under the provisions of the Private Legislation Procedure (Scotland) Act 1936, and it is requisite that the said Order should be confirmed by Parliament:

Confirmation of Order in Schedule

1. The Provisional Order contained in the Schedule hereunto annexed is hereby confirmed.

Short title

2. This Act may be cited as the Scottish Agricultural College Order Confirmation Act 1997.

SCHEDULE

Scottish Agricultural College

Provisional Order to transfer the assets of The East of Scotland College of Agriculture, The North of Scotland College of Agriculture and The West of Scotland College to The Scottish Agricultural College; and for other purposes incidental thereto.

WHEREAS—

(1) In 1989 a Report entitled A Collegiate System for Agriculture in Scotland under the chairmanship of Sir Alwyn Williams (hereinafter referred to as "the Williams Report") recommended that all the assets, functions and responsibilities of The East of Scotland College of Agriculture, The North of Scotland College of Agriculture and The West of Scotland College (hereinafter together referred to as "the regional colleges") should be merged:

(2) The Scottish Agricultural College (hereinafter referred to as "the College") was formed in 1987 as a private company limited by guarantee under the Companies Act 1985 and was originally known as Scottish Agricultural Colleges:

(3) In 1990 following the Williams Report the College increased its range of activities to include all activities previously undertaken by the regional colleges:

(4) In the events that have happened the regional colleges are now private companies limited by guarantee each having the College as its sole member:

(5) It is consistent with the recommendation of the Williams Report that the assets and liabilities of the regional colleges be transferred to the College:

(6) The purposes aforesaid cannot be effected without an Order confirmed by Parliament under the provisions of the Private Legislation Procedure (Scotland) Act 1936:

Now, therefore, in pursuance of the powers contained in the last mentioned Act, the Secretary of State orders as follows:—

Short title

1. This Order may be cited as the Scottish Agricultural College Order 1997.

Interpretation

2. In this Order, unless the subject or context otherwise requires—
"the appointed day" means such day as may be designated by the College under section 3 below;
"the College" means The Scottish Agricultural College;
"regional colleges" means The East of Scotland College of Agriculture, The North of Scotland College of Agriculture and The West of Scotland College or any of them as the case may be.

Appointed day

3.—(1) The College may designate a day to be the appointed day for the purposes of this Order.

(2) Not less than 28 days before any such day as may be designated under subsection (1) above, the College shall—
(a) give notice to the regional colleges of the day so designated; and
(b) publish in the Edinburgh Gazette a notice stating the day so designated.

Transfer of property, etc

4. All property, estate and effects, heritable and moveable, real and personal, corporeal and incorporeal, of every description and all rights, interests, powers and privileges of the regional colleges which immediately before the appointed day belonged to or were vested in or exercisable by the regional colleges shall on the appointed day, without any conveyance, transfer, disposition, assignation, or other instrument, be vested in, or be exercisable by, the College for all the right, title and interest therein of the regional colleges.

Transfer of obligations, etc

5. All debts, liabilities, responsibilities and obligations of the regional colleges existing immediately before the appointed day shall on the appointed day be transferred to and vested in the College and shall thereafter be discharged and satisfied by the College.

Savings for agreements, deeds, actions, etc

6. All agreements, appointments, awards, contracts, deeds and other instruments, and all actions and proceedings and causes of action, which immediately before the appointed day were existing or pending in favour of, or against, the regional colleges shall on and from the appointed day continue and may be carried into effect, enforced and prosecuted by, or in favour of, or against, the College to the same extent and in like manner as if the College instead of the regional colleges had been party to, or interested in, the same respectively.

Transfer of interests in heritable and other property

7. It is hereby declared that the vesting of any property in the College by virtue of this Order shall not—

    (a) constitute an assignation, assignment, transfer, devolution, parting with possession or other disposition of property or of an interest in property for the purposes of any provision relating to assignation, assignment, transfer, devolution, parting with possession or other disposition contained in any deed or other instrument or document concerning that property or that interest; or

    (b) operate as a breach of any undertaking, obligation, covenant or condition against alienation; or

    (c) give rise to any forfeiture or irritancy; or

    (d) invalidate or discharge any contract or security; or

    (e) operate so as to merge any leasehold interest (being the interest of the lessee of land under a lease or the interest of the sublessee of land under a sublease) in the interest of the immediate landlord under the lease or sublease.

Construction of bequests, etc

8. Any scheme, will, trust deed, settlement, appointment, deed or other instrument, whether made or executed before, on or after the appointed day, which contains any bequest, legacy, gift, endowment or trust or other benefit in favour of or connected with the regional colleges shall, on and after the appointed day, be read and have effect as if the College were named therein instead of the regional colleges.

Transfer of powers to appoint or nominate

9. Any power or right of the regional colleges or of any officer or employee of or of the holder of any position in relation to the regional colleges to appoint or nominate a member of any education authority or of the governing body of any educational, charitable or other institution or to appoint or nominate a trustee or to be a trustee of any trust, settlement, endowment or scheme or to exercise any power of appointment in relation to the purposes or funds of any trust, settlement, endowment or scheme, shall on the appointed day be transferred to, and may be exercised by, the College or by the officer or employee of the College who in the opinion of the directors of the College most nearly performs the functions formerly performed by the former officer, employee or holder of any position in question.

PENSIONS MEASURE 1997

(1997 No. 1)

A Measure passed by the General Synod of the Church of England to make further provision in relation to pensions and related benefits for certain persons who are or have been in the service of the Church of England and their widows, widowers and dependants. [21st March 1997]

General provisions as to pension schemes

Past service and funded schemes

1.—(1) There shall be two schemes with respect to the pensions and lump sum payments payable to clerks, deaconesses and licensed lay workers and their widows, widowers and dependants, as follows—
   (a) a scheme related exclusively to past service, to be known as "the Church of England Pensions Scheme" and referred to in this Measure as "the past service scheme";
   (b) a scheme related to future service, to be known as "the Church of England Funded Pensions Scheme" and referred to in this Measure as "the funded scheme".

(2) The past service scheme shall comprise provisions contained in the Church of England Pensions Regulations 1988, the Clergy Pensions (Lump Sum Payments) Rules 1988 and any further regulations or rules relating to the past service scheme, whether made before or after the passing of this Measure.

(3) The funded scheme shall be established by deed by the Pensions Board (hereinafter referred to as "the Board").

Funded Scheme Rules

2.—(1) The funded scheme shall provide for the making of rules as to the nature and amount of the pensions and lump sum payments payable under the funded scheme and for the making of amending rules.

(2) Any such rules shall be laid before the General Synod and shall not come into operation until they have been approved by the Synod.

(3) Where the Standing Committee of the General Synod determine that any such rules do not need to be debated by the Synod, then, unless—

(a) notice is given by a member of the Synod in accordance with its Standing Orders that he wishes the rules to be debated; or

(b) notice is so given by any such member that he wishes to move an amendment to the rules,

the rules shall for the purposes of subsection (2) above be deemed to have been approved by the Synod without amendment.

Funded scheme

Establishment of pensions fund

3.—(1) The funded scheme shall provide for the constitution and maintenance by the Board of a fund, to be known as "the Church of England Pensions Fund", and the Board shall pay into that fund—

(a) all contributions received by the Board under section 4 below;

(b) all other moneys received by the Board for the purposes of the funded scheme.

(2) All payments in respect of pensions and lump sum payments arising or to be provided under the funded scheme shall be made by the Board out of the Pensions Fund.

Contributions to pensions fund

4.—(1) It shall be the duty of each responsible body to make contributions for the purposes of the funded scheme by paying to the Board in respect of each scheme member for whom the body is responsible such sums as the Board may determine in accordance with the regulations.

(2) Before making any determination under subsection (1) above the Board shall obtain the advice of an actuary, and the determination shall be consistent with that advice.

(3) The payments mentioned in subsection (1) above shall be made at such times as may be prescribed by the regulations.

(4) In this section and in section 6 below "responsible body" means—

(a) in the case of a diocesan bishop or a dean, provost or residentiary canon in receipt of a stipend or other emoluments under section 28 of the Cathedrals Measure 1963, the Church Commissioners (hereinafter referred to as "the Commissioners");

(b) in the case of a scheme member in receipt of a stipend paid from a diocesan stipends fund income account kept by the Commissioners under section 1 of the Diocesan Stipends Fund Measure 1953, the Diocesan Board of Finance of the diocese concerned;

(c) in the case of a scheme member in receipt of a stipend paid wholly from capitular funds, the capitular body of the cathedral church concerned;

(d) in the case of a scheme member in receipt of periodical payments under section 1(1)(b) of the Ordination of Women (Financial Provisions) Measure 1993, the Commissioners;

(e) in the case of a scheme member who is—

(i) a clerk in Holy Orders employed by a World Mission Agency of the Church of England which is at the passing of this Measure an associate or full member of the Partnership for World Mission; or

      (ii) a clerk in Holy Orders employed by the Church Pastoral Aid Society,
the Commissioners;
 (f) in the case of a scheme member employed in pensionable service otherwise than as mentioned in paragraph (e) above, the employer;
 (g) in the case of any other person who is a scheme member performing pensionable service, the body primarily concerned for the time being in promoting that person's membership of the funded scheme.
(5) In its application to the Isle of Man, subsection (4) above shall have effect with the substitution for paragraph (b) of the following paragraph—

     "(b) in the case of a scheme member in receipt of a stipend paid from a diocesan stipends account kept by the Sodor and Man Diocesan Board of Finance, that Board;".

Church Commissioners

Liability of Commissioners

5.—(1) The Commissioners shall continue to be liable to meet the cost of—
 (a) any pension arising from the retirement or death of a scheme member in so far as it is attributable to past service;
 (b) any lump sum payment arising from the retirement of a scheme member in so far as it is attributable to past service;
 (c) any lump sum payment arising from the death of a scheme member occurring before the appointed day.
(2) For the purposes of subsection (1) above, the amount of any pension or lump sum payment shall include any increase in the rate or amount thereof, augmentation of an individual's pension or supplementary pension awarded under the regulations or rules, whether before or after the appointed day.
(3) The Commissioners shall not be liable to meet the cost of—
 (a) any pension arising from the retirement or death of a scheme member in so far as it is attributable to future service; or
 (b) any lump sum payment arising from the retirement of a scheme member in so far as it is attributable to future service; or
 (c) any lump sum payment arising from the death of a scheme member occurring on or after the appointed day.

Transitional grants by Commissioners for funded scheme

6. The Commissioners may, within such period as they may determine not exceeding the period of seven years following the commencement of the appointed day, make such grants to a responsible body as they may think expedient for the purpose of assisting that body in meeting the cost of any contribution due to be paid under section 4(1) above.

Application of capital

7.—(1) The Commissioners may, within such period as they may determine not exceeding the period of seven years following the commencement of the appointed day, apply capital funds for the purpose of meeting the cost of—
 (a) any pension or lump sum due to be paid under the past service scheme; or
 (b) any pension or lump sum payment payable under the Church Commissioners' Superannuation Scheme in so far as it is attributable to a period of service before the appointed day; or
 (c) any grant made under section 6 above.

(2) In this section "capital funds" means funds held by the Commissioners, the income from which forms part of the Commissioners general fund.

Pensions Board

Constitution of Board

8.—(1) For section 21(3) of the Clergy Pensions Measure 1961 there shall be substituted the following subsection—

"(3) The Board shall consist of twenty members (of whom eight shall be representative of the members of the pension schemes administered by the Board) chosen in such manner, whether by election or by appointment, as may be prescribed by regulations made under section 6 of the Clergy Pensions (Amendment) Measure 1972.".

(2) The chairman and other members of the Board in office immediately before the appointed day shall cease to hold office on that day.

Miscellaneous

Interpretation

9.—(1) In this Measure, unless the context otherwise requires—

"actuary" means a Fellow of the Institute of Actuaries or of the Faculty of Actuaries in Scotland, not being a Church Commissioner or a member of the Board or a member of the staff of the Commissioners or the Board, and includes a firm of actuaries;

"appointed day" means the day appointed under section 11(2) below for the coming into force of this Measure;

"funded scheme" means the scheme referred to in section 1(1)(b) above;

"future service" means any period of pensionable service on or after the appointed day;

"past service" means any period of pensionable service before the appointed day;

"past service scheme" means the scheme referred to in section 1(1)(a) above;

"the Pensions Fund" means the fund constituted under section 3(1) above;

"regulations" means regulations made under section 6 of the Clergy Pensions (Amendment) Measure 1972;

"rules" means, except in section 2 above, rules made under section 3 of the Clergy Pensions (Amendment) Measure 1967.

(2) For the purposes of this Measure, where the qualifying period of pensionable service performed by a scheme member comprises or is deemed to comprise a period of both past service and future service the portion attributable to past service or future service, as the case may be shall be calculated without reference to any period of service following the completion of the minimum number of years entitling him to maximum benefits.

(3) This Measure shall be construed as one with the Clergy Pensions Measure 1961.

Amendments and repeals

10.—(1) The enactments specified in Schedule 1 to this Measure shall have effect subject to the amendments specified in that Schedule, being minor amendments or amendments consequential on the preceding provisions of this Measure.

(2) The enactments specified in Schedule 2 to this Measure are hereby repealed to the extent specified in the third column of that Schedule.

(3) Without prejudice to the application of section 16 of the Interpretation Act 1978, the repeal of subsection (1A) of section 3 of the Clergy Pensions

(Amendment) Measure 1967 and rules 10 and 11 of the Church of England Pensions (Lump Sum Payments) Rules 1988 shall not apply in the case of the death of a scheme member occurring before the appointed day.

Citation, commencement and extent

11.—(1) This Measure may be cited as the Pensions Measure 1997 and this Measure may be cited with the Church of England (Pensions) Measures 1961 to 1988 as the Church of England (Pensions) Measures 1961 to 1997.

(2) This Measure shall come into force on such day as the Archbishops of Canterbury and York may jointly appoint.

(3) This Measure shall extend to the whole of the provinces of Canterbury and York except the Channel Islands, but the provisions thereof may be applied to the Channel Islands as defined in the Channel Islands (Church Legislation) Measures 1931 and 1957, or either of them, in accordance with those Measures.

SCHEDULES

Section 10(1)   SCHEDULE 1

MINOR AND CONSEQUENTIAL AMENDMENTS

PART I

AMENDMENTS TO MEASURES

Church Commissioners Measure 1947

1. The Church Commissioners Measure 1947 shall have effect subject to the following amendments.

2. In section 6 after subsection (3) there shall be inserted the following subsection—

"(3A) Before making any recommendation under subsection (3)(b) above the Assets Committee shall obtain the advice of an actuary as to the likely effect of adopting the recommendation on the Commissioners' financial position as a whole and shall have regard to that advice; and the Commissioners shall ensure that a summary of such advice is included in their annual report under section 12 of this Measure.

For the purposes of this subsection "actuary" means a Fellow of the Institute of Actuaries or of the Faculty of Actuaries in Scotland, not being a Church Commissioner or a member of the staff of the Commissioners, and includes a firm of actuaries.".

3. In section 10(6) after the words "general fund, and" there shall be inserted the words ", subject to section 7 of the Pensions Measure 1997 (which relates to the use of capital funds)".

Clergy Pensions Measure 1961

4. The Clergy Pensions Measure 1961 shall have effect subject to the following amendments.

5. In section 17 for subsections (1) and (2) there shall be substituted the following subsections—

"(1) Subject to section 7 of the Pensions Measure 1997 (which relates to the use of capital funds), all payments to be made by the Commissioners under subsection (2) below shall be made out of their general fund.

(2) The Commissioners shall pay to the Board such sums as are required by the Board for the payments to be made by them under the past service scheme."

6. In section 21(10) for the word "seven" there shall be substituted the words "six, including at least two persons representing the members of the pension schemes administered by the Board".

7. In section 22—

(a) in subsection (2)—

(i) for the word "Commissioners" there shall be substituted the word "Board";

(ii) for the words "their general fund" there shall be substituted the words "funds administered by the Board";

(b) for subsection (3) there shall be substituted the following subsection—

"(3) The Commissioners may make payments to the Board out of their general fund for the purpose of meeting so much of the administrative expenses of the Board as appears to the Board to be proportionate to the work undertaken by the Board in the administration of the past-service scheme and other matters in respect of which the Commissioners have a financial interest.".

8. In section 24—
(a) for the words from "control" to "by this Measure" there shall be substituted the words "administer the past service scheme and the funded scheme";
(b) in paragraph (a) after the word "Measure" there shall be inserted the words "or the Pensions Measure 1997";
(c) in paragraph (b) for the words from "upon the Clergy" to the end then there shall be substituted the words "in such manner and upon such terms and conditions as the Board think fit".

9. In section 25 after the word "functions" there shall be inserted the words "in connection with the past service scheme".

10. In section 34—
(a) in subsection (1)—
    (i) for the word "Treasury" in the first place where it appears there shall be substituted the word "Board";
    (ii) the words from "under section 17(2)" to the end shall be omitted;
(b) in subsection (2) for the words "at such times" there shall be substituted the word "annually" and the words from "in such form" to the end shall be omitted.

11. In section 38A(2)—
(a) for the words "the principal scheme" in the first place where they appear there shall be substituted the words "the past service scheme and the funded scheme";
(b) for the words "the principal scheme" in the second place where they appear there shall be substituted the words "those schemes".

12. In section 44 for the words from "Commissioners after" to "as the Commissioners" there shall be substituted the words "Board to such other rate as the Board".

13. In section 46(1)—
(a) in the definition of "actuary" for the words from "employed" to the end of the definition there shall be substituted the words ", not being a Church Commissioner or a member of the Board or a member of the staff of the Commissioners or the Board, and includes a firm of actuaries";
(b) after the definition of "ecclesiastical service" there shall be inserted the following definition—
    " "funded scheme" has the meaning assigned to that expression by the Pensions Measure 1997";
(c) after the definition of "licensed lay worker" there shall be inserted the following definition—
    " "past service scheme" has the meaning assigned to that expression by the Pensions Measure 1997;".

Clergy Pensions (Amendment) Measure 1967

14. In section 3(1) of the Clergy Pensions (Amendment) Measure 1967—
(a) for the word "Commissioners" there shall be substituted the word "Board";
(b) for the words from "Part II" to "1988" there shall be substituted the words "the past service scheme (within the meaning assigned to that expression by the Pensions Measure 1997)".

Clergy Pensions (Amendment) Measure 1972

15. The Clergy Pensions (Amendment) Measure 1972 shall be amended as follows.

16. In section 5(4) for the word "Commissioners" there shall be substituted the word "Board".

17. In section 6—
(a) in subsection (1) for paragraph (e) there shall be substituted the following paragraphs—
    "(e) the manner in which the amount of the contributions payable under section 4(1) of the Pensions Measure 1997 is to be determined and the times at which those contributions are to be made;
    (f) the manner in which notice is to be given as to the matters referred to in paragraph (e) above;
    (g) the manner in which elections and appointments to the Church of England Pensions Board are to be conducted and in which the chairman of the Board is to be chosen;
    (h) the period for which the chairman and other members of that Board are to hold office, the removal from office of members of that Board and the filling of casual vacancies in the membership of that Board;

      (i) the appointment by that Board of committees and the delegation of any of the Board's functions to such committees;

      (j) any matter incidental or supplementary to the matters mentioned in paragraphs (a) to (i) above.";

(b) in subsection (2) for the words "1961 to 1988" there shall be substituted the words "1961 to 1997";

(c) in subsection (3) after the words "1967" there shall be inserted the words ", sections 3 to 7 (excluding section 4(4)(e)) of the Pensions Measure 1997";

(d) in subsection (4) after the word "Commissioners" there shall be inserted the words "in so far as they relate to the past service scheme".

Deaconesses and Lay Workers (Pensions) Measure 1980

18. In section 1(1) of the Deaconesses and Lay Workers (Pensions) Measure 1980—

(a) in paragraph (a) after the word "widowers" there shall be inserted the words ", being pensions paid or payable under the past service scheme (within the meaning assigned to that expression by the Pensions Measure 1997) or in respect of service which ended before 1st December 1988";

(b) in paragraph (b) after the word "payable" there shall be inserted the words "under that scheme".

Part II

Amendments to Instruments

Church of England Pensions Regulations 1988

19. The Church of England Pensions Regulations 1988 shall have effect subject to the following amendments.

20. In regulation 2—

(a) in paragraph (1)—

      (i) in the definition of "actuary" for the words from "employed" to the end of the definition there shall be substituted the words ", not being a Church Commissioner or a member of the Board or a member of the staff of the Commissioners or the Board, and includes a firm of actuaries";

      (ii) after the definition of "the 1961 Measure" there shall be inserted the following definition—

        " "past service scheme" has the meaning assigned to that expression by the Pensions Measure 1997";

(b) at the end there shall be inserted the following paragraph—

      "(5) These regulations shall have effect subject to the provisions of the Pensions Measure 1997.".

21. In regulation 4(1) for the word "Commissioners" there shall be substituted the word "Board".

22. In regulation 6(2)—

(a) for the word "Commissioners" there shall be substituted the word "Board";

(b) for the word "Board" there shall be substituted the word "Commissioners".

23. In regulation 8 for the word "Commissioners" in both places where it appears there shall in each case be substituted the word "Board".

24. In regulation 12—

(a) in paragraph (3) for the word "Commissioners" there shall be substituted the word "Board";

(b) in paragraph (7) for the word "Commissioners" in the first place where it appears there shall be substituted the word "Board".

25. In regulation 16(3)—

(a) for the word "Commissioners" there shall be substituted the word "Board";

(b) for the word "Board" there shall be substituted the word "Commissioners".

26. For the words "principal scheme" wherever they appear in regulations 2(1) (in the definition of "pensionable service"), 5(2), 19(1), 20(1), 22, 25 and 28 there shall be substituted in each case the words "past service scheme".

Church of England Pensions (Lump Sum Payments) Rules 1988

27. The Church of England Pensions (Lump Sum Payments) Rules 1988 shall have effect subject to the following amendments.

M1–7

28. After rule 1 there shall be inserted the following rule—

    "1A. These Rules shall have effect subject to the provisions of the Pensions Measure 1997.".

29. For the word "Commissioners" wherever it appears in rules 4(1) and (2) and 5(1) and (2) there shall in each case be substituted the word "Board".

30. In rule 6 for the word "Commissioners" in the first place where it appears there shall be substituted the word "Board".

31. In rule 7—

(a) for the words "section 4(3) of the 1961 Measure" there shall be substituted the words "regulation 9(2) of the Church of England Pensions Regulations 1988";

(b) for the word "Commissioners" there shall be substituted the word "Board".

32. In rule 9 for the words from the beginning to "Board" there shall be substituted the words "The Board may, with the agreement of the Commissioners".

33. In rule 10(2)(a) for the words "section 2(4) of the 1961 Measure" there shall be substituted the words "regulation 8 of the Church of England Pensions Regulations 1988".

Section 10(2)   SCHEDULE 2

REPEALS AND REVOCATIONS

PART I

REPEALS

Chapter	Short title	Extent of repeal
1961 No. 3.	Clergy Pensions Measure 1961.	In section 21, subsections (4) to (8). Section 23. Section 33. Section 40A. In section 46, in subsection (1) the definition of "principal scheme".
1967 No. 1.	Clergy Pensions (Amendment) Measure 1967.	In section 3, subsection (A).
1988 No. 4.	Church of England (Pensions Measure) 1988.	Section 17.

PART II

REVOCATIONS

Number	Title	Extent of revocation
1988 No. 2256.	Church of England Pensions Regulations 1988.	In regulation 2, in paragraph (1) the definition of "principal scheme". In regulation 6, in paragraph (3) the words "request the "Commissioners to". In regulation 12, in paragraph (2) the words "request the Commissioners to" and in paragraph (7) the words "by the Commissioners". In regulation 29, in paragraph (1) the words "the Commissioners or" and ", as the case may be,". In regulation 30, in paragraph (1) the words ", or may authorise the Commissioners to pay,".
	Church of England Pensions (Lump Sum Payments) Rules 1988.	In rule 2(a), the definition of "maximum lump sum death payment". Rule 10. Rule 11.

CURRENT LAW STATUTES 1997

COMMENCEMENT DIARY

This table notes alphabetically by statute the commencement of statutes from January 1997 as initiated by Orders and by statutory provisions. This is up to date to **February 13, 1998** (Orders and Acts received). The full texts of the Orders can be found in the Commencement Orders section of Current Law Statutes.

Act Affected	Provision Brought Into Force	Commencement Date	Authority
Antarctic Act 1994 (c. 15)	s.5	June 1, 1997	S.I. 1997 No. 1411 (C.51)
Antarctic Act 1994 (c. 15)	s.6	October 1, 1997	S.I. 1997 No. 2298 (C.91)
Antarctic Act 1994 (c. 15)	ss.3, 4	January 14, 1998	S.I. 1997 No. 3068 (C.113)
Appropriation Act 1997 (c. 31)	All provisions	March 21, 1997	Royal Assent
Appropriation (No. 2) Act 1997 (c. 57)	All provisions	July 31, 1997	Royal Assent
Arbitration Act 1996 (c. 23)	All remaining provisions (except ss.85–87)	January 31, 1997	S.I. 1996 No. 3146 (C.96)
Architects Act 1997 (c. 22)	s.28	March 19, 1997	s.28(2)
Architects Act 1997 (c. 22)	All remaining provisions	July 21, 1997	S.I. 1997 No. 1672 (C.69)
Armed Forces Act 1996 (c. 46)	ss.5, 9, 10, 15–17, 28, 29, 35 (part), Scheds. 1, 3, 5, 6, paras. 4, 7–9, 14, 15, Sched. 7, Pts. I (part), II (part), III (part)	April 1, 1997	S.I. 1997 No. 304 (C.14)
Armed Forces Act 1996 (c. 46)	ss.20–27	October 1, 1997	S.I. 1997 No. 2164 (C.85)
Asylum and Immigration Act 1996 (c. 49)	s.8	January 27, 1997	S.I. 1996 No. 2970 (C.90)
Birds (Registration Charges) Act 1997 (c. 55)	All provisions	March 21, 1997	Royal Assent
British Nationality (Hong Kong) Act 1997 (c. 20)	All provisions	March 19, 1997	Royal Assent

Act Affected	Provision Brought Into Force	Commencement Date	Authority
Broadcasting Act 1996 (c. 55)	ss.73 (rem.), 85, 95, 106–130, 147 (rem.), 148 (rem.), Sched. 2 (rem.), 3, 4, 10 (rem.), 11 (rem.)	April 1, 1997	S.I. 1997 No. 1005 (C.34)
Building Societies Act 1997 (c. 32)	ss.40, 41, 46(1) (part), (2)(part), Sched. 8, paras. 9, 10, Sched. 9 (part)	March 21, 1997	s.47(3)
Building Societies Act 1997 (c. 32)	s.46 so far as relates to and including; Sched. 8, para. 1	May 21, 1997	S.I. 1997 No. 1307 (C.45)
Building Societies Act 1997 (c. 32)	ss.11, 16, 17, 18, 19, 20, 23 (part), 24 (part), 31, 32, 33, 37, 42, 43 (part), 44, 45(1), Sched. 4, Sched. 7, paras. 5, 6, 7(1), 8, 9, 17(1), 12(1), (3), 13(2), 14(1)(part), 17(5)(c), (6), (7), (8), 18, 19(1), (2), (4), 20, 26, 27(2), (3), 28, 29(2), 33(2), 37, 38, 45(1), (4), 51, 53(1)(b), (d), (3)(a), 55, 56(9), 58, 60(1)	June 9, 1997	S.I. 1997 No. 1427 (C.53)
Building Societies Act 1997 (c. 32)	All remaining provisions (Pt. II in accordance with arts. 2(2), (3), (5); Pt. III in accordance with art. 2(6))	December 1, 1997	S.I. 1997 No. 2668 (C.99)
Building Societies (Distributions) Act 1997 (c. 41)	All provisions	March 21, 1997	Royal Assent
Carriage by Air and Road Act 1979 (c. 28)	ss.4(1), (4) (part), 5 (part), 6(1)(a) (part), (3) (part)	December 1, 1997	S.I. 1997 No. 2565 (C.97)

Act Affected	Provision Brought Into Force	Commencement Date	Authority
Children (Scotland) Act 1995 (c. 36)	All remaining provisions (except s.98, Sched. 2, para. 25 insertion of s.51A into the Adoption (Scotland) Act 1978, Sched. 5 (part), 101, Sched. 4, para. 26(8), Sched. 5 relating to the Trusts (Scotland) Act 1921, relating to s.103 of the Children Act 1975)	April 1, 1997	S.I. 1996 No. 3201 (C.102) (S.241) amended by S.I. 1997 No. 744 (C.27) (S.70)
Children (Scotland) Act 1995 (c. 36)	s.98, Sched. 2, para. 25 (insertion of s.51A into the Adoption (Scotland) Act 1978)	April 1, 1998	S.I. 1996 No. 3201 (C.102) (S.241)
Civil Evidence Act 1995 (c. 38)	All provisions except ss.10, 16(5)	January 31, 1997	S.I. 1996 No. 3217 (C.7)
Civil Procedure Act 1997 (c. 12)	s.10 (part)	March 14, 1997	S.I. 1997 No. 841 (C.30)
Civil Procedure Act 1997 (c. 12)	ss.1–9, 10 (part)	April 27, 1997	S.I. 1997 No. 841 (C.30)
Community Care (Direct Payments) Act 1996 (c. 30)	ss.1–5, 7	April 1, 1997	S.I. 1997 No. 756 (C.28)
Confiscation of Alcohol (Young Persons) Act 1997 (c. 33)	s.2	March 21, 1997	Royal Assent
Confiscation of Alcohol (Young Persons) Act 1997 (c. 33)	s.1	August 1, 1997	S.I. 1997 No. 1725 (C.73)
Consolidated Fund Act 1997 (c. 15)	All provisions	March 19, 1997	Royal Assent
Contract (Scotland) Act 1997 (c. 34)	All provisions	June 21, 1997	s.4(2)
Crime and Punishment (Scotland) Act 1997 (c. 48)	ss.45, 46	March 21, 1997	s.65(2)

Act Affected	Provision Brought Into Force	Commencement Date	Authority
Crime and Punishment (Scotland) Act 1997 (c. 48)	ss.12, 14, 17, 20 (part), 21, 23, 24 (part), 26–32, 47(1)(a), (b), (d), (2)–(5), 55, 56, 57, 58, 59, 60, 61, 62 (part), 63(1)(a)(iii), (c), (2), 64, 65(1), (5) (7), Sched. 1, paras. 2, 6, 8, 9(1), (3)(b), (4)–(6), (10)–(14), 10(1), (2)(b), 11, 12(1), (7), 16, 17, 18(1), (2)(b), (3)–(8), 19, 20, 21(1), (2), (4), (9)–(15), (17) (19)– (22), (30), (32), 34(b), Sched. 3, various repeals	August 1, 1997	S.I. 1997 No. 1712 (C.72) (S.128)
Crime and Punishment (Scotland) Act 1997 (c. 48)	ss.49 (part), 50 (part), 51 (part), 52 (part), 53 (part), 54 (part), 62(1) (part), 63(1)(b)	October 1, 1997	S.I. 1997 No. 2323 (C.89) (S.155)
Crime and Punishment (Scotland) Act 1997 (c. 48)	ss.2, 3 (part), 5 (part), 15 (part), 16 (part), 18 (part), 19 (part), 62 (part), 63(1)(a)(i), Sched. 1, paras. 10(3), 12(5), (6), 14(1), (2)(b), (3)(a)–(d), (8), (10)(b), (11)(a), (18), 21(23) (part), (25) (part), (31) (part), (33)(a), Sched. 3 (part)	October 20, 1997	S.I. 1997 No. 2323 (C.89) (S.155)
Crime and Punishment (Scotland) Act 1997 (c. 48)	ss.47 (rem.), 48, 62(2) (part), Sched. 3 (part)	November 17, 1997	S.I. 1997 No. 2694 (C.101)
Crime and Punishment (Scotland) Act 1997 (c. 48)	ss.6, 7, 8, 9, 10, 11, 15, 22, 42, 43, 44, 62 (part), Sched. 1, paras. 9(2), (3)(a), (8), (9), (15), (16), 13(1), (2), (4), 15, 21(5)–(8), (35), Sched. 3 (part)	January 1, 1998	S.I. 1997 No. 2323 (C.89) (S.155)
Crime and Punishment (Scotland) Act 1997 (c. 48)	ss.25, 62(1), 63 (part), Sched. 1, paras. 4, 5, 7	January 1, 1998	S.I. 1997 No. 3004 (C.110) (S.190)

Act Affected	Provision Brought Into Force	Commencement Date	Authority
Crime and Punishment (Scotland) Act 1997 (c. 48)	s.49 (part)	April 1, 1998	S.I. 1997 No. 2323 (C.89) (S. 155)
Crime and Punishment (Scotland) Act 1997 (c. 48)	ss.5, 24, 62 (part)	July 1, 1998	S.I. 1997 No. 2323 (C.89) (S. 155)
Crime and Punishment (Scotland) Act 1997 (c. 48)	s.49 (part)	October 1, 1998	S.I. 1997 No. 2323 (C.89) (S. 155)
Crime (Sentences) Act 1997 (c. 43)	Sched. 1, paras. 14, 19	June 25, 1997	S.I. 1997 No. 1581 (C.64)
Crime (Sentences) Act 1997 (c. 43)	ss.1(1) (part), (2) (part), 2, 3(1)–(5), (6) (part), 5 (part), 6 (part), 7, 28–34, 36, 38, 41 (rem.), 42, 44–47, 48, 49, 51–54, 55(1), (2)(a) (part), (b), 56(1), (2), 57, Sched. 1 (rem.), Sched. 2, paras. 1–3, 5–7, 9–11, Scheds. 3, 4 (part), 5, paras. 5, 7–13, Sched. 6 (part)	October 1, 1997	S.I. 1997 No. 2200 (C.87)
Crime (Sentences) Act 1997 (c. 43)	ss.35, 37, 39(1), (2) (part), (3)–(6), 40, 43, Sched. 4, para. 10(2)	January 1, 1998	S.I. 1997 No. 2200 (C.87)
Crime (Sentences) Act 1997 (c. 43)	s.50	March 1, 1998	S.I. 1997 No. 2200 (C.87)
Criminal Appeal Act 1995 (c. 35)	s.8 (rem.), 31(1)(a), Sched. 1, paras. 1 (rem.), 3–11, Sched. 2, paras. 7–11	January 1, 1997	S.I. 1996 No. 3149 (C.97)
Criminal Appeal Act 1995 (c. 35)	All remaining provisions (ss.3, 5, 7 (rem.), 9–25, 29 (rem.), Scheds. 2 (rem.), 3 (rem.)	March 31, 1997	S.I. 1997 No. 402 (C.20)
Criminal Evidence (Amendment) Act 1997 (c. 17)	All provisions	March 19, 1997	Royal Assent
Criminal Justice and Public Order Act 1994 (c. 33)	ss.158(2), (5), (6), (7), (8), 159(5)	April 1, 1997	S.I. 1997 No. 882 (C.31)

Act Affected	Provision Brought Into Force	Commencement Date	Authority
Criminal Procedure and Investigations Act 1996 (c. 25)	s.52	February 1, 1997 [Appointed Day]	S.I. 1997 No. 36 (C.3)
Criminal Procedure and Investigations Act 1996 (c. 25)	Pt. I, ss.51, 69 (provisions extend to England and Wales only)	April 1, 1997	S.I. 1997 No. 682 (C.25)
Criminal Procedure and Investigations Act 1996 (c. 25)	ss.61, 63	April 1, 1997	S.I. 1997 No. 682 (C.25)
Criminal Procedure and Investigations Act 1996 (c. 25)	ss.28, 54, Sched. 3	April 15, 1997 [Appointed Day]	S.I. 1997 No. 1019 (C.36)
Criminal Procedure and Investigations Act 1996 (c. 25)	s.65 (part), Scheds. 1 (part), 2 (part)	March 8, 1997	S.I. 1997 No. 683 (C.26)
Criminal Procedure and Investigations Act 1996 (c. 25)	ss.54, 61 (provisions extend to Northern Ireland only)	June 30, 1997 [Appointed Day]	S.I. 1997 No. 1504 (C.59)
Criminal Procedure and Investigations Act 1996 (c. 25)	s.49	October 1, 1997 [Appointed Day]	S.I. 1997 No. 2199 (C.86)
Criminal Procedure and Investigations Act 1996 (c. 25)	Pt. I, ss.43, 69 (Northern Ireland only)	January 1, 1998	S.I. 1997 No. 3108 (C.115)
Crown Agents Act 1995 (c. 24)	s.1(1)	March 21, 1997 [Appointed Day]	S.I. 1997 No. 1139 (C.41)
Dangerous Dogs (Amendment) Act 1997 (c. 53)	All provisions	June 8, 1997	S.I. 1997 No. 1151 (C.42)
Education Act 1996 (c. 56)	s.317(6) (All remaining provisions)	January 1, 1997	S.I. 1996 No. 2904 (C.86)
Education Act 1996 (c. 56)	s.528 (England only)	August 1, 1997	S.I. 1997 No. 1623 (C.67)
Education Act 1996 (c. 56)	ss.8, 348, 582(1) (part), (2) (part), Sched. 37, Pt. II, Sched. 38, Pt. II	September 1, 1997	S.I. 1997 No. 1623 (C.67)
Education Act 1996 (c. 56)	s.517(6)	September 1, 1997 [Appointed Day]	S.I. 1997 No. 1623 (C.67)
Education Act 1996 (c. 56)	s.528 (in relation to Wales only)	October 30, 1997	S.I. 1997 No. 2352 (C.90)

Act Affected	Provision Brought Into Force	Commencement Date	Authority
Education Act 1997 (c. 44)	ss.50, 54, 57(1) (part), 58, Sched. 7, para. 48(2)	March 21, 1997	s.58(4)
Education Act 1997 (c. 44)	ss.1, 57(4) (part), Sched. 8 (repeal)	April 4, 1997	S.I. 1997 No. 1153 (C.43)
Education Act 1997 (c. 44)	ss.20, 55, 56, 57(1) (part), (4) (part), Sched. 7, paras. 15, 18, 20(a), 37, 39, 41, 42, 43, 44 (part), 45, Sched. 8 (part)	June 14, 1997	S.I. 1997 No. 1468 (C.57)
Education Act 1997 (c. 44)	ss.10–12, 14 (part), 34, 35, 37(1)–(4), 38–42, 44–46, 51, 52(4), 57(1) (part), (4) (part), 57(2), (3), Sched. 2, Sched. 3 (part), Sched. 6, Sched. 7, paras. 5, 9, 31 (part), 32, 33, 34 (part), 44 (rem.), 49(1), (3) (part), Sched. 8 (part)	September 1, 1997	S.I. 1997 No. 1468 (C.57)
Education Act 1997 (c. 44)	ss.21–32, 49(1) (part), (2), (3), 53, 57(1) (part), (4) (part), Scheds. 4, 5, Sched. 7, paras. 1, 2 (part), 3(1) (part), 4 (part), 6, 7, 26 (part), 27–29, 30(a), Sched. 8 (part)	October 1, 1997	S.I. 1997 No. 1468 (C.57)
Education Act 1997 (c. 44)	ss.15, 16(2), (3), (4) (England only), (6), 17(4), (8), 18	November 1, 1997	S.I. 1997 No. 1468 (C.57)
Education Act 1997 (c. 44)	ss.36, 48	December 1, 1997	S.I. 1997 No. 1468 (C.57)
Education (Schools) Act 1997 (c. 59)	ss.3, 4, 5(1), 6(2), 7	March 31, 1997	s.7(3)(b)
Education (Schools) Act 1997 (c. 59)	ss.1, 2, 6(1), (3) (part), Sched., Pt. I	September 1, 1997	s.7(3)(a)
Education (Schools) Act 1997 (c. 59)	ss.5, 5(2), 6(3) (so far as it relates to Sched. Pt. II), Sched. Pt. II	December 1, 1997	S.I. 1997 No. 2774 (C.105)
Education (Scotland) Act 1996 (c. 43)	All remaining provisions	April 1, 1997 [Appointed Day]	S.I. 1997 No. 365 (C.17) (S.30)

Act Affected	Provision Brought Into Force	Commencement Date	Authority
Energy Conservation Act 1996 (c. 38)	All provisions (England and Wales)	January 14, 1997 [for the purpose of giving directions and guidance]	S.I. 1997 No. 47 (C.4)
Energy Conservation Act 1996 (c. 38)	All remaining provisions (for all other purposes in England and Wales)	April 1, 1997	S.I. 1997 No. 47 (C.4)
Environment Act 1995 (c. 25)	ss.96(1), (5), (6), 96(3), (4) (part), 120(3) (part), Scheds. 13, 14	January 1, 1997 [extends only to Scotland]	S.I. 1996 No. 2857 (C.84) (S.219)
Environment Act 1995 (c. 25)	ss.78 (part), 120(3) (part), Sched. 7, para. 7(2)	April 1, 1997	S.I. 1996 No. 2560 (C.71)
Environment Act 1995 (c. 25)	ss.60(3), (4), (5)(a), (7), 116 (part)	July 1, 1997	S.I. 1997 No. 1626 (C.68)
Environment Act 1995 (c. 25)	ss.105 (part), 120(2) (part) (3) (part)	January 1, 1999	S.I. 1995 No. 1988 (C.40)
Environment Act 1995 (c. 25)	ss.82–86, 90 (rem.), 120(1) (part), Sched. 11 (rem.)	December 23, 1997	S.I. 1997 No. 3044 (C.112)
Family Law Act 1996 (c. 27)	ss.1, 22, Pt. III (ss.26–29), 66(1) (part), (3) (part), Sched. 8, Pt. II	March 21, 1997	S.I. 1997 No. 1077 (C.38)
Family Law Act 1996 (c. 27)	s.57, Sched. 9, paras. 3, 4	July 28, 1997	S.I. 1997 No. 1892 (C.76)
Family Law Act 1996 (c. 27)	ss.30–59, 61–63, 66(1) (part), (2) (part), (3) (part)	October 1, 1997	S.I. 1997 No. 1892 (C.76)
Finance Act 1989 (c. 26)	s.178(1)	December 9, 1997	S.I. 1997 No. 2708 (C.102)
Finance Act 1996 (c. 8)	Sched. 35, para. 7(2)	January 31, 1997	S.I. 1997 No. 133 (C.8)
Finance Act 1996 (c. 8)	s.197(1), (6)	April 1, 1997 [Appointed Day]	S.I. 1997 No. 1015 (C.35)
Finance Act 1997 (c. 16)	All provisions	March 19, 1997	Royal Assent
Finance Act 1997 (c. 16)	Sched. 6	June 1, 1997 [Appointed Day]	S.I. 1997 No. 1305 (C.44)
Finance Act 1997 (c. 16)	ss.52, 53	July 1, 1997 [Appointed Day]	S.I. 1997 No. 1432 (C.54)

Act Affected	Provision Brought Into Force	Commencement Date	Authority
Finance Act 1997 (c. 16)	Sched. 1, para. 13(1) — ceases to have effect	July 1, 1997 [Appointed Day]	S.I. 1997 No. 1433 (C.55)
Finance Act 1997 (c. 16)	Sched. 18, Pt. V(2) (part)	July 1, 1997 [Appointed Day]	S.I. 1997 No. 1433 (C.55)
Finance Act 1997 (c. 16)	Sched. 10, paras. 7(1), 16(1), (2)	July 1, 1997 [Appointed Day]	S.I. 1997 No. 991 (C.33)
Finance Act 1997 (c. 16)	s.110	July 2, 1997 [Appointed Day]	S.I. 1997 No. 1603 (C.66)
Finance Act 1997 (c. 16)	s.7	August 15, 1997	S.I. 1997 No. 1960 (C.80)
Finance Act 1997 (c. 16)	s.20	October 8, 1997	S.I. 1997 No. 2392 (C.93)
Finance Act 1997 (c. 16)	ss.97, 98, 102, 103	October 20, 1997 [Appointed Day]	S.I. 1997 No. 2428 (C.95)
Finance (No. 2) Act 1997 (c. 58)	s.11	July 2, 1997 (1800 hrs)	s.11(5)
Finance (No. 2) Act 1997 (c. 58)	s.49	July 8, 1997	s.49(7)
Finance (No. 2) Act 1997 (c. 58)	All provisions (except ss.7, 8, 9, 10, 11, 12, 49)	July 31, 1997	Royal Assent
Finance (No. 2) Act 1997 (c. 58)	s.12	December 1, 1997	s.12(2)
Finance (No. 2) Act 1997 (c. 58)	s.7	January 1, 1998	s.7(2)
Finance (No. 2) Act 1997 (c. 58)	s.8	January 1, 1998	s.8(2)
Finance (No. 2) Act 1997 (c. 58)	s.9	January 1, 1998	s.9(2)
Finance (No. 2) Act 1997 (c. 58)	s.10	January 1, 1998	s.10(2)
Firearms (Amendment) Act 1997 (c. 5)	ss.16, 17, 18	March 17, 1997	S.I. 1997 No. 1076 (C.37)
Firearms (Amendment) Act 1997 (c. 5)	ss.15, 51	June 10, 1997	S.I. 1997 No. 1535 (C.60)

Act Affected	Provision Brought Into Force	Commencement Date	Authority
Firearms (Amendment) Act 1997 (c. 5)	ss.1, 2, 3, 4, 5, 6, 7, 8, 9, 10, 16 (rem.), 17 (rem.), 18 (rem.), 37, 38, 40, 41, 42, 43, 47, 48, 49, 50, 52 (part), Sched. 2, paras. 1, 2, 4, 7, 8, 10, 11, 12, 14, 15, 16, 17, 18, 19, 20, Sched. 3 (part)	July 1, 1997	S.I. 1997 No. 1535 (C.60)
Firearms (Amendment) Act 1997 (c. 5)	ss.32, 33, 34, 35, 36, 39, 44, 45, 52 (part), Sched. 2, paras. 3, 5, 6, Sched. 3 (part)	October 1, 1997	S.I. 1997 No. 1535 (C.60)
Firearms (Amendment) (No. 2) Act 1997 (c. 64)	s.2 (part), Sched. (part) (both with savings)	December 17, 1997	S.I. 1997 No. 3114 (C.116)
Firearms (Amendment) (No. 2) Act 1997 (c. 64)	ss.1, 2 (rem.), Sched. (rem.)	February 1, 1998	S.I. 1997 No. 3114 (C.116)
Firearms (Amendment) (No. 2) Act 1997 (c. 64)	ss.1, 2 (rem.), Sched. (rem.) (for certain certificate or permit holders and registered firearms dealers)	March 1, 1998	S.I. 1997 No. 3114 (C.116)
Flood Prevention and Land Drainage (Scotland) Act 1997 (c. 36)	ss.6(1), 7, 9	March 21, 1997	s.9(2)
Flood Prevention and Land Drainage (Scotland) Act 1997 (c. 36)	All remaining provisions (except s.2 and s.8, so far as it relates to and including, Sched. (repeals))	May 26, 1997	S.I. 1997 No. 1322 (C.47) (S.106)
Flood Prevention and Land Drainage (Scotland) Act 1997 (c. 36)	s.2	July 28, 1997	S.I. 1997 No. 1322 (C.47) (S.106)
Flood Prevention and Land Drainage (Scotland) Act 1997 (c. 36)	s.6(2)	April 1, 1999	s.9(3)
Flood Prevention and Land Drainage (Scotland) Act 1997 (c. 36)	s.8, so far as it relates to and including, Sched. (repeals)	April 1, 1999	S.I. 1997 No. 1322 (C.47) (S.106)
Home Energy Conservation Act 1995 (c. 10)	ss.3(1), 4(1), (2)	January 10, 1997	S.I. 1996 No. 3181 (C.100)

Act Affected	Provision Brought Into Force	Commencement Date	Authority
Home Energy Conservation Act 1995 (c. 10)	All remaining provisions (Wales only)	April 1, 1997	S.I. 1996 No. 3181 (C.100)
Horserace Totalisator Board Act 1997 (c. 1)	All provisions	February 27, 1997	Royal Assent
Housing Act 1996 (c. 52)	ss.175, 176, 177 (rem.), 178–181, 183 (rem.), 184, 185 (rem.), 186–188, 189 (rem.), 190–193, 194 (rem.), 195–197, 198 (rem.), 199 (rem.), 200–202, 203 (rem.), 204–206, 207 (rem.), 208, 209, 210 (rem.), 211–214, 216, 227 (part)	January 20, 1997	S.I. 1996 No. 2959 (C.88)
Housing Act 1997 (c. 52)	ss.124–128, 129(1), (2), (5), (6), 130–134, 136, 137, 138 (1)–(3), 141(1), 144–146, 147 (rem.)	February 12, 1997	S.I. 1997 No. 66 (C.5)
Housing Act 1996 (c. 52)	ss.96 (rem.), 97–104, 148–151, 227 (so far as relates to Sched. 19, Pt. IV)	February 28, 1997	S.I. 1997 No. 225 (C.12)
Housing Act 1996 (c. 52)	Pt. II; ss.65–80 (rem. except s.73)	March 3, 1997	S.I. 1997 No. 350 (C.16)
Housing Act 1996 (c. 52)	s.227 (so far as relates to repeals in Sched. 19, Pt. II)	March 3, 1997	S.I. 1997 No. 596 (C.21)
Housing Act 1996 (c. 52)	ss.159, 160(1)–(3), 161 (rem.), 162 (rem.), 163 (rem.), 164, 165 (rem.), 166, 167 (rem.), 168, 170, 171, 173, 227 (part)	April 1, 1997	S.I. 1996 No. 2959 (C.88)
Housing Act 1996 (c. 52)	ss.16, 18 (rem.), 19, 20 (rem.), 21 (rem.), 24 (rem.), 25 (rem.), 26, 27–29 (rem.), 35(1), (2), (3), (5), 51(1) (part), (2)–(6), 55 (part), 106 (rem.), 118, 121–123, 227 (part), Sched. 2 (part)	April 1, 1997	S.I. 1997 No. 618 (C.22)

Act Affected	Provision Brought Into Force	Commencement Date	Authority
Housing Act 1996 (c. 52)	ss.83 (rem.), 86 (rem.), 152–154, 155(1), (2) (except subs. (2)(b)), 157, 158, 227 (part)	September 1, 1997	S.I. 1997 No.1851 (C.75)
Housing Act 1996 (c. 52)	s.35(4)	April 1, 1998	S.I. 1997 No. 618 (C.22)
Housing Grants, Construction and Regeneration Act 1996 (c. 53)	ss.118–125 (rem.), s.147 (part), Sched. 2	April 1, 1997	S.I. 1996 No. 2842 (C.83)
Housing Grants, Construction and Regeneration Act 1996 (c. 53)	ss.131–135 (rem.), 136–138, 139–140 (rem.)	December 16, 1997	S.I. 1997 No. 2846 (C.108)
Justices of the Peace Act 1997 (c. 25)	All provisions (subject to s.74(2) and Sched. 4, paras. 7(2)(f), 8)	June 19, 1997	s.74(1)
Knives Act 1997 (c. 21)	s.11	March 19, 1997	Royal Assent
Knives Act 1997 (c. 21)	ss.1–7, 9, 10	September 1, 1997	S.I. 1997 No. 1906 (C.77)
Land Registration Act 1997 (c. 2)	All provisions (except s.1, 4(1) (part), (2) (part), Sched. 1, Pt. I, Sched. 2, Pt. I)	April 27, 1997	s.5(2), (3)
Land Registration Act 1997 (c. 2)	All remaining provisions	April 1, 1998	S.I. 1997 No. 3036 (C.111)
Land Registration (Scotland) Act 1979 (c. 33)	ss.2(1) (part), (2) (part), 3(3) (part)	April 1, 1997	S.I. 1996 No. 2490 (C.66) (S.195)
Law Officers Act 1997 (c. 60)	All provisions	September 30, 1997	s.3(3)
Law Reform (Miscellaneous Provisions) (Scotland) Act 1990 (c. 40)	ss.17 (rem.), 18 (rem.), 20, 21, 22 (part), 74 (part), Sched. 1, Pt. II, Sched. 8, paras. 19, 20, 22(1) (part), 22(2), 24, 25, 29(5) (part), 6(b) (part), Sched. 9 (repeals)	March 1, 1997	S.I. 1996 No. 2966 (C.89) (S.226) amending S.I. 1996 No. 2894 (C.85) (S.222)
Lieutenancies Act 1997 (c. 23)	All provisions	July 1, 1997	s.9(2)

Act Affected	Provision Brought Into Force	Commencement Date	Authority
Local Government and Rating Act 1997 (c. 29)	ss.32, 34, 35	March 19, 1997	s.34(3)
Local Government and Rating Act 1997 (c. 29)	ss.2, 33(1) (part), Sched. 3, para. 2, 22 (part), 23	April 1, 1997	S.I. 1997 No. 1097 (C.40)
Local Government and Rating Act 1997 (c. 29)	Pt. III, s.33 (part), Sched. 3, paras. 1, 11–16, Sched. 4 (repeals–part)	May 19, 1997	S.I. 1997 No. 1097 (C.40)
Local Government and Rating Act 1997 (c. 29)	Pt. II; ss.9–25, Sched. 3, paras. 4–10, 21	May 19, 1997	s.34(2)
Local Government and Rating Act 1997 (c. 29)	s.1	November 18, 1997	S.I. 1997 No. 2752 (C.103)
Local Government and Rating Act 1997 (c. 29)	ss.5 (part), 8, 33(1) (part), Sched. 2 (part), Sched. 3, para. 29(b)	December 1, 1997	S.I. 1997 No. 2826 (C.106) (S.179)
Local Government (Contracts) Act 1997 (c. 65)	ss.3(2)(3), (f), 3(3) (as far as they confer power to make regulations)	December 1, 1997	S.I. 1997 No. 2843 (C.107)
Local Government (Contracts) Act 1997 (c. 65)	s.3 (part) (Scotland only)	December 2, 1997	S.I. 1997 No. 2878 (C.109) (S.182)
Local Government (Contracts) Act 1997 (c. 65)	ss.2, 3 (rem.), 4–9 (England and Wales only)	December 30, 1997	S.I. 1997 No. 2843 (C.107)
Local Government (Contracts) Act 1997 (c. 65)	ss.2, 4–9 (Scotland only)	January 1, 1998	S.I. 1997 No. 2878 (C.109) (S.182)
Local Government Finance (Supplementary Credit Approvals) Act 1997 (c. 63)	All provisions	November 6, 1997	Royal Assent
Local Government (Gaelic Names) (Scotland) Act 1997 (c. 6)	All provisions	April 27, 1997	s.2(2)
Marriage Ceremony (Prescribed Words) Act 1996 (c. 34)	All provisions	February 1, 1997	S.I. 1996 No. 2506 (C.67)

Act Affected	Provision Brought Into Force	Commencement Date	Authority
Medical (Professional Performance) Act 1995 (c. 51)	ss.4 (part), 7(2) (so far as relates to s.7(2)(b)), Sched. para. 1 (so far as relates to other provisions of Sched. brought into force), para. 2, para. 12 (so far as not already in force), para. 13	January 1, 1997	S.I. 1996 No. 1631 (C.34)
Medical (Professional Performance) Act 1995 (c. 51)	All remaining provisions (except ss.2, 4, 7(2), Sched., para. 3	July 1, 1997	S.I. 1997 No. 1315 (C.46)
Merchant Shipping Act 1995 (c. 21)	s.116	February 1, 1998	S.I. 1997 No. 3107 (C.114)
Merchant Shipping and Maritime Security Act 1997 (c. 28)	ss.5, 8, 11, 12, 13, 16, 24, 28, 30, 31, Sched. 2, Sched. 6, para. 16	March 19, 1997	s.31(4)
Merchant Shipping and Maritime Security Act 1997 (c. 28)	ss.1, 9 (part), 10, 29(1) (part), (2) (part), Sched. 1, paras. 1 to 5, Sched. 6, paras. 18(1), (3), (5), 19(1), (2)(b), (c), (3), 20, Sched. 7 (part)	March 23, 1997	S.I. 1997 No. 1082 (C.39)
Merchant Shipping and Maritime Security Act 1997 (c. 28)	ss.2, 3, 4, 6, 7, 14, 15, 17, 18, 19, 20, 21, 22, 23, 25, 26, 27, 29, Scheds. 3, 4, 5, 6 (rem.), 7 (rem.)	July 17, 1997	S.I. 1997 No. 1539 (C.62)
Ministerial and Other Salaries Act 1997 (c. 62)	All provisions	November 6, 1997	Royal Assent
National Health Service (Primary Care) Act 1997 (c. 46)	ss.38–40, 41(1)–(9), (13), (14)	March 21, 1997	s.41(2)
National Health Service (Private Finance) Act 1997 (c. 46)	All provisions	July 15, 1997	Royal Assent
National Health Service (Primary Care) Act 1997 (c. 46)	ss.9(1), (2), 10(1), (2), 13(1), (3)–(8), 18(1), (2) (part), 27, 28, 30, 41(10) (part), Sched. 2, Pt. I, paras. 13, 14, 20, 27, 44, 45, 51	August 15, 1997 [Appointed Day]	S.I. 1997 No. 1780 (C.74)

Act Affected	Provision Brought Into Force	Commencement Date	Authority
National Health Service (Primary Care) Act 1997 (c. 46)	s.4 (part)	August 22, 1997 [Appointed Day]	S.I. 1997 No. 1780 (C.74)
National Health Service (Primary Care) Act 1997 (c. 46)	s.31	September 1, 1997 [Appointed Day]	S.I. 1997 No. 1780 (C.74)
National Health Service (Primary Care) Act 1997 (c. 46)	s.36	October 14, 1997 [Appointed Day]	S.I. 1997 No. 2457 (C.96)
National Health Service (Primary Care) Act 1997 (c. 46)	ss.4 (rem), 16 (part)	October 30, 1997 [Appointed Day]	S.I. 1997 No. 2620 (C.98)
National Health Service (Primary Care) Act 1997 (c. 46)	ss.1, 2, 5 (part), 6 (part), 18(2)(b) (part)	November 28, 1997 [Appointed Day]	S.I. 1997 No. 2620 (C.98)
Northern Ireland Arms Decommissioning Act 1997 (c. 7)	All provisions (except s.7 by virtue of s.7(5))	February 27, 1997	Royal Assent
Northern Ireland Arms Decommissioning Act 1997 (c. 7)	s.7	September 1, 1997	S.I. 1997 No. 2111 (C.84)
Nursery Education and Grant-Maintained Schools Act 1996 (c. 50)	s.5 (so far as relates to Sched. 1, paras. 6(1)(a), 6(2) (rem.), (3) (rem.), 8(2) (rem.), 16)	January 1, 1997	S.I. 1996 No. 3192 (C.99)
Nursery Education and Grant-Maintained Schools Act 1996 (c. 50)	s.5 (so far as relates to Sched. 1, para. 14 (rem.))	April 1, 1997	S.I. 1996 No. 3192 (C.99)
Nurses, Midwives and Health Visitors Act 1997 (c. 24)	All provisions (note exception to s.6(1)(a))	June 19, 1997	s.24(2)
Offensive Weapons Act 1996 (c. 26)	s.6	January 1, 1997	S.I. 1996 No. 3063 (C.95)

Act Affected	Provision Brought Into Force	Commencement Date	Authority
Osteopaths Act 1993 (c. 21)	ss.1(1), (2) (part), (3) (part), (4) (part), 2(1), (2), (4), (5), (6), 34, 35(1), (2), (4), 36(1), (2), (4), (5), (6), 40, 41 (part), 42(1)–(6), (7) (part), Sched., Pt. I, paras. 1, 2, 4, 5, 6, 8, 11, 13, 14(2), (3) (part), 15, Pt. III	January 14, 1997 [Appointed Day]	S.I. 1997 No. 34 (C2)
Party Wall etc. Act 1996 (c. 40)	All provisions	July 1, 1997	S.I. 1997 No. 670 (C.24)
Pensions Act 1995 (c. 26)	ss.55, 78(8) (part), 80(4) (part), Sched. 2, para. 12 (part)	February 4, 1997	S.I. 1997 No. 216 (C.11)
Pensions Act 1995 (c. 26)	s.81(7)	March 6, 1997	S.I. 1997 No. 664 (C.23)
Pensions Act 1995 (c. 26)	ss.122 (part), 151 (part), 165, Sched. 3, para. 23, Sched. 5, paras. 20, 73	April 1, 1997	S.I. 1997 No. 664 (C.23)
Pensions Act 1995 (c. 26)	s.136 (rem.), Pt. III (ss.135–151)	April 6, 1997	S.I. 1996 No. 778 (C.13)
Pensions Act 1995 (c. 26)	ss.78(8) (rem.), 80(4) (rem.), Sched. 2, para. 12 (rem.)	April 6, 1997	S.I. 1997 No. 216 (C.11)
Pensions Act 1995 (c. 26)	ss.1(5), 3–15, 16–21, 22–26, 27–31, 32–38, 40, 41, 47, 48(1), (3)–(6), 49, 50, 51–54, 56–61, 67–72, 73–77, 78(4), (8), 79, 80(1), (3), (5), 81–86, 87–89, 91(1), (2), (4)–(7), 92–94, 96, 97, 98–103, 104–109, 110–114, 115, 116(2), (3), 117, 122, 123(1), (2), 125(1), 137, 138, 139, 140(1), (3), 141, 147, 149, 150, 151, 152–154, 155, 157–160, 161, 162–164, 173, 177, 178, 181, Scheds. 1, 2, 3, 5 (except para. 38), 6, 7 (part)	April 6, 1997	S.I. 1997 No. 664 (C.23)
Pharmacists (Fitness to Practise) Act 1997 (c. 19)	ss.2, 3	March 19, 1997	Royal Assent

Act Affected	Provision Brought Into Force	Commencement Date	Authority
Planning (Consequential Provisions) (Scotland) Act 1997 (c. 11)	All provisions (except repeal in Sched. 1, Pt. I)	May 27, 1997	s.6(2), (3)
Planning (Hazardous Substances) (Scotland) Act 1997 (c. 10)	All provisions	May 27, 1997	s.40(2)
Planning (Listed Buildings and Conservation Areas) (Scotland) Act 1997 (c. 9)	All provisions	May 27, 1997	s.83(2)
Plant Varieties Act 1997 (c. 66)	ss.49, 53, 54	November 27, 1997	s.54(2)
Police Act 1997 (c. 50)	ss.1 (part), 17 (part), 44, 45, 46, 47 (part), 62 (part), 89, 90, 128, 129 (part), 130, 131, 132, Scheds. 1 (part), 2 (part)	June 25, 1997	S.I. 1997 No. 1377 (C.50)
Police Act 1997 (c. 50)	ss.1 (rem.), 6, 13, 14, 15, 16, 18, 47 (rem.), 52, 58, 59, 60, 61, 63, 88 (part), 134 (part), Scheds. 1 (rem.), 2 (rem.), 9, paras. 27 (part), 28, 40, 41 (part), 88	July 23, 1997	S.I. 1997 No. 1377 (C.50)
Police Act 1997 (c. 50)	ss.2(6), 3(2)–(4), 25–27, 48(7) (part), 49(2)–(4), 70–72, 91 (except subs. (10)), 96, 109(1), (2) (part), (3), (5), 111 (part), 134 (part), Sched. 4, Sched. 6, paras. 3, 5, 10, Sched. 8, para. 1 (part), 2 (part), 4, 8(1), 9, 10 (part), 11, 18, Sched. 9, paras. 3, 8, 9, 29(3), 82, 83	September 1, 1997	S.I. 1997 No. 1930 (C.79)
Police Act 1997 (c. 50)	ss.2(6) (part), 17(1), (6), 48(7) (part), 62(1), (6), Scheds. 3, 5	October 8, 1997	S.I. 1997 No. 1930 (C.79)

Act Affected	Provision Brought Into Force	Commencement Date	Authority
Police Act 1997 (c. 50)	ss.4, 8, 9, 19, 21, 22(4)–(8), 28, 37, 38, 39, 50, 54, 55, 64, 66, 73, 81, 82, 83, 88 (part), 134 (part), Sched. 6, paras. 1, 2, 6, 9(e), 29, 32, Sched. 9, paras. 13, 14, 23, 38, 39, 43, 49–52, 55, 57, 66–68, 72, 73, 81, 86, 91	October 31, 1997	S.I. 1997 No. 2390 (C.92)
Police and Firemen's Pensions Act 1997 (c. 52)	ss.2, 3	May 21, 1997	s.4(2)
Police (Health and Safety) Act 1997 (c. 42)	ss.7, 8, 9	March 21, 1997	s.9(2)
Police (Insurance of Voluntary Assistants) Act 1997 (c. 45)	All provisions	March 21, 1997	Royal Assent
Police (Property) Act 1997 (c. 30)	All provisions	May 19, 1997	s.7(2)
Policyholders Protection Act 1997 (c. 18)	ss.20(1), (3), 22 (part), 23	March 19, 1997	Royal Assent
Prisons (Alcohol Testing) Act 1997 (c. 38)	All provisions	May 21, 1997	s.3(2)
Protection from Harrassment Act 1997 (c. 40)	ss.13, 14, 15, 16	March 21, 1997	Royal Assent
Protection from Harrassment Act 1997 (c. 40)	ss.1, 2, 4, 5, 7–12	June 16, 1997	S.I. 1997 No. 1418 (C.52)
Protection from Harrassment Act 1997 (c. 40)	ss.3(1), (2), 6	June 16, 1997	S.I. 1997 No. 1498 (C.58)
Public Entertainments Licences (Drug Misuse) Act 1997 (c. 49)	s.4	March 21, 1997	Royal Assent
Referendums (Scotland and Wales) Act 1997 (c. 61)	All provisions	July 31, 1997	Royal Assent

Act Affected	Provision Brought Into Force	Commencement Date	Authority
Reserve Forces Act 1996 (c. 14)	All provisions (except repeal in Sched. 11 (part))	April 1, 1997	S.I. 1997 No. 305 (C.15))
Road Traffic Act 1991 (c. 40)	s.43, Sched. 3 (provisions in relation to Scotland only)	June 16, 1997	S.I. 1997 No. 1580 (C.65)
Road Traffic Act 1991 (c. 40)	ss.41 (rem.), 42 (rem.) (provisions in relation to Scotland only)	October 10, 1997	S.I. 1997 No. 2260 (C.88) (S.151)
Road Traffic (New Drivers) Act 1995 (c. 13)	ss.5(1), (2), (8), (9), (10), 6 (part), 10(1), (5), Sched. 1, para. 11	March 1, 1997	S.I. 1997 No. 267 (C.13)
Road Traffic (New Drivers) Act 1995 (c. 13)	All remaining provisions	June 1, 1997	S.I. 1997 No. 267 (C.13)
Scottish Legal Services Ombudsman and Commissioner for Local Administration in Scotland Act 1997 (c. 35)	All provisions except s.8(2) (part), (3), 10 (part), Sched. (part)	May 21, 1997	s.11(1)
Sea Fisheries (Shellfish) (Amendment) Act 1997 (c. 3)	All provisions	February 27, 1997	Royal Assent
Self-Governing Schools etc. (Scotland) Act 1989 (c. 39)	s.70 (All remaining provisions)	February 19, 1997	S.I. 1997 No. 391 (C.18) (S.33)
Sex Discrimination Act 1975 (c. 65)	Codes of Practice relating to equal pay	March 26, 1997	S.I. 1997 No. 131 (C.6)
Sex Offenders Act 1997 (c. 51)	All provisions	September 1, 1997	S.I. 1997 No. 1920 (C.78)
Social Security Act 1990 (c. 27)	ss.15(11), 21(2) (part), Sched. 7 (part)	June 9, 1997 [Appointed Day]	S.I. 1997 No. 1370 (C.49) (S.107)
Social Security Administration (Fraud) Act 1997 (c. 47)	ss.23–26	March 21, 1997	Royal Assent
Social Security Administration (Fraud) Act 1997 (c. 47)	ss.1, 2, 3 (part), 4–10, 12, 13, 14, 17, 18, 22 (part), Sched. 1, paras. 1–7, 9–14, Sched. 2 (part)	July 1, 1997 [Appointed Day]	S.I. 1997 No. 1577 (C.63)

Act Affected	Provision Brought Into Force	Commencement Date	Authority
Social Security Administration (Fraud) Act 1997 (c. 47)	s.20(1)	August 25, 1997 [Appointed Day]	S.I. 1997 No. 2056 (C.82)
Social Security Administration (Fraud) Act 1997 (c. 47)	ss.11, 16 (authorising the making of regulations only)	October 8, 1997 [Appointed Day]	S.I. 1997 No. 2417 (C.94)
Social Security Administration (Fraud) Act 1997 (c. 47)	s.16	November 3, 1997 [Appointed Day]	S.I. 1997 No. 2417 (C.94)
Social Security Administration (Fraud) Act 1997 (c. 47)	s.19 (authorising the making of regulations only)	November 7, 1997	S.I. 1997 No. 2669 (C.100)
Social Security Administration (Fraud) Act 1997 (c. 47)	s.15 (authorising the making of regulations only)	November 21, 1997	S.I. 1997 No. 2766 (C.104)
Social Security Administration (Fraud) Act 1997 (c. 47)	s.19	December 1, 1997	S.I. 1997 No. 2669 (C.100)
Social Security Administration (Fraud) Act 1997 (c. 47)	ss.15 (rem.), 22 (part), Sched. 1, para. 8 (part)	December 18, 1997	S.I. 1997 No. 2766 (C.104)
Social Security (Recovery of Benefits) Act 1997 (c. 27)	ss.25, 29–32	March 19, 1997	Royal Assent
Social Security (Recovery of Benefits) Act 1997 (c. 27)	ss.1(2) (part), 4(9), 11(5), (6), 12(6), (7), 13(3), 14(2), (3), (4), 16(1), (2), 18, 19, 21(3), 23(1), (2), (5), (7)	September 3, 1997 (power to make regulations)	S.I. 1997 No. 2085 (C.83)
Social Security (Recovery of Benefits) Act 1997 (c. 27)	All remaining provisions	October 6, 1997	S.I. 1997 No. 2085 (C.83)
Telecommunications (Fraud) Act 1997 (c. 4)	All provisions	April 27, 1997	s.2(3)
Town and Country Planning (Scotland) Act 1997 (c. 8)	All provisions (except as provided by Sched. 3 to 1997 c.11)	May 27, 1997	s.278(2)
Trading Schemes Act 1996 (c. 32)	All provisions	February 6, 1997	S.I. 1997 No. 29 (C.1)

Act Affected	Provision Brought Into Force	Commencement Date	Authority
Transfer of Crofting Estates (Scotland) Act 1997 (c. 26)	All provisions	June 6, 1997	S.I. 1997 No. 1430 (C.56)
Treasure Act 1996 (c. 24)	s.11	March 13, 1997	S.I. 1997 No. 760 (C.29)
Treasure Act 1996 (c. 24)	All remaining provisions	September 24, 1997	S.I. 1997 No. 1977 (C.81)
Trusts of Land and Appointment of Trustees Act 1996 (c. 47)	All provisions	January 1, 1997	S.I. 1996 No. 2974 (C.91)
United Nations Personnel Act 1997 (c. 13)	All provisions	April 27, 1997	s.10(2)
Welsh Development Agency Act 1997 (c. 37)	All provisions	May 21, 1997	s.2(3)

FAIR TRADING
THE TRADING SCHEMES ACT 1996
(COMMENCEMENT) ORDER 1997

(S.I. 1997 No. 29 (C. 1))

Made - - - - - - *13th January 1997*

INTRODUCTION

This Order brings into force on February 6, 1997, all provisions of the Trading Schemes Act 1996. This Act amends Pt IX of the Fair Trading Act 1973, which deals with pyramid selling and similar trading schemes. Regulations come into force at the same time as the Act.

The Secretary of State, in exercise of the powers conferred upon him by section 5(2) of the Trading Schemes Act 1996 (c. 32), hereby makes the following Order:

Citation

1. This Order may be cited as the Trading Schemes Act 1996 (Commencement) Order 1997.

Appointed Day

2. The day appointed for the coming into force of the Trading Schemes Act 1996 is 6th February 1997.

John M Taylor,
Parliamentary Under-Secretary of State
for Corporate and Consumer Affairs,
13th January 1997　　　　　　　　Department of Trade and Industry

OSTEOPATHS
THE OSTEOPATHS ACT 1993 (COMMENCEMENT NO. 1 AND TRANSITIONAL PROVISION) ORDER 1997

(S.I. 1997 No. 34 (C. 2))

Made - - - - - - *13th January 1997*

INTRODUCTION

This Order brings into force on January 14, 1997, certain provisions of the Osteopaths Act 1993 which relate to the General Osteopathic Council. Section 1(1), *inter alia*, is brought into force for the purpose of establishing the Council, and s.1(2) brings into force the duty of the Council, which is to develop, promote and regulate the profession of osteopathy.

The Secretary of State for Health, in exercise of the powers conferred upon him by section 42(2), (4) and (5) of the Osteopaths Act 1993 (c. 21), hereby makes the following Order:

Citation and interpretation

1.—(1) This Order may be cited as the Osteopaths Act 1993 (Commencement No. 1 and Transitional Provision) Order 1997.

(2) In this Order "the Act" means the Osteopaths Act 1993.

Appointed day

2. 14th January 1997 is the day appointed for the coming into force of each provision of the Act specified in the first column of the Schedule to this Order (which relate to the matters mentioned in the second column of the Schedule) and, save as otherwise provided in the first column of the Schedule, those provisions shall come into force on that day for all purposes.

Transitional provision

3. Until such time as a person appointed to be the registrar under section 2(1) of the Act takes office—

(a) paragraph 5 of the Schedule to the Act shall have effect as if for the word "Registrar" there were substituted the words "Chairman of the General Council"; and

(b) paragraph 14(2) of that Schedule shall have effect as if for the word "Registrar" there were substituted the words "Privy Council".

13th January 1997

Stephen Dorrell,
Secretary of State for Health

Article 2   SCHEDULE

PROVISIONS OF THE ACT COMING INTO FORCE ON 14TH JANUARY 1997

(1) *Provision of the Act*	*(2)* *Subject matter*
In section 1—	The General Osteopathic Council
subsection (1);	
subsection (2), for the purpose of enabling the General Osteopathic Council to prepare for the exercise of any functions which may be, or if the relevant provision were in force could become, exercisable under any provision of the Act including this subsection;	
subsection (3), so far as it relates to the other provisions of the Act brought into force by this Order;	
subsection (4), so far as it relates to the following provisions of Part I of the Schedule to the Act—	
paragraphs 1, 2, 4, 5, 6, 8, 11, 13, 14(2), 14(3) except for paragraph (d), and 15; (para. 15 of the Sched. was amended by the Chiropractors Act 1994 (c. 17), Sched. 2, para. 10(2))	
subsections (8), (10), (11) and (12)	
Section 2(1), (2), (4), (5) and (6)	The Registrar of Osteopaths
Section 34	Default powers of the Privy Council
Section 35(1), (2) and (4)	Rules
Section 36(1), (2), (4), (5) and (6)	Exercise of powers by Privy Council
Section 40	Financial provisions
Section 41, so far as it provides a definition of "the General Council", "prescribed" and "the Registrar"	Interpretation
In section 42, subsections (1) to (6), and subsection (7) except for the words from "except that" to the end of that subsection	Short title, commencement, transitional provisions and extent
In the Schedule—	
in Part I, paragraphs 1, 2, 4, 5, 6, 8, 11, 13, 14(2), 14(3) except for paragraph (d), and 15; (see above)	The General Council
Part III	The General Council: transitional provisions

CRIMINAL LAW, ENGLAND AND WALES
THE CRIMINAL PROCEDURE AND INVESTIGATIONS ACT 1996
(APPOINTED DAY NO. 2) ORDER 1997

(1997 No. 36 (C. 3))

Made   -   -   -   -   -   -   *12th January 1997*

INTRODUCTION

By this Order, the Appointed Day for the purposes of s.52(1) of the Criminal Procedure and Investigations Act 1996, is February 1, 1997. This provision extends only to England and Wales, and applies where a person being remanded is charged with an offence alleged to be committed on or after that date.

The Secretary of State, in exercise of the powers conferred on him by sections 52(4) and 77(4) of the Criminal Procedure and Investigations Act 1996 (c. 25), hereby makes the following Order:

1. This Order may be cited as the Criminal Procedure and Investigations Act 1996 (Appointed Day No. 2) Order 1997.

2. 1st February 1997 is hereby appointed for the purposes of section 52 of the Criminal Procedure and Investigations Act 1996.

Home Office   *Michael Howard,*
12th January 1997   One of Her Majesty's Principal Secretaries of State

ENERGY CONSERVATION
THE ENERGY CONSERVATION ACT 1996
(COMMENCEMENT NO. 3 AND ADAPTATIONS) ORDER 1997

(S.I. 1997 No. 47 (C. 4))

Made - - - - - - *13th January 1997*

INTRODUCTION

This Order brings into force the Energy Conservation Act 1996 on January 14, 1997 for the purposes of ss.3(1) and 4(1)–(2) of the Home Energy Conservation Act 1995, and on April 1, 1997 for all other purposes. The Order only extends to those energy conservation authorities whose areas are in England or Wales.

The Secretary of State, in exercise of the powers conferred upon him by section 2(2) and (3) of the Energy Conservation Act 1996 (c. 38) and all other powers enabling him in that behalf, hereby makes the following Order—

Citation and application

1. This Order may be cited as the Energy Conservation Act 1996 (Commencement No. 3 and Adaptations) Order 1997 and applies to England and Wales.

Commencement

2. The Energy Conservation Act 1996 as respects energy conservation authorities whose areas are in England or Wales shall come into force—
  (a) on 14th January 1997 for the purposes of sections 3(1) and 4(1) and (2) of the Home Energy Conservation Act 1995 (c. 10) (power of Secretary of State to give directions and guidance); and
  (b) on 1st April 1997 for all other purposes.

Adaptation

3.—(1) The Home Energy Conservation Act 1995 is adapted in accordance with the following provisions of this article.
  (2) In section 2 (energy conservation reports),—
  (a) at the beginning of subsection (1) insert "Subject to subsection (7),"; and
  (b) at the end of the section add—
      "(7) An energy conservation authority may prepare a report on houses in multiple occupation or house-boats which is separate from the report on other residential accommodation.".
  (3) In section 3 (functions of the Secretary of State in relation to reports), after "different areas" insert "; and may set different dates for reports on houses in multiple occupation or house-boats or reports on other residential accommodation."

Signed by the authority of the Secretary of State

Robert Jones,
13th January 1997   Minister of State, Department of the Environment

HOUSING, ENGLAND AND WALES
THE HOUSING ACT 1996
(COMMENCEMENT NO. 6 AND SAVINGS) ORDER 1997

(S.I. 1997 No. 66 (C. 5))

Made   -   -   -   -   -   -   *14th January 1997*

INTRODUCTION

This Order brings into force on February 12, 1997 further provisions of the Housing Act 1996 relating to introductory tenancies and to repossession: secure tenancies. Where the provisions amend Pt. IV of the Housing Act 1985 (secure tenancies), they are made subject to the savings in the Schedule to the Order.

The Secretary of State, in exercise of the powers conferred on him by section 232(2) and (4) of the Housing Act 1996 (c. 52) and of all other powers enabling him in that behalf, hereby makes the following Order:

Citation and interpretation

1.—(1) This Order may be cited as the Housing Act 1996 (Commencement No. 6 and Savings) Order 1997.

(2) In this Order "the commencement date" means 12th February 1997.

Commencement and Savings

2. The following provisions of the Act shall come into force on the commencement date, subject to the savings in the Schedule to this Order—

sections 124 to 128,
section 129(1), (2), (5) and (6),
sections 130 to 134,
sections 136 and 137,
section 138(1) to (3),
section 141(1),
sections 144 to 146, and
section 147 to the extent that it is not already in force.

Article 2   SCHEDULE

SAVINGS

The substitution of section 83 of Housing Act 1985 and the amendments to section 84 of and Schedule 2 to that Act (c. 68 *See* ss.144, 145 and 147 of the Housing Act 1996) (repossession: secure tenancies) shall have no effect in a case where a notice under section 83 of that Act (notice of proceedings for possession or termination) has been served before the commencement date.

Signed by authority of the Secretary of State

David Curry,
Minister of State,
Department of the Environment

14th January 1997

SEX DISCRIMINATION
THE CODE OF PRACTICE ON EQUAL PAY
(APPOINTED DAY) ORDER 1997

(S.I. 1997 No. 131 (C. 6))

Made -	-	-	-	-	-	-	*21st January 1997*
Laid before Parliament		-	-	-			*24th January 1997*
Coming into force		-	-	-			*26th March 1997*

INTRODUCTION

Section 56A(1) and (7) of the Sex Discrimination Act 1975 provides for the Equal Opportunities Commission to issue codes of practice containing guidance for the elimination of discrimination in the field of employment and the promotion of equality of opportunity in that field between men and women. This Order provides that the day appointed for a Code of Practice on Equal Pay to come into effect, is March 26, 1997.

Whereas—

(1) in pursuance of section 56A(1) of the Sex Discrimination Act 1975 (c. 65; s.56A was inserted by the Race Relations Act 1976 (c. 74), Sched. 4, para. 1 and amended by the Trade Union Reform and Employment Rights Act 1993 (c. 19) Sched. 7, para. 15) (hereinafter referred to as "the Act") the Equal Opportunities Commission (hereinafter referred to as "the Commission") may issue codes of practice containing such practical guidance as the Commission think fit for either or both of the following purposes, namely, the elimination of discrimination in the field of employment and the promotion of equality of opportunity in that field between men and women;

(2) in pursuance of section 56A(2) of the Act the Commission prepared and published a draft code of practice for the said purposes so far as relating to equal pay, considered representations that were made to them about the draft and modified the draft in the light of those representations;

(3) in pursuance of section 56A(3) of the Act the Commission consulted with such organisations or associations representative of employers or of workers and such other organisations or bodies as appeared to the Commission to be appropriate;

(4) in pursuance of section 56A(4) of the Act the Commission transmitted the draft code of practice, as modified, to the Secretary of State who approved of it and laid it before both Houses of Parliament on 23rd October 1996;

(5) in accordance with section 56A(5) of the Act the modified draft code of practice lay before each House of Parliament for a period of forty days during which period neither House resolved that no further proceedings should be taken on it;

(6) in pursuance of section 56A(7) of the Act the Commission is to issue the code of practice in the form of the modified draft on 25th March 1997;

Now, therefore, the Secretary of State, in exercise of the power conferred on her by section 56A(7) of the Act, hereby orders as follows:

Citation and Commencement

1. This Order may be cited as the Code of Practice on Equal Pay (Appointed Day) Order 1997 and shall come into force on 26th March 1997.

Appointed Day

2. The day appointed as the day on which the Code of Practice on Equal Pay (ISBN number: 1 870358 64 3), to be issued by the Commission on 25th March 1997 under subsections (1) and (7) of section 56A of the Act in the form of the modified draft laid before Parliament on 23rd October 1996, shall come into effect is 26th March 1997.

Gillian Shephard,
21st January 1997   Secretary of State for Education and Employment

INCOME TAX

THE FINANCE ACT 1996, SCHEDULE 35, (APPOINTED DAY) ORDER 1997

(S.I. 1997 No. 133 (C. 8))

Made   -   -   -   -   -   -   *23rd January 1997*

INTRODUCTION

This Order appoints January 31, 1997 for the purposes of Sched. 35, para. 7(2) to the Finance Act 1996. Schedule 35 amends ss.33A to 33F of the Capital Allowances Act 1990 (as inserted by the Finance Act 1995), to make provision in relation to balancing charges in respect of ship disposals taking place on or after April 21, 1994. Schedule 35, para. 7(1) provides that the Schedule shall have effect subject to para. 7(2) in relation to any case in which the ship disposal occurs on or after April 29, 1996. Paragraph 7(2) provides that the Schedule shall not apply for the purposes of claims, assessments and adjustments made on or after April 29, 1996 but before such day as the Treasury may by order appoint; namely January 31, 1997.

The Treasury, in exercise of the powers conferred on them by paragraph 7(2) of Schedule 35 to the Finance Act 1996 (c. 8), hereby make the following Order:

1. This Order may be cited as the Finance Act 1996, Schedule 35, (Appointed Day) Order 1997.

2. The day appointed for the purposes of paragraph 7(2) of Schedule 35 to the Finance Act 1996 is 31st January 1997.

Bowen Wells
Richard Ottaway
23rd January 1997   Two of the Lords Commissioners of
Her Majesty's Treasury

EMPLOYMENT AND TRAINING
THE EMPLOYMENT ACT 1989
(COMMENCEMENT NO. 2) ORDER 1997

(S.I. 1997 No. 134 (C. 9))

Made   -   -   -   -   -   -   *23rd January 1997*

INTRODUCTION

This Order brings into force on March 3, 1997 all provisions of the Employment Act 1989 not already brought into force. These remaining provisions repeal s.119A of the Factories Act 1961 and enactments relating to it, and amend s.176(5) of that Act.

The Secretary of State, in exercise of the powers conferred on him by section 30(4) of the Employment Act 1989 (c. 38), ("the 1989 Act"), hereby makes the following order:

Citation

1. This order may be cited as the Employment Act 1989 (Commencement No. 2) Order 1997.

Commencement

2. The 1989 Act, so far as not already in force (*see* s.30(2) and (3) of the 1989 Act; S.I. 1990 No. 189), shall come into force on 3rd March 1997.

Signed by authority of the Secretary of State.

Paul Beresford,
Parliamentary Under Secretary of State,
23rd January 1997   Department of the Environment

CHILDREN AND YOUNG PERSONS

THE CHILDREN (SCOTLAND) ACT 1995 (COMMENCEMENT NO. 2 AND TRANSITIONAL PROVISIONS) (AMENDMENT) ORDER 1997

(S.I. 1997 No. 137 (C. 10) (S. 9))

Made - - - - - -   *19th January 1997*

INTRODUCTION

This Order amends the Children (Scotland) Act 1995 (Commencement No. 2 and Transitional Provisions) Order 1996 (S.I. 1996 No. 2203). A transitional provision relating to the Social Work (Scotland) Act 1968 is inserted into Art. 5.

The Secretary of State in exercise of the powers conferred upon him by section 105(1) and (2) of the Children (Scotland) Act 1995 (c. 36) and of all other powers enabling him in that behalf, hereby makes the following order:

Citation and interpretation

1.—(1) This Order may be cited as the Children (Scotland) Act 1995 (Commencement No. 2 and Transitional Provisions) (Amendment) Order 1997.

(2) In this Order "the second commencement order" means the Children (Scotland) Act 1995 (Commencement No. 2 and Transitional Provisions) Order 1996 (S.I. 1996 No. 2203 as amended by S.I. 1996 No. 2708).

Amendment of the second commencement order

2. In the second commencement order after article 5 there shall be inserted the following:

"5A. From 20th January 1997 until 1st April 1997 the reference in section 30(2) of the 1968 Act to a guardian shall be construed to include in relation to a child any person who, in the opinion of the court or children's hearing having cognizance of any case in relation to the child or in which the child is concerned, has for the time being the custody or charge of or control over the child.".

St Andrew's House,   *James-Douglas Hamilton*
Edinburgh   Minister of State,
19th January 1997   Scottish Office

PENSIONS

THE PENSIONS ACT 1995 (COMMENCEMENT NO. 9) ORDER 1997

(S.I. 1997 No. 216 (C. 11))

Made - - - - - - *3rd February 1997*

INTRODUCTION

This Order appoints February 4, 1997 for the coming into force of s.80(4) of, and Sched. 2, para. 12 to the Pensions Act 1995 for regulation making purposes only. Section 78(8) is also brought into force insofar as it relates to para. 12. These provisions are brought into force on April 6, 1997 for all other purposes. Section 55 is also brought into force on February 4, 1997.

The Secretary of State for Social Security, in exercise of the powers conferred on him by section 180(1) of the Pensions Act 1995 (c. 26) and of all other powers enabling him in that behalf, hereby makes the following Order:

Citation and interpretation

1.—(1) This Order may be cited as the Pensions Act 1995 (Commencement No. 9) Order 1997.

(2) In this Order "the Act" means the Pensions Act 1995.

Appointed days

2.—(1) The day appointed for the coming into force of section 80(4) of the Act (review of decisions of the Pensions Compensation Board), paragraph 12 of Schedule 2 to the Act and section 78(8) of the Act insofar as it relates to that paragraph (proceedings of the Pensions Compensation Board)—

(a) for the purpose only of authorising the making of regulations, is 4th February 1997, and

(b) for all other purposes, is 6th April 1997.

(2) The day appointed for the coming into force of section 55 of the Act (end of annual increase in GMP) is 4th February 1997.

Signed by authority of the Secretary of State for Social Security.

Oliver Heald
Parliamentary Under-Secretary of State,
3rd February 1997   Department of Social Security

HOUSING, ENGLAND AND WALES

THE HOUSING ACT 1996
(COMMENCEMENT NO. 7 AND SAVINGS) ORDER 1997

(S.I. 1997 No. 225 (C. 12))

Made   -   -   -   -   -   -   *28th January 1997*

INTRODUCTION

   This Order brings into force on February 28, 1997 provisions of the Housing Act 1996 relating to assured tenancies. Where certain of these provisions amend ss.8 and 21(1) and (4) of and Sched. 2 to the Housing Act 1988 they are commenced subject to the savings in the Schedule to this Order.

The Secretary of State, in exercise of the powers conferred on him by section 232(3) and (4) of the Housing Act 1996 (c. 52) and of all other powers enabling him in that behalf, hereby makes the following Order:

Citation and interpretation

   1.—(1) This Order may be cited as the Housing Act 1996 (Commencement No. 7 and Savings) Order 1997.

   (2) In this Order "the commencement date" means 28th February 1997.

Commencement and Savings

   2. The following provisions of the Housing Act 1996 shall come into force on the commencement date, subject to the savings in the Schedule to this Order—

      section 96 to the extent that it is not already in force,

      sections 97 to 104,

      sections 148 to 151, and

      section 227 in so far as it relates to the repeals in Part IV of Schedule 19.

SCHEDULE   Article 2

SAVINGS

   1. The insertion of section 8A in the Housing Act 1988 and the amendment to section 8 of and Schedule 2 to that Act (c. 50. *See* ss.101, 102, 148, 149, 150 and 151 of the Housing Act 1996) (repossession: assured tenancies) shall have no effect in a case where—

    (a) a notice under section 8 of that Act (notice of proceedings for possession) has been served before the commencement date; or

    (b) the court has dispensed with the requirement of such a notice and the proceedings for possession were started before the commencement date.

   2. The amendments to section 21(1) and (4) of the Housing Act 1988 (*see* s.98 of the Housing Act 1996) (recovery of possession on expiry or termination of assured shorthold tenancy) shall have no effect in a case where a landlord has served a notice under section 8 of that Act (notice of proceedings for possession) before the commencement date.

Signed by authority of the Secretary of State

James Clappison
Parliamentary Under-Secretary of State,
Department of the Environment

28th January 1997

ROAD TRAFFIC

THE ROAD TRAFFIC (NEW DRIVERS) ACT 1995 (COMMENCEMENT) ORDER 1997

(S.I. 1997 No. 267 (C. 13))

Made - - - - - - *5th February 1997*

INTRODUCTION

This Order brings into force on March 1, 1997 provisions of the Road Traffic (New Drivers) Act 1995 some of which confer powers on the Secretary of State to make regulations. All remaining provisions of the Act are brought into force on June 1, 1997.

The Secretary of State for Transport, in exercise of the powers conferred by section 10(2) of the Road Traffic (New Drivers) Act 1995 (c. 13), hereby makes the following Order:

1.—(1) This Order may be cited as the Road Traffic (New Drivers) Act 1995 (Commencement) Order 1997.

(2) In this Order "the Act" means the Road Traffic (New Drivers) Act 1995.

2.—(1) The following provisions of the Act shall come into force on 1st March 1997—

section 5(1), (2), (8), (9) and (10),

section 6, in so far as it gives effect to paragraph 11 of Schedule 1,

section 10(1) and (5), and

paragraph 11 of Schedule 1.

(2) Except as provided in paragraph (1) above, the Act shall come into force on 1st June 1997.

Signed by authority of the Secretary of State for Transport

John Bowis,
Parliamentary Under-Secretary of State
5th February 1997   Department of Transport

DEFENCE

THE ARMED FORCES ACT 1996 (COMMENCEMENT NO. 2) ORDER 1997

(S.I. 1997 No. 304 (C. 14))

Made - - - - - - *12th February 1997*

INTRODUCTION
   This Order brings into force on April 1, 1997, various provisions of the Armed Forces Act 1996 subject to the transitional provisions contained in Sched. 2 to the Order which relate to prosecutions under the Army Act 1955, Air Force Act 1955 and the Naval Discipline Act 1957.

The Secretary of State, in exercise of the powers conferred on him by section 36(2) and (5) of the Armed Forces Act 1996 (c. 46), hereby makes the following Order:

1. This Order may be cited as the Armed Forces Act 1996 (Commencement No. 2) Order 1997.

2. Subject to article 3 of this Order, the following provisions of the Armed Forces Act 1996 ("the Act") shall come into force on 1st April 1997—

   section 5 and Schedule 1;

   sections 9 and 10 and Schedule 3;

   sections 15 to 17 and Schedule 5;

   sections 28 and 29;

   section 35 so far as is necessary to bring into force Schedules 6 and 7 to the extent specified below;

   in Schedule 6, paragraphs 4, 7 to 9, 14 and 15;

   in Schedule 7, Parts I and II, and Part III so far as it relates to the provisions specified in Schedule 1 to this Order.

3.—(1) Nothing in article 2 of this Order insofar as it relates to section 5 of and Schedule 1 to the Act shall have effect in relation to—

   (a) any summary dealing or summary trial,

   (b) any trial by a court-martial or a standing civilian court, or

   (c) the hearing of any appeal by the Courts-Martial Appeal Court,

which commenced before 1st April 1997.

   (2) Nothing in article 2 of this Order insofar as it relates to sections 15 to 17 of and Schedule 5 to the Act shall have effect in relation to any finding made, sentence passed or punishment awarded before 1st April 1997.

   (3) Nothing in article 2 insofar as it relates to provisions which repeal, amend or substitute provisions in enactments shall affect the validity of anything done before 1st April 1997 under the authority of the provisions which have been repealed, amended or substituted.

4. The transitional provisions contained in Schedule 2 to this Order shall have effect.

Nicholas Soames
12th February 1997   Minister of State, Ministry of Defence

SCHEDULE 1   **Article 2**

REPEALS IN PART III OF SCHEDULE 7
TAKING EFFECT ON 1ST APRIL 1997

Chapter	Short title	Extent of repeal
1955 c. 18.	Army Act 1955.	Section 108.
1955 c. 19.	Air Force Act 1955.	Section 108.
1957 c. 53.	Naval Discipline Act 1957.	Section 72.
1968 c. 20.	Courts-Martial (Appeals) Act 1968.	In section 8, subsection (1A)(a), in subsection (2)(a) the words from "or (if" to "annulled" and subsection (5). In section 32(2)(a), the words from "under" to "1968". Section 53. In section 57(1), the words "and" after the definition of "prescribed".
1968 c. 27.	Firearms Act 1968.	Section 11(3).
1976 c. 52.	Armed Forces Act 1976.	In Schedule 3, in paragraph 19, the words from "but" to "period".
1995 c. 35.	Criminal Appeal Act 1995.	In Schedule 2, paragraphs 1 and 2.

TRANSITIONAL PROVISIONS

General

1. Subject to paragraphs 2 to 5 below, where apart from this paragraph anything done under or for the purposes of any provision which is repealed, amended or substituted by the Act would cease to have effect by virtue of that repeal, amendment or substitution it shall have effect as if it had been done under or for the purposes of the corresponding provision in the 1955 Act or the 1957 Act, as the case may be, as amended by the Act.

Prosecutions under the 1955 Act

2. A person who has been remanded for trial by court-martial and served with a copy of the charge sheet and summary (or abstract) of evidence before 1st April 1997 shall be treated as if the prosecuting authority had preferred any charge contained in the charge sheet under section 83B(4) of the 1955 Act and the person had been notified by his commanding officer under section 83B(6) of the 1955 Act that he is to be tried by court-martial.

3. A person who has been remanded for trial by court-martial before 1st April 1997 but has not been served with a copy of the charge sheet and summary (or abstract) of evidence shall be treated as if a case in respect of him had been referred to the prosecuting authority under section 76A(1) of the 1955 Act and the prosecuting authority has considered under section 83B(4) of the 1955 Act that court-martial proceedings should be instituted.

Prosecutions under the 1957 Act

4. A person who has been remanded for trial by court-martial and served with a copy of the charge sheet before 1st April 1997 shall be treated as if the prosecuting authority had preferred any charge contained in the charge sheet under section 52I(4) of the 1957 Act and the person had been notified by his commanding officer under section 52I(5) of the 1957 Act that he is to be tried by court-martial.

5. A person who has been remanded for trial by court-martial before 1st April 1997 but has not been served with a copy of the charge sheet shall be treated as if a case in respect of him had been referred to the prosecuting authority under section 52C(1) of the 1957 Act and the prosecuting authority has considered under secction 52I(4) of the 1957 Act that court-martial proceedings should be instituted.

Interpretation

6. In this Schedule—
"the 1995 Act" means—
    (a) where the accused is being prosecuted under the Army Act 1955 (c. 18), that Act;
    (b) where the accused is being prosecuted under the Air Force Act 1955 (c. 19), that Act; and
"the 1957 Act" means the Naval Discipline Act 1957 (c. 53).

DEFENCE

THE RESERVE FORCES ACT 1996
(COMMENCEMENT NO. 1) ORDER 1997

(S.I. 1997 No. 305 (C. 15))

Made   -   -   -   -   -   -   *19th February 1997*

INTRODUCTION

This Order brings into force on April 1, 1997 all remaining provisions of the Reserve Forces Act 1996 except Sched. 11 to the extent that it provides for the repeal of certain provisions of the Reserve Forces Act 1980. Schedule 11 expressly excludes the repeal, by the coming into force of the 1996 Act, of ss.48, 55, 130 to 138, 140, 151, 156 to 158 of the 1980 Act.

The Secretary of State, in exercise of the powers conferred on him by section 132(4) of the Reserve Forces Act 1996 (c. 14), hereby makes the following Order:

1. This Order may be cited as the Reserve Forces Act 1996 (Commencement No. 1) Order 1997.

2.—(1) Subject to paragraph (2) below, the Reserve Forces Act 1996 shall come into force on 1st April 1997.

(2) The repeal by Schedule 11 to the 1996 Act of provisions of the Reserve Forces Act 1980 (c. 9) shall not be brought into force by paragraph (1) above so far as it relates to the following provisions of the 1980 Act, namely, sections 10, 11, 13(2) to (4), 16, 17, 18(1) and (2), 19, 20(1), 21, 22, 24 to 26, 28, 29, 30(1) and (2), 31, 32, 34(1) to (3), 35, 36, 38, 39(1)(a) and (b), 40 to 42, 44, 47, 50, 57, 58, 63, 67, 69, 70, 83(1) and (2), 87, 93, 100, 101, 120, 139(1), 141 to 144, 145(1)(b) and (2), 146(1)(b) and (2), 154(1), 155, Schedule 2 and Schedule 8, paragraphs 1, 4, 5(1) and (3), 6 to 8, 10 to 15, 16(2), (3) and (5) to (10), 17, 19 and 20.

Nicholas Soames
19th February 1997   Minister of State for the Armed Forces

HOUSING, ENGLAND AND WALES

THE HOUSING ACT 1996 (COMMENCEMENT NO. 8) ORDER 1997

(S.I. 1997 No. 350 (C. 16))

Made   -   -   -   -   -   -   *13th February 1997*

INTRODUCTION

This Order brings into force Pt. II (ss.65–80 except s.73) of the Housing Act 1996 on March 3, 1997, so far as it is not already in force. This Part of the Act concerns houses in multiple occupation and the repeal of Pt. XII of the Housing Act 1985 which relates to common lodging houses.

The Secretary of State, in exercise of the powers conferred on him by section 232(3) of the Housing Act 1996 (c. 52) and of all other powers enabling him in that behalf, hereby makes the following Order:

Citation and commencement

1. This Order may be cited as the Housing Act 1996 (Commencement No. 8) Order 1997.

Commencement

2. Part II of the Housing Act 1996, so far as not already brought into force, except section 73, shall come into force on 3rd March 1997.

Signed by authority of the Secretary of State

James Clappison,
Parliamentary Under-Secretary of State
13th February 1997   Department of the Environment

EDUCATION, SCOTLAND

THE EDUCATION (SCOTLAND) ACT 1996 (COMMENCEMENT NO. 2) ORDER 1997

(S.I. 1997 No. 365 (C. 17) (S.30))

Made - - - - - - *10th February 1997*

INTRODUCTION

This Order brings into force on April 1, 1997, all remaining provisions of the Education (Scotland) Act 1996 which have not already been brought into force. These provisions confer substantive functions on the Scottish Qualifications Authority which will take up such functions on that day.

The Secretary of State, in exercise of the powers conferred on him by section 37(2) of the Education (Scotland) Act 1996 (c. 43) and of all other powers enabling him in that behalf, hereby makes the following Order:

Citation

1. This Order may be cited as the Education (Scotland) Act 1996 (Commencement No. 2) Order 1997.

Day appointed

2. 1st April 1997 is the day appointed for the coming into force of the Education (Scotland) Act 1996, so far as it is not already in force.

Raymond S Robertson
St Andrew's House, Edinburgh   Parliamentary Under-Secretary of State,
10th February 1997   Scottish Office

EDUCATION, SCOTLAND

THE SELF-GOVERNING SCHOOLS ETC. (SCOTLAND) ACT 1989 (COMMENCEMENT NO. 3) ORDER 1997

(S.I. 1997 No. 391 (C. 18) (S. 33))

Made   -   -   -   -   -   -   *18th February 1997*

INTRODUCTION

    This Order brings into force on February 19, 1997, s.70 of the Self-Governing Schools etc. (Scotland) Act 1989 which relates to the appraisal of teachers. All other provisions of the Act except Sched. 10, para. 10, are now in force.

The Secretary of State, in exercise of the powers conferred on him by section 81(2) of the Self-Governing Schools etc. (Scotland) Act 1989 (c. 39), and of all other powers enabling him in that behalf, hereby makes the following Order:

Citation

    1. This Order may be cited as the Self-Governing Schools etc. (Scotland) Act 1989 (Commencement No. 3) Order 1997.

    2. Section 70 of the Self-Governing Schools etc. (Scotland) Act 1989 (appraisal of teachers) shall come into force on 19th February 1997.

                                             M B Forsyth

London   Secretary of State,

18th February 1997   Scottish Office

HARBOURS, DOCKS, PIERS AND FERRIES

THE DOCKYARD SERVICES (ROSYTH) (DESIGNATION AND APPOINTED DAY) (REVOCATION) ORDER 1997

(S.I. 1997 No. 151 (C. 19))

Made	-	-	-	-	-	*20th February 1997*
Laid before Parliament			-	-		*21st February 1997*
Coming into force		-	-	-		*24th February 1997*

INTRODUCTION

This Order revokes the Dockyard Services (Rosyth) (Designation and Appointed Day) Order 1986 (S.I. 1986 No. 2244). That Order designated Rosyth Royal Dockyard and certain services provided therein for the purposes of s.1(1) of the Dockyard Services Act 1986 and appointed a day for the purposes of the section.

The Secretary of State, in exercise of the powers conferred on him by section 1(1) of the Dockyard Services Act 1986 (c. 52), and of all other enabling powers, hereby makes the following Order:

1. This Order may be cited as the Dockyard Services (Rosyth) (Designation and Appointed Day) (Revocation) Order 1997 and shall come into force on 24th February 1997.

2. The Dockyard Services (Rosyth) (Designation and Appointed Day) Order 1986 (S.I. 1986 No. 2244) is hereby revoked.

James Arbuthnot
Minister of State for Defence Procurement,
Ministry of Defence

20th February 1997

CRIMINAL LAW, ENGLAND AND WALES
CRIMINAL LAW, NORTHERN IRELAND

THE CRIMINAL APPEAL ACT 1995 (COMMENCEMENT NO. 4 AND TRANSITIONAL PROVISIONS) ORDER 1997

(S.I. 1997 No. 402 (C. 20))

Made   -   -   -   -   -   -   *17th February 1997*

INTRODUCTION

This Order brings into force on March 31, 1997 all remaining provisions of the Criminal Appeal Act 1995 subject to the transitional provisions and savings contained in Art. 4 of the Order. The provisions mostly relate to powers of the Criminal Cases Review Commission which was established under s.8 of the Act, to consider claims of miscarriages of justice.

In exercise of the powers conferred on him by section 32 of the Criminal Appeal Act 1995 (c. 35) the Secretary of State hereby makes the following Order:

1. This Order may be cited as the Criminal Appeal Act 1995 (Commencement No. 4 and Transitional Provisions) Order 1997.

2. In this Order—
"the 1968 Act" means the Criminal Appeal Act 1968 (c. 19),
"the 1980 Act" means the Criminal Appeal (Northern Ireland) Act 1980 (c. 47),
"the 1995 Act" means the Criminal Appeal Act 1995.

3. Subject to article 4 below, the following provisions of the 1995 Act shall come into force on 31st March 1997—
(a) sections 3 and 5;
(b) section 7, to the extent not already in force;
(c) sections 9 to 25;
(d) section 29 insofar as, to being provisions in Schedules 2 and 3 into force, it is not already in force;
(e) Schedule 2, to the extent not already in force; and
(f) Schedule 3, to the extent not already in force.

4.—(1) In relation to the exercise before 31st March 1997 of the power to make a reference in respect of any person to the Court of Appeal under section 17 of the 1968 Act or section 14 of the 1980 Act, paragraph 7 of Schedule 3 to the Parliamentary Commissioner Act 1967 (c. 13) shall continue to have effect as if this Order had not been made.

(2) In relation to a reference made by the Secretary of State under section 17(1)(b) of the 1968 Act or section 14(1)(b) of the 1980 Act in which the opinion of the Court of Appeal on the point referred has not been furnished when the repeal of that section takes effect, section 14(3) of the 1995 Act shall apply as if the reference had been made by the Commission under the said section 14(3).

(3) In relation to a reference made under section 17 of the 1968 Act or section 14 of the 1980 Act before 31st March 1997, section 133 of the Criminal Justice Act 1988 (c. 33) shall continue to have effect as if this Order had not been made.

Home Office   *Michael Howard*
17th February 1997   One of Her Majesty's Principle Secretaries of State

HOUSING, ENGLAND AND WALES

THE HOUSING ACT 1996 (COMMENCEMENT NO. 9) ORDER 1997

(S.I. 1997 No. 596 (C. 21))

Made - - - - - - *26th February 1997*

INTRODUCTION

This Order brings into force on March 3, 1997, s.227 of the Housing Act 1996 so far as it relates to repeals contained in Sched. 19, Pt. II to the Act. These repeals relate to the control of houses in multiple occupation.

The Secretary of State, in exercise of the powers conferred on him by section 232(3) of the Housing Act 1996 (c. 52) and all other powers enabling him in that behalf, hereby makes the following Order—

Citation

1. This Order may be cited as the Housing Act 1996 (Commencement No. 9) Order 1997.

Commencement

2. Section 227 of the Housing Act 1996 in so far as it relates to the repeals in Part II of Schedule 19 to that Act shall come into force on 3rd March 1997.

Signed by authority of the Secretary of State

James Clappison
Parliamentary Under Secretary of State,
26th February 1997   Department of the Environment

HOUSING, ENGLAND AND WALES

SOCIAL SECURITY

THE HOUSING ACT 1996 (COMMENCEMENT NO. 10 AND TRANSITIONAL PROVISIONS) ORDER 1997

(S.I. 1997 No. 618 (C. 22))

Made - - - - - - - *5th March 1997*

INTRODUCTION

This Order brings into force further provisions of the Housing Act 1996 subject to transitional provisions and savings contained in the Schedule below. The following provisions come into force on April 1, 1997: the remaining provisions of Pt. I (social rented sector), ss.106 (low rent test for leasehold enfranchisement: extension of rights), 118 (estate management schemes in connection with enfranchisement by virtue of s.106), Pt. IV (housing benefit and related matters) (except s.120), and s.227 so far as it relates to the repeals specified in art. 2.

Section 35(4) will come into force on April 1, 1998.

The Secretary of State, in exercise of the powers conferred on him by section 232(3) and (4) of the Housing Act 1996 (c. 52), and of all other powers enabling him in that behalf, hereby makes the following Order:

Citation and interpretation

1.—(1) This Order may be cited as the Housing Act 1996 (Commencement No. 10 and Transitional Provisions) Order 1997.

(2) In this Order—

"the Act" means the Housing Act 1996;

"benefit" means housing benefit, council tax benefit or community charge benefits as prescribed pursuant to section 123(1) (income related benefits) of the Social Security Contributions and Benefits Act 1992 (c. 4; s.123(1) was amended by the Local Government Finance Act 1992 (c. 14), Sched. 9, para. 1); and

"benefit subsidy" means subsidy under sections 135(1) (rate rebate, rent rebate and allowance subsidy) and 140 (community charge benefit subsidy) of the Social Security Administration Act 1992 (c. 5; s.140 was amended by the Local Government Finance Act 1992, Sched. 9, para. 21, to make provision for council tax benefit subsidy but remains in force as originally enacted by virtue of the Local Government Finance Act 1992 (Community Charge Benefit) Savings and Transitional Order 1993 (S.I. 1993 No. 232)), section 30(1A) of the Social Security Act 1986 (c. 50; s.30(1A) was inserted by S.I. 1988 No. 1483; subsidy under that section was only payable in respect of Scotland in 1988/89) and under the Social Security and Housing Benefit Act 1982 (c. 24; the provisions as to subsidy were in ss.32 and 33 and were amended by the Social Security Act 1985 (c. 53), s.22, and by the Local Government Act 1985 (c. 51), s.102 and Sched. 17; they were repealed by the Social Security Act 1986, Sched. 11).

Commencement on 1st April 1997

2.—(1) Subject to the transitional provisions and savings in the Schedule to this Order, the following provisions of the Act shall come into force on 1st April 1997—

section 16,

section 18 to the extent that it is not already in force,

section 19,

sections 20 and 21 to the extent that they are not already in force,

sections 24 and 25 to the extent that they are not already in force,
section 26,
sections 27 to 29 to the extent that they are not already in force,
section 35(1), (2), (3) and (5),
section 51(1) in so far as it relates to the provisions of Schedule 2 that are not already in force, subject to the limitation in paragraph (2) of this article,
section 51(2) to (6),
section 55 in so far as it relates the provisions of Schedule 3 which are not already in force,
section 106 to the extent not already in force,
section 118,
sections 121 to 123, and
section 227 in so far as it relates to the repeal in section 39(3) of the Leasehold Reform, Housing and Urban Development Act 1993 (c. 52) contained in Part V of Schedule 19 and to Part VI of Schedule 19.

(2) The provisions of Schedule 2 which came into force by virtue of paragraph (1) of this article shall not come into force in relation to any complaint against any social landlord which is or at any time was registered with Housing for Wales.

Commencement on 1st April 1998

3. Section 35(4) of the Act shall come into force on 1st April 1998.

Signed by authority of the Secretary of State

David Curry
Minister of State,
5th March 1997   Department of the Environment

Article 2   SCHEDULE

TRANSITIONAL PROVISIONS AND SAVINGS

1. Section 16(2)(c) (right of tenant to acquire dwelling) of the Act does not apply in a case where the dwelling has been acquired after the commencement of this Order by a registered social landlord pursuant to an option which was created or a contract which was entered into before 1st April 1997.

2.—(1) Section 106 (low rent test: extension of rights) of the Act ("section 106") shall not have effect in the following cases.

(2) In so far as it relates to the amendments made to the Leasehold Reform Act 1967 (c. 88) by paragraphs 1 and 2 of Schedule 9 to the Act, section 106 shall not have effect in a case where the house and premises are held under a tenancy which—
(a) is a shared ownership lease within the meaning of section 622 of the Housing Act 1985 (c. 68), and
(b) was granted by a housing association,
whether or not the interest of the landlord still belongs to such an association.

(3) Section 106 shall not have effect in a case where, before 1st April 1997,—
(a) a notice has been given under section 8 of the Leasehold Reform Act 1967 (notice of claim), or
(b) an application has been made under section 27 of that Act (enfranchisement where landlord cannot be found), or
(c) a notice has been given under section 13 or 42 of the Leasehold Reform, Housing and Urban Development Act 1993 (notice of claim), or
(d) an application has been made under section 26 or 50 of that Act (applications where landlord cannot be found).

3. Section 118 (estate management schemes in connection with enfranchisement by virtue of section 106) of the Act shall not have effect in a case where, before 1st April 1997, an application has been made to the leasehold valuation tribunal under any of sections 70 to 73 of the Leasehold Reform, Housing and Urban Development Act 1993 (applications for approval of proposed estate management scheme).

4. The provisions repealed by Part VI of Schedule 19 (repeals) to the Act shall continue in force, not withstanding their repeal by this Order, for the purposes of any benefit subsidy in relation to any benefit paid or claimed in respect of any period before 1st April 1997.

5. In relation to paragraph 4 of Schedule 12 (administration of housing benefit etc) to the Act, any power in relation to subsidy therein may be exercised in relation to any benefit subsidy paid or claimed in respect of any benefit paid before 1st April 1997.

6. The repeal of section 121 (rent officers: additional functions relating to housing benefit etc) of the Housing Act 1988 (c. 50. Subsection (1) of s.121 was amended by the Local Government and Housing Act 1989 (c. 42), s.110(3) and further amended by the Housing Grants, Construction and Regeneration Act 1996 (c. 53), Sched. 1, para. 13. Subsections (4) to (6) were repealed, and subs. (7) was substituted by the Social Security (Consequential Provisions) Act 1992 (c. 4), Sched. 1 and Sched. 2, para. 4 respectively) contained in Part VI of Schedule 19 to the Act shall not have effect in so far as that section has effect for the purposes of section 31 (determination of amount of grant in case of landlord's application) of the Housing Grants, Construction and Regeneration Act 1996 (c. 53).

PENSIONS

THE PENSIONS ACT 1995 (COMMENCEMENT NO. 10) ORDER 1997

(S.I. 1997 No. 664 (C. 23))

Made - - - - - - - *6th March 1997*

<small>INTRODUCTION</small>
This Order appoints certain days for the coming into force of provisions of the Pensions Act 1995. Section 81(7) comes into force on March 6, 1997 for the purpose of making regulations relating to the compensation provisions. So far as they are not already in force, the provisions specified in Pt. I of the Schedule to this Order come into force on April 1, 1997. The remaining provisions of the Act come into force on April 6, 1997 except for ss.48(2), (7) to (13), 95, 145, Sched. 5, para. 38 and a corresponding reference in Sched. 7.

The Secretary of State for Social Security, in exercise of the powers conferred on him by section 180(1) and (4) of the Pensions Act 1995 (c. 26) and of all other powers enabling him in that behalf, hereby makes the following Order:

Citation, interpretation and appointed days

Citation and interpretation

1.—(1) This Order may be cited as the Pensions Act 1995 (Commencement No. 10) Order 1997.

(2) In this Order—
"the 1993 Act" means the Pension Schemes Act 1993 (c. 48);
"the 1995 Act" means the Pensions Act 1995;
"the Authority" means the Occupational Pensions Regulatory Authority (see s.1 of the Pensions Act 1995); and
"the Board" means the Occupational Pensions Board (see s.2 of the Pension Schemes Act 1993).

Appointed days

2.—(1) For the purposes of making regulations relating to the compensation provisions (see s.81(3) of the Pensions Act 1995) the day appointed for the coming into force of section 81(7) of the 1995 Act is the day on which this Order is made.

(2) The day appointed for the coming into force of the provisions specified in Part I of the Schedule to this Order, insofar as they are not already in force, is 1st April 1997.

(3) The day appointed for the coming into force of the provisions specified in Part II of the Schedule to this Order, insofar as they are not already in force, is 6th April 1997.

Transitional adaptations, modifications and savings

Revaluation of earnings factors: early leavers

3. Section 16(3) of the 1993 Act (revaluation of earnings factors: early leavers) shall continue to have effect as if this Order had not come into force in relation to an earner whose service in contracted-out employment in relation to the scheme in question has terminated before the principal appointed day (April 6, 1997: see s.135 of the Pensions Act 1995 and the Pensions Act 1995 (Commencement No. 3) Order 1996, S.I. 1996 No. 778 (C. 13)).

Termination of contracted-out or appropriate scheme status and state scheme premiums

4.—(1) Any function of the Board under section 50 of the 1993 Act (powers of Board to approve arrangements for scheme ceasing to be certified) which fell to be exercised before the principal appointed day but has not been exercised may be exercised by the Secretary of State and, for the purposes of determining the date on which any state scheme premium has become payable, any certificate issued under subsection (2) of that section shall be taken to have had effect from the date specified by the Secretary of State.

(2) Sections 55 to 68, 170(1) and 171(1) of the 1993 Act (state scheme premiums) shall continue to have effect as if this Order had not come into force in relation to any state scheme premium which has been paid before the principal appointed day or is payable immediately before that day, and nothing in this Order shall affect the operation of any other provision of the 1993 Act or any provision of any other Act in relation to any such premium.

(3) Any function of the Board in relation to state scheme premiums under the provisions referred to in paragraph (2) falling to be exercised after the principal appointed day shall be exercised by the Secretary of State.

Transfer Values—extensions granted by the Board

5. Section 99 of the 1993 Act (trustees' duties after exercise of option under section 95) shall have effect in relation to any extension granted or refused by the Board under subsection (4) of that section before the principal appointed day as though it had been granted or refused by the Authority.

Payments to employers

6. For the purposes of—
(a) any payment to the employer out of funds held for the purposes of a scheme where an application to modify the scheme rules for the purposes of making that payment has been made in accordance with the Occupational Pension Schemes (Modification) Regulations 1990 (S.I. 1990 No. 2021; the relevant amending instruments are S.I. 1994 No. 1062 and S.I. 1996 No. 2156) before the principal appointed day; or
(b) any distribution of excess assets to the employer in relation to a scheme which begins to be wound up before the principal appointed day,
section 108 of the 1993 Act (no payments to employers from non-complying schemes) shall continue to have effect as if this Order had not come into force.

Actuarial statements pending the first minimum funding requirement valuation

7. Section 114 of the 1993 Act and regulations 8 and 9 of the Occupational Pension Schemes (Disclosure of Information) Regulations 1986 shall, in so far as they relate to the actuarial statement, remain in force in respect of a scheme to which section 56 of the 1995 Act applies until such time as the trustees or managers of the scheme are required by regulation 30 of the Occupational Pension Schemes (Minimum Funding Requirement and Actuarial Valuations) Regulations 1996 to obtain the first valuation.

Preservation—determinations of the Board

8. Where, before the principal appointed day, the Board has determined in accordance with section 134 of the 1993 Act that any provision of Chapter I of Part IV of the 1993 Act (the preservation requirements) shall not apply to a scheme, that determination shall continue to have effect as if this Order had not come into force until there is an alteration to the rules of the scheme relating to any requirement imposed by that provision.

Modification of schemes

9. Nothing in this Order shall affect the operation of sections 136 to 140 of the 1993 Act (application to modify schemes other than public service schemes) in relation to an application made to the Board before the principal appointed day, and any functions of the Board exercisable after the principal appointed day under those sections as saved by this article shall be exercised by the Authority.

Minimum payments and minimum contributions payable before the principal appointed day

10. Notwithstanding section 140(3) of the 1995 Act, section 48 of the 1993 Act shall remain in force in respect of minimum payments and minimum contributions paid or payable before the principal appointed day.

Winding up

11.—(1) Sections 73 and 74 of the 1995 Act (preferential liabilities on winding up and discharge of liabilities by insurance, etc.) do not apply to any scheme which has begun to be wound up before the principal appointed day; and for the purposes of this paragraph the time when a scheme begins to be wound up shall be determined in accordance with regulation 2 of the Occupational Pension Schemes (Winding Up) Regulations 1996 (S.I. 1996 No. 3126).

(2) At the end of paragraph 31 of Schedule 5 to the 1995 Act insert the words "and for the purposes of this paragraph the time when a scheme begins to be wound up shall be determined in accordance with regulation 2 of the Occupational Pension Schemes (Winding Up) Regulations 1996".

(3) Section 144 of the 1993 Act (which is repealed by the 1995 Act, Schedule 7, Part I) shall remain in force as regards schemes that began to wind up before 19th December 1996 and in respect of debts which arose at any applicable time before 6th April 1997.

Schedules of payments to money purchase schemes

12.—(1) The trustees or managers of an occupational pension scheme to which section 87 of the 1995 Act (schedules of payments to money purchase schemes) applies, shall not be obliged to secure the preparation, maintenance or revision of a payment schedule in respect of any period before the beginning of the first scheme year which begins on or after 6th April 1997.

(2) In paragraph (1) above "scheme year" has the same meaning as in the Occupational Pension Schemes (Scheme Administration) Regulations 1996 (S.I. 1996 No. 1715).

The National Insurance (Non-participation-Certificates) Regulations 1959—functions of the Board

13. Any function of the Board under the National Insurance (Non-participation-Certificates) Regulations 1959 (S.I. 1959 No. 1860; the relevant amending instruments are S.I. 1961 No. 2176, S.I. 1963 No. 676, S.I. 1965 No. 40 and S.I. 1983 No. 118) falling to be exercised on or after the principal appointed day, or which fell to be exercised before that day but which has not been exercised may be exercised by the Secretary of State.

Property, rights and liabilities of the Board

14. All property, rights and liabilities to which the Board is entitled or subject immediately before the principal appointed day shall become the property, rights and liabilities of the Secretary of State.

Signed by authority of the Secretary of State for Social Security.

Oliver Heald
Parliamentary Under-Secretary of State,
6th March 1997   Department of Social Security

Article 2   SCHEDULE

PART I

PROVISIONS OF THE 1995 ACT COMING INTO FORCE ON 1ST APRIL 1997 INSOFAR AS THEY ARE NOT ALREADY IN FORCE

Provisions of the 1995 Act	*Subject matter*
section 165	levy
Schedule 3, paragraph 23 and section 122 insofar as it relates to that paragraph	provision of information by the Registrar of Occupational and Personal Pension Schemes
Schedule 5, paragraph 20 and section 151 insofar as it relates to that paragraph	Occupational Pensions Regulatory Authority as Registrar of Occupational and Personal Pension Schemes
Schedule 5, paragraph 73 and section 151 insofar as it relates to that paragraph	minor amendments to section 174 of the 1993 Act

PART II

PROVISIONS OF THE 1995 ACT COMING INTO FORCE ON 6TH APRIL 1997 INSOFAR AS THEY ARE NOT ALREADY IN FORCE

Provisions of the 1995 Act	*Subject matter*
section 1(5)	constitution, procedure, etc. of the Occupational Pensions Regulatory Authority
sections 3 to 15	supervision by the Occupational Pensions Regulatory Authority
sections 16 to 21	member-nominated trustees and directors
sections 22 to 26	independent trustees
sections 27 to 31	trustees: general
sections 32 to 38	functions of trustees
sections 40 and 41	functions of trustees or managers
sections 47 and 48(1) and (3) to (6)	advisers
section 49	receipts, payments and records
section 50	resolution of disputes
sections 51 to 54	indexation
sections 56 to 61	minimum funding requirement

Provisions of the 1995 Act	*Subject matter*
sections 67 to 72	modification of schemes
sections 73 to 77	winding up
sections 78(4) and (8), 79 and 80(1) to (3) and (5)	the Pensions Compensation Board
sections 81 to 86	the compensation provisions
sections 87 to 89	money purchase schemes
sections 91(1) and (2) and (4) to (7) and 92 to 94	assignment, forfeiture, bankruptcy, etc.
sections 96 and 97	questioning the decisions of the Authority
sections 98 to 103	gathering information: the Authority
sections 104 to 109	disclosure of information: the Authority
sections 110 to 114	gathering information: the Compensation Board
sections 115, 116(2) and (3), 117, 122, 123(1) and (2) and 125(1)	general (Part I)
section 137	state scheme contributions and rebates
sections 138, 139 and 140(1) and (3)	reduction in state scheme contributions, payments of rebates and reduction in state scheme benefits
section 141	premiums and return to state scheme
sections 147, 149 and 150	miscellaneous
section 151	minor and consequential amendments
sections 152 to 154	transfer values
section 155	penalties
sections 157 to 160	Pensions Ombudsman
section 161	modification and winding up of schemes
sections 162 to 164	personal pensions
section 173	general minor and consequential amendments
sections 177, 178 and 181	general (Part IV)
Schedule 1	Occupational Pensions Regulatory Authority
Schedule 2	Pensions Compensation Board
Schedule 3	Amendments consequential on Part I
Schedule 5 (except paragraph 38)	Amendments relating to Part III
Schedule 6	General minor and consequential amendments
Schedule 7 (except the references to sections 35 and 36 of the 1993 Act)	Repeals

BUILDING AND BUILDINGS

THE PARTY WALL ETC. ACT 1996
(COMMENCEMENT) ORDER 1997

(S.I. 1997 No. 670 (C. 24))

Made - - - - - - - *6th March 1997*

INTRODUCTION
This Order brings into force on July 1, 1997, all provisions of the Party Wall etc. Act 1996.

The Secretary of State in exercise of the powers conferred upon him by section 22 of the Party Wall etc. Act 1996 (c. 40) and of all other powers enabling him in that behalf, hereby makes the following Order:

Citation and commencement

1. This Order may be cited as the Party Wall etc. Act 1996 (Commencement) Order 1997.
2. In this Order "the Act" means the Party Wall etc. Act 1996.
3. The Act shall come into force on 1st July 1997.

Transitional Provisions

4. Sections 1, 2 and 6 of the Act shall not apply to any work commenced before 1st September 1997 in accordance with any agreement, easement or right, other than a right arising under or by virtue of the Act.
5. Nothing in this article 4 shall apply to land situated in any part of Greater London where, prior to the coming into force of the Act, Part VI of the London Building Acts (Amendment) Act 1939 (2 & 3 Geo. 6C xcvii) applied.

Signed by authority of the Secretary of State

James Clappison
Parliamentary Under-Secretary of State,
6th March 1997   Department of the Environment

CRIMINAL LAW, ENGLAND AND WALES
CRIMINAL LAW, SCOTLAND

THE CRIMINAL PROCEDURE AND INVESTIGATIONS ACT 1996 (APPOINTED DAY NO. 3) ORDER 1997

(S.I. 1997 No. 682 (C. 25))

Made - - - - - - - *8th March 1997*

INTRODUCTION

This Order appoints April 1, 1997 for the purposes of Pt. I and ss.51, 61, 63 and 69 of the Criminal Procedure and Investigations Act 1996. The appointment of that date for the purposes of Pt. I and ss.51, 69 extends to England and Wales only.

The Secretary of State, in exercise of the powers conferred on him by sections 1(5), 51(3), 61(2), 63(4) and 69(3) of the Criminal Procedure and Investigations Act 1996 (c. 25), hereby makes the following Order.

1.—(1) This Order may be cited as the Criminal Procedure and Investigations Act 1996 (Appointed Day No. 3) Order 1997.

(2) Subject to article 2(2) below, this Order extends to England and Wales and Scotland only.

2.—(1) 1st April 1997 is hereby appointed for the purposes of—
(a) Part I of, and
(b) sections 51, 61, 63 and 69 of,
the Criminal Procedure and Investigations Act 1996 ("the Act").

(2) Sub-paragraph (a) and, so far as it relates to sections 51 and 69 of the Act, sub-paragraph (b) of paragraph (1) above extend to England and Wales only.

Home Office   *Michael Howard*
8th March 1997   One of Her Majesty's Principal Secretaries of State

CRIMINAL LAW, ENGLAND AND WALES

THE CRIMINAL PROCEDURE AND INVESTIGATIONS ACT 1996 (COMMENCEMENT) (SECTION 65 AND SCHEDULES 1 AND 2) ORDER 1997

(S.I. 1997 No. 683 (C. 26))

Made -   -   -   -   -   -   -   *8th March 1997*

INTRODUCTION
   This Order brings into force on March 8, 1997, s.65 of, and Scheds. 1 and 2 to, the Criminal Procedure and Investigations Act 1996. These provisions shall have effect in relation to any alleged offence in relation to which Pt. I of the Act applies.

The Secretary of State, in exercise of the powers conferred on him by section 65(4) of the Criminal Procedure and Investigations Act 1996 (c. 25), and by paragraph 39 of Schedule 1 to that Act and paragraph 7 of Schedule 2 to that Act, hereby makes the following Order.

Citation and commencement

   1.—(1) This Order may be cited as the Criminal Procedure and Investigations Act 1996 (Commencement) (Section 65 and Schedules 1 and 2) Order 1997.
   (2) Section 65 of, and Schedules 1 and 2 to, the Criminal Procedure and Investigations Act 1996 shall have effect in relation to any alleged offence in relation to which Part I of that Act applies.

Home Office   *Michael Howard*
                                      One of Her Majesty's Principal
8th March 1997   Secretaries of State

CHILDREN AND YOUNG PERSONS

THE CHILDREN (SCOTLAND) ACT 1995 (COMMENCEMENT NO. 3) (AMENDMENT AND TRANSITIONAL PROVISIONS) ORDER 1997

(S.I. 1997 No. 744 (C. 27) (S. 70))

Made -   -   -   -   -   -   -   *7th March 1997*

INTRODUCTION

This Order amends the Children (Scotland) Act 1995 (Commencement No. 3) Order 1996 (S.I. 1996 No. 3201). Provision is made by this Order to exclude s.101 of the Children (Scotland) Act 1995 from being brought into effect on April 1, 1997. The Order also excludes from repeal, s.103 of the Children Act 1975.

The Secretary of State in exercise of the powers conferred upon him by section 105(1) of the Children (Scotland) Act 1995 (c. 36) and of all other powers enabling him in that behalf, hereby makes the following Order:

Citation and interpretation

1.—(1) This Order may be cited as the Children (Scotland) Act 1995 (Commencement No. 3) (Amendment and Transitional Provisions) Order 1997.

(2) In this Order "the third commencement order" means the Children (Scotland) Act 1995 (Commencement No. 3) Order 1996 (S.I. 1996 No. 3201).

Amendment of the third commencement order

2. In the third commencement order for Article 3(7) there shall be substituted the following—

"(7) The provisions of the Act, insofar as not already in force, shall come into force on 1st April 1997 except—

(a) section 98 of and paragraph 25 of Schedule 2 to the Act insofar as they insert new section 51A into the Adoption (Scotland) Act 1978, which shall come into force on 1st April 1998;

(b) section 101 of the Act;

(c) the entry in Schedule 5 to the Act relating to the Trusts (Scotland) Act 1921 (c. 58); and

(d) the entries in Schedule 4, paragraph 26(8), and in Schedule 5 to the Act relating to section 103 of the Children Act 1975 (c. 72).".

3. After Article 3 of the third commencement order there shall be inserted the following—

"Transitional provisions

4.—(1) Subject to paragraphs (2) and (3) and notwithstanding the provisions of paragraph 3 of Schedule 3 to the Act, where the parental rights and powers in respect of a child have, by resolution under section 16 of the Social Work (Scotland) Act 1968 (c. 49), vested in a local authority or, as the case may be, a voluntary organisation and immediately prior to 1st April 1997 those rights remain so vested, provided—

(a) the period of one month after the serving of a notice under section 16(5) of that Act has not yet expired and no counter-notice under section 16(7) of that Act has been served on the local authority; or

(b) a counter-notice under section 16(7) of that Act has been served, but there still remains unexpired part of the 14 days referred to in section 16(8) without the local authority having made a summary application to the sheriff under section 16(8) of that Act, then the provisions of the Social Work (Scotland) Act 1968 shall continue to apply to the resolution under s.16 of the Social Work (Scotland) Act 1968 for the duration of whichever of the unexpired periods referred to in paragraphs (a) and (b) applies.

(2) If a counter-notice referred to in sub-paragraph (1)(a) is served within the one month period specified in that sub-paragraph, the provisions of the Social Work (Scotland) Act 1968 shall apply not for the remaining unexpired part of the month but for a further 14 days from the date of the serving of the notice or, if a summary application is made within that period, until the determination of that application by the sheriff.

(3) If a summary application referred to in sub-paragraph (1)(b) is made within the unexpired part of the 14 days referred to in that sub-paragraph, the provisions of the Social Work (Scotland) Act 1968 shall apply not for the remaining unexpired part of the 14 days but until the determination of the summary application by the sheriff.

(4) If a summary application has been served before 1st April 1997 and is at that date still pending, the provisions of the Social Work (Scotland) Act 1968 shall apply until the determination of that application by the sheriff.

5. Where prior to 1st April 1997 there has been lodged under Part II of the Adoption (Scotland) Act 1978 (c. 28) any application for an adoption order or for a freeing for adoption order, the provisions of that Act shall apply to those proceedings after 1st April 1997 notwithstanding any amendment or repeal of any provisions of that Act by the Children (Scotland) Act 1995.

6. Notwithstanding the terms of regulations 3 and 9 of the Arrangements to Look After Children (Scotland) Regulations 1996 (S.I. 1996 No. 3262) where on 1st April 1997 the child is looked after by the local authority for the purposes of section 17(6) of the Act the local authority must make a care plan in respect of the child and carry out a review of the child's case within 6 months from 1st April 1997.".

St Andrew's House, Edinburgh
7th March 1997

James Douglas-Hamilton
Minister of State,
Scottish Office

SOCIAL SERVICES

THE COMMUNITY CARE (DIRECT PAYMENTS) ACT 1996 (COMMENCEMENT) ORDER 1997

(S.I. 1997 No. 756 (C. 28))

Made - - - - - - - *10th March 1997*

INTRODUCTION

This Order brings into force on April 1, 1997, remaining provisions of the Community Care (Direct Payments) Act 1996 (ss.1–5 and 7). Section 6 was brought into force on the date of Royal Assent. The Act empowers a local authority to pay an individual a sum to be used by him to make his own arrangements to purchase care which would otherwise have been arranged by the authority.

The Secretary of State for Health, in exercise of the powers conferred by section 7(2) of the Community Care (Direct Payments) Act 1996 (c. 30) and of all other powers enabling him in that behalf, hereby makes the following Order—

Citation

1. This Order may be cited as the Community Care (Direct Payments) Act 1996 (Commencement) Order 1997.

Day appointed

2. 1st April 1997 is the day appointed for the coming into force of sections 1 to 5 and 7 of the Community Care (Direct Payments) Act 1996.

Stephen Dorrell
One of Her Majesty's Principal
10th March 1997   Secretaries of State

TREASURE

THE TREASURE ACT 1996 (COMMENCEMENT NO. 1) ORDER 1997

(S.I. 1997 No. 760 (C. 29))

Made - - - - - - - *12th March 1997*

INTRODUCTION
This Order brings into force on March 13, 1997, s.11 of the Treasure Act 1996. The section deals with codes of practice relating to treasure which the Secretary of State must prepare.

The Secretary of State, in exercise of the power conferred by section 15(2) of the Treasure Act 1996 (c. 24), hereby makes the following Order:

1. This Order may be cited as the Treasure Act 1996 (Commencement No. 1) Order 1997.

2. Section 11 of the Treasure Act 1996 shall come into force on 13th March 1997.

Lord Inglewood
Parliamentary Under-Secretary of State
12th March 1997   Department for National Heritage

SUPREME COURT OF ENGLAND AND WALES
COUNTY COURTS

THE CIVIL PROCEDURE ACT 1997
(COMMENCEMENT NO. 1) ORDER 1997

(S.I. 1997 No. 841 (C. 30))

Made - - - - - - - *14th March 1997*

INTRODUCTION

This Order brings into force various provisions of the Civil Procedure Act 1997 (c. 12). Section 10 is brought into force on March 14, 1997, so far as it relates to Sched. 2, para. 3(a). Paragraph 3(a) amends s.40 of the Matrimonial and Family Proceedings Act 1984 (c. 42) to allow Family Proceedings Rules to make different provision for different cases or areas.

The remaining provisions of the Civil Procedure Act 1997 are brought into force on April 27, 1997, with the exception of some minor and consequential amendments relating to the Supreme Court Act 1981 and the County Courts Act 1984 (Sched. 2 to the Act). When those two Acts are replaced by the Civil Procedure Rules made under the Civil Procedure Act 1997, the amendments can take effect.

The Lord Chancellor, in exercise of the powers conferred on him by section 11(2) of the Civil Procedure Act 1997 (c. 12) hereby makes the following Order—

1. This Order may be cited as the Civil Procedure Act 1997 (Commencement No. 1) Order 1997.

2. Section 10 of the Civil Procedure Act 1997 (minor and consequential amendments), so far as it relates to paragraph 3(a) of Schedule 2 to the Act, shall come into force forthwith.

3. The following provisions of the Civil Procedure Act 1997 shall come into force on 27th April 1997—
(a) sections 1 to 9; and
(b) section 10 (minor and consequential amendments) so far as it relates to the entries in Schedule 2 referred to in article 4.

4. The entries in Schedule 2 referred to in article 3(b) are—
(a) paragraph 1(1) and (2) (amendment of section 18 of the Supreme Court Act 1981 (c. 54));
(b) paragraph 1(4)(c) (amendment of section 84 of the Supreme Court Act 1981);
(c) paragraph 2(1) and (2) (amendment of the County Courts Act 1984 (c. 28));
(d) paragraph 2(4) (amendment of section 1 of the County Courts Act 1984);
(e) paragraph 2(5) (amendment of section 3 of the County Courts Act 1984); and
(f) paragraph 4 (amendment of section 120 of the Courts and Legal Services Act 1990 (c. 41)).

Dated 14th March 1997 *Mackay of Clashfern, C.*

**CRIMINAL LAW, ENGLAND AND WALES
CRIMINAL LAW, SCOTLAND
CRIMINAL LAW, NORTHERN IRELAND**

**THE CRIMINAL JUSTICE AND PUBLIC ORDER ACT 1994
(COMMENCEMENT NO. 11 AND TRANSITIONAL PROVISION)
ORDER 1997**

(S.I. 1997 No. 882 (C. 31))

Made - - - - - - - *15th March 1997*

INTRODUCTION

This Order brings into force on April 1, 1997, ss.158(2), (5), (6), (7), (8), 159(5) of the Criminal Justice and Public Order Act 1994. These provisions amend the procedures to be followed at committal hearings under the Extradition Act 1989 and before a magistrates' court under the Banking of Warrants (Republic of Ireland) Act 1965.

In exercise of the power conferred upon him by section 172(2) and (3) of the Criminal Justice and Public Order Act 1994 (c. 33), the Secretary of State hereby makes the following Order:

1. This Order may be cited as the Criminal Justice and Public Order Act 1994 (Commencement No. 11 and Transitional Provision) Order 1997.

2. Section 158(2), (6) and (7) (extradition procedures) and section 159(5) (backing of warrants: Republic of Ireland) shall come into force on 1st April 1997.

3.—(1) Subject to paragraph (2) below, section 158(5) and (8) shall come into force on 1st April 1997.

(2) In relation to a case where, before 1st April 1997, the Secretary of State has received either an extradition request under section 7 of the Extradition Act 1989, or, as the case may be, a requisition for the surrender of a fugitive criminal under paragraph 4(1) of Schedule 1 to that Act, section 9 of and Schedule 1 to the Extradition Act 1989 shall continue to apply on and after that date as if this Order had not been made.

Home Office
15th March 1997

Michael Howard
One of Her Majesty's
Principal Secretaries of State

HARBOURS, DOCKS, PIERS AND FERRIES

**THE DOCKYARD SERVICES (DEVONPORT)
(DESIGNATION AND APPOINTED DAY)
(REVOCATION) ORDER 1997**

(S.I. 1997 No. 152 (C. 32))

Made	-	-	-	-	-	-	*18th March 1997*
Laid before Parliament		-	-	-		*18th March 1997*
Coming into force		-	-	-	-		*20th March 1997*

INTRODUCTION

This Order revokes the Dockyard Services (Devonport) (Designation and Appointed Day) Order 1986 (S.I. 1986 No. 2243) on March 20, 1997. The revoked order had designating Devonport Royal Dockyard and the dockyard services provided therein, and appointed a day for the purposes of s.1 of the Dockyard Services Act 1986.

The Secretary of State, in exercise of the powers conferred on him by section 1(1) of the Dockyard Services Act 1986 (c. 52), and of all other enabling powers, hereby makes the following Order:

1. This Order may be cited as the Dockyard Services (Devonport) (Designation and Appointed Day) (Revocation) Order 1997 and shall come into force on 20th March 1997.

2. The Dockyard Services (Devonport) (Designation and Appointed Day) Order 1986 (S.I. 1986 No. 2243) is hereby revoked.

James Arbuthnot
Minister of State for Defence Procurement,
Ministry of Defence

18th March 1997

INCOME TAX

THE FINANCE ACT 1997, SCHEDULE 10, (APPOINTED DAY) ORDER 1997

(S.I. 1997 No. 991 (C. 33))

Made -   -   -   -   -   -   -   *20th March 1997*

INTRODUCTION

This Order appoints July 1, 1997, for the purposes of Sched. 10, paras. 7(1) (stock lending arrangements, transfers under such arrangements, and manufactured payments in stock lending cases), 16(1) (manufactured payments), (2) (information powers) to the Finance Act 1997.

The Treasury, in exercise of the powers conferred on them by paragraphs 7(1) and 16(1) and (2) of Schedule 10 to the Finance Act 1997 (c. 16), hereby make the following Order:

1. This Order may be cited as the Finance Act 1997, Schedule 10, (Appointed Day) Order 1997.

2. The day appointed for the purposes of paragraphs 7(1) and 16(1) and (2) of Schedule 10 to the Finance Act 1997 is 1st July 1997.

Roger Knapman
Richard Ottaway
Two of the Lords Commissioners
of Her Majesty's Treasury

20th March 1997

BROADCASTING

THE BROADCASTING ACT 1996 (COMMENCEMENT NO. 2) ORDER 1997

(S.I. 1997 No. 1005 (C. 34))

Made - - - - - - - *21st March 1997*

INTRODUCTION

This Order brings into force on April 1, 1997, various provisions of the Broadcasting Act 1996. These provisions relate to restricted services, the Gaelic Broadcasting Fund and the establishment of the Broadcasting Standards Commission. The Order also appoints April 1, 1997 as the transfer date for the purposes of s.128(2) of the Act.

The Secretary of State, in exercise of the powers conferred on her by sections 128(2) and 149(2) of the Broadcasting Act 1996 (c. 55), hereby makes the following Order:

1. This Order may be cited as the Broadcasting Act 1996 (Commencement No. 2) Order 1997.

2. In this Order, "the 1996 Act" means the Broadcasting Act 1996.

3. The transfer date appointed for the purposes of section 128(2) of the 1996 Act shall be 1st April 1997.

4. The following provisions of the 1996 Act shall come into force on 1st April 1997:

Section 73, so far as it is not yet in force
Section 85
Section 95
Sections 106 to 130
Section 147, so far as it is not yet in force
Section 148, so far as it is not yet in force
Schedule 2, so far as it is not yet in force
Schedule 3
Schedule 4
Schedule 10, so far as it is not yet in force
Schedule 11, so far as it is not yet in force.

Virginia Bottomley
21st March 1997   Secretary of State for National Heritage

CUSTOMS AND EXCISE
INSURANCE PREMIUM TAX
VALUE ADDED TAX
LANDFILL TAX

THE FINANCE ACT 1996,
SECTION 197, (APPOINTED DAY) ORDER 1997

(S.I. 1997 No. 1015 (C. 35))

Made - - - - - - - *20th March 1997*

INTRODUCTION

This Order appoints April 1, 1997 as the day from which s.197(1) and (6) of the Finance Act 1996 shall have effect in relation to air passenger duty, insurance premium tax, VAT and landfill tax.

The Treasury, in exercise of the powers conferred on them by section 197(7) of the Finance Act 1996 (c.8) and of all other powers enabling them in that behalf, hereby make the following Order:

1. This Order may be cited as the Finance Act 1996, section 197, (Appointed Day) Order 1997.

2. Subsections (1) and (6) of section 197 of the Finance Act 1996 shall have effect for periods beginning on or after 1st April 1997.

Bowen Wells
Roger Knapman
Two of the Lords Commissioners
of Her Majesty's Treasury

20th March 1997

CRIMINAL LAW, ENGLAND AND WALES
CRIMINAL LAW, SCOTLAND

THE CRIMINAL PROCEDURE AND INVESTIGATIONS ACT 1996 (APPOINTED DAY NO. 4) ORDER 1997

(S.I. 1997 No. 1019 (C. 36))

Made - - - - - - - *21st March 1997*

INTRODUCTION

This Order appoints April 15, 1997, for the purposes of ss.28 (preparatory hearings) and 54 (tainted acquittals) of, and Sched. 3 (fraud) to the Criminal Procedure and Investigations Act 1996. The Order does not extend to Northern Ireland.

The Secretary of State, in exercise of the powers conferred on him by sections 28(2) and 54(8) of and paragraph 8(2) of Schedule 3 to the Criminal Procedure and Investigations Act 1996 (c. 25), hereby makes the following Order:

1.—(1) This Order may be cited as the Criminal Procedure and Investigations Act 1996 (Appointed Day No. 4) Order 1997.

(2) This Order extends to England and Wales and Scotland only.

2. 15th April 1997 is hereby appointed for the purposes of sections 28 and 54 of and Schedule 3 to the Criminal Procedure and Investigations Act 1996.

Home Office   *Michael Howard*
21st March 1997   One of Her Majesty's Principal Secretaries of State

ARMS AND AMMUNITION

THE FIREARMS (AMENDMENT) ACT 1997 (COMMENCEMENT) (NO. 1) ORDER 1997

(S.I. 1997 No. 1076 (C. 37))

Made - - - - - - - *15th March 1997*

INTRODUCTION

This Order brings into force on March 17, 1997, ss.16, 17 and 18 of the Firearms (Amendment) Act 1997 for the purpose of making a compensation scheme. The Secretary of State is to make a compensation scheme for persons who will effectively be deprived of their firearms. Any such scheme is to provide compensation for persons whose ancillary equipment for such firearms has no practicable use in relation to other firearms. For a scheme to be made, a draft of it must be laid before Parliament and approved by both Houses.

The Secretary of State, in exercise of the powers conferred on him by section 53(3) and (4) of the Firearms (Amendment) Act 1997 (c. 5), hereby makes the following Order:

1. This Order may be cited as the Firearms (Amendment) Act 1997 (Commencement) (No. 1) Order 1997.

2. Sections 16 (Payments in respect of prohibited small firearms and ammunition), 17 (Payments in respect of ancillary equipment) and 18 (Parliamentary control of compensation schemes) of the Firearms (Amendment) Act 1997 shall, for the purposes only of making a compensation scheme, come into force on 17th March 1997.

Home Office   *Michael Howard*
15th March 1997   One of Her Majesty's Principal Secretaries of State

FAMILY LAW

THE FAMILY LAW ACT 1996 (COMMENCEMENT NO. 1) ORDER 1997

(S.I. 1997 No. 1077 (C. 38))

Made - - - - - - - *21st March 1997*

INTRODUCTION

This Order brings into force on March 21, 1997 various provisions of the Family Law Act 1996 (c. 27).

The Lord Chancellor, in exercise of the powers conferred on him by section 67 of the Family Law Act 1996 (c. 27) hereby makes the following Order—

1. This Order may be cited as the Family Law Act 1996 (Commencement No. 1) Order 1997.

2. The following provisions of the Family Law Act 1996 shall come into force forthwith—
  (a) Part I (principles of Parts II and III);
  (b) section 22 (marriage support services);
  (c) Part III (legal aid for mediation in family matters);
  (d) section 66(1) (minor and consequential amendments) so far as it relates to Part II of Schedule 8; and
  (e) section 66(3) (repeals) so far as it relates to the entry in Schedule 10 in respect of the Legal Aid Act 1988 (c. 34).

Dated 21st March 1997   *Mackay of Clashfern,* C.

MERCHANT SHIPPING

THE MERCHANT SHIPPING AND MARITIME SECURITY ACT 1997 (COMMENCEMENT NO. 1) ORDER 1997

(S.I. 1997 No. 1082 (C. 39))

Made - - - - - - - *22nd March 1997*

INTRODUCTION

This Order brings into force on March 23, 1997, various provisions of the Merchant Shipping and Maritime Security Act 1997 (c. 28). The provisions relate to temporary exclusion zones, powers of inspection and detention, powers to require ships to be moved, and various related amendments and repeals of the Merchant Shipping Act 1995.

The Secretary of State for Transport, in exercise of the powers conferred by section 31(3) of the Merchant Shipping and Maritime Security Act 1997 (c. 28), hereby makes the following Order:

1. This Order may be cited as the Merchant Shipping and Maritime Security Act 1997 (Commencement No. 1) Order 1997.

2. The provisions of the Act specified in the first column of the Schedule to this Order (which relate to the matters specified in the second column of that Schedule) shall come into force on 23rd March 1997.

George Young
22nd March 1997   Secretary of State for Transport

Article 2   SCHEDULE

PROVISIONS COMING INTO FORCE ON 23RD MARCH 1997

Provision of the Act	Subject matter of provision
Section 1	Temporary exclusion zone
Section 9, to the extent that it relates to paragraphs 1 to 5 of Schedule 1	Inspection and detention of ships
Section 10	Power to require ships to be moved
Section 29(1), to the extent that it relates to the provisions of Schedule 6 specified below	Minor and consequential amendments
Section 29(2), to the extent that it relates to the provisions of Schedule 7 specified below	Repeals
Schedule 1, paragraphs 1 to 5	Inspection and detention of ships
Schedule 6, paragraphs 18(1), (3) and (5), 19(1), (2)(b) and (c) and (3) and 20	Minor and consequential amendments
Schedule 7, to the extent that it relates to the repeals set out in the Appendix to this Schedule	Enactments repealed

APPENDIX TO THE SCHEDULE

Chapter	Short title	Extent of repeal
1995 c. 21.	The Merchant Shipping Act 1995.	In section 85(3) the words from "and regulations" to "relates to safety". Section 86(5) and (6).

RATING AND VALUATION
LOCAL GOVERNMENT, ENGLAND AND WALES

THE LOCAL GOVERNMENT AND RATING ACT 1997
(COMMENCEMENT NO. 1) ORDER 1997

(S.I. 1997 No. 1097 (C. 40))

Made - - - - - - - *26th March 1997*

INTRODUCTION

This Order brings into force various provisions of the Local Government and Rating Act 1997. Provisions relating to the abolition of rates on sporting rights, and applications for discretionary rate relief come into force on April 1, 1997. The provisions of Pt. III confer powers on parish and community councils, and come into force on May 19, 1997.

The Secretary of State, in exercise of the powers conferred on him by section 34(1) of the Local Government and Rating Act 1997 (c. 29) and of all other powers enabling him in that behalf, hereby makes the following Order:

Citation

1. This Order may be cited as the Local Government and Rating Act 1997 (Commencement No. 1) Order 1997.

Commencement of certain rating provisions

2. The following provisions of the Local Government and Rating Act 1997 ("the Act") shall come into force on 1st April 1997:
  (a) section 2;
  (b) section 33(1), in so far as it relates to the provisions mentioned in paragraph (c) below;
  (c) in Schedule 3—
       paragraph 2;
       paragraph 22 in so far as it relates to paragraph 23;
       paragraph 23.

Parish and community council powers and minor amendments

3. The following provisions of the Act shall come into force on 19th May 1997—
  (a) Part III;
  (b) section 33, in so far as it relates to the provisions mentioned in paragraphs (c) and (d) below;
  (c) in Schedule 3, paragraphs 1 and 11 to 16;
  (d) in Schedule 4, the repeals set out in the Schedule to this Order.

Signed by authority of the Secretary of State

David Curry
Minister of State,
Department of the Environment

26th March 1997

SCHEDULE

REPEALS

Chapter	Short Title	Extent of repeal
1854 c.91.	The Lands Valuation (Scotland) Act 1854.	Section 20. Sections 24 to 26.
1867 c.80.	The Valuation of Lands (Scotland) Amendment Act 1867.	The whole Act.
1894 c.36.	The Valuation of Lands (Scotland) Acts Amendment Act 1894.	The whole Act.
1928 c.44.	The Rating and Valuation (Apportionment) Act 1928.	The whole Act.
1929 c.25.	The Local Government (Scotland) Act 1929.	Section 46.
1930 c.24.	The Railways (Valuation for Rating) Act 1930.	The whole Act.
1934 c.22.	The Accessor of Public Undertakings (Scotland) Act 1934.	The whole Act.
1948 c.26.	The Local Government Act 1948.	Sections 108 and 124.
1952 c.47.	The Rating and Valuation (Scotland) Act 1952.	Section 1. Section 3. Section 4. Section 5. In section 6(1) the words from "section" where it first appears to "1854,". Section 7. Section 8(1). The First Schedule.
1954 c.70.	The Mines and Quarries Act 1954.	Section 191(7).
1961 c.34.	The Factories Act 1961.	In section 184(1), the words from the beginning to "aforesaid".
1966 c.51.	The Local Government (Scotland) Act 1966.	Section 18.
1972 c.11.	The Superannuation Act 1972.	In Schedule 6, paragraph 24.
1973 c.65.	The Local Government (Scotland) Act 1973.	In Schedule 9, paragraphs 37 and 40 to 43.
1975 c.30.	The Local Government (Scotland) Act 1975.	In section 1, in subsection (2), the words from "(including" to "Assessor")" and in subsection (6), paragraph (e). In section 2(1), paragraph (c)(i) and paragraph (g). In section 3(2) the words from "other" to "Act" where it first appears. Section 5. In section 37(1) the definition of "the Assessor". In Schedule 6, in Part I, paragraph 1 and in Part II, paragraphs 2, 3, 7, 8, 9, 17 and 18.
1976 c.64.	The Valuation and Rating (Exempted Classes) (Scotland) Act 1976.	In section 2, in subsections (1) and (2), paragraph (b) and in subsection (3), the words "or, as the case may be, the Assessor of Public Undertakings (Scotland)".

Chapter	Short Title	Extent of repeal
1984 c.31.	The Rating and Valuation (Amendment) (Scotland) Act 1984.	In Schedule 2, paragraphs 2 to 5, 8, 10, 13(2) and 16.
1984 c.54.	The Roads (Scotland) Act 1984.	In Schedule 9, paragraph 26.
1986 c.44.	The Gas Act 1986.	In Schedule 7, paragraph 7.
1995 c.45.	The Gas Act 1995.	In Schedule 4, paragraph 8.

CROWN AGENTS FOR OVERSEA GOVERNMENTS AND ADMINISTRATIONS

THE CROWN AGENTS ACT 1995 (APPOINTED DAY) ORDER 1997

(S.I. 1997 No. 1139 (C. 41))

Made - - - - - - - *20th March 1997*

INTRODUCTION

This Order appoints March 21, 1997 for the purposes of s.1(1) of the Crown Agents Act 1995. On this day all property, rights and liabilities to which the Crown Agents for Oversea Governments and Administrations were entitled or subject immediately before that day shall become property, rights and liabilities of the successor company (nominated under a separate Order).

The Secretary of State in exercise of the power conferred on him by section 1(1) of the Crown Agents Act 1995 (c. 24) hereby makes the following Order:

1. This Order may be cited as the Crown Agents Act 1995 (Appointed Day) Order 1997.

2. The day appointed under section 1(1) of the Crown Agents Act 1995 shall be 21st March 1997.

Malcolm Rifkind
One of Her Majesty's
20th March 1997   Principal Secretaries of State

DOGS

**THE DANGEROUS DOGS (AMENDMENT) ACT 1997
(COMMENCEMENT) ORDER 1997**

(S.I. 1997 No. 1151 (C. 42))

Made - - - - - - - *3rd April 1997*

INTRODUCTION

This Order brings into force on June 8, 1997, all provisions of the Dangerous Dogs (Amendment) Act 1997.

In exercise of the power conferred upon him by section 6(3) of the Dangerous Dogs (Amendment) Act 1997 (c. 53), the Secretary of State hereby makes the following Order:

1. This Order may be cited as the Dangerous Dogs (Amendment) Act 1997 (Commencement) Order 1997.

2. The Dangerous Dogs (Amendment) Act 1997 shall come into force on 8th June 1997.

Home Office　　　　　　　　　　　　　　　　　　*Tom Sackville*
3rd April 1997　　　　　　　Parliamentary Under-Secretary of State

EDUCATION, ENGLAND AND WALES

THE EDUCATION ACT 1997
(COMMENCEMENT NO. 1) ORDER 1997

(S.I. 1997 No. 1153 (C. 43))

Made - - - - - - -   *3rd April 1997*

INTRODUCTION

This Order brings into force on April 4, 1997, s.1 of the Education Act 1996 and an associated repeal contained in Sched. 4. These provide for the extension of the assisted places scheme to schools providing only primary education.

In exercise of the powers conferred on the Secretary of State by sections 54(3) and 58(3) of the Education Act 1997 (c. 44) the Secretary of State for Education and Employment hereby makes the following Order:

1. This Order may be cited as the Education Act 1997 (Commencement No. 1) Order 1997.

2. The following provisions of the Education Act 1997 shall come into force on 4th April 1997:

section 1; and
in Schedule 8 the repeal in section 479(2) of the Education Act 1996 of the words "providing secondary education", and section 57(4) insofar as it relates thereto.

Cheryl Gillan,
Parliamentary Under Secretary of State,
Department for Education and Employment

3rd April 1997

CUSTOMS AND EXCISE

THE FINANCE ACT 1997, SCHEDULE 6, PARAGRAPH 7, (APPOINTED DAY) ORDER 1997

(S.I. 1997 No. 1305 (C. 44))

Made - - - - - - - *16th May 1997*

INTRODUCTION

The appointed day for bringing into force Sched. 6 to the Finance Act 1997 (c. 16) is June 1, 1997. Schedule 6 modifies and changes various excise duty statutory provisions in order to enable the Commissioner of Customs and Excise to assess certain amounts of excise duty due.

The Commissioners of Customs and Excise, in exercise of the powers conferred on them by paragraph 7 of Schedule 6 to the Finance Act 1997 (c. 16), and of all other powers enabling them in that behalf, hereby make the following Order:

Citation

1. This Order may be cited as the Finance Act 1997, Schedule 6, Paragraph 7, (Appointed Day) Order 1997.

Commencement

2. The day appointed as the day on which Schedule 6 of the Finance Act 1997 comes into force is 1st June 1997.

New King's Beam House
22 Upper Ground
London
SE1 9PJ

D. J. Howard
16th May 1997   Commissioner of Customs and Excise

BUILDING SOCIETIES

THE BUILDING SOCIETIES ACT 1997 (COMMENCEMENT NO. 1) ORDER 1997

(S.I. 1997 No. 1307 (C. 45))

Made - - - - - - - *15th May 1997*

INTRODUCTION

This Order brings into force on May 21, 1997, provisions of the Building Societies Act 1997 (c. 32). Schedule 8, para. 1 and related provisions in s.46 contain transitional provisions which relate to the alteration of societies' purpose, powers and rules.

The Treasury, in exercise of the powers conferred on them by section 47(3) of the Building Societies Act 1997 (c. 32), hereby make the following Order:

Citation

1. This Order may be cited as the Building Societies Act 1997 (Commencement No. 1) Order 1997.

Coming into force of provisions

2. The following provisions of the Building Societies Act 1997 shall come into force on 21st May 1997, namely, paragraph 1 of Schedule 8 and section 46 so far as it relates to that paragraph.

Bob Ainsworth
John McFall
Two of the Lords Commissioners
15th May 1997 of Her Majesty's Treasury

MEDICAL PROFESSION

THE MEDICAL (PROFESSIONAL PERFORMANCE) ACT 1995 (COMMENCEMENT NO. 3) ORDER 1997

(S.I. 1997 No. 1315 (C. 46))

Made - - - - - - -   *20th May 1997*

At the Court at Buckingham Palace, the 20th day of May 1997

Present,

The Queen's Most Excellent Majesty in Council

INTRODUCTION

This Order appoints July 1, 1997 as the day on which the remaining provisions (except ss.2, 4, 7(2), Sched., para. 3) of the Medical (Professional Performance) Act 1995 (c. 51) shall come into force. The provisions not being commenced relate to the powers of the General Medical Council to make regulations providing for voluntary removal from the register of medical practitioners.

Her Majesty, in exercise of the powers conferred upon Her by section 6 of the Medical (Professional Performance) Act 1995 (c. 51), and of all other powers enabling Her in that behalf, is pleased, by and with the advice of Her Privy Council, to order, and it is hereby ordered, as follows:

Citation and interpretation

1.—(1) This Order may be cited as the Medical (Professional Performance) Act 1995 (Commencement No. 3) Order 1997.

(2) In this Order, "the Act" means the Medical (Professional Performance) Act 1995.

Appointed Day

2. 1st July 1997 is the day appointed for the coming into force of the whole of the Act so far as it is not already in force, except section 2 (voluntary removal from the register) and, in the Schedule (supplementary and consequential amendments to the Medical Act 1983 (c. 54)), paragraph 3 (which amends section 32 of that Act), and sections 4 (which introduces the Schedule) and 7(2) (extent) so far as they relate to those provisions.

N. H. Nicholls
Clerk of the Privy Council

LOCAL GOVERNMENT, SCOTLAND
LAND DRAINAGE

THE FLOOD PREVENTION AND LAND DRAINAGE (SCOTLAND) ACT 1997 (COMMENCEMENT) ORDER 1997

(S.I. 1997 No. 1322 (C. 47) (S. 106))

Made - - - - - - - *14th May 1997*

INTRODUCTION

This Order brings into force on May 26, 1997, all remaining provisions of the Flood Prevention and Land Drainage (Scotland) Act 1997, with the exception of s.2 (July 28, 1997) and certain repeals in the Schedule (April 1, 1999).

The Secretary of State, in exercise of the powers conferred on him by section 9(4) of the Flood Prevention and Land Drainage (Scotland) Act 1997 (c. 36) and of all other powers enabling him in that behalf, hereby makes the following Order:

Citation and interpretation

1.—(1) This Order may be cited as the Flood Prevention and Land Drainage (Scotland) Act 1997 (Commencement) Order 1997.

(2) In this Order, "the Act" means the Flood Prevention and Land Drainage (Scotland) Act 1997.

Commencement of Act

2.—(1) Subject to paragraphs (2) and (3) below and to section 9(3) of the Act, the Act, so far as not already in force, shall come into force on 26th May 1997.

(2) Section 2 of the Act shall come into force on 28th July 1997.

(3) The following provisions of the Act shall come into force on 1st April 1999:

   (a) the Schedule, so far as it repeals—
      (i) provisions in the Land Drainage (Scotland) Act 1930 (c. 20); and
      (ii) the Land Drainage (Scotland) Act 1941 (c. 13); and
   (b) section 8, so far as it relates to the provisions specified in sub-paragraph (a) above.

Lord Sewel
St Andrew's House, Edinburgh   Parliamentary Under Secretary of State,
14th May 1997   Scottish Office

ENERGY CONSERVATION

THE SOCIAL SECURITY ACT 1990 (COMMENCEMENT NO. 6) ORDER 1997

(S.I. 1997 No. 1370 (C. 49) (S. 107))

Made - - - - - - - *21st May 1997*

INTRODUCTION

This Order appoints June 9, 1997, as the day on which certain provisions of the Social Security Act 1990 (c. 27) shall come into force. These provisions, listed in art. 2, relate to the repeal of ss.252 and 253 of the Housing (Scotland) Act 1987.

The Secretary of State, in exercise of the powers conferred by section 23(2) of the Social Security Act 1990 (c. 27) and of all other powers enabling him in that behalf, hereby makes the following Order:

Citation

1. This Order may be cited as the Social Security Act 1990 (Commencement No. 6) Order 1997.

Appointed day

2. 9th June 1997 is appointed as the day for the coming into force of the following provisions of the Social Security Act 1990:
- (a) section 15(11);
- (b) Schedule 7, so far as relating to the repeal of sections 252 and 253 of the Housing (Scotland) Act 1987 (c. 26); and
- (c) section 21(2), so far as relating to the provisions mentioned in paragraph (b) above.

St Andrew's House, Edinburgh
21st May 1997

Malcolm Chisholm
Parliamentary Under Secretary of State,
Scottish Office

POLICE

THE POLICE ACT 1997 (COMMENCEMENT NO. 1 AND TRANSITIONAL PROVISIONS) ORDER 1997

(S.I. 1997 No. 1377 (C. 50))

Made - - - - - - -	*29th May 1997*
Laid before Parliament - - - -	*4th June 1997*
Coming into force - - - - -	*25th June 1997*

INTRODUCTION

This Order brings into force on June 25, 1997, various provisions of Pts. I and II of the Police Act 1997 for specific purposes. These provisions concern the National Criminal Intelligence Service and National Crime Squad. The provisions listed in art. 3 are brought into force for the purpose of appointing members of the service authorities for the NCIS and NCS.

Article 4 brings into force on July 23, 1997, provisions which relate to the service authorities for the NCIS and NCS, its financing and appointment of staff, officers and Director Generals.

In exercise of the powers conferred upon him by section 135 of the Police Act 1977 (c. 50), the Secretary of State hereby makes the following Order:

Citation, commencement and interpretation

1.—(1) This Order may be cited as the Police Act 1997 (Commencement No. 1 and Transitional Provisions) Order 1997.

(2) This Order shall come into force on 25th June 1997.

(3) In this Order "the Act" means the Police Act 1997.

Commencement on 25th June 1997

2.—(1) The provisions of the Act which are listed in paragraph (2) below shall come into force on 25th June 1997.

(2) The provisions referred to in paragraph (1) above are—

(a) section 17, except subsections (1) and (6), (power to issue levies);

(b) section 44 (orders governing NCIS Service Authority);

(c) section 45 (orders and regulations);

(d) section 46 (interpretation of Part I);

(e) section 62, except subsections (1) and (6), (power to issue levies);

(f) section 89 (orders and regulations);

(g) section 90 (interpretation of Part II);

(h) section 128 (regulations for special constables and police cadets);

(i) section 129, except paragraph (a), (change of name or description of certain police areas);

(j) section 130 (members of RUC engaged on service outside their force);

(k) section 131 (regulations requiring use of specified facilities or services); and

(l) section 132 (expenditure by Secretary of State for police purposes).

Commencement on 25th June 1997 for certain purposes only

3.—(1) Subject to the modifications set out in paragraphs (3) and (4) below, the provisions of the Act which are listed in paragraph (2) below shall come into force on 25th June 1997 for the purposes of the appointment, as soon as possible thereafter, of members of the Service Authority for the National Criminal Intelligence Service and members of the Service Authority for the National Crime Squad.

(2) The provisions referred to in paragraph (1) are—

(a) section 1 (the Service Authority for the National Criminal Intelligence Service);

(b) section 47 (the Service Authority for the National Crime Squad);

(c) Schedule 1 (appointment of members of Service Authorities); and

(d) Schedule 2 (other provisions about members of Service Authorities).

(3) In paragraph 13 to Schedule 1 for the words "clerk to a Service Authority" there shall be substituted "Secretary of State".

(4) Schedule 2 shall have effect as if there was inserted after paragraph 15 the following:

"15A.—(1) The first meeting of the Service Authority shall be—

(a) held within 21 days after appointments to it have been made under Schedule 1; and

(b) treated as being the annual meeting of the authority in the year in which it is held.

(2) The provisions of article 5 of the Police Act 1997 (Commencement No. 1 and Transitional Provisions) Order 1997 shall have effect in relation to the first meeting of a Service Authority".

Commencement on 23rd July 1997

4.—(1) The provisions of the Act which are listed in paragraph (2) below shall come into force on 23rd July 1997.

(2) The provisions referred to in paragraph (1) are—

(a) sections 1 and 47 and Schedules 1 and 2, for the purposes for which they are not already in force;

(b) section 6 (appointment of Director General);

(c) section 13 (officers and employees);

(d) section 14 (appointment of clerk);

(e) section 15 (appointment of persons not employed by the NCIS Service Authority);

(f) section 16 (NCIS Service Fund);

(g) section 18 (initial financing of the NCIS Service Authority);

(h) section 52 (appointment of Director General);

(i) section 58 (officers and employees);

(j) section 59 (appointment of clerk);

(k) section 60 (appointment of persons not employed by the NCS Service Authority);

(l) section 61 (NCS Service Fund);

(m) section 63 (initial financing of NCS Service Authority);

(n) section 88 (application to NCS Service Authority of local authority enactments), so far as it relates to paragraphs 3, 5 and 10 of Schedule 6;

(o) section 134 (minor and consequential amendments) so far as it relates to paragraphs 27, 40 and 88 of Schedule 9;

(p) paragraphs 27 and 41 of Schedule 9 (ineligibility for jury service of certain persons concerned with the administration of justice), so far as they relate to the members of the service authorities for the National Criminal Intelligence Service and the National Crime Squad;

(q) paragraphs 28 and 40 of Schedule 9 (disqualification in certain cases of justices who are members of local authorities); and

(r) paragraph 88 of Schedule 9 (right to time off for public duties).

First meeting of Service Authorities

5.—(1) The first meeting of a Service Authority shall be convened, and held at a time and place appointed by the Secretary of State.

(2) The regulation of the proceedings and the business of the meeting shall be determined by the chairman.

Home Office
29th May 1997

Alun Michael
Minister of State

ANTARCTICA

THE ANTARCTIC ACT 1994 (COMMENCEMENT) ORDER 1997

(S.I. 1997 No. 1411 (C. 51))

Made - - - - - - - *26th May 1997*

INTRODUCTION

This Order brings into force on June 1, 1997, s.5 of the Antarctic Act 1994 (c. 15), which provides for permits for British vessels and aircraft entering Antarctica.

The Secretary of State, in exercise of the powers conferred on him by section 35 of the Antarctic Act 1994 (c. 15), and of all other powers enabling him in that behalf, hereby makes the following Order:

Citation

1. This Order may be cited as the Antarctic Act 1994 (Commencement) Order 1997.

Commencement of Section 5 of the Antarctic Act 1994

2. Section 5 of the Antarctic Act 1994 shall come into force on 1st June 1997.

Tony Lloyd
For the Secretary of State
26th May 1997   for Foreign and Commonwealth Affairs

CRIMINAL LAW, ENGLAND AND WALES
CRIMINAL LAW, SCOTLAND

DELICT

THE PROTECTION FROM HARASSMENT ACT 1997
(COMMENCEMENT) (NO. 1) ORDER 1997

(S.I. 1997 No. 1418 (C. 52))

Made - - - - - - - *4th June 1997*

INTRODUCTION

This Order brings into force on June 16, 1997, sections 1, 2, 4, 5, 7 to 12 of the Protection from Harassment Act 1997 (c. 40).

In exercise of the power conferred upon him by section 15(1) of the Protection from Harassment Act 1997 (c. 40), the Secretary of State hereby makes the following Order:

1. This Order may be cited as the Protection from Harassment Act 1997 (Commencement) (No. 1) Order 1997.

2. Sections 1, 2, 4, 5 and 7 to 12 of the Protection from Harassment Act 1997 shall come into force on 16th June 1997.

Home Office
4th June 1997

Alun Michael
Minister of State

BUILDING SOCIETIES

THE BUILDING SOCIETIES ACT 1997 (COMMENCEMENT NO. 2) ORDER 1997

(S.I. 1997 No. 1427 (C. 53))

Made　-　-　-　-　-　-　-　*5th June 1997*

INTRODUCTION

This Order brings into force on June 9, 1997, various provisions of the Building Societies Act 1997, as listed in art. 2 of this Order.

The Treasury, in exercise of the powers conferred on them by section 47(3) of the Building Societies Act 1997 (c. 32), hereby make the following Order:

Citation and interpretation

1.—(1) This Order may be cited as the Building Societies Act 1997 (Commencement No. 2) Order 1997.

(2) In this Order "the 1986 Act" means the Building Societies Act 1986 (c. 53).

Coming into force

2. The following provisions of the Building Societies Act 1997 shall come into force on 9th June 1997, namely:

(a) section 11 (restriction on creation of floating charges);

(b) section 16 and paragraph 13(2) of Schedule 7 (which relate to the imposition or variation of conditions in urgent cases);

(c) sections 17 and 18, Schedule 4 and, so far as it relates to a direction under section 42B(1) of the 1986 Act, paragraph 14(1) of Schedule 7 (which relate to the power of the Building Societies Commission to direct transfers of engagements or business);

(d) sections 19 and 20 and paragraph 51 of Schedule 7 (which relate to supplementary directions on revocation of a society's authorisation);

(e) sections 23 and 24 (which concern appeals), so far as they relate to conditions imposed or varied under section 42A of the 1986 Act (which applies in urgent cases) or directions under section 42B(1) or 43A of the 1986 Act (directions of the kinds described in paragraphs (c) and (d) above);

(f) section 31 and paragraph 45(1) of Schedule 7 (which relate to increases in the remuneration of directors on a transfer of business);

(g) section 32 (power to amalgamate the building society and banking protection schemes);

(h) section 33 (which relates to the liability of an insolvent building society in respect of payments made by the Investor Protection Board);

(i) section 37 (which relates to access to registers of members);

(j) section 42 (which relates to the registration of charges by building societies);

(k) section 43 (amendments of the 1986 Act), so far as it relates to paragraphs 13(2), 14(1) to the extent specified in paragraph (c) above, 45(1) and 51 of Schedule 7 and the provisions of that Schedule listed in paragraph (n) below;

(l) section 44 (financial provision);

(m) section 45(1) (amendment of the Bankers' Book Evidence Act 1879 (c. 11)); and

(n) in Schedule 7—

   (i) paragraphs 5, 6, 7(1), 8, 9 and 17(1) (which relate to the Building Societies Investor Protection Scheme);

   (ii) paragraphs 12(1) and (3) (which relate to the Building Societies Commission's power to direct a building society to apply for the renewal of its authorisation);

   (iii) paragrahs 17(5)(c), (6), (7) and (8), 18, 19(1), (2) and (4) and 20 (which relate to obtaining information and documents and to confidentiality);

   (iv) paragraph 26 (which relates to records of loans etc for directors);

   (v) paragraph 27(2) and (3) (which relates to records of income of related businesses);

   (vi) paragraph 28 (which relates to the interpretation of Part VII);

   (vii) paragraph 29(2) (which relates to systems of business control);

   (viii) paragraph 33(2) (which relates to summary financial statements);

   (ix) paragraph 37 (which relates to the settlement of disputes);

   (x) paragraph 38 (which relates to dissolution);

   (xi) paragraph 45(4) (which relates to transfers of business);

   (xii) paragraph 53(1)(b) and (d) (which contains definitions), for the purpose of construing "connected undertaking" in section 43A(3)(c) or 52(5A), (6) or (9) of the 1986 Act;

   (xiii) paragraph 53(3)(a) (which relates to the interpretation of references to the value of a person's shareholding);

   (xiv) paragraph 55 (which relates to the Building Societies Commission);

   (xv) paragraph 56(9) (which relates to changes of principal office);

   (xvi) paragraph 58 (which relates to the Building Societies Investor Protection Board); and

   (xvii) paragraph 60(1) (which relates to requisite particulars of income of related businesses).

Bob Ainsworth
Graham Allen
Two of the Lords Commissioners
of Her Majesty's Treasury

5th June 1997

CUSTOMS AND EXCISE
VALUE ADDED TAX
INSURANCE PREMIUM TAX
LANDFILL TAX

THE FINANCE ACT 1997, SECTIONS 52 AND 53, (APPOINTED DAY) ORDER 1997

(S.I. 1997 No. 1432 (C. 54))

Made   -   -   -   -   -   -   -   *9th June 1997*

INTRODUCTION

This Order appoints July 1, 1997, as the day on which ss.52 and 53 of the Finance Act 1997 (c. 16) shall come into force.

The Commissioners of Customs and Excise, in exercise of the powers conferred on them by sections 52(7) and 53(9) of the Finance Act 1997 (c. 16) and of all other powers enabling them in that behalf, hereby make the following Order.

1. This Order may be cited as the Finance Act 1997, sections 52 and 53, (Appointed Day) Order 1997.

2. The day appointed as the day on which sections 52 (enforcement by diligence) and 53 (amendments consequential on sections 51 and 52) of the Finance Act 1997 come into force is 1st July 1997.

New King's Beam House
22 Upper Ground
London
SE1 9PJ

E. Woods
9th June 1997   Commissioner of Customs and Excise

CUSTOMS AND EXCISE
VALUE ADDED TAX
INSURANCE PREMIUM TAX
LANDFILL TAX

THE FINANCE ACT 1997
(REPEAL OF DISTRESS AND DILIGENCE ENACTMENTS)
(APPOINTED DAY) ORDER 1997

(S.I. 1997 No. 1433 (C. 55))

Made - - - - - - - *9th June 1997*

INTRODUCTION

This Order appoints July 1, 1997, as the day on which Sched. 1, para. 13(1) to the Finance Act 1997 (c. 16) shall cease to have effect, and the repeals of the distress and diligence enactments specified in Sched. 18, Pt. V(2) shall come into force. Certain of those repealed enactments have been re-enacted with amendments in ss.51 and 52 of the Act. Sections 51 and 53 (amendments consequential on ss.51 and 52) are brought into force on the same day (by virtue of S.I. 1997 No. 1432).

The Commissioners of Customs and Excise, in exercise of the powers conferred on them by paragraph 13(2) of Schedule 1 and the note to Part V(2) of Schedule 18 to the Finance Act 1997 (c. 16) and of all other powers enabling them in that behalf, hereby make the following Order:

1. This Order may be cited as the Finance Act 1997 (Repeal of Distress and Diligence enactments) (Appointed Day) Order 1997.

2. The day appointed as the day on which paragraph 13(1) of Schedule 1 to the Finance Act 1997 ceases to have effect and the repeals of the enactments specified in Part V(2) of Schedule 18 to that Act come into force, is 1st July 1997.

New King's Beam House
22 Upper Ground
London
SE1 9PJ

9th June 1997

E. Woods
Commissioner of Customs and Excise

CROFTERS, COTTARS AND SMALL LANDHOLDERS

THE TRANSFER OF CROFTING ESTATES (SCOTLAND) ACT 1997 COMMENCEMENT ORDER 1997

(S.I. 1997 No. 1430 (C. 56) (S. 110))

Made   -   -   -   -   -   -   -   *2nd June 1997*

INTRODUCTION

   This Order brings into force on June 6, 1997, all provisions of the Transfer of Crofting Estates (Scotland) Act 1997 (c. 26).

The Secretary of State, in exercise of the powers conferred on him by section 8(2) of the Transfer of Crofting Estates (Scotland) Act 1997 (c. 26) and of all other powers enabling him in that behalf, hereby makes the following Order:

   1. The Transfer of Crofting Estates (Scotland) Act 1997 shall come into force on 6th June 1997.

Sewel
St Andrew's House, Edinburgh   Parliamentary Under Secretary of State,
2nd June 1997   Scottish Office

EDUCATION, ENGLAND AND WALES

THE EDUCATION ACT 1997 (COMMENCEMENT NO. 2 AND TRANSITIONAL PROVISIONS) ORDER 1997

(S.I. 1997 No. 1468 (C. 57))

Made - - - - - - - *5th June 1997*

INTRODUCTION

This Order brings into force various provisions of the Education Act 1997 (c. 44) on different days and for different purposes. Schedule 1 to the Order lists in Pts. I to V these provisions, which will come into force on June 14, 1997, September 1, 1997, October 1, 1997, November 1, 1997, and December 1, 1997 respectively.

In exercise of the powers conferred on the Secretary of State by section 54(3) and 58(3) of the Education Act 1997 (c. 44), the Secretary of State for Education and Employment as respects England and the Secretary of State for Wales as respects Wales hereby make the following Order:

1.—(1) This Order may be cited as the Education Act 1997 (Commencement No. 2 and Transitional Provisions) Order 1997.

(2) In this Order

"the 1996 Act" means the Education Act 1996 (c. 56);

"the 1997 Act" means the Education Act 1997;

"the Inspections Act" means the School Inspections Act 1996 (c. 57);

"NCVQ" means the National Council for Vocational Qualifications;

"QCA" means the Qualifications and Curriculum Authority; and

"SCAA" means the School Curriculum and Assessment Authority.

2.—(1) The provisions of the 1997 Act specified in Part I of Schedule 1 to this Order shall come into force on 14th June 1997.

(2) The provisions of the 1997 Act specified in Part II of that Schedule shall come into force on 1st September 1997.

(3) The provisions of the 1997 Act specified in Part III of that Schedule shall come into force on 1st October 1997.

(4) The provisions of the 1997 Act specified in Part IV of that Schedule shall come into force on 1st November 1997.

(5) The provisions of the 1997 Act specified in Part V of that Schedule shall come into force on 1st December 1997.

3. Unless otherwise specified in Schedule 1 to this Order the provisions referred to in Article 2 above shall come into force for all purposes.

4.—(1) Part I of Schedule 2 to this Order shall have effect for the purpose of making transitional provisions in connection with paragraphs 4, 5 and 7 of Schedule 6 to the 1997 Act (which are brought into force on 1st September 1997 by Article 2(2)).

(2) Part II of Schedule 2 to this Order shall have effect for the purpose of making transitional provisions in connection with paragraphs 6, 7, 27 and 28 of Schedule 7 to the 1997 Act (which are brought into force on 1st October 1997 by Article 2(3)).

SCHEDULE 1

PART I

PROVISIONS COMING INTO FORCE ON 14TH JUNE 1997

Section 20.
Section 55.
Section 56.
Section 57(1) and (4) to the extent that those subsections relate to the provisions of Schedules 7 and 8 specified below.
In Schedule 7—
   paragraph 15;
   paragraph 18;
   paragraph 20(a);
   paragraph 37;
   paragraph 39;
   paragraph 41;
   paragraph 42;
   paragraph 43;
   paragraph 44 to the extent that it inserts the reference to "school year" into section 580 of the 1996 Act; and
   paragraph 45.
In Schedule 8 the repeal of—
   section 571(2) of the 1996 Act; and
   the definition of "school year" and the "and" preceding it in section 355(5) of the 1996 Act.

PART II

PROVISIONS COMING INTO FORCE ON 1ST SEPTEMBER 1997

Sections 10 to 12.
Section 14 to the extent that it relates to paragraphs 3 and 4 of the Schedule inserted as Schedule 33B to the 1996 Act set out in Schedule 3.
Sections 34 and 35.
Section 37(1) to (4).
Sections 38 to 42.
Sections 44 to 46.
Section 51.
Section 52(4).
Section 57(1) and (4) to the extent that those subsections relate to the provisions of Schedules 7 and 8 specified below.
Section 57(2) and (3).
Schedule 2.
In Schedule 3, paragraphs 3 and 4 of the Schedule inserted as Schedule 33B to the 1996 Act.
Schedule 6.
In Schedule 7—
   paragraph 5;
   paragraph 9;
   paragraph 31 except so far as sub-paragraph (2) inserts the words "section 413B(3) (home-school partnership documents)";
   paragraph 32;
   paragraph 33;
   paragraph 34—
      (i) except so far as sub-paragraph (a) substitutes "413A and 413B" for "413"; and
      (ii) except for sub-paragraphs (b) and (c);
   paragraph 44 insofar as it is not already in force;
   paragraph 49(1); and
   paragraph 49(3) except for paragraph (a) of paragraph 6(2A) to be inserted into Schedule 23 to the 1996 Act.
In Schedule 8 the repeal of section 423(6) of the 1996 Act.

PART III

PROVISIONS COMING INTO FORCE ON 1ST OCTOBER 1997

Sections 21 to 32.
Section 49(1) to the extent that it relates to section 49(2) and (3).
Section 49(2) and (3).
Section 53.
Sections 57(1) and (4) to the extent that those subsections relate to the provisions of Schedules 7 and 8 specified below.
Schedule 4.
Schedule 5.
In Schedule 7—
paragraph 1;
paragraph 2 except so far as sub-paragraph (1) provides that "public body" shall cease to include SCAA;
paragraph 3(1) except so far as it omits the entry relating to SCAA;
paragraph 4 except so far as it omits the entry relating to SCAA;
paragraphs 6 and 7;
paragraph 26 so far as it omits sections 360 and 361;
paragraphs 27 to 29; and
paragraph 30(a).
In Schedule 8 the repeal of—
the provisions in the Superannuation Act 1972 (c. 11) specified to the extent that they relate to the Curriculum and Assessment Authority for Wales;
the provisions in the House of Commons Disqualification Act 1975 (c. 24) specified to the extent that they relate to the Curriculum and Assessment Authority for Wales;
sections 360 and 361 of the 1996 Act;
Schedule 30 to the 1996 Act; and
the provisions of Schedule 37 to the 1996 Act specified except so far as they relate to SCAA.

PART IV

PROVISIONS COMING INTO FORCE ON 1ST NOVEMBER 1997

Section 15.
Section 16(2) and (3).
Section 16(4) in its application to England.
Section 16(6).
Section 17(4) and (8).
Section 18.

PART V

PROVISIONS COMING INTO FORCE ON 1ST DECEMBER 1997

Section 36.
Section 48.

Article 4 SCHEDULE 2

TRANSITIONAL PROVISIONS

PART I

1. The amendment of section 8(2)(d) of the Inspections Act made by paragraph 4 of Schedule 6 to the 1997 Act shall not have effect in any case where the report of an inspection mentioned in section 8(2)(d) is produced by a registered inspector before 1st September 1997.

2. The amendment of paragraph 9(2)(d) of Schedule 1 to the Nursery Education and Grant-Maintained Schools Act 1996 (c. 50) made by paragraph 5 of Schedule 6 to the 1997 Act shall not have effect in any case where the report of an inspection mentioned in paragraph 9(2)(d) is produced by a registered nursery education inspector before 1st September 1997.

3. The amendment of either of sections 16(4)(c) and 20(4)(c) of the Inspections Act made by paragraph 7 of Schedule 6 to the 1997 Act shall not have effect in any case where an inspection report mentioned in subsection (1) of that section is received by the appropriate authority (as defined in section 11(4) or (5) of the Inspections Act) before 1st September 1997.

PART II

4. Notwithstanding the coming into force on 1st October 1997 of paragraph 6 of Schedule 7 to the 1997 Act, which provides for the substitution of paragraph (a)(i) of section 32 of the Finance Act 1991 (c. 31) (relief in respect of a qualifying course of vocational qualification), a course of vocational training accredited as a National Vocational Qualification by the NCVQ before that date shall continue to be treated as a qualifying course of vocational training for the purposes of section 32 until such time as QCA or (as the case may be) the Qualifications, Curriculum and Assessment Authority for Wales decide that that accreditation should cease to have effect.

5. Notwithstanding the coming into force on 1st October 1997 of paragraph 7(a) of Schedule 7 to the 1997 Act, which provides for the substitution of paragraph (da) of Schedule 2 to the Charities Act 1993 (c. 10) (exempt charities), SCAA shall remain an exempt charity for the purposes of that Act until the coming into force of section 33 of the 1997 Act (dissolution of SCAA and NCVQ).

6.—(1) Notwithstanding the coming into force on 1st October 1997 of paragraphs 27 and 28 of Schedule 7 to the 1997 Act—

    (a) anything done by or in relation to SCAA prior to that date in connection with the provisions to which this paragraph applies, shall have effect as if done by or in relation to QCA; and

    (b) anything which is in the process of being done by or in relation to SCAA as at that date may, so far as it relates to those provisions, be continued by or in relation to QCA.

(2) This paragraph applies to section 362 of the 1996 Act (development work and experiments) and section 368 of that Act (procedure for making certain orders and regulations).

Stephen Byers
Minister of State,
Department for Education
4th June 1997   and Employment

Peter Hain
Parliamentary Under Secretary of State
5th June 1997   Welsh Office

TORTS

THE PROTECTION FROM HARASSMENT ACT 1997 (COMMENCEMENT NO. 2) ORDER 1997

(S.I. 1997 No. 1498 (C. 58))

Made   -   -   -   -   -   -   -   *10th June 1997*

INTRODUCTION

This Order brings into force on June 16, 1997, certain provisions of the Protection from Harassment Act 1997. The Protection from Harassment Act 1997 (Commencement) (No. 1) Order 1997 (S.I. 1997 No. 1418 (C. 52)) made before this Order, brings ss.1, 3, 4, 5, 7 to 12 into force on the same day.

The remaining provisions still to be brought into force after that date are subs. (3) to (9) of s.3 (ss.13 to 16 came into force on the date of Royal Assent).

The Lord Chancellor, in exercise of the powers conferred on him by section 15(2) of the Protection from Harassment Act 1997 (c. 40), hereby makes the following Order:

1. This Order may be cited as the Protection from Harassment Act 1997 (Commencement) (No. 2) Order 1997.

2. Sections 3(1) and (2) and 6 of the Protection from Harassment Act 1997 shall come into force on 16th June 1997.

Dated 10th June 1997   *Irvine of Lairg*, C.

CRIMINAL LAW, NORTHERN IRELAND

THE CRIMINAL PROCEDURE AND INVESTIGATIONS ACT 1996 (APPOINTED DAY NO. 5) ORDER 1997

(S.I. 1997 No. 1504 (C. 59))

Made   -   -   -   -   -   -   -   *9th June 1997*

INTRODUCTION

This Order extends to Northern Ireland only. The appointed day is June 30, 1997, for the purposes of ss.54 (tainted acquittals) and 61 (relates to the application of s.58 and concerns the reporting of derogatory assertions) of the Criminal Procedure and Investigations Act 1996.

The Secretary of State, in exercise of the powers conferred on her by sections 54(8) and 61(2) of the Criminal Procedure and Investigations Act 1996 (c. 25), hereby makes the following Order:

1.—(1) This Order may be cited as the Criminal Procedure and Investigations Act 1996 (Appointed Day No. 5) Order 1997.

(2) This Order extends to Northern Ireland only.

2. 30th June 1997 is hereby appointed for the purposes of sections 54 and 61 of the Criminal Procedure and Investigations Act 1996.

Northern Ireland Office   *Marjorie Mowlam*
9th June 1997   One of Her Majesty's
                              Principal Secretaries of State

ARMS AND AMMUNITION

THE FIREARMS (AMENDMENT) ACT 1997 (COMMENCEMENT) (NO. 2) ORDER 1997

(S.I. 1997 No. 1535 (C. 60))

Made - - - - - - - *10th June 1997*

INTRODUCTION

This Order brings into force further provisions of the Firearms (Amendment) Act 1997. The provisions specified in Pt. I of the Order come into force on July 1, 1997, and those in Pt. II come into force on October 1, 1997. In addition, ss.15 and 51 are brought into force on June 10, 1997. These sections enable the Secretary of State to make arrangements for the orderly surrender of firearms and other transitional, consequential and saving provisions.

In exercise of the powers conferred on me by section 53(3) and (4) of the Firearms (Amendment) Act 1997 (c. 5), I hereby make the following Order:

1. This Order may be cited as the Firearms (Amendment) Act 1997 (Commencement) (No. 2) Order 1997.

2. In this Order "the 1968 Act" means the Firearms Act 1968 (c. 27) and "the 1997 Act" means the Firearms (Amendment) Act 1997.

3. Subject to the provisions of this Order—
(a) sections 15 (surrender of prohibited small firearms and ammunition) and 51 (power to make transitional, consequential etc. provisions) of the 1997 Act shall come into force on 10th June 1997;
(b) the provisions of the 1997 Act specified in Part I of the Schedule to this Order shall come into force on 1st July 1997, and
(c) the provisions of the 1997 Act specified in Part II of that Schedule shall come into force on 1st October 1997.

4. Sections 1(2) (prohibition of certain small firearms) and 9 (prohibition of expanding ammunition) of the 1997 Act shall not have effect until 1st October 1997 in relation to the possession, sale or transfer of a firearm or ammunition by a person who, immediately before 1st July 1997,
(a) has the firearm or ammunition in his possession by virtue of a firearm certificate or a visitor's firearm permit;
(b) has the firearm or ammunition in his possession by virtue of a permit issued under section 7 of the 1968 Act, or
(c) has the firearm in his possession by virtue of being a registered firearms dealer.

5. Section 1(3) of the 1997 Act (amendment of prohibition of self-loading and pump-action rifles) shall not have effect in relation to weapons prohibited by section 5(1)(aba) of the 1968 Act (inserted by s.1(2) of the 1997 Act).

6. Section 41 of the 1997 Act (appeals) shall not have effect in relation to a decision made by a chief officer of police before 1st July 1997.

Home Office   *Jack Straw*
10th June 1997   One of Her Majesty's Principal Secretaries of State

SCHEDULE

PART I

PROVISIONS OF THE 1997 ACT COMING INTO FORCE ON 1ST JULY 1997

Provision of the Act	*Subject matter of provisions*
Section 1	Extension of s.5 of the Firearms Act 1968 to prohibit certain small firearms etc.
Section 2	Exemption for slaughtering instruments
Section 3	Exemption for firearms used for humane killing of animals
Section 4	Exemption for shot pistols used for shooting vermin
Section 5	Exemption for races at athletic meetings
Section 6	Exemption for trophies of war
Section 7	Exemption for firearms of historic interest
Section 8	Exemption for weapons and ammunition used for treating animals
Section 9	General prohibition of expanding ammunition etc.
Section 10	Expanding ammunition etc.; exemptions from prohibition
Section 16 (insofar as it is not already in force)	Payments in respect of prohibited small firearms and ammunition
Section 17 (insofar as it is not already in force)	Payments in respect of ancillary equipment
Section 18 (insofar as it is not already in force)	Parliamentary control of compensation schemes
Section 37	Applications for certificates and referees
Section 38	Grant of firearm certificates
Section 40	Revocation of certificates
Section 41	Appeals
Section 42	Authorised dealing with firearms by registered firearms dealers
Section 43	Power of search with warrant
Section 47	Museums eligible for a museum firearms licence
Section 48	Firearms powered by compressed carbon dioxide
Section 49	Financial provisions
Section 50	Interpretation and supplementary provisions
Section 52 (insofar as it relates to the provisions of Schedules 2 and 3 mentioned immediately below)	Minor and consequential amendments and repeals
In Schedule 2— paragraphs 1, 2, 4, 7, 8, 10, 11, 12, 14, 15, 16, 17, 18, 19 and 20	Consequential and minor amendment

Provision of the Act	*Subject matter of provisions*
In Schedule 3— the entries relating to sections 5, 5A, 23 and 28 of the Firearms Act 1968, the entries relating to sections 9, 10 and 12 of the Firearms (Amendment) Act 1988 and the entry relating to the Firearms (Amendment) Act 1992	Repeals

PART II

PROVISIONS OF THE 1997 ACT COMING INTO FORCE ON 1ST OCTOBER 1997

Provisions of the Act	*Subject matter of provisions*
Section 32	Transfers of firearms etc. to be in person
Section 33	Notification of transfers including firearms
Section 34	Notification of de-activation, destruction or loss of firearms etc.
Section 35	Notification of events taking place outside Great Britain involving firearms etc.
Section 36	Penalty for offences under sections 32 to 35
Section 39	Register of holders of shotgun and firearm certificates
Section 44	Firearm certificates for certain firearms used for target shooting: special conditions
Section 45	Approved rifle clubs and muzzle-loading pistol clubs
Section 52 (insofar as it relates to the provisions of Schedules 2 and 3 mentioned below)	Minor and consequential amendments and repeals
In Schedule 2— paragraphs 3, 5 and 6	Consequential and minor amendments
In Schedule 3— the entries relating to sections 42 and 54 of, and Schedule 6 to, the Firearms Act 1968, and the entry relating to section 4 of the Firearms (Amendment) Act 1988	Repeals

ARMS AND AMMUNITION

THE FIREARMS (AMENDMENT) ACT 1997 (COMMENCEMENT) (NO. 2) (AMENDMENT) ORDER 1997

(S.I. 1997 No. 1536 (C. 61))

Made - - - - - - - *18th June 1997*

Introduction
This Order amends the Firearms (Amendment) Act 1997 (Commencement) (No. 2) Order 1997 (S.I. 1997 No. 1535 (C. 60)). Article 4 of that Order is substituted by new arts. 4 and 4A with the result that prohibition of firearms by s.1(2) of the 1997 Act will not have effect until October 1, 1997 in relation to the acquisition or purchase of a firearm by a registered firearms dealer.

In exercise of the powers conferred on me by section 53(3) and (4) of the Firearms (Amendment) Act 1997 (c. 5), I hereby make the following Order:

Citation and commencement

1. This Order may be cited as the Firearms (Amendment) Act 1997 (Commencement) (No. 2) (Amendment) Order 1997.

2. For article 4 of the Firearms (Amendment) Act 1997 (Commencement) (No. 2) Order 1997 (S.I. 1997 No. 1535) there shall be substituted:
    "**4.** Sections 1(2) (prohibition of certain small firearms) and 9 (prohibition of expanding ammunition) of the 1997 Act shall not have effect until 1st October 1997 in relation to the possession, sale or transfer of a firearm or ammunition by a person who, immediately before 1st July 1997, has the firearm or ammunition in his possession by virtue of:
    (a) a firearm certificate or a visitor's firearm permit, or
    (b) a permit issued under section 7 of the 1968 Act.

    4A. Section 1(2) of the 1997 Act shall not have effect until 1st October 1997 in relation to the possession, purchase, acquisition, sale or transfer of a firearm by a registered firearms dealer.".

Home Office   *Jack Straw*
18th June 1997   One of Her Majesty's Principal Secretaries of State

MERCHANT SHIPPING

THE MERCHANT SHIPPING AND MARITIME SECURITY ACT 1997 (COMMENCEMENT NO. 2) ORDER 1997

(S.I. 1997 No. 1539 (C. 62))

Made - - - - - - - *19th June 1997*

INTRODUCTION

This Order brings into force on July 17, 1997, further provisions of the Merchant Shipping and Maritime Security Act 1997 which are listed in the Schedule to this Order. The only provisions of the Act which have not yet been brought into force are s.9 (partially) and Sched. 1, para. 6.

The Secretary of State for Transport, in exercise of the powers conferred by section 31(3) of the Merchant Shipping and Maritime Security Act 1997 (c. 28), hereby makes the following Order:

1. This Order may be cited as the Merchant Shipping and Maritime Security Act 1997 (Commencement No. 2) Order 1997.

2. The provisions of the Act specified in the first column of the Schedule to this Order (which relate to the matters specified in the second column of that Schedule) shall come into force on 17th July 1997.

Signed by authority of the
Secretary of State for Transport

Glenda Jackson
Parliamentary Under-Secretary of State,
Department of the Environment,
19th June 1997 Transport and the Regions

Article 2   SCHEDULE

PROVISIONS COMING INTO FORCE ON 17TH JULY 1997

Provisions of the Act	Subject matter of provision
Section 2	Powers of intervention where shipping accident threatens pollution
Section 3	Powers of intervention in cases of pollution by substances other than oil
Section 4	Powers of fire authorities
Section 6	Indemnities in connection with counter-pollution measures
Section 7	Increased penalty for causing pollution, etc.
Section 14	Carriage of hazardous and noxious substances
Section 15	Limitation of liability
Section 17	Financial assistance for training
Section 18	Discharge books
Section 19	Powers of general lighthouse authorities

Provisions of the Act	*Subject matter of provision*
Section 20	Disclosure of information to general lighthouse authorities
Section 21	Certain duties not to apply to RNLI
Section 22	Disposal of unclaimed wreck
Section 23	Retention of documents by Registrar General
Section 25	Amendments of Aviation and Maritime Security Act 1990
Section 26	Piracy
Section 27	Application of section 1 of International Organisations Act 1968 to International Oil Pollution Compensation Fund
Section 29	Minor and consequential amendments, etc.
Schedule 3	Provisions to be inserted as Schedule 5A to the Merchant Shipping Act 1995
Schedule 4	Amendments of Part III of Aviation and Maritime Security Act 1990
Schedule 5	Provisions of United Nations Convention on the Law of the Sea to be treated as part of the law of nations
Schedule 6 so far as it is not already in force	Minor and consequential amendments
Schedule 7 so far as it is not already in force	Repeals and Revocations

SOCIAL SECURITY

THE SOCIAL SECURITY ADMINISTRATION (FRAUD) ACT 1997 (COMMENCEMENT NO. 1) ORDER 1997

(S.I. 1997 No. 1577 (C. 63))

Made - - - - - - - *24th June 1997*

INTRODUCTION

This Order appoints July 1, 1997 as the day on which certain provisions (listed in the Schedule) of the Social Security Administration (Fraud) Act 1997 shall come into force. Sections 5 to 10 relate to the administration of housing benefit and council tax benefit; ss.13 and 14 relate to offences.

The Secretary of State for Social Security, in exercise of the powers conferred on her by section 25(1) and (2) of the Social Security Administration (Fraud) Act 1997 (c. 47) and of all other powers enabling her in that behalf, hereby makes the following Order:

Citation and interpretation

1.—(1) This Order may be cited as the Social Security Administration (Fraud) Act 1997 (Commencement No. 1) Order 1997.

(2) In this Order, references to "the Act" are references to the Social Security Administration (Fraud) Act 1997 and, except where the context otherwise requires, references to sections and Schedules are references to sections of, and Schedules to, the Act.

Appointed day

2. The day appointed for the coming into force of the provisions of the Act specified in the Schedule to this Order is 1st July 1997.

Signed by authority of the Secretary of State for Social Security.

John Y. Denham
Parliamentary Under-Secretary of State,
24th June 1997   Department of Social Security

Article 2   SCHEDULE

PROVISIONS OF THE ACT COMING INTO FORCE ON 1ST JULY 1997

Provisions of the Act	Subject Matter
section 1	Information held by tax authorities
section 2	Other government information
section 3 except in so far as it inserts section 122E(3) and (4) into the Social Security Administration Act 1992 (c. 5)	Authorities administering housing benefit or council tax benefit
section 4	Unauthorised disclosure by officials
section 5	Overseeing of administration by Secretary of State
section 6	Role of Audit Commission

Provisions of the Act	Subject Matter
section 7	Role of Accounts Commission for Scotland
section 8	Directions by Secretary of State
section 9	Enforcement of directions
section 10	Adjustment of subsidy
section 12	Inspectors appointed by authorities
section 13	Offence of dishonest representation for obtaining benefit
section 14	Extension of offence of false representation for obtaining benefit
section 17	Reviews initiated by Secretary of State
section 18	Medical examinations of persons awarded certain benefits
Paragraphs 1 to 7 and 9 to 14 of Schedule 1 and section 22 in so far as it relates to those paragraphs	Minor and consequential amendments
Schedule 2 and section 22 in so far as it relates to that Schedule except for the repeal of section 128A of the Social Security Administration Act 1992 (inserted by s.28(2) of the Jobseekers Act 1995 (c. 18)) and the heading preceding that section	Repeals

CRIMINAL LAW, ENGLAND AND WALES
CRIMINAL LAW, NORTHERN IRELAND
CRIMINAL LAW, SCOTLAND

THE CRIME (SENTENCES) ACT 1997
(COMMENCEMENT) (NO. 1) ORDER 1997

(S.I. 1997 No. 1581 (C. 64))

Made - - - - - - - *23rd June 1997*

INTRODUCTION

This Order brings into force on June 25, 1997, Sched. 1, paras. 14 and 19 to the Crime (Sentences) Act 1997. These provisions relate to the transfer of prisoners in relation to the Isle of Man, and restricted transfers between any part of the U.K. and the Channel Islands respectively.

The Secretary of State, in exercise of the powers conferred upon him by section 57(2) of the Crime (Sentences) Act 1997 (c. 43), hereby makes the following Order:

1. This Order may be cited as the Crime (Sentences) Act 1997 (Commencement) (No. 1) Order 1997.

2. Paragraphs 14 and 19 of Schedule 1 to the Crime (Sentences) Act 1997 shall come into force on 25th June 1997.

Home Office   *Joyce Quin*
23rd June 1997   Minister of State

ROAD TRAFFIC

THE ROAD TRAFFIC ACT 1991 (COMMENCEMENT NO. 13) (SCOTLAND) ORDER 1997

(S.I. 1997 No. 1580 (C. 65) (S. 121))

Made - - - - - - - *13th June 1997*

INTRODUCTION

This Order brings into force on June 16, 1997, certain provisions of the Road Traffic Act 1991 insofar as they relate to Scotland and have not already been brought into force. Section 43 and Sched. 3 relate to the establishment of permitted parking areas and special parking areas outside London.

The Secretary of State, in exercise of the powers conferred on him by section 84 of the Road Traffic Act 1991 (c. 40) and of all other powers enabling him in that behalf, hereby makes the following Order:

Citation and interpretation

1.—(1) This Order may be cited as the Road Traffic Act 1991 (Commencement No. 13) (Scotland) Order 1997.

(2) In this Order—
"the Act" means the Road Traffic Act 1991.

Commencement of certain provisions of the Act

2. The following provisions of the Act shall come into force on the 16th June 1997, insofar as they relate to Scotland and have not already been commenced:—

(a) Section 43; and
(b) Schedule 3.

Malcolm Chisholm
St Andrew's House, Edinburgh　　Parliamentary Under Secretary of State,
13th June 1997　　　　　　　　　　　　　　　Scottish Office

INCOME TAX
TAXES

THE FINANCE ACT 1997, SECTION 110, (APPOINTED DAY) ORDER 1997

(S.I. 1997 No. 1603 (C. 66))

Made   -   -   -   -   -   -   -   *26th June 1997*

INTRODUCTION

This Order appoints July 2, 1997, for the purposes of s.110 of the Finance Act 1997 (c. 16). Thereby, the section permits information held by social security authorities to be supplied to the Commissioners of Customs and Excise, the Commissioners of Inland Revenue, or persons providing services to either of those Commissioners, as from July 2, 1997.

The Treasury, in exercise of the powers conferred on them by section 110(7) of the Finance Act 1997 (c. 16), hereby make the following Order:

1. This Order may be cited as the Finance Act 1997, Section 110, (Appointed Day) Order 1997.

2. The day appointed for the purposes of section 110 of the Finance Act 1997 is 2nd July 1997.

Graham Allen
Bob Ainsworth
Two of the Lords Commissioners
of Her Majesty's Treasury

26th June 1997

EDUCATION, ENGLAND AND WALES

THE EDUCATION ACT 1996 (COMMENCEMENT NO. 2 AND APPOINTED DAY) ORDER 1997

(S.I. 1997 No. 1623 (C. 67))

Made - - - - - - -   *30th June 1997*

INTRODUCTION

This Order brings into force on August 1, 1997, s.528 of the Education Act 1996, as it applies to England. This section provides that local education authorities have a duty to publish disability statements relating to further education.

Certain other provisions (listed in art. 2(2)), shall come into force on September 1, 1997. These relate to, *inter alia*, compulsory school age.

This Order also provides that September 1, 1997 is the appointed day for the purposes of s.517(6) and all the provisions referred to in that subsection (payment of fees at non-maintained schools).

In exercise of the powers conferred on the Secretary of State by sections 517(6) and 583(3) and (5)(b) of the Education Act 1996 (c. 56), the Secretary of State for Education and Employment hereby makes the following Order:

1.—(1) This Order may be cited as the Education Act 1996 (Commencement No. 2 and Appointed Day) Order 1997.

(2) In this Order "the Act" means the Education Act 1996.

2.—(1) Section 528 of the Act in its application to England shall come into force on 1st August 1997.

(2) The following provisions of the Act shall come into force on 1st September 1997—

Section 8.

Section 348.

Part II of Schedule 37 and section 582(1) so far as relating thereto.

Part II of Schedule 38 and section 582(2) so far as relating thereto.

3. 1st September 1997 is hereby appointed for the purposes of section 517(6) of the Act and that day is appointed for all the provisions referred to in that subsection and for all purposes.

Andrew Smith
Minister of State,
30th June 1997   Department for Education and Employment

ENVIRONMENTAL PROTECTION

THE ENVIRONMENT ACT 1995 (COMMENCEMENT NO. 9 AND TRANSITIONAL PROVISIONS) ORDER 1997

(S.I. 1997 No. 1626 (C. 68))

Made - - - - - - - *27th June 1997*

INTRODUCTION

This Order brings into force on July 1, 1997, further provisions of the Environment Act 1995 relating to anti-pollution works and operations and water resources management.

The Secretary of State, in exercise of the powers conferred on him by section 125(3) and (4) of the Environment Act 1995 (c. 25), hereby makes the following Order:

Citation

1. This Order may be cited as the Environment Act 1995 (Commencement No. 9 and Transitional Provisions) Order 1997.

Provisions coming into force on 1st July 1997

2. The following provisions of the Environment Act 1995 shall come into force on 1st July 1997—
  (a) section 60(3), (4), (5)(a) and (7); and
  (b) section 116 in so far as it relates to paragraph 2(4) of Schedule 21 except for the purposes of the application of the substituted section 222 of the Water Resources Act 1991 (c. 57) to Part II of that Act.

Transitional provisions

3.—(1) Any application by the Crown for a consent for the purposes of section 88(1)(a) of the Water Resources Act 1991 made before 1st July 1997, and anything done before that date in relation to that application, shall be treated on and after that date as if it had been made or done under the relevant provisions of Schedule 10 (substituted by Sched. 22, para. 183 to the Environment Act 1995) to that Act or the Control of Pollution (Applications, Appeals and Registers) Regulations 1996 (S.I. 1996 No. 2971).
  (2) Where—
  (a) any application to which paragraph (1) above applies has not been finally disposed of before 1st July 1997; and
  (b) the application relates to discharges which are substantially the same as discharges lawfully made by the Crown before that date without a consent,
the Environment Agency shall be deemed to have given unconditionally the consent applied for and the deemed consent shall continue in force until the application is finally disposed of.
  (3) An application shall be treated as finally disposed of for the purposes of paragraph (2) above—
  (a) on the date on which the Agency gives the consent applied for unconditionally or the application is withdrawn;
  (b) if the Agency gives its consent subject to conditions or refuses its consent, on the expiration of the time limit for appealing against that decision; or
  (c) if an appeal is duly made against the Agency's decision, on the date on which that appeal is determined or withdrawn.

Signed by authority of the Secretary of State

Angela Eagle
Parliamentary Under Secretary of State,
Department of the Environment,
Transport and the Regions

27th June 1997

ARCHITECTS

THE ARCHITECTS ACT 1997 (COMMENCEMENT) ORDER 1997

(S.I. 1997 No. 1672 (C. 69))

Made   -   -   -   -   -   -   -   *9th July 1997*

INTRODUCTION

This Order brings into force on July 21, 1997, all remaining provisions of the Architects Act 1997 (c. 22).

The Secretary of State, in exercise of the powers conferred by section 28(2) of the Architects Act 1997 (c. 22) hereby makes the following Order:

Citation

1. This Order may be cited as the Architects Act 1997 (Commencement) Order 1997.

Commencement

2. The Architects Act 1997, except for section 28 (short title, commencement and extent (see s.28 which came into force at Royal Assent), shall come into force on 21st July 1997.

Signed by authority of the Secretary of State

Nick Raynsford
Parliamentary Under Secretary of State,
Department of the Environment,
9th July 1997   Transport and the Regions

ENVIRONMENTAL PROTECTION

THE NOISE ACT 1996 (COMMENCEMENT NO. 2) ORDER 1997

(S.I. 1997 No. 1695 (C. 70))

Made - - - - - - - *10th July 1997*

INTRODUCTION
This Order brings into force on July 23, 1997, all remaining provisions of the Noise Act 1996. These provisions relate to the summary procedure for dealing with noise at night and supplementary matters (including powers of entry and seizure).

The Secretary of State, in exercise of the powers conferred on him by section 14(2) of the Noise Act 1996 (c. 37) and of all other powers enabling him in that behalf, hereby makes the following Order:

Citation

1. This Order may be cited as the Noise Act 1996 (Commencement No. 2) Order 1997.

Provisions coming into force on 23rd July 1997

2. The Noise Act 1996, so far as not already brought into force by the Noise Act 1996 (Commencement No. 1) Order 1996 (S.I. 1996 No. 2219), shall come into force on 23rd July 1997.

Signed by authority of the Secretary of State

Angela Eagle
Parliamentary Under Secretary of State,
10th July 1997   Department of the Environment

POLICE

THE POLICE ACT 1997 (COMMENCEMENT NO. 2) ORDER 1997

(S.I. 1997 No. 1696 (C. 71))

Made - - - - - - - *14th July 1997*

INTRODUCTION

This Order brings into force on August 5, 1997, s.101 of the Police Act 1997 (c. 50), requiring the Secretary of State to issue a code of practice in connection with the performance of functions under Pt.III of the Act, by persons other than the Commissioners appointed under s.91.

In exercise of the powers conferred upon him by section 135(1) of the Police Act 1997 (c. 50), the Secretary of State hereby makes the following Order:

1. This Order may be cited as the Police Act 1997 (Commencement No. 2) Order 1997.

2. Section 101 (code of practice in connection with authorisation of action in respect of property) of the Police Act 1997 shall come into force on 5th August 1997.

Home Office 14th July 1997

Alun Michael Minister of State

CRIMINAL LAW, SCOTLAND

THE CRIME AND PUNISHMENT (SCOTLAND) ACT 1997 (COMMENCEMENT AND TRANSITIONAL PROVISIONS) ORDER 1997

(S.I. 1997 No. 1712 (C. 72) (S. 128))

Made - - - - - - - *10th July 1997*

INTRODUCTION

This Order brings into force on August 1, 1997, various provisions of the Crime and Punishment (Scotland) Act 1997 (c. 48) which are listed in the Schedule to the Order.

The Secretary of State, in exercise of the powers conferred on him by section 65(2) and (4) of the Crime and Punishment (Scotland) Act 1997 (c. 48) and of all other powers enabling him in that behalf, hereby makes the following Order:

Citation

1. This Order may be cited as the Crime and Punishment (Scotland) Act 1997 (Commencement and Transitional Provisions) Order 1997.

Interpretation

2. In this Order—
"the Act" means the Crime and Punishment (Scotland) Act 1997;
"the 1995 Act" means the Criminal Procedure (Scotland) Act 1995 (c. 46).

Commencement of provisions

3. Subject to articles 4 and 5 below, the provisions of the Act which are specified in column 1 of the Schedule to this Order and described by reference to the subject matter in column 2 of that Schedule shall come into force on 1st August 1997 but, where a particular purpose is specified in relation to any provision in column 3 of that Schedule, that provision shall come into force on that day only for that purpose.

Transitional Provisions

4. The coming into force of section 14 of the Act shall not affect the penalty for an offence committed before 1st August 1997.

5. Section 67A of the 1995 Act as inserted by section 57 of the Act shall apply only in the case of a citation served on or after 1st August 1997.

St Andrew's House, Edinburgh
10th July 1997

Henry B McLeish
Minister of State,
Scottish Office

Article 3   SCHEDULE

The Provisions of the Act Which Come into Force on 1st August 1997

Column (1) *Provision of the Act*	Column (2) *Subject Matter*	Column 3 *Purpose*
Section 12	Sentence calculation where remand spent in hospital	
Section 14	Increase in maximum penalty for certain sexual offences	
Section 17	Right of appeal	
Section 20	Transfer of rights of appeal of deceased person	Only for the purpose of inserting sections 303A(1) and (2) and (4) to (6) after section 303 of the 1995 Act.
Section 21	Increased rights of appeal of prosecutor	
Section 23	Appeals against orders under section 49 of the 1995 Act	
Section 24	Suspension of certain sentences pending determination of appeal	Only for the purpose of inserting sections 121A(1) to (3) and (4)(a) to (c) and 193A(1) to (3) and (4)(a) to (c) into the 1995 Act.
Sections 26–32	Evidential provisions	
Section 47(1)(a), (b) and (d) and (2) to (5)	Record of evidence taken from external parts of body	
Section 55	Liberation of child by police	
Section 56	Powers of court on remand or commital of children and young persons	
Section 57	Precognitions	
Section 58	Information concerning jurors	
Section 59	Certification of previous convictions in criminal proceedings	
Section 60	Grants for forensic medical services	
Section 61	Confiscation of alochol from persons under 18	
Section 62	Amendments and repeals	Only for the purpose of bringing into force the provisions of Schedules 1 and 3 specified or referred to in column 1 below.
Section 63(1)(a)(iii), and (c) and (2)	Financial provisions	
Section 64	Interpretation	
Section 65(1), (5) and (7)	Short title commencement and extent	
In Schedule 1, paragraphs 2, 6, 8, 9(1), (3)(b), (4) to (6) and (10) to (14), 10(1) and (2)(b), 11, 12(1) and (7), 16, 17, 18(1), (2)(b), (3) to (8), 19, 20, 21(1), (2), (4) and (9) to (15), (17), (19) to (22), (30), (32) and (34)(b)	Amendment of Enactments	
In Schedule 3, the repeals specified in the Table below	Repeals	

TABLE

Chapter	Short title	Extent of Repeals
1967 c. 77.	The Police (Scotland) Act 1967	Section 6(2).
1968 c. 49.	The Social Work (Scotland) Act 1968	In section 27(1)(b), the word "and" where it appears after subparagraph (iv).
1976 c. 67.	The Sexual Offences (Scotland) Act 1976	The whole Act.
1993 c. 24.	The Video Recordings Act 1993	Section 5.
1995 c. 20.	The Criminal Justice (Scotland) Act 1995	Section 66.
1995 c. 25.	The Environment Act 1995	In Schedule 22, paragraph 35.
1995 c. 36.	The Children (Scotland) Act 1995	In Schedule 4, paragraph 35(6).
1995 c. 40.	The Criminal Procedure (Consequential Provisions) (Scotland) Act 1995	In Part II of Schedule 2, the entry relating to section 1(1) of the Protection of Animals (Scotland) Act 1912. In Schedule 4, paragraphs 6(4)(a) and (d), 16, 50(7)(b) and 53(3).
1995 c. 46.	The Criminal Procedure (Scotland) Act 1995	In section 19(4)(b), the words ", print or impression". In section 74(4), the word "and" after paragraph (a). In section 81(6), the word ", signed". In section 85(1), the words from "but" to the end. Section 101(5). In section 104(1)(b), the word "additional". In section 118(4)(b), the word "additional". Section 140(3). In section 141(3), the words "signed by the prosecutor and". Section 154. In section 179(2), the word "additional". In section 182(5)(b), the word "additional". In section 189(1)(b), the word "additional". In section 204(2), the words from "and" to the end. In section 234A, subsection (5).

POLICE

THE CONFISCATION OF ALCOHOL (YOUNG PERSONS) ACT 1997 (COMMENCEMENT) ORDER 1997

(S.I. 1997 No. 1725 (C. 73))

Made - - - - - - - *18th July 1997*

INTRODUCTION

This Order brings into force on August 1, 1997, s.1 of the Confiscation of Alcohol (Young Persons) Act 1997 (c. 33). The remainder of the Act has already been brought into force on March 21, 1997, by virtue of Royal Assent.

In exercise of the power conferred upon him by section 2(2) of the Confiscation of Alcohol (Young Persons) Act 1997 (c. 33), the Secretary of State hereby makes the following Order:

1. This Order may be cited as the Confiscation of Alcohol (Young Persons) Act 1997 (Commencement) Order 1997.

2. Section 1 of the Confiscation of Alcohol (Young Persons) Act 1997 shall come into force on 1st August 1997.

Home Office　　　　　　　　　　　　　　　　*Alun Michael*
18th July 1997　　　　　　　　　　　　　Minister of State

**NATIONAL HEALTH SERVICE, ENGLAND AND WALES
NATIONAL HEALTH SERVICE, SCOTLAND
OPTICIANS**

**THE NATIONAL HEALTH SERVICE (PRIMARY CARE) ACT 1997
(COMMENCEMENT NO. 1) ORDER 1997**

(S.I. 1997 No. 1780 (C. 74))

Made - - - - - - - *23rd July 1997*

INTRODUCTION

This Order brings into force on various dates, provisions of the National Health Service (Primary Care) Act 1997 (c. 46). The provisions brought into force on August 15 and August 22, 1997, relate to pilot schemes. Provisions brought into force on September 1, 1997, relate to the provision of certain optical and pharmaceutical services under NHS contracts.

The Secretary of State, in exercise of the powers conferred by section 41(3) of the National Health Service (Primary Care) Act 1997 (c. 46) and of all other powers enabling him in that behalf, hereby makes the following Order:—

Citation and interpretation

1.—(1) This Order may be cited as the National Health Service (Primary Care) Act 1997 (Commencement No. 1) Order 1997.

(2) In this Order, "the Act" means the National Health Service (Primary Care) Act 1997.

Appointed days

2.—(1) 15th August 1997 is the day appointed for the coming into force of the provisions of the Act specified in column (1) of the Schedule to this Order (the subject matter of each provision being mentioned in column (2)).

(2) 22nd August 1997 is the day appointed for the coming into force of section 4 of the Act (proposals for pilot schemes), in so far as it relates to pilot schemes under which personal medical services are provided.

(3) 1st September 1997 is the day appointed for the coming into force of section 31 of the Act (provision of certain services under NHS contracts).

Frank Dobson
One of Her Majesty's Principal Secretaries of State,
23rd July 1997   Department of Health

Article 2(1)   SCHEDULE

PROVISIONS OF THE ACT COMING INTO FORCE ON 15TH AUGUST 1997

Column (1) Provision of the Act	Column (2) Subject Matter
Section 9(1) and (2)	Relationship between provisions of the Act and the National Health Service Act 1977.
Section 10(1) and (2)	Relationship between provisions of the Act and the National Health Service (Scotland) Act 1978.
Section 13(1) and (3) to (8)	Preferential treatment on transfer to medical lists.
Section 18(1), (2) (except for paragraph (b)) and (3)	Funding of preparatory work.
Section 27	Provision of additional pharmaceutical services.

Column (1) Provision of the Act	Column (2) Subject Matter
Section 28	Terms and conditions for additional pharmaceutical services.
Section 30	Duty of registered opticians to refer certain persons to registered medical practitioners.
Section 41(10), in so far as it relates to the provisions of Schedule 2 to the Act mentioned below	Introduction of Part I of Schedule 2.
Schedule 2, Part I, paragraphs 13, 14, 20, 27, 44, 45 and 51	Minor and consequential amendments relating to additional pharmaceutical services and regulations and directions under the 1977 Act and the 1978 Act.

HOUSING, ENGLAND AND WALES

THE HOUSING ACT 1996 (COMMENCEMENT NO. 11 AND SAVINGS) ORDER 1997

(S.I. 1997 No. 1851 (C. 75))

Made   -   -   -   -   -   -   -   *25th July 1997*

INTRODUCTION

   This Order brings into force on September 1, 1997, ss.83, 86, 152–154, 155(1) and (2)(part), 157, 158 of the Housing Act 1996 (c. 52), subject to the savings in the Schedule to the Order.

The Secretary of State, in exercise of the powers conferred on him by section 232(3) and (4) of the Housing Act 1996 (c. 52) and all other powers enabling him in that behalf, hereby makes the following Order:

Citation and interpretation

   1.—(1) This Order may be cited as the Housing Act 1996 (Commencement No. 11 and Savings) Order 1997.

   (2) In this Order "the commencement date" means 1st September 1997.

Commencement

   2. Subject to the savings in the Schedule to this Order, the following provisions of the Housing Act 1996 shall come into force on the commencement date—

(a) section 83 to the extent that it is not already in force,
(b) section 86 to the extent that it is not already in force,
(c) sections 152 to 154,
(d) section 155(1) and (2) (except for subsection (2)(b)),
(e) sections 157 and 158, and
(f) section 227 in so far as it relates to the repeals to the Landlord and Tenant Act 1985 (c. 70) and the Arbitration Act 1996 (c. 23) in Part III of Schedule 19 to that Act.

Signed by authority of the Secretary of State

Hilary Armstrong
Minister of State,
Department of the Environment,
Transport and the Regions

25th July 1997

SCHEDULE

SAVINGS

Service charges

1. Section 83 of the Housing Act 1996 (determination of reasonableness of service charges) and the repeals referred to in article 2(f) (consequential repeals) shall not have effect in relation to any matter relating to—
   (a) a service charge (within the meaning of section 18 of the Landlord and Tenant Act 1985); or
   (b) paragraph 8 of the Schedule to the Landlord and Tenant Act 1985 (right to challenge landlord's choice of insurers)
where, before the commencement date, court proceedings have been begun, or a reference to arbitration has been made, in respect of that matter.

Appointment of manager

2. Section 86 of the Housing Act 1996 (appointment of manager: transfer of jurisdiction to leasehold valuation tribunal) shall not have effect—
   (a) in a case where an application is made to court for an order under section 24 of the Landlord and Tenant Act 1987 (c. 31) (appointment of manager), which is not an application for an order varying or discharging a previous order under that section, and—
      (i) notice has been served under section 22 of that Act (preliminary notice by tenant) before the commencement date, or
      (ii) an application has been made to the court before the commencement date for the requirement to serve such a notice to be dispensed with; or
   (b) in a case where an application for an order varying or discharging an order under section 24 is made before the commencement date.

FAMILY LAW

THE FAMILY LAW ACT 1996
(COMMENCEMENT NO. 2) ORDER 1997

(S.I. 1997 No. 1892 (C. 76))

Made   -   -   -   -   -   -   -   *28th July 1997*

INTRODUCTION

This Order brings into force certain provisions of the Family Law Act 1996 (c. 27). Section 57 and Sched. 9, paras. 3 and 4 are brought into force forthwith (July 28, 1997). The Order also brings into force on October 1, 1997, Pt. IV (except s.60) and Scheds. 4 to 7 of the Act which relate to Family Homes and Domestic Violence together with s.66(2) (partially).

The Lord Chancellor, in exercise of the powers conferred on him by sections 65 and 67 of the Family Law Act 1996 (c. 27), hereby makes the following Order:

1. This Order may be cited as the Family Law Act 1996 (Commencement No. 2) Order 1997.

2. Section 57 (jurisdiction of courts) of, and paragraphs 3 and 4 of Schedule 9 (modifications of enactments) to, the Family Law Act 1996 shall come into force forthwith.

3.—(1) The following provisions of the Family Law Act 1996 shall come into force on 1st October 1997:

(a) Part IV (Family Homes and Domestic Violence) except section 60,

(b) section 66(1) (minor and consequential amendments), so far as it relates to Part III of Schedule 8,

(c) section 66(2) (transitional provisions), so far as it relates to paragraphs 7 to 15 of Schedule 9, and

(d) section 66(3) (repeals), so far as it relates to the entries in Schedule 10 in respect of—

    (i) the Domestic Violence and Matrimonial Proceedings Act 1976 (c. 50),

    (ii) sections 16 to 18 and 28(2) of, and paragraph 53 of Schedule 2 to, the Domestic Proceedings and Magistrates' Courts Act 1978 (c. 22),

    (iii) the Matrimonial Homes Act 1983 (c. 19),

    (iv) section 34(2) of, and paragraph 37 of Schedule 2 to, the Administration of Justice Act 1985 (c. 61),

    (v) paragraph 56 of Schedule 2 to the Housing (Consequential Provisions) Act 1985 (c. 71),

    (vi) paragraphs 33 and 34 of Schedule 17 to the Housing Act 1988 (c. 50),

    (vii) section 8(4) of the Children Act 1989 (c. 41),

    (viii) section 58(10) of, and paragraph 21 of Schedule 18 to, the Courts and Legal Services Act 1990 (c. 41), and

    (ix) paragraph 3 of the Schedule to the Private International Law (Miscellaneous Provisions) Act 1995 (c. 42).

(2) Until such time as Part II of the Family Law Act 1996 is brought into force, section 22(2) of the Matrimonial and Family Proceedings Act 1984 (c. 42) (as substituted by paragraph 52 of Schedule 8 to the 1996 Act) shall be

modified by substituting for the words from "if -(a) a divorce order" to "made or granted", the words "if a decree of divorce, a decree of nullity of marriage or a decree of judicial separation has been granted".

4. Until such time as Part II of the Family Law Act 1996 is brought into force, paragraphs 2(2), 7(3), (4) and (6), 12 and 13(1) of Schedule 7 to that Act shall be modified as follows:—

(a) for paragraph 2(2) there shall be substituted the following:

"(2) On granting a decree of divorce, a decree of nullity of marriage or a decree of judicial separation or at any time thereafter (whether, in the case of a decree of divorce or nullity of marriage, before or after the decree is made absolute), the court may make a Part II order.";

(b) in paragraph 7(3) and (4) the words "(or, in the case of judicial separation, his spouse)" shall be substituted for the words "(or, if a separation order is in force, his spouse)";

(c) paragraph 7(6) shall be omitted;

(d) in paragraph 12(1) the words "divorce or" shall be inserted after the words "decree of" and paragraph 12(2) shall be omitted; and

(e) in paragraph 13(1):

(i) the words "the making of a divorce order or" and "the making of that order or" shall be omitted, and

(ii) the words, "dissolving or" shall be inserted after the words "grant of a decree".

Irvine of Lairg, C.

Dated 28th July 1997

CRIMINAL LAW, ENGLAND AND WALES
CRIMINAL LAW, SCOTLAND
CRIMINAL LAW, NORTHERN IRELAND

THE KNIVES ACT 1997
(COMMENCEMENT) (NO. 1) ORDER 1997

(S.I. 1997 No. 1906 (C. 77))

Made - - - - - - - *25th July 1997*

INTRODUCTION

This Order brings into force on September 1, 1997, ss.1–7, 9 and 10 of the Knives Act 1997 (c. 21). Section 11 was brought into force on the date of Royal Assent.

In exercise of the power conferred upon him by section 11(3) of the Knives Act 1997 (c. 21), the Secretary of State hereby makes the following Order:

1. This Order may be cited as the Knives Act 1997 (Commencement) (No. 1) Order 1997.

2. Sections 1 to 7, 9 and 10 of the Knives Act 1997 shall come into force on 1st September 1997.

Home Office   *Alun Michael*
25th July 1997   Minister of State

**CRIMINAL LAW, ENGLAND AND WALES
CRIMINAL LAW, SCOTLAND
CRIMINAL LAW, NORTHERN IRELAND**

**THE SEX OFFENDERS ACT 1997
(COMMENCEMENT) ORDER 1997**

(S.I. 1997 No. 1920 (C. 78))

Made -   -   -   -   -   -   -   *2nd August 1997*

INTRODUCTION

This Order brings into force on September 1, 1997, all provisions of the Sex Offenders Act 1997 (c. 51).

In exercise of the power conferred upon him by section 10(2) of the Sex Offenders Act 1997 (c. 51), the Secretary of State hereby makes the following Order:

1. This Order may be cited as the Sex Offenders Act 1997 (Commencement) Order 1997.

2. The Sex Offenders Act 1997 shall come into force on 1st September 1997.

Home Office   *Alun Michael*
2nd August 1997   Minister of State

POLICE

THE POLICE ACT 1997 (COMMENCEMENT NO. 3 AND TRANSITIONAL PROVISIONS) ORDER 1997

(S.I. 1997 No. 1930 (C. 79))

Made - - - - - - -	*1st August 1997*
Laid before Parliament - - -	*11th Aguust 1997*
Coming into force - - - -	*1st September 1997*

INTRODUCTION

This Order brings into force on September 1, 1997 and October 8, 1997, various provisions of the Police Act 1997 (c. 50) which relate to the National Criminal Intelligence Service, the National Crime Squad and the Police Information Technology Organisation.

In exercise of the powers conferred upon me by section 135 of the Police Act 1997 (c. 50), I hereby make the following Order:

Citation, commencement and interpretation

1. This Order may be cited as the Police Act 1997 (Commencement No. 3 and Transitional Provisions) Order 1997 and shall come into force on 1st September 1997.

2. In this Order "the 1997 Act" means the Police Act 1997.

Commencement on 1st September 1997

3.—(1) Subject to the modifications set out in paragraph (3) below, the provisions of the 1997 Act which are listed in paragraph (2) below shall come into force on 1st September 1997.

(2) The provisions referred to in paragraph (1) above are—

(a) section 2(6), so far as it relates to any directions given under section 27;
(b) section 3(2) to (4);
(c) sections 25 to 27.
(d) section 48(7), so far as it relates to any directions given under section 72;
(e) section 49(2) to (4);
(f) sections 70 to 72;
(g) section 91, except subsection (10);
(h) section 96, for the purpose of making orders;
(i) section 109(1);
(j) section 109(2), so far as it relates to paragraphs 1, (except sub-paragraph (6)), 2 (except sub-paragraphs (3)(e) and (f)), 4, 8(1), 9, 10 (except the reference to paragraph 1(3)(e) in sub-paragraph (1)(a) and the reference to paragraphs 1(3)(f) in sub-paragraph (1)(b)), 11 and 18 of Schedule 8;
(k) section 109(3) and (5), for the purpose of making orders;
(l) section 111, except subsections (1)(c) and (d), (2)(d) and (e) and (3)(c) and (d);
(m) Schedule 4;
(n) paragraphs 3, 5 and 10 of Schedule 6;
(o) paragraph 1 of Schedule 8; except sub-paragraph (3)(e) and (f);
(p) paragraph 2 of Schedule 8, except sub-paragraph (6);
(q) paragraph 4 of Schedule 8;
(r) paragraph 8(1) of Schedule 8;
(s) paragraph 9 of Schedule 8;
(t) paragraph 10 of Schedule 8, except the reference to paragraph 1(3)(e) in sub-paragraph (1)(a) and the reference to paragraph 1(3)(f) in sub-paragraph (1)(b);

(u) paragraph 11 of Schedule 8;

(v) paragraph 18 of Schedule 8;

(w) section 134, so far as it relates to paragraphs 3, 8, 9, 28 29(3), 41, 72, 81, 82 and 83 of Schedule 9;

(x) paragraphs 3, 8, 9, 29(3), 82 and 83 of Schedule 9.

(3) Notwithstanding the provisions of section 111 of the 1997 Act, in paragraph 1(2) of Schedule 8 to that Act the reference to "police authorities" shall not include the Police Authority for Northern Ireland and the reference to "chief officers of police" shall not include the Chief Constable of the Royal Ulster Constabulary.

Commencement on 8th October 1997

3.—(1) The provisions of the 1997 Act which are listed in paragraph (2) below shall come into force on 8th October 1997.

(2) The provisions referred to in paragraph (1) above are—

(a) section 2(6), so far as it relates, to any directions given under Schedule 3;

(b) section 17(1) and (6);

(c) section 48(7), so far as it relates to any directions given under Schedule 5;

(d) section 62(1) and (6); and

(e) Schedules 3 and 5.

Transitional provision about Director General

4.—(1) Prior to the Director General appointed under sections 6 or 52 of the 1997 Act taking up this post, the Secretary of State may designate a person to carry out the functions of the Director General of NCIS and the Director General of National Crime Squad.

(2) Sections 3(4)(a), 26(2)(b) and (f), 49(4)(a) and 71(2)(b) and (f) of, and paragraph 1(4)(a) of Schedules 3 and 5 to, the 1997 Act shall have effect as if the references to the Director General of NCIS and the Director General of the National Crime Squad were references to the person designated to carry out the functions of the Director General of NCIS under paragraph (1) above and the person designated to carry out the functions of the Director General of NCS under paragraph (1) above respectively.

Home Office   *Jack Straw*

1st August 1997   One of Her Majesty's Principal Secretaries of State

CUSTOMS & EXCISE

THE FINANCE ACT 1997, SECTION 7(10), (APPOINTED DAY) ORDER 1997

(S.I. 1997 No. 1960 (C. 80))

Made -   -   -   -   -   -   -   *6th August 1997*

INTRODUCTION

This Order appoints August 15, 1997 as the day on which s.7 of the Finance Act 1997 (c. 16) comes into force. This section introduces a new category of heavy oil (ultra low sulphur diesel) for excise duty purposes into the Hydrocarbon Oil Duties Act 1979 (c. 5).

The Commissioners of Customs and Excise, in exercise of the powers conferred on them by section 7(10) of the Finance Act 1997 (c. 16), hereby make the following Order:

Citation

1. This Order may be cited as the Finance Act 1997, section 7(10), (Appointed Day) Order 1997.

Commencement

2. The day appointed as the day on which section 7 of the Finance Act 1997 comes into force is 15th August 1997.

New King's Beam House
22 Upper Ground
London
SE1 9PJ

6th August 1997

D. J. Howard
Commissioner of Customs and Excise

TREASURE

THE TREASURE ACT 1996 (COMMENCEMENT NO. 2) ORDER 1997

(S.I. 1997 No. 1977 (C. 81))

Made -   -   -   -   -   -   -   *7th August 1997*

INTRODUCTION

This Order brings into force on September 24, 1997, the remaining provisions of the Treasure Act 1996 (c. 24). Section 11 has already been brought into force on March 13, 1997 (S.I. 1997 No. 760 (C. 29)).

The Secretary of State, in exercise of the power conferred by section 15(2) of the Treasure Act 1996 (c. 24), hereby makes the following Order:

1. This Order may be cited as the Treasure Act 1996 (Commencement No. 2) Order 1997.

2. The provisions of the Treasure Act 1996 not already in force shall come into force on 24th September 1997.

Signed by authority of the
Secretary of State for National Heritage

7th August 1997   *Mark Fisher*
Parliamentary Under-Secretary of State

SOCIAL SECURITY

THE SOCIAL SECURITY ADMINISTRATION (FRAUD) ACT 1997 (COMMENCEMENT NO. 2) ORDER 1997

(S.I. 1997 No. 2056 (C. 82))

Made -   -   -   -   -   -   -   24th August 1997

INTRODUCTION

This Order appoints August 25, 1997, as the day on which s.20(1) of the Social Security Administration (Fraud) Act 1997 (c. 47) shall come into force. This provision concerns the return of social security post in the London Boroughs of Richmond and Hounslow.

The Secretary of State for Social Security, in exercise of the powers conferred on her by section 25(1) and (4) of the Social Security Administration (Fraud) Act 1997 (c. 47) and of all other powers enabling her in that behalf, hereby makes the following Order:

Citation

1. This Order may be cited as the Social Security Administration (Fraud) Act 1997 (Commencement No. 2) Order 1997.

Appointed day

2. The day appointed for the coming into force of section 20(1) of the Social Security Administration (Fraud) Act 1997 (return of social security post) in relation to the area falling within the London Borough of Richmond and the area falling within the London Borough of Hounslow is 25th August 1997.

Signed by authority of the Secretary of State for Social Security.

Patricia Hollis
Parliamentary Under-Secretary of State,
24th August 1997   Department of Social Security

SOCIAL SECURITY

THE SOCIAL SECURITY (RECOVERY OF BENEFITS) ACT 1997 (COMMENCEMENT) ORDER 1997

(S.I. 1997 No. 2085 (C. 83))

Made - - - - - - *1st September 1997*

INTRODUCTION

This Order brings into force on September 3, 1997, certain provisions of the Social Security (Recovery of Benefits) Act 1997 (c. 27) for the purpose of allowing the Secretary of State to make regulations. The remaining provisions of the Act, so far as not already in force, shall come into effect on October 6, 1997.

The Secretary of State for Social Security, in exercise of the power conferred upon her by section 34(2) of the Social Security (Recovery of Benefits) Act 1997 (c. 27), hereby makes the following Order:

Citation and interpretation

1.—(1) This Order may be cited as the Social Security (Recovery of Benefits) Act 1997 (Commencement) Order 1997.

(2) In this Order, "the 1997 Act" means the Social Security (Recovery of Benefits) Act 1997.

Appointed days

2.—(1) The following provisions of the 1997 Act shall come into force on 3rd September 1997 for the purpose of conferring on the Secretary of State the powers to make regulations:

section 1(2) insofar as it relates to paragraphs 4 and 8 of Part I of Schedule 1
section 4(9)
section 11(5) and (6)
section 12(6) and (7)
section 13(3)
section 14(2), (3) and (4)
section 16(1) and (2)
section 18
section 19
section 21(3)
section 23(1), (2), (5) and (7).

(2) The 1997 Act to the extent it is not already in force shall come into force on 6th October 1997.

Signed by authority of the Secretary of State for Social Security

Patricia Hollis
Parliamentary Under-Secretary of State
1st September 1997 Department of Social Security

ARMS AND AMMUNITION
EXPLOSIVES

THE NORTHERN IRELAND ARMS DECOMMISSIONING ACT 1997 (COMMENCEMENT OF SECTION 7) ORDER 1997

(S.I. 1997 No. 2111 (C. 84))

Made -   -   -   -   -   -   -   29th August 1997

INTRODUCTION

This Order provides for s.7 of the Northern Ireland Arms Decommissioning Act 1997 (c. 7), to be brought into force on September 1, 1997. This section allows the Secretary of State power to confer certain powers, immunities and privileges on an independent Commission, its members and others, established by agreement, in connection with the affairs of Northern Ireland, between the United Kingdom and the Republic of Ireland to facilitate the decommissioning of firearms, ammunition and explosives.

In exercise of the powers conferred upon her by section 7(5) of the Northern Ireland Arms Decommissioning Act 1997 (c. 7), and after consulting the Minister for Justice of the Republic of Ireland (on 9th July, 1997, the title of the Minister was altered to that of the Minister for Justice, Equality and Law Reform ((Republic of Ireland) S.I. 1997 No. 298), the Secretary of State hereby makes the following Order:

1. This Order may be cited as the Northern Ireland Arms Decommissioning Act 1997 (Commencement of Section 7) Order 1997.

2. Section 7 of the Northern Ireland Arms Decommissioning Act 1997 (independent organisation established by agreement with the Government of the Republic of Ireland to facilitate the decommissioning of firearms, ammunition and explosives) shall come into force on 1st September 1997.

Northern Ireland Office   *Marjorie Mowlam*
29th August 1997   One of Her Majesty's Principal Secretaries of State

DEFENCE

THE ARMED FORCES ACT 1996 (COMMENCEMENT NO. 3 AND TRANSITIONAL PROVISIONS) ORDER 1997

(S.I. 1997 No. 2164 (C. 85))

Made - - - - - - - *29th August 1997*

INTRODUCTION
This Order brings into force on October 1, 1997, ss.20 to 27 of the Armed Forces Act 1996 which relate to applications for redress of complaints and complaints to industrial tribunals.

The Secretary of State, in exercise of the powers conferred on him by section 36(2) and (5) of the Armed Forces Act 1996 (c. 46) hereby makes the following Order:—

1. This Order may be cited as the Armed Forces Act 1996 (Commencement No. 3 and Transitional Provisions) Order 1997.

2. Sections 20 to 27 of the Armed Forces Act 1996 shall come into force on 1st October 1997.

3. The transitional provisions contained in the Schedule to this Order shall have effect.

John Reid
29th August 1997   Minister of State, Ministry of Defence

Article 3   SCHEDULE

TRANSITIONAL PROVISIONS

Sex discrimination
1. The amendments made by—
(a) section 21(4) of the Armed Forces Act 1996 ("the 1996 Act") to section 84 of the Sex Discrimination Act 1975 (c. 65; s.85(4) was amended by S.I. 1994 No. 3276) ("the 1975 Act"), and
(b) section 22(4) of the 1996 Act to Article 82 of the Sex Discrimination (Northern Ireland) Order 1976 (S.I. 1976 No. 1042 (N.I. 15); Art. 82(5) was amended by S.R. (N.I.) 1995 No. 318),
shall not have effect in relation to any complaint of discrimination contrary to Part II or IV of the 1975 Act, or (as the case may be) Part II or IV of that Order, where the act complained of was done before 1st October 1997.

Racial discrimination
2. The amendments made by section 23 of the 1996 Act to section 75 of the Race Relations Act 1976 (c. 74) shall not have effect in relation to any complaint of discrimination contrary to Part II or IV of that Act where the act complained of was done before 1st October 1997.

Equal treatment
3.—(1) Section 7A(5) of the Equal Pay Act 1970 (c. 41) (as inserted by section 24(2) of the 1996 Act) shall not have effect in relation to any complaint in respect of a claim falling within section 7A(3) of that Act, if the period of service during which the claim arose ended before 1st October 1997.
(2) Section 6A(5) of the Equal Pay Act (Northern Ireland) 1970 (c. 32 (N.I.)) (as inserted by section 25(2) of the 1996 Act) shall not have effect in relation to any complaint in respect of a claim falling within section 6A(3) of that Act, if the period of service during which the claim arose ended before 1st October 1997.

CRIMINAL LAW, ENGLAND AND WALES

THE CRIMINAL PROCEDURE AND INVESTIGATIONS ACT 1996 (APPOINTED DAY NO. 6) ORDER 1997

(S.I. 1997 No. 2199 (C. 86))

Made - - - - - - *8th September 1997*

INTRODUCTION

This Order appoints October 1, 1997, as the day on which s.49 of the Criminal Procedure and Investigations Act 1996 (c. 25) is brought into force. This section relates to the accused's intention to plea in either way offences.

The Secretary of State, in exercise of the powers conferred on him by sections 49(7) and 77(4) of the Criminal Procedure and Investigations Act 1996 (c. 25), hereby makes the following Order:

1. This Order may be cited as the Criminal Procedure and Investigations Act 1996 (Appointed Day No. 6) Order 1997.

2. 1st October 1997 is hereby appointed for the purposes of section 49 of the Criminal Procedure and Investigations Act 1996.

Home Office   *Jack Straw*
8th September 1997   One of Her Majesty's Principal Secretaries of State

CRIMINAL LAW, ENGLAND AND WALES
CRIMINAL LAW, NORTHERN IRELAND
CRIMINAL LAW, SCOTLAND

THE CRIME (SENTENCES) ACT 1997 (COMMENCEMENT NO. 2 AND TRANSITIONAL PROVISIONS) ORDER 1997

(S.I. 1997 No. 2200 (C. 87))

Made - - - - - - *8th September 1997*

INTRODUCTION

This Order brings into force various provisions of the Crime (Sentences) Act 1997 (c. 43). Sections 1 to 3, 5 to 7 and 28 to 57 together with specified provisions in Scheds. 1 to 6 come into force on October 1, 1997. Sections 35, 37, 39, 40, 43, 50 and Sched. 4, para. 10(2) come into force on January 1, 1998. Section 50 comes into force on March 1, 1998.

The Secretary of State, in exercise of the powers conferred on him by section 57(2) and (3) of the Crime (Sentences) Act 1997 (c. 43), hereby makes the following Order:

1.—(1) This Order may be cited as the Crime (Sentences) Act 1997 (Commencement No. 2 and Transitional Provisions) Order 1997.

(2) In this Order "the 1997 Act" means the Crime (Sentences) Act 1997.

2.—(1) Subject to the transitional provisions and savings made by article 5 below, the following provisions of the 1997 Act shall come into force on 1st October 1997, namely—

(a) in section 1, subsections (1) and (2) and, so far as relating to section 3, subsection (3);

(b) section 2;

(c) in section 3, subsections (1) to (5) and, so far as relating to that section, subsection (6);

(d) section 5 so far as relating to sentences imposed under section 2(2) or 3(2);

(e) section 6 so far as relating to serious offences within the meaning of section 2 or class A drug trafficking offences within the meaning of section 3;

(f) sections 7, 28 to 34, 36 and 38;

(g) section 41 and Schedule 1 so far as not already in force;

(h) section 42 and, in Schedule 2, paragraphs 1 to 3, 5 to 7 and 9 to 11;

(i) sections 44 to 47;

(j) section 48 and Schedule 3;

(k) sections 49 and 51 to 54;

(l) section 55(1) and the provisions of Schedule 4 mentioned in paragraph (2) below;

(m) in section 55(2), paragraph (a) so far as relating to sentences falling to be imposed under section 2(2) or 3(2), and paragraph (b);

(n) section 56(1) and paragraphs 5 and 7 to 13 of Schedule 5;

(o) section 56(2) and Schedule 6 so far as relating to the repeals in the Criminal Justice Act 1961 (c. 39), the 1973 Act, the 1983 Act and sections 4(1) and 12 of, and paragraph 14 of Schedule 2 to, the 1991 Act;

(p) section 56(2) and Schedule 6 so far as they repeal the provisions of the 1991 Act mentioned in paragraph (3) below; and

(q) section 57.

(2) The provisions of Schedule 4 to the 1997 Act referred to in paragraph (1)(l) above are—

(a) in each of paragraphs 1 to 3, sub-paragraph (1) so far as relating to offences whose corresponding civil offences are offences to which section 2 would apply, and sub-paragraphs (2) and (4);

   (b) paragraphs 4 and 5;

   (c) in paragraph 6, sub-paragraph (1)(a);

   (d) in paragraph 8, sub-paragraphs (1) to (3) so far as relating to offences the sentences for which fall to be imposed under section 2(2) or 3(2), and sub-paragraph (4);

   (e) in paragraph 10, sub-paragraph (1);

   (f) in paragraph 12, sub-paragraph (1), sub-paragraph (2) so far as relating to offences the sentences for which would otherwise fall to be imposed under section 3(2), and sub-paragraphs (3) and (5) to (19);

   (g) paragraph 13 so far as relating to sentences required by section 2(2) or 3(2);

   (h) in paragraph 15, sub-paragraphs (1), (8) and (9) so far as relating to offences the sentences for which fall to be imposed under section 2(2) or 3(2), sub-paragraph (4) so far as relating to section 3(2), sub-paragraph (5) so far as relating to sentences falling to be imposed under section 3(2), and sub-paragraphs (2), (3), (6), (7) and (10) to (13);

   (i) paragraph 16; and

   (j) paragraph 17 so far as relating to offences the sentences for which fall to be imposed under section 3(2).

(3) The provisions of the 1991 Act referred to in paragraph (1)(p) above are—

   (a) section 34;

   (b) in section 35, subsections (2) and (3);

   (c) in section 36, subsection (1) so far as relating to life prisoners and, in subsection (2), the words "or life";

   (d) in section 37, subsection (3) and, so far as relating to life prisoners, subsections (4) and (5);

   (e) in section 39, in subsection (1), the words "or life" and, in subsection (5), paragraph (a), the word "other" in paragraph (b) and the words "direction or";

   (f) in section 43, subsection (2) and, in subsection (3), the words "(whether short-term, long-term or life prisoners)" and the words "or (2)";

   (g) section 48; and

   (h) in section 51, in subsection (1), the definitions of "discretionary life prisoner" and "life "prisoner", and subsection (3).

(4) In paragraph (3) above "life prisoner" has the same meaning as in Part II of the 1991 Act.

3. Subject to the transitional provisions and saving made by article 5 below, the following provisions of the 1997 Act shall come into force on 1st January 1998, namely—

   (a) sections 35 and 37;

   (b) in section 39, subsections (1) and (3) to (6) and, so far as relating to offences the sentences for which are fixed by law or fall to be imposed under section 2(2) or 3(2), subsection (2);

   (c) sections 40 and 43; and

   (d) paragraph 10(2) of Schedule 4.

4. Section 50 of the 1997 Act shall come into force on 1st March 1998.

5.—(1) The following provisions of the 1997 Act shall not apply where the offence in question was committed before 1st October 1997, namely—

   (a) sections 38, 44, 46 and 52;

   (b) paragraph 15(2) and (11) to (13) of Schedule 4; and

   (c) Schedule 6 so far as relating to the repeals in sections 2(3) and 14(2) of the 1973 Act and sections 4(1) and 12 of, and paragraph 14 of Schedule 2 to, the 1991 Act.

(2) Sections 39 and 43 of the 1997 Act shall not apply where the offence in question was committed before 1st January 1998.

(3) In relation to any time before the commencement of Chapter I of Part II of the 1997 Act—

    (a) section 31(6) of that Act shall have effect as if for the words "section 24(2) above" there were substituted the words "section 46(3) of the 1991 Act";

    (b) section 56(2) of the Criminal Justice Act 1967 (c. 80) (as amended by paragraph 5(1)(b) of Schedule 4 to the 1997 Act) shall have effect as if for the words "section 17(3) of the Crime (Sentences) Act 1997 (committal for breach of conditions of release supervision order)" there were substituted the words "section 40(3)(b) of the Criminal Justice Act 1991 (committal for sentence for offence committed during currency of original sentence)"; and

    (c) section 32 of the 1991 Act (as amended by paragraphs 15(10) of Schedule 4 to the 1997 Act) shall have effect as if—

        (i) in subsection (1), for the words "the functions conferred by Part II of the Crime (Sentences) Act 1997 ("Part II")" there were substituted the words "the functions conferred by this Part in respect of long-term and short-term prisoners and by Chapter II of Part II of the Crime (Sentences) Act 1997 ("Chapter II") in respect of life prisoners within the meaning of that Chapter"; and

        (ii) in subsections (3), (4) and (6), for the words "Part II" there were substituted the words "this Part or Chapter II".

(4) Without prejudice to the operation of section 17 of the Interpretation Act 1978 (c. 30), in relation to prisoners repatriated to England and Wales for offences committed before the commencement of Chapter I of Part II of the 1997 Act, any reference in the Repatriation of Prisoners Act 1984 (c. 47) (whether or not as modified by Schedule 2 to the 1997 Act) to a provision of Part II of the 1991 Act applicable to life prisoners (withing the meaning of that Part) shall be construed as including a reference to the equivalent provision of Chapter II of Part II of the 1997 Act.

(5) A certificate issued under subsection (1) of section 48 of the 1991 Act in respect of a person who is a transferred life prisoner within the meaning of that section shall, after 30th September 1997, have effect as if—

    (a) it had been issued under subsection (1) of section 33 of the 1997 Act; and

    (b) the person where a transferred life prisoner within the meaning of that section.

(6) Schedule 1 to the 1997 Act and, so far as relating to the repeal of Part III of the Criminal Justice Act 1961, Schedule 6 to that Act shall not apply in respect of any person who on 1st October 1997 is in any part of the United Kingdom or any of the Channel Islands or the Isle of Man by virtue of an order made under that Part, for so long as that order has effect under that Part.

Jack Straw

Home Office   One of Her Majesty's
8th September 1997   Principal Secretaries of State

ROAD TRAFFIC

THE ROAD TRAFFIC ACT 1991 (COMMENCEMENT NO. 14) (SCOTLAND) ORDER 1997

(S.I. 1997 No. 2260 (C. 88) (S. 151))

Made - - - - - -   *3rd September 1997*

INTRODUCTION

This Order brings into force on October 10, 1997, ss.41 and 42 of the Road Traffic Act 1991 (c. 40) in relation to Scotland and so far as they are not already commenced.

The Secretary of State, in exercise of the powers conferred upon him by section 84 of the Road Traffic Act 1991 (c. 40), and of all other powers enabling him in that behalf, hereby makes the following Order:

Citation and interpretation

1.—(1) This Order may be cited as the Road Traffic Act 1991 (Commencement No. 14) (Scotland) Order 1997.

(2) In this Order—

"the Act" means the Road Traffic Act 1991.

Commencement of certain provisions of the Act

2. The following provisions of the Act shall come into force on 10th October 1997, insofar as they relate to Scotland and have not already been commenced—

(a) section 41; and

(b) section 42.

Malcolm Chisholm
St Andrew's House, Edinburgh   Parliamentary Under Secretary of State,
3rd September 1997   The Scottish Office

CRIMINAL LAW, SCOTLAND
LEGAL AID AND ADVICE, SCOTLAND
PRISONS

THE CRIME AND PUNISHMENT (SCOTLAND) ACT 1997 (COMMENCEMENT NO. 2 AND TRANSITIONAL AND CONSEQUENTIAL PROVISIONS) ORDER 1997

(S.I. 1997 No. 2323 (C. 89) (S. 155))

Made - - - - - - *24th September 1997*

INTRODUCTION

This Order brings into force Part V of the Crime and Punishment (Scotland) Act 1997 (c. 48) on various dates which are set out in Sched. 3 to the Order. This part of the Act amends the Legal Aid (Scotland) Act 1986 (c. 47) to provide for criminal assistance, employment of solicitors in relation to criminal legal assistance, fixed payments for criminal legal assistance and powers of investigation of the Scottish Legal Aid Board. Appointed days are also set for various provisions listed in the Schedules to the Order.

The Secretary of State, in exercise of the powers conferred upon him by section 65(2), (3) and (4) of the Crime and Punishment (Scotland) Act 1997 (c. 48) and of all other powers enabling him in that behalf, hereby makes the following Order:

Citation

1. This Order may be cited as the Crime and Punishment (Scotland) Act 1997 (Commencement No. 2 and Transitional and Consequential Provisions) Order 1997.

Interpretation

2. In this Order—
"the Act" means the Crime and Punishment (Scotland) Act 1997; and
"the 1995 Act" means the Criminal Procedure (Scotland) Act 1995 (c. 46).

Commencement of provisions of Parts I, II, III and VI

3. The provisions of Parts I, II and VI of the Act specified in column 1 of Schedule 1 to this Order and whose subject matter is specified in column 2 of that Schedule shall, in so far as they are not then in force, come into force on 20th October 1997, but, where a particular purpose is specified in relation to any provision in column 3 of that Schedule, that provision shall come into force on that day only for that purpose.

4. Subject to article 7 below, the provisions of Parts I, II, III and VI of the Act specified in column 1 of Schedule 2 to this Order and whose subject matter is specified in column 2 of that Schedule shall, in so far as they are not then in force, come into force on 1st January 1998 but, where a particular purpose is specified in relation to any provision in column 3 of that Schedule, that provision shall come into force on that day only for that purpose.

5.—(1) Sections 5 and 24 of the Act shall, in so far as they are not then in force, come into force on 1st July 1998.

(2) Section 62 of the Act shall come into force on 1st July 1998 for the purpose of bringing into force the amendments made to the 1995 Act by paragraphs 21(27) and (28) of Schedule 1 to the Act.

Commencement of Parts V and VI and consequential provisions

6.—(1) The provisions of Part V of the Act specified in column 1 of Schedule 3 to this Order shall, in so far as they are not then in force, come into force on the date specified in column 2 of that Schedule so as to enable the provisions of the 1986 Act which are specified in column 3 to the Schedule to come into force on that date for the purpose specified in column 4 of that Schedule.

(2) Section 62(1) of the Act shall come into force on 1st October 1997 for the purpose of bringing into force the amendments to the 1986 Act which are made by paragraphs 12(2) to (4) and (8) to (10) of Schedule 1 to the Act.

(3) Section 63(1)(b) of the Act shall come into force on 1st October 1997.

(4) Where the name of a solicitor and any firm with which he is connected is not entered on the Register on 1st October 1998, the solicitor shall, in accordance with arrangements approved by the Board, forthwith and without waiting for the resolution of any appeal under section 25A(13) (s.25A was inserted by s.49 of the Act) of the 1986 Act, transfer—

(a) any work currently being undertaken by him for any client by way of criminal legal assistance; and

(b) notwithstanding any lien to which he might otherwise be entitled, any documents connected with any such work,

to a registered solicitor.

(5) For the purposes of this article and Schedule 3 to this Order—

"the 1986 Act" means the Legal Aid (Scotland) Act 1986 (c. 47);

"the Board" means the Scottish Legal Aid Board;

"criminal legal assistance" means criminal legal aid and advice and assistance in relation to criminal matters;

"document" includes information recorded in any form;

"firm" includes an incorporated practice, a sole solicitor and a law centre;

"the Register" means the Register established and maintained under section 25A of the 1986 Act;

"registered firm" means a firm whose name appears on the Register; and

"registered solicitor" means a solicitor whose name appears on the Register.

Transitional Provisions

7. Sections 248A and 248B of the 1995 Act as inserted by section 15 of the Act shall not apply in relation to any offence committed before 1st January 1998.

St Andrew's House, Edinburgh
24th September 1997

Henry B McLeish
Minister of State,
Scottish Office

Article 3   SCHEDULE 1

The Provisions of Parts I, II and VI of the Act which come into force on 20th October 1997

Column 1 Provision of Act	Column 2 Subject matter	Column 3 Purpose
Section 2	Minimum sentence for third conviction of certain offences relating to drug trafficking	
Section 3	Meaning of conviction	Only for the purpose of inserting section 205C(1) into the 1995 Act for the purpose of the interpretation of section 205B of the 1995 Act.
Section 5	Restriction of liberty orders	Only for the purposes of enabling the Secretary of State to make regulations, notify courts and make arrangements, including contractual arrangements, under sections 245A, 245B and 245C of the 1995 Act.
Section 15	Driving disqualifications	Only for the purpose of enabling the Secretary of State to make an order under section 248C of the 1995 Act.
Section 16	Designated life prisoners	For all purposes, except for the purpose of substituting into section 2(1) of the Prisoners and Criminal Proceedings (Scotland) Act 1993 a reference to sentences imposed under section 205A(2) of the 1995 Act.
Section 18	Automatic sentences; jurisdiction and appeals	For all purposes except for the purpose of inserting references to section 205A and 209(1A) into the 1995 Act.
Section 19	Appeal against automatic sentence where earlier conviction quashed	For all purposes except for the purposes of inserting— (a) section 106A(1) into the 1995 Act; and (b) section 106A(3) in so far as it refers to section 205A(2) of the 1995 Act.
Section 62	Amendments and repeals	Only for the purpose of bringing into force the provisions of Schedules 1 and 3 specified or referred to in column 1 below.
Section 63(1)(a)(i)	Financial provisions	
In Schedule 1, paragraphs 10(3), 12(5) and (6), 14(1), (2)(b), (3)(a) to (d), (8), (10)(b), (11)(a) and (18) and 21(33)(a)	Amendments	
In Schedule 1, paragraphs 21(23), (25) and (31)	Amendments	For all purposes except for the purpose of inserting references to section 205A into the 1995 Act.

Column 1 *Provision of Act*	Column 2 *Subject matter*	Column 3 *Purpose*
In Schedule 3, the Repeals specified in the Table below	Repeals	

TABLE

Column 1 *Chapter*	Column 2 *Short Title*	Column 3 *Extent of Repeals*
1984 c. 47	The Repatriation of Prisoners Act 1984	In section 3(9), the words "or section 10" in the second place where they occur.
1993 c. 9	The Prisoners and Criminal Proceedings (Scotland) Act 1993	In section 2(2), the word "and".

Article 4   SCHEDULE 2

The Provisions of Parts I, II, III and VI of the Act which come into force on 1st January 1998

Column 1 *Provision of Act*	Column 2 *Subject matter*	Column 3 *Purpose*
Section 6	Disposal in cases of mentally disordered offenders	
Section 7	Effect of hospital direction	
Section 8	Remand of persons suffering from mental disorder to private hospital	
Section 9	Power to specify hospital unit	
Section 10	Medical evidence in relation to mentally disordered offenders	
Section 11	Increase in maximum period of interim hospital orders	
Section 15	Driving disqualifications	
Section 22	Appeal by prosecutor against hospital orders etc	
Section 42	Testing of prisoners for alcohol	
Section 43	Medical services in prisons	
Section 44	Unlawful disclosure of information	
Section 62	Amendments and repeals	Only for the purpose of bringing into force the provisions of Schedules 1 and 3 specified or referred to in column 1 below.
In Schedule 1, paragraphs 9(2), (3)(a), (8), (9), (15) and (16), 13(1), (2) and (4), 15, 21(5) to (8) and (35)	Amendments	
In Schedule 3, the repeals specified in the Table below	Repeals	

TABLE

Column 1 Chapter	Column 2 Short Title	Column 3 Extent of Repeals
1984 c. 36	The Mental Health (Scotland) Act 1984	In section 65(2), the words after paragraph (b). In section 70(1), the words "(not being a private hospital)".
1989 c. 45	The Prisons (Scotland) Act 1989	In section 3(1), the words from "including" to the end.
1995 c. 46	The Criminal Procedure (Scotland) Act 1995	In section 53, in subsection (1), the words "subsection (2) below and", and subsection (2). In section 63, subsection (1)(d) and in subsection (2)(b)(ii) the words "or (d)". In section 252(2), the word "and", in the third place where it occurs.

Article 6   SCHEDULE 3

COMMENCEMENT OF PART V OF THE ACT

Column 1 Provision of Act	Column 2 Date in Force	Column 3 Provision of 1986 Act	Column 4 Purpose for which provision of 1986 Act comes into force on date
Section 49	1 October 1997	Section 25A(5) and (6) (Criminal Legal Assistance Register)	Only for the purpose of enabling the Board to determine the form of the application for entry on the Register and to specify the documents which are to accompany the application.
Section 49	1 October 1997	Section 25B (Code of Practice in relation to Criminal legal assistance)	For all purposes.
Section 49	1 April 1998	Section 25A(1) and (5) to (15) (Criminal Legal Assistance Register)	For all purposes.
Section 49	1 April 1998	Section 25F(1) (Publication of Register)	For all purposes.
Section 49	1 October 1998	Section 25A(2) to (4) (Criminal Legal Assistance Register)	For all purposes.
Section 49	1 October 1998	Sections 25C to E (Supervision of registered solicitors and firms, removal of name from Register following failure to comply with code and further provisions as to removal of name from Register)	For all purposes.
Section 49	1 October 1998	Section 25F(2) and (3) (Publication of Register)	For all purposes.

Column 1 *Provision of Act*	Column 2 *Date in Force*	Column 3 *Provision of 1986 Act*	Column 4 *Purpose for which provision of 1986 Act comes into force on date*
Section 50	1 October 1997	Section 28A (Employment of solicitors in relation to criminal legal assistance)	For all purposes.
Section 51	1 October 1997	Section 33(3A) and (3B) (Fixed payments)	For all purposes.
Section 52	1 October 1997	Section 33A (Contracts for the provision of criminal legal assistance)	For all purposes.
Section 53	1 October 1997	Section 35A to C (Power of Board to require information, to enter premises and investigate and suspend payments to a solicitor)	For all purposes.
Section 54	1 October 1997	Section 41A (Regulations in relation to criminal legal assistance)	For all purposes.

EDUCATION, ENGLAND AND WALES

THE EDUCATION ACT 1996
(COMMENCEMENT NO. 3) ORDER 1997

(S.I. 1997 No. 2352 (C. 90))

Made - - - - - -	*26th September 1997*
Laid before Parliament - - -	*6th October 1997*
Coming into force - - - -	*30th October 1997*

INTRODUCTION

This Order brings into force on October 30, 1997, s.528 of the Education Act 1996 (c. 56) so far as it applies to Wales. Under this section, local education authorities are placed under a duty to publish disability statements relating to further education.

In exercise of the powers conferred on the Secretary of State by section 583(3) and (5)(b) of the Education Act 1996 (c. 56) the Secretary of State for Wales hereby makes the following Order:

1. This Order may be cited as the Education Act 1996 (Commencement No. 3) Order 1997.

2. Section 528 of the Education Act 1996, in its application to Wales, shall come into force on 30th October 1997.

Signed by authority of the Secretary of State for Wales

Win Griffiths
Parliamentary Under Secretary of State,
26th September 1997   Welsh Office

ANTARCTICA

THE ANTARCTIC ACT 1994 (COMMENCEMENT) (NO. 2) ORDER 1997

(S.I. 1997 No. 2298 (C. 91))

Made - - - - - - *22nd September 1997*

INTRODUCTION

This Order brings into force on October 1, 1997, s.6 of the Antarctic Act 1994 (c. 15). The section prohibits mineral resource activities in Antarctica by U.K. nationals except for certain limited purposes.

The Secretary of State, in exercise of the powers conferred on him by section 35 of the Antarctic Act 1994 (c. 15), and of all other powers enabling him in that behalf, hereby makes the following Order:

Citation

1. This Order may be cited as the Antarctic Act 1994 (Commencement) (No. 2) Order 1997.

Commencement of Section 6 of the Antarctic Act 1994

2. Section 6 of the Antarctic Act 1994 shall come into force on 1st October 1997.

Derek Fatchett
For the Secretary of State for
22nd September 1997   Foreign and Commonwealth Affairs

POLICE

THE POLICE ACT 1997 (COMMENCEMENT NO. 4 AND TRANSITIONAL PROVISIONS) ORDER 1997

(S.I. 1997 No. 2390 (C. 92))

Made - - - - - - -	*3rd October 1997*
Laid before Parliament - -	*10th October 1997*
Coming into force - - - -	*31st October 1997*

INTRODUCTION

This Order brings into force on October 31, 1997, certain provisions in Pts. I and II of the Police Act 1997 (c. 50) which relate to the National Criminal Intelligence Service and the National Crime Squad.

In exercise of the powers conferred upon him by section 135 of the Police Act 1997 (c. 50), the Secretary of State hereby makes the following Order:

Citation, commencement and interpretation

1.—(1) This Order may be cited as the Police Act 1997 (Commencement No. 4 and Transitional Provisions) Order 1997.

(2) This Order shall come into force on 31st October 1997.

(3) In this Order "the 1997 Act" means the Police Act 1997.

Commencement on 31st October 1997

2.—(1) Subject to articles 3 to 7 below, the provisions of the 1997 Act which are listed in paragraph (2) below shall come into force on 31st October 1997.

(2) The provisions referred to in paragraph (1) above are:

(a) section 4 (service plans);
(b) section 8 (Deputy Director General);
(c) section 9 (members of NCIS);
(d) section 19 (charges);
(e) section 21 (pensions and gratuities);
(f) section 22(4) to (8) (collaboration agreements);
(g) section 28 (Codes of Practice);
(h) section 37 (discipline regulations);
(i) section 38 (appeals), for the purpose of making orders;
(j) section 39 (complaints);
(k) section 50 (service plans);
(l) section 54 (Deputy Director General);
(m) section 55 (members of the National Crime Squad);
(n) section 64 (charges);
(o) section 66 (pensions and gratuities);
(p) section 73 (Codes of Practice);
(q) section 81 (discipline regulations);
(r) section 82 (appeals), for the purpose of making orders;
(s) section 83 (complaints);
(t) section 88 (application to NCS Service Authority of local authority enactments), so far as it relates to paragraphs 1, 2, 6, 9(e), 29 and 32 of Schedule 6;
(u) section 134 (amendments and repeals), so far as it relates to paragraphs 13, 14, 23, 38, 39, 43, 49 to 52, 55, 57, 66 to 68, 73, 86 and 91 of Schedule 9;

    (v) paragraphs 1, 2, 6, 9(e), 29 and 32 of Schedule 6;
   (w) paragraphs 13, 14, 23, 38, 39, 43, 49 to 52, 55, 57, 66 to 68, 72, 73, 81, 86, and 91 of Schedule 9.

Transitional provision about the Directors General

3. The references to the Director General of NCIS and the Director General of the National Crime Squad in sections 4(3), (4) and (5)(e), 8(1) and (2), 9(6), (8), (9)(b) and (10) (in the first place where it occurs), 50(3), (4) and (5)(e), 54(1) and (2), and 55(6), (8), (9)(b) and (10) (in the first place where it occurs) of the 1997 Act shall have effect as if they were respectively references to the person designated to carry out the functions of the Director General of NCIS and the person designated to carry out the functions of the Director General of the National Crime Squad under article 4(1) of the Police Act 1997 (Commencement No. 3 and Transitional Provisions) Order 1997 (S.I. 1997 No. 1930 (C. 79)).

Transitional provision about the Deputy Directors General

4. Sections 8(1) and 54(1) of the 1997 Act shall have effect as if the references to a member of NCIS and a member of National Crime Squad appointed under section 9 and section 55 respectively were references to an appointment made which takes effect on 1st April 1998.

Transitional provision about collaboration agreements

5.—(1) Section 22(5)(a) of the 1997 Act shall be omitted.
(2) Section 22(6) of the 1997 Act shall have effect as if "(1) or" were omitted.
(3) Section 22(7) of the 1997 Act shall have effect as if "(1)," were omitted.

Transitional provision about Local Government Act 1972

6. Paragraph 6 of Schedule 6 to the 1997 Act shall have effect as if, in section 146A(1AA) of the Local Government Act 1972 (application to police authorities of miscellaneous powers of local authorities), as inserted by sub-paragraph (4) of that paragraph, for the words from "shall" to the end there were substituted the words "shall be treated as a principal council for the purposes of section 120 above only and as local authority for the purposes of section 135 above only".

Transitional provision about the Local Government and Housing Act 1989

7. Paragraph 29 of Schedule 6 to the 1997 Act (definition of local authority for purposes of various provisions relating to their members, officers, staff and committees etc.) shall have effect as if for the words from "inserted" to the end there were substituted the words "inserted" "or, in sections 7, 19 and 20 only, the Service Authority for the National Crime Squad.".

Repeals

8. Article 3(3) of the Police Act 1997 (Commencement No. 1 and Transitional Provisions) Order 1997 (S.I. 1997 No. 1377 (C. 50)) is hereby repealed.

Home Office   *Alun Michael*
3rd October 1997   Minister of State

ROAD TRAFFIC

THE FINANCE ACT 1997 (COMMENCEMENT NO. 1) ORDER 1997

(S.I. 1997 No. 2392 (C. 93))

Made - - - - - - -   3rd October 1997

INTRODUCTION

  This Order brings into force on October 8, 1997, s.20 of the Finance Act 1997 (c. 16) which relates to the removal and disposal of vehicles on public roads.

The Secretary of State for Transport, in exercise of the power conferred by section 20(4) of the Finance Act 1997 (c. 16), hereby makes the following Order:

  1. This Order may be cited as the Finance Act 1997 (Commencement No. 1) Order 1997.

  2. Section 20 of the Finance Act 1997 (removal and disposal of vehicles) shall come into force on 8th October 1997.

Signed by authority of the Secretary of State

Helene Hayman
Parliamentary Under-Secretary of State,
Department of the Environment,
3rd October 1997   Transport and the Regions

SOCIAL SECURITY

THE SOCIAL SECURITY ADMINISTRATION (FRAUD) ACT 1997 (COMMENCEMENT NO. 3) ORDER 1997

(S.I. 1997 No. 2417 (C. 94))

Made - - - - - - - *7th October 1997*

INTRODUCTION

This Order brings into force on October 8, 1997, s.11 of the Social Security Administration (Fraud) Act 1997 (c. 47). Section 16 is also brought into force on that date for the purpose of making regulations and for all other purposes on November 3, 1997.

The Secretary of State for Social Security, in exercise of the powers conferred on her by section 25(1) and (2) of the Social Security Administration (Fraud) Act 1997 (c. 47) and of all other powers enabling her in that behalf, hereby makes the following Order:

Citation and interpretation

1.—(1) This Order may be cited as the Social Security Administration (Fraud) Act 1997 (Commencement No. 3) Order 1997.

(2) In this Order, references to "the Act" are references to the Social Security Administration (Fraud) Act 1997.

Appointed days

2.—(1) The day appointed for the coming into force of section 11 of the Act (information from landlords and agents) is 8th October 1997.

(2) The day appointed for the coming into force of section 16 of the Act (recovery of overpaid housing benefit)—

(a) for the purposes only of authorising the making of regulations is 8th October 1997; and

(b) for all other purposes is 3rd November 1997.

Signed by authority of the Secretary of State for Social Security

John Y. Denham
Parliamentary Under-Secretary of State,
7th October 1997
Department of Social Security

TAXES

THE FINANCE ACT 1997 (STAMP DUTY AND STAMP DUTY RESERVE TAX) (APPOINTED DAY) ORDER 1997

(S.I. 1997 No. 2428 (C. 95))

Made - - - - - - - *8th October 1997*

INTRODUCTION

This Order appoints October 20, 1997 as the day on which certain sections of the Finance Act 1997 (c. 16) come into force. These sections introduce new rules conferring relief from stamp duty and stamp duty reserve tax for intermediate trading in U.K. securities.

The Treasury, in exercise of the powers conferred on them by sections 97(6), 98(4), 102(6) and 103(8) of the Finance Act 1997 (c. 16), hereby make the following Order:

1. This Order may be cited as the Finance Act 1997 (Stamp Duty and Stamp Duty Reserve Tax) (Appointed Day) Order 1997.

2.—(1) The day appointed for the purposes of each of the enactments specified in paragraph (2) is 20th October 1997.

(2) The enactments specified are sections 97, 98, 102 and 103 of the Finance Act 1997.

Jim Dowd
Graham Allen
Two of the Lords Commissioners of
8th October 1997 Her Majesty's Treasury

NATIONAL HEALTH SERVICE, ENGLAND AND WALES

THE NATIONAL HEALTH SERVICE (PRIMARY CARE) ACT 1997 (COMMENCEMENT NO. 2) ORDER 1997

(S.I. 1997 No. 2457 (C. 96))

Made - - - - - - *13th October 1997*

INTRODUCTION

This Order appoints October 14, 1997, as the day on which s.36 of the National Health (Primary Care) Act 1997 (c. 46) shall come into force. This section relates to expenditure of Health Authorities and amends s.97 of the National Health Service Act 1977 (c. 49) as substituted by the Health Authorities Act 1995 (c. 17).

The Secretary of State, in exercise of powers conferred on him by section 41(3) and (4) of the National Health Service (Primary Care) Act 1997 (c. 46) and of all other powers enabling him in that behalf, hereby makes the following Order:

Citation

1. This Order may be cited as the National Health Service (Primary Care) Act 1997 (Commencement No. 2) Order 1997.

Appointed day

2. The day appointed for the coming into force of section 36 of the National Health Service (Primary Care) Act 1997 (expenditure of Health Authorities) is 14th October 1997.

Saving

3. Notwithstanding article 2, in relation to—
(a) expenditure of Health Authorities in respect of a financial year ending on 31st March 1998 or before; and
(b) amounts allotted to Health Authorities in respect of such a financial year,
section 97 of the National Health Service Act 1977 (c. 49. Section 97 was substituted by the Health Authorities Act 1995 (c. 17), Sched. 1, para. 47) shall continue to have effect as if this Order had not been made.

Frank Dobson
One of Her Majesty's Principal Secretaries of State
13th October 1997   Department of Health

CIVIL AVIATION

THE CARRIAGE BY AIR AND ROAD ACT 1979 (COMMENCEMENT NO. 2) ORDER 1997

(S.I. 1997 No. 2565 (C. 97))

Made - - - - - - *30th October 1997*

At the Court at Buckingham Palace, the 30th day of October 1997

Present,

The Queen's Most Excellent Majesty in Council

INTRODUCTION

This Order brings into force on December 1, 1997, various provisions of the Carriage by Air and Road Act 1979 (c. 28). The commencement of these provisions is as a consequence of the entry into force on February 15, 1996, of Additional Protocol No. 2 to the Warsaw Convention as amended at the Hague, 1955 (which introduces a new unit of account).

Her Majesty, in exercise of the powers conferred upon Her by section 7(2) of the Carriage by Air and Road Act 1979 (c. 28), is pleased, by and with the advice of Her Privy Council, to order, and it is hereby ordered, as follows:

1. This Order may be cited as the Carriage by Air and Road Act 1979 (Commencement No. 2) Order 1997.

2. The provisions of the Carriage by Air and Road Act 1979 which are listed in column (1) of the Schedule to this Order and which relate to the matters respectively specified in relation to those provisions in column (2) thereof shall (to the extent stated in the Schedule) come into force on 1st December 1997.

N. H. Nicholls
Clerk of the Privy Council

Article 2   SCHEDULE

(1) *Provisions of the Act*	(2) *Subject matter of the provisions*
Section 4(1)	Replacement of gold francs by special drawing rights for the purposes of the Carriage by Air Act 1961 (c. 27) (the Act of 1961)
Section 4(4) (so far as it relates to the enactments amended by section 4(1))	Effect of amendments made by section 4(1) upon judgments in respect of liability which arises before the amendments come into force
Section 5 (so far as it relates to the enactments amended by section 4(1))	Conversion of special drawing rights into sterling
Section 6(1) (a) (so far as it relates to sections 9 and 10 of the Act of 1961)	Supplemental
Section 6(3) (so far as it relates to the provisions specified above in this Schedule)	Supplemental

NATIONAL HEALTH SERVICE, ENGLAND AND WALES
NATIONAL HEALTH SERVICE, SCOTLAND

THE NATIONAL HEALTH SERVICE (PRIMARY CARE) ACT 1997 (COMMENCEMENT NO. 3) ORDER 1997

(S.I. 1997 No. 2620 (C. 98))

Made - - - - - - *29th October 1997*

INTRODUCTION

This Order brings into force various provisions of the National Health Service (Primary Care) Act 1997 (c. 46). Provisions are brought into force on October 30, 1997 which relate to the preparation of proposals for pilot schemes for the provision of personal dental services, and to the status of contacts entered into by those who provide personal medical services under a pilot scheme.

On November 28, 1997, provisions are brought into force in relation to the approval and making of pilot schemes for personal medical services and the funding of work preparatory to the provision of such services.

The Secretary of State, in exercise of powers conferred on him by section 41(3) of the National Health Service (Primary Care) Act 1997 (c. 46) and of all other powers enabling him in that behalf, hereby makes the following Order:—

Citation and interpretation

1.—(1) This Order may be cited as the National Health Service (Primary Care) Act 1997 (Commencement No. 3) Order 1997.

(2) In this Order, "the Act" means the National Health Service (Primary Care) Act 1997.

Appointed days

2.—(1) 30th October 1997 is the day appointed for the coming into force of the following provisions of the Act—

(a) section 4 (proposals for pilot schemes), in so far as it is not already in force; and

(b) section 16 (NHS contracts), in so far as it relates to pilot schemes under which personal medical services are provided.

(2) 28th November 1997 is the day appointed for the coming into force of the following provisions of the Act—

(a) section 1 (pilot schemes) and section 2 (provision of personal medical services under a pilot scheme); and

(b) section 5 (approval of pilot schemes), section 6 (making of pilot schemes) and section 18(2)(b) (funding of preparatory work), in so far as those sections relate to pilot schemes under which personal medical services are provided.

Frank Dobson
One of Her Majesty's Principal Secretaries of State,
Department of Health

29th October 1997

BUILDING SOCIETIES

THE BUILDING SOCIETIES ACT 1997 (COMMENCEMENT NO. 3) ORDER 1997

(S.I. 1997 No. 2668 (C. 99))

Made - - - - - - *5th November 1997*

INTRODUCTION

This Order brings into force all remaining provisions of the Building Societies Act 1997 (c. 32). The provisions listed in Pt. I of the Schedule to the Order will come into force on December 1, 1997. Part II provisions will come into force in accordance with art. 2(2), (3) and (5) and those in Pt. III in accordance with art. 2(6).

The Treasury, in exercise of the powers conferred on them by section 47(3) of the Building Societies Act 1997 (c. 32), hereby make the following Order:

Citation and interpretation

1.—(1) This Order may be cited as the Building Societies Act 1997 (Commencement No. 3) Order 1997.

(2) In this Order "the Act" means the Building Societies Act 1997 and "the 1986 Act" means the Building Societies Act 1986 (c. 53).

Coming into force of provisions

2.—(1) The provisions of the Act specified in Part I of the Schedule to this Order shall come into force, subject to paragraph (7) below, on 1st December 1997.

(2) In the case of any existing building society which sends the central office a record of alterations to its purpose or principal purpose, its powers and its rules, in accordance with paragraph 1(1) of Schedule 8 to the Act, where—

(a) the alterations are specified as taking effect on or before 1st December 1997; and

(b) the record of the alterations is registered by the central office under paragraph 1(3) of Schedule 8 to the Act on or before 1st December 1997,

the provisions of the Act specified in Part II of the Schedule to this Order shall come into force for all purposes, subject to paragraph (7) below, on 1st December 1997.

(3) In the case of any other existing building society, the provisions of the Act specified in Part II of the Schedule to this Order shall come into force for all purposes, except for the purpose and to the extent stated in paragraph (4) below and subject to paragraph (7) below, on the date on which the record of alterations to its purpose or principal purpose, its powers and its rules takes effect under paragraph 1(5) or 2(6) of Schedule 8 to the Act, or as the case may be, is registered under paragraph 3(3)(a) of that Schedule.

(4) For the purpose of ending the period mentioned in paragraph 1(1) of Schedule 8 to the Act and of construing the definitions of "existing building society" and "the transitional period" in paragraph 2(7) or 3(6) of that Schedule, sections 1 and 2 of the Act shall come into force in the case of a building society falling within paragraph (3) above on 1st December 1997.

(5) In the case of any building society registered after 30th November 1997 the provisions of the Act specified in Part II of the Schedule to this Order shall come into force for all purposes, subject to paragraph (7) below, on 1st December 1997.

(6) The provisions of the Act specified in Part III of the Schedule to this Order shall come into force on the day after the transitional period defined in paragraph 2(7) of Schedule 8 to the Act ends.

(7) Where an entry in the Schedule is stated to come into force for specified purposes or to a specified extent, it shall come into force only for those purposes or to that extent.

Jon Owen Jones
John McFall
Two of the Lords Commissioners
of Her Majesty's Treasury

5th November 1997

Article 2   THE SCHEDULE

PART I

PROVISIONS COMING INTO FORCE ON 1ST DECEMBER 1997

Provision		*Subject matter*
(a)	Section 7 and Schedule 2.	Discharge of mortgages.
(b)	Section 12(1)(a), so far as it relates to section 13(7) of and Schedule 4 to the 1986 Act.	Superseded provisions of 1986 Act (supplementary provisions as to mortgages).
(c)	Section 12(2) and (4).	Superseded provisions of 1986 Act (duties of mortgagee).
(d)	Section 22.	Statements of principles etc. by Commission.
(e)	Section 30 and Schedule 5.	Information about transfers or proposed transfers of business.
(f)	Section 34.	Recognised schemes for investigation of complaints.
(g)	Section 35.	Persons entitled to have complaints investigated.
(h)	Section 36.	Registered and business names.
(i)	Section 39 and Schedule 6.	Application of certain insolvency legislation.
(j)	Section 43, so far as it relates to the provisions of Schedule 7 specified in this Part of this Schedule.	Amendments of the 1986 Act.
(k)	Section 46, so far as it relates to the provisions of Schedule 8 and 9 specified in this Part of this Schedule.	Transitional provisions, savings and repeals, etc.
(l)	In Schedule 7—	
(i)	Paragraph 3(4).	Authorisation to raise funds and borrow money.
(ii)	Paragraph 4.	The Building Societies Investor Protection Board.
(iii)	Paragraph 7(2), (3) and (4).	Payments to investors.
(iv)	Paragraph 10.	Power to obtain information.
(v)	Paragraph 14, so far as not already in force.	Revocation of authorisation.
(vi)	Paragraph 15(2).	Reauthorisation.
(vii)	Paragraph 36.	Investigation of complaints: supplementary provisions.
(viii)	Paragraph 41(a).	Amalgamations.
(ix)	Paragraph 43.	Mergers: provisions supplementing sections 93 and 94.

Provision		Subject matter
(x)	Paragraph 44.	Mergers: compensation for loss of office etc.
(xi)	Paragraph 46.	Regulated terms: compensation for loss of office etc.
(xii)	Paragraph 48.	Power to amend etc. to assimilate to company law.
(xiii)	Paragraph 50.	Power to require building society to change misleading name.
(xiv)	Paragraph 53, so far as not already in force, for the purpose of defining expressions used in provisions falling within this Part of this Schedule.	Interpretation.
(xv)	Paragraph 61.	Auditors: appointment, tenure and qualifications.
(xvi)	Paragraph 62.	Schemes for investigation of complaints.
(xvii)	Paragraph 63.	Recognition etc. of schemes for investigation of complaints.
(xviii)	Paragraph 64(5).	Settlement of disputes.
(xix)	Paragraph 65.	Application of companies winding up legislation to building societies.
(xx)	Paragraph 66(1)(b), (2), (3) and (4).	Mergers: supplementary provisions.
(xxi)	Paragraph 67(b), so far as it relates to paragraphs 2 to 4 and 18 of Schedule 20 to the 1986 Act.	Transitional and saving provisions.

(m) In Schedule 8—

(i)	Paragraph 2.	Alteration of purpose, powers and rules.
(ii)	Paragraph 3.	Default powers.

(n) In Schedule 9, the repeal and revocation of the following provisions—

    (i)   Section 86 of the Solicitors Act 1974 (c. 47).

    (ii)   Regulation 41(5) of the Credit Institutions (Protection of Depositors) Regulations 1995 (S.I. 1995 No. 1442).

(o) In Schedule 9, the repeals of the following provisions of the 1986 Act—

    (i)   In Part III, section 13(7) and Schedule 4.

    (ii)   In section 28(2), the words "as in respect of a contractual debt incurred immediately before the institution began to be wound up".

    (iii)   In section 41, subsections (14) to (16).

Provision	Subject matter
(iv)	Section 84(1).
(v)	In section 95, subsections (7) to (9).
(vi)	Section 108.
(vii)	In section 119(3)(a), the words "by him" and "to him".
(viii)	In Schedule 12, Part II.
(ix)	In Schedule 16, paragraph 1(5).
(x)	In Schedule 20, paragraphs 2 to 4 and 18.

PART II

PROVISIONS COMING INTO FORCE IN ACCORDANCE WITH ARTICLE 2(2), (3) AND (5)

Provision	Subject matter
(a) Section 1.	Principal purpose and powers.
(b) Section 2.	Membership and liability of members.
(c) Section 3 and Schedule 1.	Capacity etc.
(d) Section 4.	The lending limit.
(e) Section 5.	Loans secured on land.
(f) Section 6.	Loans fully secured on land.
(g) Section 8.	The funding limit.
(h) Section 9.	Raising funds and borrowing.
(i) Section 10.	Restrictions on certain transactions.
(j) Section 12(1), so far as not already in force, and (3).	Superseded provisions of the 1986 Act.
(k) Section 13 and Schedule 3.	Power to direct restructuring of business etc.
(l) Section 14.	Power to make prohibition orders.
(m) Section 15.	Power to petition for winding up etc.
(n) Section 21.	The criteria of prudent management.
(o) Section 23, so far as not already in force.	Rights of appeal.
(p) Section 24, so far as not already in force.	Determination of appeals.
(q) Section 25.	Special meeting on members' requisition.
(r) Section 26.	Failure to comply with members' requisition.
(s) Section 27.	Election of directors: general.
(t) Section 28.	Election of directors: supplementary.
(u) Section 29.	Acquisition or establishment of a business.
(v) Section 38.	Transactions with directors and persons connected with them.

Provision		Subject matter
(w)	Section 43, so far as it relates to the provisions of Schedule 7 specified in this Part of this Schedule.	Amendments of the 1986 Act.
(x)	Section 45(2).	Amendment of the Finance Act 1988 (c. 39).
(y)	Section 46, so far as it relates to the provisions of Schedules 8 and 9 specified in this Part of this Schedule.	Transitional provisions, savings and repeals etc.
(z)	In Schedule 7—	
	(i) Paragraph 1.	The Building Societies Commission.
	(ii) Paragraph 3(1), (2) and (3).	Authorisation to raise funds and borrow money.
	(iii) Paragraph 11.	Voluntary schemes.
	(iv) Paragraph 12(2), (4) and (5).	Power to direct application to renew authorisation.
	(v) Paragraph 13(1).	Imposition of conditions on current authorisation.
	(vi) Paragraph 15(1), (3) and (4).	Reauthorisation.
	(vii) Paragraph 16.	Powers to avoid apparent association with other bodies.
	(viii) Paragraph 17, so far as not already in force.	Powers to obtain information and documents etc.
	(ix) Paragraph 19(3).	Confidentiality of information obtained by the Commission.
	(x) Paragraph 21.	Investigation on behalf of the Commission.
	(xi) Paragraph 22.	Inspections and special meetings: general.
	(xii) Paragraph 23.	Inspections: supplementary provisions.
	(xiii) Paragraph 24.	Restrictions on loans etc. to directors.
	(xiv) Paragraph 25.	Directors etc. not to accept commissions in connection with loans.
	(xv) Paragraph 27(1).	Records of income of related business.
	(xvi) Paragraph 29(1), (3) and (4).	Accounting records and systems of business control etc.
	(xvii) Paragraph 30.	Contents and form of annual accounts.
	(xviii) Paragraph 31.	Duty of directors to prepare annual business statement.
	(xix) Paragraph 32.	Directors' Report.
	(xx) Paragraph 33(1).	Summary financial statement for members and depositors.
	(xxi) Paragraph 34.	Auditor's report and powers.
	(xxii) Paragraph 35.	Auditor's duties to Commission and related rights.
	(xxiii) Paragraph 39.	Winding up: grounds and petitioners.
	(xxiv) Paragraph 40.	Winding up or dissolution: supplementary.
	(xxv) Paragraph 41(b).	Amalgamations.

Provision		Subject matter
(xxvi)	Paragraph 42.	Transfer of engagements.
(xxvii)	Paragraph 45(2) and (3).	Transfer of business to commercial company.
(xxviii)	Paragraph 47.	Distribution and share rights.
(xxix)	Paragraph 49.	Limited power to anticipate future statutory instrument powers.
(xxx)	Paragraph 52.	Qualifying asset holding for certain powers.
(xxxi)	Paragraph 53, so far as not already in force.	Interpretation.
(xxxii)	Paragraph 54.	Northern Ireland.
(xxxiii)	Paragraph 56, so far as not already in force.	Establishment, incorporation and constitution.
(xxxiv)	Paragraph 57.	Meetings, resolutions and postal ballots.
(xxxv)	Paragraph 59.	Directors: requisite particulars of restricted transactions.
(xxxvi)	Paragraph 60(2) and (3).	Requisite particulars of income of related business.
(xxxvii)	Paragraph 64(1), (2), (3) and (4).	Settlement of disputes.
(xxxviii)	Paragraph 66(1)(a).	Mergers: supplementary provisions.
(xxxix)	Paragraph 67(a) and, so far as it relates to paragraphs 7 to 13, 15 and 17 of Schedule 20 to the 1986 Act, (b).	Transitional and saving provisions.

(aa) In Schedule 8—

(i)	Paragraph 4.	Existing members to whom advances have been made.
(ii)	Paragraph 5.	Existing borrowing members which are corporations.
(iii)	Paragraph 6.	Existing fully secured loans.
(iv)	Paragraph 7.	Existing shareholders.
(v)	Paragraph 8.	Existing depositors and shareholders.

(bb) In Schedule 9, the repeals and revocation of the following provisions—

(i)	Section 3(1)(b) of the House Purchase Assistance and Housing Corporation Guarantee Act 1978 (c. 27).	

Provision	*Subject matter*
(ii)	Article 155 of the Housing (Northern Ireland) Order 1981 (S.I. 1981 No. 156 (N.I. 3)).
(iii)	Section 450 of the Housing Act 1985 (c. 68).
(iv)	In the Banking Act 1987 (c. 22), paragraph 26(1) and (8) of Schedule 6.
(v)	In the Deregulation and Contracting Out Act 1994 (c. 40), sections 16 and 17 and paragraph 7(6) of Schedule 11.
(cc) In Schedule 9, the repeals of the following provisions of the 1986 Act—	
(i)	In section 9(3), paragraph (d) and the word "or" immediately preceding that paragraph.
(ii)	Part III, so far as not already repealed.
(iii)	Section 33.
(iv)	Part V.
(v)	Sections 38 to 40.
(vi)	Section 51.
(vii)	Section 52(3).
(viii)	In section 60(17), the definition of "ordinary resolution".
(ix)	In section 65(10), the word "and" immediately following the definition of "provision of funds".
(x)	Section 71(10A).
(xi)	Section 79(5).
(xii)	In section 82, in subsection (2), paragraph (c) and the word "and" immediately preceding that paragraph and, in subsection (3), paragraph (d).
(xiii)	In section 97(3), the words from "and for the purposes" to the end.
(xiv)	Section 105.

Provision	Subject matter
(xv)	Section 118.
(xvi)	In section 119, in subsection (1), the definitions of "adopt", "adopted", "adoptable powers", "advance secured on land", "advance fully secured on land", "advance secured on third party land", "mobile home loan", "qualifying asset holding", "subsidiary" and "total commercial assets".
(xvii)	In section 122(1), the words "section 15,".
(xviii)	In Schedule 2, paragraph 2(5), in paragraph 4(4), the words "subject to paragraph 19 below" and, in paragraph 30(3), the words "has been duly given".
(xix)	In Schedule 10, in paragraphs 1, 2, 5 and 6, the words "under section 6, 10, 17 or 19".
(xx)	In Schedule 18, paragraphs 18(4) and 23(3).
(xxi)	In Schedule 20, in paragraph 1, the definitions of "existing society" and "existing rules", and paragraphs 7 to 13, 15 and 17.

PART III

PROVISIONS COMING INTO FORCE IN ACCORDANCE WITH ARTICLE 2(6)

Provision	Subject matter
(a) Section 43, so far as not already in force.	
(b) Section 46, so far as not already in force.	
(c) In Schedule 7, paragraph 2.	Annual report of the Commission.
(d) In Schedule 7, paragraph 67(b), so far as it relates to paragraph 14 of Schedule 20 to the 1986 Act.	Transitional and saving provisions.
(e) In Schedule 9, the repeal of section 4(2) of the 1986 Act.	
(f) In Schedule 9, the repeal of paragraph 14 of Schedule 20 to the 1986 Act.	

SOCIAL SECURITY

THE SOCIAL SECURITY ADMINISTRATION (FRAUD) ACT 1997 (COMMENCEMENT NO. 4) ORDER 1997

(S.I. 1997 No. 2669 (C. 100))

Made -   -   -   -   -   -   6th November 1997

INTRODUCTION
  This Order brings into force on November 7, 1997, s.19 of the Social Security Administration (Fraud) Act 1997 (c. 47) for the purpose of making regulations. This section, which concerns a requirement to state national insurance number, comes into force for all other purposes on December 1, 1997.

The Secretary of State for Social Security, in exercise of the powers conferred on her by section 25(1) and (2) of the Social Security Administration (Fraud) Act 1997 (c. 47) and of all other powers enabling her in that behalf, hereby makes the following Order:

Citation

  1. This Order may be cited as the Social Security Administration (Fraud) Act 1997 (Commencement No. 4) Order 1997.

Appointed days

  2. The day appointed for the coming into force of section 19 of the Act (requirement to state national insurance number)—
  (a) for the purposes only of authorising the making of regulations is 7th November 1997; and
  (b) for all other purposes is 1st December 1997.

Signed by authority of the Secretary of State for Social Security.

John Y. Denham
Parliamentary Under-Secretary of State,
Department of Social Security

6th November 1997

CRIMINAL LAW, SCOTLAND

THE CRIME AND PUNISHMENT (SCOTLAND) ACT 1997 (COMMENCEMENT NO. 3) ORDER 1997

(S.I. 1997 No. 2694 (C. 101) (S. 170))

Made - - - - - - *10th November 1997*

INTRODUCTION

This Order brings into force on November 17, 1997, ss.47 (remainder) (record of evidence taken from external parts of body), 48 (samples, etc. from persons convicted of sexual and violent offences) and a related repeal specified in Sched. 3 to, the Crime and Punishment (Scotland) Act 1997 (c. 48).

The Secretary of State, in exercise of the powers conferred upon him by section 65(2) of the Crime and Punishment (Scotland) Act 1997 (c. 48) and of all other powers enabling him in that behalf, hereby makes the following Order:

Citation and interpretation

1.—(1) This Order may be cited as the Crime and Punishment (Scotland) Act 1997 (Commencement No. 3) Order 1997.

(2) In this Order "the Act" means the Crime and Punishment (Scotland) Act 1997.

Commencement

2.—(1) The provisions of the Act which are listed in paragraph (2) below shall come into force on 17th November 1997.

(2) The provisions referred to in paragraph (1) above are—

(a) section 47 (record of evidence taken from external parts of body) insofar as not already in force;

(b) section 48 (samples etc. from persons convicted of sexual and violent offences);

(c) section 62(2) (repeals) so far as it relates to the entry referred to in sub-paragraph (d) below; and

(d) in Schedule 3 (repeals) the entry in respect of section 18(7) of the Criminal Procedure (Scotland) Act 1995 (c. 46).

St Andrew's House, Edinburgh
10th November 1997

Henry B McLeish
Minister of State,
Scottish Office

INCOME TAX
INHERITANCE TAX
TAXES

THE FINANCE ACT 1989, SECTION 178(1), (APPOINTED DAY) ORDER 1997

(S.I. 1997 No. 2708 (C. 102))

Made - - - - - - *17th November 1997*

INTRODUCTION

This Order appoints December 9, 1997, as the day for periods beginning on or after which s.178(1) of the Finance Act 1989 (c. 26) shall have effect for the purposes of s.118F of the Income and Corporation Taxes Act 1988 (c. 1).

The Treasury, in exercise of the powers conferred on them by section 178(7) of the Finance Act 1989 (c. 26; s.178 was amended by para. 107 of Sched. 2 to the Social Security (Consequential Provisions) Act 1992 (c. 6), para. 19(4) of Sched. 10 to the Taxation of Chargeable Gains Act 1992 (c. 12), para. 5 of Sched. 11 to the Finance (No. 2) Act 1992 (c. 48), para. 44 of Sched. 19 to the Finance Act 1994 (c. 9), and by para. 30 of Sched. 7, para. 13 of Sched. 18, para. 8 of Sched. 29 and Pt. V(2) and (8) of Sched. 41, to the Finance Act 1996 (c. 8)), hereby make the following Order:

1. This Order may be cited as the Finance Act 1989, section 178(1), (Appointed Day) Order 1997.

2. The day appointed for section 118F of the Income and Corporation Taxes Act 1988 (c. 1; ss.118A to 118K were inserted by para. 1 of Sched. 29 to the Finance Act 1996) for periods beginning on or after which section 178(1) of the Finance Act 1989 shall have effect is 9th December 1997.

Bob Ainsworth
Jon Owen Jones
Two of the Lords Commissioners
17th November 1997   of Her Majesty's Treasury

RATING AND VALUATION

THE LOCAL GOVERNMENT AND RATING ACT 1997 (COMMENCEMENT NO. 2) ORDER 1997

(S.I. 1997 No. 2752 (C. 103))

Made - - - - - - *18th November 1997*

INTRODUCTION

This Order brings into force on November 19, 1997, s.1 of and Sched. 1 to, the Local Government and Rating Act 1997 (c. 29), which provide for mandatory and discretionary relief from non-domestic rates for certain hereditaments in rural settlements in England and Wales. The relief will become available in the financial year beginning on April 1, 1998.

The Secretary of State, in exercise of the powers conferred on him by section 34(1) and (4) of the Local Government and Rating Act 1997 (c. 29) and of all other powers enabling him in that behalf, hereby makes the following Order:

Citation

1. This Order may be cited as the Local Government and Rating Act 1997 (Commencement No. 2) Order 1997.

Commencement of rural settlement provisions in England and Wales

2.—(1) Section 1 of the Local Government and Rating Act 1997 (which introduces Schedule 1) shall come into force on the day following the making of this Order.

(2) Notwithstanding paragraph (1) above, no rural settlement list shall have effect for a financial year before that beginning on 1st April 1998.

Signed by authority of the Secretary of State

Hilary Armstrong
Minister of State,
Department of the Environment,
Transport and the Regions

18th November 1997

SOCIAL SECURITY

THE SOCIAL SECURITY ADMINISTRATION (FRAUD) ACT 1997 (COMMENCEMENT NO. 5) ORDER 1997

(S.I. 1997 No. 2766 (C. 104))

Made -   -   -   -   -   -   *20th November 1997*

INTRODUCTION

This Order provides for the coming into force of s.15 of the Social Security Administration (Fraud) Act 1997 (c. 47), which concerns a penalty as an alternative to prosecution, for the purposes of making regulations on November 21, 1997, and for all other purposes on December 18, 1997. The Order also provides for the coming into force of a consequential amendment in Sched. 1, para. 8 on December 18, 1997.

The Secretary of State for Social Security, in exercise of the powers conferred on her by section 25(1) and (2) of the Social Security Administration (Fraud) Act 1997 (c. 47) and of all other powers enabling her in that behalf, hereby makes the following Order:

Citation and interpretation

1.—(1) This Order may be cited as the Social Security Administration (Fraud) Act 1997 (Commencement No. 5) Order 1997.

(2) In this Order, references to "the Act" are references to the Social Security Administration (Fraud) Act 1997.

Appointed days

2.—(1) The day appointed for the coming into force of section 15 of the Act (penalty as alternative to prosecution)—

(a) for the purposes only of authorising the making of regulations is 21st November 1997; and

(b) for all other purposes is 18th December 1997.

(2) The day appointed for the coming into force of paragraph 8 of Schedule 1 to the Act and section 22 of the Act in so far as it relates to that paragraph is 18th December 1997.

Signed by authority of the Secretary of State for Social Security.

John Y. Denham
Parliamentary Under-Secretary of State,
20th November 1997   Department of Social Security

EDUCATION, SCOTLAND

THE EDUCATION (SCHOOLS) ACT 1997 (COMMENCEMENT) ORDER 1997

(S.I. 1997 No. 2774 (C. 105) (S. 173))

Made -   -   -   -   -   -   *18th November 1997*

INTRODUCTION

This Order brings into force on December 1, 1997, the Education (Schools) Act 1997 (c. 59), ss.5(2) and 6(3) (in part) and Part II of the Schedule to the Act, which revokes provisions of the Education (Scotland) Act 1980 (c. 44) made redundant by the phasing out of the Assisted Places Scheme.

The Secretary of State, in exercise of the powers conferred on him by section 7(3)(b) of the Education (Schools) Act 1997 (c. 59) and of all other powers enabling him in that behalf, hereby makes the following Order:

Citation

1. This Order may be cited as the Education (Schools) Act 1997 (Commencement) Order 1997.

Commencement of provisions

2. The following provisions of the Education (Schools) Act 1997 shall come into force on 1st December 1997:
     section 5(2),
     section 6(3) so far as relating to Part II of the Schedule, and
     Part II of the Schedule.

St Andrew's House, Edinburgh
18th November 1997

Brian Wilson
Minister of State,
Scottish Office

RATING AND VALUATION

THE LOCAL GOVERNMENT AND RATING ACT 1997 (COMMENCEMENT NO. 3) ORDER 1997

(S.I. 1997 No. 2826 (C. 106) (S. 179))

Made -   -   -   -   -   -   *21st November 1997*

INTRODUCTION

  This Order brings into force on December 1, 1997, certain provisions of the Local Government and Rating Act 1997 (c. 29), which relate to Scotland only, concerning the new system of mandatory and discretionary relief from non-domestic rates for general stores and other rural settlements.

The Secretary of State, in exercise of the powers conferred on him by section 34(1) and (4) of the Local Government and Rating Act 1997 (c. 29) and of all other powers enabling him in that behalf, hereby makes the following Order:

Citation

  1. This Order may be cited as the Local Government and Rating Act 1997 (Commencement No. 3) Order 1997.

Commencement of provisions

  2. Subject to article 3 below, the following provisions of the Local Government and Rating Act 1997 shall come into force on 1st December 1997:
  (a) section 5 and Schedule 2 (relief from non-domestic rates for general stores etc. in rural settlements: Scotland);
  (b) section 8 (orders under section 6 and Schedule 2);
  (c) section 33(1) (minor and consequential amendments), insofar as it relates to the provision mentioned in paragraph (d) below; and
  (d) paragraph 29(b) of Schedule 3 (amendment of Schedule 12 to the Local Government Finance Act 1992 (c. 14)).

Transitional provision

  3. Nothing in article 2(a) above shall result in a rural settlement list having effect for a financial year which commenced prior to 1st April 1998.

Malcolm Chisholm

St Andrew's House, Edinburgh   Parliamentary Under Secretary of State,
21st November 1997   Scottish Office

LOCAL GOVERNMENT, ENGLAND AND WALES

THE LOCAL GOVERNMENT (CONTRACTS) ACT 1997 (COMMENCEMENT NO. 1) ORDER 1997

(S.I. 1997 No. 2843 (C. 107))

Made - - - - - - *28th November 1997*

INTRODUCTION

This Order brings into force ss.2 to 9 of the Local Government (Contracts) Act 1997 (c. 65) which make provision for safeguarding the interests of persons who enter into certain contracts with a local authority. Article 2(1) of the Order brings into force on December 1, 1997 certain powers for the Secretary of State to make regulations under s.3 of the Act. Article 2(2) brings into force on December 30, 1997 the other provisions of s.3 and ss.2 and 4 to 9 of the Act.

The Order extends only to England and Wales.

The Secretary of State, in exercise of the powers conferred on him by section 12(2) of the Local Government (Contracts) Act 1997 (c. 65) and of all other powers enabling him in that behalf, hereby makes the following Order:

Citation

1. This Order may be cited as the Local Government (Contracts) Act 1997 (Commencement No. 1) Order 1997.

Commencement

2.—(1) Sections 3(2)(e) and (f) and 3(3) of the Local Government (Contracts) Act 1997, in so far as they confer power on the Secretary of State to make regulations, shall come into force in England and Wales on 1st December 1997.

(2) Sections 2 and 4 to 9 of that Act, and section 3 of that Act except in so far as it is brought into force by paragraph (1), shall come into force in England and Wales on 30th December 1997.

Signed by authority of the Secretary of State

Hilary Armstrong
Minister of State,
Department of the Environment,
28th November 1997   Transport and the Regions

HOUSING, ENGLAND AND WALES

THE HOUSING GRANTS, CONSTRUCTION AND REGENERATION ACT 1996 (COMMENCEMENT NO. 3) ORDER 1997

(S.I. 1997 No. 2846 (C. 108))

Made - - - - - - *1st December 1997*

INTRODUCTION

This Order brings ss.131–140 of the Housing Grants, Construction and Regeneration Act 1996 (c. 53) into force on December 16, 1997, (insofar as they are not already in force). The sections concern relocation grants.

The Secretary of State, in exercise of the powers conferred on him by section 150(3) of the Housing Grants, Construction and Regeneration Act 1996 (c. 53), and of all other powers enabling him in that behalf, hereby makes the following Order:

Citation

1. This Order may be cited as the Housing Grants, Construction and Regeneration Act 1996 (Commencement No. 3) Order 1997.

Commencement

2. The following provisions of the Housing Grants, Construction and Regeneration Act 1996 shall come into force on 16th December 1997:
sections 131 to 135 insofar as they are not already in force,
sections 136 to 138, and
sections 139 and 140 insofar as they are not already in force.

Signed by authority of the Secretary of State

Hilary Armstrong
Minister of State,
Department of the Environment,
1st December 1997   Transport and the Regions

LOCAL GOVERNMENT, SCOTLAND

THE LOCAL GOVERNMENT (CONTRACTS) ACT 1997 (COMMENCEMENT NO. 2) ORDER 1997

(S.I. 1997 No. 2878 (C. 109) (S. 182))

Made - - - - - - *1st December 1997*

INTRODUCTION

This Order brings ss.2–9 (insofar as they are not already in force) of the Local Government (Contracts) Act 1997 (c. 65) into force in Scotland on December 2, 1997 and January 1, 1998. These sections concern the safeguarding of persons who enter into certain contracts with a local authority. The Act is now fully in force in consequence of this Order.

The Secretary of State, in exercise of the powers conferred on him by section 12(2) of the Local Government (Contracts) Act 1997 (c. 65) and of all other powers enabling him in that behalf, hereby makes the following Order:

Citation

1. This Order may be cited as the Local Government (Contracts) Act 1997 (Commencement No. 2) Order 1997.

Commencement

2.—(1) Subsections (2)(e) and (f) and (3) of section 3 of the Local Government (Contracts) Act 1997, insofar as they confer power on the Secretary of State to make regulations, shall come into force in Scotland on 2nd December 1997.

(2) Sections 2 and 4 to 9 of that Act, and section 3 of that Act except insofar as it is brought into force by paragraph (1) above, shall come into force in Scotland on 1st January 1998.

Malcolm Chisholm
St Andrew's House, Edinburgh   Parliamentary Under Secretary of State,
1st December 1997   Scottish Office

CRIMINAL LAW, SCOTLAND

THE CRIME AND PUNISHMENT (SCOTLAND) ACT 1997 (COMMENCEMENT NO. 4) ORDER 1997

(S.I. 1997 No. 3004 (C. 110) (S. 190))

Made - - - - - - *12th December 1997*

INTRODUCTION

This Order brings into force on January 1, 1998 s.25 of the Crime and Punishment (Scotland) Act 1997 (c. 48) which inserts certain provisions into the Criminal Procedure (Scotland) Act 1995 (c. 46) which relate to the setting up of the Scottish Criminal Cases Review Commission and s.63(1)(a)(ii) which relates to the finance of the Commission. It also brings into force s.62(1) and various paragraphs of Schedule 1 which concern consequential amendments.

The Secretary of State, in exercise of the powers conferred upon him by section 65(2) of the Crime and Punishment (Scotland) Act 1997 (c. 48) and of all other powers enabling him in that behalf, hereby makes the following Order:

Citation and interpretation

1.—(1) This Order may be cited as the Crime and Punishment (Scotland) Act 1997 (Commencement No. 4) Order 1997.

(2) In this Order—

"the Act" means the Crime and Punishment (Scotland) Act 1997; and

"the 1995 Act" means the Criminal Procedure (Scotland) Act 1995 (c. 46).

Commencement of provisions

2. The provisions of the Act which are specified in column 1 of the Schedule to this Order and whose subject matter is specified in column 2 of that Schedule shall, insofar as they are not then in force, come into force on 1st January 1998, but where a particular purpose is specified in relation to any provision in column 3 of that Schedule that provision shall come into force on that day only for that purpose.

Henry McLeish
St Andrew's House, Edinburgh   Minister of State,
12th December 1997   Scottish Office

Article 2   SCHEDULE

THE PROVISIONS OF THE ACT WHICH COME INTO FORCE ON 1ST JANUARY 1998

Column 1 *Provision of Act*	Column 2 *Subject Matter*	Column 3 *Purpose*
Section 25	Scottish Criminal Cases Review Commission	Only for the purpose of inserting sections 194A, 194E and 194G and Schedule 9A into the 1995 Act
Section 62(1)	Amendments	Only for the purpose of bringing into force the provisions of Schedule 1 to the Act specified or referred to in this Schedule
Section 63(1)(a)(ii) In Schedule 1, paragraphs 4, 5 and 7	Financial provisions Amendment of enactments	

LAND REGISTRATION

THE LAND REGISTRATION ACT 1997
(COMMENCEMENT) ORDER 1997

(S.I. 1997 No. 3036 (C. 111))

Made - - - - -	*9th December 1997*
Coming into force - - - -	*1st April 1998*

INTRODUCTION
  This Order brings into force the remaining provisions of the Land Registration Act 1997 (c. 2) on April 1, 1998.

The Lord Chancellor, in exercise of the powers conferred on him by section 5(2) of the Land Registration Act 1997 (c. 2), hereby makes the following Order—

1. This Order may be cited as the Land Registration Act 1997 (Commencement) Order 1997.

2. The following provisions of the Land Registration Act 1997—
(a) section 1,
(b) Part I of Schedule 1 and section 4(1) so far as relating thereto, and
(c) Part I of Schedule 2 and section 4(2) so far as relating thereto,
shall come into force on 1st April 1998.

3. Part I of Schedule 1 to, and section 4(1) (so far as relating thereto) of, the Land Registration Act 1997 shall apply only in relation to dispositions made on or after 1st April 1998.

Dated 9th December 1997

Irvine of Lairg, C.

ENVIRONMENTAL PROTECTION

THE ENVIRONMENT ACT 1995 (COMMENCEMENT NO. 10) ORDER 1997

(S.I. 1997 No. 3044 (C. 112))

Made - - - - - - *16th December 1997*

INTRODUCTION

This Order brings into force on December 23, 1997, all provisions of the Environment Act 1995 (c. 25) Part IV which are not already in force, and also s.4(4A) of the Environmental Protection Act 1990 (c. 43) requiring local authorities to have regard to the National Air Quality Strategy published under s.50 of the 1995 Act in relation to their powers to enforce air pollution controls.

The Secretary of State, in exercise of his powers under section 125(3) of the Environment Act 1995 (c. 25), hereby makes the following Order:

Citation

1. This Order may be cited as the Environment Act 1995 (Commencement No. 10) Order 1997.

Provisions coming into force on 23rd December 1997

2. The following provisions of the Environment Act 1995 shall come into force on 23rd December 1997:
    sections 82 to 86;
    section 90 and Schedule 11 insofar as they are not already in force;
    section 120(1) insofar as it relates to paragraph 46(5) of Schedule 22.

Signed by authority of the Secretary of State,

Michael Meacher
Minister of State,
Department of the Environment,
Transport and the Regions

16th December 1997

ANTARCTICA

THE ANTARCTIC ACT 1994 (COMMENCEMENT) (NO. 3) ORDER 1997

(S.I. 1997 No. 3068 (C. 113))

Made - - - - - *22nd December 1997*

INTRODUCTION

This Order brings into force ss.3 and 4 of the Antarctic Act 1994 (c. 15) on January 14, 1998 which relate to permits for Antarctic expeditions organised in or departing from the United Kingdom and permits for manned British stations in Antarctica. As from January 14, 1998 the whole Act will be in force.

The Secretary of State, in exercise of the powers conferred on him by section 35 of the Antarctic Act 1994 (c. 15), and of all other powers enabling him in that behalf, hereby makes the following Order:

Citation

1. This Order may be cited as the Antarctic Act 1994 (Commencement) (No. 3) Order 1997.

Commencement of Sections 3 and 4 of the Antarctic Act 1994

2. Sections 3 and 4 of the Antarctic Act 1994 shall come into force on 14th January 1998.

Tony Lloyd
For the Secretary of State for
Foreign and Commonwealth Affairs

22nd December 1997

MERCHANT SHIPPING

THE MERCHANT SHIPPING ACT 1995 (APPOINTED DAY NO. 2) ORDER 1997

(S.I. 1997 No. 3107 (C. 114))

Made - - - - - - *17th December 1997*

INTRODUCTION

This Order brings into force s.116 of the Merchant Shipping Act 1995 (c. 21) on February 1, 1998 which concerns the production of crew certificates and other documents of qualification.

The Secretary of State for Transport, in exercise of the power conferred by paragraph 5 of Schedule 14 of the Merchant Shipping Act 1995 (c. 21), hereby makes the following Order:

1. This Order may be cited as the Merchant Shipping Act 1995 (Appointed Day No. 2) Order 1997.

2. The day appointed for section 116 of the Merchant Shipping Act 1995 to come into force is 1st February 1998.

Signed by authority of the
Secretary of State for Transport

Glenda Jackson
Parliamentary Under Secretary of State,
Department of Environment,
17th December 1997
Transport and the Regions

CRIMINAL LAW, NORTHERN IRELAND

THE CRIMINAL PROCEDURE AND INVESTIGATIONS ACT 1996 (APPOINTED DAY NO. 7) ORDER 1997

(S.I. 1997 No. 3108 (C. 115))

Made - - - - - - *29th December 1997*

INTRODUCTION

This Order appoints January 1, 1998 for the purposes of Part I and ss.43 and 69 of the Criminal Procedure and Investigations Act 1996 (c. 25). It extends to Northern Ireland only. Part I relates to alleged offences into which no criminal investigation had begun before January 1, 1998; s.43 relates to pre-trial hearings beginning on or after January 1, 1998; and s.69 concerns statements tendered in evidence on or after January 1, 1998.

The Secretary of State, in exercise of the powers conferred on her by Sections 1(5), 43(2) and 69(3) of the Criminal Procedure and Investigations Act 1996 (c. 25), hereby makes the following Order:

1.—(1) This Order may be cited as the Criminal Procedure and Investigations Act 1996 (Appointed Day No. 7) Order 1997.

(2) This Order extends to Northern Ireland only.

2. 1st January 1998 is hereby appointed for the purposes of—

(a) Part I of, and

(b) Sections 43 (application of Part IV of the Act) and 69 of, the Criminal Procedure and Investigations Act 1996.

Northern Ireland Office
29th December 1997

Marjorie Mowlam
One of Her Majesty's
Principal Secretaries of State

ARMS AND AMMUNITION

THE FIREARMS (AMENDMENT) (NO. 2) ACT 1997 (COMMENCEMENT) ORDER 1997

(S.I. 1997 No. 3114 (C. 116))

Made - - - - - - *17th December 1997*

INTRODUCTION

This Order brings into force the provisions of the Firearms (Amendment) (No. 2) Act 1997 (c. 64). S.2 (part) and Sch. (part) shall come into force on December 17, 1997 subject to savings and ss.1, 2 (remainder) and Sch. (remainder) shall come into force on February 1, 1998. However, the latter provisions do not have effect until March 1, 1998 in the case of certain certificate or permit holders and registered firearms dealers.

The Secretary of State, in exercise of the powers conferred upon him by section 3(3) and (4) of the Firearms (Amendment) (No. 2) Act 1997 (c. 64), hereby makes the following Order:

1. This Order may be cited as the Firearms (Amendment) (No. 2) Act 1997 (Commencement) Order 1997.

2. In this Order "the 1997 (No. 2) Act" means the Firearms (Amendment) (No. 2) Act 1997.

3. The provisions of the 1997 (No. 2) Act specified in Part I of the Schedule to this Order shall come into force on 17th December 1997, save that:
  (a) subsections (3) and (4) of section 2 shall come into force on that date for the purposes only of making a compensation scheme, and
  (b) subsection (7) of section 2 shall come into force on that date to the extent only that it relates to the repeals listed in the said Part I.

4. Subject to article 5 below the provisions of the 1997 (No. 2) Act specified in Part II of the Schedule to this Order shall come into force on 1st February 1998.

5. The provisions referred to in article 4 above shall not have effect until 1st March 1998 in relation to—
  (a) the possession, sale or transfer of a small-calibre pistol by a person who, immediately before 1st February 1998, has the pistol in his possession by virtue of:
     (i) a firearm certificate or a visitor's firearm permit, or
     (ii) a permit issued under section 7 of the Firearms Act 1968 (c. 27), or
  (b) the possession, purchase, acquisition, sale or transfer of a small-calibre pistol by a registered firearms dealer.

Home Office   *Jack Straw*
17th December 1997   One of Her Majesty's Principal Secretaries of State

CURRENT LAW STATUTES

NUMERICAL TABLE OF STATUTORY INSTRUMENTS 1997

DOCUMENT DELIVERY

Copies of 1997 Statutory Instruments can be obtained from Legal Information Resources Ltd (part of Sweet & Maxwell). Please telephone for current rates and direct any orders to LIR on fax no. 01422 888001 or tel. no. 01422 888000.

This table details in numerical order Statutory Instruments released in 1997 and 1998. The table is up to date to **February 13, 1998** (Orders received). For brief digests of Statutory Instruments see the Current Law Monthly Digest.

1997

446...............City of Westminster (Trunk Roads) Red Route (Bus Lanes)
Traffic Order 1997
447...............Northampton Community Healthcare National Health Service Trust (Transfer of Trust Property) Order 1997
448...............Princess Alexandra Hospital National Health Service Trust
(Transfer of Trust Property) Order 1997
449...............London Borough of Haringey (Trunk Roads) Red Route (Bus
Lanes) Traffic Order 1997
450...............London Borough of Enfield (Trunk Roads) Red Route (Bus
Lanes) Traffic Order 1997
451...............Infant Formula and Follow-on Formula (Amendment) Regulations 1997
452 (S.34)....Non-domestic Rates (Levying) (Scotland) Regulations 1997
453...............Birmingham Heartlands and Solihull (Teaching) National
Health Service Trust (Transfer of Trusts Property) Order
1997
454...............Social Security (Miscellaneous Amendments) Regulation
1997
455...............Local Government Act 1988 (Defined Activities) (Exemption) (Lichfield District Council) Order 1997
456...............Wiltshire County Council (Borough of Thamesdown) (Staff
Transfer) Order 1997
457...............Guaranteed Minimum Pensions Increase Order 1997
458...............Dorset County Council (Boroughs of Poole and Bourne-
mouth) (Staff Transfer) Order 1997
459...............Derbyshire County Council (City of Derby) (Staff Transfer)
Order 1997
460...............Durham County Council (Borough of Darlington) (Staff
Transfer) Order 1997
461...............East Sussex County Council (Boroughs of Brighton and
Hove) (Staff Transfer) Order 1997
463...............London Borough of Camden (Trunk Roads) Red Route (Bus
Lanes) Traffic Order 1997
464...............A10 Trunk Road (Haringey) Red Route Traffic Order 1997
465...............A13 Trunk Road (Newham) Red Route Traffic Order 1997
466...............A13 Trunk Road (Tower Hamlets) Red Route Traffic Order
1997
467...............A41 Trunk Road (Barnet) Red Route Traffic Order 1997
468...............Hampshire County Council (Cities of Portsmouth and Southampton) (Staff Transfer) Order 1997
469...............Staffordshire County Council (City of Stoke-on-Trent) (Staff
Transfer) Order 1997
470...............Personal Pension Schemes (Appropriate Schemes) Regulations 1997
471...............Friendly Societies (Modification of the Corporation Tax Acts)
(Amendment) Regulations 1997
472...............Friendly Societies (Taxation of Transfers of Business)
(Amendment) Regulations 1997
473...............Friendly Societies (Modification of the Corporation Tax Acts)
Regulations 1997
474...............Friendly Societies (Provisional Repayments for Exempt Business) (Amendment) Regulations 1997
475...............Friendly Societies (Gilt-edged Securities) (Periodic Accounting for Tax on Interest) (Amendment) Regulations 1997
476...............Leicestershire County Council (City of Leicester and District
of Rutland) (Staff Transfer) Order 1997
477...............Injuries in War (Shore Employments) Compensation
(Amendment) Scheme 1997

624................Housing (Right to Acquire or Enfranchise) (Designated Rural Areas in the North East) Order 1997
625................Housing (Right to Acquire or Enfranchise) (Designated Rural Areas in the South East) Order 1997
626................Housing (Right to Acquire) (Discount) Order 1997
627................Housing Act 1996 (Consequential Amendments) (No. 2) Order 1997
628................Homelessness (Persons Subject to Immigration Control) (Amendment) Order 1997
629................Electricity and Pipe-line Works (Assessment of Environmental Effects) (Amendment) Regulations 1997
630................Measuring Instruments (EEC Requirements) (Fees) (Amendment) Regulations 1997
631................Allocation of Housing and Homelessness (Amendment) Regulations 1997
632................Street Litter Control Notices (Amendment) Order 1997
633................Litter Control Areas (Amendment) Order 1997
634................Pensions Increase (Review) Order 1997
635................Vocational Training (Public Financial Assistance and Disentitlement to Tax Relief) (Amendment) Regulations 1997
636................Divorce etc. (Pensions) (Amendment) Regulations 1997
637................Family Proceedings (Amendment) Rules 1997
638................Medicines (Medicated Animal Feeding Stuffs) (Amendment) Regulations 1997
639................Animals (Third Country Imports) (Charges) Regulations 1997
640................Leasehold Reform (Notices) Regulations 1997
641 (S.39)....New Town (Irvine) Dissolution Order 1997
642 (S.40)....New Town (Livingston) Dissolution Order 1997
643 (S.41)....New Town (Cumbernauld) Dissolution Order 1997
645................Child Maintenance Bonus (Northern Ireland Reciprocal Arrangements) Regulations 1997
646................National Health Service (Injury Benefits) Amendment Regulations 1997
647................Merchant Shipping (Ro-Ro Passenger Ship Survivability) Regulations 1997
648................Producer Responsibility Obligations (Packaging Waste) Regulations 1997
649................Adoption Agencies and Children (Arrangements for Placement and Reviews) (Miscellaneous Amendments) Regulations 1997
650................Motor Cars (Driving Instruction) (Amendment) Regulations 1997
651................Financial Assistance for Environmental Purposes Order 1997
652................National Health Service Trusts (Originating Capital Debt) Order 1997
653................Insurance (Fees) Regulations 1997
654................Good Laboratory Practice Regulations 1997
655................Plant Health (Fees) (Forestry) (Great Britain) (Amendment) Regulations 1997
656................Council Tax (Chargeable Dwellings, Exempt Dwellings and Discount Disregards) Amendment Order 1997
657................Council Tax (Additional Provisions for Discount Disregards) Amendment Regulations 1997
658................Wine and Made-wine (Amendment) Regulations 1997
659................Cider and Perry (Amendment) Regulations 1997
660................Capital Allowances (Corresponding Northern Ireland Grants) Order 1997

697 (S.56) ....National Health Service (Charges for Drugs and Appliances) (Scotland) Amendment Regulations 1997

698 (L.4)......Crown Court (Criminal Procedure and Investigations Act 1996) (Disclosure) Rules 1997

699 (L.5)......Crown Court (Criminal Procedure and Investigations Act 1996) (Confidentiality) Rules 1997

700 (L.6)......Crown Court (Advance Notice of Expert Evidence) (Amendment) Rules 1997

701 (L.7)......Crown Court (Amendment) Rules 1997

702 (L.8)......Criminal Appeal (Amendment) Rules 1997

703 (L.9)......Magistrates' Courts (Criminal Procedure and Investigations Act 1996) (Disclosure) Rules 1997

704 (L.10)....Magistrates' Courts (Criminal Procedure and Investigations Act 1996) (Confidentiality) Rules 1997

705 (L.11)....Magistrates' Courts (Advance Notice of Expert Evidence) Rules 1997

706 (L.12)....Magistrates' Courts (Amendment) Rules 1997

707...............Magistrates' Courts (Forms) (Amendment) Rules 1997

708 (L.13)....Magistrates' Court (Notices of Transfer) (Amendment) Rules 1997

709 (L.14)....Magistrates' Courts (Notice of Transfer) (Children's Evidence) (Amendment) Rules 1997

710 (L.15)....Justices' Clerks (Amendment) Rules 1997

711 (L.16)....Indictments (Procedure) (Amendment) Rules 1997

712...............Electricity Generating Stations and Overhead Lines and Pipe-Lines (Inquiries Procedure) (Amendment) Rules 1997

713...............Land Registration (Conduct of Business) Regulations 1997

714 (S.57) ....Reporters (Conduct of Proceedings before the Sheriff) (Scotland) Regulations 1997

715 (S.58) ....Grants for Pre-school Education (Scotland) Amendment Regulations 1997

716 (S.59) ....Registration of Births, Deaths, Marriages and Divorces (Fees) (Scotland) Regulations 1997

717 (S.60) ....Registration of Births, Deaths and Marriages (Fees) (Scotland) Order 1997

718 (S.61) ....Legal Aid in Contempt of Court Proceedings (Scotland) (Fees) Amendment Regulations 1997

719 (S.62) ....Criminal Legal Aid (Scotland) (Fees) Amendment Regulations 1997

720 (S.63) ....Local Government (Amendment of Regulations for Compensation on Reorganisation) (Scotland) Regulations 1997

721 (S.64) ....Police Grant (Scotland) Order 1997

722 (S.65) ....Rural Diversification Programme (Scotland) Amendment Regulations 1997

723...............Food Premises (Registration) Amendment Regulations 1997

724...............Pensions Compensation Board (Determinations and Review Procedure) Regulations 1997

725...............Combined Probation Areas (Cleveland-Teesside) Order 1997

726 (S.66) ....Advice and Assistance (Scotland) Amendment Regulations 1997

727 (S.67) ....Civil Legal Aid (Scotland) Amendment Regulations 1997

728 (S.68) ....Council Tax (Exempt Dwellings) (Scotland) Order 1997

729 (S.69) ....Reporters (Appeals against Dismissal) (Scotland) Regulations 1997

730...............National Health Service (General Medical Services) Amendment Regulations 1997

731...............Workmen's Compensation (Supplementation) (Amendment) Scheme 1997

732................Local Government Residuary Body (England) (Amendment) Order 1997
733................Dairy Produce Quotas Regulations 1997
734................Community Care (Direct Payments) Regulations 1997
735................Offshore Installations (Safety Zones) Order 1997
736................Severn Trent Water Limited (Extension of Byelaws) Order 1997
737................Criminal Justice Act 1987 (Notice of Transfer) (Amendment) Regulations 1997
738................Criminal Justice Act 1991 (Notice of Transfer) (Amendment) Regulations 1997
739................Prosecution of Offences (Revocation) Regulations 1997
740................Building Societies (General Charge and Fees) Regulations 1997
741................Friendly Societies (General Charge and Fees) Regulations 1997
742................Industrial and Provident Societies (Credit Unions) (Amendment of Fees) Regulations 1997
743................Industrial and Provident Societies (Amendment of Fees) Regulations 1997
744 (C.27) (S.70) Children (Scotland) Act 1995 (Commencement No.3) (Amendment and Transitional Provisions) Order 1997
745 (S.71) ....Divorce etc. (Pensions) (Scotland) Amendment Regulations 1997
746................United Kingdom Central Council for Nursing, Midwifery and Health Visiting (Electoral Scheme) Variation Order 1997
747................NHS (Fund-holding Practices) Amendment Regulations 1997
748................National Health Service (Travelling Expenses and Remission of Charges) Amendment Regulations 1997
749 (S.72) ....Town and Country Planning (General Development Procedure) (Scotland) Amendment Regulations 1997
750 (S.73) ....Town and Country Planning Appeals (Determination by Appointed Person) (Inquiries Procedure) (Scotland) Rules 1997
751................Legal Advice and Assistance (Amendment) Regulations 1997
752................Legal Aid in Criminal and Care Proceedings (General) (Amendment) Regulations 1997
753................Civil Legal Aid (Assessment of Resources) (Amendment) Regulations 1997
754................Legal Aid in Criminal and Care Proceedings (Costs) (Amendment) Regulations 1997
755................Education (School Teachers' Pay and Conditions) Order 1997
756 (C.28)....Community Care (Direct Payments) Act 1996 (Commencement) Order 1997
757................Enzootic Bovine Leukosis Order 1997
758................Brucellosis Order 1997
759................Isles of Scilly (Direct Payments Act) Order 1997
760 (C.29)....Treasure Act 1996 (Commencement No.1) Order 1997
761................City of Manchester (Egerton Street Service Bridge Scheme) 1994 Confirmation Instrument 1997
762................City of Manchester (Egerton Street West Bridge Scheme) 1994 Confirmation Instrument 1997
763................A127 Trunk Road (M25 to Rayleigh Section and Slip Roads) (Detrunking) Order 1997
774................Parliamentary Elections (Returning Officer's Charges) (Northern Ireland) Order 1997
775................Borough of Thurrock (Electoral Changes) Order 1997
776................District of the Medway Towns (Parishes and Electoral Changes) Order 1997

814................Sweeteners in Food (Amendment) Regulations 1997
815................Motor Vehicle Tyres (Safety) (Amendment) Regulations 1997
816................Financial Services Act 1986 (Corporate Debt Exemption) Order 1997
817................Banking Act 1987 (Exempt Transactions) Regulations 1997
818................National Health Service (Optical Charges and Payments) Regulations 1997
819................Occupational Pension Schemes (Reference Scheme and Miscellaneous Amendments) Regulations 1997
820................Social Security (Contributions) Amendment (No.3) Regulations 1997
821................Channel Tunnel Rail Link (Planning Appeals) Regulations 1997
822................Channel Tunnel Rail Link (Fees for Requests for Planning Approval) Regulations 1997
823................Workmen's Compensation (Supplementation) (Amendment) (No. 2) Scheme 1997
824................Pneumoconiosis, Byssinosis and Miscellaneous Diseases Benefit (Amendment) Scheme 1997
826................Gas (Extent of Domestic Supply Licences) Order 1997
827................Social Security and Child Support (Miscellaneous Amendments) Regulations 1997
828................Farm Woodland (Amendment) Scheme 1997
829................Farm Woodland Premium Scheme 1997
830 (S.77)....Loch Ewe, Isle of Ewe, Wester Ross, Scallops Several Fishery Order 1997
831................Lifts Regulations 1997
832................West Cheshire National Health Service Trust Dissolution Order 1997
833................Wirral and West Cheshire Community National Health Service Trust (Establishment) Order 1997
834................Wirral Community Healthcare National Health Service Trust Dissolution Order 1997
835................Calderdale Healthcare National Health Service Trust (Establishment) Amendment Order 1997
836................Worcester Royal Infirmary National Health Service Trust (Establishment) Amendment Order 1997
837................Carlisle Hospitals National Health Service Trust (Establishment) Amendment Order 1997
838................Caribbean Development Bank (Further Payments) Order 1997
839................African Development Fund (Seventh Replenishment) Order 1997
840................International Development Association (Interim Trust Fund) Order 1997
841 (C.30)....Civil Procedure Act 1997 (Commencement No.1) Order 1997
842................A406 London North Circular Trunk Road (East London River Crossing (A13 to A2)) Orders 1988 and 1991, Revocation Order 1997
844................Registration of Births and Deaths (Amendment) Regulations 1997
845................Local Government Act 1988 (Defined Activities) (Exemption) (Rushcliffe Borough Council) Order 1997
846................Motor Vehicles (Driving Licences) (Amendment) (No.3) Regulations 1997
847................M4 Motorway (Heathrow Airport Spur Road) (Bus Lane) Regulations 1997

883................Sea Fishing (Enforcement of Community Quota Measures) Order 1997

884................Plant Protection Products (Fees) (Amendment) Regulations 1997

886................Public Telecommunication System Designated (ACC Long Distance UK Ltd) Order 1997

887................Public Telecommunication System Designated (AT & T Communications (UK) Ltd) Order 1997

888................Public Telecommunication System Designated (CableTel (UK) Ltd) Order 1997

889................Public Telecommunication System Designated (COLT Telecommunications) Order 1997

890................Public Telecommunication System Designation (Communicorp (UK) Ltd) Order 1997

891................Public Telecommunication System Designation (Concert Communications Company) Order 1997

892................Public Telecommunication System Designation (Convergence Ventures Ltd) Order 1997

893................Public Telecommunication System Designation (Energis Communications Ltd) Order 1997

894................Public Telecommunication System Designation (Esat Telecommunications (UK) Ltd) Order 1997

895................Public Telecommunication System Designation (Esprit Telecom UK Ltd) Order 1997

896................Public Telecommunication System Designation (Eurotunnel) Order 1997

897................Public Telecommunication System Designation (Facilicom International (UK) Ltd) Order 1997

898................Public Telecommunication System Designation (Frontel Newco Ltd) Order 1997

899................Public Telecommunication System Designation (Global One Communications Holding Ltd) Order 1997

900................Public Telecommunication System Designation (Hermes Europe Railtel B.V.) Order 1997

901................Public Telecommunication System Designation (Spacetel International Ltd) Order 1997

902................Public Telecommunication System Designation (Scottish Power Telecommunications Ltd) Order 1997

903................Public Telecommunication System Designation (RSL Communications Ltd) Order 1997

904................Public Telecommunication System Designation (Racal Telecommunications Ltd) Order 1997

905................Public Telecommunication System Designation (Primus Telecommunications Ltd) Order 1997

906................Public Telecommunication System Designation (MCI Telecommunications Ltd) Order 1997

907................Public Telecommunication System Designation (National Transcommunications Ltd) Order 1997

908................Public Telecommunication System Designation (MFS Telecommunications Ltd) Order 1997

909................Public Telecommunication System Designation (L D I Communications Ltd) Order 1997

910................Public Telecommunication System Designation (Pacific Gateway Exchange (UK) Ltd) Order 1997

911................Public Telecommunication System Designation (Interoute Networks Ltd) Order 1997

912................Public Telecommunication System Designation (Incom (UK) Ltd) Order 1997

1015 (C.35)....Finance Act 1996, section 197, (Appointed Day) Order 1997
1016...............Air Passenger Duty and other Indirect Taxes (Interest Rate) Regulations 1997
1019 (C.36)....Criminal Procedure and Investigations Act 1996 (Appointed Day No.4) Order 1997
1033...............Criminal Procedure and Investigations Act 1996 (Code of Practice) (No. 2) Order 1997
1034...............Parliamentary Elections (Returning Officers' Charges) Order 1997
1045...............Social Security (Contributions) Amendment (No.4) Regulations 1997
1046...............Northern Ireland (Entry to Negotiations, etc) Act 1996 (Cessation of Section 3) Order 1997
1048 (S.93)....British Gas plc (Rateable Values) (Scotland) Amendment Order 1997
1049 (S.94)....Education Authority Bursaries and Students' Allowances (Scotland) Amendment Regulations 1997
1050 (S.95)....Act of Sederunt (Rules of the Court of Session Amendment No. 4) (Miscellaneous) 1997
1051 (L.19)....Criminal Justice Act 1987 (Preparatory Hearings) Rules 1997
1052 (L.20)....Criminal Procedure and Investigations Act 1996 (Preparatory Hearings) Rules 1997
1053 (L.21)....Criminal Procedure and Investigations Act 1996 (Preparatory Hearings) (Interlocutory Appeals) Rules 1997
1054 (L.22)....Crown Court (Criminal Procedure and Investigations Act 1996) (Tainted Acquittals) Rules 1997
1055 (L.23)....Magistrates' Courts (Criminal Procedure and Investigations Act 1996) (Tainted Acquittals) Rules 1997
1056 (L.24)....Family Proceedings (Amendment No. 2) Rules 1997
1059...............Combined Probation Areas (West Midlands) Order 1997
1060...............Data Protection (Regulation of Financial Services etc) (Subject Access Exemption) (Amendment) Order 1997
1071...............Licensed Betting Offices (Amendment) Regulations 1997
1072...............Gaming (Records of Cheques and Debit Card Payments) Regulations 1997
1073...............Deregulation (Football Pools) Order 1997
1074...............Deregulation (Betting and Bingo Advertising etc) Order 1997
1075...............Deregulation (Casinos and Bingo Clubs: Debit Cards) Order 1997
1076 (C.37)....Firearms (Amendment) Act 1997 (Commencement) (No. 1) Order 1997
1077 (C.38)....Family Law Act 1996 (Commencement No. 1) Order 1997
1078...............Legal Aid (Mediation in Family Matters) Regulations 1997
1079...............Civil Legal Aid (General) (Amendment No. 2) Regulations 1997
1080 (L.25)....Family Proceedings Fees (Amendment) (No. 2) Order 1997
1081...............Timeshare Regulations 1997
1082 (C.39)....Merchant Shipping and Maritime Security Act 1997 (Commencement No. 1) Order 1997
1083...............Essex and Herts Community National Health Service Trust (Transfer of Trust Property) Order 1997
1084 (S.96)....Reporters (Conduct of Proceedings before the Sheriff) (Scotland) (Amendment) Regulations 1997
1085...............Civil Courts (Amendment) (No. 2) Order 1997
1086...............Value Added Tax (Amendment) Regulations 1997
1091...............Sheffield Development Corporation (Dissolution) Order 1997
1092...............Local Government Act 1988 (Defined Activities) (Exemption) (Daventry District Council) Order 1997

1306................Southern Sea Fisheries District (Constitution of Committee and Expenses) (Variation) Order 1997

1307 (C.45)....Building Societies Act 1997 (Commencement No. 1) Order 1997

1308................Wiltshire Health Authority (Transfers of Trust Property) Order 1997

1313................Companies Overseas Branch Registers (Hong Kong) Order 1997

1314................Consular Fees Order 1997

1315 (C.46)....Medical (Professional Performance) Act 1995 (Commencement No. 3) Order 1997

1316................Criminal Justice Act 1988 (Designated Countries and Territories) (Amendment) Order 1997

1317................Criminal Justice (International Co-operation) Act 1990 (Enforcement of Overseas Forfeiture Orders) (Amendment) Order 1997

1318................Drug Trafficking Act 1994 (Designated Countries and Territories) (Amendment) Order 1997

1319................European Convention on Cinematographic Co-production (Amendment) (No. 2) Order 1997

1320................Merchant Shipping (Safe Manning, Hours of Work and Watchkeeping) Regulations 1997

1322 (C.47) (S.106) Flood Prevention and Land Drainage (Scotland) Act 1997 (Commencement) Order 1997

1325................Leicestershire Ambulance and Paramedic Service National Health Service (Establishment) Amendment Order 1997

1326................Gloucestershire Health Authority (Transfers of Trust Property) Order 1997

1328................British Nationality (Fees) (Amendment) Order 1997

1329................Stock Transfer (Gilt-edged Securities) (CGO Service) (Amendment) Regulations 1997

1330................A501 Trunk Road (Euston Road, Camden and Westminster) Red Route (Prescribed Route and Prohibited Turn) Traffic Order 1997

1331................Surface Waters (Fishlife) (Classification) Regulations 1997

1332................Surface Waters (Shellfish) (Classification) Regulations 1997

1333................Listed Events (Prescribed Multiplier) Order 1997

1334................Hong Kong Economic and Trade Office (Exemptions and Reliefs) Order 1997

1335................Novel Foods and Novel Food Ingredients Regulations 1997

1336................Novel Foods and Novel Food Ingredients Regulations (Fees) 1997

1337................Home-Grown Cereals Authority (Rate of Levy) Order 1997

1340................Road Vehicles (Construction and Use) (Amendment) (No. 3) Regulations 1997

1341................Merchant Shipping (Mandatory Ships' Routeing) Regulations 1997

1342................Road Traffic (Special Parking Area) (London Borough of Croydon) Order 1997

1349................Medicines (Registered Homoeopathic Veterinary Medicinal Products) (General Sale List) Order 1997

1350................Medicines (Pharmacy and General Sale-Exemption) (Amendment) Order 1997

1354................BBC World Service Transfer Scheme (Capital Allowances) Order 1997

1359................Anglian Regional Flood Defence Committee Order 1997

1360................Northumbria Regional Flood Defence Committee Order 1997

1361................Severn-Trent Regional Flood Defence Committee Order 1997

1362................Southern Regional Flood Defence Committee Order 1997
1363................Thames Regional Flood Defence Committee Order 1997
1364................Wessex Regional Flood Defence Committee Order 1997
1365................Motor Vehicles (Type Approval for Goods Vehicles) (Great Britain) (Amendment) Regulations 1997
1366................Motor Vehicles (Approval) (Amendment) Regulations 1997
1367................Motor Vehicles (Type Approval) (Great Britain) (Amendment) Regulations 1997
1368................Education (Individual Pupils' Achievements) (Information) Regulations 1997
1369................Road Traffic (Special Parking Area) (City of Westminster) (Amendment) Order 1997
1370 (C.49) (S.107) Social Security Act 1990 (Commencement No. 6) Order 1997
1372................Control of Trade in Endangered Species (Enforcement) Regulations 1997
1373................Local Government Superannuation (Scotland) Amendment (No.2) Regulations 1997
1375................Solihull Healthcare National Health Service (Transfer of Trust Property) Order 1997
1376................Horizon National Health Service Trust (Establishment) Amendment Order 1997
1377 (C.50)....Police Act 1997 (Commencement No. 1 and Transitional Provisions) Order 1997
1396................Atomic Weapons Establishment Act 1991 Amendment Order 1997
1399................Education (Funding for Teacher Training) Designation (No. 2) Order 1997
1400................West Yorkshire Metropolitan Ambulance Service National Health Service Trust (Establishment) Amendment Order 1997
1401................Portsmouth Health Care National Health Service Trust (Transfer of Trust Property) Order 1997
1402................Immigration (Exemption from Control) (Amendment) Order 1997
1403................Northern Ireland (Emergency Provision) Act 1996 (Amendment) Order 1997
1405................Register of Occupational and Personal Pension Schemes (Amendment) Regulations 1997
1410................Northern Ireland (Entry to Negotiations etc) Act 1996 (Revival of Section 3) Order 1997
1411 (C.51)....Antarctic Act 1994 (Commencement) Order 1997
1413................Miscellaneous Food Additives (Amendment) Regulations 1997
1414................Eggs (Marketing Standards) (Amendment) Regulations 1997
1415................Seeds (Fees) (Amendment) Regulations 1997
1418 (C.52)....Protection from Harassment Act 1997 (Commencement) (No. 1) Order 1997
1420................Local Government Act 1988 (Defined Activities) (Exemption) (Dacorum Borough Council) Order 1997
1421................Control of Trade in Endangered Species (Fees) Regulations 1997
1427 (C.53)....Building Societies Act 1997 (Commencement No.2) Order 1997
1428................Hydrographic Office Trading Fund (Variation) Order 1997
1429................Police Pensions (Amendment) Regulations 1997
1430 (C.56) (S.110) Transfer of Crofting Estates (Scotland) Act 1997 Commencement Order 1997

1526 (S.119) ..Act of Adjournal (Criminal Procedure Rules Amendment No.2) (Non-harassment Order) 1997
1527 (S.120) ..Act of Sederunt (Rules of the Court of Session Amendment No.6) (Actions of Harassment) 1997
1528................Protection of Wrecks (Designation) Order 1997
1529................General Medical Council (Professional Performance) Rules Order of Council 1997
1530................Unichem Limited (Allotment of Shares) Revocation Order 1997
1531................Railways (Heathrow Express Temporary Network) (Exemptions) Order 1997
1532................North Yorkshire (Coroners' Districts) Order 1997
1533................Registration of Births and Deaths (Amendment No.2) Regulations 1997
1534................Land Registration (District Registries) Order 1997
1535 (C.60)....Firearms (Amendment) Act 1997 (Commencement) (No.2) Order 1997
1536 (C.61)....Firearms (Amendment) Act 1997 (Commencement) (No.2) (Amendment) Order 1997
1537................Firearms (Amendment) Act 1997 (Firearms of Historic Interest) Order 1997
1538................Firearms (Amendment) Act 1997 (Transitional Provisions and Savings) Regulations 1997
1539................Merchant Shipping and Maritime Security Act 1997 (Commencement No.2) Order 1997
1543................Fertilisers (Amendment) Regulations 1997
1544................Road Vehicles (Construction and Use) (Amendment) (No.5) Regulations 1997
1545................A21 Trunk Road (Morleys Interchange Slip Roads) (Trunking) Order 1997
1565................Food Protection (Emergency Prohibitions) (Paralytic Shellfish Poisoning) Order 1997
1572................Hong Kong (Colonial Probates Act) Order 1997
1573................Potato Marketing Board (Residuary Functions) Regulations 1997
1576................Public Lending Right Scheme 1982 (Commencement of Variations) Order 1997
1577 (C.63)....Social Security Administration (Fraud) Act 1997 (Commencement No.1) Order 1997
1578................Bermuda (Territorial Sea) (Amendment) Order 1997
1579................Transfer of Prisoners (Isle of Man) Order 1997
1580................Road Traffic Act 1991 (Commencement No.13) (Scotland) Order 1997
1581 (C.64)....Crime (Sentences) Act 1997 (Commencement) (No.1) Order 1997
1584................Water (Prevention of Pollution) (Code of Practice) (Scotland) Order 1997
1585................Police Act 1997 (Provisions in Relation to the NCIS Service Authority) (No.1) Order 1997
1588................British Coal Corporation (Change of Quorum) Regulations 1997
1603................Finance Act 1997, section 110, (Appointed Day) Order 1997
1604................Horserace Betting Levy (Bookmakers' Committee) Regulations 1997
1607................A41 Trunk Road (Camden) Red Route Experimental (No.2) Traffic Order 1997 Variation (No.2) Order 1997
1608................A406 Trunk Road (Barnet) Red Route Traffic Order 1997
1611................International Monetary Fund (Limit on Lending) Order 1997

1612................Local Government Pension Scheme Regulations 1997
1613................Local Government Pension Scheme (Transitional Provisions) Regulations 1997
1614................Value Added Tax (Amendment) (No.3) Regulations 1997
1615................Value Added Tax (Cars) (Amendment) Order 1997
1616................Value Added Tax (Special Provisions) (Amendment) Order 1997
1618................Avon Health Authority (Transfers of Trust Property) Order 1997
1619................North and East Devon Health Authority (Transfer of Trust Property) Order 1997
1620................Worcestershire Community Healthcare National Health Service Trust (Transfer of Trust Property) Order 1997
1621................Housing (Change of Landlord) (Payment of Disposal Cost by Instalments) (Amendment) (No.2) Regulations 1997
1623................Education Act 1996 (Commencement No.2 and Appointed Day) Order 1997
1624................Energy Information (Combined Washer-dryers) Regulations 1997
1625................Education (Disability Statements for Local Education Authorities) (England) Regulations 1997
1626................Environment Act 1995 (Commencement No.9 and Transitional Provisions) Order 1997
1627................Insurance Premium Tax (Taxable Insurance Contracts) Order 1997
1628................Value Added Tax (Increase of Registration Limits) Order 1997
1629................Third Country Fishing (Enforcement) (Amendment) Order 1997
1630................Fishing Boats (Specified Countries) Designation (Variation) Order 1997
1631................Local Authorities etc. (Allowances) (Scotland) Amendment Regulations 1997
1632................A12 Trunk Road (Redbridge) Red Route Traffic Order 1997 Variation Order 1997
1633................Education (School Performance Information) (Wales) Regulations 1997
1638................Grants for School Education (Early Intervention and Alternatives to Exclusion) (Scotland) Regulations 1997
1639................Royal Parks and Other Open Spaces Regulations 1997
1640................St Mary's Music School (Aided Places) Amendment Regulations 1997
1641................Education (Assisted Places) (Scotland) Amendment Regulations 1997
1652................Contracting Out (Functions in relation to the provision of Guardians Ad Litter and Reporting Officers Panels) Order 1997
1653................Civil Aviation (Route Charges for Navigation Services) (Third Amendment) Regulations 1997
1654................Recreation Grounds (Revocation of Parish Council Byelaws) Order 1997
1655................Offshore Installations (Safety Zones) (No.3) Order 1997
1662................Guardians Ad Litter and Reporting Officers (Panels) (Amendment) Regulations 1997
1666................Local Government Act 1988 (Defined Activities) (Exemption) (Craven, Kerrier and Mid-Devon District Councils and Middlesbrough Borough Council) Order 1997
1671................Social Security (Miscellaneous Amendments) (No.3) Regulations 1997

1672................Architects Act 1997 (Commencement) Order 1997
1673................International Carriage of Perishable Foodstuffs (Amendment) Regulations 1997
1674................Merchant Shipping (Compensation to Seamen - War Damage to Effects) (Revocation) Scheme 1997
1675................Education (Student Loans) Regulations 1997
1676................Safety of Sports Grounds (Designation) Order 1997
1677................Football Spectators (Seating) Order 1997
1678................National Health Service (Fund-Holding Practices) Amendment (No. 2) Regulations 1997
1679................Motor Vehicles (Tests) (Amendment) (No. 2) Regulations 1997
1680 (S.127)..Registration of Births, Deaths, Marriages and Divorces (Fees) (Scotland) Amendment Regulations 1997
1681................Taxes (Interest Rate) (Amendment) Regulations 1997
1682................Satellite Television Service Regulations 1997
1687................Judicial Pensions (Miscellaneous) (Amendment) Regulations 1997
1688................Golden Valley Railway Order 1997
1690................Northern Ireland Act 1974 (Interim Period Extension) Order 1997
1691................Pneumoconiosis etc. (Workers' Compensation) (Payment of Claims) Amendment Regulations 1997
1692................Firearms (Museums) Order 1997
1693................Education (Mandatory Awards) (Amendment) Regulations 1997
1694................Dual-use and Related Goods (Export Control) (Amendment No.3) Regulations 1997
1695 (C.70)....Noise Act 1996 (Commencement No.2) Order 1997
1696 (C.71)....Police Act 1997 (Commencement No.2) Order 1997
1697................Local Authorities (Direct Labour Organisations) (Competition) (Wales) (Amendment) Regulations 1997
1698................Local Government Act 1988 (Defined Activities) (Exemption) (Wales) (Amendment) Regulations 1997
1699................Local Government Act 1988 (Competition) (Wales) Regulations 1997
1700................Local Government Act 1988 (Defined Activities) (Works Contracts) (Exemptions) (Wales) Regulations 1997
1701................Local Government Act 1988 (Defined Activities) (Housing Management) (Exemptions) (Wales) (Amendment) Order 1997
1702................Local Government Act 1988 (Direct Service Organisations) (Accounts etc.) (Extension) (Wales) (Amendment) Order 1997
1709................Government Stock (Amendment) Regulations 1997
1710................Land Registration Fees (No.2) Order 1997
1711................Charities (The Peabody Donation Fund) Order 1997
1712................(C.72) (S.128) Crime and Punishment (Scotland) Act 1997 (Commencement and Transitional Provisions) Order 1997
1713................Confined Spaces Regulations 1997
1714................Betting and Gaming Duties Act 1981 (Bingo Prize Limit) Order 1997
1715................Open-ended Investment Companies (Tax) Regulations 1997
1716................Personal Equity Plan (Amendment No.2) Regulations 1997
1717................Protection of Wrecks (Designation No.2) Order 1997
1718................Protection of Wrecks (Designation No.3) Order 1997
1719................Return of Cultural Objects (Amendments) Regulations 1997
1720................(S.129) Act of Sederunt (Rules of the Court of Session Amendment No.7) (Judicial Factors) 1997

1721...............(S.130) Liquor Licensing (Fees) (Scotland) Order 1997
1723...............Nurses, Midwives and Health Visitors (Supervisors of Midwives) Amendment Rules Approval Order 1997
1724...............James Paget Hospital National Health Service Trust (Change of Name) Order 1997
1725 (C.73)....Confiscation of Alcohol (Young Persons) Act 1997 (Commencement) Order 1997
1726...............Council Tax Limitation (England) (Maximum Amounts) Order 1997
1727...............Medicines (Stilbenes and Thyrostatic Substances Prohibition) (Revocation) Order 1997
1728...............Medicines (Control of Substances for Manufacture) (Revocation) Order 1997
1729...............Animals and Animal Products (Examination for Residues and Maximum Residue Limits) Regulations 1997
1731...............Legal Advice and Assistance (Scope) (Amendment) (No.2) Regulations 1997
1736...............Contracting Out (Metropolitan Police and Civil Staffs Pensions) Order 1997
1738...............London Docklands Development Corporation (Alteration of Boundaries) Order 1997
1739...............Food Protection (Emergency Prohibitions) (Paralytic Shellfish Poisoning) Order 1997 Partial Revocation Order 1997
1740...............Supply of Beer (Tied Estate) (Amendment) Order 1997
1741...............Homelessness (Suitability of Accommodation) (Amendment) Order 1997
1742...............European Communities (Designation) (No.2) Order 1997
1743...............European Convention on Cinematographic Co-production (Amendment) (No.3) Order 1997
1744...............Secretary of State for Culture, Media and Sport Order 1997
1745...............Army, Air Force and Naval Discipline Acts (Continuation) Order 1997
1746...............Air Navigation (Overseas Territories) (Amendment) Order 1997
1747...............Child Abduction and Custody (Parties to Conventions) (Amendment) Order 1997
1748...............Environment Protection (Overseas Territories) (Amendment) Order 1997
1749...............Transfer of Functions (International Development) Order 1997
1750...............Fishery Limits Order 1997
1751...............United Nations (International Tribunal) (Rwanda) (Amendment) Order 1997
1752...............United Nations (International Tribunal) (Former Yugoslavia) (Amendment) Order 1997
1753...............United Nations (International Tribunal) (Former Yugoslavia and Rwanda) (Dependent Territories) (Amendment) Order 1997
1754 (N.I.13).Appropriation (No.2) (Northern Ireland) Order 1997
1755...............Broadcasting Act 1996 (British Broadcasting Corporation—Transmission Network) (Guernsey) Order 1997
1756...............Broadcasting Act 1996 (British Broadcasting Corporation—Transmission Network) (Isle of Man) Order 1997
1757...............Broadcasting Act 1996 (British Broadcasting Corporation—Transmission Network) (Jersey) Order 1997
1758 (N.I.14).Commissioner for Complaints (Amendment) (Northern Ireland) Order 1997
1759...............European Convention on Extradition Order 1990 (Amendment) Order 1997

1760................Extradition (Aviation Security) Order 1997
1761................Extradition (Designated Commonwealth Countries) Order 1991 (Amendment) Order 1997
1762................Extradition (Drug Trafficking) Order 1997
1763................Extradition (Hijacking) Order 1997
1764................Extradition (Internationally Protected Persons) Order 1997
1765................Extradition (Protection of Nuclear Material) Order 1997
1766................Extradition (Safety of Maritime Navigation) Order 1997
1767................Extradition (Taking of Hostages) Order 1997
1768................Extradition (Tokyo Convention) Order 1997
1769................Extradition (Torture) Order 1997
1770................Food and Environment Protection Act 1985 (Guernsey) (Amendment) Order 1997
1771................Food and Environment Protection Act 1985 (Jersey) (Amendment) Order 1997
1772 (N.I.15)...Further Education (Northern Ireland) Order 1997
1773................Merchant Shipping (Salvage Convention) (Jersey) Order 1997
1774 (N.I.16)...Police (Health and Safety) (Northern Ireland) Order 1997
1775................Transfer of Prisoners (Isle of Man) (No.2) Order 1997
1776................Transfer of Prisoners (Restricted Transfers) (Channel Islands and Isle of Man) Order 1997
1777................Double Taxation Relief (Taxes on Income) (Argentina) Order 1997
1778................Social Security (United States of America) Order 1997
1779................Visiting Forces (Designation) Order 1997
1780 (C.74)....National Health Service (Primary Care) Act 1997 (Commencement No.1) Order 1997
1781 (S.131)..Valuation Timetable (Scotland) Amendment Order 1997
1782 (S.132)..Registration of Births, Still-births and Deaths (Prescription of Errors) (Scotland) Regulations 1997
1783................Lotteries (Gaming Board Fees) Order 1997
1787................Sports Grounds and Sporting Events (Designation) (Scotland) Amendment Order 1997
1788................Act of Adjournal (Criminal Procedure Rules Amendment No.3) 1997
1789................Education (School Teachers' Pay and Conditions) (No.2) Order 1997
1790................Social Security (Lone Parents) (Amendment) Regulations 1997
1791................Birmingham Health Authority (Transfer of Trust Property) Order 1997
1820................Oil Pollution (Compulsory Insurance) Regulations 1997
1821................National Health Service Pilot Schemes (Financial Assistance for Preparatory Work) Regulations 1997
1824................A316 Trunk Road (Richmond) Red Route Traffic Order 1997
1828................Gaming Act (Variation of Monetary Limits) Order 1997
1829................Firemen's Pensions (Provision of Information) Regulations 1997
1830................Prescription Only Medicines (Human Use) Order 1997
1831................Medicines (Sale or Supply) (Miscellaneous Provisions) Amendment Regulations 1997
1832................Education (School Information) (Wales) Regulations 1997
1833................Education (School Inspection) (Wales) (No.2) (Amendment) Regulations 1997
1834................Act of Adjournal (Criminal Procedure Rules Amendment No.4) 1997
1835................Local Authorities (Goods and Services) (Public Bodies) (English Heritage) Order 1997

1836................Value Added Tax (Terminal Markets) (Amendment) Order 1997
1837................(L.27) County Court (Amendment) Rules 1997
1838................(L.28) County Court (Forms) (Amendment) Rules 1997
1839................Social Security (Attendance Allowance and Disability Living Allowance) (Miscellaneous Amendments) Regulations 1997
1840................Fire Precautions (Workplace) Regulations 1997
1841................Council Tax Benefit (General) Amendment Regulations 1997
1842................Wireless Telegraphy (Control of Interference from Video-senders) Order 1997
1844................West Mercia (Police Area and Authority) Order 1997
1845................Cheshire (Police Area and Authority) Order 1997
1846................Cambridgeshire (Police Area and Authority) Order 1997
1847................Essex (Police Area and Authority) Order 1997
1848................Thames Valley (Police Authority) Order 1997
1849................Devon and Cornwall (Police Area and Authority) Order 1997
1850................Nottinghamshire (Police Area and Authority) Order 1997
1851 (C.75)....Housing Act 1996 (Commencement No.11 and Savings) Order 1997
1852................Leasehold Valuation Tribunals (Fees) Order 1997
1853................Leasehold Valuation Tribunals (Service Charges, Insurance or Appointment of Managers Applications) Order 1997
1854................Rent Assessment Committee (England and Wales) (Leasehold Valuation Tribunal) (Amendment) Regulations 1997
1855................Lancashire (Police Area and Authority) Order 1997
1856................Broadcasting (Technical Services) Order 1997
1857................Kent (Police Area and Authority) Order 1997
1858................Savings Contracts (Amendment) Regulations 1997
1859................Savings Certificates (Amendment) Regulations 1997
1860................Savings Certificates (Children's Bonus Bonds) (Amendment) Regulations 1997
1861................General Medical Council (Legal Assessors) (Amendment) Rules 1997
1862................Premium Savings Bonds (Amendment) Regulations 1997
1863................Savings Certificates (Yearly Plan) (Amendment) Regulations 1997
1864................National Savings Stock Register (Amendment) Regulations 1997
1866................Banking Act 1987 (Exempt Transactions) (Amendment) Regulations 1997
1869................Merchant Shipping (Prevention of Pollution: Substances Other than Oil) (Intervention) Order 1997
1870................(S.136) Environmental Assessment (Scotland) Amendment Regulations 1997
1871................(S.137) Town and Country Planning (General Permitted Development) (Scotland) Amendment Order 1997
1872................(S.138) Building Standards (Relaxation by Local Authorities) (Scotland) Regulations 1997
1873................Corn Returns Regulations 1997
1881................Fish Health Regulations 1997
1884................General Medical Council (Registration Fees) (Amendment) Regulation Order of Council 1997
1885................Wireless Telegraphy (Licence Charges) (Amendment No.2) Regulations 1997
1886................Telecommunications (Voice Telephony) Regulations 1997
1887................Trading Schemes (Exclusion) (Amendment) Regulations 1997

1888................National Health Service Pension Scheme (Amendment) Regulations 1997
1889................Ecclesiastical Judges and Legal Officers (Fees) Order 1997
1890................Legal Officers (Annual Fees) Order 1997
1891................Parochial Fees Order 1997
1892................(C.76) Family Law Act 1996 (Commencement No.2) Order 1997
1893................(L.29) Family Proceedings (Amendment No.3) Rules 1997
1894................(L.30) Family Proceedings Courts (Matrimonial Proceedings etc.) (Amendment) Rules 1997
1895................(L.31) Family Proceedings Courts (Children Act 1989) (Amendment) Rules 1997
1896................(L.32) Family Law Act 1996 (Part IV) (Allocation of Proceedings) Order 1997
1897................(L.33) Children (Allocation of Proceedings) (Amendment) Order 1997
1898................(L.34) Family Law Act 1996 (Modifications of Enactments) Order 1997
1899................(L.35) Family Proceedings Fees (Amendment) (No.3) Order 1997
1900................Genetically Modified Organisms (Deliberate Release and Risk Assessment—Amendment) Regulations 1997
1901................Cattle Identification (Enforcement) Regulations 1997
1902................Allocation of Housing (Reasonable and Additional Preference) Regulations 1997
1903................Housing (Prescribed Forms) (Amendment) (No.2) Regulations 1997
1904................Building Regulations (Amendment) Regulations 1997
1905................Bovines and Bovine Products (Despatch Prohibition and Production Restriction) Regulations 1997
1906 (C.77)....Knives Act 1997 (Commencement) (No.1) Order 1997
1907................Knives (Forfeited Property) Regulations 1997
1908................Police (Property) Regulations 1997
1909................Jobseeker's Allowance (Workskill Courses) Pilot (No.2) Regulations 1997
1910................Merchant Shipping (Prevention of Oil Pollution) (Amendment) Regulations 1997
1911................Merchant Shipping (Training, Certification and Safe Manning) (Amendment) Regulations 1997
1912................Police Pensions (Provision of Information) Regulations 1997
1913................Local Government Act 1988 (Defined Activities) (Exemption) (Hackney and Southwark London Borough Councils and Liverpool City Council) Order 1997
1914................Dartford-Thurrock Crossing Tolls Order 1997
1915................Dartford-Thurrock Crossing (Amendment) Regulations 1997
1916................(S.139) National Health Service Superannuation Scheme (Scotland) Amendment (No.2) Regulations 1997
1920................(C.78) Sex Offenders Act 1997 (Commencement) Order 1997
1921................Sex Offenders (Certificate of Caution) Order 1997
1924................Fishing Vessels (Decommissioning) Scheme 1997
1929................Church of England Pensions Regulations 1997
1930................(C.79) Police Act 1997 (Commencement No.3 and Transitional Provisions) Order 1997
1931................Education (National Curriculum) (Assessment Arrangements for the Core Subjects) (Key Stage 1) (England) (Amendment) Order 1997
1937................Partnerships (Unrestricted Size) No.12 Regulations 1997
1939................(S.140) Electronic Fingerprinting etc. Device Approval (Scotland) Order 1997

1940...............Local Government Act 1988 (Defined Activities) (Exemption) (Christchurch Borough Council) Order 1997
1941...............Energy Efficiency (Refrigerators and Freezers) Regulations 1997
1949...............Sea Fishing (Enforcement of Community Conservation Measures) Order 1997
1951...............Transport and Works (Guided Transport Modes) (Amendment) Order 1997
1952...............Inverness Harbour Revision Order 1997
1953...............Cromarty Firth Port Authority Harbour Revision Order 1997
1954...............Nursery Education (Amendment) Regulations 1997
1960...............(C.80) Finance Act 1997, section 7(10), (Appointed Day) Order 1997
1961...............Plant Passport (Plant Health Fees) (England and Wales) (Amendment) Regulations 1997
1962...............Agricultural Holdings (Units of Production) Order 1997
1963...............National Board for Nursing, Midwifery and Health Visiting for England (Constitution and Administration) Amendment Order 1997
1964...............Land Registration (Matrimonial Home Rights) Rules 1997
1965...............Lands Tribunal (Amendment) Rules 1997
1966...............Education (School Inspection) Regulations 1997
1967...............Education (Grants) (Music, Ballet and Choir Schools) (Amendment) Regulations 1997
1968...............Education (Assisted Places) Regulations 1997
1969...............Education (Assisted Places) (Incidental Expenses) Regulations 1997
1970...............Education (School Leaving Date) Order 1997
1972...............Education (Fees and Awards) Regulations 1997
1974...............Housing Benefit (General) Amendment (No.2) Regulations 1997
1975...............Housing Benefit (General) Amendment (No.3) Regulations 1997
1976...............Protection of Wrecks (SS Castilian) Order 1997
1977...............(C.81) Treasure Act 1996 (Commencement No.2) Order 1997
1978...............Food Protection (Emergency Prohibitions) (Paralytic Shellfish Poisoning) Order 1997
1979...............(S.141) Accounts Commission for Scotland (Financial Year) Order 1997
1980...............(S.142) Local Authority Accounts (Scotland) Amendment Regulations 1997
1981...............(S.143) Local Government (Publication of Performance Information) (Scotland) Order 1997
1984...............Rent Officers (Housing Benefit Functions) Order 1997
1985...............Legal Aid in Criminal and Care Proceedings (General) (Amendment) (No.3) Regulations 1997
1986...............Veal (Marketing Payment) Regulations 1997
1987...............Anglian Harbours National Health Service Trust Dissolution Order 1997
1988...............A180 Trunk Road (A180/A1136 Junction Improvement Slip Roads) Order 1997
1990...............Education (London Residuary Body) (Suspense Account Properties) Order 1997
1991...............European Bank for Reconstruction and Development (Further Payments to Capital Stock) Order 1997
1992...............Local Government Changes for England (Lord-Lieutenants and Sheriffs) Order 1997
1993...............Offshore Electricity and Noise Regulations 1997

2176................Education (National Curriculum) (Assessment Arrangements for Key Stages 1, 2 and 3) (England) (Amendment) Order 1997

2177................Public Telecommunication System Designation (ACC Long Distance UK Limited) (No.2) Order 1997

2178................Public Telecommunication System Designation (Coventry Cable Limited) Order 1997

2179................Public Telecommunication System Designation (Diamond Cable Communications (UK) Limited) Order 1997

2180................Public Telecommunication System Designation (Advanced Radio Telecom Limited) Order 1997

2181................Public Telecommunication System Designation (RadioTel Systems Limited) Order 1997

2182................Foods Intended for Use in Energy Restricted Diets for Weight Reduction Regulations 1997

2196................Gaming Duty Regulations 1997

2197................Income-related Benefits and Jobseeker's Allowance (Amendment) (No.2) Regulations 1997

2199................(C.86) Criminal Procedure and Investigations Act 1996 (Appointed Day No.6) Order 1997

2200................(C.87) Crime (Sentences) Act 1997 (Commencement No.2 and Transitional Provisions) Order 1997

2203................Waste Management Licensing (Amendment) Regulations 1997

2204................Registration of Marriages (Amendment) Regulations 1997

2205................Social Security (Recovery of Benefits) Regulations 1997

2206................Food Protection (Emergency Prohibition) (Oil and Chemical Pollution of Fish and Plants) (Revocation) Order 1997

2207................Immigration (Exemption from Control) (Amendment) (No.2) Order 1997

2231................Northern Ireland Arms Decommissioning Act 1997 (Immunities and Privileges) Order 1997

2232................Bicester (Tibbett & Britten Consumer Limited Siding) Order 1997

2237................Social Security (Recovery of Benefits) (Appeals) Regulations 1997

2238................Food (Pistachios From Iran) (Emergency Control) Order 1997

2239................Social Security (Claims and Payments and Adjudication) Amendment Regulations 1997

2240................Charities (Clergy Orphan Corporation) Order 1997

2258................Education (Funding for Teacher Training) Designation (No.3) Order 1997

2259................Local Government Act 1988 (Defined Activities) (Exemption) (Brent London Borough Council and Harrogate Borough Council) Order 1997

2260 (C.88; S.151) Road Traffic Act 1991 (Commencement No.14) (Scotland) Order 1997

2261 (S.152)..Local Authorities' Variation of Charges at Off–street and Designated Parking Places (Notice Procedure) (Scotland) Regulations 1997

2262................Mid-Norfolk Railway Order 1997

2276................Portsmouth Health Care National Health Service Trust (Transfer of Trust Property) (No.2) Order 1997

2281................A127 Trunk Road (Southend Arterial Road, Havering) (50 MPH Speed Limit) Order 1997

2282................Motor Cycle (EC Type Approval) (Amendment) Regulations 1997

2349 (S.158)..Marriages (Prescription of Forms) (Scotland) Regulations 1997
2351...............Curfew Order (Responsible Officer) Order 1997
2352 (C.90)....Education Act 1996 (Commencement No.3) Order 1997
2353...............Education (Disability Statements for Local Education Authorities) (Wales) Regulations 1997
2354 (S.156)..Prevention of Water Pollution (Loch Lomond) (Extension of Period of Byelaws) Order 1997
2364...............Education (School Performance Information) (England) (Amendment) (No.2) Regulations 1997
2365...............Bovine Spongiform Encephalopathy Compensation (Amendment) Order 1997
2366...............Merchant Shipping (Carriage of Cargoes) (Amendment) Regulations 1997
2367...............Merchant Shipping (Dangerous Goods and Marine Pollutants) Regulations 1997
2385...............A4 Trunk Road (Hillingdon) Red Route (Clearway) Traffic Order 1996 Variation Order 1997
2386...............A406 Trunk Road (Ealing and Hounslow) Red Route Traffic Order 1997
2387...............Bovine Spongiform Encephalopathy (No.2) (Amendment) Order 1997
2388...............Personal Pension Schemes (Establishment of Schemes) Order 1997
2389...............Airports (Groundhandling) Regulations 1997
2390 (C.92)....Police Act 1997 (Commencement No.4 and Transitional Provisions) Order 1997
2391...............Police Act 1997 (Provisions in relation to NCIS Service Authority) (No.2) Order 1997
2392 (C.93)....Finance Act 1997 (Commencement No.1) Order 1997
2393...............National Health Service (Travelling Expenses and Remission of Charges) Amendment (No.2) Regulations 1997
2394...............Legal Aid in Family Proceedings (Remuneration) (Amendment) Regulations 1997
2395...............Education (Grants for Education Support and Training) (Wales) (Amendment) Regulations 1997
2400...............Zebra, Pelican and Puffin Pedestrian Crossings Regulations and General Directions 1997
2401...............A406 Trunk Road (North Circular Road, Hounslow) Red Route (Prescribed Route) Traffic Order 1997
2402...............A205 Trunk Road (Hounslow) Red Route (Bus Lanes) Traffic Order 1997
2403...............A30 Trunk Road (Great South West Road, Hounslow) (Temporary Prohibition of Traffic) Order 1997
2416...............Police Authorities (Standing Orders) Regulations 1997
2417 (C.94)....Social Security Administration (Fraud) Act 1997 (Commencement No.3) Order 1997
2420 (L.37)....Magistrates' Courts (Children and Young Persons) (Amendment) Rules 1997
2421 (L.38)....Magistrates' Courts (Forms) (Amendment) (No.2) Rules 1997
2427...............Gas Act 1986 (Exemption) Order 1997
2428 (C.95)....Finance Act 1997 (Stamp Duty and Stamp Duty Reserve Tax) (Appointed Day) Order 1997
2429...............Stamp Duty and Stamp Duty Reserve Tax (Investment Exchanges and Clearing Houses) Regulations 1997
2430...............Stamp Duty Reserve Tax (Amendment) Regulations 1997
2434...............Housing Benefit and Council Tax Benefit (General) Amendment (No.2) Regulations 1997

2435................Housing Benefit (Recovery of Overpayments) Regulations 1997
2436................Housing Benefit (Information from Landlords and Agents) Regulations 1997
2437................Value Added Tax (Amendment) (No.4) Regulations 1997
2439................Vehicle Excise Duty (Immobilisation, Removal and Disposal of Vehicles) Regulations 1997
2440................Education (Individual Performance Information) (Prescribed Bodies and Persons) Regulations 1997
2441................Potatoes Originating in the Netherlands Regulations 1997
2452 (S.159)..Prescription as "Persons in Need" (Persons Subject to Immigration Control) (Scotland) Order 1997
2453................Oxleas National Health Service Trust (Transfer of Trust Property) Order 1997
2454................A205 Trunk Road (Lewisham) Red Route (Bus Lane) (No.2) Experimental Traffic Order 1997
2455 (S.160)..National Health Service (Travelling Expenses and Remission of Charges) (Scotland) Amendment (No.2) Regulations 1997
2456................Local Government Changes for England (Direct Labour Organisations) (County of Leicestershire and District of Rutland) Order 1997
2457 (C.96)....National Health Service (Primary Care) Act 1997 (Commencement No.2) Order 1997
2458................Local Government Act 1988 (Defined Activities) (Exemption) (Chichester District Council and Mole Valley District Council) Order 1997
2464................Export of Goods (United Nations Sanctions) (Sierra Leone) Order 1997
2465................North Tyneside Steam Railway Order 1997
2466................Railtrack (Ammanford Level Crossings) Order 1997
2467................Local Government Pension Scheme (Burnley and Pendle Transport Company Limited) Regulations 1997
2468................National Health Service (General Medical Services) Amendment (No.3) Regulations 1997
2469 (S.161)..National Health Service (Fund-holding Practices Audit) (Scotland) Regulations 1997
2470 (S.162)..Surface Waters (Shellfish) (Classification) (Scotland) Regulations 1997
2471 (S.163)..Surface Waters (Fishlife) (Classification) (Scotland) Regulations 1997
2488................National Health Service (Optical Charges and Payments) Amendment Regulations 1997
2489................A1 Trunk Road (Barnet) Red Route (Clearway) Traffic Order 1997
2491................Income Tax (Payments on Account) (Amendment) Regulations 1997
2492 (S.164)..National Health Service (Optical Charges and Payments) (Scotland) Amendment (No.2) Regulations 1997
2498................Offshore Installations (Safety Zones) (No.4) Order 1997
2499................Plant Protection Products (Amendment) (No.2) Regulations 1997
2500................Sheep Annual Premium (Amendment) Regulations 1997
2501................Licensing (Fees) (Variation) Order 1997
2502................Local Government Act 1988 (Defined Activities) (Exemption) (Reigate and Banstead Borough Council, Vale of White Horse District Council and Aylesbury Vale District Council) Order 1997

2605...............Nevill Hall and District National Health Service Trust (Establishment) Amendment Order 1997
2618...............Local Authorities (Armorial Bearings) (No.2) Order 1997
2619...............Housing Benefit (Recovery of Overpayments) (No.2) Regulations 1997
2620 (C.98)....National Health Service (Primary Care) Act 1997 (Commencement No.3) Order 1997
2621...............City of Stoke-on-Trent Birches Head Road Canal Footbridge Scheme 1997
2622...............Food Protection (Emergency Prohibitions) (Dounreay Nuclear Establishment) Order 1997
2623...............Combined Probation Areas (Bedfordshire) Order 1997
2624...............Education (Pupil Registration) (Amendment) Regulations 1997
2634 (S.167)..Scottish Examination Board and Scottish Vocational Education Council (Dissolution) (Scotland) Order 1997
2646...............Gilt Strips (Consequential Amendments) Regulations 1997
2647...............Legal Aid in Criminal and Care Proceedings (General) (Amendment) (No.4) Regulations 1997
2648...............Local Government Act 1988 (Defined Activities) (Exemptions) (Wales) (Amendment) Order 1997
2649...............Local Government Act 1988 (Competition) (Wales) (No. 2) Regulations 1997
2651...............Rhondda Health Care National Health Service Trust (Transfer of Trust Property) Order 1997
2652...............East Glamorgan National Health Service Trust (Transfer of Trust Property) Order 1997
2653 (S.168)..Act of Adjournal (Criminal Procedure Rules Amendment No.7) 1997
2655...............A316 Trunk Road (Hounslow) Red Route Experimental Traffic Order 1997
2656...............A315 Trunk Road (Hounslow and Richmond) Red Route (Clearway) Traffic Order 1997
2657...............A4 Trunk Road (Hounslow and Hammersmith & Fulham) Red Route (Clearway) Traffic Order 1997
2658...............Smoke Control Areas (Authorised Fuels) (Amendment) Regulations 1997
2666...............Air Navigation (Dangerous Goods) (Second Amendment) Regulations 1997
2667...............Judicial Pensions (Requisite Surviving Spouses' Benefits etc.) Order 1997
2668 (C.99)....Building Societies Act 1997 (Commencement No.3) Order 1997
2669 (C.100)..Social Security Administration (Fraud) Act 1997 (Commencement No.4) Order 1997
2670 (L.39)....County Court Fees (Amendment) (No.2) Order 1997
2671 (L.40)....Family Proceedings Fees (Amendment) (No.4) Order 1997
2672 (L.41)....Supreme Court Fees (Amendment) Order 1997
2673...............Food Industry Development Scheme 1997
2674...............Food Industry Development Scheme (Specification of Activities) Order 1997
2675...............Coast Protection (Variation of Excluded Waters) Regulations 1997
2676...............Social Security (National Insurance Number Information: Exemption) Regulations 1997
2677...............Jobseeker's Allowance (Amendment) (No.2) Regulations 1997
2678...............Teacher Training Agency (Additional Functions) Order 1997

2735................Food Protection (Emergency Prohibitions) (Oil and Chemical Pollution of Fish) Order 1997 (Partial Revocation) Order 1997
2743................City of Westminster (A41 Trunk Road) Red Route (Bus Lanes) Traffic Order 1997
2744................Value Added Tax (Drugs, Medicines and Aids for the Handicapped) Order 1997
2746................Local Government Act 1988 (Defined Activities) (Exemptions) Order 1997
2747................Local Government Act 1988 (Competition) (Revocations) Regulations 1997
2748................Local Government Act 1988 (Defined Activities) (Exemptions) (Schools) Order 1997
2749................A23 Trunk Road (Croydon) Red Route Traffic Order 1997 Variation Order 1997
2750................Mink (Keeping) (Amendment) Regulations 1997
2751................Coypus (Special Licence) (Fees) Regulations 1997
2752 (C.103)..Local Government and Rating Act 1997 (Commencement No.2) Order 1997
2756................Local Government (Direct Labour Organisations) (Competition) (Amendment) Regulations 1997
2757................Sole, Plaice, etc. (Specified Seas Areas) (Prohibition of Fishing) Order 1997
2758................Export of Goods (Control) (Amendment No. 3) Order 1997
2759................Dual-use and Related Goods (Export Control) (Amendment No. 4) Regulations 1997
2760................Lancashire Fire Services (Combination Scheme) Order 1997
2761................Nottinghamshire Fire Services (Combination Scheme) Order 1997
2762................Civil Courts (Amendment No.4) Order 1997
2763................Public Bodies (Admission to Meetings) (National Health Service Trusts) Order 1997
2764................Relocation Grants Regulations 1997
2765................M40 Motorway (Wheatley Service Area Access) Connecting Roads Scheme 1997
2766 (C.104)..Social Security Administration (Fraud) Act 1997 (Commencement No.5) Order 1997
2767................South Yorkshire Metropolitan Ambulance and Paramedic Service National Health Service Trust (Establishment) Amendment Order 1997
2768................Public Telecommunication System Designation (Atlantic Telecommunications Limited) Order 1997
2769................Public Telecommunication System Designation (Worldxchange Communications Limited) Order 1997
2770................Public Telecommunication System Designation (First Telecom plc) Order 1997
2771................Public Telecommunication System Designation (American Telemedia Limited) Order 1997
2772................Public Telecommunication System Designation (TotalTel International Inc.) Order 1997
2773 (S.172)..Education (Assisted Places) (Scotland) Amendment (No.2) Regulations 1997
2774 (C.105; S.173) Education (Schools) Act 1997 (Commencement) Order 1997
2776................Diving at Work Regulations 1997
2777 (NI.18)..Industrial Pollution Control (Northern Ireland) Order 1997
2778 (NI.19)..Waste and Contaminated Land (Northern Ireland) Order 1997

2779 (NI.20)..Shops (Sunday Trading &c.) (Northern Ireland) Order 1997

2780 (S.174) ..Civil Jurisdiction and Judgments Act 1982 (Provisional and Protective Measures) (Scotland) Order 1997

2781................Transfer of Functions (Insurance) Order 1997

2782................A1 Trunk Road (Islington High Street) Red Route (Prohibited Turn) Traffic Order 1997

2783................A1 Trunk Road (Islington) Red Route Traffic Order 1993 Variation Order 1997

2784................London Borough of Islington (Trunk Roads) Red Route (Bus Lanes) Experimental Traffic Order 1997

2785................A4 Trunk Road (Hammersmith & Fulham and Kensington & Chelsea) Red Route Experimental Traffic Order 1997

2786................A41 Trunk Road (Camden) (Temporary Prohibition of Traffic) (No.3) Order 1997

2787................National Health Service (Vocational Training) Amendment Regulations 1997

2788................Staffordshire Ambulance Service National Health Service Trust (Establishment) Amendment Order 1997

2789................Horse Passports Order 1997

2790 (S.175) ..Grants for School Improvements (Scotland) Regulations 1997

2791 (S.176) ..Police Cadets (Scotland) Amendment Regulations 1997

2792................Non-Domestic Rating (Rural Settlements) (England) Order 1997

2793................Income-related Benefits (Miscellaneous Amendments) Regulations 1997

2813................Social Security (Penalty Notice) Regulations 1997

2814................Social Security (National Insurance Number Information: Exemption) (No.2) Regulations 1997

2815................Occupational Pensions (Revaluation) Order 1997

2816................Education (School Performance Information) (England) (Amendment) (No.3) Regulations 1997

2817................National Health Service (Vocational Training for General Medical Practice) Regulations 1997

2818................Combined Fire Authorities (Protection from Personal Liability) (Wales) Order 1997

2819................Combined Fire Authorities (Protection from Personal Liability) (England) Regulations 1997

2820................A205 Trunk Road (Perry Vale and Waldram Crescent, Lewisham) Red Route (Prohibited Turns) Traffic Order 1997

2821................Public Telecommunication System Designation (Cable Thames Valley Limited) Order 1997

2822................Public Telecommunication System Designation (General Telecommunications Limited) Order 1997

2823................Public Telecommunication System Designation (Eurobell (Holdings) Plc) Order 1997

2824 (S.177) ..Act of Sederunt (Fees of Sheriff Officers) 1997

2825 (S.178) ..Act of Sederunt (Fees of Messengers-at-Arms) 1997

2826 (C.106; S.179) Local Government and Rating Act 1997 (Commencement No.3) Order 1997

2827 (S.180) ..Non-Domestic Rating (Rural Areas and Rateable Value Limits) (Scotland) Order 1997

2840................Building Societies (Members' Resolutions) Order 1997

2841................Sea Fishing (Enforcement of Community Conservation Measures) (Amendment) Order 1997

2842................Local Government Changes for England (Property Transfer) (Humberside) Order 1997

2843 (C.107)..Local Government (Contracts) Act 1997 (Commencement No.1) Order 1997

2910................Public Telecommunication System Designation (Shropshire Cable and Telecoms Limited) Order 1997

2911................Insurance Companies (Accounts and Statements) (Amendment) Regulations 1997

2912................Civil Aviation (Air Travel Organiser's Licensing) (Second Amendment) Regulations 1997

2913................Courses for Drink-drive Offenders (Designation of Areas) Order 1997

2914................Cosmetic Products (Safety) (Amendment) Regulations 1997

2915................Motor Vehicles (Driving Licences) (Amendment) (No.5) Regulations 1997

2916................Minibus and Other Section 19 Permit Buses (Amendment) Regulations 1997

2917................Community Bus (Amendment) Regulations 1997

2918................Education (Particulars of Independent Schools) Regulations 1997

2919................Education (Student Loans) (Amendment) Regulations 1997

2920................Civil Aviation (Route Charges for Navigation Services) Regulations 1997

2921................A205 Trunk Road (Southwark) Red Route (Bus Lanes) Experimental Traffic Order 1997

2922................A23 Trunk Road (Lambeth) Red Route Experimental Traffic Order 1997

2928................European Specialist Medical Qualifications Amendment Regulations 1997

2929................National Health Service (Pilot Schemes–Health Service Bodies) Regulations 1997

2930................Telecommunications (Licensing) Regulations 1997

2931................Telecommunications (Interconnection) Regulations 1997

2932................Telecommunications (Open Network Provision and Leased Lines) Regulations 1997

2933................Motor Vehicles (Type Approval) (Great Britain) (Amendment) (No. 3) Regulations 1997

2934................Motor Vehicles (Approval) (Amendment) (No. 2) Regulations 1997

2935................Road Vehicles (Construction and Use) (Amendment) (No. 6) Regulations 1997

2936................Motor Vehicles (Type Approval for Goods Vehicles) (Great Britain) (Amendment) (No. 2) Regulations 1997

2937................Civil Aviation (Joint Financing) Regulations 1997

2938................Southend Health Care Services National Health Service Trust (Change of Name) Order 1997

2939................Registration of Births, Deaths and Marriages (Fees) Order 1997

2940 (S.185) ..Disqualification from Driving (Prescribed Courts) (Scotland) Order 1997

2941 (S.186) ..Invergarry–Kyle of Lochalsh Trunk Road (A87) Extension (Skye Bridge Crossing) Toll Order (Variation) Order 1997

2942 (S.187) ..Removal of Vehicles (Prescribed Charges) (Scotland) Regulations 1997

2943 (S.188) ..Child Support (Written Agreements) (Scotland) Order 1997

2944................Restrictive Trade Practices (Non-notifiable Agreements) (Turnover Threshold) Amendment Order 1997

2945................Restrictive Trade Practices (Non-notifiable Agreements) (Sale and Purchase, Share Subscription and Franchise Agreements) Order 1997

2946................London Docklands Development Corporation (Planning Functions) Order 1997

2947................Severn Bridge Tolls Order 1997
2948 (S.189)..Dundee Teaching Hospitals National Health Service Trust (Establishment) Amendment Order 1997
2949................Portland Harbour Revision Order 1997
2950................A102(M) Motorway (Port Greenwich Development Connecting Roads) Scheme 1997
2951................A102 Trunk Road (Port Greenwich Development Slip Roads) Order 1997
2954................Local Government Changes for England (Valuation Tribunals) Regulations 1997
2959................Beef Bones Regulations 1997
2960................Highway Litter Clearance and Cleaning (Transfer of Responsibility) Order 1997
2961................Education (Grant) (Amendment) (No. 2) Regulations 1997
2962................Merchant Shipping and Fishing Vessels (Health and Safety at Work) Regulations 1997
2964................Specified Risk Material Order 1997
2965................Specified Risk Material Regulations 1997
2966................Antarctic (Guernsey) Regulations 1997
2967................Antarctic (Jersey) Regulations 1997
2968................Antarctic (Isle of Man) Regulations 1997
2969................Arable Area Payments (Amendment) Regulations 1997
2971................Secretary of State for the Environment, Transport and the Regions Order 1997
2972................European Communities (Definition of Treaties) (European Police Office) Order 1997
2973................European Communities (Immunities and Privileges of the European Police Office) Order 1997
2974................Falkland Islands Constitution (Amendment) (No.2) Order 1997
2975................OSPAR Commission (Immunities and Privileges) Order 1997
2976................Criminal Justice Act 1988 (Designated Countries and Territories) (Amendment) (No.2) Order 1997
2977................Criminal Justice (International Co-operation) Act 1990 (Enforcement of Overseas Forfeiture Orders) (Amendment) (No.2) Order 1997
2978................Deep Sea Mining (Temporary Provisions) Act 1981 (Guernsey) Order 1997
2979................Deep Sea Mining (Temporary Provisions) Act 1981 (Jersey) Order 1997
2980................Drug Trafficking Act 1994 (Designated Countries and Territories) (Amendment) (No.2) Order 1997
2981................Immigration (European Economic Area) (Amendment) Order 1997
2982................Summer Time Order 1997
2983 (NI.21)..Civil Evidence (Northern Ireland) Order 1997
2984 (NI.22)..Deregulation (Northern Ireland) Order 1997
2985................Double Taxation Relief (Taxes on Income) (Falkland Islands) Order 1997
2986................Double Taxation Relief (Taxes on Income) (Lesotho) Order 1997
2987................Double Taxation Relief (Taxes on Income) (Malaysia) Order 1997
2988................Double Taxation Relief (Taxes on Income) (Singapore) Order 1997
2989................Aviation Security (Guernsey) Order 1997

3046...............Food (Pistachios from Iran) (Emergency Control) (Amendment) Order 1997

3047...............Criminal Procedure and Investigations Act 1996 (Code of Practice) (Northern Ireland) Order 1997

3048 (S.192)..Local Government Superannuation (Scotland) Amendment (No. 4) Regulations 1997

3049 (S.193)..Homeless Persons (Priority Need) (Scotland) Order 1997

3050...............Wireless Telegraphy Apparatus Approval and Examination Fees Order 1997

3051...............Electromagnetic Compatibility (Wireless Telegraphy Apparatus) Certification and Examination Fees Regulations 1997

3052...............Combined Probation Areas (North Wales) Order 1997

3053...............Traffic Signs (Temporary Obstructions) Regulations 1997

3054...............Sole, etc. (Specified Sea Areas) (Prohibition of Fishing) Order 1997

3055...............Conservation (Natural Habitats, &c.) (Amendment) Regulations 1997

3056...............Road Traffic (Special Parking Area) (London Borough of Bromley) (Amendment) Order 1997

3057...............Road Traffic (Special Parking Area) (London Borough of Haringey) (Amendment) Order 1997

3058...............Road Traffic (Vehicle Emissions) (Fixed Penalty) Regulations 1997

3059 (S.191)..Act of Sederunt (Rules of the Court of Session Amendment No. 9) (Solicitors and Notaries Public) 1997

3060 (S.194)..Town and Country Planning (General Permitted Development) (Scotland) Amendment (No. 2) Order 1997

3061 (S.195)..Town and Country Planning (Use Classes) (Scotland) Order 1997

3062...............Specified Risk Material (Amendment) Regulations 1997

3063...............Vehicle Excise Duty (Immobilisation, Removal and Disposal of Vehicles) (Amendment) Regulations 1997

3066...............A205 Trunk Road (Lewisham) Red Route Experimental Traffic Order 1997 Variation Order 1997

3067...............Local Government (Changes for the Registration Service in Berkshire, Cambridgeshire, Cheshire, Devon, Essex, Hereford and Worcester, Kent, Lancashire, Nottinghamshire and Shropshire) Order 1997

3068 (C.113)..Antarctic Act 1994 (Commencement) (No. 3) Order 1997

3069 (S.196)..Criminal Legal Aid (Scotland) (Prescribed Proceedings) Regulations 1997

3070 (S.197)..Advice and Assistance (Assistance by Way of Representation) (Scotland) Regulations 1997

3107 (C.114)..Merchant Shipping Act 1995 (Appointed Day No. 2) Order 1997

3108 (C.115)..Criminal Procedure and Investigations Act 1996 (Appointed Day No. 7) Order 1997

3114 (C.116)..Firearms (Amendment) (No. 2) Act 1997 (Commencement) Order 1997

1998

1...............Road Vehicles (Construction and Use) (Amendment) Regulations 1998

3...............National Health Service (Proposals for Pilot Schemes) and (Miscellaneous Amendments) Amendment Regulations 1998

4 (S.1)......National Health Service (General Medical Services) (Scotland) Amendment Regulations 1998

ALPHABETICAL TABLE OF STATUTES

This is an alphabetical table of statutes from 1700–1997. It comprises a listing of Acts printed in the edition of the Record Commissioners known as Statutes of the Realm so far as it extends (1713), the Acts printed in Ruffhead's Edition so far as it extends (1785) and thereafter all Acts printed by the King's or Queen's Printer as Public Acts or (since 1797) Public General Acts. It should be noted that from 1797 Public Acts were divided into two series, Public General and Public Local and Personal Acts, prior to that date Acts which might now be classified as local were included in the definition Public Acts. Such Acts are therefore included in this list. For 1998 statutes see the most recent table in the Contents section of the Service File.

Abandonment of Animals Act 1960 (c.43)
Abandonment of Railways Act 1850 (c.83)
Abandonment of Railways Act 1869 (c.114)
Aberbrothock Beer Duties Act 1737 (c.4)
Aberbrothock Beer Duties Act 1763 (c.28)
Aberbrothock Beer Duties Act 1787 (c.46)
Aberdare Canal Act 1793 (c.95)
Aberdeen Beer Duties Act 1730 (c.13)
Aberdeen Commissary Court Records Act 1721 (c.28)
Aberdeen Harbour Act 1772 (c.29)
Aberdeen Harbour Act 1795 (c.41)
Aberdeen Harbour Act 1796 (c.68)
Aberdeen: Harbour Improvement Act 1797 (c.101)
Aberdeen Improvements Act 1795 (c.76)
Aberdeen Records Act 1722 (c.25)
Aberdeen Roads Act 1795 (c.161)
Abergavenny: Improvement Act 1794 (c.106)
Abergele and Rhydlan: Drainage Act 1794 (c.110)
Aberystwyth Harbour Act 1780 (c.26)
Abingdon: Improvement Act 1794 (c.89)
Abingdon to Swinford Roads Act 1768 (c.61)
Abingdon to Trowbridge Canal Act 1795 (c.52)
Abnormal Importations (Customs Duties) Act 1931 (c.1)
Abolition of Domestic Rates Etc. (Scotland) Act 1987 (c.47)
Abolition of Offices in Courts of Law Act 1845 (c.78)
Abolition of Slave Trade Act 1807 (c.36)
Abolition of Slavery Act 1836 (c.5)
Abolition of Slavery Act 1836 (c.16)
Abolition of Slavery Act 1836 (c.82)
Abolition of Slavery Act 1837 (c.3)
Abolition of Slavery Act 1838 (c.19)
Abolition of Slavery Act 1841 (c.18)
Abortion Act 1967 (c.87)
Absconding Debtors Act 1870 (c.76)
Access to Health Records Act 1990 (c.23)
Access to Medical Reports Act 1988 (c.28)
Access to Mountains Act 1939 (c.30)
Access to Neighbouring Land Act 1992 (c.23)
Access to Personal Files Act 1987 (c.37)
Accession Declaration Act 1910 (c.29)
Accessories and Abettors Act 1861 (c.94)
Accommodation Agencies Act 1953 (c.23)

Account of Civil List Revenues Act 1815 (c.15)
Accountant General in Chancery Act 1804 (c.82)
Accountant General of Court of Chancery Act 1813 (c.14)
Accounting for Certain Debentures Act 1706 (c.33)
Accounts, etc., of Barrack Master General Act 1807 (c.13)
Accounts of Barrack Office Act 1808 (c.89)
Accounts of Colonial Revenues Act 1814 (c.184)
Accounts of Expenditure in France Act 1814 (c.98)
Accounts of Expenditure in West Indies Act 1808 (c.91)
Accounts of Paymaster General Act 1808 (c.49)
Accumulations Act 1800 (c.98)
Accumulations Act 1892 (c.58)
Achurch Parish Church 1778 (c.9)
Acknowledgement of Deeds by Married Women Act 1854 (c.75)
Acknowledgement of Deeds by Married Women (Ireland) Act 1878 (c.23)
Acquisition of Land Act 1981 (c.67)
Acquisition of Land (Assessment of Compensation) Act 1919 (c.57)
Acquisition of Land (Assessment of Compensation) (Scotland) Act 1931 (c.11)
Acquisition of Land (Authorisation Procedure) Act 1946 (c.49)
Acquisition of Land (Authorisation Procedure) (Scotland) Act 1947 (c.42)
Act of Marriage 1929 (c.36)
Act of Settlement 1700 (c.2)
Act of Uniformity 1662 (c.4)
Act of Uniformity Amendment Act 1872 (c.35)
Actions Against Certain Spiritual Persons Act 1803 (c.34)
Actions Against Spiritual Persons Act 1813 (c.6)
Actions, etc., for Buying Oak Bark, etc. Act 1806 (c.152)
Actions for Gaming Act 1844 (c.3)
Actions for Gaming Act 1844 (c.58)
Activity Centres (Young Persons' Safety) Act 1995 (c.15)

Acts of Common Council, London Act 1745 (c.8)

Acts of Parliament (Commencement) Act 1793 (c.13)

Acts of Parliament (Expiration) 1808 (c.106)

Acts of Parliament (Mistaken References) Act 1837 (c.60)

Acts of Parliament Numbering and Citation Act 1962 (c.34)

Adam Buildings Act 1772 (c.75)

Aden, Perim and Kuria Muria Islands Act 1967 (c.71)

Addenbrooke's Hospital, Cambridge Act 1767 (c.99)

Adderbury and Oxford Road Act 1797 (c.170)

Addingham to Black Lane End Road Act 1781 (c.99)

Additional Income Tax Act 1884 (c.1)

Additional Taxes Act 1795 (c.14)

Admeasurement of Coals Act 1780 (c.34)

Administration Act 1868 (c.90)

Administration of Estates Act 1798 (c.87)

Administration of Estates Act 1869 (c.46)

Administration of Estates Act 1925 (c.23)

Administration of Estates Act 1971 (c.25)

Administration of Estates (Probate) Act 1800 (c.72)

Administration of Estates (Small Payments) Act 1965 (c.32)

Administration of Intestates' Estates Act 1856 (c.94)

Administration of Justice Act 1705 (c.3)

Administration of Justice Act 1813 (c.24)

Administration of Justice Act 1920 (c.81)

Administration of Justice Act 1925 (c.28)

Administration of Justice Act 1928 (c.26)

Administration of Justice Act 1932 (c.55)

Administration of Justice Act 1956 (c.46)

Administration of Justice Act 1960 (c.65)

Administration of Justice Act 1964 (c.42)

Administration of Justice Act 1965 (c.2)

Administration of Justice Act 1968 (c.5)

Administration of Justice Act 1969 (c.58)

Administration of Justice Act 1970 (c.31)

Administration of Justice Act 1973 (c.15)

Administration of Justice Act 1977 (c.38)

Administration of Justice Act 1982 (c.53)

Administration of Justice Act 1985 (c.61)

Administration of Justice (Appeals) Act 1934 (c.40)

Administration of Justice (Emergency Provisions) Act 1939 (c.78)

Administration of Justice (Emergency Provisions) Act 1939 (c.105)

Administration of Justice (Emergency Provisions) (Scotland) Act 1939 (c.79)

Administration of Justice (Emergency Provisions) (Scotland) Act 1979 (c.19)

Administration of Justice in Certain Boroughs Act 1836 (c.105)

Administration of Justice (Judges and Pensions) Act 1960 (c.3)

Administration of Justice (Miscellaneous Provisions) Act 1933 (c.36)

Administration of Justice (Miscellaneous Provisions) Act 1938 (c.63)

Administration of Justice, New South Wales, etc. Act 1838 (c.50)

Administration of Justice (Pensions) Act 1950 (c.11)

Administration of Justice (Scotland) Act 1809 (c.119)

Administration of Justice (Scotland) Act 1933 (c.41)

Administration of Justice (Scotland) Act 1948 (c.10)

Administration of Justice (Scotland) Act 1972 (c.59)

Administration of Justice, West Indies Act 1836 (c.17)

Admiralty and Prize Courts Act 1810 (c.118)

Admiralty and War Office Regulation Act 1878 (c.53)

Admiralty Court Act 1840 (c.65)

Admiralty Court Act 1861 (c.10)

Admiralty, etc. Acts Repeal Act 1865 (c.112)

Admiralty, etc., Courts, (Scotland) Act 1786 (c.47)

Admiralty Jurisdiction (Indian) Act 1860 (c.88)

Admiralty Lands Act 1843 (c.58)

Admiralty Lands and Works Act 1864 (c.57)

Admiralty Offences Act 1826 (c.38)

Admiralty Offences Act 1844 (c.2)

Admiralty Offences (Colonial) Act 1849 (c.96)

Admiralty Offences (Colonial) Act 1860 (c.122)

Admiralty Pensions Act 1921 (c.39)

Admiralty Powers etc. Act 1865 (c.124)

Admiralty Suits Act 1868 (c.78)

Admission of Vassals (Scotland) Act 1751 (c.20)

Adoption Act 1950 (c.26)

Adoption Act 1958 (c.5)

Adoption Act 1960 (c.59)

Adoption Act 1964 (c.57)

Adoption Act 1968 (c.53)

Adoption Act 1976 (c.36)

Adoption of Children Act 1926 (c.29)

Adoption of Children Act 1949 (c.98)

Adoption of Children (Regulation) Act 1939 (c.27)

Adoption of Children (Scotland) Act 1930 (c.37)

Adoption of Children (Workmen's Compensation) Act 1934 (c.34)

Adoption (Scotland) Act 1978 (c.28)

Adulteration of Coffee Act 1718 (c.11)

Adulteration of Food and Drugs Act 1872 (c.74)

Adulteration of Hops Act 1733 (c.19)

Adulteration of Seeds Act 1869 (c.112)

Adulteration of Seeds Act 1878 (c.17)

Adulteration of Tea Act 1730 (c.14)

Adulteration of Tea Act 1776 (c.29)

Adulteration of Tea and Coffee Act 1724 (c.30)

Advance by Bank of England Act 1781 (c.60)

Advance by Bank of England Act 1816 (c.7)

Advance by Bank of England Act 1816 (c.14)

Advance from Bank of England Act 1808 (c.3)

Advance of Money to Foreign States Act 1729 (c.5)

Advance of Unclaimed Dividends, etc. Act 1808 (c.4)

Advance of Unclaimed Dividends, etc. Act 1816 (c.97)

Advance Petroleum Revenue Tax Act 1986 (c.68)

Advance to Boyed, Benfield and Co. Act 1805 (c.78)

Advances by Bank of Ireland Act 1811 (c.35)

Advances for Public Works Act 1837 (c.51)

Advances for Public Works Act 1838 (c.88)

Advances for Public Works Act 1840 (c.10)

Advances for Public Works Act 1842 (c.9)

Advances for Public Works Act 1861 (c.80)

Advances for Public Works Act 1862 (c.30)

Advances for Railways (Ireland) Act 1847 (c.73)

Advances to County of Mayo Acts 1854 (c.110)

Advertisements (Hire Purchase) Act 1957 (c.41)

Advertisements (Hire-Purchase) Act 1967 (c.42)

Advertisements Regulation Act 1907 (c.27)

Advertisements Regulation Act 1925 (c.52)

Advertising Stations (Rating) Act 1889 (c.27)

Advowsons Act 1707 (c.18)

Aerial Navigation Act 1911 (c.4)

Aerial Navigation Act 1913 (c.22)

Affidavits in County of Durham Act 1763 (c.21)

Affidavits in County of Lancaster Act 1743 (c.7)

Affiliation Orders Act 1914 (c.6)

Affiliation Orders Act 1952 (c.41)

Affiliation Orders (Increase of Maximum Payment) Act 1918 (c.49)

Affiliation Proceedings Act 1957 (c.55)

Affiliation Proceedings (Amendment) Act 1972 (c.49)

Affirmation by Quakers Act 1701 (c.4)

Affirmations Act 1861 (c.66)

Affirmations by Quakers etc. Act 1859 (c.10)

Affirmations (Scotland) Act 1855 (c.25)

Affirmations (Scotland) Act 1865 (c.9)

African Company Act 1711 (c.34)

African Company Act 1750 (c.49)

African Company Act 1751 (c.40)

African Company Act 1783 (c.65)

African Slave Trade Act 1862 (c.40)

African Slave Trade Act 1862 (c.90)

African Slave Trade Treaty Act 1863 (c.34)

Age of Legal Capacity (Scotland) Act 1991 (c.50)

Age of Majority (Scotland) Act 1969 (c.39)

Age of Marriage Act 1929 (c.36)

Agent General for Volunteers, etc. Act 1812 (c.152)

Agent General for Volunteers, etc. Act 1815 (c.170)

Aggravated Vehicle-Taking Act 1992 (c.11)

Agricultural and Technical Instruction (Ireland) - Northern Irish Act 1899 (c.50)

Agricultural and Forestry Associations Act 1962 (c.29)

Agricultural and Forestry (Financial Provisions) Act 1991 (c.33)

Agricultural Children Act 1873 (c.67)

Agricultural Credits Act 1923 (c.34)

Agricultural Credits Act 1928 (c.43)

Agricultural Credits Act 1931 (c.35)

Agricultural Credits (Scotland) Act 1929 (c.13)

Agricultural Development Act 1939 (c.48)

Agricultural Development (Ploughing up of Land) Act 1946 (c.32)

Agricultural Gangs Act 1867 (c.130)

Agricultural Holdings Act 1900 (c.50)

Agricultural Holdings Act 1906 (c.56)

Agricultural Holdings Act 1908 (c.28)

Agricultural Holdings Act 1913 (c.21)

Agricultural Holdings Act 1914 (c.7)

Agricultural Holdings Act 1923 (c.9)

Agricultural Holdings Act 1948 (c.63)

Agricultural Holdings Act 1984 (c.41)

Agricultural Holdings Act 1986 (c.5)

Agricultural Holdings (Amendment) Act 1990 (c.15)

Agricultural Holdings (Amendment) (Scotland) Act 1983 (c.46)

Agricultural Holdings (England) Act 1875 (c.92)

Agricultural Holdings (England) Act (1875) Amendment Act 1876 (c.74)

Agricultural Holdings (England) Act 1883 (c.61)

Agricultural Holdings (Notices to Quit) Act 1977 (c.12)

Agricultural Holdings (Scotland) Act 1883 (c.62)

Agricultural Holdings (Scotland) Act 1889 (c.20)

Agricultural Holdings (Scotland) Act 1908 (c.64)

Agricultural Holdings (Scotland) Act 1923 (c.10)

Agricultural Holdings (Scotland) Act 1949 (c.75)

Agricultural Holdings (Scotland) Act 1991 (c.55)

Agricultural Holdings (Scotland) Amendment Act 1910 (c.30)

Agricultural Improvement Grants Act 1959 (c.31)

Agricultural Land (Removal of Surface Soil) Act 1953 (c.10)

Agricultural Land Sales (Restriction of Notice to Quit) Act 1919 (c.63)

Agricultural Land (Utilisation) Act 1931 (c.41)

Agricultural Marketing Act 1931 (c.42)

Agricultural Marketing Act 1933 (c.31)

Agricultural Marketing Act 1949 (c.38)
Agricultural Marketing Act 1958 (c.47)
Agricultural Marketing Act 1983 (c.3)
Agricultural Marketing (No. 2) Act 1933 (c.1)
Agricultural (Miscellaneous Provisions) Act 1949 (c.37)
Agricultural (Miscellaneous Provisions) Act 1950 (c.17)
Agricultural Mortgage Corporation Act 1956 (c.38)
Agricultural Mortgage Corporation Act 1958 (c.2)
Agricultural Produce (Grading and Marking) Act 1928 (c.19)
Agricultural Produce (Grading and Marking) Amendment Act 1931 (c.40)
Agricultural Rates Act 1896 (c.16)
Agricultural Rates Act, 1896, etc., Continuance Act 1901 (c.13)
Agricultural Rates Act, 1896, etc., Continuance Act 1905 (c.8)
Agricultural Rates Act 1923 (c.39)
Agricultural Rates Act 1929 (c.26)
Agricultural Rates (Additional Grant) Continuance Act 1925 (c.10)
Agricultural Rates, Congested Districts, and Burgh Land Tax Relief (Scotland) 1896 (c.37)
Agricultural Research Act 1955 (c.28)
Agricultural Research etc. (Pensions) Act 1961 (c.9)
Agricultural Returns Act 1925 (c.39)
Agricultural Statistics Act 1979 (c.13)
Agricultural Tenancies Act 1995 (c.8)
Agricultural Training Board Act 1982 (c.9)
Agricultural Training Board Act 1985 (c.36)
Agricultural Training Board Act 1987 (c.29)
Agricultural Wages Act 1948 (c.47)
Agricultural Wages (Regulation) Act 1924 (c.37)
Agricultural Wages (Regulation) Act 1947 (c.15)
Agricultural Wages (Regulation) Amendment Act 1939 (c.17)
Agricultural Wages (Regulation) (Scotland) Act 1937 (c.53)
Agricultural Wages (Regulation) (Scotland) Act 1939 (c.27)
Agricultural Wages (Scotland) Act 1949 (c.30)
Agriculture Act 1920 (c.76)
Agriculture Act 1937 (c.70)
Agriculture Act 1947 (c.48)
Agriculture Act 1957 (c.57)
Agriculture Act 1958 (c.71)
Agriculture Act 1967 (c.22)
Agriculture Act 1970 (c.40)
Agriculture Act 1986 (c.49)
Agriculture Act 1993 (c.37)
Agriculture (Amendment) Act 1921 (c.17)
Agriculture (Amendment) Act 1923 (c.25)
Agriculture (Amendment) Act 1984 (c.20)
Agriculture and Horticulture Act 1964 (c.28)

Agriculture and Technical Instruction (Ireland) Act 1902 (c.3)
Agriculture and Technical Instruction (Ireland) (No. 2) Act 1902 (c.33)
Agriculture (Artificial Insemination) Act 1946 (c.29)
Agriculture (Calf Subsidies) Act 1952 (c.62)
Agriculture (Emergency Payments) Act 1947 (c.32)
Agriculture (Fertilisers) Act 1952 (c.15)
Agriculture (Improvement of Roads) Act 1955 (c.20)
Agriculture (Miscellaneous Provisions) Act 1940 (c.14)
Agriculture (Miscellaneous Provisions) Act 1941 (c.50)
Agriculture (Miscellaneous Provisions) Act 1943 (c.16)
Agriculture (Miscellaneous Provisions) Act 1944 (c.28)
Agriculture (Miscellaneous Provisions) Act 1949 (c.37)
Agriculture (Miscellaneous Provisions) Act 1950 (c.17)
Agriculture (Miscellaneous Provisions) Act 1954 (c.39)
Agriculture (Miscellaneous Provisions) Act 1963 (c.11)
Agriculture (Miscellaneous Provisions) Act 1968 (c.34)
Agriculture (Miscellaneous Provisions) Act 1972 (c.62)
Agriculture (Miscellaneous Provisions) Act 1976 (c.55)
Agriculture (Miscellaneous War Provisions) Act 1940 (c.14)
Agriculture (Miscellaneous War Provisions) (No.2) Act 1940 (c.50)
Agriculture Mortgage Corporation Act 1956 (c.38)
Agriculture (Ploughing Grants) Act 1952 (c.35)
Agriculture (Poisonous Substances) Act 1952 (c.60)
Agriculture (Safety, Health and Welfare Provisions) Act 1956 (c.49)
Agriculture (Scotland) Act 1948 (c.45)
Agriculture (Small Farmers) Act 1959 (c.12)
Agriculture (Spring Traps) (Scotland) Act 1969 (c.26)
Agriculture and Horticulture Act 1964 (c.28)
Aid to Government of France Act 1794 (c.9)
Aid to Russia, etc. Act 1813 (c.13)
AIDS Control Act 1987 (c.33)
Air Corporations Act 1949 (c.91)
Air Corporations Act 1960 (c.13)
Air Corporations Act 1962 (c.5)
Air Corporations Act 1966 (c.11)
Air Corporations Act 1967 (c.33)
Air Corporations Act 1968 (c.30)
Air Corporations Act 1969 (c.43)
Air Corporations Act 1971 (c.5)
Air Force Act 1955 (c.19)

Air Force (Constitution) Act 1917 (c.51)

Air Force Reserve Act 1950 (c.33)

Air Force Reserve (Pilots and Observers) Act 1934 (c.5)

Air Guns and Shot Guns, etc. Act 1962 (c.49)

Air Ministry (Heston and Kenley Aerodromes Extension) Act 1939 (c.59)

Air Ministry (Kenley Common Acquisition) Act 1922 (c.40)

Air Navigation Act 1919 (c.3)

Air Navigation Act 1920 (c.80)

Air Navigation Act 1936 (c.44)

Air Navigation Act 1947 (c.18)

Air Navigation (Financial Provisions) Act 1938 (c.33)

Air Raid Precaution (Postponement of Financial Investigations) Act 1941 (c.10)

Air Raid Precautions Act 1937 (c.6)

Air Transport (Subsidy Agreements) Act 1930 (c.30)

Air Travel Reserve Fund Act 1975 (c.36)

Aircraft and Shipbuilding Industries Act 1977 (c.3)

Aire and Calder, Navigation Act 1774 (c.96)

Airports Act 1986 (c.31)

Airport Authority Act 1965 (c.16)

Airports Authority Act 1972 (c.8)

Airports Authority Act 1975 (c.78)

Airways Corporations Act 1949 (c.57)

Alcoholic Liquor Duties Act 1979 (c.4)

Alderney Harbour (Transfer) Act 1874 (c.92)

Alderney (Transfer of Property etc.) Act 1923 (c.15)

Alford to Cowbridge Road Act 1784 (c.62)

Aldwork Bridge, Ure Act 1772 (c.87)

Alehouses Act 1753 (c.31)

Alehouses Act 1756 (c.12)

Alexander Wilson (Provost of Edinburgh) Act 1736 (c.34)

Alice Holt Forest Act 1812 (c.72)

Aliens Act 1746 (c.44)

Aliens Act 1793 (c.4)

Aliens Act 1794 (c.82)

Aliens Act 1795 (c.24)

Aliens Act 1796 (c.109)

Aliens Act 1797 (c.92)

Aliens Act 1798 (c.50)

Aliens Act 1798 (c.77)

Aliens Act 1800 (c.24)

Aliens Act 1802 (c.92)

Aliens Act 1803 (c.155)

Aliens Act 1814 (c.155)

Aliens Act 1815 (c.54)

Aliens Act 1816 (c.86)

Aliens Act 1844 (c.66)

Aliens Act 1847 (c.83)

Aliens Act 1848 (c.20)

Aliens Act 1905 (c.13)

Aliens' Employment Act 1955 (c.18)

Aliens Restriction Act 1914 (c.12)

Aliens Restriction (Amendment) Act 1919 (c.92)

Alkali Act 1863 (c.124)

Alkali Act 1874 (c.43)

Alkali Act Perpetuation Act 1868 (c.36)

Alkali, etc., Works Regulation Act 1881 (c.37)

Alkali, etc., Works Regulation Act 1892 (c.30)

Alkali, etc., Works Regulation Act 1906 (c.14)

Alkali, etc., Works Regulation (Scotland) Act 1951 (c.21)

All Saints' Church, Newcastle Act 1786 (c.117)

All Saints' Church, Southampton Act 1791 (c.71)

All Saints' Church, Southampton Act 1793 (c.101)

Allied Forces Act 1939 (c.51)

Allied Powers (Maritime Courts) Act 1941 (c.21)

Allied Powers (War Service) Act 1942 (c.29)

Alloa Beer Duties Act 1754 (c.35)

Alloa Harbour Act 1786 (c.13)

Allotments Act 1887 (c.48)

Allotments Act 1890 (c.65)

Allotments Act 1922 (c.51)

Allotments Act 1925 (c.61)

Allotments Act 1950 (c.31)

Allotments and Cottage Gardens Compensation for Crops Act 1887 (c.26)

Allotments Extension Act 1882 (c.80)

Allotments Rating Exemption Act 1891 (c.33)

Allotments (Scotland) Act 1892 (c.54)

Allotments (Scotland) Act 1922 (c.52)

Allotments (Scotland) Act 1926 (c.5)

Allotments (Scotland) Act 1950 (c.38)

Allowance for Mint Prosecutions Act 1772 (c.52)

Allowance of Duty to Meux & Co. Act 1815 (c.189)

Allowance to Brewers Act 1785 (c.73)

Allowance to Distillers (Scotland) Act 1790 (c.39)

Allowances to Foreign Officers Act 1815 (c.126)

Allowing Time for First Meetings Act 1757 (c.13)

Alteration of Terms in Scotland Act 1708 (c.15)

Altrincham and Warrington Roads Act 1796 (c.145)

Alvingham, Lincoln, Navigation Act 1763 (c.39)

Amendment of c.10 of this Session Act 1800 (c.19)

Amendment of cc.26, 28 of this Session Act 1808 (c.71)

Amendment of c.29 of this Session Act 1793 (c.51)

American and European Payments (Financial Provisions) Act 1949 (c.17)

American Colonies Act 1766 (c.12)

American Loan Act 1915 (c.81)

American Loyalists Act 1783 (c.80)

American Loyalists Act 1785 (c.76)

American Loyalists Act 1786 (c.68)

American Loyalists Act 1787 (c.39)

American Loyalists Act 1788 (c.44)
American Loyalists Act 1789 (c.62)
American Loyalists Act 1790 (c.34)
American Prizes Act 1813 (c.63)
American Rebellion Act 1774 (c.39)
American Rebellion Act 1774 (c.45)
American Rebellion Act 1778 (c.13)
American Treaty Commissioners Act 1803 (c.135)
Amlwch Harbour Act 1793 (c.125)
Anatomy Act 1832 (c.75)
Anatomy Act 1871 (c.16)
Anatomy Act 1984 (c.14)
Anchors and Chain Cables Act 1899 (c.23)
Ancient Monument Act 1931 (c.16)
Ancient Monuments and Archaeological Areas Act 1979 (c.46)
Ancient Monuments Consolidation and Amendment Act 1913 (c.32)
Ancient Monuments Protection Act 1882 (c.73)
Ancient Monuments Protection Act 1900 (c.34)
Ancient Monuments Protection Act 1910 (c.3)
Ancient Monuments Protection (Ireland) Act 1892 (c.46)
Andover Canal Act 1789 (c.72)
Anglesey: Drainage, etc. Act 1788 (c.71)
Anglesey: Drainage Act 1790 (c.59)
Anglesey Roads Act 1765 (c.56)
Anglo-French Convention Act 1904 (c.33)
Anglo-French Treaty (Defence of France) Act 1919 (c.34)
Anglo-German Agreement Act 1890 (c.32)
Anglo-Italian Treaty (East African Territories) Act 1925 (c.9)
Anglo-Persian Oil Company (Acquisition of Capital) Act 1914 (c.37)
Anglo-Persian Oil Company (Acquisition of Capital) (Amendment) Act 1919 (c.86)
Anglo-Persian Oil Company (Payment of Calls) Act 1922 (c.26)
Anglo-Portuguese Commercial Treaty Act 1914 (c.1)
Anglo-Portuguese Commercial Treaty Act 1916 (c.39)
Anglo-Turkish (Armaments Credit) Agreement 1938 (c.60)
Anglo-Venezuelan Treaty (Island of Patos) Act 1942 (c.17)
Anguilla Act 1971 (c.63)
Anguilla Act 1980 (c.67)
Animal Boarding Establishments Act 1963 (c.43)
Animal Health Act 1981 (c.22)
Animal Health and Welfare Act 1984 (c.40)
Animals Act 1948 (c.35)
Animals Act 1971 (c.22)
Animals (Anaesthetics) Act 1919 (c.54)
Animals (Cruel Poisons) Act 1962 (c.26)
Animals (Restriction of Importation) Act 1964 (c.61)
Animals (Scientific Procedures) Act 1986 (c.14)

Animals (Scotland) Act 1987 (c.9.)
Annoyance Jurors, Westminster Acts 1861 (c.78)
Annual Revision of Rateable Property (Ireland) Amendment Act 1860 (c.4)
Annual Turnpike Acts Continuance Act 1850 (c.79)
Annual Turnpike Acts Continuance Act 1851 (c.37)
Annual Turnpike Acts Continuance Act 1853 (c.135)
Annual Turnpike Acts Continuance Act 1854 (c.58)
Annual Turnpike Acts Continuance Act 1859 (c.51)
Annual Turnpike Acts Continuance Act 1860 (c.73)
Annual Turnpike Acts Continuance Act 1861 (c.64)
Annual Turnpike Acts Continuance Act 1862 (c.72)
Annual Turnpike Acts Continuance Act 1863 (c.94)
Annual Turnpike Acts Continuance Act 1864 (c.75)
Annual Turnpike Acts Continuance Act 1865 (c.107)
Annual Turnpike Acts Continuance Act 1866 (c.105)
Annual Turnpike Acts Continuance Act 1867 (c.121)
Annual Turnpike Acts Continuance Act 1867 (c.129)
Annual Turnpike Acts Continuance Act 1868 (c.99)
Annual Turnpike Acts Continuance Act 1869 (c.90)
Annual Turnpike Acts Continuance Act 1870 (c.73)
Annual Turnpike Acts Continuance Act 1871 (c.115)
Annual Turnpike Acts Continuance Act 1872 (c.85)
Annual Turnpike Acts Continuance Act 1873 (c.90)
Annual Turnpike Acts Continuance Act 1874 (c.95)
Annual Turnpike Acts Continuance Act 1876 (c.39)
Annual Turnpike Acts Continuance Act 1877 (c.64)
Annual Turnpike Acts Continuance Act 1878 (c.62)
Annual Turnpike Acts Continuance Act 1879 (c.46)
Annual Turnpike Acts Continuance Act 1880 (c.12)
Annual Turnpike Acts Continuance Act 1881 (c.31)
Annual Turnpike Acts Continuance Act 1882 (c.52)
Annual Turnpike Acts Continuance Act 1883 (c.21)

Annual Turnpike Acts Continuance Act 1884 (c.52)
Annual Turnpike Acts Continuance Act 1885 (c.37)
Annuities Act 1704 (c.2)
Annuities Act 1799 (c.29)
Annuities Act 1799 (c.30)
Annuities, etc. Act 1702 (c.14)
Annuities, etc. Act 1704 (c.14)
Annuities (Ireland) Act 1807 (c.21)
Annuities (Prince of Wales, etc.) Act 1863 (c.1)
Annuities to Branches of Royal Family Act 1807 (c.39)
Annuities to Duke and Princess Mary of Cambridge Act 1850 (c.77)
Annuities to Duke, etc., of York 1792 (c.13)
Annuities to Duke of Sussex etc. Act 1802 (c.48)
Annuities to Lady Abercromby, etc. Act 1801 (c.59)
Annuities to Princesses Act 1812 (c.57)
Annuities to Retired Judges (Scotland) Act 1814 (c.94)
Annuities to Royal Family Act 1806 (c.145)
Annuity, Duchess of Mecklenburgh Strelitz Act 1843 (c.25)
Annuity, Duke of Albany Act 1882 (c.5)
Annuity, Duke of Edinburgh Act 1866 (c.8)
Annuity, Duke of Marlborough; Pension Act 1706 (c.6)
Annuity, etc., to Duke of Wellington Act 1814 (c.161)
Annuity (Heirs of Sir T. Clarges) Act 1799 (c.84)
Annuity, Lady Mayo Act 1872 (c.56)
Annuity (Lady of Havelock) Act 1858 (c.2)
Annuity (Lord Amherst) Act 1803 (c.159)
Annuity (Lord and Lady Raglan) Act 1855 (c.64)
Annuity, Lord Exmouth Act 1814 (c.164)
Annuity, Lord Gough Act 1846 (c.32)
Annuity Lord Hardinge Act 1846 (c.31)
Annuity (Lord Napier) Act 1868 (c.91)
Annuity (Lord Rodney) Act 1793 (c.77)
Annuity (Penn's Descendants) Act 1790 (c.46)
Annuity, Princess Beatrice Act 1885 (c.24)
Annuity, Princess Helena Act 1866 (c.7)
Annuity, Princess Mary of Cambridge Act 1866 (c.48)
Annuity, Princess Royal Act 1857 (c.2)
Annuity (Sir H. Brand) Act 1884 (c.1)
Annuity Tax in Edinburgh and Montrose Act 1860 (c.50)
Annuity Tax in Edinburgh and Montrose, etc. Act 1870 (c.87)
Annuity to Admiral Duckworth Act 1806 (c.40)
Annuity to Admiral Saumanez Act 1803 (c.37)
Annuity to Brook Watson, Esq. Act 1786 (c.93)
Annuity to Brook Watson, Esq. Act 1788 (c.43)

Annuity to Dr. Willis Act 1790 (c.44)
Annuity to Duchess of Brunswick Wolfenbuttel Act 1808 (c.59)
Annuity to Duke and Duchess of Edinburgh Act 1873 (c.80)
Annuity to Duke of Atholl, etc. Act 1805 (c.123)
Annuity to Duke of Brunswick Act 1810 (c.37)
Annuity to Duke of Clarence Act 1791 (c.34)
Annuity to Duke of Connaught Act 1871 (c.64)
Annuity to Duke of Gloucester Act 1785 (c.53)
Annuity to Duke of St. Albans Act 1788 (c.41)
Annuity to Duke of Wellington, etc. Act 1810 (c.8)
Annuity to Duke of Wellington, etc. Act 1812 (c.37)
Annuity to Family of Lord Kilwarden Act 1804 (c.76)
Annuity to Family of Sir G. Carlton Act 1788 (c.42)
Annuity to Lady Elgin Act 1864 (c.31)
Annuity to Lady Maria Carlton Act 1786 (c.88)
Annuity to Lady Nelson Act 1806 (c.4)
Annuity to Lord Beresford, etc. Act 1814 (c.162)
Annuity to Lord Camperdown Act 1797 (c.22)
Annuity to Lord Collingwood, etc. Act 1806 (c.13)
Annuity to Lord Combermere, etc. Act 1814 (c.163)
Annuity to Lord Hill Act 1814 (c.165)
Annuity to Lord Hutchinson, etc. Act 1802 (c.113)
Annuity to Lord Keane, etc. Act 1841 (c.1)
Annuity to Lord Lynedoch Act 1814 (c.166)
Annuity to Lord Nelson, etc. Act 1798 (c.1)
Annuity to Lord Rodney Act 1783 (c.86)
Annuity to Lord Rodney Act 1806 (c.147)
Annuity to Lord St. Vincent Act 1797 (c.21)
Annuity to Lord St. Vincent Act 1806 (c.50)
Annuity to Lord Walsingham Act 1815 (c.18)
Annuity to Major-Gen. Sir J. Stuart Act 1807 (c.4)
Annuity to Prince Leopold Act 1874 (c.65)
Annuity to Prince of Wales, etc. Act 1803 (c.26)
Annuity to Princess Alice Act 1861 (c.15)
Annuity to Princess Louise Act 1871 (c.1)
Annuity to Princess of Wales Act 1814 (c.160)
Annuity to Right Hon. Charles Shaw Lefevre Act 1857 (c.9)
Annuity to Sir G.A. Elliott Act 1783 (c.85)
Annuity to Sir J. Marriott Act (c.58)
Annuity to Sir J. Skynner Act 1787 (c.12)
Annuity to Sir R. Strachan Act 1806 (c.5)
Annuity to Sir Sidney Smith Act 1801 (c.5)
Annuity to Sir W.F. Williams Act 1856 (c.30)
Annuity to Viscount Lake, etc. Act 1808 (c.13)
Anstruther Easter Beer Duties Act 1748 (c.10)
Anstruther Easter Beer Duties Act 1775 (c.48)

Anstruther Union Harbour Act 1860 (c.39)
Antarctic Act 1994 (c.15)
Antarctic Minerals Act 1989 (c.21)
Antarctic Treaty Act 1967 (c.65)
Anthrax Prevention Act 1919 (c.23)
Antigua and Barbuda Act 1859 (c.13)
Anwick: Inclosure Act 1791 (c.93)
"Anzac" (Restriction on Trade Use of Word) Act 1916 (c.51)
Apothecaries Act 1702 (c.5)
Apothecaries Act 1815 (c.194)
Apothecaries Act Amendment Act 1874 (c.34)
Appeal (Forma Pauperis) Act 1893 (c.22)
Appeal in Revenue Cases (Ireland) Act 1812 (c.78)
Appeals on Civil Bills, Dublin Act 1848 (c.34)
Appellate Jurisdiction Act 1876 (c.59)
Appellate Jurisdiction Act 1887 (c.70)
Appellate Jurisdiction Act 1908 (c.51)
Appellate Jurisdiction Act 1913 (c.21)
Appellate Jurisdiction Act 1929 (c.8)
Appellate Jurisdiction Act 1947 (c.11)
Application of Bounties on Linen, etc. Act 1812 (c.96)
Application of Highway Rates to Turnpikes Act 1841 (c.59)
Appointment Act 1834 (c.22)
Appointment of a Judge at Bombay Act 1864 (c.16)
Appointment of Judges in Vacation Act 1799 (c.113)
Appointment of Revising Barristers Act 1872 (c.84)
Appointment of Superintending Magistrates, etc. Act 1814 (c.131)
Appointment of Vice-Chancellor Act 1851 (c.4)
Appointments in Cathedral Churches Act 1839 (c.14)
Apportionment Act 1820 (c.108)
Apportionment Act 1834 (c.22)
Apportionment Act 1870 (c.35)
Appraisers Licences Act 1806 (c.43)
Apprehension of Certain Offenders Act 1853 (c.118)
Apprehension of Endorsed Warrants Act 1750 (c.55)
Apprehension of Housebreakers Act 1706 (c.31)
Apprehension of Offenders Act 1804 (c.92)
Apprehension of Offenders Act 1814 (c.186)
Apprehension of Offenders Act 1843 (c.34)
Apprentices Act 1814 (c.96)
Apprentices (Settlement) Act 1757 (c.11)
Apprenticeship Indentures Act 1801 (c.22)
Appropriation Act 1775 (c.12)
Appropriation Act 1775 (c.42)
Appropriation Act 1776 (c.47)
Appropriation Act 1776 (c.49)
Appropriation Act 1778 (c.54)
Appropriation Act 1779 (c.71)
Appropriation Act 1780 (c.62)

Appropriation Act 1781 (c.57)
Appropriation Act 1782 (c.67)
Appropriation Act 1783 (c.78)
Appropriation Act 1784 (c.44)
Appropriation Act 1786 (c.61)
Appropriation Act 1787 (c.33)
Appropriation Act 1788 (c.26)
Appropriation Act 1789 (c.61)
Appropriation Act 1790 (c.32)
Appropriation Act 1791 (c.41)
Appropriation Act 1792 (c.35)
Appropriation Act 1793 (c.72)
Appropriation Act 1794 (c.49)
Appropriation Act 1795 (c.120)
Appropriation Act 1796 (c.126)
Appropriation Act 1797 (c.144)
Appropriation Act 1798 (c.90)
Appropriation Act 1799 (c.114)
Appropriation Act 1800 (c.14)
Appropriation Act 1802 (c.120)
Appropriation Act 1803 (c.162)
Appropriation Act 1804 (c.110)
Appropriation Act 1805 (c.129)
Appropriation Act 1806 (c.149)
Appropriation Act 1807 (c.76)
Appropriation Act 1808 (c.148)
Appropriation Act 1809 (c.128)
Appropriation Act 1810 (c.115)
Appropriation Act 1811 (c.117)
Appropriation Act 1812 (c.154)
Appropriation Act 1813 (c.136)
Appropriation Act 1814 (c.167)
Appropriation Act 1815 (c.187)
Appropriation Act 1835 (c.80)
Appropriation Act 1836 (c.98)
Appropriation Act 1837 (c.79)
Appropriation Act 1838 (c.111)
Appropriation Act 1839 (c.89)
Appropriation Act 1840 (c.112)
Appropriation Act 1841 (c.11)
Appropriation Act 1841 (c.53)
Appropriation Act 1842 (c.121)
Appropriation Act 1843 (c.99)
Appropriation Act 1844 (c.104)
Appropriation Act 1845 (c.130)
Appropriation Act 1846 (c.116)
Appropriation Act 1848 (c.126)
Appropriation Act 1849 (c.98)
Appropriation Act 1850 (c.107)
Appropriation Act 1851 (c.101)
Appropriation Act 1852 (c.82)
Appropriation Act 1853 (c.110)
Appropriation Act 1854 (c.121)
Appropriation Act 1855 (c.129)
Appropriation Act 1856 (c.105)
Appropriation Act 1857 (c.20)
Appropriation Act 1857 (c.69)
Appropriation Act 1858 (c.107)
Appropriation Act 1859 (c.23)
Appropriation Act 1859 (c.55)
Appropriation Act 1860 (c.131)
Appropriation Act 1861 (c.103)
Appropriation Act 1862 (c.71)

Appropriation Act 1863 (c.99)
Appropriation Act 1865 (c.123)
Appropriation Act 1866 (c.91)
Appropriation Act 1867 (c.120)
Appropriation Act 1868 (c.85)
Appropriation Act 1869 (c.93)
Appropriation Act 1870 (c.96)
Appropriation Act 1871 (c.89)
Appropriation Act 1872 (c.87)
Appropriation Act 1873 (c.79)
Appropriation Act 1874 (c.56)
Appropriation Act 1875 (c.78)
Appropriation Act 1876 (c.60)
Appropriation Act 1877 (c.61)
Appropriation Act 1878 (c.65)
Appropriation Act 1879 (c.51)
Appropriation Act 1880 (c.13)
Appropriation Act 1881 (c.56)
Appropriation Act 1882 (c.71)
Appropriation Act 1883 (c.50)
Appropriation Act 1884 (c.73)
Appropriation Act 1885 (c.64)
Appropriation Act 1886 (c.26)
Appropriation Act 1887 (c.50)
Appropriation Act 1888 (c.61)
Appropriation Act 1889 (c.70)
Appropriation Act 1890 (c.72)
Appropriation Act 1891 (c.55)
Appropriation Act 1892 (c.33)
Appropriation Act 1893 (c.60)
Appropriation Act 1894 (c.59)
Appropriation Act 1895 (c.6)
Appropriation Act 1895 (c.31)
Appropriation Act 1896 (c.46)
Appropriation Act 1897 (c.67)
Appropriation Act 1898 (c.61)
Appropriation Act 1899 (c.1)
Appropriation Act 1899 (c.49)
Appropriation Act 1900 (c.2)
Appropriation Act 1900 (c.57)
Appropriation Act 1901 (c.21)
Appropriation Act 1902 (c.27)
Appropriation Act 1903 (c.32)
Appropriation Act 1904 (c.17)
Appropriation Act 1905 (c.17)
Appropriation Act 1906 (c.26)
Appropriation Act 1907 (c.20)
Appropriation Act 1908 (c.30)
Appropriation Act 1909 (c.5)
Appropriation Act 1910 (c.14)
Appropriation Act 1911 (c.15)
Appropriation Act 1912 (c.7)
Appropriation Act 1913 (c.27)
Appropriation Act 1913 (c.35)
Appropriation Act 1914 (c.24)
Appropriation Act 1915 (c.77)
Appropriation Act 1916 (c.71)
Appropriation Act 1917 (c.52)
Appropriation Act 1918 (c.56)
Appropriation Act 1919 (c.88)
Appropriation Act 1921 (c.46)
Appropriation Act 1922 (c.3)
Appropriation Act 1922 (c.32)

Appropriation Act 1923 (c.35)
Appropriation Act 1924 (c.31)
Appropriation Act 1925 (c.57)
Appropriation Act 1926 (c.23)
Appropriation Act 1927 (c.11)
Appropriation Act 1928 (c.18)
Appropriation Act 1929 (c.22)
Appropriation Act 1930 (c.27)
Appropriation Act 1931 (c.29)
Appropriation Act 1931 (c.50)
Appropriation Act 1933 (c.34)
Appropriation Act 1934 (c.44)
Appropriation Act 1935 (c.28)
Appropriation Act 1936 (c.37)
Appropriation Act 1937 (c.55)
Appropriation Act 1938 (c.47)
Appropriation Act 1939 (c.46)
Appropriation Act 1939 (c.52)
Appropriation Act 1941 (c.38)
Appropriation Act 1942 (c.27)
Appropriation Act 1943 (c.31)
Appropriation Act 1944 (c.25)
Appropriation Act 1944 (c.30)
Appropriation Act 1946 (c.65)
Appropriation Act 1947 (c.52)
Appropriation Act 1948 (c.50)
Appropriation Act 1949 (c.48)
Appropriation Act 1950 (c.16)
Appropriation Act 1951 (c.44)
Appropriation Act 1952 (c.38)
Appropriation Act 1953 (c.35)
Appropriation Act 1954 (c.45)
Appropriation Act 1955 (c.16)
Appropriation Act 1956 (c.55)
Appropriation Act 1957 (c.63)
Appropriation Act 1959 (c.59)
Appropriation Act 1960 (c.45)
Appropriation Act 1961 (c.59)
Appropriation Act 1962 (c.45)
Appropriation Act 1963 (c.26)
Appropriation Act 1964 (c.62)
Appropriation Act 1965 (c.23)
Appropriation Act 1966 (c.3)
Appropriation Act 1967 (c.59)
Appropriation Act 1968 (c.43)
Appropriation Act 1969 (c.31)
Appropriation Act 1970 (c.25)
Appropriation Act 1971 (c.67)
Appropriation Act 1972 (c.56)
Appropriation Act 1973 (c.40)
Appropriation Act 1974 (c.2)
Appropriation Act 1975 (c.44)
Appropriation Act 1976 (c.43)
Appropriation Act 1977 (c.35)
Appropriation Act 1978 (c.57)
Appropriation Act 1979 (c.24)
Appropriation Act 1980 (c.54)
Appropriation Act 1981 (c.51)
Appropriation Act 1982 (c.40)
Appropriation Act 1983 (c.27)
Appropriation Act 1983 (c.48)
Appropriation Act 1984 (c.44)
Appropriation Act 1985 (c.55)

Appropriation Act 1986 (c.42)
Appropriation Act 1987 (c.17)
Appropriation Act 1988 (c.38)
Appropriation Act 1989 (c.25)
Appropriation Act 1990 (c.28)
Appropriation Act 1991 (c.32)
Appropriation Act 1992 (c.22)
Appropriation Act 1993 (c.33)
Appropriation Act 1994 (c.24)
Appropriation Act 1995 (c.19)
Appropriation Act 1996 (c.45)
Appropriation Act 1997 (c.31)
Appropriation Acts Amendment Act 1842 (c.1)
Appropriation, etc. Act 1785 (c.60)
Appropriation, etc. Act 1801 (c.84)
Appropriation (No. 2) Act 1902 (c.30)
Appropriation (No. 2) Act 1910 (c.38)
Appropriation (No. 2) Act 1915 (c.86)
Appropriation (No. 2) Act 1921 (c.63)
Appropriation (No. 2) Act 1925 (c.78)
Appropriation (No. 2) Act 1926 (c.33)
Appropriation (No. 2) Act 1927 (c.25)
Appropriation (No. 2) Act 1931 (c.50)
Appropriation (No. 2) Act 1939 (c.63)
Appropriation (No. 2) Act 1941 (c.43)
Appropriation (No. 2) Act 1942 (c.33)
Appropriation (No. 2) Act 1943 (c.41)
Appropriation (No. 2) Act 1944 (c.37)
Appropriation (No. 2) Act 1955 (c.3)
Appropriation (No. 2) Act 1966 (c.26)
Appropriation (No. 2) Act 1970 (c.48)
Appropriation (No. 2) Act 1974 (c.31)
Appropriation (No. 2) Act 1979 (c.51)
Appropriation (No. 2) Act 1983 (c.48)
Appropriation (No. 2) Act 1987 (c.50)
Appropriation (No. 2) Act 1992 (c.47)
Appropriation (No. 2) Act 1997 (c.57)
Appropriation (No. 3) Act 1942 (c.34)
Appropriation of Certain Duties Act 1799 (c.11)
Appropriation of Revenue Act 1700 (c.12)
Appropriation (Session 2) Act 1880 (c.40)
Appropriation (Session 2) Act 1886 (c.1)
Arbitration Act 1889 (c.49)
Arbitration Act 1934 (c.14)
Arbitration Act 1950 (c.27)
Arbitration Act 1975 (c.3)
Arbitration Act 1979 (c.42)
Arbitration Act 1996 (c.23)
Arbitration Clauses (Protocol) Act 1924 (c.39)
Arbitration (Foreign Awards) Act 1930 (c.15)
Arbitration (International Investment Disputes) Act 1966 (c.41)
Arbitration (Masters and Workmen) Act 1872 (c.46)
Arbitration (Scotland) Act 1894 (c.13)
Arbitrations Act 1844 (c.93)
Archbishops' etc., House of Residence Act 1839 (c.18)
Archbishops' Palace, Dublin Act 1804 (c.63)
Archdeaconries and Rural Deaneries Act 1874 (c.63)
Archdeaconry of Cornwall Act 1897 (c.9)
Archdeaconry of London (Additional Endowment) Act 1897 (c.45)

Archdeaconry of Rochester Act 1861 (c.131)
Architects Act 1997 (c.22)
Architects Registration Act 1938 (c.54)
Architects (Registration) Act 1931 (c.33)
Architects (Registration) Act 1934 (c.38)
Argentine Treaty Act 1842 (c.40)
Argyll Roads and Bridges Act 1775 (c.63)
Argyllshire Valuation Act 1748 (c.29)
Architects Registration (Amendment) Act 1969 (c.42)
Argyllshire Valuation Act 1748 (c.29)
Arklow Harbour Act 1882 (c.13)
Armed Forces Act 1966 (c.45)
Armed Forces Act 1971 (c.33)
Armed Forces Act 1976 (c.52)
Armed Forces Act 1981 (c.55)
Armed Forces Act 1986 (c.21)
Armed Forces Act 1991 (c.62)
Armed Forces Act 1996 (c.46)
Armed Forces (Conditions of Service) Act 1939 (c.68)
Armed Forces (Housing Loans) Act 1949 (c.77)
Armed Forces (Housing Loans) Act 1953 (c.3)
Armed Forces (Housing Loans) Act 1958 (c.1)
Armed Forces (Housing Loans) Act 1965 (c.9)
Armorial Bearings Act 1798 (c.53)
Armorial Bearings Act 1799 (c.8)
Arms and Gunpowder (Ireland) Act 1807 (c.8)
Arms and Gunpowder (Ireland) Act 1836 (c.39)
Arms and Gunpowder (Ireland) Act 1838 (c.71)
Arms Control and Disarmament (Inspections) Act 1991 (c.41)
Arms Control and Disarmament (Privileges and Immunities) Act 1988 (c.2)
Arms, etc. (Ireland) Act 1843 (c.74)
Arms (Ireland) Act 1810 (c.109)
Arms (Ireland) Act 1813 (c.78)
Army Act 1774 (c.54)
Army Act 1811 (c.106)
Army Act 1812 (c.27)
Army Act 1812 (c.120)
Army Act 1881 (c.58)
Army Act 1955 (c.18)
Army Act 1992 (c.39)
Army (Amendment) Act 1915 (c.26)
Army (Amendment) No. 2 Act 1915 (c.58)
Army and Air Force Act 1961 (c.52)
Army and Air Force (Annual) Act 1921 (c.9)
Army and Air Force (Annual) Act 1922 (c.6)
Army and Air Force (Annual) Act 1923 (c.3)
Army and Air Force (Annual) Act 1924 (c.5)
Army and Air Force (Annual) Act 1925 (c.25)
Army and Air Force (Annual) Act 1926 (c.6)
Army and Air Force (Annual) Act 1927 (c.7)
Army and Air Force (Annual) Act 1928 (c.7)
Army and Air Force (Annual) Act 1929 (c.20)
Army and Air Force (Annual) Act 1930 (c.22)
Army and Air Force (Annual) Act 1931 (c.14)

Army and Air Force (Annual) Act 1932 (c.22)
Army and Air Force (Annual) Act 1933 (c.11)
Army and Air Force (Annual) Act 1934 (c.11)
Army and Air Force (Annual) Act 1935 (c.17)
Army and Air Force (Annual) Act 1936 (c.14)
Army and Air Force (Annual) Act 1937 (c.26)
Army and Air Force (Annual) Act 1938 (c.20)
Army and Air Force (Annual) Act 1939 (c.17)
Army and Air Force (Annual) Act 1940 (c.18)
Army and Air Force (Annual) Act 1941 (c.17)
Army and Air Force (Annual) Act 1942 (c.15)
Army and Air Force (Annual) Act 1943 (c.15)
Army and Air Force (Annual) Act 1944 (c.18)
Army and Air Force (Annual) Act 1945 (c.22)
Army and Air Force (Annual) Act 1946 (c.47)
Army and Air Force (Annual) Act 1947 (c.25)
Army and Air Force (Annual) Act 1948 (c.28)
Army and Air Force (Annual) Act 1949 (c.28)
Army and Air Force (Annual) Act 1950 (c.3)
Army and Air Force (Annual) Act 1951 (c.24)
Army and Air Force (Annual) Act 1952 (c.24)
Army and Air Force (Annual) Act 1953 (c.31)
Army and Air Force (Annual) Act 1954 (c.35)
Army and Air Force (Women's Service) Act 1948 (c.21)
Army and Navy Act 1797 (c.6)
Army and Navy Act 1798 (c.4)
Army and Navy Act 1800 (c.16)
Army and Navy Act 1800 (c.29)
Army and Navy Act 1800 (c.100)
Army and Navy Act 1807 (c.15)
Army and Navy Audit Act 1889 (c.31)
Army (Annual) Act 1882 (c.7)
Army (Annual) Act 1883 (c.6)
Army (Annual) Act 1884 (c.8)
Army (Annual) Act 1885 (c.8)
Army (Annual) Act 1886 (c.8)
Army (Annual) Act 1887 (c.2)
Army (Annual) Act 1888 (c.4)
Army (Annual) Act 1889 (c.3)
Army (Annual) Act 1890 (c.4)
Army (Annual) Act 1891 (c.5)
Army (Annual) Act 1892 (c.2)
Army (Annual) Act 1893 (c.4)
Army (Annual) Act 1894 (c.3)
Army (Annual) Act 1895 (c.7)
Army (Annual) Act 1896 (c.2)
Army (Annual) Act 1897 (c.3)
Army (Annual) Act 1898 (c.1)
Army (Annual) Act 1899 (c.3)
Army (Annual) Act 1900 (c.5)
Army (Annual) Act 1901 (c.2)
Army (Annual) Act 1902 (c.2)
Army (Annual) Act 1903 (c.4)
Army (Annual) Act 1904 (c.5)
Army (Annual) Act 1905 (c.2)
Army (Annual) Act 1906 (c.2)
Army (Annual) Act 1907 (c.2)
Army (Annual) Act 1908 (c.2)
Army (Annual) Act 1909 (c.3)
Army (Annual) Act 1910 (c.6)
Army (Annual) Act 1911 (c.3)
Army (Annual) Act 1912 (c.5)

Army (Annual) Act 1913 (c.2)
Army (Annual) Act 1914 (c.2)
Army (Annual) Act 1915 (c.25)
Army (Annual) Act 1916 (c.5)
Army (Annual) Act (1916) Amendment 1917 (c.10)
Army (Annual) Act 1917 (c.9)
Army (Annual) Act 1918 (c.6)
Army (Annual) Act 1919 (c.11)
Army Chaplains Act 1868 (c.83)
Army (Conditions of Enlistment) Act 1957 (c.50)
Army (Courts of Inquiry) Act 1916 (c.33)
Army Discipline and Regulation Act 1879 (c.33)
Army Discipline and Regulation (Annual) Act 1880 (c.9)
Army Discipline and Regulation (Annual) Act 1881 (c.9)
Army Enlistment Act 1849 (c.73)
Army Enlistment Act 1855 (c.4)
Army Enlistment Act 1858 (c.55)
Army Enlistment Act 1867 (c.34)
Army in Ireland Act 1768 (c.13)
Army Pensions Act 1830 (c.41)
Army Pensions Act 1914 (c.83)
Army Prize Money Act 1814 (c.86)
Army Prize Money Act 1848 (c.103)
Army Prize (Shares of Deceased) Act 1864 (c.36)
Army Reserve Act 1950 (c.32)
Army Reserve Act 1962 (c.10)
Army Reserve Act 1969 (c.23)
Army Schools Act 1891 (c.16)
Army (Supply of Food, Forage and Stores) Act 1914 (c.26)
Army (Suspension of Sentences) Act 1915 (c.23)
Army (Suspension of Sentences) Amendment Act 1916 (c.103)
Army (Transfer) Act 1915 (c.43)
Arrangements Between Debtors and Creditors Act 1844 (c.70)
Arranmore Polling District Act 1878 (c.75)
Arrears of Crown, etc., Rents (Ireland) Act 1816 (c.71)
Arrears of Crown Rents (Ireland) Act 1811 (c.91)
Arrears of Rent (Ireland) Act 1882 (c.47)
Arrest for Debtors Act 1851 (c.52)
Arrest in Personal Actions (Ireland) Act 1841 (c.17)
Arsenic Act 1851 (c.13)
Art Act 1866 (c.16)
Art Unions Act 1846 (c.48)
Art Unions Indemnity Act 1844 (c.109)
Art Unions Indemnity Act 1845 (c.57)
Arthur Jenkins Indemnity Act 1941 (c.1)
Articles of Commerce (Returns, &c.) Act 1914 (c.65)
Artificers Act 1718 (c.27)
Artificers etc. Act 1749 (c.13)
Artificial Cream Act 1929 (c.32)

Artillery and Rifle Ranges Act 1885 (c.36)

Artillery Corps, etc. Act 1795 (c.83)

Artizans and Labourers Dwellings Act 1868 (c.130)

Artizans and Labourers Dwellings Act (1868) Amendment 1879 (c.64)

Artizans' and Labourers' Dwellings Improvement Act 1875 (c.36)

Artizans and Labourers Dwellings Improvement Act 1879 (c.63)

Artizans and Labourers Dwellings Improvement (Scotland) Act 1875 (c.49)

Artizans and Labourers Dwellings Improvement (Scotland) Act 1880 (c.2)

Artizans' Dwellings Act (1868) Amendment Act (1879) Amendment 1880 (c.8)

Artizans Dwellings Act 1882 (c.54)

Arun, Sussex: Navigation Act 1785 (c.100)

Arundel: Improvement Act 1785 (c.90)

Ascertaining of Strength of Spirits Act 1791 (c.44)

Ashburton Roads Act 1776 (c.79)

Assaulting a Privy Counsellor Act 1710 (c.21)

Assaults (Ireland) Act 1814 (c.181)

Assaults (Ireland) Act 1815 (c.88)

Assaults (Ireland) Act 1839 (c.77)

Assaults (Ireland) Act 1844 (c.23)

Assaults (Ireland) Act 1849 (c.38)

Assaults with Intent to Rob Act 1733 (c.21)

Assay of Imported Watch-Cases (Existing Stocks Exemption) Act 1907 (c.8)

Assay of Plate Act 1702 (c.3)

Assessed Rates Act 1879 (c.10)

Assessed Taxes Act 1791 (c.5)

Assessed Taxes Act 1805 (c.13)

Assessed Taxes Act 1805 (c.105)

Assessed Taxes Act 1806 (c.78)

Assessed Taxes Act 1810 (c.104)

Assessed Taxes Act 1811 (c.72)

Assessed Taxes Act 1812 (c.93)

Assessed Taxes Act 1812 (c.147)

Assessed Taxes Act 1816 (c.66)

Assessed Taxes Act 1837 (c.61)

Assessed Taxes Act 1840 (c.38)

Assessed Taxes Act 1841 (c.26)

Assessed Taxes Act 1845 (c.36)

Assessed Taxes Act 1851 (c.33)

Assessed Taxes Act 1854 (c.1)

Assessed Taxes Composition Act 1850 (c.96)

Assessed Taxes and Income Tax Act 1846 (c.56)

Assessed Taxes, etc. Act 1839 (c.35)

Assessed Taxes, etc. (Ireland) Act 1807 (c.11)

Assessed Taxes, etc. (Ireland) Act 1816 (c.57)

Assessed Taxes (Ireland) Act 1807 (c.21)

Assessed Taxes (Ireland) Act 1808 (c.42)

Assessed Taxes (Ireland) Act 1815 (c.61)

Assessed Taxes (Ireland) Act 1815 (c.67)

Assessed Taxes (Ireland) Act 1815 (c.140)

Assessed Taxes, Property Tax and Duty on Pensions and Offices of Profit Act 1844 (c.46)

Assessionable Manors Award Act 1848 (c.83)

Assessment of Taxes Act 1808 (c.141)

Assessments in Edinburgh Act 1861 (c.27)

Assessor of Public Undertakings (Scotland) Act 1934 (c.22)

Assise and Making of Bread, London Act 1797 (c.98)

Assise of Bread Act 1798 (c.62)

Assise of Fuel Act 1710 (c.20)

Assise of Fuel Act 1711 (c.5)

Assistant Postmaster-General Act 1909 (c.14)

Assizes Act 1839 (c.72)

Assizes and Quarter Sessions Act 1908 (c.41)

Assizes for Cornwall Act 1715 (c.45)

Assizes (Ireland) Act 1825 (c.51)

Assizes (Ireland) Act 1835 (c.26)

Assizes (Ireland) Act 1850 (c.85)

Assizes (Ireland) Act 1850 (c.88)

Assizes Relief Act 1889 (c.12)

Association of County Councils (Scotland) Act 1946 (c.77)

Assurance Companies Act 1909 (c.49)

Assurance Companies Act 1946 (c.28)

Assurance Companies (Winding Up) Act 1933 (c.9)

Assurance Companies (Winding Up) Act 1935 (c.45)

Assurance on French Ships Act 1747 (c.4)

Asthall to Buckland Road Act 1777 (c.105)

Asylum and Immigration Act 1996 (c.49)

Asylum and Immigration Appeals Act 1993 (c.23)

Asylums and Certified Institutions (Officers Pensions) Act 1918 (c.33)

Asylums' Officers Superannuation Act 1909 (c.48)

Atomic Energy Act 1946 (c.80)

Atomic Energy Act 1989 (c.7)

Atomic Energy Authority Act 1954 (c.32)

Atomic Energy Authority Act 1959 (c.5)

Atomic Energy Authority Act 1971 (c.11)

Atomic Energy Authority Act 1986 (c.3)

Atomic Energy Authority Act 1995 (c.37)

Atomic Energy Authority (Special Constables) Act 1976 (c.23)

Atomic Energy Authority (Weapons Group) Act 1973 (c.4)

Atomic Energy (Miscellaneous Provisions) Act 1981 (c.48)

Atomic Weapons Establishment Act 1991 (c.46)

Attachment of Earnings Act 1971 (c.32)

Attachment of Goods (Ireland) Act 1850 (c.73)

Attainder of Bishop of Rochester Act 1722 (c.17)

Attainder of David Ogilvy: Disabilities Removed on Pardon Act 1783 (c.34)

Attainder of Duke of Ormonde Act 1714 (c.17)

Attainder of Earl of Kellie and Others Act 1745 (c.26)

Attainder of Earl of Mar and Others Act 1715 (c.32)

Attainder of Earl of Marischal and Others Act 1715 (c.42)

Attainder of George Kelley Act 1722 (c.16)

Attainder of John Plunket Act 1722 (c.15)

Attainder of Thomas Forster and Others Act 1715 (c.53)

Attainder of Viscount Bolingbroke Act 1714 (c.16)

Attempted Rape Act 1948 (c.19)

Attendance of Witnesses Act 1854 (c.34)

Attorneys Act 1809 (c.28)

Attorneys and Solicitors Act 1728 (c.23)

Attorneys and Solicitors Act 1732 (c.27)

Attorneys and Solicitors Act (1860) Amendment 1872 (c.81)

Attorneys and Solicitors Act 1870 (c.28)

Attorneys and Solicitors Act 1874 (c.68)

Attorneys and Solicitors (Ireland) Act 1866 (c.84)

Auction Duties Act 1815 (c.142)

Auction Duties, etc. Act 1779 (c.56)

Auction Duties (Ireland) Act 1807 (c.17)

Auction Duties (Ireland) Act 1814 (c.82)

Auction Duty Act 1792 (c.41)

Auction Duty Act 1807 (c.65)

Auction Duty Act 1812 (c.53)

Auction Duty, etc. Act 1790 (c.26)

Auctioneers Act 1845 (c.15)

Auctioneers' Licences Act 1776 (c.50)

Auctions (Bidding Agreements) Act 1927 (c.12)

Auctions (Bidding Agreements) Act 1969 (c.56)

Auctions Duties (Ireland) Act 1809 (c.100)

Audit (Local Authorities) Act 1927 (c.31)

Audit (Local Authorities etc.) Act 1922 (c.14)

Audit (Miscellaneous Provisions) Act 1996 (c.10)

Audit of Accounts Act 1813 (c.100)

Audit of Accounts, etc. Act 1813 (c.150)

Audit of Military Accounts (Ireland) Act 1812 (c.51)

Audit of Public Accounts Act 1780 (c.40)

Audit of Public Accounts Act 1780 (c.45)

Audit of Public Accounts Act 1780 (c.54)

Audit of Public Accounts Act 1782 (c.50)

Audit of Public Accounts Act 1784 (c.13)

Audit of Public Accounts Act 1785 (c.52)

Audit of Public Accounts Act 1785 (c.68)

Audit of Public Accounts Act 1786 (c.67)

Audit of Public Accounts Act 1794 (c.59)

Audit of Public Accounts Act 1805 (c.55)

Audit of Public Accounts Act 1806 (c.141)

Audit of Public Accounts (Ireland) Act 1812 (c.52)

Auditing of Public Accounts Act 1805 (c.91)

Auditing of Public Accounts Act 1809 (c.95)

Auditing of the Public Accounts Act 1783 (c.68)

Auditor of the Exchequer Act (1806) (c.1)

Auditors of Land Revenue Act 1799 (c.83)

Augmentation of Benefices Act 1854 (c.84)

Augmentation of 60th Regiment Act 1797 (c.13)

Augmentation of 60th Regiment Act 1799 (c.104)

Augmentation of 60th Regiment Act 1813 (c.12)

Australia Act 1986 (c.2)

Australian Colonies Act 1801 (c.44)

Australian Colonies Duties Act 1873 (c.22)

Australian Colonies Duties Act 1895 (c.3)

Australian Colonies, Waste Lands Act 1842 (c.36)

Australian Constitution (Public Record Copy) Act 1990 (c.17)

Australian Constitutions Act 1842 (c.76)

Australian Constitutions Act 1844 (c.74)

Australian Constitutions Act 1850 (c.59)

Australian Constitutions Act 1862 (c.11)

Australian Passengers Act 1861 (c.52)

Australian States Constitution Act 1907 (c.7)

Australian Waste Lands Act 1855 (c.56)

Austrian Loan Guarantee Act 1931 (c.5)

Austrian State Treaty Act 1955 (c.1)

Auxiliary Air Force and Air Force Reserve Act 1924 (c.15)

Auxiliary and Reserve Forces Act 1949 (c.96)

Auxiliary Forces Act 1953 (c.50)

Average Price of Brown Sugar Act 1809 (c.43)

Aviation and Maritime Security Act 1990 (c.31)

Aviation Security Act 1982 (c.36)

Axminster Roads Act 1754 (c.32)

Aylesbury Gaol and Shire Hall: Rate in Buckinghamshire Act 1736 (c.10)

Aylesbury to West Wycombe Road Act 1795 (c.149)

Ayre and Lamark Roads Act 1771 (c.90)

Ayr Bridge Act 1785 (c.37)

Ayr (County) Roads Act 1797 (c.162)

Ayr Harbour Act 1772 (c.22)

Ayr Harbour Act 1794 (c.99)

Ayr Roads Act 1757 (c.57)

Ayr Roads Act 1767 (c.106)

Ayr Roads Act 1774 (c.109)

Ayr Roads Act 1789 (c.79)

Ayr Roads Act 1791 (c.95)

Ayr Roads Act 1791 (c.107)

Ayr Roads Act 1792 (c.121)

Backing of Warrants (Republic of Ireland) Act 1965 (c.45)

Bacon Industry Act 1938 (c.71)

Bacon Industry (Amendment) Act 1939 (c.10)

Badgers Act 1973 (c.57)

Badgers Act 1991 (c.36)

Badgers (Further Protection) Act 1991 (c.35)

Badgers (Protection) Act 1992 (c.51)

Bagshot to Hertford Bridge Hill Road Act 1777 (c.84)
Bagshot to Winchester Road Act 1773 (c.88)
Bahama Islands (Constitution) Act 1963 (c.56)
Bahama Islands Trade Act 1812 (c.99)
Bahamas Independence Act 1973 (c.27)
Bail Act 1898 (c.7)
Bail Act 1976 (c.63)
Bail (Amendment) Act 1993 (c.26)
Bail Bonds Act 1808 (c.58)
Bail etc. (Scotland) Act 1980 (c.4)
Bail in Cases of Forgery, etc. (Scotland) Act 1835 (c.73)
Bail in Criminal Cases (Scotland) Act 1724 (c.26)
Bail in Criminal Cases (Scotland) Act 1799 (c.49)
Bail in Error Act 1845 (c.68)
Bail in Error Act 1853 (c.32)
Bail (Scotland) Act 1888 (c.36)
Bails Act 1869 (c.38)
Bakehouse Regulation Act 1863 (c.40)
Baking Industry (Hours of Work) Act 1938 (c.41)
Baking Industry (Hours of Work) Act 1954 (c.57)
Baking Trade Act 1810 (c.73)
Baking Trade, Dublin Act 1802 (c.8)
Balby to Worksop Road Act 1765 (c.67)
Balby to Worksop Road Act 1787 (c.84)
Bale and Dolgelly Roads Act 1796 (c.147)
Ballot Act 1872 (c.33)
Banbury Church Act 1790 (c.72)
Banbury Road Act 1780 (c.67)
Banbury to Lutterworth Road Act 1785 (c.128)
Bancroft's Patent Act 1785 (c.38)
Bangladesh Act 1973 (c.49)
Bank Act 1892 (c.48)
Bank Charter Act 1844 (c.32)
Bank Holiday (Ireland) Act 1903 (c.1)
Bank Holidays Act 1871 (c.17)
Bank Notes (Scotland) Act 1765 (c.49)
Bank Notes Act 1833 (c.83)
Bank Notes Act 1841 (c.50)
Bank Notes Act 1852 (c.2)
Bank Notes Act 1853 (c.2)
Bank Notes Forgery Act 1801 (c.57)
Bank Notes (Forgery) Act 1805 (c.89)
Bank Notes Forgery (Scotland) Act 1820 (c.92)
Bank Notes (Ireland) Act 1864 (c.78)
Bank Notes (Scotland) Act 1765 (c.49)
Bank Notes (Scotland) Act 1845 (c.38)
Bank of Ayr Act 1774 (c.21)
Bank of Bombay Failure Commissioners Act 1868 (c.63)
Bank of England Act 1694 (c.20)
Bank of England Act 1696 (c.20)
Bank of England Act 1707 (c.59)
Bank of England Act 1708 (c.30)
Bank of England Act 1709 (c.1)

Bank of England Act 1710 (c.7)
Bank of England Act 1716 (c.8)
Bank of England Act 1727 (c.8)
Bank of England Act 1728 (c.3)
Bank of England Act 1741 (c.13)
Bank of England Act 1745 (c.6)
Bank of England Act 1750 (c.4)
Bank of England Act 1784 (c.32)
Bank of England Act 1785 (c.83)
Bank of England Act 1791 (c.33)
Bank of England Act 1800 (c.28)
Bank of England Act 1833 (c.98)
Bank of England Act 1854 (c.1)
Bank of England Act 1861 (c.3)
Bank of England Act 1946 (c.27)
Bank of England (Advance) Act 1816 (c.96)
Bank of England Buildings Act 1764 (c.49)
Bank of England: Buildings Act 1766 (c.76)
Bank of England (Election of Directors) Act 1872 (c.34)
Bank of England Notes Act 1773 (c.79)
Bank of England Notes Act 1797 (c.28)
Bank of England Site Act 1793 (c.15)
Bank of England Stock Act 1796 (c.90)
Bank of Ireland Act 1808 (c.103)
Bank of Ireland Act 1860 (c.31)
Bank of Ireland Act 1865 (c.16)
Bank of Ireland Advances Act 1837 (c.59)
Bank of Ireland Advances Act 1838 (c.81)
Bank of Ireland Advances Act 1839 (c.91)
Bank of Ireland Charter Act 1872 (c.5)
Bank of Ireland, Transfer of Stocks Act 1862 (c.21)
Bank of Scotland Act 1774 (c.32)
Bank of Scotland Act 1784 (c.12)
Bank of Scotland Act 1792 (c.25)
Bank of Scotland Act 1794 (c.19)
Bank Post Bills Composition (Ireland) Act
Bank (Scotland) Act 1797 (c.40)
Bank (Scotland) Act 1797 (c.137)
Bankers' Books Evidence Act 1876 (c.48)
Bankers' Books Evidence Act 1879 (c.11)
Bankers' Composition Act 1856 (c.20)
Bankers' Composition (Scotland) Act 1853 (c.63)
Bankers' (Scotland) Act 1854 (c.73)
Bankers' Debt Act 1703 (c.9)
Bankers (Ireland) Act 1845 (c.37)
Bankers (Northern Ireland) Act 1928 (c.15)
Banking Act 1979 (c.37)
Banking Act 1987 (c.22)
Banking and Financial Dealings Act 1971 (c.80)
Banking Companies' (Shares) Act 1867 (c.29)
Banking Copartnerships Act 1864 (c.32)
Bankrupt and Insolvent Act 1857 (c.60)
Bankruptcy Act 1621 (c.18)
Bankruptcy Act 1716 (c.12)
Bankruptcy Act 1836 (c.27)
Bankruptcy Act 1839 (c.29)
Bankruptcy Act 1839 (c.86)
Bankruptcy Act 1842 (c.122)

Bankruptcy Act 1845 (c.48)
Bankruptcy Act 1852 (c.77)
Bankruptcy Act 1854 (c.119)
Bankruptcy Act 1861 (c.134)
Bankruptcy Act 1862 (c.99)
Bankruptcy Act 1869 (c.71)
Bankruptcy Act 1883 (c.52)
Bankruptcy Act 1890 (c.71)
Bankruptcy Act 1914 (c.59)
Bankruptcy (Agricultural Labourers' Wages) Act 1886 (c.28)
Bankruptcy Amendment Act 1868 (c.104)
Bankruptcy (Amendment) Act 1926 (c.7)
Bankruptcy and Cessio (Scotland) Act 1881 (c.22)
Bankruptcy and Deeds of Arrangement Act 1913 (c.34)
Bankruptcy and Real Securities (Scotland) Act 1857 (c.19)
Bankruptcy Appeals (County Courts) Act 1884 (c.9)
Bankruptcy Court Act 1853 (c.81)
Bankruptcy (Discharge and Closure) Act 1887 (c.66)
Bankruptcy Disqualification Act 1871 (c.50)
Bankruptcy, etc. Act 1847 (c.102)
Bankruptcy, etc. (Ireland) Act 1859 (c.62)
Bankruptcy Frauds and Disabilities (Scotland) Act 1884 (c.16)
Bankruptcy (Ireland) Act 1836 (c.14)
Bankruptcy (Ireland) Act 1837 (c.48)
Bankruptcy (Ireland) Act 1849 (c.107)
Bankruptcy (Ireland) Amendment Act 1872 (c.58)
Bankruptcy Law Consolidation Act 1849 (c.106)
Bankruptcy (Office Accommodation) Act 1885 (c.47)
Bankruptcy (Office Accommodation) Act 1886 (c.12)
Bankruptcy Repeal and Insolvent Court Act 1869 (c.83)
Bankruptcy (Scotland) Act 1839 (c.41)
Bankruptcy (Scotland) Act 1853 (c.53)
Bankruptcy (Scotland) Act 1856 (c.79)
Bankruptcy (Scotland) Act 1875 (c.26)
Bankruptcy (Scotland) Act 1913 (c.20)
Bankruptcy (Scotland) Act 1985 (c.66)
Bankruptcy (Scotland) Act 1993 (c.6)
Bankruptcy (Scotland) Amendment Act 1860 (c.33)
Bankrupts Act 1705 (c.4)
Bankrupts Act 1706 (c.22)
Bankrupts Act 1711 (c.25)
Bankrupts Act 1718 (c.24)
Bankrupts Act 1720 (c.19)
Bankrupts Act 1720 (c.31)
Bankrupts Act 1731 (c.30)
Bankrupts Act 1742 (c.27)
Bankrupts Act 1745 (c.32)
Bankrupts Act 1763 (c.33)
Bankrupts Act 1772 (c.47)
Bankrupts Act 1794 (c.57)

Bankrupts Act 1797 (c.124)
Bankrupts Act 1806 (c.135)
Bankrupts (England) and (Ireland) Act 1809 (c.121)
Bankrupts, etc. Act 1763 (c.36)
Bankrupts Release Act 1848 (c.86)
Banks (Scotland) Act 1797 (c.62)
Baptismal Fees Abolition Act 1872 (c.36)
Barbados Independence Act 1966 (c.37)
Barbed Wire Act 1893 (c.32)
Barking Act 1786 (c.115)
Barmouth Harbour Act 1797 (c.50)
Barnsley Canal Act 1793 (c.110)
Barnsley Canal Act 1793 (c.115)
Barnstaple Roads Act 1763 (c.35)
Barnstaple Roads Act 1783 (c.31)
Barrack Lane, Windsor Act 1867 (c.109)
Barracks Act 1890 (c.25)
Barristers Admission (Ireland) Act 1885 (c.20)
Barristers Admission, Stamp Duty Act 1874 (c.19)
Barristers (Qualifications for Office) Act 1961 (c.44)
Barthomley Church, Chester Act 1789 (c.11)
Basingstoke Canal Act 1778 (c.75)
Basingstoke Canal Act 1793 (c.16)
Basingstoke Roads Act 1797 (c.169)
Basingstoke to Winchester Road Act 1795 (c.162)
Basses Lights Act 1869 (c.77)
Basses Lights Act 1872 (c.55)
Bastard Children Act 1732 (c.31)
Bastard Children Act 1839 (c.85)
Bastards Act 1810 (c.51)
Bastards (Scotland) Act 1836 (c.22)
Bastardy Act 1809 (c.68)
Bastardy Act 1845 (c.10)
Bastardy Act 1923 (c.23)
Bastardy (Ireland) Act 1863 (c.21)
Bastardy Laws Act Amendment 1872 (c.65)
Bastardy Laws Amendment Act 1873 (c.9)
Bastardy Orders Act 1880 (c.32)
Bastardy (Witness Process) Act 1929 (c.38)
Bath City Prison Act 1871 (c.46)
Bath Highway, Streets, etc. Act 1707 (c.42)
Bath Highway, Streets, etc. Act 1720 (c.19)
Bath Hospital Act 1738 (c.31)
Bath Hospital Act 1779 (c.23)
Bath: Improvement Act 1766 (c.70)
Bath: Improvement Act 1789 (c.73)
Bath Roads Act 1757 (c.67)
Bath Roads Act 1758 (c.51)
Bath Roads Act 1760 (c.31)
Bath Roads Act 1793 (c.144)
Bath Roads, Streets, etc. Act 1738 (c.20)
Bath (Streets, Buildings, Watch etc.) 1757 (c.65)
Baths and Washhouses Act 1846 (c.74)
Baths and Washhouses Act 1847 (c.61)
Baths and Washhouses Act 1878 (c.14)
Baths and Washhouses Act 1882 (c.30)
Baths and Washhouses Act 1896 (c.59)

15

Baths and Washhouses Act 1899 (c.29)
Baths and Washhouses (Ireland) Act 1846 (c.87)
Bathwick Roads and Bridges, etc. Act 1769 (c.95)
Battersea Bridge Act 1766 (c.66)
Battersea Bridge and Embankment, etc. Act 1846 (c.39)
Battersea Parish Church Act 1774 (c.95)
Battersea Park Act 1846 (c.38)
Battersea Park Act 1851 (c.77)
Battersea Park Act 1853 (c.47)
Battle-axe Guards (Ireland) Act 1813 (c.54)
Bawtry to Markham Road Act 1793 (c.136)
Bawtry by Selby Road Act 1793 (c.166)
Beaconsfield and Redhill Road Act 1750 (c.32)
Beaconsfield and Stokenchurch Road Act 1759 (c.37)
Beaconsfield to Stokenchurch Road Act 1775 (c.70)
Beaconsfield to Stokenchurch Road Act 1794 (c.142)
Beccles: Improvement Act 1796 (c.51)
Bedford and Buckingham Highways Act 1708 (c.25)
Bedford and Buckingham Highways Act 1709 (c.25)
Bedford and Buckingham Roads Act 1727 (c.10)
Bedford and Buckingham Roads Act 1754 (c.21)
Bedford and Buckingham Roads Act 1754 (c.34)
Bedford and Buckingham Roads Act 1780 (c.68)
Bedford and Buckingham Roads Act 1790 (c.114)
Bedford and Hertford Roads Act 1742 (c.42)
Bedford and Hertford Roads Act 1775 (c.72)
Bedford and Hertford Roads Act 1786 (c.130)
Bedford and Hertford Roads Act 1795 (c.163)
Bedford and Hunts. Roads Act 1770 (c.83)
Bedford and Hunts. Roads Act 1791 (c.96)
Bedford and Northants Roads Act 1754 (c.33)
Bedford and Woburn Road Act 1796 (c.151)
Bedford Level Act 1754 (c.19)
Bedford Level Act 1756 (c.9)
Bedford Level Act 1772 (c.9)
Bedford Level Act 1780 (c.25)
Bedford Level Act 1783 (c.25)
Bedford Level Act 1789 (c.22)
Bedford Level Act 1796 (c.73)
Bedford Level and Swaffham Drainage Act 1767 (c.53)
Bedford Level: Drainage Act 1757 (c.18)
Bedford Level: Drainage Act 1771 (c.78)
Bedford Level: Drainage Act 1772 (c.40)
Bedford Level: Drainage Act 1772 (c.45)
Bedford Level: Drainage Act 1772 (c.49)
Bedford Level: Drainage Act 1775 (c.12)
Bedford Level: Drainage Act 1777 (c.65)

Bedford Level: Drainage Act 1779 (c.24)
Bedford Level: Drainage Act 1796 (c.33)
Bedford Roads Act 1731 (c.26)
Bedford Roads Act 1772 (c.89)
Bedford Roads Act 1772 (c.107)
Bedford Roads Act 1777 (c.94)
Bedford Roads Act 1793 (c.178)
Bedford: Poor Relief Act 1794 (c.98)
Bedford to Kimbolton Road Act 1795 (c.148)
Bedfordshire and Buckinghamshire Roads Act 1706 (c.4)
Bedfordshire and Buckinghamshire Roads Act 1739 (c.9)
Bedfordshire and Hertfordshire Roads Act 1763 (c.27)
Bedfordshire Highways Act 1706 (c.13)
Bedfordshire Roads Act 1724 (c.20)
Bedfordshire Roads Act 1736 (c.24)
Bedfordshire Roads Act 1753 (c.41)
Bee Pest Prevention (Ireland) Act 1908 (c.34)
Beef and Veal Customs Duties Act 1937 (c.8)
Beer Act 1761 (c.14)
Beer Act 1816 (c.58)
Beer and Malt (Ireland) Act 1809 (c.57)
Beer Dealers Retail Licences Act 1880 (c.6)
Beer Dealers, Retail Licences (Amendment) Act 1882 (c.34)
Beer, Devon, Harbour Act 1792 (c.92)
Beer Duties, Borrowstoness Act 1743 (c.21)
Beer Duties, Borrowstoness Act 1767 (c.90)
Beer Duties: Borrowstoness Act 1794 (c.91)
Beer, etc., Licences (Great Britain) Act 1816 (c.113)
Beer Licences Regulation (Ireland) Act 1877 (c.4)
Beer Retailers etc., Retail Licences (Ireland) Act 1900 (c.30)
Beerhouse Act 1840 (c.61)
Beerhouse Act 1870 (c.111)
Beerhouses (Ireland) Act 1864 (c.35)
Beerhouses (Ireland) Act (1864) Amendment 1871 (c.111)
Bees Act 1980 (c.12)
Behring Sea Award Act 1894 (c.2)
Belfast Borough Extension Act 1853 (c.114)
Belfast Commission Act 1886 (c.4)
Belfast Constabulary Act 1866 (c.46)
Belfast Custom House Act 1852 (c.30)
Belize Act 1981 (c.52)
Benefice (Ireland) Act 1865 (c.82)
Benefices Act 1807 (c.75)
Benefices Act 1808 (c.5)
Benefices Act 1898 (c.48)
Benefices (England) Act 1803 (c.84)
Benefices (England) Act 1803 (c.109)
Benefices (Ireland) Act 1808 (c.66)
Benefices (Ireland) Act 1860 (c.72)
Benefices (Scotland) Act 1843 (c.61)
Benefit Building Societies Act 1836 (c.32)
Benthall Bridge, Severn Act 1776 (c.17)
Berkshire Act 1751 (c.21)
Berkshire and Oxford Roads Act 1765 (c.55)
Berkshire and Southampton Roads Act 1772 (c.78)

Berkshire and Southampton Roads Act 1794 (c.141)

Berkshire and Wiltshire Roads Act 1770 (c.100)

Berkshire and Wiltshire Roads Act 1771 (c.97)

Berkshire and Wiltshire Roads Act 1781 (c.91)

Berkshire and Wiltshire Roads Act 1781 (c.101)

Berkshire and Wiltshire Roads Act 1793 (c.138)

Berkshire Highways Act 1713 (c.28)

Berkshire, Oxford, Buckinghamshire and Hertford Roads Act 1787 (c.81)

Berkshire Roads Act 1732 (c.16)

Berkshire Roads Act 1738 (c.11)

Berkshire Roads Act 1746 (c.6)

Berkshire Roads Act 1751 (c.21)

Berkshire Roads Act 1756 (c.77)

Berkshire Roads Act 1756 (c.81)

Berkshire Roads Act 1771 (c.70)

Berkshire Roads Act 1772 (c.104)

Berkshire Roads Act 1778 (c.99)

Berkshire Roads Act 1783 (c.100)

Berkshire Roads Act 1790 (c.106)

Berkshire Roads Act 1791 (c.105)

Berkshire Roads Act 1794 (c.132)

Bermuda Constitution Act 1967 (c.63)

Bermondsey, etc.: Streets Act 1785 (c.23)

Bermondsey (Poor Relief) Act 1757 (c.45)

Bermondsey: Poor Relief Act 1791 (c.19)

Bermuda Trade Act 1813 (c.50)

Berwick and Durham Roads Act 1793 (c.185)

Berwick-on-Tweed Act 1836 (c.103)

Berwick Roads Act 1753 (c.82)

Berwick Roads Act 1766 (c.73)

Berwick Roads Act 1772 (c.97)

Berwick Roads Act 1779 (c.79)

Berwick Roads Act 1781 (c.91)

Berwick Roads Act 1787 (c.89)

Berwick Roads Act 1792 (c.149)

Berwickshire County Town Act 1903 (c.5)

Berwickshire Courts Act 1853 (c.27)

Bethnal Green and Shoreditch: Improvement Act 1793 (c.88)

Bethnal Green: Completion of Church and Poor Relief Act 1745 (c.15)

Bethnal Green: Parish Act 1742 (c.28)

Bethnal Green: Poor Relief Act 1763 (c.40)

Bethnal Green: Poor Relief Act 1772 (c.53)

Bethnal Green Road Act 1756 (c.43)

Bethnal Green Road Act 1767 (c.105)

Betting Act 1853 (c.119)

Betting Act 1874 (c.15)

Betting and Gaming Act 1960 (c.60)

Betting and Gaming Duties Act 1972 (c.25)

Betting and Gaming Duties Act 1981 (c.63)

Betting and Loans (Infants) Act 1892 (c.4)

Betting and Lotteries Act 1934 (c.58)

Betting Duties Act 1963 (c.3)

Betting, Gaming and Lotteries Act 1963 (c.2)

Betting, Gaming and Lotteries Act 1964 (c.78)

Betting, Gaming and Lotteries (Amendment) Act 1969 (c.17)

Betting, Gaming and Lotteries (Amendment) Act 1971 (c.26)

Betting, Gaming and Lotteries (Amendment) Act 1980 (c.18)

Betting, Gaming and Lotteries (Amendment) Act 1984 (c.25)

Betting, Gaming and Lotteries (Amendment) Act 1985 (c.18)

Betting (Juvenile Messengers) (Scotland) Act 1928 (c.27)

Betting Levy Act 1961 (c.17)

Beverley and Kexby Bridge Road Act 1764 (c.76)

Beverley Improvement Act 1726 (c.4)

Beverley Improvement Act 1744 (c.13)

Beverley to Kexby Bridge Road Act 1785 (c.110)

Bewdley Bridge Act 1795 (c.78)

Bewdley Roads Act 1753 (c.39)

Bewdley Roads Act 1774 (c.112)

Bicester and Aylesbury Road Act 1770 (c.72)

Bicester Roads Act 1793 (c.180)

Bicester to Aylesbury Road Act 1791 (c.101)

Bicester to Aynho Road Act 1791 (c.103)

Bideford Roads Act 1764 (c.87)

Bideford Roads Act 1785 (c.119)

Bigamy Act 1795 (c.67)

Billiards (Abolition of Restrictions) Act 1987 (c.19)

Bill Chamber Procedure Act 1857 (c.18)

Bill of Exchange Act 1702 (c.8)

Bill of Exchange Act 1704 (c.8)

Bill of Exchange Act 1776 (c.30)

Bill of Exchange Act 1800 (c.42)

Bill of Exchange Act 1808 (c.88)

Bill of Exchange (Scotland) Act 1772 (c.72)

Bill of Sale Act 1891 (c.35)

Billeting of Civilians Act 1917 (c.20)

Bills and Notes Metropolis Act 1852 (c.1)

Bills and Notes Metropolis Act 1863 (c.2)

Bills Confirming Provisional Orders Act 1870 (c.1)

Bills of Exchange Act 1836 (c.58)

Bills of Exchange Act 1871 (c.74)

Bills of Exchange Act 1878 (c.13)

Bills of Exchange Act 1882 (c.61)

Bills of Exchange Act 1914 (c.82)

Bills of Exchange Act (1882) Amendment Act 1932 (c.44)

Bills of Exchange (Crossed Cheques) Act 1906 (c.17)

Bills of Exchange, etc. Act 1783 (c.7)

Bills of Exchange (Ireland) Act 1828 (c.24)

Bills of Exchange (Ireland) Act 1862 (c.23)

Bills of Exchange (Ireland) Act 1864 (c.7)

Bills of Exchange (Scotland) Act 1772 (c.72)

Bills of Exchange (Time of Noting) Act 1917 (c.48)

Bills of Lading Act 1855 (c.111)

Bills of Sale Act 1854 (c.36)

Bills of Sale (Ireland) Act 1854 (c.55)

Bills of Sale Act 1866 (c.96)
Bills of Sale Act 1878 (c.31)
Bills of Sale Act (1878) Amendment Act 1882 (c.43)
Bills of Sale Act 1890 (c.53)
Bills of Sale (Ireland) Act 1879 (c.50)
Bills of Sale (Ireland) Act (1879) Amendment Act 1883 (c.7)
Bingo Act 1992 (c.10)
Biological Standards Act 1975 (c.4)
Biological Weapons Act 1974 (c.6)
Birds (Registration Charges) Act 1997 (c.55)
Birkenhead Enfranchisement Act 1861 (c.112)
Birmingham and Chesterfield Roads Act 1786 (c.149)
Birmingham and Stratford Roads Act 1825 (c.6)
Birmingham and Wednesbury Roads Act 1726 (c.14)
Birmingham Canal Act 1769 (c.53)
Birmingham Canal, Navigation Act 1768 (c.38)
Birmingham Canal, Navigation Act 1771 (c.67)
Birmingham Canal, Navigation Act 1783 (c.92)
Birmingham Canal, Navigation Act 1784 (c.4)
Birmingham Canal: Navigation Act 1785 (c.99)
Birmingham Canal: Navigation Act 1792 (c.81)
Birmingham Canal: Navigation Act 1794 (c.25)
Birmingham Canal: Navigation Act 1794 (c.87)
Birmingham Chapels Act 1772 (c.64)
Birmingham: Improvement Act 1769 (c.83)
Birmingham: Improvement Act 1772 (c.36)
Birmingham Police Act 1839 (c.88)
Birmingham: Poor Relief Act 1783 (c.54)
Birmingham to Edghill Road Act 1757 (c.58)
Birmingham to Stratford Roads Act 1725 (c.6)
Birmingham to Stratford Road Act 1771 (c.74)
Birmingham and Wednesbury Roads Act 1726 (c.14)
Birmingham Canal, Navigation Act 1784 (c.4)
Birstall to Huddersfield Roads Act 1786 (c.140)
Births and Deaths Registration Act 1836 (c.86)
Births and Deaths Registration Act 1837 (c.22)
Births and Deaths Registration Act 1858 (c.25)
Births and Deaths Registration Act 1874 (c.88)
Births and Deaths Registration Act 1901 (c.26)
Births and Deaths Registration Act 1926 (c.48)
Births and Deaths Registration Act 1947 (c.12)
Births and Deaths Registration Act 1953 (c.20)
Births and Deaths Registration (Ireland) Act 1880 (c.13)

Bishop of Calcutta Act 1874 (c.13)
Bishop of Quebec Act 1852 (c.53)
Bishopric of Bristol Act 1884 (c.66)
Bishopric of Bristol Amendment Act 1894 (c.21)
Bishopric of Bristol Amendment Act 1896 (c.29)
Bishopric of Christ Church, New Zealand Act 1852 (c.88)
Bishopric of St. Albans Act 1875 (c.34)
Bishopric of Southwark and Birmingham Act 1904 (c.30)
Bishopric of Truro Act 1876 (c.54)
Bishoprics Act 1878 (c.68)
Bishoprics, etc., in West Indies Act 1842 (c.4)
Bishoprics of Bradford and Coventry Act 1918 (c.57)
Bishoprics of Sheffield, Chelmsford and for the County of Suffolk Act 1913 (c.36)
Bishoprics of Southwark and Birmingham Act 1904 (c.30)
Bishops in Foreign Countries Act 1841 (c.6)
Bishops of London and Durham Act 1856 (c.115)
Bishops Trusts Substitution Act 1858 (c.71)
Bishops Resignation Act 1869 (c.111)
Bishops Resignation Act 1875 (c.19)
Bishops Resignation Act Continuance 1872 (c.40)
Bishopsgate: Poor Relief Act 1795 (c.61)
Black Game in Somerset and Devon Act 1810 (c.67)
Blackburn and Addingham Road Act 1796 (c.137)
Blackburn Roads Act 1776 (c.75)
Blackburn Roads Act 1796 (c.144)
Blackburn to Burscough Bridge Road Act 1793 (c.134)
Blackfriars Bridge Act 1756 (c.86)
Blackfriars Bridge Act 1756 (c.86)
Blackfriars Bridge (Sunday Tolls) Act 1786 (c.37)
Blackfriars Sewer Act 1795 (c.131)
Blackheath, etc., Small Debts Act 1770 (c.29)
Blackwater Bridge Act 1867 (c.57)
Blackwater Bridge Act 1873 (c.46)
Blackwater Bridge Debt Act 1873 (c.47)
Blandford Forum (Rebuilding after the Fire) Act 1731 (c.16)
Bleaching and Dyeing Works Act 1860 (c.78)
Bleaching and Dyeing Works Act Amendment Act 1863 (c.38)
Bleaching and Dyeing Works Act Ext. 1864 (c.98)
Bleaching Powder Act 1815 (c.38)
Bleaching Works Act 1862 (c.8)
Blind Persons Act 1938 (c.11)
Blind Voters Act 1933 (c.27)
Bloomsbury Churches Act 1730 (c.19)

Bloomsbury: Poor Relief Act 1774 (c.62)

Bloomsbury: Poor Relief Act 1774 (c.108)

Blything, Suffolk: Poor Relief, etc. Act 1764 (c.56)

Blything, Suffolk (Poor Relief, Guardians, etc.) Act 1793 (c.126)

Board of Agriculture Act 1889 (c.30)

Board of Agriculture and Fisheries Act 1903 (c.31)

Board of Agriculture and Fisheries Act 1909 (c.15)

Board of Education Act 1899 (c.33)

Board of Education (Scotland) Act 1877 (c.38)

Board of Trade Act 1909 (c.23)

Board of Trade Arbitrations etc. Act 1874 (c.40)

Boards of Guardians (Default) Act 1926 (c.20)

Boards of Management of Poor Law District Schools (Ireland) Act 1892 (c.41)

Bodies Corporate (Joint Tenancy) Act 1899 (c.20)

Bodmin Canal Act 1797 (c.29)

Bodmin Gaol Act 1778 (c.17)

Bodmin Roads Act 1769 (c.69)

Bodmin Roads Act 1786 (c.129)

Bogs (Ireland) Act 1811 (c.122)

Bogs (Ireland) Act 1812 (c.74)

Boiler Explosions Act 1882 (c.22)

Boiler Explosions Act 1890 (c.35)

Bolton and Nightingale's Road Act 1763 (c.31)

Bolton and Nightingale's Road Act 1763 (c.40)

Bolton and St. Helens Road Act 1796 (c.149)

Bolton, Blackburn and Twisey Roads Act 1797 (c.173)

Bolton Grammar School Act 1788 (c.81)

Bolton Police Act 1839 (c.95)

Bombay Civil Fund Act 1882 (c.45)

Bonded Corn Act 1842 (c.92)

Bonded Corn Act 1845 (c.103)

Bonded Warehouses Act 1805 (c.87)

Bonded Warehouses Act 1848 (c.122)

Bonding of Coffee, etc. Act 1807 (c.48)

Bonding of Spirits Act 1806 (c.27)

Bonding of Spirits (Ireland) Act 1804 (c.104)

Bonding of Sugar Act 1804 (c.36)

Bonding of Wine Act 1803 (c.103)

Bonding of Wines Act 1803 (c.14)

Bonding Warehouses Act 1806 (c.137)

Bonding Warehouses (Ireland) Act 1808 (c.32)

Bonded Warehouses (Ireland) Act 1810 (c.38)

Bonds of East India Company Act 1803 (c.3)

Booth's Charity, Salford Act 1776 (c.55)

Booth's Patent Act 1792 (c.73)

Borders Rivers (Prevention of Pollution) Act 1951 (c.7)

Borough and Local Courts of Record Act 1872 (c.86)

Borough and Watch Rates Act 1845 (c.110)

Borough Charters Confirmation Act 1842 (c.111)

Borough Clerks of the Peace (Ireland) Act 1868 (c.98)

Borough Constables Act 1883 (c.44)

Borough Coroners (Ireland) Act 1860 (c.74)

Borough Councillors (Alteration of Number) Act 1925 (c.11)

Borough Courts (England) Act 1839 (c.27)

Borough Electors Act 1868 (c.41)

Borough Fund in Certain Boroughs Act 1836 (c.104)

Borough Funds Act 1872 (c.91)

Borough Funds Act 1903 (c.14)

Borough Funds (Ireland) Act 1888 (c.53)

Borough Justices Act 1850 (c.91)

Borough of Hanley Act 1857 (c.10)

Borough Police Act 1848 (c.14)

Borough Quarter Sessions Act 1877 (c.17)

Borough Rates (England) Act 1854 (c.71)

Borough Recorders' Deputies Act 1869 (c.23)

Borough Watch Rates Act 1839 (c.28)

Boroughbridge and Darlington Road Act 1744 (c.8)

Boroughs, Relief from County Expenditure Act 1849 (c.82)

Borrowing (Control and Guarantees) Act 1946 (c.58)

Borrowstoness Canal Act 1783 (c.5)

Bosmere and Claydon, Suffolk (Poor Relief) Act 1764 (c.57)

Boston: Improvement Act 1792 (c.80)

Boston Pilotage Act 1776 (c.23)

Boston Pilotage Act 1792 (c.79)

Boston: Streets Act 1776 (c.25)

Boston Water Supply Act 1711 (c.44)

Botswana Independence Act 1966 (c.23)

Boundaries of Burghs Extension (Scotland) Act 1857 (c.70)

Boundaries of Burghs Extension (Scotland) Act 1861 (c.36)

Boundary Act 1868 (c.46)

Boundary Commissions Act 1992 (c.55)

Boundary Survey (Ireland) Act 1854 (c.17)

Boundary Survey (Ireland) Act 1857 (c.45)

Boundary Survey (Ireland) Act 1859 (c.8)

Bounties Act 1779 (c.27)

Bounties Act 1780 (c.40)

Bounties Act 1783 (c.21)

Bounties Act 1795 (c.21)

Bounties Act 1796 (c.56)

Bounties Act 1801 (c.13)

Bounties Act 1801 (c.34)

Bounties Act 1801 (c.92)

Bounties Act 1802 (c.59)

Bounties and Drawbacks Act 1805 (c.24)

Bounties and Drawbacks Act 1808 (cc.16, 17)

Bounties, etc., on Sugar Act 1809 (cc.10, 11)

Bounties, etc., on Sugar Act 1812 (c.15)

Bounties, etc., on Sugar Act 1813 (c.24)

Bounties for Destroying Spanish Ships Act 1785 (c.29)

Bounties for Destroying Spanish Ships Act 1786 (c.35)

Bounties (Great Britain) Act 1807 (c.29)

Bounties on Exportation Act 1744 (c.25)

Bounties on Importation Act 1800 (c.10)

Bounties on Importation Act 1800 (c.29)

Bounties on Pilchards Act 1812 (c.42)

Bounties on Sugar Act 1807 (c.22)

Bounties on Sugar Act 1808 (c.12)

Bounty for Taking L'Amazone Act 1784 (c.28)

Bounty of Exportation Act 1766 (c.45)

Bounty of Raw Sugar Act 1810 (c.9)

Bounty on British Calicoes Act 1807 (c.64)

Bounty on British Sail Cloth Exported Act 1797 (c.30)

Bounty on Certain Linens Exported Act 1799 (c.28)

Bounty on Cordage Exported Act 1786 (c.85)

Bounty on Corn Act 1780 (c.31)

Bounty on Corn, etc. Act 1750 (c.56)

Bounty on Exportation Act 1797 (c.76)

Bounty on Exportation Act 1806 (c.99)

Bounty on Exportation Act 1810 (c.40)

Bounty on Hemp Act 1779 (c.37)

Bounty on Importation Act 1800 (c.35)

Bounty on Pilchards Act 1797 (c.94)

Bounty on Pilchards Act 1799 (c.65)

Bounty on Pilchards Act 1808 (c.68)

Bounty on Rye Act 1800 (c.53)

Bounty on Silk Manufactures Act 1806 (c.110)

Bounty on Sugar Act 1816 (c.19)

Bounty on Sugar, etc. Act 1806 (c.109)

Bounty to Garrison of Gibraltar Act 1783 (c.16)

Bounty upon Importation Act 1763 (c.26)

Board of Trade (Parliamentary Secretary) Act 1867 (c.72)

Bourn, Lincs.: Navigation Act 1780 (c.22)

Bradford and Wakefield Road Act 1753 (c.83)

Bradford-on-Avon (Additional Overseer) Act 1783 (c.20)

Bradford to Idle Canal Act 1771 (c.89)

Bradford, Yorks: Water Supply Act 1790 (c.63)

Branding of Herrings (Northumberland) Act 1891 (c.28)

Brandon and Sams Cut Drain: Drainage Act 1757 (c.35)

Brandon and Waveney: Navigation Act 1750 (c.12)

Brazilian Slave Trade Repeal Act 1869 (c.2)

Bread Act 1762 (c.6)

Bread Act 1762 (c.11)

Bread Act 1772 (c.62)

Bread Act 1793 (c.37)

Bread Act 1836 (c.37)

Bread Acts Amendment Act 1922 (c.28)

Bread (Ireland) Act 1838 (c.28)

Brecknock and Abergavenny Canal Act 1793 (c.96)

Brecknock Forest Act 1815 (c.190)

Brecknock Water Supply Act 1776 (c.56)

Brecon Roads Act 1767 (c.60)

Brecon Roads Act 1772 (c.105)

Brecon Roads Act 1787 (c.75)

Brecon Roads Act 1793 (c.154)

Breeding of Dogs Act 1973 (c.60)

Breeding of Dogs Act 1991 (c.64)

Brent Bridge to Plymouth Road Act 1777 (c.81)

Brentford Road Act 1791 (c.124)

Bretton Woods Agreements Act 1945 (c.19)

Brewers' Licensing Act 1850 (c.67)

Brewn Roads Act 1772 (c.105)

Bribery at Elections Act 1842 (c.102)

Brick Duties Repeal Act 1850 (c.9)

Brick Making Act 1725 (c.35)

Brickmaking Act 1728 (c.15)

Brickmaking Act 1730 (c.22)

Bricks and Tiles Act 1770 (c.49)

Bricks and Tiles Act 1776 (c.42)

Bridewell Hospital Act 1780 (c.27)

Bridgeford Lane, Notts. to Kettering Road 1754 (c.39)

Bridges Act 1670 (c.12)

Bridges Act 1702 (c.12)

Bridges Act 1740 (c.33)

Bridges Act 1803 (c.59)

Bridges Act 1812 (c.110)

Bridges Act 1814 (c.90)

Bridges Act 1815 (c.143)

Bridges Act 1850 (c.64)

Bridges Act 1929 (c.33)

Bridges (Ireland) Act 1843 (c.42)

Bridges (Ireland) Act 1850 (c.4)

Bridges (Ireland) Act 1851 (c.21)

Bridges (Ireland) Act 1867 (c.50)

Bridges (Ireland) Act 1875 (c.46)

Bridges (Ireland) Act 1813 (c.77)

Bridges (Scotland) Act 1813 (c.117)

Bridgewell Hospital Act 1783 (c.27)

Bridgnorth Bridge Act 1797 (c.58)

Bridgnorth Church Act 1792 (c.30)

Bridgwater and Beverly Disfranchisement Act 1870 (c.21)

Bridgwater Canal Act 1795 (c.44)

Bridgwater Markets Act 1779 (c.36)

Bridgwater: Navigation Act 1794 (c.105)

Bridgwater Roads Act 1730 (c.34)

Bridgwater Roads Act 1779 (c.100)

Bridlington Pier Act 1715 (c.49)

Bridlington Pier Act 1718 (c.10)

Bridlington Pier Act 1789 (c.23)

Bridlington Piers Act 1720 (c.16)

Bridlington Piers Act 1753 (c.10)

Bridlington Roads Act 1767 (c.89)

Bridport, Dorset, Harbour Act 1721 (c.11)

Bridport: Improvement Act 1785 (c.91)

Brighton: Streets Act 1772 (c.34)

Brine Pumping (Compensation for Subsidence) Act 1891 (c.40)

Bringing of Coals, etc., to London, etc. Act 1805 (c.128)

Bringing of Coals, etc., to London Act 1807 (c.34)

Bringing of Coals, etc., to London, etc. Act 1808 (c.95)

Bringing of Coals, etc., to London, etc. Act 1810 (c.110)

Bringing of Coals, etc., to London Act 1811 (c.29)

Bringing of Coals, etc., to London, etc. Act 1817 (c.114)

Bringing of Coals to London, etc. Act 1806 (c.104)

Bringing of Coals to London, etc. Act 1813 (c.135)

Bringing of Coals to London, etc. 1815 (c.175)

Bringing of Coals to London, etc. Act 1816 (c.124)

Bristol and Exeter Railway Act 1836 (c.36)

Bristol Bridge Act 1759 (c.52)

Bristol Bridge Act 1786 (c.111)

Bristol: Building Act 1788 (c.66)

Bristol Charities Act 1858 (c.30)

Bristol Charities Act 1858 (c.31)

Bristol Churches Act 1750 (c.37)

Bristol Dock Act 1776 (c.33)

Bristol Gaol Act 1792 (c.82)

Bristol Guildhall, etc. Act 1788 (c.67)

Bristol Hospitals Act 1744 (c.38)

Bristol: Improvement Act 1788 (c.65)

Bristol Museum Act 1766 (c.18)

Bristol (Nightly Watch) Act 1755 (c.32)

Bristol, Paving, etc. Act 1748 (c.20)

Bristol, Poor Relief Act 1713 (c.32)

Bristol (Poor Relief) Act 1757 (c.56)

Bristol Roads Act 1726 (c.12)

Bristol Roads Act 1730 (c.22)

Bristol Roads Act 1748 (c.28)

Bristol Roads Act 1779 (c.117)

Bristol Roads Act 1797 (c.178)

Bristol Streets Act 1766 (c.34)

Bristol Theatre Act 1778 (c.8)

Bristol Watch Act 1756 (c.47)

British Aerospace Act 1980 (c.26)

British Airways Board Act 1977 (c.13)

British Calicoes Act 1811 (c.33)

British Caribbean Federation Act 1956 (c.63)

British Coal and British Rail (Transfer Proposals) Act 1993 (c.2)

British Columbia Act 1866 (c.67)

British Columbia Boundaries Act 1863 (c.83)

British Columbia Government Act 1858 (c.99)

British Columbia Government Act 1870 (c.66)

British Columbia (Loan) Act 1892 (c.52)

British Council and Commonwealth Institute Superannuation Act 1986 (c.51)

British Empire Exhibition (Amendment) Act 1922 (c.25)

British Empire Exhibition (Guarantee) Act 1920 (c.74)

British Empire Exhibition (Guarantee) Act 1925 (c.26)

British Ferries Society Act 1799 (c.100)

British Film Institute Act 1949 (c.35)

British Fisheries Act 1795 (c.56)

British Fisheries Act 1798 (c.58)

British Fisheries Act 1800 (c.85)

British Fisheries Act 1804 (c.86)

British Fisheries Act 1806 (c.34)

British Fisheries Act 1806 (c.156)

British Fisheries Act 1807 (c.51)

British Fisheries Act 1808 (c.86)

British Fisheries Act 1810 (c.54)

British Fisheries, etc. Act 1802 (c.79)

British Fisheries Society Act 1786 (c.106)

British Fishing Boats Act 1983 (c.8)

British Forces in India Act 1862 (c.27)

British Guiana Act 1928 (c.5)

British Honduras (Court of Appeal) Act 1881 (c.36)

British Hydrocarbon Oils Production Act 1934 (c.4)

British Industries Fair (Guarantees and Grants) Act 1954 (c.26)

British Kaffrania Act 1865 (c.5)

British Law Ascertainment Act 1859 (c.63)

British Leyland Act 1975 (c.43)

British Library Act 1972 (c.54)

British Mercantile Marine Uniform Act 1919 (c.62)

British Museum Act 1700 (c.7)

British Museum Act 1706 (c.30)

British Museum Act 1753 (c.22)

British Museum Act 1766 (c.18)

British Museum Act 1805 (c.127)

British Museum Act 1807 (c.36)

British Museum Act 1816 (c.99)

British Museum Act 1839 (c.10)

British Museum Act 1878 (c.55)

British Museum Act 1902 (c.12)

British Museum Act 1924 (c.23)

British Museum Act 1930 (c.46)

British Museum Act 1931 (c.34)

British Museum Act 1932 (c.34)

British Museum Act 1938 (c.62)

British Museum Act 1946 (c.56)

British Museum Act 1955 (c.23)

British Museum Act 1962 (c.18)

British Museum Act 1963 (c.24)

British Museum (Purchase of Land) Act 1894 (c.34)

British Nationality Act 1730 (c.21)

British Nationality Act 1772 (c.21)

British Nationality Act 1948 (c.56)

British Nationality Act 1958 (c.10)

British Nationality Act 1964 (c.22)

British Nationality Act 1965 (c.34)

British Nationality Act 1981 (c.61)

British Nationality and Status of Aliens Act 1918 (c.38)

British Nationality and Status of Aliens Act 1922 (c.44)

British Nationality and Status of Aliens Act 1933 (c.49)

British Nationality and Status of Aliens Act 1943 (c.14)

British Nationality (Falkland Islands) Act 1983 (c.6)

British Nationality (Hong Kong) Act 1990 (c.34)

British Nationality (Hong Kong) Act 1997 (c.20)

British Nationality (No. 2) Act 1964 (c.54)

British North America Act 1840 (c.35)

British North America Act 1867 (c.3)

British North America Act 1870 (c.28)

British North America Act 1871 (c.28)

British North America Act 1886 (c.35)

British North America Act 1907 (c.11)

British North America Act 1915 (c.45)

British North America Act 1916 (c.19)

British North America Act 1930 (c.26)

British North America Act 1939 (c.36)

British North America Act 1940 (c.36)

British North America Act 1943 (c.30)

British North America Act 1946 (c.63)

British North America Act 1949 (c.22)

British North America Act 1951 (c.32)

British North America Act 1960 (c.2)

British North America Act 1964 (c.73)

British North America (No. 2) Act 1949 (c.81)

British North America (Quebec) Act 1774 (c.83)

British Overseas Airways Act 1939 (c.61)

British Railways Board (Finance) Act 1991 (c.63)

British Sailcloth, etc. Act 1793 (c.49)

British Settlements Act 1887 (c.54)

British Settlements Act 1945 (c.7)

British Settlements in Africa, etc. Act 1764 (c.44)

British Shipbuilders Act 1983 (c.15)

British Shipbuilders (Borrowing Powers) Act 1983 (c.58)

British Shipbuilders (Borrowing Powers) Act 1986 (c.19)

British Shipbuilders (Borrowing Powers) Act 1987 (c.52)

British Shipping (Assistance) Act 1935 (c.7)

British Shipping (Continuance of Subsidy) Act 1936 (c.12)

British Shipping (Continuance of Subsidy) Act 1937 (c.21)

British Ships Act 1772 (c.26)

British Ships Captured by the Enemy Act 1808 (c.70)

British Ships (Transfer Restriction) Act 1915 (c.21)

British Ships (Transfer Restriction) Act 1916 (c.42)

British Standard Time Act 1968 (c.45)

British Steel Act 1988 (c.35)

Btitish Subjects Act 1751 (c.39)

British Subjects in China Act 1843 (c.80)

British Sugar Industry (Assistance) Act 1931 (c.35)

British Sugar (Subsidy) Act 1925 (c.12)

British Sugar (Subsidy) Act 1934 (c.39)

British Sugar (Subsidy) Act 1935 (c.37)

British Technology Group Act 1991 (c.66)

British Telecommunications Act 1981 (c.38)

British White Herring Fishery Act 1811 (c.101)

British White Herring Fishery Act 1812 (c.153)

British White Herring Fishery Act 1814 (c.102)

Brixton: Small Debts Act 1757 (c.23)

Broadcasting Act 1980 (c.64)

Broadcasting Act 1981 (c.68)

Broadcasting Act 1987 (c.10)

Broadcasting Act 1990 (c.42)

Broadcasting Act 1996 (c.55)

Broadstairs Pier Act 1792 (c.86)

Brokers, Bristol Act 1730 (c.31)

Bromsgrove and Birmingham Roads Act 1776 (c.15)

Bromsgrove to Birmingham Road Act 1790 (c.101)

Brown Linen Manufacture (Ireland) Act 1815 (c.25)

Brunei and Maldives Act 1985 (c.3)

Brunei Appeals Act 1989 (c.36)

Bruntisland Beer Duties Act 1746 (c.26)

Bruntisland Beer Duties Act 1776 (c.20)

Bruntisland Beer Duties Act 1794 (c.8)

Bruton Roads Act 1756 (c.50)

Bubble Schemes, Colonies Act 1740 (c.37)

Bubwith Bridge Act 1793 (c.106)

Buckingham and Hanwell Road Act 1792 (c.134)

Buckingham and Middlesex Roads Act 1779 (c.83)

Buckingham and Oxford Roads Act 1770 (c.58)

Buckingham and Oxford Roads Act 1785 (c.127)

Buckingham to Banbury Road Act 1791 (c.133)

Buckingham to Hanwell Road Act 1769 (c.52)

Buckingham to Warmington Road Act 1743 (c.43)

Buckinghamshire and Oxford Roads Act 1769 (c.88)

Buckinghamshire and Oxford Roads Act 1791 (c.136)

Buckinghamshire Assizes Act 1747 (c.12)

Buckinghamshire Assizes Act 1849 (c.6)

Buckinghamshire Highways Act 1722 (c.13)

Buckinghamshire Roads Act 1720 (c.24)

Buckinghamshire Roads Act 1735 (c.11)

Buckinghamshire Roads Act 1735 (c.21)

Buckinghamshire Roads Act 1741 (c.5)

Buckinghamshire Roads Act 1741 (c.6)

Buckinghamshire Roads Act 1759 (c.43)

Buckinghamshire Roads Act 1767 (c.61)

Buckinghamshire Roads Act 1777 (c.82)

Bude Canal Act 1774 (c.53)

Building Act 1984 (c.55)

Building Control Act 1966 (c.27)

Building Materials and Housing Act 1945 (c.20)

Building of Churches, etc. (Ireland) Act 1809

Building of Churches, London and Westminster Act 1714 (c.23)

Building Restrictions (War-Time Contraventions) Act 1946 (c.35)
Building (Scotland) Act 1959 (c.24)
Building (Scotland) Act 1970 (c.38)
Building Sites for Religious and Other Purposes Act 1868 (c.44)
Building Societies Act 1874 (c.42)
Building Societies Act 1875 (c.9)
Building Societies Act 1877 (c.63)
Building Societies Act 1884 (c.41)
Building Societies Act 1894 (c.47)
Building Societies Act 1939 (c.55)
Building Societies Act 1960 (c.64)
Building Societies Act 1962 (c.37)
Building Societies Act 1986 (c.53)
Building Societies Act 1997 (c.32)
Building Societies (Distributions) Act 1997 (c.41)
Building Societies (Joint Account Holders) Act 1995 (c.5)
Bunhill Fields Burial Ground Act 1867 (c.38)
Burford Charities Act 1861 (c.22)
Burford to Preston Road Act 1780 (c.76)
Burgesses Qualification (Scotland) Act 1876 (c.12)
Burgesses (Scotland) Act 1860 (c.47)
Burgh Council Elections (Scotland) Act 1853 (c.26)
Burgh Customs (Scotland) Act 1870 (c.42)
Burgh Gas Supply (Scotland) Amendment Act 1918 (c.45)
Burgh Harbours (Scotland) Act 1853 (c.93)
Burgh Police (Amendment) (Scotland) Act 1964 (c.33)
Burgh Police, etc. (Scotland) Act 1847 (c.39)
Burgh Police (Scotland) Act 1892 (c.55)
Burgh Police (Scotland) Act 1892, Amendment 1894 (c.18)
Burgh Police (Scotland) Act 1893 (c.25)
Burgh Police (Scotland) Act 1903 (c.33)
Burgh Police (Scotland) Amendment Act 1911 (c.51)
Burgh Registers (Scotland) Act 1926 (c.50)
Burgh, Scotland (Petty Customs) Act 1879 (c.13)
Burgh Sewerage, Drainage and Water Supply (Scotland) Act 1901 (c.24)
Burgh Trading Act 1846 (c.17)
Burgh Voters' Registration (Scotland) Act 1856 (c.58)
Burgh Wards (Scotland) Act 1876 (c.25)
Burghs Gas Supply (Scotland) Act 1876 (c.49)
Burghs Gas Supply (Scotland) Act 1893 (c.52)
Burghs of Barony (Scotland) Act 1795 (c.122)
Burghs (Scotland) Act 1852 (c.33)
Burglaries, etc. Act 1706 (c.9)
Burglary Act 1837 (c.86)
Burglary Act 1896 (c.57)
Burial Act 1852 (c.85)
Burial Act 1853 (c.134)
Burial Act 1854 (c.87)
Burial Act 1855 (c.128)
Burial Act 1857 (c.81)
Burial Act 1859 (c.1)

Burial Act 1860 (c.64)
Burial Act 1862 (c.100)
Burial Act 1871 (c.33)
Burial Act 1900 (c.15)
Burial Act 1906 (c.44)
Burial and Registration Acts (Doubts Removal) Act 1881 (c.2)
Burial Boards (Contested Elections) Act 1885 (c.21)
Burial Grounds (Ireland) Act 1856 (c.98)
Burial Grounds (Ireland) Act 1860 (c.76)
Burial Grounds (Scotland) Act 1855 (c.68)
Burial Grounds (Scotland) Act, 1855, Amendment Act 1881 (c.27)
Burial Grounds (Scotland) Act 1857 (c.42)
Burial Grounds (Scotland) Amendment Act 1886 (c.21)
Burial in Burghs (Scotland) Act 1866 (c.46)
Burial (Ireland) Act 1868 (c.103)
Burial Laws Amendment Act 1880 (c.41)
Burial of Drowned Persons Act 1808 (c.75)
Burial of Drowned Persons Act 1886 (c.20)
Burma Independence Act 1947 (c.3)
Burma Legislature Act 1946 (c.57)
Burning of Buildings, etc. Act 1837 (c.89)
Burning of Farm Buildings Act 1844 (c.62)
Burning of Houses (Dublin) Act 1841 (c.10)
Burning of Land (Ireland) Act 1814 (c.115)
Burnley Roads Act 1795 (c.146)
Burnt Fen (Northampton): Drainage Act 1797 (c.89)
Bursledon Bridge, Southampton Act 1797 (c.131)
Burton-upon-Trent and Derby Road Act 1753 (c.59)
Burton-upon-Trent and Derby Road Act 1764 (c.51)
Burton-upon-Trent: Improvement Act 1779 (c.39)
Burtry Ford to Burnstone Road 1794 (c.125)
Bury and Bolton Roads Act 1797 (c.174)
Bury and Stratton Road Act 1755 (c.35)
Bury St. Edmunds (Poor Relief) Act 1749 (c.21)
Bury to Church Kirk Canal Act 1794 (c.77)
Burying in Woollen Act 1814 (c.108)
Bus Fuel Grants Act 1966 (c.46)
Bushey Heath to Aylesbury Road Act 1783 (c.93)
Business Names Act 1985 (c.7)
Butter and Cheese Trade Act 1844 (c.48)
Butter and Margarine Act 1907 (c.21)
Butter Trade (Ireland) Act 1812 (c.134)
Butter Trade (Ireland) Act 1813 (c.46)
Buxton and Manchester Road Act 1753 (c.53)
Buxton to Manchester Road Act 1729 (c.4)
Buxton to Manchester Road Act 1748 (c.12)
Byron's Shorthand Act 1741 (c.23)

Cable and Broadcasting Act 1984 (c.46)
Cable and Wireless Act 1946 (c.82)

Caddington Church Act 1740 (c.26)
Caithness Roads Act 1793 (c.120)
Calder and Hebb: Navigation Act 1769 (c.71)
Calder Canal Act 1774 (c.13)
Calder Navigation Act 1757 (c.72)
Caldey Island Act 1990 (c.44)
Caldon Canal Act 1797 (c.36)
Caledonian and Crinan Canals Amendment Act 1860 (c.46)
Caledonian Canal Act 1803 (c.102)
Caledonian Canal Act 1804 (c.62)
Caledonian Canal Act 1840 (c.41)
Caledonian Canal Act 1848 (c.54)
Caledonian Canal Act 1857 (c.27)
Calendar Act 1750 (c.30)
Calendar (New Style) Act 1750 (c.23)
Callington Roads Act 1764 (c.48)
Camberwell and Peckham: Streets Act 1776 (c.26)
Camberwell, Bristol and Nottingham Elections (Validation) Act 1946 (c.43)
Camberwell: Streets Act 1787 (c.52)
Cambrics Act 1744 (c.36)
Cambrics Act 1747 (c.26)
Cambridge and Arrington Roads Act 1797 (c.179)
Cambridge and Ely Roads Act 1763 (c.36)
Cambridge and Newmarket Road Act 1763 (c.30)
Cambridge and Norfolk Roads Act 1770 (c.97)
Cambridge Commissioners Act 1873 (c.73)
Cambridge: Improvement Act 1788 (c.64)
Cambridge: Improvement Act 1794 (c.104)
Cambridge Roads Act 1723 (c.12)
Cambridge Roads Act 1724 (c.14)
Cambridge Roads Act 1730 (c.37)
Cambridge Roads Act 1755 (c.36)
Cambridge Roads Act 1765 (c.74)
Cambridge Roads Act 1765 (c.76)
Cambridge Roads Act 1765 (c.79)
Cambridge Roads Act 1766 (c.84)
Cambridge Roads Act 1773 (c.110)
Cambridge Roads Act 1790 (c.94)
Cambridge Roads Act 1792 (c.129)
Cambridge to Royston Road Act 1793 (c.130)
Cambridge University Act 1856 (c.88)
Cambridge University Act 1858 (c.11)
Cambridge University, etc. Act 1859 (c.34)
Cambridgeshire Roads Act 1730 (c.24)
Cambridgeshire Roads Act 1741 (c.16)
Camps Act 1939 (c.22)
Camps Act 1945 (c.26)
Canada Act 1775 (c.40)
Canada Act 1982 (c.11)
Canada Civil List Act 1847 (c.71)
Canada Company's Amendment Act 1856 (c.23)
Canada Copyright Act 1875 (c.53)
Canada Defences Loan Act 1870 (c.82)
Canada Loan Guarantee Act 1842 (c.118)
Canada (Ontario Boundary) Act 1889 (c.28)
Canada (Public Works) Loan Act 1873 (c.45)

Canada Railway Loan Act 1867 (c.16)
Canada (Rupert's Land) Loan Act 1869 (c.101)
Canada Union Act 1848 (c.56)
Canadian Speaker (Appointment of Deputy) Act 1895 (c.3)
Canadian Stock Stamp Act 1874 (c.26)
Canal Boats Act 1877 (c.60)
Canal Boats Act 1884 (c.75)
Canal, Carmarthen Act 1766 (c.55)
Canal Carriers Act 1845 (c.42)
Canal (Carriers) Act 1847 (c.94)
Canal Tolls Act 1845 (c.28)
Canals (Continuance of Charging Powers) Act 1922 (c.27)
Canals (Continuance of Charging Powers) Act 1924 (c.2)
Canals, etc. (Scotland) Act 1806 (c.155)
Canals (Ireland) Act 1816 (c.55)
Canals (Offences) Act 1840 (c.50)
Canals Protection (London) Act 1898 (c.16)
Canals: Trent and Mersey Act 1797 (c.81)
Cancer Act 1939 (c.13)
Canterbury Association (New Zealand) Act 1850 (c.70)
Canterbury Association (New Zealand) Act 1851 (c.84)
Canterbury: Church of St. Andrew Act 1763 (c.49)
Canterbury: Poor Relief Act 1727 (c.20)
Canterbury: Streets Act 1787 (c.14)
Canterbury to Whitstable Road Act 1783 (c.97)
Canvey Island, Sea Defences Act 1792 (c.23)
Cape of Good Hope (Advance) Act 1885 (c.7)
Cape of Good Hope Trade Act 1796 (c.21)
Cape of Good Hope Trade Act 1806 (c.30)
Cape of Good Hope Trade Act 1807 (c.11)
Cape of Good Hope Trade Act 1808 (c.105)
Cape of Good Hope Trade Act 1809 (c.17)
Cape of Good Hope Trade Act 1816 (c.8)
Cape Race Lighthouse Act 1886 (c.13)
Cape Rock Lighthouse (Scotland) Act 1806 (c.132)
Capital Allowances Act 1968 (c.3)
Capital Allowances Act 1990 (c.1)
Capital Expenditure (Money) Act 1904 (c.21)
Capital Gains Tax Act 1979 (c.14)
Capital Punishment, etc. Act 1823 (c.46)
Capital Punishment Abolition Act 1835 (c.81)
Capital Punishment Abolition Act 1836 (c.4)
Capital Punishment Amendment Act 1868 (c.24)
Capital Punishment (Ireland) Act 1842 (c.28)
Capital Transfer Tax Act 1984 (c.51)
Captive Birds Shooting (Prohibition) Act 1921 (c.13)
Captures Act 1776 (c.40)
Car Tax (Abolition) Act 1992 (c.58)
Car Tax Act 1983 (c.53)
Caravan Sites Act 1968 (c.52)
Caravan Sites and Control of Development Act 1960 (c.62)

Caravans (Standard Community Charge and Rating) Act 1991 (c.2)

Cardiff Bay Barrage Act 1993 (c.42)

Cardiff: Improvement Act 1774 (c.9)

Cardigan Roads Act 1770 (c.55)

Cardigan Roads Act 1791 (c.97)

Care and Treatment of Lunatics Act 1853 (c.96)

Care, etc., of Lunatics Act 1841 (c.4)

Care of King During His Illness, etc. Act 1811 (c.1)

Care of King's Estate During His Illness Act 1812 (c.14)

Carers (Recognition and Services) Act 1995 (c.12)

Carlford, Suffolk: Poor Relief Act 1756 (c.79)

Carlford, Suffolk (Poor Relief) Act 1764 (c.58)

Carlisle and Eamont Bridge Road Act 1753 (c.40)

Carlisle and Newcastle Road Act 1750 (c.25)

Carlton Bridge, Yorks. Act 1774 (c.63)

Carmarthen and Pembroke Roads Act 1763 (c.34)

Carmarthen: Improvement Act 1792 (c.104)

Carmarthen Roads Act 1765 (c.76)

Carmarthen Roads Act 1779 (c.102)

Carmarthen Roads Act 1779 (c.103)

Carmarthen Roads Act 1783 (c.33)

Carmarthen Roads Act 1786 (c.150)

Carmarthen Roads Act 1788 (c.109)

Carmarthen Roads Act 1792 (c.156)

Carnarvon Harbour Act 1793 (c.123)

Carnarvon Roads Act 1769 (c.77)

Carnarvon Roads Act 1795 (c.143)

Carriage and Deposit of Dangerous Goods Act 1866 (c.69)

Carriage by Air Act 1931 (c.36)

Carriage by Air Act 1961 (c.27)

Carriage by Air and Road Act 1979 (c.28)

Carriage by Air (Supplementary Provisions) Act 1962 (c.43)

Carriage by Railway Act 1972 (c.33)

Carriage Duties Act 1795 (c.109)

Carriage of Corn, etc. Act 1702 (c.20)

Carriage of Goods by Road Act 1965 (c.37)

Carriage of Goods by Sea Act 1924 (c.22)

Carriage of Goods by Sea Act 1971 (c.19)

Carriage of Goods by Sea Act 1992 (c.50)

Carriage of Gunpowder (Great Britain) Act 1814 (c.152)

Carriage of Passengers by Road Act 1974 (c.35)

Carriers Act 1830 (c.68)

Carriers Act Amendment Act 1865 (c.94)

Carrying of Knives etc. (Scotland) Act 1993 (c.13)

Carts on Highways Act 1744 (c.33)

Casting Away of Vessels, etc. Act 1803 (c.113)

Castle Stewart and Nairn Road Assessment Act 1860 (c.37)

Casual Poor Act 1882 (c.36)

Catering Wages Act 1943 (c.24)

Cathedral Acts Amendment 1873 (c.39)

Cathedral Churches, etc. Act 1853 (c.35)

Cathedral Statutes Act 1707 (c.75)

Cathedrals Act 1864 (c.70)

Catterick Bridge to Durham Road Act 1788 (c.90)

Cattle Assurance Act 1866 (c.34)

Cattle Disease Act 1866 (c.15)

Cattle Disease (Ireland) Act 1866 (c.4)

Cattle Disease (Ireland) Act 1876 (c.51)

Cattle Disease (Ireland) Acts Amendment 1874 (c.6)

Cattle Disease (Ireland) Amendment Act 1872 (c.16)

Cattle Diseases (Ireland) Amendment Act 1870 (c.36)

Cattle Disease Prevention Amendment Act 1866 (c.110)

Cattle Diseases Prevention Act 1866 (c.2)

Cattle Distemper, Vagrancy, Marshalsea Prison Act 1753 (c.34)

Cattle Industry Act 1936 (c.46)

Cattle Industry (Emergency Provisions) Act 1934 (c.54)

Cattle Industry (Emergency Provisions) Act 1935 (c.12)

Cattle Industry (Emergency Provisions) (No. 2) Act 1935 (c.39)

Cattle sheds in Burghs (Scotland) Act 1866 (c.17)

Cattle Stealing Act 1740 (c.6)

Cattle Stealing Act 1741 (c.34)

Cattle Theft (Scotland) Act 1747 (c.34)

Catwater Harbour and Sutton Pool, Plymouth Act 1709 (c.4 (b))

Causey, Yarmouth to Caistor Act 1723 (c.8)

Cawdle Fen. etc. Drainage Act 1737 (c.34)

Cayman Islands Act 1863 (c.31)

Cayman Islands and Turks and Caicos Islands Act 1958 (c.13)

Celluloid and Cinematograph Film Act 1922 (c.35)

Cemeteries Clauses Act 1847 (c.65)

Census Act 1800 (c.15)

Census Act 1841 (c.7)

Census Act 1841 (c.9)

Census Act 1860 (cc.61, 62)

Census Act 1880 (c.37)

Census Act 1920 (c.41)

Census (Confidentiality) Act 1991 (c.6)

Census (England) Act 1870 (c.107)

Census (England and Wales) Act 1890 (c.61)

Census (Great Britain) Act 1811 (c.6)

Census (Great Britain) Act 1840 (c.99)

Census, Great Britain Act 1850 (c.53)

Census (Great Britain) Act 1900 (c.4)

Census (Great Britain) Act 1910 (c.27)

Census (Ireland) Act 1812 (c.133)

Census (Ireland) Act 1815 (c.120)

Census (Ireland) Act 1840 (c.100)

Census (Ireland) Act 1850 (c.44)

Census (Ireland) Act 1870 (c.80)

Census (Ireland) Act 1880 (c.28)

Census (Ireland) Act 1890 (c.46)
Census (Ireland) Act 1900 (c.6)
Census (Ireland) Act 1910 (c.11)
Census of Production Act 1906 (c.49)
Census of Production Act 1917 (c.2)
Census of Production Act 1939 (c.15)
Census (Scotland) Act 1860 (c.98)
Census (Scotland) Act 1870 (c.108)
Census (Scotland) Act 1880 (c.38)
Census (Scotland) Act 1890 (c.38)
Central Criminal Court Act 1837 (c.77)
Central Criminal Court Act 1846 (c.24)
Central Criminal Court Act 1856 (c.16)
Central Criminal Court (Prisons) Act 1881 (c.64)
Central Criminal Lunatic Asylum (Ireland) Act 1845 (c.107)
Cereals Marketing Act 1965 (c.14)
Certain Export Duties Repeal Act 1845 (c.7)
Certain Mutinous Crews Act 1797 (c.71)
Certain Parliamentary Grants Act 1801 (c.73)
Certificates for Killing Hares Act 1791 (c.21)
Certificates of Attorneys, etc. Act 1804 (c.59)
Cessio (Scotland) Act 1836 (c.56)
Cestui que Vie Act 1707 (c.72)
Ceylon Independence Act 1947 (c.7)
Chaff-Cutting Machines (Accidents) Act 1897 (c.60)
Chain Cable and Anchor Act 1864 (c.27)
Chain Cable and Anchor Act 1871 (c.101)
Chain Cable and Anchor Act 1872 (c.30)
Chain Cables and Anchors Act 1874 (c.51)
Chairman of District Councils Act 1896 (c.22)
Chairman of Quarter Sessions (Ireland) Act 1858 (c.88)
Chairman of Quarter Sessions (Ireland) Jurisdiction Act 1876 (c.71)
Chairman of Traffic Commissioners etc. (Tenure of Office) Act 1937 (c.52)
Chancel Repairs Act 1931 (c.20)
Chancery Amendment Act 1858 (c.27)
Chancery and Common Law Offices (Ireland) Act 1867 (c.129)
Chancery Appeal Court (Ireland) Act 1856 (c.92)
Chancery Court Act 1838 (c.54)
Chancery (Ireland) Act 1834 (c.78)
Chancery (Ireland) Act 1835 (c.16)
Chancery (Ireland) Act 1851 (c.15)
Chancery (Ireland) Act 1867 (c.44)
Chancery of Lancaster Act 1890 (c.23)
Chancery Receivers (Ireland) Act 1856 (c.77)
Chancery Regulation Act 1862 (c.42)
Chancery Regulation (Ireland) Act 1862 (c.46)
Chancery Rules and Orders Act 1860 (c.128)
Chancery Taxing Master (Ireland) Act 1845 (c.115)
Channel Tunnel Act 1987 (c.53)
Channel Tunnel (Initial Finance) Act 1973 (c.66)
Channel Tunnel Rail Link Act 1996 (c.61)
Chapel of Ease, Yarmouth Act 1713 (c.16(d))

Chapels of Ease Act 1836 (c.31)
Chapels of Ease, etc. (Ireland) Act 1849 (c.99)
Chaplains in Gaols, etc. (England) Act 1815 (c.48)
Chaplains in the Navy (1820) (c.106)
Charge of Certain Annuities Act 1813 (c.156)
Charge of Loan Act 1807 (c.55)
Charge of Loan Act 1811 (c.61)
Charges of Loan, etc., of Present Session Act 1810 (c.71)
Charge of Loans Act 1809 (c.92)
Charging Orders Act 1979 (c.53)
Charitable Corporation Act 1732 (c.2)
Charitable Corporation (Arrangements with Creditors) Act 1732 (c.36)
Charitable Corporation (Claims and Disputes) Act 1731 (c.31)
Charitable Corporation Frauds Act 1731 (c.3)
Charitable Corporation Lottery Act 1733 (c.11)
Charitable Corporation Lottery Act 1734 (c.14)
Charitable Donations and Bequest (Ireland) Act 1867 (c.54)
Charitable Donations and Bequests (Ireland) Act 1844 (c.97)
Charitable Donations and Bequests (Ireland) Act 1871 (c.102)
Charitable Donations Registration Act 1812 (c.102)
Charitable Funds Investment Act 1870 (c.34)
Charitable Loan Societies (Ireland) Act 1844 (c.38)
Charitable Loan Societies (Ireland) Act 1900 (c.25)
Charitable Loan Societies (Ireland) Act 1906 (c.23)
Charitable Pawn Offices (Ireland) Act 1842 (c.75)
Charitable Trust (Recovery) Act 1891 (c.17)
Charitable Trustees Incorporation Act 1872 (c.24)
Charitable Trusts Act 1853 (c.137)
Charitable Trusts Act 1860 (c.136)
Charitable Trusts Act 1862 (c.112)
Charitable Trusts Act 1869 (c.110)
Charitable Trusts Act 1887 (c.49)
Charitable Trusts Act 1914 (c.56)
Charitable Trusts Act 1925 (c.27)
Charitable Trusts Amendment Act 1855 (c.124)
Charitable Trusts Deeds Enrolment Act 1866 (c.57)
Charitable Trusts (Places of Religious Worship) Amendment Act 1894 (c.35)
Charitable Trusts (Validation) Act 1954 (c.58)
Charitable Uses Act 1735 (c.36)
Charitable Uses Act 1861 (c.9)
Charitable Uses Act 1862 (c.17)
Charities Act 1960 (c.58)
Charities Act 1985 (c.20)
Charities Act 1992 (c.41)

Charities Act 1993 (c.10)

Charities (Amendment) Act 1995 (c.48)

Charities (Enrolment of Deeds) Act 1864 (c.13)

Charities (Fuel Allotments) Act 1939 (c.26)

Charities Inquiries Commission Expenses Act 1837 (c.4)

Charities Inquiries (England) Act 1835 (c.71)

Charities of John Pierrepont Act 1708 (c.10)

Charities of Thomas Guy Act 1724 (c.12)

Charities Procedure Act 1812 (c.101)

Charities (Service of Notice) Act 1851 (c.56)

Charity Inquiries Expenses Act 1892 (c.15)

Charity Lands Act 1863 (c.106)

Charles Beattie Indemnity Act 1956 (c.27)

Charles Radcliffe's Estates Act 1788 (c.63)

Charlwood and Horley Act 1974 (c.11)

Charter Trustees Act 1985 (c.45)

Chartered and Other Bodies (Resumption of Elections) Act 1945 (c.6)

Chartered and Other Bodies (Temporary Provisions) Act 1939 (c.119)

Chartered and Other Bodies (Temporary Provisions) Act 1941 (c.19)

Chartered Associations (Protection of Names and Uniforms) Act 1926 (c.26)

Chartered Companies Act 1837 (c.73)

Chartered Companies Act 1884 (c.56)

Charterhouse Governors (Quorum) Act 1721 (c.29)

Charterhouse Square: Rates Act 1742 (c.6)

Chatham and Sheerness Stipendiary Magistrate Act 1867 (c.63)

Chatham and Sheerness Stipendiary Magistrate Act 1929 (c.30)

Chatham Dockyard Act 1861 (c.41)

Chatham Fortifications Act 1780 (c.49)

Chatham: Improvement Act 1776 (c.58)

Chatham Lands Purchase Act 1857 (c.30)

Chatham Roads Act 1797 (c.155)

Chatham: Streets Act 1772 (c.18)

Cheap Trains Act 1883 (c.34)

Cheap Trains and Canal Carriers Act 1858 (c.75)

Checkweighing in Various Industries Act 1919 (c.51)

Chelmsford and Blackwater Canal Act 1793 (c.93)

Chelmsford Gaol Act 1770 (c.28)

Chelmsford: Improvement Act 1789 (c.44)

Chelmsford Roads Act 1794 (c.137)

Chelsea and Greenwich Out-Pensioners Act 1847 (c.54)

Chelsea and Greenwich Out-Pensioners, etc. Act 1848 (c.84)

Chelsea and Kilmainham Hospitals Act 1826 (c.16)

Chelsea Bridge Act 1858 (c.66)

Chelsea Hospital Act 1755 (c.1)

Chelsea Hospital Act 1812 (c.109)

Chelsea Hospital Act 1815 (c.125)

Chelsea Hospital Act 1843 (c.31)

Chelsea Hospital Act 1858 (c.18)

Chelsea Hospital Act 1876 (c.14)

Chelsea Hospital Out-Pensioners Act 1842 (c.70)

Chelsea Hospital Out-Pensioners Act 1843 (c.95)

Chelsea Hospital Purchase Act 1855 (c.21)

Chelsea and Greenwich Hospitals Act 1815 (c.133)

Chelsea Pensions (Abolition of Poundage) Act 1847 (c.4)

Cheltenham Roads Act 1785 (c.125)

Cheltenham: Streets Act 1786 (c.116)

Chemical Weapons Act 1996 (c.6)

Chequers Estate Act 1917 (c.55)

Chequers Estate Act 1958 (c.60)

Cheques Act 1957 (c.36)

Cheques Act 1992 (c.32)

Cheshire Roads Act 1730 (c.3)

Cheshire Roads Act 1753 (c.62)

Cheshire Roads Act 1774 (c.100)

Cheshire Roads Act 1781 (c.82)

Cheshire Roads Act 1786 (c.139)

Chest of Greenwich Act 1806 (c.101)

Chester and Derby Roads Act 1770 (c.97)

Chester and Derby Roads Act 1789 (c.93)

Chester and Derby Roads Act 1790 (c.88)

Chester and Lancaster Roads Act 1770 (c.89)

Chester and Stafford Roads Act 1783 (c.101)

Chester and Stafford Roads Act 1788 (c.104)

Chester and Whitchurch Roads Act 1778 (c.86)

Chester Courts Act 1867 (c.36)

Chester Highways Act 1705 (c.26)

Chester: Improvement Act 1788 (c.82)

Chester, Lancaster and Yorks. Roads Act 1765 (c.100)

Chester Lighthouse Act 1776 (c.61)

Chester–Nantwich Canal Act 1772 (c.75)

Chester (Poor Relief, etc.) Act 1762 (c.45)

Chester Roads Act 1753 (c.84)

Chester Roads Act 1765 (c.98)

Chester Roads Act 1769 (c.65)

Chester Roads Act 1777 (c.76)

Chester Roads Act 1779 (c.113)

Chester Roads Act 1787 (c.93)

Chester Roads Act 1788 (c.111)

Chester Roads Act 1789 (c.99)

Chester Roads Act 1791 (c.125)

Chester Theatre Act 1776 (c.14)

Chester to Birmingham Road Act 1759 (c.51)

Chesterfield to Stockwith (Trent) Canal Act 1771 (c.75)

Chesterfield to Worksop Road Act 1786 (c.152)

Chevening Estate Act 1959 (c.49)

Chevening Estate Act 1987 (c.20)

Chichester Paving and Improvement Act 1791 (c.63)

Chichester: Poor Relief, etc. Act 1753 (c.100)

Chief Justice's Salary Act 1851 (c.41)

Chief Superintendent in China Act 1859 (c.9)

Child Abduction Act 1984 (c.37)

Child Abduction and Custody Act 1985 (c.60)
Child Benefit Act 1975 (c.61)
Child Care Act 1980 (c.5)
Child Stealing Act 1814 (c.101)
Child Support Act 1991 (c.48)
Child Support Act 1995 (c.34)
Children Act 1908 (c.67)
Children Act 1921 (c.4)
Children Act 1948 (c.43)
Children Act 1958 (c.65)
Children Act 1972 (c.44)
Children Act 1975 (c.72)
Children Act 1989 (c.41)
Children Act (1908) Amendment Act 1910 (c.25)
Children and Young Persons Act 1931 (c.46)
Children and Young Persons Act 1932 (c.46)
Children and Young Persons Act 1933 (c.12)
Children and Young Persons Act 1938 (c.40)
Children and Young Persons Act 1956 (c.24)
Children and Young Persons Act 1963 (c.37)
Children and Young Persons Act 1969 (c.54)
Children and Young Persons Act 1952 (c.50)
Children and Young Persons (Amendment) Act 1986 (c.28)
Children and Young Persons (Harmful Publications) Act 1955 (c.28)
Children and Young Persons (Protection from Tobacco) Act 1991 (c.23)
Children and Young Persons (Scotland) Act 1931 (c.47)
Children and Young Persons (Scotland) Act 1937 (c.37)
Children (Employment Abroad) Act 1913 (c.7)
Children (Scotland) Act 1995 (c.36)
Children's Dangerous Performances Act 1879 (c.34)
Children's (Employment Abroad) Act 1930 (c.21)
Children's Homes Act 1982 (c.20)
Chimney Sweepers Act 1788 (c.48)
Chimney Sweepers Act 1875 (c.70)
Chimney Sweepers Act 1894 (c.51)
Chimney Sweepers Acts (Repeal) Act 1938 (c.58)
Chimney Sweepers and Chimneys Regulation Act 1840 (c.85)
Chimney Sweepers Regulations Act 1864 (c.37)
China (Currency Stabilisation) Act 1939 (c.14)
China Indemnity (Application) Act 1925 (c.41)
China Indemnity (Application) Act 1931 (c.7)
Chinese Passengers Act 1855 (c.104)
Chippenham Roads Act 1726 (c.13)
Chiropractors Act 1994 (c.17)
Cholera, etc. Protection (Ireland) Act 1884 (c.69)
Cholera Hospitals (Ireland) Act 1883 (c.48)
Cholera Hospitals (Ireland) Act 1884 (c.59)
Cholera Hospitals (Ireland) Act 1885 (c.39)
Cholera Hospitals (Ireland) Act 1893 (c.13)

Chorley and Rufford Chapels, Lancaster Act 1793 (c.24)
Christ Church, Oxford Act 1867 (c.76)
Christ Church, Surrey Act 1737 (c.21)
Christ College of Brecknock Act 1853 (c.82)
Christchurch, Middlesex Act 1772 (c.38)
Christchurch, Middlesex: Improvement Act 1788 (c.60)
Christchurch, Middlesex: Light and Watch Act 1737 (c.35)
Christchurch, Stepney: Poor Relief Act 1753 (c.98)
Christchurch, Stepney: Poor Relief Act 1778 (c.74)
Christchurch, Surrey: Improvement Act 1791 (c.61)
Christchurch, Surrey, Streets Act 1793 (c.90)
Christmas Islands Act 1958 (c.25)
Chronically Sick and Disabled Persons Act 1970 (c.44)
Chronically Sick and Disabled Persons (Amendment) Act 1976 (c.49)
Chronically Sick and Disabled Persons (Northern Ireland) Act 1978 (c.53)
Chronically Sick and Disabled Persons (Scotland) Act 1972 (c.51)
Church at Coventry Act 1733 (c.27)
Church at Gravesend Act 1730 (c.20)
Church at Limerick Act 1844 (c.89)
Church at Woolwich Act 1731 (c.4)
Church, Buckingham Act 1776 (c.32)
Church Building Act 1818 (c.45)
Church Building Act 1819 (c.134)
Church Building Act 1822 (c.72)
Church Building Act 1824 (c.103)
Church Building Act 1827 (c.72)
Church Building Act 1831 (c.38)
Church Building Act 1832 (c.61)
Church Building Act 1837 (c.75)
Church Building Act 1838 (c.107)
Church Building Act 1839 (c.49)
Church Building Act 1840 (c.60)
Church Building Act 1845 (c.70)
Church Building Act 1848 (c.37)
Church Building Act 1851 (c.97)
Church Building Act 1854 (c.32)
Church Building Acts Amendment Act 1871 (c.82)
Church Building (Banns and Marriages) Act 1844 (c.56)
Church Building (Burial Service in Chapels) Act 1846 (c.68)
Church Building Commission Act 1848 (c.71)
Church Building Commission Act 1854 (c.14)
Church Building Commissioners (Transfer of Powers) Act 1856 (c.55)
Church Building etc. (Ireland) Act 1808 (c.65)
Church Building (Ireland) Act 1814 (c.117)
Church Discipline Act 1840 (c.86)
Church in Sheffield Act 1739 (c.12)
Church in Strand on Maypole Site: Stepney Advowsons Act 1712 (c.17)
Church, Macclesfield Act 1779 (c.7)

Church of Abthorpe and Foxcoate, Northants Act 1736 (c.21)
Church of Allhallows, City Act 1765 (c.65)
Church of Allhallows, City Act 1766 (c.75)
Church of All Saints, Worcester Act 1737 (c.5)
Church of England 1706 (c.8)
Church of England Act 1966 (c.2)
Church of England Assembly (Powers) Act 1919 (c.76)
Church of Ireland Act 1858 (c.59)
Church of Ireland Act 1863 (c.123)
Church of Ireland Acts Repeal Act 1851 (c.71)
Church of Ireland Act 1851 (c.72)
Church of Scotland Act 1921 (c.29)
Church of Scotland, etc. Act 1748 (c.21)
Church of Scotland Courts Act 1863 (c.47)
Church of Scotland (Property and Endowments) Act 1925 (c.33)
Church of Scotland (Property and Endowments) Amendment Act 1933 (c.44)
Church of St. George, Southwark Act 1732 (c.8)
Church of St. John, Wapping Act 1756 (c.89)
Church of St. Leonard, Shoreditch Act 1734 (c.27)
Church of St. Olave, Southwark Act 1736 (c.18)
Church of Scotland, etc. Act 1743 (c.11)
Church of Scotland (Property and Endowments) Act 1925 (c.33)
Church of Scotland (Property and Endowments) Act 1957 (c.30)
Church of Scotland (Property and Endowments) Amendment Act 1933 (c.44)
Church Patronage Act 1737 (c.17)
Church Patronage Act 1846 (c.88)
Church Patronage Act 1870 (c.39)
Church Patronage (Scotland) Act 1711 (c.21)
Church Patronage (Scotland) Act 1718 (c.29)
Church Patronage (Scotland) Act 1874 (c.82)
Church Seats Act 1872 (c.49)
Church Services (Wales) Act 1863 (c.82)
Church Temporalities Act 1854 (c.11)
Church Temporalities Act 1860 (c.150)
Church Temporalities (Ireland) Act 1836 (c.99)
Church Temporalities (Ireland) Act 1840 (c.101)
Church Temporalities (Ireland) Act 1867 (c.137)
Churches in London and Westminster Act 1711 (c.20 (c))
Churches (Scotland) Act 1905 (c.12)
Cider and Perry Act 1763 (c.7)
Cinemas Act 1985 (c.13)
Cinematograph Act 1909 (c.30)
Cinematograph Act 1952 (c.68)
Cinematograph (Amendment) Act 1982 (c.33)
Cinematograph Films Act 1927 (c.29)
Cinematograph Films Act 1937 (c.17)
Cinematograph Films Act 1948 (c.23)
Cinematograph Films Act 1957 (c.21)

Cinematograph Films Act 1960 (c.14)
Cinematograph Films Act 1975 (c.73)
Cinematograph Films (Animals) Act 1937 (c.59)
Cinematograph Film Production (Special Loans) Act 1949 (c.20)
Cinematograph Film Production (Special Loans) Act 1950 (c.18)
Cinematograph Film Production (Special Loans) Act 1952 (c.20)
Cinematograph Film Production (Special Loans) Act 1954 (c.15)
Cinque Ports Act 1811 (c.36)
Cinque Ports Act 1855 (c.48)
Cinque Ports Act 1857 (c.1)
Cinque Ports Act 1869 (c.53)
Cinque Ports Pilots Act 1813 (c.140)
Circulation of Notes, etc., Issued in France Act 1793 (c.1)
Circuit Clerks (Scotland) Act 1898 (c.40)
Circuit Courts and Criminal Procedure (Scotland) Act 1925 (c.81)
Circuit Courts (Scotland) Act 1828 (c.29)
Circuit Courts (Scotland) Act 1709 (c.16)
Circuits Courts Act 1711 (c.40)
Cirencester Roads Act 1726 (c.11)
Cirencester to Birdlip Hill Road Act 1795 (c.141)
Cirencester to Cricklade Road Act 1779 (c.116)
Citation Amendment (Scotland) Act 1871 (c.42)
Citation Amendment (Scotland) Act 1882 (c.77)
Citations (Scotland) Act 1846 (c.67)
City of London Burial Act 1857 (c.35)
City of London Elections Act 1724 (c.18)
City of London (Garbling of Spices and Admission of Brokers) Act 1707 (c.68)
City of London: Improvement Act 1759 (c.38)
City of London: Improvement Act 1765 (c.91)
City of London: Improvement Act 1785 (c.97)
City of London Militia Act 1662 (c.3)
City of London Militia Act 1813 (c.17)
City of London Militia Act 1813 (c.38)
City of London Parochial Charities Act 1883 (c.36)
City of London Sewerage Act 1771 (c.29)
City Streets Act 1783 (c.46)
Civic Amenities Act 1967 (c.69)
Civic Government (Scotland) Act 1982 (c.45)
Civic Restaurants Act 1947 (c.22)
Civil Aviation Act 1946 (c.70)
Civil Aviation Act 1949 (c.67)
Civil Aviation Act 1968 (c.61)
Civil Aviation Act 1971 (c.75)
Civil Aviation Act 1978 (c.8)
Civil Aviation Act 1980 (c.60)
Civil Aviation Act 1982 (c.16)
Civil Aviation (Air Navigation Charges) Act 1989 (c.9)
Civil Aviation (Amendment) Act 1982 (c.1)
Civil Aviation (Amendment) Act 1996 (c.39)

Civil Aviation Authority (Borrowing Powers) Act 1990 (c.2)
Civil Aviation (Declaratory Provisions) Act 1971 (c.6)
Civil Aviation (Eurocontrol) Act 1962 (c.8)
Civil Aviation (Eurocontrol) Act 1983 (c.11)
Civil Aviation (Licensing) Act 1960 (c.38)
Civil Bill Court (Ireland) Act 1865 (c.1)
Civil Bill Courts (Ireland) Act 1836 (c.75)
Civil Bill Courts (Ireland) Act 1851 (c.57)
Civil Bill Courts (Ireland) Act 1874 (c.66)
Civil Bill Courts Procedure Amendment (Ireland) Act 1864 (c.99)
Civil Bill Courts Procedure Amendment (Ireland) Act 1871 (c.99)
Civil Bill Decrees (Ireland) Act 1842 (c.33)
Civil Contingencies Fund Act 1919 (c.6)
Civil Contingencies Fund Act 1952 (c.2)
Civil Defence Act 1939 (c.31)
Civil Defence Act 1948 (c.6)
Civil Defence Act 1949 (c.5)
Civil Defence (Armed Forces) Act 1954 (c.66)
Civil Defence (Electricity Undertakings) Act 1954 (c.19)
Civil Defence (Suspension of Powers) Act 1945 (c.12)
Civil Evidence Act 1968 (c.64)
Civil Evidence Act 1972 (c.30)
Civil Evidence Act 1995 (c.38)
Civil Evidence (Family Mediation) (Scotland) Act 1995 (c.6)
Civil Evidence (Scotland) Act 1988 (c.32)
Civil Imprisonment (Scotland) Act 1882 (c.42)
Civil Jurisdiction and Judgments Act 1982 (c.27)
Civil Jurisdiction and Judgments Act 1991 (c.12)
Civil Liability (Contribution) Act 1978 (c.47)
Civil List Act 1714 (c.1)
Civil List Act 1727 (c.1)
Civil List Act 1760 (c.1)
Civil List Act 1776 (c.21)
Civil List Act 1785 (c.61)
Civil List Act 1804 (c.80)
Civil List Act 1837 (c.2)
Civil List Act 1901 (c.4)
Civil List Act 1910 (c.28)
Civil List Act 1936 (c.15)
Civil List Act 1937 (c.32)
Civil List Act 1952 (c.37)
Civil List Act 1972 (c.7)
Civil List Act 1975 (c.82)
Civil List and Secret Service Money Act 1782 (c.82)
Civil List Audit Act 1816 (c.46)
Civil List, During King's Illness Act 1812 (c.6)
Civil List (Ireland) Act 1805 (c.76)
Civil Procedure Act 1997 (c.12)
Civil Procedure Acts Repeal 1879 (c.59)
Civil Protection in Peacetime Act 1986 (c.22)
Civil Rights of Convicts Act 1828 (c.32)
Civil Service, India Act 1837 (c.70)
Civil Service (Management Functions) Act 1992 (c.61)

Civil Service Superannuation Act 1857 (c.37)
Clackmannan and Perth Roads Act 1794 (c.139)
Clackmannan and Perth Roads Act 1797 (c.166)
Clan Gregour (Scotland) Act 1775 (c.29)
Clandestine Marriages Act 1753 (c.33)
Clandestine Running of Goods, etc. Act 1810 (c.10)
Clapham Church Act 1774 (c.12)
Clapham: Streets Act 1785 (c.88)
Claremont Estate Purchase (Grant of Life Interest) Act 1816 (c.115)
Clean Air Act 1956 (c.52)
Clean Air Act 1968 (c.62)
Clean Air Act 1993 (c.11)
Clean Rivers (Estuaries and Tidal Waters) Act 1960 (c.54)
Cleansing of Persons Act 1897 (c.31)
Clearance of Vessels, London Act 1811 (c.24)
Clergy Discipline Act 1892 (c.32)
Clergy Endowments (Canada) Act 1791 (c.31)
Clergy Ordination Act 1804 (c.43)
Clergy Reserves in Canada Act 1840 (c.78)
Clergy Residences Repair Act 1776 (c.53)
Clergy Residences Repair Act 1781 (c.66)
Clergymen Ordained Abroad Act 1863 (c.121)
Clerical Disabilities Act 1870 (c.91)
Clerical Subscription Act 1865 (c.122)
Clerkenwell Church Act 1788 (c.10)
Clerkenwell: Poor Relief Act 1775 (c.23)
Clerkenwell: Poor Relief Act 1783 (c.44)
Clerkenwell: Streets Act 1774 (c.24)
Clerkenwell: Streets Act 1777 (c.63)
Clerkenwell: Watching, etc. Act 1771 (c.33)
Clerk of Assize (Ireland) Act 1821 (c.54)
Clerk of the Crown (Ireland) Act 1832 (c.48)
Clerk of the Council Act 1859 (c.1)
Clerk of the Crown in Chancery Act 1844 (c.77)
Clerk of the Hanaper Act 1749 (c.25)
Clerks of Assize, etc. Act 1869 (c.89)
Clerks of Session (Scotland) Regulation Act 1889 (c.54)
Clerks of Session (Scotland) Regulation Act 1913 (c.23)
Clerks of the Peace (Removal) Act 1864 (c.65)
Cloth Manufacture Act 1733 (c.25)
Cloth Manufacture Act 1737 (c.28)
Cloth Manufacture Act 1740 (c.35)
Cloth Manufacturer Act 1724 (c.24)
Cloth Manufacture, Yorkshire Act 1765 (c.51)
Cloth Manufacture, Yorkshire Act 1766 (c.23)
Clothing of the Army, etc. Act 1810 (c.107)
Clubs (Temporary Provisions) Act 1915 (c.84)
Clyde Bridge Act 1758 (c.62)
Clyde Marine Society Act 1786 (c.109)
Clyde, Navigation Act 1774 (c.103)

Coaches, Bond Street Act 1792 (c.62)
Coadjutors to Bishops in Ireland Act 1812 (c.62)
Coal Act 1938 (c.52)
Coal Act 1943 (c.38)
Coal (Concurrent Leases) Act 1942 (c.19)
Coal Consumers' Councils (Northern Irish Interests) Act 1962 (c.22)
Coal Duty, Dublin Act 1811 (c.11)
Coal Duty, London Act 1845 (c.101)
Coal Industry Act 1949 (c.53)
Coal Industry Act 1951 (c.41)
Coal Industry Act 1956 (c.61)
Coal Industry Act 1960 (c.17)
Coal Industry Act 1961 (c.5)
Coal Industry Act 1962 (c.6)
Coal Industry Act 1965 (c.82)
Coal Industry Act 1967 (c.91)
Coal Industry Act 1971 (c.16)
Coal Industry Act 1973 (c.8)
Coal Industry Act 1975 (c.56)
Coal Industry Act 1977 (c.39)
Coal Industry Act 1980 (c.50)
Coal Industry Act 1982 (c.15)
Coal Industry Act 1983 (c.60)
Coal Industry Act 1985 (c.27)
Coal Industry Act 1987 (c.3)
Coal Industry Act 1990 (c.3)
Coal Industry Act 1992 (c.17)
Coal Industry Act 1994 (c.21)
Coal Industry Commission Act 1919 (c.1)
Coal Industry Nationalisation Act 1946 (c.59)
Coal Industry (No. 2) Act 1949 (c.79)
Coal Loading: Newcastle and Sunderland Act 1766 (c.22)
Coal Loading: Newcastle and Sunderland Act 1772 (c.22)
Coal Measurement, London Act 1776 (c.13)
Coal Metage, etc., London Act 1766 (c.23)
Coal Mines Act 1855 (c.107)
Coal Mines Act 1862 (c.79)
Coal Mines Act 1886 (c.40)
Coal Mines Act 1911 (c.50)
Coal Mines Act 1914 (c.22)
Coal Mines Act 1919 (c.48)
Coal Mines Act 1926 (c.17)
Coal Mines Act 1930 (c.34)
Coal Mines Act 1931 (c.27)
Coal Mines Act 1932 (c.29)
Coal Mines (Check Weigher) Act 1894 (c.52)
Coal Mines Control Agreement (Confirmation) Act 1918 (c.56)
Coal Mines (Decontrol) Act 1921 (c.6)
Coal Mines (Employment of Boys) Act 1937 (c.62)
Coal Mines Inspection Act 1850 (c.100)
Coal Mines (Minimum Wage) Act 1912 (c.2)
Coal Mines Regulation Act 1872 (c.76)
Coal Mines Regulation Act 1887 (c.58)
Coal Mines Regulation Act (1887) Amendment 1903 (c.7)
Coal Mines Regulation Act 1896 (c.43)
Coal Mines Regulation Act 1908 (c.57)

Coal Mines Regulation (Amendment) Act 1917 (c.8)
Coal Mines (Weighing of Minerals) Act 1905 (c.9)
Coal Mining (Subsidence) Act 1950 (c.23)
Coal Mining (Subsidence) Act 1957 (c.59)
Coal Mining Subsidence Act 1991 (c.45)
Coal (Registration of Ownership) Act 1937 (c.56)
Coal Trade Act 1710 (c.30)
Coal Trade Act 1730 (c.26)
Coal Trade Act 1730 (c.30)
Coal Trade Act 1788 (c.53)
Coal Trade Act 1836 (c.109)
Coal Trade, London Act 1745 (c.35)
Coal Trade, London Act 1758 (c.27)
Coal Trade, London Act 1786 (c.83)
Coal Trade, London Act 1796 (c.61)
Coal Trade: Westminster Act 1766 (c.35)
Coal Trade, Westminster Act 1786 (c.108)
Coal Vendors Act 1843 (c.2)
Coalport Bridge over Severn (Tolls, etc.) Act 1776 (c.12)
Coals Act 1743 (c.35)
Coals, Newcastle Act 1782 (c.32)
Coalwhippers, London Act 1851 (c.78)
Coalwhippers, Port of London Act 1846 (c.36)
Coast Protection Act 1939 (c.39)
Coast Protection Act 1949 (c.74)
Coast Trade Act 1792 (c.50)
Coastal Flooding (Emergency Provisions) Act 1953 (c.18)
Coastguard Act 1925 (c.88)
Coastguard Service Act 1856 (c.83)
Coasting Trade Act 1805 (c.81)
Coasting Trade Act 1854 (c.5)
Coatbridge and Springburn Elections (Validation) Act 1945 (c.3)
Cobham, Leatherhead and Godalming Bridges Act 1782 (c.17)
Cockburnspath Bridge, Berwick Act 1789 (c.42)
Cockermouth and Workington Road Act 1779 (c.105)
Cockerton Bridge to Staindrop Road Act 1793 (c.146)
Cockfighting Act 1952 (c.59)
Cocos Islands Act 1955 (c.5)
Codbreck Brook, Navigation Act 1767 (c.95)
Coffee and Cocoa-Nuts Act 1783 (c.79)
Coffee, etc. Act 1812 (c.149)
Coffee, etc. Act 1814 (c.47)
Coin Act 1732 (c.26)
Coin Act 1774 (c.70)
Coin Act 1816 (c.68)
Coin Act 1849 (c.41)
Coinage Act 1708 (c.24)
Coinage Act 1859 (c.30)
Coinage Act 1870 (c.10)
Coinage Act 1889 (c.58)
Coinage Act 1891 (c.72)
Coinage Act 1893 (c.1)
Coinage Act 1946 (c.74)

Coinage Act 1971 (c.24)
Coinage (Colonial Offences) Act 1853 (c.48)
Coinage Duties Act 1730 (c.12)
Coinage Duties Act 1738 (c.5)
Coinage Duties Act 1745 (c.14)
Coinage Duties Act 1760 (c.16)
Coinage Duties Act 1769 (c.25)
Coinage Duties, etc. Act 1754 (c.11)
Coinage in American Plantations Act 1707 (c.57)
Coinage Offences Act 1861 (c.99)
Coinage Offences Act 1936 (c.16)
Colewort Barracks, Portsmouth Act 1860 (c.49)
Collecting Societies and Industrial Assurance Companies Act 1896 (c.26)
Collection of Charity Money Act 1705 (c.25)
Collection of Malt Duties, etc. Act 1805 (c.53)
Collection of Revenue, etc. (Ireland) Act 1803 (c.98)
Collection of Revenue (Ireland) Act 1803 (c.43)
Collection of Revenue (Ireland) Act 1803 (c.97)
Collection of Revenue (Ireland) Act 1804 (c.105)
Collection of Revenues (Ireland) Act 1802 (c.36)
College Charter Act 1871 (c.63)
College of Physicians (Ireland) Act 1862 (c.15)
Collegiate Church of Manchester Act 1728 (c.29)
Collieries and Mines Act 1800 (c.77)
Collieries (Ireland) Act 1807 (c.45)
Colliers Act 1775 (c.28)
Colliers (Scotland) Act 1799 (c.56)
Collingham to York Road Act 1792 (c.142)
Colneis and Carlford Hundreds, Suffolk: Poor Relief Act 1790 (c.22)
Colne Oyster Fishery Act 1757 (c.71)
Colne River, Essex: Navigation Act 1718 (c.31)
Colonial Acts Confirmation Act 1863 (c.84)
Colonial Acts Confirmation Act 1894 (c.72)
Colonial Acts Confirmation Act 1901 (c.29)
Colonial Affidavits Act 1859 (c.12)
Colonial and Other Territories (Divorce Jurisdiction) Act 1950 (c.20)
Colonial Attorneys Relief Act 1857 (c.39)
Colonial Attorneys Relief Act 1874 (c.41)
Colonial Attorneys Relief Amendment Act 1884 (c.24)
Colonial Bishops Act 1852 (c.52)
Colonial Bishops Act 1853 (c.49)
Colonial Boundaries Act 1895 (c.34)
Colonial Branch Mint Act 1866 (c.65)
Colonial Clergy Act 1874 (c.77)
Colonial Copyright Act 1847 (c.95)
Colonial Courts of Admiralty Act 1890 (c.27)
Colonial Development Act 1929 (c.5)
Colonial Development and Welfare Act 1939 (c.40)

Colonial Development and Welfare Act 1944 (c.20)
Colonial Development and Welfare Act 1949 (c.49)
Colonial Development and Welfare Act 1950 (c.4)
Colonial Development and Welfare Act 1955 (c.6)
Colonial Development and Welfare Act 1959 (c.71)
Colonial Docks Loans Act 1865 (c.106)
Colonial Duties Act 1842 (c.49)
Colonial Fortifications Act 1877 (c.23)
Colonial Governors (Pensions) Act 1865 (c.113)
Colonial Governors (Pensions) Act 1872 (c.29)
Colonial Inland Post Office Act 1849 (c.66)
Colonial Laws Validity Act 1865 (c.63)
Colonial Leave of Absence Act 1782 (c.75)
Colonial Letters Patent Act 1863 (c.76)
Colonial Loans Act 1899 (c.36)
Colonial Loans Act 1949 (c.50)
Colonial Loans Act 1952 (c.1)
Colonial Loans Act 1962 (c.41)
Colonial Marriages Act 1865 (c.64)
Colonial Marriages (Deceased Wife's Sister) Act 1906 (c.30)
Colonial Naval Defence Act 1865 (c.14)
Colonial Naval Defence Act 1909 (c.19)
Colonial Naval Defence Act 1931 (c.9)
Colonial Naval Defence Act 1949 (c.18)
Colonial Officers (Leave of Absence) Act 1894 (c.17)
Colonial Offices Act 1830 (c.4)
Colonial Prisoners Removal Act 1869 (c.10)
Colonial Prisoners Removal Act 1884 (c.31)
Colonial Probates Act 1892 (c.6)
Colonial Probates (Protected States and Mandated Territories) Act 1927 (c.43)
Colonial Shipping Act 1868 (c.129)
Colonial Solicitors Act 1900 (c.14)
Colonial Stock Act 1877 (c.59)
Colonial Stock Act 1892 (c.35)
Colonial Stock Act 1900 (c.62)
Colonial Stock Act 1934 (c.47)
Colonial Stock Act 1948 (c.1)
Colonial Trade Act 1730 (c.28)
Colonial Trade Act 1734 (c.19)
Colonial Trade Act 1738 (c.30)
Colonial Trade Act 1760 (c.9)
Colonial Trade Act 1763 (c.27)
Colonial Trade Act 1768 (c.22)
Colonial Trade Act 1769 (c.27)
Colonial Trade Act 1812 (c.98)
Colonial War Risks Insurance (Guarantees) Act 1941 (c.35)
(Colonies) Evidence Act 1843 (c.22)
Colony of New York Act 1770 (c.35)
Colouring of Porter Act 1811 (c.87)
Combination of Workmen Act 1796 (c.111)
Combinations of Workmen Act 1801 (c.38)
Combination of Workmen Act 1859 (c.34)

Commerce with Certain Countries Act 1721 (c.8)

Commerce with Spain Act 1739 (c.27)

Commerce with Sweden Act 1716 (c.1)

Commerce with United States Act 1816 (c.15)

Commerce with United States Act 1816 (c.51)

Commercial Treaty with Portugal Act 1811 (c.47)

Commissariat Accounts Act 1821 (c.121)

Commissary Court of Edinburgh Act 1815 (c.97)

Commissary Court of Edinburgh, etc. Act 1836 (c.41)

Commissioners Clauses Act 1847 (c.16)

Commissioners for Oaths Act 1853 (c.78)

Commissioners for Oaths Act 1855 (c.42)

Commissioners for Oaths Act 1889 (c.10)

Commissioners for Oaths Act 1891 (c.50)

Commissioners for Oaths Amendment Act 1890 (c.7)

Commissioners for Oaths, Bail in Error, etc. Act 1859

Commissioners for Oaths, Bail in Error, etc. Act 1859 (c.16)

Commissioners for Oaths (Ireland) Act 1872 (c.75)

Commissioners for Oaths (Prize Proceedings) Act 1907 (c.25)

Commissioners of Customs Act 1845 (c.85)

Commissioners of Sewers (City of London) Act 1708 (c.32)

Commissioners of Supply Meetings (Scotland) Act 1865 (c.38)

Commissioners of Supply (Scotland) Act 1856 (c.93)

Commissioners of Supply (Scotland) Act 1857 (c.11)

Commissioners of the Treasury Act 1807 (c.20)

Commissioners of Woods (Audit) Act 1844 (c.89)

Commissioners of Woods (Thames Piers) Act 1879 (c.73)

Commissioners of Works Act 1852 (c.28)

Commissioners of Works Act 1894 (c.23)

Commissions of Sewers Act 1708 (c.33)

Commissions of the Peace Continuance Act 1837 (c.1)

Commissions to Foreign Protestants Act 1756 (c.5)

Commissions and Salaries of Judges Act 1760 (c.23)

Commission of Assize in County Palatine of Lancaster Act 1855 (c.45)

Common Informers Act 1951 (c.39)

Common Land (Rectification of Registers) Act 1989 (c.18)

Common Law Chambers Act 1867 (c.68)

Common Law Courts Act 1852 (c.73)

Common Law Courts (Fees) Act 1865 (c.45)

Common Law Courts (Fees and Salaries) Act 1866 (c.101)

Common Law Courts (Ireland) Act 1851 (c.17)

Common Law Offices (Ireland) Act 1844 (c.107)

Common Law Procedure Act 1838 (c.45)

Common Law Procedure Act 1852 (c.76)

Common Law Procedure Act 1854 (c.125)

Common Law Procedure Act 1860 (c.126)

Common Law Procedure Act 1864 (c.28)

Common Law Procedure Amendment (Ireland) Act 1853 (c.113)

Common Law Procedure Amendment (Ireland) Act 1856 (c.102)

Common Law Procedure Amendment (Ireland) Act 1870 (c.109)

Common Law Procedure (Ireland) Act 1855 (c.7)

Common Law Procedure (Ireland) Act 1860 (c.82)

Common Lodging House Act 1853 (c.41)

Common Lodging Houses Act 1851 (c.28)

Common Lodging Houses (Ireland) Act 1860 (c.26)

Common Pleas of Lancaster Act 1794 (c.46)

Common Pleas of Lancaster Act 1800 (c.105)

Common Pleas at Lancaster Amendment Act 1869 (c.37)

Common Recoveries, etc. Act 1740 (c.20)

Commonable Rights Compensation Act 1882 (c.15)

Commons Act 1876 (c.56)

Commons Act 1879 (c.37)

Commons Act 1899 (c.30)

Commons Act 1908 (c.44)

Commons (Expenses) Act 1878 (c.56)

Commons Registration Act 1965 (c.64)

Commonwealth Development Act 1963 (c.40)

Commonwealth Development Corporation Act 1978 (c.2)

Commonwealth Development Corporation Act 1982 (c.54)

Commonwealth Development Corporation Act 1986 (c.25)

Commonwealth Development Corporation Act 1995 (c.9)

Commonwealth Development Corporation Act 1996 (c.28)

Commonwealth Immigrants Act 1962 (c.21)

Commonwealth Immigration Act 1968 (c.9)

Commonwealth (India (Consequential) Provisions) Act 1949 (c.92)

Commonwealth Institute Act 1958 (c.16)

Commonwealth of Australia Constitution Act 1900 (c.12)

Commonwealth Scholarships Act 1959 (c.6)

Commonwealth Scholarships (Amendment) Act 1963 (c.6)

Commonwealth Secretariat Act 1966 (c.10)

Commonwealth Settlement Act 1957 (c.8)

Commonwealth Settlement Act 1962 (c.17)

Commonwealth Settlement Act 1967 (c.31)

Commonwealth Teachers Act 1960 (c.40)

Commonwealth Telecommunications Act 1968 (c.24)

Commonwealth Telegraphs Act 1949 (c.39)

Communications from Marylebone to Charing Cross Act 1813 (c.121)

Community Care (Direct Payments) Act 1996 (c.30)

Community Care (Residential Accommodation) Act 1992 (c.49)

Community Charges (General Reduction) Act 1991 (c.9)

Community Charges (Substitute Setting) Act 1991 (c.8)

Community Health Councils (Access to Information) Act 1988 (c.24)

Community Land Act 1975 (c.77)

Community Service by Offenders (Scotland) Act 1978 (c.49)

Companies Act 1862 (c.89)

Companies Act 1867 (c.131)

Companies Act 1877 (c.26)

Companies Act 1879 (c.76)

Companies Act 1880 (c.19)

Companies Act 1883 (c.28)

Companies Act 1886 (c.23)

Companies Act 1898 (c.26)

Companies Act 1900 (c.48)

Companies Act 1907 (c.50)

Companies Act 1908 (c.12)

Companies Act 1913 (c.25)

Companies Act 1928 (c.45)

Companies Act 1929 (c.23)

Companies Act 1947 (c.47)

Companies Act 1948 (c.38)

Companies Act 1967 (c.81)

Companies Act 1976 (c.69)

Companies Act 1980 (c.22)

Companies Act 1981 (c.62)

Companies Act 1985 (c.6)

Companies Act 1989 (c.40)

Companies (Beneficial Interests) Act 1983 (c.50)

Companies Clauses Act 1863 (c.118)

Companies Clauses Act 1869 (c.48)

Companies Clauses Consolidation Act 1845 (c.16)

Companies Clauses Consolidation Act 1888 (c.48)

Companies Clauses Consolidation Act 1889 (c.37)

Companies Clauses Consolidation (Scotland) Act 1845 (c.17)

Companies (Colonial Registers) Act 1883 (c.30)

Companies (Consolidation) Act 1908 (c.69)

Companies Consolidation (Consequential Provisions) Act 1985 (c.9)

Companies (Converted Societies) Act 1910 (c.23)

Companies (Defence) Act 1939 (c.75)

Companies (Floating Charges and Receivers) (Scotland) Act 1972 (c.67)

Companies (Floating Charges) (Scotland) Act 1961 (c.46)

Companies (Foreign Interests) Act 1917 (c.18)

Companies (Memorandum of Association) Act 1890 (c.62)

Companies (Particulars as to Directors) Act 1917 (c.28)

Companies (Winding-up) Act 1890 (c.63)

Companies (Winding-up) Act 1893 (c.58)

Company Directors (Disqualification) Act 1986 (c.46)

Company Seals Act 1864 (c.19)

Company Securities (Insider Dealing) Act 1985 (c.8)

Compassionate List of the Navy, etc. Act 1809 (c.45)

Compensation (Defence) Act 1939 (c.75)

Compensation for Injuries to Mills etc. Act 1801 (c.24)

Compensation for Works at Portsmouth Act 1815 (c.123)

Compensation of Displaced Officers (War Service) Act 1945 (c.10)

Compensation to American Loyalists, etc. Act 1788 (c.40)

Compensation to Patentee Officers (Ireland) Act 1808 (c.108)

Competency of Witnesses Act 1787 (c.29)

Competition Act 1980 (c.21)

Competition and Service (Utilities) Act 1992 (c.43)

Completing St. Paul's, etc. Act 1702 (c.12)

Completion of Somerset House Act 1780 (c.40)

Composition for a Certain Crown Debt Act 1770 (c.12)

Composition for a Crown Debt Act 1774 (c.35)

Composition for a Crown Debt Act 1775 (c.19)

Composition for a Crown Debt Act 1776 (c.31)

Composition for a Crown Debt Act 1776 (c.49)

Composition for a Crown Debt Act 1779 (c.77)

Composition for a Crown Debt Act 1784 (c.14)

Composition for a Crown Debt Act 1801 (c.60)

Compound Householders Act 1851 (c.14)

Comptroller of the Exchequer, etc. Act 1865 (c.93)

Compulsory Church Date Abolition 1868 (c.109)

Compulsory Purchase Act 1965 (c.56)

Compulsory Purchase (Vesting Declarations) Act 1981 (c.66)

Computer Misuse Act 1990 (c.18)

Concealment of Birth (Scotland) Act 1809 (c.14)

Concessionary Travel for Handicapped Persons (Scotland) Act 1980 (c.29)

Conciliation Act 1896 (c.30)

Concorde Aircraft Act 1973 (c.7)

Confirmation and Probate Amendment Act 1859 (c.30)

Confirmation of Certain Marriages Act 1781 (c.53)

Confirmation of Certain Marriages Act 1858 (c.46)

Confirmation of Certain Marriages Act 1889 (c.38)

Confirmation of Certain Proceedings Act 1842 (c.43)

Confirmation of Executors (Scotland) Act 1823 (c.98)

Confirmation of Executors (Scotland) Act 1858 (c.56)

Confirmation of Executors (War Service) (Scotland) Act 1917 (c.27)

Confirmation of Executors (War Service) (Scotland) Act 1939 (c.41)

Confirmation of Executors (War Service) (Scotland) Act 1940 (c.41)

Confirmation of Marriages Act 1853 (c.122)

Confirmation of Marriages Act 1854 (c.88)

Confirmation of Marriages Act 1855 (c.66)

Confirmation of Marriages Act 1856 (c.70)

Confirmation of Marriages Act 1857 (c.29)

Confirmation of Marriages Act 1859 (c.24)

Confirmation of Marriages Act 1859 (c.64)

Confirmation of Marriages Act 1860 (c.1)

Confirmation of Marriages Act 1861 (c.16)

Confirmation of Marriages, Blakedown Chapel Act 1868 (c.113)

Confirmation of Marriages (Cove Chapel) Act 1873 (c.1)

Confirmation of Marriages on Her Majesty's Ships Act 1879 (c.29)

Confirmation of Provision Order (Land Drainage) Act 1867 (c.22)

Confirmation of Provisional Orders, Turnpike Trusts Act 1867 (c.66)

Confirmation of Sales etc., by Trustees Act 1862 (c.108)

Confirmation to Small Estates (Scotland) Act 1979 (c.22)

Confiscation of Alcohol (Young Persons) Act 1997 (c.33)

Congenital Disabilities (Civil Liability) Act 1976 (c.28)

Congested Districts Board (Ireland) Act 1893 (c.35)

Congested Districts Board (Ireland) Act 1894 (c.50)

Congested Districts Board (Ireland) Act 1899 (c.18)

Congested Districts Board (Ireland) Act 1901 (c.34)

Congested Districts (Scotland) Act 1897 (c.53)

Conjugal Rights (Scotland) Amendment Act 1861 (c.86)

Conjugal Rights (Scotland) Amendment Act 1874 (c.31)

Consecration of Bishops Abroad Act 1786 (c.84)

Consecration of Churchyards Act 1867 (c.133)

Consecration of Churchyards Act 1868 (c.47)

Conservation of Seals Act 1970 (c.30)

Conservation of Wild Creatures and Wild Plants Act 1975 (c.48)

Consolidated Annuities (Ireland) Act 1853 (c.75)

Consolidated Fund Act 1806 (c.44)

Consolidated Fund Act 1816 (c.98)

Consolidated Fund Act 1947 (c.17)

Consolidated Fund Act 1950 (c.1)

Consolidated Fund Act 1951 (c.12)

Consolidated Fund Act 1952 (c.16)

Consolidated Fund Act 1953 (c.6)

Consolidated Fund Act 1954 (c.22)

Consolidated Fund Act 1955 (c.3)

Consolidated Fund Act 1956 (c.32)

Consolidated Fund Act 1957 (c.7)

Consolidated Fund Act 1958 (c.7)

Consolidated Fund Act 1960 (c.10)

Consolidated Fund Act 1963 (c.1)

Consolidated Fund Act 1965 (c.1)

Consolidated Fund Act 1966 (c.1)

Consolidated Fund Act 1968 (c.1)

Consolidated Fund Act 1969 (c.3)

Consolidated Fund Act 1970 (c.1)

Consolidated Fund Act 1971 (c.1)

Consolidated Fund Act 1972 (c.13)

Consolidated Fund Act 1973 (c.1)

Consolidated Fund Act 1974 (c.1)

Consolidated Fund Act 1975 (c.1)

Consolidated Fund Act 1976 (c.2)

Consolidated Fund Act 1977 (c.1)

Consolidated Fund Act 1978 (c.7)

Consolidated Fund Act 1979 (c.20)

Consolidated Fund Act 1980 (c.14)

Consolidated Fund Act 1981 (c.4)

Consolidated Fund Act 1982 (c.8)

Consolidated Fund Act 1983 (c.1)

Consolidated Fund Act 1984 (c.1)

Consolidated Fund Act 1985 (c.1)

Consolidated Fund Act 1986 (c.4)

Consolidated Fund Act 1987 (c.8)

Consolidated Fund Act 1988 (c.6)

Consolidated Fund Act 1989 (c.2)

Consolidated Fund Act 1990 (c.4)

Consolidated Fund Act 1991 (c.7)

Consolidated Fund Act 1992 (c.1)

Consolidated Fund Act 1993 (c.4)

Consolidated Fund Act 1994 (c.4)

Consolidated Fund Act 1995 (c.2)

Consolidated Fund Act 1996 (c.4)

Consolidated Fund Act 1997 (c.15)

Consolidated Fund (Civil List Provisions) Act 1951 (c.50)

Consolidated Fund (No. 1) Act 1879 (c.2)

Consolidated Fund (No. 1) Act 1880 (c.5)

Consolidated Fund (No. 1) Act 1881 (c.1)

Consolidated Fund (No. 1) Act 1882 (c.1)

Consolidated Fund (No. 1) Act 1883 (c.2)

Consolidated Fund (No. 1) Act 1884 (c.2)

Consolidated Fund (No. 1) Act 1884 (c.4)

Consolidated Fund (No. 1) Act 1886 (c.4)

Consolidated Fund (No. 1) Act 1887 (c.1)

Consolidated Fund (No. 1) Act 1888 (c.1)

Consolidated Fund (No. 1) Act 1889 (c.1)
Consolidated Fund (No. 1) Act 1890 (c.1)
Consolidated Fund (No. 1) Act 1891 (c.6)
Consolidated Fund (No. 1) Act 1892 (c.3)
Consolidated Fund (No. 1) Act 1893 (c.3)
Consolidated Fund (No. 1) Act 1894 (c.1)
Consolidated Fund (No. 1) Act 1895 (c.4)
Consolidated Fund (No. 1) Act 1896 (c.3)
Consolidated Fund (No. 1) Act 1897 (c.4)
Consolidated Fund (No. 1) Act 1898 (c.3)
Consolidated Fund (No. 1) Act 1899 (c.2)
Consolidated Fund (No. 1) Act 1900 (c.1)
Consolidated Fund (No. 1) Act 1901 (c.1)
Consolidated Fund (No. 1) Act 1902 (c.1)
Consolidated Fund (No. 1) Act 1903 (c.3)
Consolidated Fund (No. 1) Act 1904 (c.1)
Consolidated Fund (No. 1) Act 1905 (c.1)
Consolidated Fund (No. 1) Act 1906 (c.1)
Consolidated Fund (No. 1) Act 1907 (c.1)
Consolidated Fund (No. 1) Act 1908 (c.1)
Consolidated Fund (No. 1) Act 1909 (c.1)
Consolidated Fund (No. 1) Act 1910 (c.4)
Consolidated Fund (No. 1) Act 1911 (c.1)
Consolidated Fund (No. 1) Act 1912 (c.1)
Consolidated Fund (No. 1) Act 1913 (c.1)
Consolidated Fund (No. 1) Act 1914 (c.1)
Consolidated Fund (No. 1) Act 1916 (c.1)
Consolidated Fund (No. 1) Act 1917 (c.1)
Consolidated Fund (No. 1) Act 1918 (c.1)
Consolidated Fund (No. 1) Act 1919 (c.5)
Consolidated Fund (No. 1) Act 1921 (c.2)
Consolidated Fund (No. 1) Act 1922 (c.1)
Consolidated Fund (No. 1) Act 1923 (c.1)
Consolidated Fund (No. 1) Act 1924 (c.2)
Consolidated Fund (No. 1) Act 1925 (c.8)
Consolidated Fund (No. 1) Act 1926 (c.1)
Consolidated Fund (No. 1) Act 1927 (c.2)
Consolidated Fund (No. 1) Act 1928 (c.1)
Consolidated Fund (No. 1) Act 1928 (c.2)
Consolidated Fund (No. 1) Act 1929 (c.10)
Consolidated Fund (No. 1) Act 1932 (c.1)
Consolidated Fund (No. 1) Act 1932 (c.14)
Consolidated Fund (No. 1) Act 1934 (c.3)
Consolidated Fund (No. 1) Act 1935 (c.4)
Consolidated Fund (No. 1) Act 1936 (c.8)
Consolidated Fund (No. 1) Act 1937 (c.7)
Consolidated Fund (No. 1) Act 1938 (c.9)
Consolidated Fund (No. 1) Act 1939 (c.12)
Consolidated Fund (No. 1) Act 1940 (c.11)
Consolidated Fund (No. 1) Act 1941 (c.6)
Consolidated Fund (No. 1) Act 1943 (c.4)
Consolidated Fund (No. 1) Act 1944 (c.1)
Consolidated Fund (No. 1) Act 1944 (c.4)
Consolidated Fund (No. 1) Act 1945 (c.4)
Consolidated Fund (No. 1) Act 1946 (c.33)
Consolidated Fund (No. 1) Act 1948 (c.18)
Consolidated Fund (No. 1) Act 1949 (c.24)
Consolidated Fund (No. 1) (Session 2) Act 1880 (c.3)
Consolidated Fund (No. 1) (Session 2) Act 1914 (c.6)
Consolidated Fund (No. 1) (Session 2) Act 1931 (c.1)

Consolidated Fund (No. 1) (Session 2) Act 1941 (c.2)
Consolidated Fund (No. 2) Act 1879 (c.7)
Consolidated Fund (No. 2) Act 1881 (c.8)
Consolidated Fund (No. 2) Act 1882 (c.4)
Consolidated Fund (No. 2) Act 1883 (c.5)
Consolidated Fund (No. 2) Act 1884 (c.15)
Consolidated Fund (No. 2) Act 1885 (c.6)
Consolidated Fund (No. 2) Act 1886 (c.7)
Consolidated Fund (No. 2) Act 1887 (c.14)
Consolidated Fund (No. 2) Act 1888 (c.16)
Consolidated Fund (No. 2) Act 1889 (c.2)
Consolidated Fund (No. 2) Act 1890 (c.28)
Consolidated Fund (No. 2) Act 1891 (c.27)
Consolidated Fund (No. 2) Act 1892 (c.20)
Consolidated Fund (No. 2) Act 1893 (c.16)
Consolidated Fund (No. 2) Act 1894 (c.7)
Consolidated Fund (No. 2) Act 1895 (c.15)
Consolidated Fund (No. 2) Act 1896 (c.7)
Consolidated Fund (No. 2) Act 1898 (c.32)
Consolidated Fund (No. 2) Act 1900 (c.3)
Consolidated Fund (No. 2) Act 1901 (c.6)
Consolidated Fund (No. 2) Act 1905 (c.6)
Consolidated Fund (No. 2) Act 1909 (c.2)
Consolidated Fund (No. 2) Act 1910 (c.9(a))
Consolidated Fund (No. 2) Act 1911 (c.5)
Consolidated Fund (No. 2) Act 1913 (c.5)
Consolidated Fund (No. 2) Act 1915 (c.33)
Consolidated Fund (No. 2) Act 1916 (c.3)
Consolidated Fund (No. 2) Act 1917 (c.7)
Consolidated Fund (No. 2) Act 1918 (c.11)
Consolidated Fund (No. 2) Act 1919 (c.49)
Consolidated Fund (No. 2) Act 1921 (c.3)
Consolidated Fund (No. 2) Act 1922 (c.3)
Consolidated Fund (No. 2) Act 1924 (c.4)
Consolidated Fund (No. 2) Act 1929 (c.10)
Consolidated Fund (No. 2) Act 1930 (c.14)
Consolidated Fund (No. 2) Act 1931 (c.10)
Consolidated Fund (No. 2) Act 1933 (c.3)
Consolidated Fund (No. 2) Act 1935 (c.10)
Consolidated Fund (No. 2) Act 1936 (c.11)
Consolidated Fund (No. 2) Act 1937 (c.20)
Consolidated Fund (No. 2) Act 1939 (c.39)
Consolidated Fund (No. 2) Act 1941 (c.9)
Consolidated Fund (No. 2) Act 1942 (c.12)
Consolidated Fund (No. 2) Act 1943 (c.11)
Consolidated Fund (No. 2) Act 1944 (c.17)
Consolidated Fund (No. 2) Act 1945 (c.4)
Consolidated Fund (No. 2) Act 1957 (c.10)
Consolidated Fund (No. 2) Act 1958 (c.18)
Consolidated Fund (No. 2) Act 1961 (c.12)
Consolidated Fund (No. 2) Act 1962 (c.11)
Consolidated Fund (No. 2) Act 1963 (c.8)
Consolidated Fund (No. 2) Act 1964 (c.17)
Consolidated Fund (No. 2) Act 1965 (c.8)
Consolidated Fund (No. 2) Act 1967 (c.6)
Consolidated Fund (No. 2) Act 1968 (c.15)
Consolidated Fund (No. 2) Act 1969 (c.9)
Consolidated Fund (No. 2) Act 1970 (c.12)
Consolidated Fund (No. 2) Act 1971 (c.14)
Consolidated Fund (No. 2) Act 1972 (c.23)
Consolidated Fund (No. 2) Act 1973 (c.10)
Consolidated Fund (No. 2) Act 1974 (c.12)

Consolidated Fund (No. 2) Act 1975 (c.12)
Consolidated Fund (No. 2) Act 1976 (c.84)
Consolidated Fund (No. 2) Act 1977 (c.52)
Consolidated Fund (No. 2) Act 1978 (c.59)
Consolidated Fund (No. 2) Act 1979 (c.56)
Consolidated Fund (No. 2) Act 1980 (c.68)
Consolidated Fund (No. 2) Act 1981 (c.70)
Consolidated Fund (No. 2) Act 1983 (c.5)
Consolidated Fund (No. 2) Act 1984 (c.61)
Consolidated Fund (No. 2) Act 1985 (c.11)
Consolidated Fund (No. 2) Act 1986 (c.67)
Consolidated Fund (No. 2) Act 1987 (c.54)
Consolidated Fund (No. 2) Act 1988 (c.55)
Consolidated Fund (No. 2) Act 1989 (c.46)
Consolidated Fund (No. 2) Act 1990 (c.46)
Consolidated Fund (No. 2) Act 1991 (c.10)
Consolidated Fund (No. 2) Act 1992 (c.21)
Consolidated Fund (No. 2) Act 1993 (c.7)
Consolidated Fund (No. 2) Act 1994 (c.41)
Consolidated Fund (No. 2) Act 1995 (c.54)
Consolidated Fund (No. 2) Act 1996 (c.60)
Consolidated Fund (No. 2) Act 1997 (c.67)
Consolidated Fund (No. 2) (Session 2) Act 1880 (c.30)
Consolidated Fund (No. 3) Act 1879 (c.14)
Consolidated Fund (No. 3) Act 1881 (c.15)
Consolidated Fund (No. 3) Act 1882 (c.8)
Consolidated Fund (No. 3) Act 1883 (c.13)
Consolidated Fund (No. 3) Act 1885 (c.14)
Consolidated Fund (No. 3) Act 1888 (c.26)
Consolidated Fund (No. 3) Act 1889 (c.15)
Consolidated Fund (No. 3) Act 1893 (c.28)
Consolidated Fund (No. 3) Act 1894 (c.29)
Consolidated Fund (No. 3) Act 1915 (c.53)
Consolidated Fund (No. 3) Act 1916 (c.16)
Consolidated Fund (No. 3) Act 1917 (c.17)
Consolidated Fund (No. 3) Act 1918 (c.37)
Consolidated Fund (No. 3) Act 1930 (c.18)
Consolidated Fund (No. 3) Act 1939 (c.52)
Consolidated Fund (No. 3) Act 1941 (c.26)
Consolidated Fund (No. 3) Act 1942 (c.22)
Consolidated Fund (No. 3) Act 1943 (c.20)
Consolidated Fund (No. 3) Act 1944 (c.20)
Consolidated Fund (No. 3) Act 1945 (c.13)
Consolidated Fund (No. 3) Act 1951 (c.1)
Consolidated Fund (No. 3) Act 1953 (c.2)
Consolidated Fund (No. 3) Act 1971 (c.79)
Consolidated Fund (No. 3) Act 1972 (c.78)
Consolidated Fund (No. 3) Act 1974 (c.15)
Consolidated Fund (No. 3) Act 1975 (c.79)
Consolidated Fund (No. 3) Act 1983 (c.57)
Consolidated Fund (No. 3) Act 1985 (c.74)
Consolidated Fund (No. 3) Act 1987 (c.55)
Consolidated Fund (No. 3) Act 1991 (c.68)
Consolidated Fund (No. 3) Act 1992 (c.59)
Consolidated Fund (No. 3) Act 1993 (c.52)
Consolidated Fund (No. 4) Act 1879 (c.20)
Consolidated Fund (No. 4) Act 1881 (c.50)
Consolidated Fund (No. 4) Act 1882 (c.28)
Consolidated Fund (No. 4) Act 1883 (c.23)
Consolidated Fund (No. 4) Act 1893 (c.46)
Consolidated Fund (No. 4) Act 1915 (c.80)
Consolidated Fund (No. 4) Act 1916 (c.30)
Consolidated Fund (No. 4) Act 1917 (c.33)

Consolidated Fund (No. 4) Act 1974 (c.57)
Consolidated Fund (No. 5) Act 1916 (c.48)
Consolidated Fund (No. 5) Act 1917 (c.49)
Consolidated Fund (Permanent Charges Redemption) Act 1873 (c.57)
Consolidated Fund (Permanent Charges Redemption) Act 1883 (c.1)
Consolidation of Enactments (Procedure) Act 1949 (c.33)
Conspiracy and Protection of Property Act 1875 (c.86)
Constables Expenses Act 1801 (c.78)
Constables Near Public Works (Scotland) Act 1845 (c.3)
Constables Protection Act 1750 (c.44)
Constables (Scotland) Act 1875 (c.47)
Constabulary and Police (Ireland) Act 1883 (c.14)
Constabulary and Police (Ireland) Act 1914 (c.54)
Constabulary and Police (Ireland) Act 1916 (c.59)
Constabulary and Police (Ireland) Act 1918 (c.53)
Constabulary and Police (Ireland) Act 1919 (c.68)
Constabulary (Ireland) Act 1836 (c.13)
Constabulary (Ireland) Act 1846 (c.97)
Constabulary (Ireland) Act 1848 (c.72)
Constabulary (Ireland) Act 1851 (c.85)
Constabulary (Ireland) Act 1857 (c.17)
Constabulary (Ireland) Act 1859 (c.22)
Constabulary (Ireland) Act 1866 (c.103)
Constabulary (Ireland) Act 1875 (c.44)
Constabulary (Ireland) Act 1877 (c.20)
Constabulary (Ireland) Act 1897 (c.64)
Constabulary (Ireland) Act 1908 (c.60)
Constabulary (Ireland) Act 1922 (c.55)
Constabulary (Ireland) Amendment Act 1865 (c.70)
Constabulary (Ireland) Amendment) Act 1870 (c.83)
Constabulary (Ireland) Amendment Act 1882 (c.63)
Constabulary (Ireland) (Consular Advances) Act 1825 (c.87)
Constabulary (Ireland) (No. 2) Act 1836 (c.36)
Constabulary (Ireland) Redistribution Act 1885 (c.12)
Consular Conventions Act 1949 (c.29)
Consular Fees Act 1980 (c.23)
Consular Marriage Act 1868 (c.61)
Consular Marriages Act 1849 (c.68)
Consular Relations Act 1968 (c.18)
Consular Salaries and Fees Act 1891 (c.36)
Consuls in Ottoman Dominions Act 1836 (c.78)
Consumer Arbitration Agreements Act 1988 (c.21)
Consumer Credit Act 1974 (c.39)
Consumer Protection Act 1961 (c.40)
Consumer Protection Act 1971 (c.15)

Consumer Protection Act 1987 (c.43)
Consumer Safety Act 1978 (c.38)
Consumer Safety (Amendment) Act 1986 (c.29)
Consumption of Malt Liquors (Ireland) Act 1810 (c.46)
Contagious Diseases Act 1866 (c.35)
Contagious Diseases Act 1869 (c.96)
Contagious Diseases Acts Repeal 1886 (c.10)
Contagious Diseases (Animals) Act 1853 (c.62)
Contagious Diseases, Animals Act 1856 (c.101)
Contagious Diseases (Animals) Act 1867 (c.125)
Contagious Diseases (Animals) Act 1869 (c.70)
Contagious Diseases (Animals) Act 1878 (c.74)
Contagious Diseases (Animals) Act 1884 (c.13)
Contagious Diseases (Animals) Act 1886 (c.32)
Contagious Diseases (Animals) Act 1892 (c.47)
Contagious Diseases (Animals) Act 1893 (c.43)
Contagious Diseases (Animals) (Pleuro pneumonia) Act 1890 (c.14)
Contagious Diseases (Animals) (Scotland) Act 1875 (c.75)
Contagious Diseases (Animals) Transfer of Parts of Districts Act 1884 (c.47)
Contagious Diseases (Ireland) Amendment Act 1868 (c.80)
Contagious Diseases of Sheep Act 1858 (c.62)
Contagious Diseases Prevention Act 1864 (c.85)
Contagious Disorders (Sheep), etc. Act 1848 (c.107)
Contempt of Court Act 1981 (c.49)
Continental Shelf Act 1964 (c.29)
Continental Shelf Act 1989 (c.35)
Contingencies Fund Act 1970 (c.56)
Contingencies Fund Act 1974 (c.18)
Contingent Remainders Act 1877 (c.33)
Continuance etc. of Acts Act 1735 (c.18)
Continuance etc., of Acts Act 1757 (c.42)
Continuance etc. of Acts Act 1763 (c.25)
Continuance of Acts Act 1702 (c.13)
Continuance of Acts Act 1706 (c.34)
Continuance of Acts Act 1711 (c.24(e))
Continuance of Acts Act 1718 (c.25)
Continuance of Acts Act 1726 (c.27)
Continuance of Acts Act 1734 (c.18)
Continuance of Acts Act 1737 (c.18)
Continuance of Acts Act 1740 (c.34)
Continuance of Acts Act 1746 (c.47)
Continuance of Acts Act 1750 (c.57)
Continuance of Acts Act 1756 (c.28)
Continuance of Acts Act 1759 (c.16)

Continuance of Acts Act 1797 (c.9)
Continuance of Acts Act 1780 (cc.4, 5)
Continuance of Acts Act 1799 (c.9)
Continuance of Acts Act 1799 (c.12)
Continuance of Acts Act 1799 (c.38)
Continuance of Acts Act 1801 (c.45)
Continuance of Acts, etc. Act 1722 (c.8)
Continuance of Acts, etc. Act 1723 (c.17)
Continuance of Acts, etc. Act 1724 (c.29)
Continuance of Acts, etc. Act 1739 (c.28)
Continuance of Acts, etc. Act 1749 (c.26)
Continuance of Acts, etc. Act 1753 (c.32)
Continuance of Acts, etc. Act 1754 (c.18)
Continuance of Acts, etc. Act 1757 (c.1)
Continuance of Acts. etc. Act 1757 (c.35)
Continuance of Certain Duties, etc. Act 1708 (c.31)
Continuance of Certain Laws Act 1772 (c.56)
Continuance of Certain Laws, etc. Act 1771 (c.51)
Continuance of Criminal Law Act 1722 Act 1725 (c.30)
Continuance of Laws Act 1734 (c.21)
Continuance of Laws Act 1763 (c.11)
Continuance of Laws Act 1763 (c.12)
Continuance of Laws Act 1766 (c.44)
Continuance of Laws Act 1768 (c.1)
Continuance of Laws Act 1774 (c.67)
Continuance of Laws Act 1774 (c.80)
Continuance of Laws Act 1774 (c.86)
Continuance of Laws Act 1776 (c.44)
Continuance of Laws Act 1776 (c.54)
Continuance of Laws Act 1778 (c.45)
Continuance of Laws Act 1779 (c.22)
Continuance of Laws Act 1780 (c.19)
Continuance of Laws Act 1782 (c.13)
Continuance of Laws Act 1783 (c.6)
Continuance of Laws Act 1786 (c.53)
Continuance of Laws Act 1786 (c.80)
Continuance of Laws Act 1787 (c.36)
Continuance of Laws Act 1788 (cc.23, 24)
Continuance of Laws Act 1789 (c.55)
Continuance of Laws Act 1790 (c.18)
Continuance of Laws Act 1791 (c.43)
Continuance of Laws Act 1792 (c.36)
Continuance of Laws Act 1793 (c.40)
Continuance of Laws Act 1794 (c.36)
Continuance of Laws Act 1795 (c.38)
Continuance of Laws Act 1796 (c.40)
Continuance of Laws Act 1796 (c.108)
Continuance of Laws Act 1797 (c.35)
Continuance of Laws Act 1797 (c.99)
Continuance of Laws Act 1800 (c.5)
Continuance of Laws Act 1800 (c.20)
Continuance of Laws Act 1803 (c.4)
Continuance of Laws Act 1803 (c.29)
Continuance of Laws Act 1805 (c.80)
Continuance of Laws Act 1806 (c.29)
Continuance of Laws, etc. Act 1714 (c.26)
Continuance of Laws, etc. Act 1742 (c.26)
Continuance of Laws, etc. Act 1748 (c.46)
Contract (India Office) Act 1903 (c.11)
Contract (Scotland) Act 1997 (c.34)
Contracts (Applicable Law) Act 1990 (c.36)

Contracts of Employment Act 1963 (c.49)
Contracts of Employment Act 1972 (c.53)
Controlled Drugs (Penalties) Act 1985 (c.39)
Control of Employment Act 1939 (c.104)
Control of Food Premises (Scotland) Act 1977 (c.28)
Control of Liquid Fuel Act 1967 (c.57)
Control of Office and Industrial Development Act 1965 (c.33)
Control of Office Development Act 1977 (c.40)
Control of Pollution Act 1974 (c.40)
Control of Pollution (Amendment) Act 1989 (c.14)
Control of Smoke Pollution Act 1989 (c.17)
Controverted Elections Act 1788 (c.52)
Controverted Elections Act 1796 (c.59)
Controverted Elections Act 1801 (c.101)
Controverted Elections Act 1802 (c.84)
Controverted Elections Act 1802 (c.106)
Controverted Elections Act 1807 (c.1)
Controverted Elections Act 1813 (c.71)
Controverted Elections Act 1841 (c.58)
Controverted Elections Act 1842 (c.73)
Controverted Elections Act 1843 (c.47)
Controverted Elections Act 1844 (c.103)
Controverted Elections, etc. Act 1792 (c.1)
Controverted Elections (Ireland) Act 1807 (c.14)
County Rates Act 1738 (c.29)
Convention (Ireland) Act Repeal 1879 (c.28)
Convention of Royal Burghs (Scotland) Act 1879 (c.27)
Convention of Royal Burghs (Scotland) Act 1879, Amendment Act 1895 (c.6)
Convention with United States Act 1855 (c.77)
Conversion of India Stock Act 1887 (c.11)
Conveyance by Release Without Lease Act 1841 (c.21)
Conveyance of Mails Act 1893 (c.38)
Conveyance of Prisoners (Ireland) Act 1815 (c.158)
Conveyance of Prisoners (Ireland) Act 1837 (c.6)
Conveyance of Real Property Act 1845 (c.119)
Conveyancers (Ireland) Act 1864 (c.8)
Conveyancing Act 1881 (c.41)
Conveyancing Act 1882 (c.39)
Conveyancing Act 1911 (c.37)
Conveyancing Amendment (Scotland) Act 1938 (c.24)
Conveyancing and Feudal Reform (Scotland) Act 1970 (c.35)
Conveyancing and Law of Property Act 1892 (c.13)
Conveyancing (Scotland) Act 1874 (c.94)
Conveyancing (Scotland) Act, 1874, Amendment 1879 (c.40)
Conveyancing (Scotland) Act 1924 (c.27)
Conveyancing (Scotland) Acts (1874 and 1879) Amendment 1887 (c.69)

Convict Prisons Act 1850 (c.39)
Convict Prisons Act 1853 (c.121)
Convict Prisons Abroad Act 1859 (c.25)
Convict Prisons Act 1854 (c.76)
Convict Prisons Returns Act 1876 (c.42)
Convicted Prisoners Removal, etc. Act 1853
Conway's Patent Kiln Act 1795 (c.68)
Conwy Tunnel (Supplementary Powers) Act 1983 (c.7)
Co-operative Development Agency 1978 (c.21)
Co-operative Development Agency and Industrial Development Act 1984 (c.57)
Copyhold Act 1843 (c.23)
Copyhold Act 1852 (c.51)
Copyhold Act 1887 (c.73)
Copyhold Act 1894 (c.46)
Copyhold Commission Act 1846 (c.53)
Copyhold Commission Act 1847 (c.101)
Copyhold Commission Act 1858 (c.53)
Copyhold Commission Cont. Act 1860 (c.81)
Copyhold, etc., Commission Act 1853 (c.124)
Copyhold, etc., Commission Act 1855 (c.52)
Copyhold, etc., Commission Act 1857 (c.8)
Copyhold, etc., Commission Cont. Act 1862 (c.73)
Copyhold Lands Act 1844 (c.55)
Copyholds Act 1722 (c.29)
Copyholds Act 1853 (c.57)
Copyholds Act 1858 (c.94)
Copyright Act 1709 (c.21(i))
Copyright Act 1775 (c.53)
Copyright Act 1798 (c.71)
Copyright Act 1801 (c.107)
Copyright Act 1814 (c.156)
Copyright Act 1836 (c.110)
Copyright Act 1842 (c.45)
Copyright Act 1911 (c.46)
Copyright Act 1956 (c.74)
Copyright Act 1956 (Amendment) Act 1982 (c.35)
Copyright (Amendment) Act 1983 (c.42)
Copyright (British Museum) Act 1915 (c.38)
Copyright (Computer Software) Amendment Act 1985 (c.41)
Copyright, Designs and Patents Act 1988 (c.48)
Copyright (Musical Compositions) Act 1882 (c.40)
Copyright (Musical Compositions) Act 1888 (c.17)
Copyright of Designs Act 1839 (c.13)
Copyright of Designs Act 1839 (c.17)
Copyright of Designs Act 1842 (c.100)
Copyright of Designs Act 1843 (c.65)
Copyright of Designs Act 1850 (c.104)
Copyright of Designs Act 1858 (c.70)
Copyright of Designs Act 1861 (c.73)
Copyright of Designs Act 1875 (c.93)
Cordage for Shipping Act 1785 (c.56)
Cork Infirmary Act 1861 (c.29)
Corn Act 1731 (c.12)
Corn Act 1766 (c.17)

Corn Act 1770 (c.39)
Corn Act 1774 (c.64)
Corn Act 1780 (c.50)
Corn Accounts and Returns Act 1864 (c.87)
Corn Duties Act 1847 (c.1)
Corn, etc. Act 1801 (c.13)
Corn Exportation Act 1737 (c.22)
Corn Production Act 1917 (c.46)
Corn Production Acts (Repeal) Act 1921 (c.48)
Corn Production (Amendment) Act 1918 (c.36)
Corn Rents Act 1963 (c.14)
Corn Returns Act 1882 (c.37)
Corn Sales Act 1921 (c.35)
Corneal Grafting Act 1952 (c.28)
Corneal Tissue Act 1986 (c.18)
Cornwall and Devon Roads Act 1770 (c.87)
Cornwall and Devon Roads Act 1777 (c.79)
Cornwall Duchy Act 1760 (c.11)
Cornwall Duchy Act 1793 (c.78)
Cornwall Duchy Act 1810 (c.6)
Cornwall Roads Act 1759 (c.42)
Cornwall Roads Act 1760 (c.27)
Cornwall Roads Act 1760 (c.32)
Cornwall Roads Act 1762 (c.46)
Cornwall Roads Act 1763 (c.52)
Cornwall Roads Act 1781 (c.78)
Cornwall Roads Act 1781 (c.90)
Cornwall Roads Act 1782 (c.104)
Cornwall Roads Act 1783 (c.27)
Cornwall Roads Act 1785 (c.108)
Cornwall Roads Act 1785 (c.114)
Cornwall Submarine Mines Act 1858 (c.109)
Coroners Act 1751 (c.29)
Coroners Act 1836 (c.89)
Coroners Act 1843 (c.12)
Coroners Act 1843 (c.83)
Coroners Act 1844 (c.92)
Coroners Act 1887 (c.71)
Coroners Act 1892 (c.56)
Coroners Act 1921 (c.30)
Coroners Act 1954 (c.31)
Coroners Act 1980 (c.38)
Coroners Act 1988 (c.13)
Coroners (Amendment) Act 1926 (c.59)
Coroners (Emergency Provisions) Act 1917 (c.19)
Coroners (Emergency Provisions Continuance) Act 1922 (c.2)
Coroners' Inquests, Bail Act 1859 (c.33)
Coroners' Inquests Expenses Act 1837 (c.68)
Coroners (Ireland) Act 1846 (c.37)
Coroners (Ireland) Act 1881 (c.35)
Coroners (Ireland) Act 1908 (c.37)
Coroners' Juries Act 1983 (c.31)
Corporate Bodies' Contracts Act 1960 (c.46)
Corporation of Dublin Act 1850 (c.55)
Corporations Act 1718 (c.6)
Correspondence with Enemies Act 1704 (c.13)
Correspondence with Enemies Act 1793 (c.27)

Correspondence with Foreign Parts Act 1801 (c.11)
Correspondence with James the Pretender (High Treason) Act 1701 (c.3)
Corrupt and Illegal Practices Prevention Act 1883 (c.51)
Corrupt and Illegal Practices Prevention Act 1895 (c.40)
Corrupt Practice (Municipal Elections) Act 1872 (c.60)
Corrupt Practices Act 1856 (c.84)
Corrupt Practices Act 1858 (c.87)
Corrupt Practices Act 1859 (c.48)
Corrupt Practices Act 1861 (c.122)
Corrupt Practices Act 1862 (c.109)
Corrupt Practices 1854 Act, Continuation Act 1860 (c.99)
Corrupt Practices at Elections Act 1735 (c.38)
Corrupt Practice Commission Expenses Act 1869 (c.21)
Corrupt Practices at Parliamentary Elections Act 1728 (c.24)
Corrupt Practices, Dublin City 1869 (c.65)
Corrupt Practices Prevention Act 1854 (c.102)
Corrupt Practices Prevention Act 1863 (c.29)
Corrupt Practices (Suspension of Election) Act 1882 (c.68)
Corrupt Practices (Suspension of Elections) Act 1881 (c.42)
Corrupt Practices (Suspension of Elections) Act 1883 (c.46)
Corrupt Practices (Suspension of Elections) Act 1884 (c.78)
Corruption of Blood Act 1814 (c.145)
Corsham to Bath Easton Bridge Road Act 1779 (c.112)
Cosford, Suffolk: Poor Relief Act 1779 (c.30)
Cosham to Chichester Road Act 1762 (c.84)
Cosham to Chichester Road Act 1783 (c.32)
Costs Act 1803 (c.46)
Costs in Criminal Cases Act 1952 (c.48)
Costs in Criminal Cases Act 1908 (c.15)
Costs in Criminal Cases Act 1973 (c.14)
Costs of Action of Trespass Act 1840 (c.24)
Costs of Leases Act 1958 (c.52)
Cottier Tenant (Ireland) Act 1856 (c.65)
Cottingham, Yorks: Inclosure Act 1791 (c.20)
Cotton Act 1954 (c.24)
Cotton Association (Emergency Action) Act 1915 (c.69)
Cotton (Centralised Buying) Act 1947 (c.26)
Cotton Cloth Factories Act 1889 (c.62)
Cotton Cloth Factories Act 1897 (c.58)
Cotton Industry Act 1923 (c.22)
Cotton Industry Act 1928 (c.11)
Cotton Industry Act 1933 (c.30)
Cotton Industry Act 1938 (c.15)
Cotton Industry Act 1939 (c.9)
Cotton Industry Act 1959 (c.48)
Cotton Industry (Reorganisation) Act 1939 (c.54)
Cotton Industry (Reorganisation) (Postponement) Act 1939 (c.116)

Cotton Manufacture (Scotland) Act 1803 (c.151)

Cotton Manufacturing Industry (Temporary Provisions) Act 1934 (c.30)

Cotton Spinning Industry Act 1936 (c.21)

Cotton Spinning (Re-equipment Subsidy) Act 1948 (c.31)

Cotton Statistics Act 1868 (c.33)

Cotton Trade (Ireland) Act 1813 (c.75)

Council of India Act 1876 (c.7)

Council of India Act 1907 (c.35)

Council of India Reduction Act 1889 (c.65)

Councils of Conciliation Act 1867 (c.105)

Counter Inflation Act 1973 (c.9)

Counter Inflation (Temporary Provisions) Act 1972 (c.74)

Counterfeit Currency (Convention) Act 1935 (c.25)

Counterfeit Dollars and Tokens Act 1804 (c.71)

Counterfeit Medal Act 1883 (c.45)

Counterfeiting Act 1702 (c.3)

Counterfeiting Bank of England Tokens Act 1811 (c.110)

Counterfeiting Bank of Ireland Silver Tokens, etc. Act 1805 (c.42)

Counterfeiting Coin Act 1741 (c.28)

Counterfeiting Coin Act 1797 (c.126)

Counterfeiting, etc., of Gold Coin Act 1772 (c.71)

Counterfeiting of Bank of Ireland Tokens Act 1813 (c.106)

Counterfeiting of Copper Coin Act 1771 (c.40)

Counterfeiting of Tokens, etc. Act 1808 (c.31)

Counterfeiting of Tokens, etc. Act 1812 (c.138)

Countervailing Duties Act 1802 (c.27)

Countervailing Duties Act 1804 (c.27)

Countervailing Duties (Ireland) Act 1807 (c.18)

Countervailing Duties on Spirit Mixtures, etc. Act 1836 (c.72)

Countervailing Duty Act 1803 (c.154)

Counties and Boroughs (Ireland) Act 1840 (c.109)

Counties (Detached Parts) Act 1839 (c.82)

Counties (Detached Parts) Act 1844 (c.61)

Counties of Cities Act 1798 (c.52)

Counties of Cities Act 1811 (c.100)

Counties of Drogheda and Meath Act 1845 (c.121)

Countryside Act 1968 (c.41)

Countryside (Scotland) Act 1967 (c.86)

Countryside (Scotland) Act 1981 (c.44)

County and Borough Councils (Qualification) Act 1914 (c.21)

County and Borough Police Act 1856 (c.69)

County and Borough Police Act 1859 (c.32)

County and Borough Police Act 1919 (c.84)

County and City of Dublin Grand Juries Act 1873 (c.65)

County Boundaries (Ireland) Act 1872 (c.48)

County Bridges Act 1841 (c.49)

County Bridges Loans Extension Act 1880 (c.5)

County Buildings Act 1837 (c.24)

County Buildings Act 1847 (c.28)

County Buildings (Loans) Act 1872 (c.7)

County Cessation (Ireland) Act 1848 (c.32)

County Cessation (Ireland) Act 1849 (c.36)

County Cessation (Ireland) Act 1850 (c.1)

County Cessation (Ireland) Act 1859 (c.23)

County Cessation (Ireland) Act 1861 (c.58)

County Common Juries Act 1910 (c.17)

County Contributions to Prisons, etc. Act 1861 (c.12)

County Coroners Act 1860 (c.116)

County Council Association Expenses (Amendment) Act 1937 (c.27)

County Council (Elections) Act 1891 (c.68)

County Councils Association Expenses Act 1890 (c.3)

County Councils Association Expenses (Amendment) Act 1947 (c.13)

County Councils Association (Scotland) Expenses Act 1894 (c.5)

County Councils (Bills in Parliament) Act 1903 (c.9)

County Councils (Elections) Amendment Act 1900 (c.13)

County Councils Mortgages Act 1909 (c.38)

County Court Amendment (Ireland) Act 1882 (c.29)

County Court Appeals (Ireland) Act 1889 (c.48)

County Court (Buildings) Act 1870 (c.15)

County Court (Costs and Salaries) Act 1882 (c.57)

County Court Districts (England) Act 1858 (c.74)

County Court Judges Act 1859 (c.57)

County Court Judges (Retirement Pensions and Deputies) Act 1919 (c.70)

County Court Jurisdiction in Lunacy (Ireland) Act 1880 (c.39)

County Court (Penalties for Contempt) Act 1983 (c.45)

County Courts Act 1849 (c.101)

County Courts Act 1850 (c.61)

County Courts Act 1852 (c.54)

County Courts Act 1854 (c.16)

County Courts Act 1856 (c.108)

County Courts Act 1857 (c.36)

County Courts Act 1866 (c.14)

County Courts Act 1867 (c.142)

County Courts Act 1875 (c.50)

County Courts Act 1888 (c.43)

County Courts Act 1903 (c.42)

County Courts Act 1919 (c.73)

County Courts Act 1924 (c.17)

County Courts Act 1934 (c.53)

County Courts Act 1955 (c.8)

County Courts Act 1959 (c.22)

County Courts Act 1984 (c.28)

County Courts Admiralty Jurisdiction Act 1868 (c.71)

County Courts Admiralty Jurisdiction Amendment Act 1869 (c.51)

County Courts (Amendment) Act 1934 (c.17)

County Courts (Equity Jurisdiction) Act 1865 (c.99)

County Courts (Expenses) Act 1887 (c.3)

County Courts (Investment) Act 1900 (c.47)

County Courts (Jurisdiction) Act 1963 (c.5)

County Courts Westminster and Southwark Act 1859 (c.8)

County Debentures Act 1873 (c.35)

County Dublin Baronies Act 1838 (c.115)

County Dublin Grand Jury Act 1844 (c.106)

County Dublin Surveyors Act 1897 (c.2)

County Elections Act 1788 (c.36)

County Elections Act 1789 (c.13)

County Elections Act 1789 (c.18)

County Elections (Ireland) Act 1862 (c.62)

County Elections (Scotland) Act 1853 (c.28)

County Electors Act 1888 (c.10)

County Fermanagh Baronies Act 1837 (c.82)

County General Assessment (Scotland) Act 1868 (c.82)

County Infirmaries (Ireland) Act 1805 (c.111)

County Infirmaries (Ireland) Act 1807 (c.50)

County Infirmaries (Ireland) Act 1814 (c.62)

County Institutions (Ireland) Act 1838 (c.116)

County Law Procedure Act 1848 (c.31)

County of Clare Treasurer Act 1838 (c.104)

County of Dublin Jurors and Voters' Revision Act 1884 (c.35)

County of Durham Coroners Act 1837 (c.64)

County of Hertford Act 1878 (c.50)

County of Hertford and Liberty of St. Albans Act 1874 (c.45)

County of Roscommon Act 1840 (c.76)

County of Sussex Act 1865 (c.37)

County Officers and Courts (Ireland) Act 1877 (c.56)

County Officers and Courts (Ireland) Amendment Act 1885 (c.71)

County Palatine of Chester Act 1787 (c.43)

County Police Act 1839 (c.93)

County Police Act 1840 (c.88)

County Police Act 1856 (c.2)

County Property Act 1858 (c.92)

County Property Act 1871 (c.14)

County Rate Act 1866 (c.78)

County Rates Act 1815 (c.51)

County Rates Act 1816 (c.49)

County Rates Act 1844 (c.33)

County Rates Act 1845 (c.111)

County Rates Act 1852 (c.81)

County Rates (England) Act 1858 (c.33)

County Rates Within Boroughs Act 1849 (c.65)

County Surveyors, etc. (Ireland) Act 1861 (c.63)

County Surveyors (Ireland) Act 1862 (c.106)

County Surveyors (Ireland) Act 1893 (c.49)

County Surveyors (Ireland) Act 1900 (c.18)

County Surveyors Superannuation (Ireland) - Northern Irish Act 1875 (c.56)

County, Town and Parish Councils (Qualification) (Scotland) Act 1914 (c.39)

County Treasurers (Ireland) Act 1837 (c.54)

County Treasurers (Ireland) Act 1838 (c.53)

County Treasurers (Ireland) Act 1867 (c.46)

County Voters Registration Act 1865 (c.36)

County Votes Registration (Scotland) Act 1861 (c.83)

County Works (Ireland) Act 1846 (c.2)

County Works (Ireland) Act 1846 (c.78)

Court Funds Act 1829 (c.13)

Court House (Ireland) Act 1813 (c.131)

Court Houses (Ireland) Act 1815 (c.89)

Court Houses (Ireland) Act 1840 (c.102)

Court Houses (Ireland) Act 1841 (c.31)

Court-martial on Admiral Keppel Act 1779 (c.6)

Court of Admiralty Act 1854 (c.78)

Court of Admiralty (Ireland) Act 1867 (c.114)

Court of Admiralty (Ireland) Amendment Act 1876 (c.28)

Court of Appeal in Chancery Act 1867 (c.64)

Court of Appeal in Chancery Act 1868 (c.11)

Court of Bankruptcy (Ireland) Officers and Clerks Act 1881 (c.23)

Court of Chancery Act 1738 (c.24)

Court of Chancery Act 1763 (c.32)

Court of Chancery Act 1765 (c.28)

Court of Chancery Act 1769 (c.19)

Court of Chancery Act 1774 (c.43)

Court of Chancery Act 1806 (c.129)

Court of Chancery Act 1840 (c.94)

Court of Chancery Act 1841 (c.5)

Court of Chancery Act 1841 (c.52)

Court of Chancery Act 1842 (c.103)

Court of Chancery Act 1845 (c.105)

Court of Chancery Act 1848 (c.10)

Court of Chancery Act 1851 (c.83)

Court of Chancery Act 1852 (c.87(a))

Court of Chancery Act 1854 (c.100)

Court of Chancery Act 1855 (c.134)

Court of Chancery Act 1860 (c.149)

Court of Chancery and Exchequer Funds (Ireland) Act 1868 (c.88)

Court of Chancery Act 1852 (c.80)

Court of Chancery (England) Act 1850 (c.35)

Court of Chancery (England) Act 1853 (c.98)

Court of Chancery Examiners Act 1853 (c.22)

Court of Chancery (Funds) Act 1872 (c.44)

Court of Chancery (Ireland) Act 1823 (c.61)

Court of Chancery (Ireland) Act 1836 (c.74)

Court of Chancery (Ireland) Reg. Act 1850 (c.89)

Court of Chancery of Lancaster Act 1850 (c.43)

Court of Chancery of Lancaster Act 1854 (c.82)

Court of Chancery of Lancaster Act 1952 (c.49)

Court of Chancery of Lancaster (Amendment) Act 1961 (c.38)

Court of Chancery (Officers) Act 1867 (c.87)

Court of Chancery Offices Act 1848 (c.94)

Court of Chancery Procedure Act 1852 (c.86)
Court of Common Pleas Act 1850 (c.75)
Court of Common Pleas Act 1862 (c.96)
Court of Exchequer Chamber (Ireland) Act 1857 (c.6)
Court of Exchequer, Equity Side Act 1836 (c.112)
Court of Exchequer (Ireland) Act 1816 (c.122)
Court of Exchequer (Ireland) Act 1855 (c.50)
Court of Exchequer (Scotland) Act 1806 (c.154)
Court of Exchequer (Scotland) Act 1836 (c.73)
Court of Justice Act Act 1866 (c.63)
Court of Justiciary (Scotland) Act 1864 (c.30)
Court of Justiciary (Scotland) Act 1868 (c.95)
Court of Pleas of Durham Act 1839 (c.16)
Court of Probate Act 1857 (c.77)
Court of Probate Act 1858 (c.95)
Court of Probate Act (Ireland) 1859 (c.31)
Court of Probate (Ireland) Act 1861 (c.111)
Court of Queen's Bench Act 1843 (c.20)
Court of Session Act 1723 (c.19)
Court of Session Act 1808 (c.151)
Court of Session Act 1810 (c.112)
Court of Session Act 1813 (c.64)
Court of Session Act 1821 (c.38)
Court of Session Act 1825 (c.120)
Court of Session Act 1830 (c.69)
Court of Session Act 1838 (c.86)
Court of Session Act 1839 (c.36)
Court of Session Act 1850 (c.36)
Court of Session Act 1857 (c.56)
Court of Session Act 1868 (c.100)
Court of Session Act 1988 (c.36)
Court of Session Adjournment Act 1762 (c.27)
Court of Session Consignations (Scotland) Act 1895 (c.19)
Court of Session (Extracts) Act 1916 (c.49)
Court of Session (No. 2) Act 1838 (c.118)
Court of Session (Records) Act 1815 (c.70)
Court of Session (Scotland) Act 1745 (c.7)
Courts Act 1672 (c.40)
Courts Act 1971 (c.23)
Courts and Legal Services Act 1990 (c.41)
Courts Baron of High Peak and Castleton Act 1759 (c.31)
Courts Baron, Sheffield Act 1756 (c.37)
Courts (Colonial) Jurisdiction Act 1874 (c.27)
Courts (Emergency Powers) Act 1914 (c.78)
Courts (Emergency Powers) Act 1917 (c.25)
Courts (Emergency Powers) Act 1919 (c.64)
Courts (Emergency Powers) Act 1939 (c.67)
Courts (Emergency Powers) Act 1940 (c.37)
Courts (Emergency Powers) Act 1943 (c.19)
Courts (Emergency Powers) (Amendment) Act 1916 (c.13)
Courts (Emergency Powers) Amendment Act 1942 (c.36)
Courts (Emergency Powers) (Ireland) Act 1914 (c.19)
Courts (Emergency Power) (No. 2) Act 1916 (c.18)

Courts (Emergency Powers) (Scotland) Act 1939 (c.113)
Courts (Emergency Powers) (Scotland) Act 1944 (c.6)
Courts in Prince of Wales Island and India Act 1855 (c.93)
Courts in Wales and Chester Act 1732 (c.14)
Courts-Martial (Appeals) Act 1951 (c.46)
Courts-Martial (Appeals) Act 1968 (c.20)
Courts-Martial, East Indies Act 1760 (c.14)
Courts-Martial in India Act 1844 (c.18)
Courts-Martial on Troops of East India Company Act 1810 (c.87)
Courts, Newfoundland Act 1791 (c.29)
Courts, Newfoundland Act 1792 (c.46)
Courts, Newfoundland Act 1793 (c.76)
Courts, Newfoundland Act 1795 (c.25)
Courts, Newfoundland Act 1796 (c.37)
Courts, Newfoundland Act 1799 (c.16)
Courts, Newfoundland, etc. Act 1794 (c.44)
Courts of Common Law, Sittings Act 1838 (c.32)
Courts of Exchequer Act 1799 (c.67)
Courts of Judicature, India Act 1839 (c.34)
Courts of Justice (Additional Site) Act 1871 (c.57)
Courts of Justice Building Act 1865 (c.48)
Courts of Justice Building Amendment Act 1880 (c.29)
Courts of Justice, Canada Act 1803 (c.138)
Courts of Justice Concentration (Site) Act 1865 (c.49)
Courts of Justice (Salaries and Funds) Act 1869 (c.91)
Courts of Law Fees Act 1867 (c.122)
Courts of Law Fees (Scotland) Act 1868 (c.55)
Courts of Law Fees (Scotland) Act 1895 (c.14)
Covent Garden Market Act 1961 (c.49)
Covent Garden Market (Financial Provisions) Act 1977 (c.2)
Coventry Act 1842 (c.110)
Coventry Canal Act 1768 (c.36)
Coventry Canal Act 1786 (c.20)
Coventry Canal Act 1786 (c.30)
Coventry Freemen, etc. Act 1781 (c.54)
Coventry Gaol Act 1768 (c.40)
Coventry Grammar School Act 1864 (c.41)
Coventry Improvement Act 1763 (c.41)
Coventry–Oxford Canal Act 1775 (c.9)
Coventry Roads Act 1796 (c.133)
Coventry: Streets Act 1790 (c.77)
Coventry to Oxford Canal Act 1769 (c.70)
Coventry to Oxford Canal Act 1794 (c.103)
Coventry to Ticknall Canal Act 1794 (c.93)
Cowgil Parish; Marriages Confirmation, Park Gate Chapel Act 1869 (c.30)
Cowley's Charity Act 1858 (c.81)
Cran Measures Act 1908 (c.17)
Cranbourne Street Act 1864 (c.111)
Cranford and Maidenhead Road Act 1726 (c.31)

Credit-Sale Agreements (Scotland) Act 1961 (c.56)
Credit Unions Act 1979 (c.34)
Cremation Act 1902 (c.8)
Cremation Act 1952 (c.31)
Crew of a Certain Foreign Vessel Act 1786 (c.8)
Crewkerne Roads Act 1765 (c.61)
Crewkerne Roads Act 1786 (c.123)
Crime and Outrage (Ireland) Act 1850 (c.106)
Crime and Outrage (Ireland) Act 1852 (c.66)
Crime and Outrage (Ireland) Act 1853 (c.72)
Crime and Outrage (Ireland) Act 1854 (c.92)
Crime (Sentences) Act 1997 (c.43)
Crimes and Outrage (Ireland) Act 1855 (c.112)
Crime and Punishment (Scotland) Act 1997 (c.48)
Criminal and Dangerous Lunatics (Scotland) Amendment Act 1871 (c.55)
Criminal Appeal Act 1907 (c.23)
Criminal Appeal Act 1964 (c.43)
Criminal Appeal Act 1966 (c.31)
Criminal Appeal Act 1968 (c.19)
Criminal Appeal Act 1995 (c.35)
Criminal Appeal (Amendment) Act 1908 (c.46)
Criminal Appeal (Northern Ireland) Act 1930 (c.45)
Criminal Appeal (Northern Ireland) Act 1968 (c.21)
Criminal Appeal (Northern Ireland) Act 1980 (c.47)
Criminal Appeal (Scotland) Act 1926 (c.15)
Criminal Appeal (Scotland) Act 1927 (c.26)
Criminal Attempts Act 1981 (c.47)
Criminal Costs (Dublin) Act 1815 (c.91)
Criminal Court, Norfolk Island Act 1794 (c.45)
Criminal Court, Norfolk Island Act 1795 (c.18)
Criminal Damage Act 1971 (c.48)
Criminal Evidence Act 1898 (c.36)
Criminal Evidence Act 1965 (c.20)
Criminal Evidence Act 1979 (c.16)
Criminal Evidence (Amendment) Act 1997 (c.17)
Criminal Injuries Compensation Act 1995 (c.53)
Criminal Injuries (Ireland) Act 1919 (c.14)
Criminal Jurisdiction Act 1802 (c.85)
Criminal Jurisdiction Act 1975 (c.59)
Criminal Justice Act 1855 (c.126)
Criminal Justice Act 1856 (c.118)
Criminal Justice Act 1925 (c.86)
Criminal Justice Act 1948 (c.58)
Criminal Justice Act 1961 (c.39)
Criminal Justice Act 1965 (c.26)
Criminal Justice Act 1967 (c.80)
Criminal Justice Act 1972 (c.71)
Criminal Justice Act 1982 (c.48)
Criminal Justice Act 1987 (c.38)
Criminal Justice Act 1988 (c.33)
Criminal Justice Act 1991 (c.53)
Criminal Justice Act 1993 (c.36)

Criminal Justice Administration Act 1851 (c.55)
Criminal Justice Administration Act 1914 (c.58)
Criminal Justice Administration Act 1956 (c.34)
Criminal Justice Administration Act 1962 (c.15)
Criminal Justice Administration (Amendment) Act 1959 (c.41)
Criminal Justice Administration (Postponement) Act 1914 (c.9)
Criminal Justice (Amendment) Act 1925 (c.13)
Criminal Justice (Amendment) Act 1981 (c.27)
Criminal Justice and Public Order Act 1994 (c.33)
Criminal Justice (International Co-operation) Act 1990 (c.5)
Criminal Justice (Scotland) Act 1949 (c.94)
Criminal Justice (Scotland) Act 1963 (c.39)
Criminal Justice (Scotland) Act 1980 (c.62)
Criminal Justice (Scotland) Act 1987 (c.41)
Criminal Justice (Scotland) Act 1995 (c.20)
Criminal Law Act 1722 (c.22)
Criminal Law Act 1772 (c.31)
Criminal Law Act 1776 (c.43)
Criminal Law Act 1778 (c.62)
Criminal Law Act 1779 (c.54)
Criminal Law Act 1781 (cc.68, 69)
Criminal Law Act 1782 (c.40)
Criminal Law Act 1782 (c.58)
Criminal Law Act 1826 (c.64)
Criminal Law Act 1967 (c.58)
Criminal Law Act 1977 (c.45)
Criminal Law Amendment Act 1867 (c.35)
Criminal Law Amendment Act 1871 (c.32)
Criminal Law Amendment Act 1880 (c.45)
Criminal Law Amendment Act 1885 (c.69)
Criminal Law Amendment Act 1912 (c.20)
Criminal Law Amendment Act 1922 (c.56)
Criminal Law Amendment Act 1928 (c.42)
Criminal Law Amendment Act 1951 (c.36)
Criminal Law and Procedure (Ireland) Act 1887 (c.20)
Criminal Law (Consolidation) (Scotland) Act 1995 (c.39)
Criminal Law (Ireland) Act 1828 (c.54)
Criminal Law (Scotland) Act 1829 (c.38)
Criminal Law (Scotland) Act 1830 (c.37)
Criminal Lunatic Asylums Act 1860 (c.75)
Criminal Lunatics Act 1800 (c.94)
Criminal Lunatics Act 1838 (c.14)
Criminal Lunatics Act 1867 (c.12)
Criminal Lunatics Act 1869 (c.78)
Criminal Lunatics Act 1884 (c.64)
Criminal Lunatics (Ireland) Act 1838 (c.27)
Criminal Lunatics (Scotland) Act 1935 (c.32)
Criminal Procedure Act 1694 (c.43)
Criminal Procedure Act 1701 (c.6)
Criminal Procedure Act 1848 (c.46)
Criminal Procedure Act 1851 (c.100)

Criminal Procedure Act 1853 (c.30)

Criminal Procedure Act 1865 (c.18)

Criminal Procedure and Investigations Act 1996 (c.25)

Criminal Procedure (Attendance of Witnesses) Act 1965 (c.69)

Criminal Procedure (Consequential Provisions) (Scotland) Act 1995 (c.40)

Criminal Procedure (Insanity) Act 1964 (c.84)

Criminal Procedure (Insanity and Unfitness to Plead) Act 1991 (c.25)

Criminal Procedure (Right of Reply) Act 1964 (c.34)

Criminal Procedure (Scotland) Act 1887 (c.35)

Criminal Procedure (Scotland) Act 1921 (c.50)

Criminal Procedure (Scotland) Act 1938 (c.48)

Criminal Procedure (Scotland) Act 1965 (c.39)

Criminal Procedure (Scotland) Act 1975 (c.21)

Criminal Procedure (Scotland) Act 1995 (c.46)

Criminal Prosecutions Fees (Ireland) Act 1809 (c.101)

Criminal Statutes Repeal Act 1861 (c.95)

Crinan Canal Act 1793 (c.104)

Crinan Canal Act 1805 (c.85)

Cripplegate: Church Building Act 1732 (c.21)

Crofter Forestry (Scotland) Act 1991 (c.18)

Crofters Commission (Delegation of Powers) Act 1888 (c.63)

Crofters Common Grazings Regulation Act 1891 (c.41)

Crofters Common Grazings Regulation Act 1908 (c.50)

Crofters Holdings (Scotland) Act 1886 (c.29)

Crofters Holdings (Scotland) Act 1887 (c.24)

Crofters (Scotland) Act 1955 (c.21)

Crofters (Scotland) Act 1961 (c.58)

Crofters (Scotland) Act 1993 (c.44)

Crofting Reform (Scotland) Act 1976 (c.21)

Cromarty Harbour Act 1785 (c.39)

Cromford Bridge to Langley Mill Road Act 1786 (c.124)

Cromford Canal Act 1789 (c.74)

Crossbows Act 1987 (c.32)

Crossed Cheques Act 1876 (c.81)

Crossford Bridge and Altrincham Road Act 1796 (c.143)

Crown Agents Act 1979 (c.43)

Crown Agents Act 1995 (c.24)

Crown Agents (Amendment) Act 1986 (c.43)

Crown Appointments, Colonies Act 1846 (c.91)

Crown Cases Act 1848 (c.78)

Crown Debt from Late Right Hon. R. Rigby Act 1794 (c.66)

Crown Debt of Abraham Goldsmid, etc. Act 1812 (c.75)

Crown Debtors Act 1785 (c.35)

Crown Debts Act 1541 (c.39)

Crown Debts Act 1801 (c.90)

Crown Debts Act 1824 (c.111)

Crown Debts and Judgments Act 1860 (c.115)

Crown Estate Act 1956 (c.73)

Crown Estate Act 1961 (c.55)

Crown Land, Revenues Act 1854 (c.68)

Crown Lands Act 1702 (c.1)

Crown Lands Act 1775 (c.33)

Crown Lands Act 1784 (c.57)

Crown Lands Act 1800 (c.78)

Crown Lands Act 1806 (c.151)

Crown Lands Act 1810 (c.65)

Crown Lands Act 1814 (c.70)

Crown Lands Act 1841 (c.1)

Crown Lands Act 1845 (c.99)

Crown Lands Act 1848 (c.102)

Crown Lands Act 1851 (c.42)

Crown Lands Act 1852 (c.62)

Crown Lands Act 1853 (c.56)

Crown Lands Act 1855 (c.16)

Crown Lands Act 1866 (c.62)

Crown Lands Act 1873 (c.36)

Crown Lands Act 1885 (c.79)

Crown Lands Act 1894 (c.43)

Crown Lands Act 1906 (c.28)

Crown Lands Act 1913 (c.8)

Crown Lands Act 1927 (c.23)

Crown Lands Act 1936 (c.47)

Crown Lands Act 1943 (c.7)

Crown Lands at Byfleet, Weybridge, etc., Surrey Act 1804 (c.25)

Crown Lands at Catterick and Tunstall, Yorkshire Act 1790 (c.51)

Crown Lands at Egham, Exchange King and David Jebb Act 1807 (c.77)

Crown Lands at Enfield, Middlesex Act 1776 (c.17)

Crown Lands at North Scotland Yard, Middlesex Act 1785 (c.98)

Crown Lands at Richmond, Surrey Act 1772 (c.35)

Crown Lands at Richmond, Surrey Act 1772 (c.59)

Crown Lands at Shilston Bay, Devon Act 1805 (c.116)

Crown Lands (Copyholds) Act 1851 (c.46)

Crown Lands, Escheats Act 1807 (c.24)

Crown Lands (Forfeited Estates) Act 1715 (c.50)

Crown Lands—Forfeited Estates Act 1717 (c.8)

Crown Lands—Forfeited Estates Act 1718 (c.22)

Crown Lands—Forfeited Estates Act 1719 (c.24)

Crown Lands—Forfeited Estates Act 1720 (c.22)

Crown Lands—Forfeited Estates Act 1726 (c.28)

Crown Lands—Forfeited Estates Act 1727 (c.21)

Crown Lands—Forfeited Estates Act 1728 (c.33)

Crown Lands—Forfeited Estates Act 1744 (c.37)

Crown Lands—Forfeited Estates Act 1746 (c.41)

Crown Lands—Forfeited Estates Act 1748 (c.52)

Crown Lands—Forfeited Estates Act 1751 (c.41)

Crown Lands, Forfeited Estates Act 1757 (c.16)

Crown Lands, Forfeited Estates Act 1762 (c.17)

Crown Lands—Forfeited Estates Act 1774 (c.22)

Crown Lands—Forfeited Estates Act 1794 (c.101)

Crown Lands—Forfeited Estates Act 1795 (c.69)

Crown Lands (Forfeited Estates): Greenwich Hospital Act 1737 (c.30)

Crown Lands, Forfeited Estates in Ireland Act 1793 (c.46)

Crown Lands, Forfeited Estates (Ireland) Act 1702 (c.18(a))

Crown Lands, Forfeited Estates (Ireland) Act 1702 (c.25)

Crown Lands, Forfeited Estates (Ireland) Act 1706 (c.25)

Crown Lands, Forfeited Estates (Ireland) Act 1778 (c.61)

Crown Lands Grant to Jame's Archbald Stuart Act 1772 (c.44)

Crown Lands—Greenwich Hospital Act 1778 (c.29)

Crown Lands in Fenchurch Street London Act 1772 (c.19)

Crown Lands in Holborn, London Act 1772 (c.43)

Crown Lands in Meath to Vest in Gerald Fitz-gerald Act 1771 (c.56)

Crown Lands in Northamptonshire, Grant to Earl of Exeter Act 1796 (c.63)

Crown Lands in Northamptonshire, Grant to Earl of Upper Ossory Act 1795 (c.40)

Crown Lands in Northamptonshire, Grant to Earl of Westmorland Act 1796 (c.62)

Crown Lands in Privy Garden, Westminster Act 1792 (c.24)

Crown Lands (Ireland) Act 1822 (c.63)

Crown Lands - New Forest Act 1800 (c.86)

Crown Land Revenues, etc. Act 1786 (c.87)

Crown Lands, Savoy Act 1771 (c.4)

Crown Lands (Scotland) Act 1833 (c.69)

Crown Lands: Taxation Act 1801 (c.47)

Crown Lessees (Protection of Sub-Tenants) Act 1952 (c.40)

Crown Office Act 1860 (c.54)

Crown Office Act 1877 (c.41)

Crown Office Act 1890 (c.2)

Crown Pensioners Disqualification Act 1715 (c.56)

Crown Pre-Emption of Lead Ore Act 1815 (c.134)

Crown Private Estate Act 1800 (c.88)

Crown Private Estates Act 1862 (c.37)

Crown Private Estates Act 1873 (c.61)

Crown Proceedings Act 1947 (c.44)

Crown Proceedings (Armed Forces) Act 1987 (c.25)

Crown Land Revenues Act 1794 (c.75)

Crown Revenues (Colonies) Act 1852 (c.39)

Crown Suits Act 1769 (c.16)

Crown Suits Act 1855 (c.90)

Crown Suits Act 1861 (c.62)

Crown Suits, etc. Act 1865 (c.104)

Crown Suits (Isle of Man) Act 1862 (c.14)

Crown Suits (Scotland) Act 1857 (c.44)

Croydon Parish Church Act 1760 (c.38)

Cruelty to Animals Act 1849 (c.92)

Cruelty to Animals Act 1854 (c.60)

Cruelty to Animals Act 1876 (c.77)

Cruelty to Animals (Ireland) Act 1837 (c.66)

Cruelty to Animals (Scotland) Act 1850 (c.92)

Cruelty to Animals (Scotland) Act 1895 (c.13)

Cultivation, etc. of Trees Act 1766 (c.36)

Cultivation of Madder Act 1765 (c.18)

Cumberland and Westmorland Roads Act 1762 (c.81)

Cumberland and Westmorland Roads Act 1783 (c.108)

Cumberland Roads Act 1749 (c.40)

Cumberland Roads Act 1753 (c.37)

Cumberland Roads Act 1753 (c.49)

Cumberland Roads Act 1767 (c.83)

Cumberland Roads Act 1778 (c.108)

Cumberland Roads Act 1779 (c.97)

Cumberland Roads Act 1789 (c.97)

Cumberland Roads Act 1794 (c.143)

Cunard Agreement (Money) Act 1904 (c.22)

Cunard (Insurance) Agreement Act 1931 (c.2)

Curates, etc. Act 1796 (c.83)

Curragh of Kildare Act 1868 (c.60)

Curragh of Kildare Act 1870 (c.74)

Currency Act 1982 (c.3)

Currency Act 1983 (c.9)

Currency and Bank Notes Act 1914 (c.14)

Currency and Bank Notes Act 1928 (c.13)

Currency and Bank Notes Act 1939 (c.7)

Currency and Bank Notes Act 1954 (c.12)

Currency and Bank Notes (Amendment) Act 1914 (c.72)

Currency (Defence) Act 1939 (c.64)

Curriers, etc. Act 1738 (c.25)

Cursitor Baron of the Exchequer Act 1856 (c.86)

Custody of Children Act 1891 (c.3)

Custody of Children (Scotland) Act 1939 (c.4)

Custody of Infants Act 1839 (c.54)

Custody of Infants Act 1873 (c.12)

Custody of Insane Persons Act 1816 (c.117)

Custody of Napoleon Buonaparte Act 1816 (c.22)

Customs Act 1719 (c.12)

Customs Act 1722 (c.21)
Customs Act 1772 (c.50)
Customs Act 1772 (c.60)
Customs Act 1724 (c.7)
Customs Act 1736 (c.30)
Customs Act 1753 (c.12)
Customs Act 1763 (c.9)
Customs Act 1763 (c.22)
Customs Act 1766 (c.20)
Customs Act 1766 (c.28)
Customs Act 1766 (c.41)
Customs Act 1766 (c.45)
Customs Act 1766 (c.50)
Customs Act 1767 (c.58)
Customs Act 1768 (c.23)
Customs Act 1770 (c.17)
Customs Act 1770 (c.30)
Customs Act 1770 (c.43)
Customs Act 1775 (c.34)
Customs Act 1775 (c.35)
Customs Act 1775 (c.37)
Customs Act 1776 (c.12)
Customs Act 1776 (c.27)
Customs Act 1776 (c.41)
Customs Act 1776 (c.42)
Customs Act 1776 (c.43)
Customs Act 1776 (c.48)
Customs Act 1778 (c.4)
Customs Act 1778 (cc.24, 25)
Customs Act 1778 (c.27)
Customs Act 1778 (c.40)
Customs Act 1778 (c.58)
Customs Act 1779 (c.29)
Customs Act 1779 (c.41)
Customs Act 1779 (c.62)
Customs Act 1780 (c.7)
Customs Act 1780 (c.16)
Customs Act 1780 (c.25)
Customs Act 1780 (c.30)
Customs Act 1780 (c.32)
Customs Act 1782 (c.20)
Customs Act 1782 (c.21)
Customs Act 1782 (c.28)
Customs Act 1782 (c.49)
Customs Act 1782 (c.61)
Customs Act 1783 (c.11)
Customs Act 1783 (c.56)
Customs Act 1783 (c.74)
Customs Act 1784 (c.9)
Customs Act 1784 (c.16)
Customs Act 1784 (c.49)
Customs Act 1785 (c.25)
Customs Act 1785 (c.69)
Customs Act 1786 (c.42)
Customs Act 1786 (c.104)
Customs Act 1788 (c.27)
Customs Act 1788 (c.33)
Customs Act 1789 (c.59)
Customs Act 1789 (c.60)
Customs Act 1789 (c.64)
Customs Act 1790 (c.4)
Customs Act 1791 (c.15)
Customs Act 1791 (c.26)

Customs Act 1792 (c.32)
Customs Act 1792 (c.43)
Customs Act 1792 (c.54)
Customs Act 1793 (c.48)
Customs Act 1793 (c.70)
Customs Act 1793 (c.81)
Customs Act 1794 (c.51)
Customs Act 1794 (c.70)
Customs Act 1795 (c.20)
Customs Act 1796 (c.15)
Customs Act 1796 (cc.78, 79)
Customs Act 1796 (c.110)
Customs Act 1797 (c.110)
Customs Act 1798 (c.86)
Customs Act 1799 (c.61)
Customs Act 1800 (c.51)
Customs Act 1800 (c.59)
Customs Act 1800 (c.60)
Customs Act 1801 (c.87)
Customs Act 1801 (c.89)
Customs Act 1801 (c.94)
Customs Act 1802 (c.95)
Customs Act 1803 (c.68)
Customs Act 1803 (c.70)
Customs Act 1803 (c.128)
Customs Act 1803 (c.131)
Customs Act 1804 (c.53)
Customs Act 1805 (c.18)
Customs Act 1805 (c.29)
Customs Act 1805 (cc.44, 45)
Customs Act 1805 (c.88)
Customs Act 1805 (c.103)
Customs Act 1806 (c.150)
Customs Act 1807 (c.51)
Customs Act 1807 (c.61)
Customs Act 1808 (c.9)
Customs Act 1808 (c.26)
Customs Act 1808 (c.28)
Customs Act 1808 (cc.56, 57)
Customs Act 1808 (c.67)
Customs Act 1809 (c.46)
Customs Act 1809 (c.65)
Customs Act 1809 (c.98)
Customs Act 1810 (c.77)
Customs Act 1811 (c.52)
Customs Act 1811 (c.55)
Customs Act 1811 (c.71)
Customs Act 1811 (c.96)
Customs Act 1812 (c.2)
Customs Act 1812 (c.60)
Customs Act 1812 (c.89)
Customs Act 1812 (c.117)
Customs Act 1812 (c.141)
Customs Act 1813 (cc.26, 27)
Customs Act 1813 (c.29)
Customs Act 1813 (c.33)
Customs Act 1813 (c.47)
Customs Act 1813 (c.104)
Customs Act 1813 (c.105)
Customs Act 1814 (c.14)
Customs Act 1814 (c.50)
Customs Act 1814 (cc.64–66)
Customs Act 1814 (c.69)

47

Customs Act 1814 (c.77)
Customs Act 1814 (c.103)
Customs Act 1814 (c.122)
Customs Act 1815 (cc.22, 23)
Customs Act 1815 (c.24)
Customs Act 1815 (cc.32, 33)
Customs Act 1815 (c.36)
Customs Act 1815 (c.52)
Customs Act 1815 (c.95)
Customs Act 1815 (c.135)
Customs Act 1815 (c.163)
Customs Act 1815 (c.174)
Customs Act 1815 (c.181)
Customs Act 1816 (c.77)
Customs Act 1816 (c.93)
Customs Act 1835 (c.66)
Customs Act 1836 (c.60)
Customs Act 1838 (c.113)
Customs Act 1840 (c.19)
Customs Act 1840 (c.95)
Customs Act 1842 (c.47)
Customs Act 1843 (c.84)
Customs Act 1844 (c.16)
Customs Act 1844 (c.43)
Customs Act 1844 (c.73)
Customs Act 1845 (c.12)
Customs Act 1845 (c.84)
Customs Act 1845 (c.86)
Customs Act 1845 (c.92)
Customs Act 1846 (c.24)
Customs Act 1846 (c.58)
Customs Act 1846 (c.94)
Customs Act 1846 (c.102)
Customs Act 1847 (c.24)
Customs Act 1849 (c.90)
Customs Act 1850 (c.95)
Customs Act 1851 (c.62)
Customs Act 1853 (c.54)
Customs Act 1853 (c.106)
Customs Act 1854 (cc.28, 29)
Customs Act 1854 (c.122)
Customs Act 1855 (c.21)
Customs Act 1856 (c.75)
Customs Act 1857 (c.15)
Customs Act 1857 (c.62)
Customs Act 1858 (c.12)
Customs Act 1858 (c.16)
Customs Act 1859 (c.37)
Customs Act 1860 (c.22)
Customs Act 1860 (c.36)
Customs Act 1867 (c.82)
Customs Amendment Act 1842 (c.56)
Customs Amendment Act 1886 (c.41)
Customs and Excise Act 1711 (c.19)
Customs and Excise Act 1782 (c.66)
Customs and Excise Act 1787 (c.13)
Customs and Excise Act 1804 (c.67)
Customs and Excise Act 1806 (c.38)
Customs and Excise Act 1809 (c.116)
Customs and Excise Act 1814 (cc.120, 121)
Customs and Excise Act 1815 (c.118)
Customs and Excise Act 1816 (c.85)
Customs and Excise Act 1857 (c.61)

Customs and Excise Act 1952 (c.44)
Customs and Excise Duties (General Reliefs) Act 1979 (c.3)
Customs and Excise (Ireland) Act 1804 (c.103)
Customs and Excise (Ireland) Act 1805 (c.108)
Customs and Excise (Ireland) Act 1806 (c.58)
Customs and Excise (Ireland) Act 1807 (c.48)
Customs and Excise (Ireland) Act 1808 (c.62)
Customs and Excise (Ireland) Act 1816 (c.20)
Customs and Excise Management Act 1979 (c.2)
Customs and Excise Warehousing Act 1869 (c.103)
Customs and Income Tax Act 1871 (c.21)
Customs and Inland Revenue Act 1861 (c.20)
Customs and Inland Revenue Act 1863 (c.22)
Customs and Inland Revenue Act 1867 (c.23)
Customs and Inland Revenue Act 1870 (c.32)
Customs and Inland Revenue Act 1872 (c.20)
Customs and Inland Revenue Act 1873 (c.18)
Customs and Inland Revenue Act 1874 (c.16)
Customs and Inland Revenue Act 1875 (c.23)
Customs and Inland Revenue Act 1876 (c.16)
Customs and Inland Revenue Act 1878 (c.15)
Customs and Inland Revenue Act 1879 (c.21)
Customs and Inland Revenue Act 1880 (c.14)
Customs and Inland Revenue Act 1881 (c.12)
Customs and Inland Revenue Act 1882 (c.41)
Customs and Inland Revenue Act 1883 (c.10)
Customs and Inland Revenue Act 1884 (c.25)
Customs and Inland Revenue Act 1885 (c.51)
Customs and Inland Revenue Act 1886 (c.18)
Customs and Inland Revenue Act 1887 (c.15)
Customs and Inland Revenue Act 1888 (c.8)
Customs and Inland Revenue Act 1889 (c.7)
Customs and Inland Revenue Act 1890 (c.8)
Customs and Inland Revenue Act 1891 (c.25)
Customs and Inland Revenue Act 1892 (c.16)
Customs and Inland Revenue Act 1893 (c.7)
Customs and Inland Revenue Amendment Act 1877 (c.10)
Customs and Inland Revenue Buildings (Ireland) - Northern Irish Act 1882 (c.17)
Customs Buildings Act 1879 (c.36)
Customs Consolidation Act 1853 (c.107)
Customs Consolidation Act 1860 (c.110)
Customs Consolidation Act 1876 (c.36)
Customs Consolidation Act, 1876, Amendment 1887 (c.7)
Customs Consolidation Act, 1876, Amendment 1890 (c.56)
Customs Duties Act 1811 (cc.67, 68)
Customs Duties (Dumping and Subsidies) Act 1957 (c.18)
Customs Duties (Dumping and Subsidies) Act 1969 (c.16)
Customs Duties (Dumping and Subsidies) Amendment Act 1968 (c.33)
Customs Duties, etc. Act 1763 (c.15)
Customs, etc. Act 1721 (c.18)
Customs, etc. Act 1727 (c.17)

Customs, etc. Act 1728 (c.18)
Customs, etc. Act 1736 (c.27)
Customs, etc. Act 1765 (cc.29–32)
Customs, etc. Act 1765 (c.45)
Customs, etc. Act 1766 (cc.46, 47)
Customs, etc. Act 1766 (c.52)
Customs, etc. Act 1769 (c.35)
Customs, etc. Act 1769 (c.41)
Customs, etc. Act 1784 (c.7)
Customs, etc. Act 1798 (c.76)
Customs, etc. Act 1813 (c.36)
Customs, etc. Act 1814 (c.171)
Customs, etc. Act 1815 (cc.82, 83)
Customs, etc. Act 1816 (c.29)
Customs, etc. (Ireland) Act 1812 (c.76)
Customs, etc., Revenues Act 1725 (c.28)
Customs, etc., Revenues Act 1765 (c.43)
Customs, Excise and Taxes Act 1804 (c.26)
Customs (Exportation Prohibition) Act 1914 (c.64)
Customs (Exportation Restriction) Act 1914 (c.2)
Customs (Exportation Restriction) Act 1915 (c.52)
Customs (Import Deposits) Act 1968 (c.74)
Customs (Import Deposits) Act 1969 (c.64)
Customs, Inland Revenue, and Savings Banks Act 1877 (c.13)
Customs (Ireland) Act 1806 (c.87)
Customs (Ireland) Act 1807 (c.12)
Customs (Ireland) Act 1808 (c.80)
Customs (Isle of Man) Act 1870 (c.12)
Customs (Isle of Man) Tariff Act 1874 (c.46)
Customs (Manchester Bonding) Act 1850 (c.84)
Customs (Officers) Act 1881 (c.30)
Customs Refined Sugar Duties, Isle of Man Act 1870 (c.43)
Customs Rotulorum (Ireland) Act 1831 (c.17)
Customs Seizures Act 1790 (c.43)
Customs Sugar Duties (Isle of Man) Act 1873 (c.29)
Customs Tariff Act 1855 (c.97)
Customs Tariff Act 1876 (c.35)
Customs (War Powers) Act 1915 (c.31)
Customs (War Powers) Act 1916 (c.102)
Customs (War Powers) (No. 2) Act 1915 (c.71)
Customs (Wine Duty) Act 1888 (c.14)
Cutlery Trade Act 1819 (c.7)
Cycle Tracks Act 1984 (c.38)
Cyprus Act 1960 (c.52)
Czecho-Slovakia (Financial Assistance) Act 1939 (c.6)
Czecho-Slovakia (Financial Claims and Refugees) Act 1940 (c.4)
Czecho-Slovakia (Restrictions on Banking Accounts etc.) Act 1939 (c.11)

Dalkeith Beer Duties Act 1759 (c.53)
Dalkeith Beer Duties Act 1782 (c.18)
Damages Act 1996 (c.48)

Damages (Scotland) Act 1976 (c.13)
Damages (Scotland) Act 1993 (c.5)
Damaging of Hides Act 1801 (c.53)
Dangerous Dogs Act 1989 (c.30)
Dangerous Dogs Act 1991 (c.65)
Dangerous Dogs (Amendment) Act 1997 (c.53)
Dangerous Drugs Act 1925 (c.74)
Dangerous Drugs Act 1931 (c.14)
Dangerous Drugs Act 1951 (c.48)
Dangerous Drugs Act 1964 (c.36)
Dangerous Drugs Act 1965 (c.15)
Dangerous Drugs Act 1967 (c.82)
Dangerous Drugs (Amendment) Act 1950 (c.7)
Dangerous Drugs and Poisons (Amendment) Act 1923 (c.5)
Dangerous Litter Act 1971 (c.35)
Dangerous Performances Act 1897 (c.52)
Dangerous Vessels Act 1985 (c.22)
Dangerous Wild Animals Act 1976 (c.38)
Danube Works Loan Act 1868 (c.126)
Darby Court, Westminster Act 1845 (c.104)
Dartford and Strood Road Act 1760 (c.40)
Dartford Roads Act 1766 (c.98)
Dartford Roads Act 1788 (c.84)
Dartford–Thurrock Crossing Act 1988 (c.20)
Data Protection Act 1984 (c.35)
Day Industrial Schools (Scotland) Act 1893 (c.12)
Deal Act 1711 (c.43)
Deal Chapel of Ease Act 1711 (c.43)
Deal: Improvement Act 1791 (c.64)
Deal: Improvement Act 1796 (c.45)
Dealers in Excisable Articles Act 1805 (c.52)
Dean and Chapter Act 1868 (c.19)
Dean and New Forests Act 1808 (c.72)
Dean Forest (Encroachments) Act 1838 (cc.39–41)
Dean Forest Act 1861 (c.40)
Dean Forest (Mines) Act 1838 (c.43)
Dean Forest (Mines) Act 1871 (c.85)
Dean Forest (Mines) Act 1871 (c.85)
Dean Forest Roads Act 1796 (c.131)
Deanery of Manchester Act 1906 (c.19)
Deans and Canons Resignation Act 1872 (c.8)
Dean's Yard, Westminster Act 1755 (c.54)
Death Duties (Killed in War) Act 1914 (c.76)
Debenture Stock Act 1871 (c.27)
Debt of City of Edinburgh, etc. Act 1838 (c.55)
Debtors Act 1869 (c.62)
Debtors Act 1878 (c.54)
Debtors and Creditors Act 1860 (c.147)
Debtors and Imprisonment Act 1758 (c.28)
Debtors Imprisonment Act 1758 (c.28)
Debtors (Ireland) Act 1840 (c.105)
Debtors (Ireland) Act 1872 (c.57)
Debtors, Middlesex Act 1785 (c.45)
Debtors' Prison, Devonshire Act 1753 (c.57)
Debtors Relief Act 1793 (c.5)
Debtors Relief Act 1801 (c.64)
Debtors Relief Act 1812 (c.34)

Debtors (Scotland) Act 1838 (c.114)
Debtors (Scotland) Act 1880 (c.34)
Debtors (Scotland) Act 1987 (c.18)
Debts Clearing Offices Act 1948 (c.2)
Debts Clearing Offices and Import Restrictions Act 1934 (c.31)
Debts Due to Swiss Government Act 1798 (c.45)
Debts Due to the Army Act 1702 (c.24)
Debts Due to the Army Act 1711 (c.38)
Debts Due to the Army Act 1714 (c.24)
Debts Due to the Army Act 1715 (c.35)
Debts Due to the Army Act 1716 (c.17)
Debts Due to the Army Act 1720 (c.30)
Debts Due to the Army, etc. Act 1701 (c.1)
Debts Due to the Army, etc. Act 1717 (c.9)
Debts Due to the Army, etc. Act 1718 (c.14)
Debts Due to the Army, etc. Act 1719 (c.17)
Debts Due to the United Provinces, etc. Act 1797 (c.28)
Debts of East India Company Act 1812 (c.121)
Debts of Traders Act 1807 (c.74)
Debts Recovery Act 1839 (c.60)
Debts Recovery Act 1848 (c.87)
Debts Recovery (Scotland) Act 1867 (c.96)
Debts Securities (Scotland) Act 1856 (c.91)
Deceased Brother's Widow's Marriage Act 1921 (c.24)
Deceased Wife's Sister's Marriage Act 1907 (c.47)
Decimal Currency Act 1967 (c.47)
Decimal Currency Act 1969 (c.19)
Declaration by Quakers, etc. Act 1837 (c.5)
Declaration of Title Act 1862 (c.67)
Declarations by Quakers, etc. on Acceptance of Offices Act 1838 (c.15)
Declarations Before Taking Office Act 1866 (c.22)
Deeds of Arrangement Act 1887 (c.57)
Deeds of Arrangement Act 1914 (c.47)
Deeds of Arrangement Amendment Act 1890 (c.24)
Deep Sea Mining (Temporary Provisions) Act 1981 (c.53)
Deeping Fen Drainage Act 1737 (c.39)
Deeping Fens Act 1774 (c.23)
Deer Act 1963 (c.36)
Deer Act 1980 (c.49)
Deer Act 1987 (c.28)
Deer Act 1991 (c.54)
Deer (Amendment) (Scotland) Act 1967 (c.37)
Deer (Amendment) (Scotland) Act 1982 (c.19)
Deer (Amendment) (Scotland) Act 1996 (c.44)
Deer (Scotland) Act 1959 (c.40)
Deer (Scotland) Act 1996 (c.58)
Deer Stealers Act 1718 (c.15)
Deer Stealing (England) Act 1802 (c.107)
Deer Stealing (England) Act 1811 (c.120)
Defacing the Coin Act 1853 (c.102)

Defamation Act 1952 (c.66)
Defamation Act 1996 (c.31)
Defective Premises Act 1972 (c.35)
Defence Act 1842 (c.94)
Defence Act 1854 (c.67)
Defence Act 1859 (c.12)
Defence Act 1860 (c.112)
Defence Act 1865 (c.65)
Defence Act Amendment Act 1864 (c.89)
Defence Acts Amendment Act 1873 (c.72)
Defence (Barracks) Act 1935 (c.26)
Defence Contracts Act 1958 (c.38)
Defence Loans Act 1937 (c.13)
Defence Loans Act 1939 (c.8)
Defence of the Realm Act 1797 (c.27)
Defence of the Realm Act 1803 (c.55)
Defence of the Realm Act 1803 (c.120)
Defence of the Realm Act 1803 (c.125)
Defence of the Realm Act 1804 (c.95)
Defence of the Realm Act 1806 (c.90)
Defence of the Realm Act 1808 (c.107)
Defence of the Realm Act 1914 (c.29)
Defence of the Realm (Acquisition of Land) Act 1916 (c.63)
Defence of the Realm (Acquisition of Land) Act 1920 (c.79)
Defence of the Realm (Amendment) Act 1915 (c.34)
Defence of the Realm (Amendment) (No. 2) Act 1915 (c.37)
Defence of the Realm (Amendment) (No. 3) Act 1915 (c.42)
Defence of the Realm (Beans, Peas and Pulse Orders) Act 1918 (c.12)
Defence of the Realm Consolidation Act 1914 (c.8)
Defence of the Realm (Employment Exchanges) Act 1918 (c.58)
Defence of the Realm (England) Act 1803 (c.82)
Defence of the Realm (England) Act 1803 (c.123)
Defence of the Realm, etc. Act 1803 (c.96)
Defence of the Realm, etc. Act 1804 (c.56)
Defence of the Realm, etc. Act 1804 (c.66)
Defence of the Realm, etc. Act 1804 (c.74)
Defence of the Realm (Food Profits) Act 1918 (c.9)
Defence of the Realm (Ireland) Act 1803 (c.85)
Defence of the Realm (Ireland) Act 1806 (c.63)
Defence of the Realm, London Act 1803 (c.101)
Defence of the Realm, London Act 1804 (c.96)
Defence of the Realm, London Act 1806 (c.144)
Defence of the Realm (No. 2) Act 1914 (c.63)
Defence of the Realm (Scotland) Act 1803 (c.83)
Defence of the Realm (Scotland) Act 1803 (c.124)

Defence (Transfer of Functions) Act 1964 (c.15)

Defranchisement of Sudbury Act 1844 (c.53)

Delamere Forest Act 1856 (c.13)

Delay Act 1387 (c.10)

Delay of Cause After Issue Joined Act 1740 (c.17)

Demise of Parts of Rolls Estate Act 1836 (c.49)

Demise of the Crown Act 1727 (c.5)

Demise of the Crown Act 1830 (c.43)

Demise of the Crown Act 1837 (c.31)

Demise of the Crown Act 1901 (c.5)

Denbigh and Carnarvon Roads Act 1757 (c.69)

Denbigh and Flint Roads Act 1769 (c.45)

Denbigh and Flint Roads Act 1790 (c.110)

Denbigh, Flint and Carnarvon Roads Act 1758 (c.55)

Denbigh, Flint and Carnarvon Roads Act 1779 (c.109)

Denbigh, Flint and Carnarvon Roads Act 1780 (c.97)

Denbigh, Flint, Salop. and Chester Roads Act 1767 (c.104)

Denbigh Roads Act 1756 (c.68)

Denbigh Roads Act 1762 (c.77)

Denbigh Roads Act 1763 (c.43)

Denbigh Roads Act 1777 (c.111)

Denbigh Roads Act 1788 (c.112)

Denbigh to Rutland Road Act 1781 (c.80)

Dentists Act 1878 (c.33)

Dentists Act 1921 (c.21)

Dentists Act 1923 (c.36)

Dentists Act 1956 (c.29)

Dentists Act 1957 (c.28)

Dentists Act 1983 (c.38)

Dentists Act 1984 (c.24)

Dentists (Amendment) Act 1973 (c.31)

Denver, etc., Drainage, Norfolk Act 1771 (c.72)

Denver, etc. (Norfolk and Cambridge) Drainage Act 1748 (c.16)

Deodands Act 1846 (c.62)

Department of Science and Art Act 1875 (c.68)

Department of Scientific and Industrial Research Act 1956 (c.58)

Department of Technical Co-operation Act 1961 (c.30)

Dependency of Ireland on Great Britain Act 1719 (c.5)

Deposit of Poisonous Waste Act 1972 (c.21)

Depredations on the Thames Act 1800 (c.87)

Depredations on the Thames Act 1807 (c.37)

Depredations on the Thames Act 1814 (c.187)

Deputy Lieutenants Act 1918 (c.19)

Deputy Speaker Act 1855 (c.84)

Derby and Cheshire Roads Act 1792 (c.128)

Derby and Chester Roads Act 1782 (c.107)

Derby and Leicester Roads Act 1794 (c.120)

Derby and Nottinghamshire Roads Act 1757 (c.60)

Derby and Nottinghamshire Roads Act 1764 (c.67)

Derby and Nottinghamshire Roads Act 1780 (c.74)

Derby and Nottinghamshire Roads Act 1790 (c.113)

Derby and Sheffield Roads Act 1756 (c.82)

Derby and Stafford Roads Act 1766 (c.79)

Derby and Stafford Roads Act 1787 (c.87)

Derby and Uttoxeter Road Act 1763 (c.57)

Derby and Yorkshire Roads Act 1764 (c.65)

Derby and Yorkshire Roads Act 1776 (c.73)

Derby and Yorkshire Roads Act 1779 (c.99)

Derby Bridge Act 1788 (c.77)

Derby Canal Act 1793 (c.102)

Derby Gaol Act 1756 (c.48)

Derby: Improvement Act 1792 (c.78)

Derby, Leicester and Warwick Roads Act 1759 (c.47)

Derby, Leicester and Warwick Roads Act 1781 (c.92)

Derby Roads Act 1737 (c.33)

Derby Roads Act 1743 (c.20)

Derby Roads Act 1759 (c.33)

Derby Roads Act 1764 (c.82)

Derby Roads Act 1766 (c.69)

Derby Roads Act 1766 (c.80)

Derby Roads Act 1766 (c.87)

Derby Roads Act 1777 (c.92)

Derby Roads Act 1777 (c.101)

Derby Roads Act 1785 (c.121)

Derby Roads Act 1786 (c.151)

Derby Roads Act 1788 (c.89)

Derby Roads Act 1793 (c.152)

Derby Roads Act 1795 (c.154)

Derby to Newcastle-under-Lyme Road Act 1758 (c.60)

Derbyshire Roads Act 1724 (c.13)

Derbyshire Roads Act 1738 (c.12)

Derbyshire Roads Act 1758 (c.43)

Derbyshire Roads Act 1759 (c.39)

Derbyshire Roads Act 1769 (c.81)

Derbyshire Roads Act 1779 (c.87)

Derbyshire Roads Act 1781 (c.81)

Derbyshire Roads Act 1781 (c.83)

Deregulation and Contracting Out Act 1994 (c.40)

Derelict Land Act 1982 (c.42)

Derelict Vessels (Report) Act 1896 (c.12)

Deritend and Bordesley, Warwick: Improvement Act 1791 (c.17)

Deritend Bridge, Birmingham: Rebuilding Act 1788 (c.70)

Derwent (Yorks.) Navigation Act 1702 (c.14)

Desertion of Seamen Act 1797 (c.73)

Design Copyright Act 1968 (c.68)

Designing and Printing of Linens, etc. Act 1787 (c.38)

Designing and Printing of Linens, etc. Act 1789 (c.19)

Destruction of Coal Works Act 1739 (c.21)

Destruction of Deer (England) Act 1718 (c.28)

Destruction of Prisons by Rioters Act 1780 (c.1)

Destruction of Property (S.) Act 1789 (c.46)

Destruction of Stocking Frames, etc. Act 1812 (c.16)

Destruction of Stocking Frames, etc. Act 1813 (c.42)

Destruction of Turnpikes, etc. Act 1727 (c.19)

Destruction of Turnpikes, etc. Act 1731 (c.33)

Destruction of Turnpikes, etc. Act 1734 (c.20)

Destructive Imported Animals Act 1932 (c.12)

Destructive Insects Act 1877 (c.68)

Destructive Insects and Pests Act 1907 (c.4)

Destructive Insects and Pests Act 1927 (c.32)

Detached Parts of Counties (England) Act 1858 (c.68)

Detached Portions of Counties (Ireland) Act 1871 (c.106)

Determination of Needs Act 1941 (c.11)

Development and Road Improvement Funds Act 1909 (c.47)

Development and Road Improvement Funds Act 1910 (c.7)

Development Board for Rural Wales Act 1991 (c.1)

Development Land Tax Act 1976 (c.24)

Development (Loan Guarantees and Grants) Act 1929 (c.7)

Development of Inventions Act 1948 (c.60)

Development of Inventions Act 1954 (c.20)

Development of Inventions Act 1958 (c.3)

Development of Inventions Act 1965 (c.21)

Development of Inventions Act 1967 (c.32)

Development of Rural Wales Act 1976 (c.75)

Development of Tourism Act 1969 (c.51)

Devizes Road Act 1784 (c.65)

Devizes Roads Act 1797 (c.154)

Devizes: Streets Act 1780 (c.36)

Devon Bridges Act 1757 (c.47)

Devon: Canal Act 1796 (c.46)

Devon, Dorset and Somerset Roads Act 1792 (c.144)

Devon Gaol Act 1787 (c.59)

Devon (Poor Relief) Act 1772 (c.18)

Devon Roads Act 1755 (c.49)

Devon Roads Act 1757 (c.51)

Devon Roads Act 1758 (c.52)

Devon Roads Act 1758 (c.68)

Devon Roads Act 1760 (c.34)

Devon Roads Act 1762 (c.50)

Devon Roads Act 1762 (c.64)

Devon Roads Act 1763 (c.38)

Devon Roads Act 1765 (cc.69, 70)

Devon Roads Act 1767 (c.62)

Devon Roads Act 1772 (c.86)

Devon Roads Act 1772 (c.93)

Devon Roads Act 1780 (c.79)

Devon Roads Act 1781 (c.84)

Devon Roads Act 1783 (c.26)

Devon Roads Act 1784 (c.63)

Devon Roads Act 1784 (c.67)

Devon Roads Act 1787 (c.74)

Devon Roads Act 1791 (c.117)

Devon, Shire Hall Act 1772 (c.16)

Devonshire: Poor Relief Act 1769 (c.82)

Dewsbury to Elland Road Act 1758 (c.54)

Dewsbury to Elland Road Act 1779 (c.88)

Diet of Soldiers on a March Act 1813 (c.83)

Differential Duties on Foreign Ships Act 1852 (c.47)

Dindings Agreement (Approval) Act 1934 (c.55)

Diocesan Boundaries Act 1871 (c.14)

Diocesan Boundaries Act 1872 (c.14)

Diocese of Norwich Act 1848 (c.61)

Diplomatic and Consular Premises Act 1987 (c.46)

Diplomatic and Other Privileges Act 1971 (c.64)

Diplomatic Immunities (Commonwealth Countries and Republic of Ireland) Act 1951 (c.18)

Diplomatic Immunities (Conferences with Commonwealth Countries and Republic of Ireland) Act 1961 (c.11)

Diplomatic Immunities Restriction Act 1955 (c.22)

Diplomatic Privileges Act 1708 (c.12)

Diplomatic Privileges Act 1964 (c.81)

Diplomatic Privileges (Extension) Act 1941 (c.7)

Diplomatic Privileges (Extension) Act 1944 (c.44)

Diplomatic Privileges (Extension) Act 1946 (c.66)

Diplomatic Privileges (Extension) Act 1950 (c.7)

Diplomatic Relations with See of Rome Act 1848 (c.108)

Diplomatic Salaries, etc. Act 1869 (c.43)

Directors' Liability Act 1890 (c.64)

Disability Discrimination Act 1995 (c.50)

Disability (Grants) Act 1993 (c.14)

Disability Living Allowance and Disability Working Allowance Act 1991 (c.21)

Disabled Men (Facilities for Employment) (Master and Servant) Act 1919 (c.22)

Disabled Persons Act 1981 (c.43)

Disabled Persons Act 1986 (c.33)

Disabled Persons (Employment) Act 1944 (c.10)

Disabled Persons (Employment) Act 1958 (c.33)

Disabled Persons (Northern Ireland) Act 1989 (c.10)

Disarming the Highlands, etc. Act 1745 (c.39)

Disarming the Highlands, etc. Act 1753 (c.29)

Discharge of a Crown Debt Act 1788 (c.32)

Discharge of Certain Imprisoned Debtors Act 1808 (c.123)

Discharge to Lady A. Jekyll's Executors Act 1772 (c.53)

Discharged Prisoners Act 1774 (c.20)

Discharged Prisoners' Aid Act 1862 (c.44)

Discharged Soldiers, etc. Act 1748 (c.44)

Discontinuance of Duties Act 1757 (c.7)

Discontinuance of Duties Act 1757 (c.14)
Discontinuance of Duties Act 1758 (c.12)
Discontinuance of Duties Act 1770 (c.8)
Discontinuance of Portsdown Fair, South-ampton Act 1862 (c.34)
Discount on Newspapers Act 1809 (c.50)
Discovery of Longitude at Sea Act 1713 (c.14)
Discovery of Longitude at Sea Act 1762 (c.14)
Discovery of Longitude at Sea Act 1762 (c.18)
Discovery of Longitude at Sea Act 1765 (c.11)
Discovery of Longitude at Sea Act 1765 (c.20)
Discovery of Longitude at Sea Act 1770 (c.34)
Discovery of Longitude at Sea Act 1774 (c.66)
Discovery of Longitude at Sea Act 1790 (c.14)
Discovery of Longitude at Sea Act 1815 (c.75)
Discovery of Longitude at Sea, etc. Act 1803 (c.118)
Discovery of Longitude at Sea, etc. Act 1806 (c.77)
Discovery of Longitude at Seas Act 1753 (c.25)
Discovery of North-West Passage Act 1744 (c.17)
Discovery of Northern Passage Act 1776 (c.6)
Disease Among Cattle Act 1772 (c.51)
Diseased Sheep, etc. Act 1798 (c.65)
Diseases of Animals Act 1894 (c.57)
Diseases of Animals Act 1896 (c.15)
Diseases of Animals Act 1903 (c.43)
Diseases of Animals Act 1909 (c.26)
Diseases of Animals Act 1910 (c.20)
Diseases of Animals Act 1922 (c.8)
Diseases of Animals Act 1923 (c.3)
Diseases of Animals Act 1925 (c.63)
Diseases of Animals Act 1927 (c.13)
Diseases of Animals Act 1935 (c.31)
Diseases of Animals Act 1950 (c.36)
Diseases of Animals Act 1975 (c.40)
Diseases of Animals (Ireland) Act 1914 (c.40)
Diseases of Fish Act 1937 (c.33)
Diseases of Fish Act 1983 (c.30)
Diseases Prevention Act 1855 (c.116)
Diseases Prevention (Metropolis) Act 1883 (c.35)
Disfranchisement of Freemen, Great Yar-mouth Act 1848 (c.24)
Disfranchisement of St. Alban's Act 1852 (c.9)
Disorderly Houses Act 1751 (c.36)
Dispensary Committees (Ireland) Act 1896 (c.10)
Dispensary Houses (Ireland) Act 1879 (c.25)
Disposal of Ulysses Fitzmaurice's Intestate Estate Act 1774 (c.40)

Disposal of Uncollected Goods Act 1952 (c.43)
Disposition of Copyhold Estates by Will Act 1815 (c.192)
Disputes Between Masters and Workmen Act 1800 (c.90)
Dissolved Boards of Management and Guardians Act 1870 (c.2)
Distemper Amongst Cattle Act 1745 (c.5)
Distemper Amongst Cattle Act 1746 (c.4)
Distemper Amongst Cattle Act 1749 (c.23)
Distemper Amongst Cattle Act 1750 (c.31)
Distemper Amongst Cattle Act 1754 (c.14)
Distemper Amongst Cattle Act 1755 (c.18)
Distemper Amongst Cattle Act 1757 (c.20)
Distemper Amongst Cattle Act 1770 (c.4)
Distemper Amongst Cattle Act 1770 (c.45)
Distillation Act 1757 (c.10)
Distillation Act 1757 (c.15)
Distillation Act 1759 (c.9)
Distillation, etc. Act 1702 (c.14)
Distillation, etc. Act 1774 (c.73)
Distillation, etc. of Spirits (Ireland) Act 1813 (c.52)
Distillation from Corn, etc. Act 1812 (c.118)
Distillation from Corn Prohibition, etc. Act 1812 (c.7)
Distillation from Wheat, etc. Act 1799 (c.7)
Distillation from Wheat, etc. Act 1800 (c.21)
Distillation from Wheat, etc., Prohibition Act 1795 (c.20)
Distillation from Wheat (Ireland) Act 1801 (c.15)
Distillation (Ireland) Act 1812 (c.47)
Distillation of Spirits Act 1803 (c.11)
Distillation of Spirits Act 1805 (c.100)
Distillation of Spirits Act 1808 (c.118)
Distillation of Spirits Act 1809 (c.7)
Distillation of Spirits Act 1809 (c.24)
Distillation of Spirits Act 1810 (c.5)
Distillation of Spirits Act 1812 (c.3)
Distillation of Spirits from Sugar Act 1847 (c.6)
Distillation of Spirits from Sugar, etc. Act 1848 (c.100)
Distillation of Spirits (Ireland) Act 1813 (c.145)
Distillation of Spirits (Ireland) Act 1813 (c.148)
Distillation of Spirits (Ireland) Act 1814 (c.150)
Distillation of Spirits (Ireland) Act 1815 (c.151)
Distillation of Spirits (Ireland) Act 1816 (c.112)
Distillation of Spirits (Scotland) Act 1808 (c.10)
Distillation of Spirits (Scotland) Act 1810 (c.79)
Distillation of Spirits (Scotland) Act 1813 (c.9)
Distilleries, etc. Act 1793 (c.61)
Distillers Act 1746 (c.39)
Distillers Act 1779 (c.50)

Distillers of Spirits Act 1811 (c.42)

Distress (Costs) Act 1817 (c.93)

Distress for Rates Act 1849 (c.14)

Distress for Rent Act 1737 (c.19)

Distress for Rent Act 1960 (c.12)

Distressed Unions Advances (Ireland) Act 1850 (c.14)

Distressed Unions (Ireland) Act 1852 (c.68)

Distresses Under Justices' Warrants Act 1754 (c.20)

Distribution of Certain Monies Act 1803 (c.39)

Distribution of Industry Act 1944 (c.36)

Distribution of Industry (Industrial Finance) Act 1958 (c.41)

District Auditors Act 1879 (c.6)

District Church Tithes Act 1865 (c.42)

District Councillors and Guardians (Term of Office) Act 1900 (c.16)

District Councils (Water Supply Facilities) Act 1897 (c.44)

District Courts and Prisons Act 1842 (c.53)

District Courts and Prisons Act 1844 (c.50)

District Courts (Scotland) Act 1975 (c.20)

Distribution of Germany Enemy Property Act 1949 (c.85)

Distribution of Industry Act 1950 (c.8)

Disused Burial Grounds Act 1884 (c.72)

Disused Burial Grounds (Amendment) Act 1981 (c.18)

Disused Public Buildings (Ireland) Act 1808 (c.113)

Divided Parishes and Poor Law Amendment Act 1876 (c.61)

Divided Parishes and Poor Law Amendment Act 1882 (c.58)

Dividends Act 1978 (c.54)

Dividends and Stock Act 1869 (c.104)

Dividends and Stock Act 1870 (c.47)

Division of Deanery of St. Burian Act 1850 (c.76)

Divorce Amendment Act 1868 (c.77)

Divorce (Insanity and Desertion) Act 1958 (c.54)

Divorce Jurisdiction, Court Fees and Legal Aid (Scotland) Act 1983 (c.12)

Divorce Reform Act 1969 (c.55)

Divorce (Scotland) Act 1938 (c.50)

Divorce (Scotland) Act 1964 (c.91)

Divorce (Scotland) Act 1976 (c.39)

Dock Work Regulation Act 1976 (c.79)

Dock Workers (Pensions) Act 1960 (c.39)

Dock Workers (Regulation of Employment) Act 1946 (c.22)

Docking and Nicking of Horses Act 1949 (c.70)

Docks and Harbours Act 1966 (c.28)

Docks and Ordnance Service Act 1804 (c.79)

Docks, etc., at Chatham, etc. Act 1806 (c.130)

Dockyard Act 1865 (c.25)

Dockyard Ports Regulation Act 1865 (c.125)

Dockyard Services Act 1986 (c.52)

Dockyards, etc., Protection Act 1772 (c.24)

Dockyards Protection Act Amendment Act 1863 (c.30)

Doctrine of the Trinity Act 1813 (c.160)

Documentary Evidence Act 1868 (c.37)

Documentary Evidence Act 1882 (c.9)

Documentary Evidence Act 1895 (c.9)

Dog Licences Act 1959 (c.55)

Dog Licences Act 1867 (c.5)

Dog Racecourse Betting (Temporary Provisions) Act 1947 (c.20)

Dog Stealing Act 1770 (c.18)

Dog Stealing Act 1845 (c.47)

Dogs Act 1865 (c.60)

Dogs Act 1871 (c.56)

Dogs Act 1906 (c.32)

Dogs (Amendment) Act 1928 (c.21)

Dogs Amendment Act 1938 (c.21)

Dogs (Fouling of Land) Act 1996 (c.20)

Dogs (Ireland) Act 1862 (c.59)

Dogs (Ireland) Act 1867 (c.116)

Dogs (Protection of Livestock) Act 1953 (c.28)

Dogs Regulation (Ireland) Act 1865 (c.50)

Dogs Regulation (Ireland) Act 1919 (c.81)

Dogs (Scotland) Act 1863 (c.100)

Domestic and Appellate Proceedings (Restriction of Publicity) Act 1968 (c.63)

Domestic Proceedings and Magistrates' Courts Act 1978 (c.22)

Domestic Violence and Matrimonial Proceedings Act 1976 (c.50)

Domicile Act 1861 (c.121)

Domicile and Matrimonial Proceedings Act 1973 (c.45)

Dominica Act 1938 (c.10)

Dominica Loan Act 1860 (c.57)

Dominica Loan Act 1867 (c.91)

Doncaster and Tadcaster Road Act 1740 (c.28)

Doncaster Road and Bridges Act 1795 (c.158)

Doncaster Roads Act 1785 (c.104)

Doncaster: Small Debts, Lighting, etc. Act 1763 (c.40)

Doncaster to Bawtry Road Act 1776 (c.71)

Doncaster to Chester Road Act 1789 (c.98)

Donnington to Southall Canal Act 1788 (c.73)

Dorchester Bridge and Causeway Act 1745 (c.24)

Dorchester: Streets Act 1776 (c.27)

Dorset and Devon Roads Act 1757 (c.43)

Dorset and Devon Roads Act 1765 (c.75)

Dorset and Somerset Roads Act 1765 (c.102)

Dorset and Somerset Roads Act 1767 (c.82)

Dorset and Wilts: Canal Act 1796 (c.47)

Dorset, Devon and Somerset Roads Act 1777 (c.89)

Dorset, etc., Roads Act 1762 (c.61)

Dorset Roads Act 1758 (c.50)

Dorset Roads Act 1760 (c.24)

Dorset Roads Act 1766 (c.68)

Dorset Roads Act 1766 (c.92)

Dorset Roads Act 1769 (c.47)

Dorset Roads Act 1777 (c.103)
Dorset Roads Act 1782 (c.101)
Dorset Roads Act 1788 (c.91)
Dorset Roads Act 1790 (c.95)
Dover and Rye Harbours Act 1764 (c.72)
Dover, Deal and Sandwich Road Act 1797 (c.156)
Dover Harbour Act 1703 (c.7)
Dover Harbour Act 1717 (c.13)
Dover Harbour Act 1722 (c.30)
Dover Harbour Act 1737 (c.7)
Dover Harbour Act 1757 (c.8)
Dover Harbour Act 1786 (c.11)
Dover Harbour Act 1794 (c.112)
Dover Streets Act 1778 (c.76)
Doveridge Roads, Derby Act 1769 (c.59)
Downpatrick Election Committee Act 1815 (c.98)
Drafts on Bankers Act 1856 (c.25)
Drafts on Bankers Act 1858 (c.79)
Drainage and Improvement of Land (Ireland) Act 1866 (c.40)
Drainage and Improvement of Land (Ireland) Act 1892 (c.65)
Drainage and Improvement of Land, Supplemental (Ireland) Act 1865 (c.13)
Drainage and Improvement of Land, Supplemental (Ireland) Act 1865 (c.50)
Drainage and Improvement of Land, Supplemental (Ireland) Act 1867 (c.43)
Drainage and Improvement of Lands Amendment (Ireland) Act 1865 (c.52)
Drainage and Improvement of Lands Amendment (Ireland) Act 1869 (c.72)
Drainage and Improvement of Lands Amendment (Ireland) Act 1872 (c.31)
Drainage and Improvement of Lands Amendment (Ireland) Act 1874 (c.32)
Drainage and Improvement of Lands (Ireland) Act 1853 (c.130)
Drainage and Improvement of Lands (Ireland) Act 1855 (c.110)
Drainage and Improvement of Lands (Ireland) Act 1863 (c.88)
Drainage and Improvement of Lands (Ireland) Act 1864 (c.72)
Drainage and Improvement of Lands (Ireland) Act 1878 (c.59)
Drainage and Improvement of Lands (Ireland) Act 1880 (c.27)
Drainage and Improvement of Lands Supplemental Act 1866 (c.61)
Drainage and Improvement of Lands, Supplemental (Ireland) Act 1864 (c.107)
Drainage and Improvement of Lands, Supplemental (Ireland) Act 1867 (c.139)
Drainage: Cambridge, Isle of Ely Act 1772 (c.26)
Drainage, etc. (Ireland) Act 1847 (c.106)
Drainage (Ireland) Act 1842 (c.89)
Drainage (Ireland) Act 1846 (c.4)
Drainage (Ireland) Act 1847 (c.79)
Drainage (Ireland) Act 1856 (c.62)

Drainage: Isle of Ely Act 1772 (c.27)
Drainage Haddenham Level Act 1726 (c.18)
Drainage Maintenance Act 1866 (c.49)
Drainage of Bogs, etc. (Ireland) Act 1809 (c.102)
Drainage of Lands Act 1849 (c.100)
Drainage Rates Act 1958 (c.37)
Drainage Rates Act 1962 (c.39)
Drainage Rates Act 1963 (c.10)
Drainage Rates (Disabled Persons) Act 1986 (c.17)
Dramatic and Musical Performers' Protection Act 1925 (c.46)
Dramatic and Musical Performers' Protection Act 1958 (c.44)
Dramatic and Musical Performers' Protection Act 1972 (c.32)
Drawback Act 1795 (c.98)
Drawback Act 1795 (c.110)
Drawback Act 1796 (c.106)
Drawback Act 1806 (c.114)
Drawback Act 1807 (c.49)
Drawback, etc. on Glass Act 1812 (c.77)
Drawback of Duties Act 1795 (c.39)
Drawback of Duty on Coals Act 1811 (c.83)
Drawback on Chocolate Act 1812 (c.11)
Drawback on Coals Act 1813 (c.18)
Drawback on Linens Act 1805 (c.98)
Drawback on Paper Act 1814 (c.153)
Drawback on Wines Act 1813 (c.44)
Drawbacks Act 1802 (c.17)
Drawbacks Act 1802 (c.60)
Drawbacks Act 1803 (c.5)
Drawbacks Act 1803 (c.10)
Drawbacks Act 1807 (c.20)
Drawbacks Act 1807 (c.62)
Drawbacks Act 1808 (c.43)
Drawbacks and Bounties Act 1795 (c.18)
Drawbacks and Bounties Act 1802 (c.11)
Drawbacks and Bounties Act 1805 (c.93)
Drawbacks, etc. Act 1798 (c.61)
Drawbacks, etc. (Ireland) Act 1805 (c.23)
Drawbacks, etc., on Sugar Act 1811 (c.12)
Drawbacks, etc. on Tobacco, etc. Act 1815 (c.129)
Drawbacks (Ireland) Act 1806 (c.14)
Drawbacks (Ireland) Act 1807 (c.19)
Drawbacks on Paper Act 1814 (c.106)
Drawbacks on Spirits Act 1811 (c.121)
Drawbacks upon Sugar Act 1806 (c.10)
Drayton and Edgehill Road Act 1753 (c.78)
Drill Grounds Act 1886 (c.5)
Driving of Cattle, Metropolis Act 1774 (c.87)
Driving of Cattle, Metropolis Act 1781 (c.67)
Droitwich Roads Act 1768 (c.39)
Drought Act 1976 (c.44)
Drouly Fund Act 1838 (c.89)
Drugging of Animals Act 1876 (c.13)
Drugs (Prevention of Misuse) Act 1964 (c.64)
Drug Trafficking Act 1994 (c.37)
Drug Trafficking Offences Act 1986 (c.32)
Drury Lane Theatre Act 1776 (c.13)
Dublin Amended Carriage Act 1854 (c.45)

Dub

Alphabetical Table of Statutes

Dublin Amended Carriage Act 1855 (c.65)
Dublin and Other Roads Turnpikes Abolition Act 1855 (c.69)
Dublin Baronies Act 1842 (c.96)
Dublin Carriage Act 1853 (c.112)
Dublin, Collection of Rates Act 1849 (c.91)
Dublin Collector-General of Rates Act 1870 (c.11)
Dublin Corporation Act 1849 (c.85)
Dublin Corporation Act 1850 (c.81)
Dublin Foundling Hospital 1814 (c.128)
Dublin, Four Courts Act 1858 (c.84)
Dublin General Post Office Act 1808 (c.48)
Dublin General Post Office Act 1809 (c.70)
Dublin Grand Jury Act 1845 (c.81)
Dublin Harbour Act 1815 (c.191)
Dublin Harbour Act 1816 (c.62)
Dublin Hospitals Act 1856 (c.110)
Dublin, Hotels and Restaurants Act 1910 (c.33)
Dublin Improvement Act 1849 (c.97)
Dublin Improvement Act 1861 (c.26)
Dublin Justices Act 1840 (c.103)
Dublin Justices Act 1875 (c.20)
Dublin National Gallery Act 1865 (c.71)
Dublin Parliamentary Revising Act 1853 (c.58)
Dublin Paying, etc., Inquiry Act 1806 (c.68)
Dublin, Phoenix Park Act 1860 (c.42)
Dublin Police Act 1836 (c.29)
Dublin Police Act 1837 (c.25)
Dublin Police Act 1839 (c.78)
Dublin Police Act 1842 (c.24)
Dublin Police Act 1848 (c.113)
Dublin Police Act 1859 (c.52)
Dublin Police District Act 1838 (c.63)
Dublin Police Magistrates Act 1808 (c.140)
Dublin, Public Offices Site Act 1903 (c.16)
Dublin, Purchase of Land Act 1841 (c.16)
Dublin Reconstruction Act 1916 (c.66)
Dublin Record Office Act 1814 (c.63)
Dublin Revising Barristers Act 1857 (c.68)
Dublin Revising Barristers Act 1861 (c.56)
Dublin, Sale of Game Act 1865 (c.2)
Dublin, Sale of Property Act 1842 (c.62)
Dublin Science and Art Museum Act 1884 (c.6)
Dublin, Site of Record Office Act 1814 (c.113)
Dublin Tramways Act 1876 (c.65)
Dublin Voters Disfranchisement Act 1870 (c.54)
Duchess of Kent's Annuity Act 1838 (c.8)
Duchies of Lancaster and Cornwall (Accounts) Act 1838 (c.101)
Duchy of Cornwall Act 1700 (c.13)
Duchy of Cornwall Act 1707 (c.52)
Duchy of Cornwall Act 1713 (c.25)
Duchy of Cornwall Act 1715 (c.37)
Duchy of Cornwall Act 1750 (c.50)
Duchy of Cornwall Act 1759 (c.10)
Duchy of Cornwall Act 1768 (c.26)
Duchy of Cornwall Act 1776 (c.10)
Duchy of Cornwall Act 1812 (c.123)

Duchy of Cornwall Act 1844 (c.65)
Duchy of Cornwall Act 1860 (c.53)
Duchy of Cornwall Lands Act 1862 (c.49)
Duchy of Cornwall Leases, etc. Act 1842 (c.2)
Duchy of Cornwall (Limitation of Actions, etc.) Act 1860 (c.53)
Duchy of Cornwall Management Act 1863 (c.49)
Duchy of Cornwall Management Act 1868 (c.35)
Duchy of Cornwall Management Act 1893 (c.20)
Duchy of Cornwall Management Act 1982 (c.47)
Duchy of Cornwall (No. 2) Act 1844 (c.105)
Duchy of Cornwall Office Act 1854 (c.93)
Duchy of Lancaster Lands Act 1855 (c.58)
Duchy of Lancaster Act 1779 (c.45)
Duchy of Lancaster Act 1787 (c.34)
Duchy of Lancaster Act 1796 (c.97)
Duchy of Lancaster Act 1808 (c.73)
Duchy of Lancaster Act 1812 (c.161)
Duchy of Lancaster Act 1920 (c.51)
Duchy of Lancaster Act 1988 (c.10)
Duchy of Lancaster (Application of Capital Moneys) Act 1921 (c.45)
Duchy of Lancaster (Precinct of Savoy) Act 1772 (c.42)
Dudley Canal Act 1776 (c.66)
Dudley Canal Act 1785 (c.87)
Dudley Canal Act 1796 (c.13)
Dudley: Improvement Act 1791 (c.79)
Duke of Connaught, Annuity Act 1878 (c.46)
Duke of Connaught's Leave Act 1887 (c.10)
Duke of Grafton's Annuity Act 1806 (c.79)
Duke of Marlborough; Pension Act 1706 (c.7)
Duke of Marlborough's Annuity Act 1839 (c.94)
Duke of Richmond's Annuity Act 1800 (c.43)
Duke of Wellington, Purchase of Estate for Act 1815 (c.186)
Duke of York's School (Chapel) Act 1910 (c.16)
Dulwich College Act 1857 (c.84)
Dunbar Beer Duties Act 1718 (c.16)
Dumbarton Road and Bridges Act 1786 (c.21)
Dumfries and Roxburgh Roads Act 1764 (c.85)
Dumfries Beer Duties Act 1716 (c.6)
Dumfries Beer Duties Act 1736 (c.7)
Dumfries Beer Duties Act 1762 (c.55)
Dumfries Beer Duties Act 1787 (c.57)
Dumfries Roads Act 1777 (c.107)
Dumfries Roads Act 1785 (c.120)
Dumfries Roads Act 1788 (c.114)
Dumfries Roads Act 1789 (c.87)
Dumping at Sea Act 1974 (c.20)
Dunbar Beer Duties Act 1736 (c.4)
Dunbar Beer Duties Act 1764 (c.46)
Dunbar Harbour Loan Act 1857 (c.63)
Dunbar Water Supply Act 1768 (c.57)
Dunchurch to Southam Road Act 1794 (c.128)

Dunchurch to Stone Bridge Road Act 1770 (c.90)
Dundee Beer Duties Act 1730 (c.11)
Dundee Beer Duties Act 1746 (c.17)
Dundee Beer Duties Act 1776 (c.16)
Dunstable Highways Act 1710 (c.34)
Dunstable Highways Act 1713 (c.29)
Dunstable Roads Act 1722 (c.11)
Dunstable to Hockliffe Road Act 1792 (c.159)
Durham and Northumberland Roads Act 1792 (c.113)
Durham and Tyne Bridge Road Act 1753 (c.48)
Durham Chancery Act 1869 (c.84)
Durham (County Palatine) Act 1836 (c.19)
Durham County Palatine Act 1858 (c.45)
Durham Roads Act 1747 (c.5)
Durham Roads Act 1749 (c.27)
Durham Roads Act 1750 (c.30)
Durham Roads Act 1754 (c.29)
Durham Roads Act 1756 (c.70)
Durham Roads Act 1759 (c.56)
Durham Roads Act 1773 (c.99)
Durham Roads Act 1777 (c.110)
Durham Roads Act 1789 (c.81)
Durham Roads Act 1792 (c.127)
Durham Roads Act 1793 (c.148)
Durham Roads Act 1793 (c.161)
Durham Roads Act 1795 (c.139)
Durham: Streets Act 1790 (c.67)
Durham to Tyne Bridge Road Act 1746 (c.12)
Duties and Drawbacks Act 1799 (c.12)
Duties and Drawbacks (Ireland) Act 1806 (c.12)
Duties and Drawbacks (Ireland) Act 1806 (c.62)
Duties, Bounties, etc. (Ireland) Act 1806 (c.120)
Duties Continuance Act 1801 (c.17)
Duties Continuance Act 1802 (c.31)
Duties Continuance Act 1803 (c.24)
Duties, Drawbacks, etc. (Ireland) Act 1809 (c.74)
Duties, etc. Act 1743 (c.31)
Duties, etc., India Act 1814 (c.105)
Duties, etc. (Ireland) Act 1803 (c.92)
Duties, etc., on Coffee, etc. Act 1802 (c.83)
Duties, etc., on Foreign Liquors, etc. Act 1812 (c.159)
Duties, etc., on Glass, etc. Act 1815 (c.113)
Duties, etc., on Glass (Ireland) Act 1814 (c.87)
Duties, etc., on Malt, etc. (Ireland) Act 1807 (c.40)
Duties, etc., on Soap Act 1816 (c.44)
Duties, etc., on Sugar, etc. Act 1803 (c.42)
Duties, etc., on Tobacco (Ireland) Act 1813 (c.73)
Duties in American Colonies Act 1765 (c.12)
Duties in American Colonies Act 1766 (c.11)
Duties (Logwood, etc.) Act 1766 (c.47)
Duties of Customs Act 1845 (c.90)
Duties of Customs and Tonnage Act 1802 (c.43)

Duties of Prisage and Butlerage (Ireland) Act (c.94)
Duties on Auctioneers, etc. Act 1803 (c.130)
Duties on Auctions (Ireland) Act 1808 (c.63)
Duties on Beer, etc. Act 1802 (c.38)
Duties on Beetroot Sugar Act 1837 (c.57)
Duties on Bricks Act 1839 (c.24)
Duties on Bricks and Tiles Act 1784 (c.24)
Duties on Bricks and Tiles Act 1785 (c.66)
Duties on Bricks and Tiles Act 1794 (c.15)
Duties on Buckwheat, etc. Act 1847 (c.3)
Duties on Calicoes, etc. Act 1807 (c.47)
Duties on Candles Act 1784 (c.36)
Duties on Candles Act 1792 (c.7)
Duties on Cape Wines Act 1813 (c.84)
Duties on Carriages, etc. (Ireland) Act 1813 (c.59)
Duties on Certain Goods Act 1806 (c.42)
Duties on Certain Licences Act 1784 (c.41)
Duties on Certain Licences Act 1808 (c.143)
Duties on Certain Woods, etc. Act 1811 (c.43)
Duties on Cider, etc. Act 1766 (c.14)
Duties on Cinnamon, etc. Act 1798 (c.68)
Duties on Cinnamon, etc. Act 1802 (c.24)
Duties on Cinnamon, etc. Act 1808 (c.18)
Duties on Clocks and Watches Act 1797 (c.108)
Duties on Coach Makers' Licences, etc. 1785 (c.49)
Duties on Coals, etc. Act 1785 (c.54)
Duties on Coals, etc. Act 1812 (c.9)
Duties on Copper and Lead Act 1848 (c.127)
Duties on Corn Act 1842 (c.14)
Duties on Corn, etc. Act 1847 (c.64)
Duties on Distillation Act 1800 (c.73)
Duties on Distilleries Act 1797 (c.11)
Duties on Distilleries Act 1797 (c.31)
Duties on Distilleries Act 1799 (c.31)
Duties on Distilleries (Scotland) Act 1799 (c.78)
Duties on Distilleries (Scotland), etc. Act 1796 (c.17)
Duties on Dogs Act 1796 (c.124)
Duties on East India Goods Act 1707 (c.37)
Duties on Epsom Salts Act 1815 (c.162)
Duties on Foreign Cambrics, etc. Act 1741 (c.29)
Duties on Foreign Hops Act 1800 (c.82)
Duties on Foreign Packets Act 1816 (c.9)
Duties on Game Certificates Act 1803 (c.23)
Duties on Glass Act 1795 (c.114)
Duties on Glass Act 1805 (c.122)
Duties on Glass Act 1811 (c.69)
Duties on Glass Act 1812 (c.54)
Duties on Glass Act 1813 (c.109)
Duties on Glass Act 1839 (c.25)
Duties on Glass Act 1840 (c.22)
Duties on Glass, etc. Act 1800 (c.45)
Duties on Glass, etc. (Ireland) Act 1814 (c.7)
Duties on Glass (Great Britain) Act 1814 (c.97)
Duties on Glass (Great Britain) Act 1816 (c.1)
Duties on Hair Powder, etc. Act 1800 (c.32)

Duties on Hats, etc., Repeal (Ireland) Act 1811 (c.60)

Duties on Hides, etc. Act 1815 (c.105)

Duties on Hides, etc. (Ireland) Act 1813 (c.60)

Duties on Hops Act 1800 (c.4)

Duties on Horse Dealers' Licences Act 1795 (c.17)

Duties on Horses Act 1784 (c.31)

Duties on Horses Act 1795 (cc.15, 16)

Duties on Horses Act 1797 (c.106)

Duties on Horses and Carriage Act 1789 (c.49)

Duties on Horses, etc. Act 1802 (c.100)

Duties on Horses Let for Hire Act 1853 (c.88)

Duties on Houses, etc. Act 1779 (c.59)

Duties on Houses, etc. Act 1786 (c.79)

Duties on Importation, etc. Act 1791 (c.42)

Duties on Income Act 1799 (c.13)

Duties on Income Act 1799 (c.22)

Duties on Income Act 1799 (c.42)

Duties on Income Act 1799 (c.72)

Duties on Income Act 1800 (c.49)

Duties on Income Act 1800 (c.96)

Duties on Kid Skins Act 1800 (c.63)

Duties on Killing Game Act 1814 (c.141)

Duties on Leather Act 1815 (c.102)

Duties on Linens Act 1784 (c.40)

Duties on Linens Act 1785 (c.72)

Duties on Madder Act 1816 (c.69)

Duties on Mahogany, etc. Act 1812 (c.36)

Duties on Malt Act 1803 (c.16)

Duties on Malt Act 1805 (c.1)

Duties on Malt Act 1806 (c.2)

Duties on Malt Act 1807 (c.3)

Duties on Malt, etc. Act 1780 (c.35)

Duties on Malt, etc. Act 1795 (c.1)

Duties on Malt, etc. Act 1796 (c.1)

Duties on Malt, etc. Act 1797 (c.4)

Duties on Malt, etc. Act 1801 (c.1)

Duties on Malt, etc. Act 1802 (c.3)

Duties on Malt, etc. Act 1805 (c.22)

Duties on Malt, etc. Act 1808 (c.2)

Duties on Malt, etc. Act 1809 (c.1)

Duties on Malt, etc. Act 1810 (c.1)

Duties on Malt, etc. Act 1811 (c.2)

Duties on Malt, etc. Act 1812 (c.1)

Duties on Malt, etc. Act 1812 (c.15)

Duties on Malt, etc. Act 1813 (c.2)

Duties on Malt, etc. Act 1814 (c.3)

Duties on Malt, etc. Act 1816 (c.3)

Duties on Malt, etc. Act 1816 (c.43)

Duties on Malt (Ireland) Act 1815 (c.99)

Duties on Norway Timber Act 1811 (c.93)

Duties on Offices and Pensions Act 1836 (c.97)

Duties on Paper Act 1805 (c.106)

Duties on Paper Act 1839 (c.23)

Duties on Paper (Ireland) Act 1815 (c.112)

Duties on Paper (Ireland) Act 1816 (c.78)

Duties on Pensions, etc. Act 1798 (c.3)

Duties on Pensions, etc. Act 1799 (c.3)

Duties on Pensions, etc. Act 1801 (c.2)

Duties on Pensions, etc. Act 1802 (c.4)

Duties on Pensions, etc. Act 1803 (c.17)

Duties on Pensions, etc. Act 1805 (c.2)

Duties on Pensions, etc. Act 1806 (c.3)

Duties on Pensions, etc. Act 1807 (c.4)

Duties on Plate Act 1797 (c.24)

Duties on Post Horses, etc. Act 1785 (c.51)

Duties on Property, etc. Act 1816 (c.65)

Duties on Property, etc. (Great Britain) Act 1815 (c.53)

Duties on Rape Seed, etc. Act 1816 (c.75)

Duties on Rape Seed, etc. Act 1816 (c.79)

Duties on Rum, etc. Act 1802 (c.20)

Duties on Rum, etc. Act 1841 (c.8)

Duties on Salt Act 1703 (c.16)

Duties on Salt Act 1795 (c.19)

Duties on Salt Act 1798 (c.43)

Duties on Salt, etc. Act 1706 (c.29)

Duties on Scotch Distilleries Act 1795 (c.59)

Duties on Servants Act 1780 (c.31)

Duties on Servants Act 1785 (c.43)

Duties on Servants Act 1785 (c.70)

Duties on Servants Act 1791 (c.3)

Duties on Servants Act 1797 (c.107)

Duties on Servants Act 1798 (c.80)

Duties on Servants, etc. Act 1797 (c.41)

Duties on Servants, etc. Act 1802 (c.37)

Duties on Shops Act 1785 (c.30)

Duties on Shops Act 1786 (c.9)

Duties on Shops Act 1789 (c.9)

Duties on Smalts, etc. Act 1783 (c.75)

Duties on Soap Act 1839 (c.63)

Duties on Soap Act 1840 (c.49)

Duties on Soap, etc. Act 1776 (c.52)

Duties on Spanish Red Wine Act 1805 (c.67)

Duties on Spirit Licences Act 1787 (c.30)

Duties on Spirit Mixtures, etc. Act 1842 (c.25)

Duties on Spirits Act 1784 (c.46)

Duties on Spirits Act 1795 (c.89)

Duties on Spirits Act 1799 (c.8)

Duties on Spirits Act 1808 (c.115)

Duties on Spirits Act 1808 (c.119)

Duties on Spirits Act 1811 (c.59)

Duties on Spirits Act 1843 (c.49)

Duties on Spirits Act 1845 (c.65)

Duties on Spirits Act 1848 (c.60)

Duties on Spirits and Coffee Act 1808 (cc.121, 122)

Duties on Spirits, etc. Act 1794 (cc.3, 4)

Duties on Spirits, etc. Act 1842 (c.15)

Duties on Spirits, etc. Act 1853 (c.37)

Duties on Spirits, etc. (Scotland) Act 1815 (c.155)

Duties on Spirits, etc. (Scotland) Act 1816 (c.106)

Duties on Spirits (Great Britain) Act 1813 (c.147)

Duties on Spirits (Ireland) Act 1806 (c.56)

Duties on Spirits (Ireland) Act 1806 (c.88)

Duties on Spirits (Ireland) Act 1807 (c.17)

Duties on Spirits (Ireland) Act 1808 (c.81)

Duties on Spirits (Ireland) Act 1809 (c.73)

Duties on Spirits (Ireland) Act 1810 (c.15)

Duties on Spirits (Ireland) Act 1812 (c.46)

Duties on Spirits (Ireland) Act 1812 (c.48)
Duties on Spirits (Ireland) Act 1814 (c.88)
Duties on Spirits (Ireland) Act 1815 (c.111)
Duties on Spirits (Ireland) Act 1816 (c.111)
Duties on Spirits (Scotland) Act 1814 (c.172)
Duties on Spirituous Liquors (Ireland) Act 1805 (c.104)
Duties on Starch Act 1779 (c.40)
Duties on Starch Act 1786 (c.51)
Duties on Starch and Soap Act 1784 (c.48)
Duties on Stills, etc. (Scotland) Act 1806 (c.102)
Duties on Stone Bottles Act 1812 (c.139)
Duties on Sugar Act 1813 (c.62)
Duties on Sugar Act 1845 (c.13)
Duties on Sugar Act 1865 (c.95)
Duties on Sugar Act 1867 (c.10)
Duties on Sugar, etc. Act 1799 (c.63)
Duties on Sugar, etc. Act 1800 (c.48)
Duties on Sugar, etc. Act 1802 (c.47)
Duties on Sweets, etc. (Ireland) Act 1815 (c.110)
Duties on Tea, etc. (American Plantations) Act 1766 (c.46)
Duties on Tobacco Act 1785 (c.81)
Duties on Tobacco Act 1811 (c.56)
Duties on Tobacco and Snuff Act 1789 (c.68)
Duties on Waggons, etc. Act 1783 (c.66)
Duties on Wagons, etc. Act 1792 (c.4)
Duties on Wash Made From Sugar Act 1800 (c.61)
Duties on Wheat, etc. Act 1843 (c.29)
Duties on Windows, etc. Act 1802 (c.34)
Duties on Wines, etc. Act 1783 (c.76)
Duties on Wines, etc. Act 1796 (c.123)
Duties on Worts or Wash Act 1808 (c.152)
Duties on Worts, Spirits, etc. Act 1791 (c.1)
Duties on Worts, Wash, etc. Act 1794 (c.2)
Duties upon Candles Act 1784 (c.11)
Duties upon East India Goods Act 1814 (c.10)
Duties upon Malt, etc. Act 1798 (c.2)
Duties upon Malt, etc. Act 1799 (c.2)
Duties upon Silks Act 1808 (c.117)
Duty of Spirits, Newfoundland Act 1812 (c.106)
Duty on Almanacks Act 1781 (c.56)
Duty on Coffee, etc., Warehoused Act 1807 (c.52)
Duty on Copper Act 1811 (c.31)
Duty on Corks Act 1816 (c.34)
Duty on Cotton Stuffs, etc. Act 1774 (c.72)
Duty on Foreign Spirits Act 1815 (c.164)
Duty on Hair Powder Act 1795 (c.49)
Duty on Hats Act 1796 (c.125)
Duty on Hats, etc., Repeal (Great Britain) Act 1811 (c.70)
Duty on Hawkers, etc. Act 1789 (c.26)
Duty on Hops Act 1805 (c.94)
Duty on Horses Act 1797 (c.134)
Duty on Horses Act 1801 (c.9)
Duty on Houses Act 1806 (c.36)
Duty on Lead (Great Britain) Act 1816 (c.18)
Duty on Linen Act 1811 (c.44)

Duty on Malt Act 1812 (c.9)
Duty on Malt (Ireland) Act 1804 (c.28)
Duty on Malt (Ireland) Act 1813 (c.74)
Duty on Malt (Ireland) Act 1816 (c.59)
Duty on Oil, etc. Act 1816 (c.118)
Duty on Paper Act 1816 (c.103)
Duty on Paper Hangings, etc. (Ireland) Act 1815 (c.106)
Duty on Pensions, etc. Act 1800 (c.8)
Duty on Pensions, etc. Act 1800 (c.31)
Duty on Racehorses Act 1856 (c.82)
Duty on Racehorses Act 1857 (c.16)
Duty on Rice Act 1812 (c.10)
Duty on Salt Act 1812 (c.107)
Duty on Salt Act 1813 (c.21)
Duty on Servants Act 1778 (c.30)
Duty on Silk Handkerchiefs Act 1815 (c.93)
Duty on Spanish Red Wines Act 1805 (c.107)
Duty on Spirits Act 1788 (c.4)
Duty on Spirits (Ireland) Act 1813 (c.94)
Duty on Spirits (Ireland) Act 1815 (c.139)
Duty on Stage Carriages Act 1839 (c.66)
Duty on Sugar Act 1809 (c.61)
Duty on Sugar, etc. Act 1810 (c.61)
Duty on Taxed Carts Act 1798 (c.93)
Duty on Tiles Act 1815 (c.176)
Duty on Tobacco Act 1794 (c.55)
Duty on Tobacco and Snuff Act 1790 (c.40)
Duty on Woollen Goods Act 1805 (c.82)
Duty on Worts, etc. Act 1801 (c.5)
Dwelling-houses for the Working Classes (Scotland) Act 1855 (c.88)
Dyeing Trade Act 1726 (c.24)
Dyeing Trade (Frauds) Act 1783 (c.15)
Dyers Act 1776 (c.33)
Dyestuffs (Import Regulations) Act 1920 (c.77)
Dyestuffs (Import Regulations) Act 1934 (c.6)
Dygart Beer Duties Act 1753 (c.44)

Ealing Church Act 1738 (c.7)
Ealing Roads Act 1767 (c.75)
Earl of Clanriccard's Estates Act 1708 (c.29)
Earldom of Mar Act 1885 (c.48)
East Africa Loans Act 1926 (c.62)
East Africa Loans (Amendment) Act 1931 (c.21)
East African Protectorates (Loans) Act 1914 (c.38)
East and West Flegg: Poor Relief Act 1775 (c.13)
East Greenwich Church: Burial Act 1751 (c.11)
East Grinstead Church Act 1790 (c.79)
East India Act 1797 (c.142)
East India Annuity Funds Act 1874 (c.12)
East India Company Act 1707 (c.71)
East India Company Act 1711 (c.35)
East India Company Act 1730 (c.14)
East India Company Act 1767 (c.49)
East India Company Act 1767 (c.57)
East India Company Act 1768 (c.11)

East India Company Act 1769 (c.24)
East India Company Act 1770 (c.47)
East India Company Act 1772 (c.7)
East India Company Act 1772 (c.9)
East India Company Act 1772 (c.63)
East India Company Act 1772 (c.64)
East India Company Act 1775 (c.44)
East India Company Act 1776 (c.8)
East India Company Act 1776 (c.51)
East India Company Act 1779 (c.61)
East India Company Act 1780 (c.56)
East India Company Act 1780 (c.58)
East India Company Act 1780 (c.70)
East India Company Act 1781 (c.65)
East India Company Act 1782 (c.51)
East India Company Act 1783 (c.2)
East India Company Act 1783 (c.3)
East India Company Act 1783 (c.36)
East India Company Act 1783 (c.83)
East India Company Act 1784 (c.25)
East India Company Act 1784 (c.34)
East India Company Act 1786 (c.16)
East India Company Act 1786 (c.57)
East India Company Act 1788 (c.8)
East India Company Act 1788 (c.29)
East India Company Act 1793 (c.52)
East India Company Act 1796 (c.120)
East India Company Act 1797 (c.31)
East India Company Act 1797 (c.74)
East India Company Act 1799 (c.89)
East India Company Act 1803 (c.48)
East India Company Act 1803 (c.63)
East India Company Act 1803 (c.137)
East India Company Act 1806 (c.85)
East India Company Act 1807 (c.41)
East India Company Act 1810 (c.86)
East India Company Act 1811 (c.75)
East India Company Act 1812 (c.10)
East India Company Act 1812 (c.135)
East India Company Act 1813 (c.155)
East India Company Act 1815 (c.64)
East India Company Bonds Act 1811 (c.64)
East India Company (Money) Act 1794 (c.41)
East India Company Stock Act 1786 (c.62)
East India Company Stock Act 1789 (c.65)
East India Company (Stock) Act 1791 (c.11)
East India Company (Stock) Act 1793 (c.47)
East India Company, Warehouses Act 1787 (c.48)
East India Company's Officers Superannuation Act 1897 (c.10)
East India Contracts Act 1870 (c.59)
East India Irrigation and Canal Act 1869 (c.7)
East India Unclaimed Stock Act 1885 (c.25)
East India Loan Act 1859 (c.11)
East India Loan Act 1860 (c.130)
East India Loan Act 1861 (c.25)
East India Loan Act 1861 (c.118)
East India Loan Act 1869 (c.106)
East India Loan Act 1873 (c.32)
East India Loan Act 1874 (c.3)
East India Loan Act 1877 (c.51)
East India Loan Act 1879 (c.60)

East India Loan Act 1885 (c.28)
East India Loan Act 1893 (c.70)
East India Loan Act 1898 (c.13)
East India Loan (East Indian Railway Debentures) Act 1880 (c.10)
East India Loan (Great Indian Peninsular Railway Debentures) Act 1901 (c.25)
East India Loan (No. 2) Act 1859 (c.39)
East India Loans Act 1858 (c.3)
East India Loans Act 1908 (c.54)
East India Loans Act 1923 (c.31)
East India Loans Act 1937 (c.14)
East India Loans (Railway and Irrigation) Act 1922 (c.9)
East India Loans (Railways) Act 1905 (c.19)
East India Loans (Railways and Irrigation) Act 1910 (c.5)
East India Merchants: Land for Warehouses etc. Act 1796 (c.127)
East India Merchants: Purchase of Land in City, etc. Act 1796 (c.119)
East India Prize Goods Act 1804 (c.72)
East India Stock Act 1860 (c.102)
East India Stock Dividend Redemption Act 1873 (c.17)
East India Trade Act 1774 (c.34)
East India Trade Act 1813 (c.34)
East India Trade Act 1813 (c.35)
East India Trade Act 1840 (c.56)
East India Trade, etc. Act 1814 (c.134)
East India Unclaimed Stock Act 1885 (c.25)
East Indian Loan (Annuities) Act 1879 (c.61)
East Indian Railway (Redemption of Annuities) Act 1879 (c.43)
East Indian Railway (Redemption of Annuities) Act 1881 (c.53)
East Indies Act 1791 (c.40)
East Kent: Drainage Act 1776 (c.62)
East Stonehouse Chapel Act 1787 (c.17)
East Tarbet Harbour Act 1707 (c.79(b))
Easter Act 1928 (c.35)
Eccles, Appointments Suspension Act 1836 (c.67)
Ecclesiastical Appointments Suspension Act 1838 (c.108)
Ecclesiastical Assessments (Scotland) Act 1900 (c.20)
Ecclesiastical Buildings and Glebes (Scotland) Act 1868 (c.96)
Ecclesiastical Commissioners Act 1836 (c.77)
Ecclesiastical Commissioners Act 1840 (c.113)
Ecclesiastical Commissioners Act 1840, Amendment 1885 (c.55)
Ecclesiastical Commissioners Act 1841 (c.39)
Ecclesiastical Commissioners Act 1847 (c.108)
Ecclesiastical Commissioners Act 1850 (c.94)
Ecclesiastical Commissioners Act 1860 (c.124)

Ecclesiastical Commissioners Act 1866 (c.111)

Ecclesiastical Commissioners Act 1868 (c.114)

Ecclesiastical Commissioners Act 1873 (c.64)

Ecclesiastical Commissioners Act 1875 (c.71)

Ecclesiastical Commissioners Act 1885 (c.31)

Ecclesiastical Commissioners (Exchange of Patronage) Act 1853 (c.50)

Ecclesiastical Commissioners (Superannuation) Act 1865 (c.68)

Ecclesiastical Commissioners (Takenhill Rectory) Act 1885 (c.31)

Ecclesiastical Courts Act 1813 (c.127)

Ecclesiastical Courts Act 1840 (c.93)

Ecclesiastical Courts Act 1844 (c.68)

Ecclesiastical Courts Act 1854 (c.47)

Ecclesiastical Courts Act 1855 (c.41)

Ecclesiastical Courts and Registries (Ireland) Act 1864 (c.54)

Ecclesiastical Courts Jurisdiction Act 1860 (c.32)

Ecclesiastical Dilapidations Act 1871 (c.43)

Ecclesiastical Dilapidations Act 1872 (c.96)

Ecclesiastical Districts in Forest of Dean Act 1842 (c.65)

Ecclesiastical Fees Act 1867 (c.135)

Ecclesiastical Fees Act 1875 (c.76)

Ecclesiastical Houses of Residence Act 1842 (c.26)

Ecclesiastical Jurisdiction Act 1842 (c.58)

Ecclesiastical Jurisdiction Act 1843 (c.60)

Ecclesiastical Jurisdiction Act 1847 (c.98)

Ecclesiastical Jurisdiction Act 1848 (c.67)

Ecclesiastical Jurisdiction Act 1849 (c.39)

Ecclesiastical Jurisdiction Act 1850 (c.47)

Ecclesiastical Jurisdiction Act 1851 (c.29)

Ecclesiastical Jurisdiction Act 1852 (c.17)

Ecclesiastical Jurisdiction Act 1853 (c.108)

Ecclesiastical Jurisdiction Act 1854 (c.65)

Ecclesiastical Jurisdiction Act 1855 (c.75)

Ecclesiastical Jurisdiction Act 1857 (c.10)

Ecclesiastical Jurisdiction Act 1858 (c.50)

Ecclesiastical Jurisdiction Act 1859 (c.45)

Ecclesiastical Leases Act 1800 (c.41)

Ecclesiastical Leases Act 1836 (c.20)

Ecclesiastical Leases Act 1842 (c.27)

Ecclesiastical Leases Act 1861 (c.104)

Ecclesiastical Leases Act 1862 (c.52)

Ecclesiastical Leases Act 1865 (c.57)

Ecclesiastical Leases Act 1765 (c.17)

Ecclesiastical Leases (Amendment) Act 1836 (c.64)

Ecclesiastical Leases (Isle of Man) Act 1866 (c.81)

Ecclesiastical Leasing Act 1842 (c.108)

Ecclesiastical Leasing Act 1858 (c.57)

Ecclesiastical Patronage (Ireland) Act 1845 (c.51)

Ecclesiastical Patronage (Ireland) Act 1848 (c.78)

Ecclesiastical Patronage (Ireland) Act 1848 (c.67)

Ecclesiastical Preferments (England) Act 1839 (c.55)

Ecclesiastical Proctors (Ireland) Act 1814 (c.68)

Ecclesiastical Property (Ireland) Act 1855 (c.28)

Ecclesiastical Property Valuation (Ireland) Act 1851 (c.74)

Ecclesiastical Services (Omission of Account on War) Act 1917 (c.5)

Ecclesiastical Suits Act 1787 (c.44)

Ecclesiastical Tithe Rentcharges (Rates) Act 1922 (c.58)

Ecclesiastical Titles Act 1851 (c.60)

Ecclesiastical Titles Act 1871 (c.53)

Ecclesiastical Unions, etc. (Ireland) Act 1848 (c.41)

Economy (Miscellaneous Provisions) Act 1926 (c.9)

Eddystone Lighthouse Act 1705 (c.7)

Eddystone Lighthouse Act 1709 (c.17)

Eden River, Cumberland (Temporary Tolls for Improvement) Act 1721 (c.14)

Edinburgh and Glasgow Roads Act 1757 (c.55)

Edinburgh and Leith Road Act 1750 (c.35)

Edinburgh and Linlithgow Roads Act 1764 (c.86)

Edinburgh Beer Duties Act 1716 (c.5)

Edinburgh Beer Duties Act 1722 (c.14)

Edinburgh Beer Duties Act 1727 (c.22)

Edinburgh Beer Duties Act 1751 (c.9)

Edinburgh Bridewell Act 1791 (c.57)

Edinburgh Bridges and Highways Act 1713 (c.30)

Edinburgh Buildings Act 1753 (c.36)

Edinburgh College of Surgeons Act 1787 (c.65)

Edinburgh Debt Act 1844 (c.20)

Edinburgh, etc., Roads Act 1795 (c.150)

Edinburgh General Register House Act 1896 (c.24)

Edinburgh: Improvement Act 1772 (c.15)

Edinburgh: Improvement Act 1786 (c.113)

Edinburgh: Improvement Act 1787 (c.51)

Edinburgh: Improvements Act 1766 (c.27)

Edinburgh, Linlithgow and Lanark Roads, etc. Act 1792 (c.120)

Edinburgh Roads Act 1755 (c.39)

Edinburgh Roads Act 1783 (c.18)

Edinburgh Roads Act 1789 (c.105)

Edinburgh (Slaughter of Animals) Act 1782 (c.52)

Edinburgh: Streets Act 1771 (c.36)

Edinburgh: Streets Act 1785 (c.28)

Edinburgh University Property Arrangement Act 1861 (c.90)

Edinburgh University (Transfer of Patronage) Act 1897 (c.13)

Edinburgh Water Act 1756 (c.74)

Edington, Somerset Drainage, etc. Act 1790 (c.58)

Education Act 1901 (c.11)
Education Act 1901 (Renewal) 1902 (c.19)
Education Act 1902 (c.42)
Education Act 1918 (c.39)
Education Act 1921 (c.51)
Education Act 1936 (c.41)
Education Act 1944 (c.31)
Education Act 1946 (c.50)
Education Act 1959 (c.60)
Education Act 1962 (c.12)
Education Act 1964 (c.82)
Education Act 1967 (c.3)
Education Act 1968 (c.17)
Education Act 1973 (c.16)
Education Act 1975 (c.2)
Education Act 1976 (c.81)
Education Act 1979 (c.49)
Education Act 1980 (c.20)
Education Act 1981 (c.60)
Education Act 1986 (c.40)
Education Act 1993 (c.35)
Education Act 1994 (c.30)
Education Act 1996 (c.56)
Education Act 1997 (c.44)
Education (Administrative Provisions) Act 1907 (c.43)
Education (Administrative Provisions) Act 1909 (c.29)
Education (Administrative Provisions) Act 1911 (c.32)
Education (Amendment) Act 1986 (c.1)
Education (Amendment) (Scotland) Act 1984 (c.6)
Education and Local Taxation Account (Scotland) Act 1892 (c.51)
Education (Choice of Employment) Act 1910 (c.37)
Education Code (1890) (c.22)
Education (Compliance with Conditions of Grants) Act 1919 (c.41)
Education (Deaf Children) Act 1937 (c.25)
Education Department Act 1856 (c.116)
Education (Emergency) Act 1939 (c.111)
Education (Emergency) (Scotland) Act 1939 (c.112)
Education Endowments (Scotland) Act 1931 (c.5)
Education (Exemptions) (Scotland) Act 1947 (c.36)
Education (Fees and Awards) Act 1983 (c.40)
Education (Grants and Awards) Act 1984 (c.11)
Education (Handicapped Children) Act 1970 (c.52)
Education (Institution Children) Act 1923 (c.38)
Education (Ireland) Act 1806 (c.122)
Education (Local Authorities) Act 1931 (c.6)
Education (Local Authority Default) Act 1904 (c.18)
Education (London) Act 1903 (c.24)
Education (Mentally Handicapped Children) (Scotland) Act 1974 (c.27)

Education (Milk) Act 1971 (c.74)
Education (Miscellaneous Provisions) Act 1948 (c.40)
Education (Miscellaneous Provisions) Act 1953 (c.33)
Education (Necessity of Schools) Act 1933 (c.29)
Education (Northern Ireland) Act 1978 (c.13)
Education (No. 2) Act 1968 (c.37)
Education (No. 2) Act 1986 (c.61)
Education of Blind and Deaf Children (Scotland) Act 1890 (c.43)
Education of Defective Children (Scotland) Act 1906 (c.10)
Education of Pauper Children Act 1855 (c.34)
Education (Provision of Meals) Act 1906 (c.57)
Education (Provision of Meals) Act 1914 (c.20)
Education (Provision of Meals) (Ireland) Act 1914 (c.35)
Education (Provision of Meals) (Ireland) Act 1916 (c.10)
Education (Provision of Meals) (Ireland) Act 1917 (c.53)
Education (Provision of the Working Balances) Act 1903 (c.10)
Education Reform Act 1988 (c.40)
Education (School-Leaving Dates) Act 1976 (c.5)
Education (School Milk) Act 1970 (c.14)
Education (Schools) Act 1992 (c.38)
Education (Schools) Act 1997 (c.59)
Education (Scotland) Act 1872 (c.62)
Education (Scotland) Act 1878 (c.78)
Education (Scotland) Act 1883 (c.56)
Education (Scotland) Act 1897 (c.62)
Education (Scotland) Act 1901 (c.9)
Education (Scotland) Act 1908 (c.63)
Education (Scotland) Act 1913 (c.12)
Education (Scotland) Act 1918 (c.48)
Education (Scotland) Act 1925 (c.89)
Education (Scotland) Act 1928 (c.28)
Education (Scotland) Act 1930 (c.36)
Education (Scotland) Act 1936 (c.42)
Education (Scotland) Act 1942 (c.5)
Education (Scotland) Act 1944 (c.37)
Education (Scotland) Act 1945 (c.37)
Education (Scotland) Act 1946 (c.72)
Education (Scotland) Act 1949 (c.19)
Education (Scotland) Act 1956 (c.75)
Education (Scotland) Act 1962 (c.47)
Education (Scotland) Act 1963 (c.21)
Education (Scotland) Act 1965 (c.7)
Education (Scotland) Act 1969 (c.49)
Education (Scotland) Act 1971 (c.42)
Education (Scotland) Act 1973 (c.59)
Education (Scotland) Act 1976 (c.20)
Education (Scotland) Act 1980 (c.44)
Education (Scotland) Act 1981 (c.58)
Education (Scotland) Act 1996 (c.43)
Education (Scotland) (Glasgow Electoral Division) Act 1913 (c.13)

Education (Scotland) (Provision of Meals) Act 1914 (c.68)

Education (Scotland) (Superannuation) Act 1919 (c.17)

Education (Scotland) (Superannuation) Act 1922 (c.48)

Education (Scotland) (Superannuation) Act 1924 (c.13)

Education (Scotland) (Superannuation) Act 1925 (c.55)

Education (Scotland) (War Service Superannuation) Act 1914 (c.67)

Education (Scotland) (War Service Superannuation) Act 1939 (c.96)

Education (Small Population Grants) Act 1915 (c.95)

Education (Student Loans) Act 1990 (c.6)

Education (Student Loans) Act 1996 (c.9)

Education (Work Experience) Act 1973 (c.23)

Educational Endowments (Ireland) Act 1885 (c.78)

Educational Endowments (Scotland) Act 1882 (c.59)

Educational Endowments (Scotland) Act 1928 (c.30)

Educational Endowments (Scotland) Act 1935 (c.5)

Edw. Whitaker, Public Accountant Act 1702 (c.16)

Effects of Residents in France Act 1794 (c.79)

Egham and Bagshot Roads Act 1727 (c.6)

Egham and Bagshot Road Act 1738 (c.16)

Egham and Bagshot Road Act 1763 (c.47)

Egyptian Loan Act 1885 (c.11)

Egyptians Act 1783 (c.51)

Eire (Confirmation of Agreements) Act 1938 (c.25)

Eisteddfod Act 1959 (c.32)

Ejectment and Distress (Ireland) Act 1846 (c.111)

Elders Widows' Fund (India) Act 1878 (c.47)

Elected Authorities (Northern Ireland) Act 1989 (c.3)

Election Commissioners Act 1852 (c.57)

Election Commissioners Act 1949 (c.90)

Election Commissioners Expenses Act 1871 (c.61)

Election (Hours of Poll) Act 1884 (c.34)

Election in the Recess Act 1863 (c.20)

Election (Ireland) Act 1862 (c.92)

Election of Members During Recess Act 1858 (c.110)

Election of Members for Cheshire Act 1846 (c.44)

Election of Representative Peers (Ireland) Act 1882 (c.26)

Election Petitions Act 1794 (c.83)

Election Petitions Act 1839 (c.38)

Election Petitions Act 1848 (c.98)

Election Petitions Act 1865 (c.8)

Election Recognizances Act 1848 (c.18)

Elections and Jurors Act 1945 (c.21)

Elections and Registration Act 1915 (c.76)

Elections (Fraudulent Conveyance) Act 1711 (c.31)

Elections (Hours of Poll) Act 1885 (c.10)

Elections in Recess Act 1863 (c.20)

Elections (Northern Ireland) Act 1985 (c.2)

Elections (Scotland) (Corrupt and Illegal Practices) Act 1890 (c.55)

Elections (Welsh Forms) Act 1964 (c.31)

Electoral Disabilities (Military Service) Removal Act 1900 (c.8)

Electoral Disabilities (Naval and Military Service) Removal Act 1914 (c.25)

Electoral Disabilities Removal Act 1891 (c.11)

Electoral Registers Act 1949 (c.86)

Electoral Registers Act 1953 (c.8)

Electric Lighting Act 1882 (c.56)

Electric Lighting Act 1888 (c.12)

Electric Lighting Act 1909 (c.34)

Electric Lighting (Clauses) Act 1899 (c.19)

Electric Lighting (Scotland) Act 1890 (c.13)

Electric Lighting (Scotland) Act 1902 (c.35)

Electricity Act 1947 (c.54)

Electricity Act 1957 (c.48)

Electricity Act 1972 (c.17)

Electricity Act 1989 (c.29)

Electricity (Amendment) Act 1961 (c.8)

Electricity and Gas Act 1963 (c.59)

Electricity (Borrowing Powers) Act 1959 (c.20)

Electricity (Borrowing Powers) (Scotland) Act 1962 (c.7)

Electricity (Financial Provisions) Act 1982 (c.56)

Electricity (Financial Provisions) (Scotland) Act 1976 (c.61)

Electricity (Financial Provisions) (Scotland) Act 1982 (c.56)

Electricity (Financial Provisions) (Scotland) Act 1988 (c.37)

Electricity Reorganisation (Scotland) Act 1954 (c.60)

Electricity (Scotland) Act 1969 (c.1)

Electricity (Scotland) Act 1979 (c.11)

Electricity (Supply) Act 1919 (c.100)

Electricity (Supply) Act 1922 (c.46)

Electricity (Supply) Act 1926 (c.51)

Electricity (Supply) Act 1928 (c.4)

Electricity (Supply) Act 1933 (c.46)

Electricity Supply Act 1935 (c.3)

Electricity Supply (Meters) Act 1936 (c.20)

Electricity Supply (Meters) Act 1952 (c.32)

Elementary Education Act 1870 (c.75)

Elementary Education Act 1873 (c.86)

Elementary Education Act 1876 (c.79)

Elementary Education Act 1880 (c.23)

Elementary Education Act 1891 (c.56)

Elementary Education Act 1897 (c.16)

Elementary Education Act 1900 (c.53)

Elementary Education Act Amendment Act 1872 (c.27)

Elementary Education Amendment Act 1903 (c.13)

Elementary Education (Blind and Deaf Children) Act 1893 (c.42)
Elementary Education (Defective and Epileptic Children) Act 1899 (c.32)
Elementary Education (Defective and Epileptic Children) Act 1914 (c.45)
Elementary Education (Election) Act 1871 (c.94)
Elementary Education (Elections) Act 1872 (c.59)
Elementary Education (Fee Grant) Act 1916 (c.35)
Elementary Education (Industrial Schools) Act 1879 (c.48)
Elementary Education (Orders) Act 1874 (c.90)
Elementary Education (School Attendance) Act 1893 (c.51)
Elementary Education (School Attendance) Act (1893) Amendment 1899 (c.13)
Elementary Education (Wenlock) Act 1874 (c.39)
Elementary School Teachers (Superannuation) Act 1898 (c.57)
Elementary School Teachers (Superannuation) Act 1912 (c.12)
Elementary School Teachers Superannuation (Isle of Man) Act 1900 (c.38)
Elementary School Teachers Superannuation (Jersey) Act 1900 (c.40)
Elementary School Teachers (War Service Superannuation) Act 1914 (c.66)
Elgin Beer Duties Act 1721 (c.7)
Elizabeth Taylor's Patent Act 1776 (c.18)
Elland and Leeds Road Act 1753 (c.61)
Elland to Leeds Road Act 1777 (c.87)
Elland to Leeds Road Act 1795 (c.159)
Elland to Leeds Road Act 1740 (c.25)
Ellesmere and Chester Canal Act 1793 (c.91)
Ellesmere and Chester Canal Act 1796 (c.71)
Ellesmere and Chester Canal Act 1796 (c.96)
Ellesmere, Salop: Poor Relief Act 1791 (c.78)
Elloe, Lincoln: Small Debts Act 1775 (c.64)
Elver Fishing Act 1876 (c.34)
Ely Roads Act 1740 (c.14)
Embezzlement Act 1799 Act (c.85)
Embezzlement Act 1814 (c.60)
Embezzlement by Bankers, etc. Act 1812 (c.63)
Embezzlement by Collectors Act 1810 (c.59)
Embezzlement (Ireland) Act 1811 (c.38)
Embezzlement of Naval, etc., Stores Act 1812 (c.12)
Embezzlement of Public Stores Act 1800 (c.89)
Embezzlement of Public Stores Act (c.126)
Embezzlement of Public Stores Act 1815 (c.127)
Emergency Laws (Miscellaneous Provisions) Act 1947 (c.10)
Emergency Laws (Miscellaneous Provisions) Act 1953 (c.47)
Emergency Laws (Re-enactments and Repeals) Act 1964 (c.60)

Emergency Laws (Repeal) Act 1959 (c.19)
Emergency Laws (Transitional Provisions) Act 1946 (c.26)
Emergency Powers Act 1920 (c.55)
Emergency Powers Act 1964 (c.38)
Emergency Powers (Defence) Act 1939 (c.20)
Emergency Powers (Defence) Act 1939 (c.62)
Emergency Powers (Defence) Act 1944 (c.31)
Emergency Powers (Defence) (No. 2) Act 1939 (c.45)
Emergency Powers (Isle of Man—Defence) Act 1943 (c.36)
Emigration from Scotland Act 1851 (c.91)
Empire Settlement Act 1922 (c.13)
Empire Settlement Act 1937 (c.18)
Empire Settlement Act 1952 (c.26)
Employers and Workmen Act 1875 (c.90)
Employers' Liability Act 1880 (c.42)
Employers' Liability Act 1888 (c.58)
Employers' Liability (Compulsory Insurance) Act 1969 (c.57)
Employers' Liability (Defective Equipment) Act 1969 (c.37)
Employers' Liability Insurance Companies Act 1907 (c.46)
Employment Act 1980 (c.42)
Employment Act 1982 (c.46)
Employment Act 1988 (c.19)
Employment Act 1989 (c.38)
Employment Act 1990 (c.38)
Employment Agencies Act 1973 (c.35)
Employment and Training Act 1948 (c.46)
Employment and Training Act 1973 (c.50)
Employment and Training Act 1981 (c.57)
Employment (Continental Shelf) Act 1978 (c.46)
Employment Medical Advisory Service Act 1972 (c.28)
Employment of Children Act 1903 (c.45)
Employment of Children Act 1973 (c.24)
Employment of Poor Act 1847 (c.87)
Employment of Poor, etc. (I.) Act 1847 (c.80)
Employment of Women Act 1907 (c.10)
Employment of Women and Young Persons Act 1936 (c.24)
Employment of Women, Young Persons and Children Act 1920 (c.65)
Employment Protection Act 1975 (c.71)
Employment Protection (Consolidation) Act 1978 (c.44)
Employment Rights Act 1996 (c.18)
Employment Subsidies Act 1978 (c.6)
Encouragement of Manufacturers Act 1723 (c.11)
Encouragement of Seamen, etc. Act 1803 (c.160)
Endangered Species (Import and Export) Act 1976 (c.72)
Endowed Institutions (Scotland) Act 1869 (c.39)

Endowed Institutions (Scotland) Act 1878 (c.48)

Endowed School Acts Continuance 1879 (c.66)

Endowed Schools Act 1813 (c.107)

Endowed Schools Act 1860 (c.11)

Endowed Schools Act 1869 (c.56)

Endowed Schools Act 1868 (c.32)

Endowed Schools Act 1869 (c.56)

Endowed Schools Act 1873 (c.87)

Endowed Schools Act 1874 (c.87)

Endowed Schools Inquiries (Ireland) Act 1855 (c.59)

Endowed Schools (Ireland) Act 1813 (c.107)

Endowed Schools (Masters) Act 1908 (c.39)

Endowed Schools (Time of Address) Act 1873 (c.7)

Endowed Schools (Vested Interests) Act Continued 1875 (c.29)

Enduring Power of Attorney Act 1985 (c.29)

Enemy Property Act 1953 (c.52)

Energy Act 1976 (c.76)

Energy Act 1983 (c.25)

Energy Conservation Act 1981 (c.17)

Energy Conservation Act 1996 (c.38)

Enfranchisement of Copyholds Act 1841 (c.35)

English Industrial Estates Corporation Act 1981 (c.13)

Engraving Copyright Act 1734 (c.13)

Engraving Copyright Act 1766 (c.38)

Enlargement of Time for First Meetings Act 1757 (c.34)

Enlargement of Time for First Meetings Act 1759 (c.14)

Enlargement of Times for Executing Acts Act 1757 (c.37)

Enlargement of Times for Executing Acts Act 1765 (c.15)

Enlistment Act 1794 (c.43)

Enlistment of Foreigners Act 1804 (c.75)

Enlistment of Foreigners Act 1806 (c.23)

Enlistment of Foreigners Act 1815 (c.85)

Enlistment of Foreigners Act 1837 (c.29)

Enlistment of Foreigners Act 1855 (c.2)

Enlistment of Persons Transferred from the Indian Forces Act 1861 (c.74)

Enlistment in Foreign Service Act 1713 (c.10)

Entail Act 1838 (c.70)

Entail Amendment Act 1848 (c.36)

Entail Amendment Act 1853 (c.94)

Entail Amendment (Scotland) Act 1868 (c.84)

Entail Amendment (Scotland) Act 1875 (c.61)

Entail Amendment (Scotland) Act 1878 (c.28)

Entail Cottages Act 1860 (c.95)

Entail Improvement Act 1770 (c.51)

Entail Powers Act 1836 (c.42)

Entail (Scotland) Act 1882 (c.53)

Entail (Scotland) Act 1914 (c.43)

Entail Sites Act 1840 (c.48)

Entailed Estates Act 1800 (c.56)

Entailed Lands, etc. (Scotland) Act 1841 (c.24)

Enterprise and New Towns (Scotland) Act 1990 (c.35)

Entertainments Duty Act 1958 (c.9)

Entertainments (Increased Penalties) Act 1990 (c.20)

Environment Act 1995 (c.25)

Environment and Safety Information Act 1988 (c.30)

Environmental Protection Act 1990 (c.43)

Epidemic and Other Diseases Prevention Act 1883 (c.59)

Episcopal and Capitular Estates Act 1851 (c.104)

Episcopal and Capitular Estates Act 1854 (c.116)

Episcopal and Capitular Estates Act 1857 (c.74)

Episcopal and Capitular Estates Act 1859 (c.46)

Episcopal Church (Scotland) Act 1864 (c.94)

Episcopal Church (Scotland) Act 1964 (c.12)

Episcopal, etc., Estates Management Act 1856 (c.74)

Episcopal Jurisdiction (England) Act 1839 (c.9)

Episcopal Meeting Houses (Scotland) Act 1745 (c.38)

Epping and Ongar Road Act 1742 (c.19)

Epping and Ongar Road Act 1769 (c.63)

Epping Forest Act 1871 (c.93)

Epping Forest Act 1873 (c.5)

Epping Forest Act 1875 (c.6)

Epping Forest Act 1876 (c.3)

Epping Forest Act Amendment 1872 (c.95)

Equal Pay Act 1970 (c.41)

Equity Procedure Act 1731 (c.25)

Equivalent Act 1714 (c.27)

Equivalent Act 1716 (c.14)

Equivalent Company Act 1850 (c.63)

Equivalent Money Act 1707 (c.51)

Equivalent Money Act 1713 (c.12)

Erasures in Deeds (Scotland) Act 1836 (c.33)

Erection of Cottages Act 1775 (c.32)

Erection of Lighthouses Act 1786 (c.101)

Erection of Lighthouses Act 1788 (c.25)

Erection of Lighthouses Act 1789 (c.52)

Erewash Canal Act 1777 (c.69)

Erewash Canal Act 1790 (c.56)

Erskine Bridge Tolls Act 1968 (c.4)

Escape of Debtors from Prison Act 1702 (c.6)

Escheat (Procedure) Act 1887 (c.53)

Escrick Church, Yorks Act 1781 (c.76)

Essential Buildings and Plant (Repair of War Damage) Act 1939 (c.74)

Essential Commodities Reserves Act 1938 (c.51)

Essex and Hertfordshire Roads Act 1743 (c.9)

Essex and Hertfordshire Roads Act 1769 (c.51)

Essex and Hertfordshire Roads Act 1791 (c.99)

Essex Roads Act 1702 (c.10)

Essex Roads Act 1723 (c.9)
Essex Roads Act 1725 (c.23)
Essex Roads Act 1746 (c.7)
Essex Roads Act 1763 (c.58)
Essex Roads Act 1787 (c.69)
Essex Roads Act 1793 (c.145)
Essex Roads Act 1793 (c.149)
Essex Shire House Act 1789 (c.8)
Essex, Suffolk and Hertford Roads Act 1765 (c.60)
Established Church Act 1713 (c.7)
Estate Agents Act 1979 (c.38)
Estate of Benjamin Hopkins Act 1795 (c.103)
Estate of Hugh Naish Act 1737 (c.38)
Estates Held for the Barrack Service Act 1805 (c.69)
Estates of Duke of Wellington Act 1839 (c.4)
Estates of Grenada and St. Vincent Traders Act 1806 (c.157)
Estates of Grenada and St. Vincent Traders Act 1806 (c.158)
Estates of Intestates, etc. Act 1852 (c.3)
Estates of Lunatics Act 1803 (c.75)
Estates Vest in Heirs, etc., of Mortgages Act 1838 (c.69)
Estreats Act 1716 (c.15)
European Assembly Elections Act 1978 (c.10)
European Assembly Elections Act 1981 (c.8)
European Assembly (Pay and Pensions) Act 1979 (c.50)
European Coal and Steel Community Act 1955 (c.4)
European Communities Act 1972 (c.68)
European Communities (Amendment) Act 1986 (c.58)
European Communities (Amendment) Act 1993 (c.32)
European Communities (Finance) Act 1985 (c.64)
European Communities (Finance) Act 1988 (c.46)
European Communities (Finance) Act 1995 (c.1)
European Communities (Greek Accession) Act 1979 (c.57)
European Communities (Spanish and Portuguese Accession) Act 1985 (c.75)
European Economic Area Act 1993 (c.51)
European Forces (India) Act 1860 (c.100)
European Free Trade Association Act 1960 (c.19)
European Monetary Agreement Act 1959 (c.11)
European Parliamentary Elections Act 1993 (c.41)
European Payments Union (Financial Provisions) Act 1950 (c.8)
European Troops in India Act 1859 (c.27)
European Union (Accessions) Act 1994 (c.38)
Everton, etc. (Nottinghamshire): Drainage, etc. Act 1796 (c.99)

Evesham Roads Act 1727 (c.11)
Evesham Roads Act 1778 (c.93)
Evesham Roads Act 1789 (c.103)
Evicted Tenants (Ireland) Act 1907 (c.56)
Evicted Tenants (Ireland) Act 1908 (c.22)
Eviction (Ireland) Act 1848 (c.47)
Evidence Act 1791 (c.35)
Evidence Act 1840 (c.26)
Evidence Act 1843 (c.85)
Evidence Act 1845 (c.113)
Evidence Act 1851 (c.99)
Evidence Act 1870 (c.49)
Evidence Act 1877 (c.14)
Evidence Act 1938 (c.28)
Evidence (Amendment) Act 1853 (c.83)
Evidence (Amendment) Act 1915 (c.94)
Evidence and Powers of Attorney Act 1940 (c.28)
Evidence and Powers of Attorney Act 1943 (c.18)
Evidence by Commission Act 1843 (c.82)
Evidence by Commission Act 1859 (c.20)
Evidence by Commission Act 1885 (c.74)
Evidence (Colonial Statutes) Act 1907 (c.16)
Evidence (Foreign, Dominion and Colonial Documents) Act 1933 (c.4)
Evidence Further Amendment Act 1869 (c.68)
Evidence Further Amendment Act 1874 (c.64)
Evidence Ireland Act 1815 (c.157)
Evidence (Proceedings in Other Jurisdictions) Act 1975 (c.34)
Evidence (Scotland) Act 1840 (c.59)
Evidence (Scotland) Act 1852 (c.27)
Evidence (Scotland) Act 1853 (c.20)
Evidence (Scotland) Act 1866 (c.112)
Examination of Drugs Act 1723 (c.20)
Excessive Loading of Vehicles, London and Westminster Act 1719 (c.6)
Exchange Control Act 1947 (c.14)
Exchange, Crown and Eton College Act 1842 (c.78)
Exchange Equalisation Account Act 1933 (c.18)
Exchange Equalisation Account Act 1937 (c.41)
Exchange Equalisation Account Act 1979 (c.30)
Exchange of American Prisoners Act 1782 (c.10)
Exchange of Crown Advowsons Act 1848 (c.57)
Exchange of Crown Lands in Perthshire Act 1766 (c.33)
Exchange of Ecclesiastical Patronage Act 1859 (c.9)
Exchequer Act 1728 (c.6)
Exchequer and Audit Departments Act 1866 (c.39)
Exchequer and Audit Departments Act 1921 (c.52)
Exchequer and Audit Departments Act 1950 (c.3)

Exchequer and Audit Departments Act 1957 (c.45)
Exchequer and Audit Departments (Temporary Provisions) Act 1939 (c.101)
Exchequer and Treasury Bills Act 1885 (c.44)
Exchequer Bills Act 1700 (c.1)
Exchequer Bills Act 1786 (c.97)
Exchequer Bills Act 1787 (c.23)
Exchequer Bills Act 1793 (c.29)
Exchequer Bills Act 1796 (cc.29, 30)
Exchequer Bills Act 1798 (c.91)
Exchequer Bills Act 1799 (c.6)
Exchequer Bills Act 1800 (c.33)
Exchequer Bills Act 1800 (c.109)
Exchequer Bills Act 1802 (c.41)
Exchequer Bills Act 1803 (c.60)
Exchequer Bills Act 1803 (c.148)
Exchequer Bills Act 1804 (c.73)
Exchequer Bills Act 1805 (c.27)
Exchequer Bills Act 1806 (c.93)
Exchequer Bills Act 1807 (c.28)
Exchequer Bills Act 1808 (c.7)
Exchequer Bills Act 1808 (cc.53, 54)
Exchequer Bills Act 1808 (c.97)
Exchequer Bills Act 1808 (c.114)
Exchequer Bills Act 1809 (cc.2, 3)
Exchequer Bills Act 1809 (c.52)
Exchequer Bills Act 1809 (c.93)
Exchequer Bills Act 1809 (c.114)
Exchequer Bills Act 1810 (cc.2, 3)
Exchequer Bills Act 1810 (cc.69, 70)
Exchequer Bills Act 1810 (cc.113, 114)
Exchequer Bills Act 1811 (cc.3, 4)
Exchequer Bills Act 1811 (c.15)
Exchequer Bills Act 1811 (cc.53, 54)
Exchequer Bills Act 1811 (c.85)
Exchequer Bills Act 1811 (c.112)
Exchequer Bills Act 1812 (cc.4, 5)
Exchequer Bills Act 1812 (c.16)
Exchequer Bills Act 1812 (c.86)
Exchequer Bills Act 1812 (c.114)
Exchequer Bills Act 1812 (c.164)
Exchequer Bills Act 1813 (c.18)
Exchequer Bills Act 1813 (cc.26, 27)
Exchequer Bills Act 1813 (c.39)
Exchequer Bills Act 1813 (c.42)
Exchequer Bills Act 1813 (cc.118, 119)
Exchequer Bills Act 1813 (c.161)
Exchequer Bills Act 1814 (cc.4, 5)
Exchequer Bills Act 1814 (c.53)
Exchequer Bills Act 1814 (cc.79, 80)
Exchequer Bills Act 1814 (c.188)
Exchequer Bills Act 1815 (cc.148, 149)
Exchequer Bills Act 1816 (c.4)
Exchequer Bills Act 1816 (c.28)
Exchequer Bills Act 1816 (c.54)
Exchequer Bills Act 1836 (c.2)
Exchequer Bills Act 1836 (c.113)
Exchequer Bills Act 1837 (c.16)
Exchequer Bills Act 1837 (c.38)
Exchequer Bills Act 1838 (c.12)
Exchequer Bills Act 1838 (c.26)
Exchequer Bills Act 1838 (c.93)

Exchequer Bills Act 1839 (c.8)
Exchequer Bills Act 1839 (c.90)
Exchequer Bills Act 1840 (c.12)
Exchequer Bills Act 1840 (c.106)
Exchequer Bills Act 1841 (c.19)
Exchequer Bills Act 1842 (c.21)
Exchequer Bills Act 1842 (c.66)
Exchequer Bills Act 1842 (c.86)
Exchequer Bills Act 1842 (c.115)
Exchequer Bills Act 1843 (c.17)
Exchequer Bills Act 1844 (c.14)
Exchequer Bills Act 1845 (c.23)
Exchequer Bills Act 1845 (c.129)
Exchequer Bills Act 1846 (c.15)
Exchequer Bills Act 1847 (c.19)
Exchequer Bills Act 1848 (c.16)
Exchequer Bills Act 1849 (c.20)
Exchequer Bills Act 1850 (c.10)
Exchequer Bills Act 1850 (c.22)
Exchequer Bills Act 1851 (c.9)
Exchequer Bills Act 1852 (c.10)
Exchequer Bills Act 1853 (c.25)
Exchequer Bills Act 1854 (c.3)
Exchequer Bills Act 1854 (c.12)
Exchequer Bills Act 1855 (c.8)
Exchequer Bills Act 1856 (c.19)
Exchequer Bills Act 1857 (c.17)
Exchequer Bills Act 1858 (c.13)
Exchequer Bills Act 1859 (c.22)
Exchequer Bills Act 1860 (c.20)
Exchequer Bills Act 1861 (c.5)
Exchequer Bills Act 1862 (c.3)
Exchequer Bills and Bonds Act 1855 (c.130)
Exchequer Bills and Bonds Act 1856 (c.44)
Exchequer Bills and Bonds Act 1866 (c.25)
Exchequer Bills and Bonds Act 1877 (c.5)
Exchequer Bills and Bonds Act 1878 (c.2)
Exchequer Bills and Bonds Act 1879 (c.62)
Exchequer Bills and Bonds Act 1880 (c.16)
Exchequer Bills and Bonds (Session 2) Act 1880 (c.21)
Exchequer Bills (Great Britain) Act 1815 (c.196)
Exchequer Bonds Act 1858 (c.14)
Exchequer Bonds Act 1862 (c.13)
Exchequer Bonds Act 1863 (c.16)
Exchequer Bonds Act 1864 (c.74)
Exchequer Bonds Act 1865 (c.29)
Exchequer Bonds Act 1867 (c.31)
Exchequer Bonds Act 1868 (c.27)
Exchequer Bonds Act 1869 (c.22)
Exchequer Bonds Act 1870 (c.41)
Exchequer Bonds Act 1871 (c.52)
Exchequer Bonds Act 1873 (c.54)
Exchequer Bonds Act 1876 (c.1)
Exchequer Bonds Act 1878 (c.7)
Exchequer Bonds and Bills Act 1854 (c.23)
Exchequer Bonds and Bills Act 1860 (c.132)
Exchequer Bonds and Bills (No. 2) Act 1878 (c.64)
Exchequer Bonds (No. 1) Act 1879 (c.3)
Exchequer Bonds (No. 2) Act 1878 (c.22)
Exchequer Court (Ireland) Act 1843 (c.55)

Exchequer Court (Ireland) Act 1843 (c.78)
Exchequer Court (Scotland) Act 1707 (c.53)
Exchequer Court (Scotland) Act 1779 (c.38)
Exchequer Court (Scotland) Act 1837 (c.65)
Exchequer Court (Scotland) Act 1856 (c.56)
Exchequer Equitable Jurisdiction (Ireland) Act 1850 (c.51)
Exchequer, etc., Courts (Scotland) Act 1790 (c.17)
Exchequer Extra Receipts Act 1868 (c.9)
Exchequer (Ireland) Act 1814 (c.83)
Excisable Goods on the Thames Act 1803 (c.115)
Excisable Liquors (Scotland) Act 1804 (c.55)
Excise Act 1719 (c.21)
Excise Act 1758 (c.29)
Excise Act 1772 (c.46)
Excise Act 1781 (c.55)
Excise Act 1781 (c.64)
Excise Act 1783 (c.70)
Excise Act 1785 (c.22)
Excise Act 1785 (c.47)
Excise Act 1785 (c.74)
Excise Act 1786 (c.59)
Excise Act 1786 (c.64)
Excise Act 1786 (cc.73, 74)
Excise Act 1786 (c.77)
Excise Act 1788 (c.37)
Excise Act 1788 (c.46)
Excise Act 1789 (c.63)
Excise Act 1790 (c.37)
Excise Act 1793 (c.59)
Excise Act 1795 (cc.10–13)
Excise Act 1795 (c.13)
Excise Act 1795 (c.97)
Excise Act 1795 (c.116)
Excise Act 1796 (c.14)
Excise Act 1798 (c.42)
Excise Act 1798 (c.54)
Excise Act 1800 (c.23)
Excise Act 1801 (c.91)
Excise Act 1802 (c.93)
Excise Act 1802 (c.96)
Excise Act 1803 (c.69)
Excise Act 1803 (c.81)
Excise Act 1803 (c.129)
Excise Act 1804 (c.49)
Excise Act 1805 (c.30)
Excise Act 1806 (c.39)
Excise Act 1806 (c.75)
Excise Act 1806 (c.112)
Excise Act 1806 (cc.138, 139)
Excise Act 1807 (c.27)
Excise Act 1807 (c.37)
Excise Act 1809 (c.63)
Excise Act 1809 (c.77)
Excise Act 1809 (c.80)
Excise Act 1809 (c.81)
Excise Act 1811 (c.32)
Excise Act 1812 (c.58)
Excise Act 1812 (c.61)
Excise Act 1812 (c.94)
Excise Act 1812 (c.128)

Excise Act 1813 (cc.56, 57)
Excise Act 1813 (c.88)
Excise Act 1813 (c.103)
Excise Act 1814 (c.73)
Excise Act 1814 (c.148)
Excise Act 1814 (c.183)
Excise Act 1815 (c.27)
Excise Act 1815 (c.30)
Excise Act 1815 (c.35)
Excise Act 1815 (c.62)
Excise Act 1815 (c.63)
Excise Act 1816 (c.17)
Excise Act 1816 (c.104)
Excise Act 1816 (c.108)
Excise Act 1836 (c.52)
Excise Act 1840 (c.17)
Excise Act 1848 (c.118)
Excise Act 1854 (c.27)
Excise Act 1855 (c.94)
Excise Act 1858 (c.15)
Excise Act 1860 (c.113)
Excise and Customs Act 1815 (c.66)
Excise and Stamps Act 1808 (c.41)
Excise and Stamps (Ireland) Act 1807 (c.14)
Excise and Taxes (Ireland) Act 1805 (c.19)
Excise Duties Act 1780 (c.17)
Excise Duties Act 1789 (c.45)
Excise Duties Act 1794 (c.33)
Excise Duties Act 1855 (c.22)
Excise Duties Act 1856 (c.34)
Excise Duties Act 1862 (c.84)
Excise Duties and Drawbacks Act 1807 (c.63)
Excise Duties and Licences (Ireland) Act 1815 (c.19)
Excise Duties and Taxes (Ireland) Act 1807 (c.18)
Excise Duties (Surcharges or Rebates) Act 1979 (c.8)
Excise Duty on Malt Act 1863 (c.3)
Excise Duty on Malt Act 1865 (c.66)
Excise, etc. Act 1811 (c.95)
Excise, etc. (Great Britain) Act 1807 (c.30)
Excise, etc. Act 1816 (c.30)
Excise (Great Britain) Act 1809 (c.117)
Excise (Ireland) Act 1807 (c.35)
Excise (Ireland) Act 1808 (c.82)
Excise (Ireland) Act 1809 (c.33)
Excise Incorporation (Scotland) Act 1835 (c.72)
Excise Laws, Glass Act 1792 (c.40)
Excise Management Act 1841 (c.20)
Excise Officers Act 1810 (c.44)
Excise Officers Allowance Act 1812 (c.81)
Excise on Spirits Act 1860 (c.129)
Excise (Scotland) Act 1793 (c.69)
Exclusive Trading (Ireland) Act 1846 (c.76)
Execution Act 1844 (c.96)
Execution (Ireland) Act 1848 (c.28)
Execution of Diligence (Scotland) Act 1926 (c.16)
Execution of Sentences (Scotland) Act 1730 (c.32)

Execution of Trusts (Emergency Provisions) Act 1939 (c.114)

Execution of Trusts (War Facilities) Act 1914 (c.13)

Execution of Trusts (War Facilities) Amendment Act 1915 (c.70)

Executions for Murder Act 1836 (c.30)

Executors (Scotland) Act 1900 (c.55)

Exemption from Coal Duty Act 1787 (c.21)

Exemption from Duties Act 1809 (c.44)

Exemption from Impressment Act 1739 (c.17)

Exemption from Toll Act 1812 (c.145)

Exemption of Bankers from Penalties Act 1813 (c.139)

Exercise Act 1723 (c.10)

Exercise Act 1727 (c.16)

Exercise of Trade by Soldiers Act 1784 (c.6)

Exercise of Trade by Soldiers, etc. Act 1802 (c.69)

Exercise of Trades by Soldiers, etc. Act 1816 (c.67)

Exercises of Trades Act 1712 (c.14)

Exercising Ground, Chatham Act 1808 (c.101)

Exeter: Lighting, etc. Act 1760 (c.28)

Exeter (Poor Relief) Act 1757 (c.53)

Exeter: Poor Relief Act 1774 (c.61)

Exeter: Poor Relief Act 1785 (c.21)

Exeter: Poor Relief Act 1788 (c.76)

Exeter Roads Act 1753 (c.74)

Exeter Roads Act 1756 (c.55)

Exeter Roads Act 1769 (c.93)

Exeter Roads Act 1770 (c.73)

Exeter Roads, etc. Act 1773 (c.109)

Exeter: Small Debts Act 1772 (c.27)

Exhibition Medals Act 1863 (c.119)

Exmoor Forest Act 1815 (c.138)

Ex-Officio Justice of the Peace (Scotland) Act 1898 (c.20)

Expenditure, etc., of Office of Works, etc. Act 1812 (c.41)

Expenditure in the West Indies Act 1800 (c.22)

Expenses of Fortifications for Protecting Royal Arsenals (No. 1) Act 1867 (c.24)

Expenses of Fortifications for Protecting Royal Arsenals (No. 2) Act 1867 (c.145)

Expenses of H.M. Forces, India Act 1791 (c.10)

Expenses of Prince Regent Act 1812 (c.7)

Expiring Laws Act 1922 (c.50)

Expiring Laws Act 1925 (c.76)

Expiring Laws Act 1931 (c.2)

Expiring Laws Act 1969 (c.61)

Expiring Laws Continuance Act 1841 (c.7)

Expiring Laws Continuance Act 1863 (c.95)

Expiring Laws Continuance Act 1864 (c.84)

Expiring Laws Continuance Act 1865 (c.119)

Expiring Laws Continuance Act 1866 (c.102)

Expiring Laws Continuance Act 1867 (c.143)

Expiring Laws Continuance Act 1868 (c.111)

Expiring Laws Continuance Act 1869 (c.85)

Expiring Laws Continuance Act 1870 (c.103)

Expiring Laws Continuance Act 1871 (c.95)

Expiring Laws Continuance Act 1872 (c.88)

Expiring Laws Continuance Act 1873 (c.75)

Expiring Laws Continuance Act 1874 (c.76)

Expiring Laws Continuance Act 1875 (c.72)

Expiring Laws Continuance Act 1876 (c.69)

Expiring Laws Continuance Act 1877 (c.67)

Expiring Laws Continuance Act 1878 (c.70)

Expiring Laws Continuance Act 1879 (c.67)

Expiring Laws Continuance Act 1880 (c.48)

Expiring Laws Continuance Act 1881 (c.70)

Expiring Laws Continuance Act 1882 (c.64)

Expiring Laws Continuance Act 1883 (c.40)

Expiring Laws Continuance Act 1884 (c.53)

Expiring Laws Continuance Act 1885 (c.59)

Expiring Laws Continuance Act 1886 (c.5)

Expiring Laws Continuance Act 1887 (c.63)

Expiring Laws Continuance Act 1888 (c.38)

Expiring Laws Continuance Act 1889 (c.67)

Expiring Laws Continuance Act 1890 (c.49)

Expiring Laws Continuance Act 1891 (c.60)

Expiring Laws Continuance Act 1892 (c.60)

Expiring Laws Continuance Act 1893 (c.59)

Expiring Laws Continuance Act 1894 (c.48)

Expiring Laws Continuance Act 1895 (c.1)

Expiring Laws Continuance Act 1896 (c.39)

Expiring Laws Continuance Act 1897 (c.54)

Expiring Laws Continuance Act 1898 (c.47)

Expiring Laws Continuance Act 1899 (c.34)

Expiring Laws Continuance Act 1900 (c.37)

Expiring Laws Continuance Act 1901 (c.33)

Expiring Laws Continuance Act 1902 (c.32)

Expiring Laws Continuance Act 1903 (c.40)

Expiring Laws Continuance Act 1904 (c.29)

Expiring Laws Continuance Act 1905 (c.21)

Expiring Laws Continuance Act 1906 (c.51)

Expiring Laws Continuance Act 1907 (c.34)

Expiring Laws Continuance Act 1908 (c.18)

Expiring Laws Continuance Act 1909 (c.46)

Expiring Laws Continuance Act 1910 (c.36)

Expiring Laws Continuance Act 1911 (c.22)

Expiring Laws Continuance Act 1912 (c.18)

Expiring Laws Continuance Act 1913 (c.15)

Expiring Laws Continuance Act 1914 (c.23)

Expiring Laws Continuance Act 1915 (c.63)

Expiring Laws Continuance Act 1916 (c.29)

Expiring Laws Continuance Act 1917 (c.38)

Expiring Laws Continuance Act 1918 (c.21)

Expiring Laws Continuance Act 1919 (c.39)

Expiring Laws Continuance Act 1920 (c.73)

Expiring Laws Continuance Act 1921 (c.53)

Expiring Laws Continuance Act 1923 (c.37)

Expiring Laws Continuance Act 1924 (c.1)

Expiring Laws Continuance Act 1926 (c.49)

Expiring Laws Continuance Act 1927 (c.34)

Expiring Laws Continuance Act 1928 (c.3)

Expiring Laws Continuance Act 1929 (c.12)

Expiring Laws Continuance Act 1931 (c.4)

Expiring Laws Continuance Act 1932 (c.2)

Expiring Laws Continuance Act 1933 (c.48)

Expiring Laws Continuance Act 1934 (c.57)

Expiring Laws Continuance Act 1935 (c.4)

Expiring Laws Continuance Act 1936 (c.4)

Expiring Laws Continuance Act 1937 (c.1)
Expiring Laws Continuance Act 1938 (c.1)
Expiring Laws Continuance Act 1939 (c.1)
Expiring Laws Continuance Act 1941 (c.3)
Expiring Laws Continuance Act 1942 (c.1)
Expiring Laws Continuance Act 1943 (c.1)
Expiring Laws Continuance Act 1944 (c.2)
Expiring Laws Continuance Act 1945 (c.9)
Expiring Laws Continuance Act 1947 (c.1)
Expiring Laws Continuance Act 1948 (c.3)
Expiring Laws Continuance Act 1949 (c.71)
Expiring Laws Continuance Act 1950 (c.1)
Expiring Laws Continuance Act 1951 (c.3)
Expiring Laws Continuance Act 1952 (c.5)
Expiring Laws Continuance Act 1953 (c.9)
Expiring Laws Continuance Act 1954 (c.69)
Expiring Laws Continuance Act 1955 (c.22)
Expiring Laws Continuance Act 1957 (c.2)
Expiring Laws Continuance Act 1958 (c.4)
Expiring Laws Continuance Act 1959 (c.4)
Expiring Laws Continuance Act 1960 (c.4)
Expiring Laws Continuance Act 1961 (c.4)
Expiring Laws Continuance Act 1962 (c.3)
Expiring Laws Continuance Act 1963 (c.58)
Expiring Laws Continuance Act 1964 (c.94)
Expiring Laws Continuance Act 1965 (c.77)
Expiring Laws Continuance Act 1966 (c.40)
Expiring Laws Continuance Act 1967 (c.89)
Expiring Laws Continuance Act 1968 (c.76)
Expiring Laws Continuance Act 1970 (c.58)
Explosive Substances Act 1883 (c.3)
Explosives Act 1875 (c.17)
Explosives Act 1923 (c.17)
Explosives (Age of Purchase) Act 1976 (c.26)
Export and Investment Guarantees Act 1991 (c.67)
Export Duty Act 1804 (c.57)
Export Guarantees Act 1937 (c.61)
Export Guarantees Act 1939 (c.5)
Export Guarantees Act 1944 (c.9)
Export Guarantees Act 1948 (c.54)
Export Guarantees Act 1949 (c.14)
Export Guarantees Act 1952 (c.21)
Export Guarantees Act 1957 (c.23)
Export Guarantees Act 1959 (c.63)
Export Guarantees Act 1967 (c.11)
Export Guarantees Act 1968 (c.26)
Export Guarantees Act 1975 (c.38)
Export Guarantees Amendment Act 1975 (c.19)
Export Guarantees and Overseas Investment Act 1978 (c.18)
Export Guarantees and Payments Act 1970 (c.14)
Export Guarantees and Payments Act 1970 (c.15)
Export of Salted Beef, etc. (Ireland) Act 1807 (c.10)
Exportation Act 1705 (c.19)
Exportation Act 1707 (c.44)
Exportation Act 1709 (c.2)
Exportation Act 1709 (c.7)
Exportation Act 1730 (c.29)

Exportation Act 1740 (c.3)
Exportation Act 1753 (c.11)
Exportation Act 1753 (c.15)
Exportation Act 1756 (cc.15, 16)
Exportation Act 1757 (c.1)
Exportation Act 1757 (c.9)
Exportation Act 1757 (c.37)
Exportation Act 1758 (c.8)
Exportation Act 1759 (c.15)
Exportation Act 1759 (c.28)
Exportation Act 1768 (c.24)
Exportation Act 1769 (c.1)
Exportation Act 1770 (c.1)
Exportation Act 1770 (c.10)
Exportation Act 1770 (c.31)
Exportation Act 1770 (c.38)
Exportation Act 1771 (c.37)
Exportation Act 1771 (c.39)
Exportation Act 1772 (cc.1, 2)
Exportation Act 1774 (c.5)
Exportation Act 1774 (c.10)
Exportation Act 1774 (c.11)
Exportation Act 1774 (c.26)
Exportation Act 1774 (c.71)
Exportation Act 1775 (c.5)
Exportation Act 1776 (c.28)
Exportation Act 1776 (c.37)
Exportation Act 1778 (c.16)
Exportation Act 1780 (c.37)
Exportation Act 1780 (c.46)
Exportation Act 1783 (c.14)
Exportation Act 1783 (c.81)
Exportation Act 1785 (c.5)
Exportation Act 1785 (c.62)
Exportation Act 1785 (c.67)
Exportation Act 1786 (c.2)
Exportation Act 1786 (c.76)
Exportation Act 1786 (c.89)
Exportation Act 1788 (c.16)
Exportation Act 1788 (c.38)
Exportation Act 1788 (c.45)
Exportation Act 1792 (c.2)
Exportation Act 1792 (c.9)
Exportation Act 1793 (c.3)
Exportation Act 1794 (c.34)
Exportation Act 1795 (c.5)
Exportation Act 1796 (c.53)
Exportation Act 1797 (c.10)
Exportation Act 1797 (c.29)
Exportation Act 1797 (c.125)
Exportation Act 1798 (c.67)
Exportation Act 1799 (c.26)
Exportation Act 1799 (c.96)
Exportation Act 1800 (c.1)
Exportation Act 1800 (c.2)
Exportation Act 1800 (c.91)
Exportation Act 1801 (c.21)
Exportation Act 1803 (c.49)
Exportation Act 1803 (c.105)
Exportation Act 1804 (c.22)
Exportation Act 1804 (c.70)
Exportation Act 1804 (c.101)
Exportation Act 1806 (c.11)

Exportation Act 1806 (c.17)
Exportation Act 1806 (c.115)
Exportation Act 1806 (c.116)
Exportation Act 1807 (c.9)
Exportation Act 1807 (c.30)
Exportation Act 1807 (c.49)
Exportation Act 1808 (c.29)
Exportation Act 1808 (cc.33–35)
Exportation Act 1808 (c.44)
Exportation Act 1808 (c.69)
Exportation Act 1809 (c.23)
Exportation Act 1809 (cc.30, 31)
Exportation Act 1810 (c.26)
Exportation Act 1810 (c.34)
Exportation Act 1810 (c.60)
Exportation Act 1810 (c.63)
Exportation Act 1810 (c.64)
Exportation Act 1811 (c.50)
Exportation Act 1811 (c.57)
Exportation Act 1812 (c.25)
Exportation Act 1812 (c.45)
Exportation Act 1812 (c.140)
Exportation Act 1813 (c.7)
Exportation Act 1813 (c.30)
Exportation Act 1813 (cc.31, 32)
Exportation Act 1813 (c.38)
Exportation Act 1813 (c.40)
Exportation Act 1813 (c.45)
Exportation Act 1813 (c.98)
Exportation Act 1813 (c.125)
Exportation Act 1814 (c.57)
Exportation Act 1814 (c.100)
Exportation Act 1814 (c.127)
Exportation Act 1814 (c.142)
Exportation Act 1814 (c.185)
Exportation Act 1815 (c.180)
Exportation Act 1815 (c.183)
Exportation Act 1816 (c.76)
Exportation Act 1816 (c.92)
Exportation Act 1816 (c.109)
Exportation Act 1816 (c.127)
Exportation and Importation Act 1768 (cc.1–3)
Exportation and Importation Act 1795 (c.3)
Exportation and Importation Act 1795 (c.4)
Exportation and Importation Act 1796 (c.7)
Exportation and Importation Act 1797 (c.83)
Exportation and Importation Act 1803 (c.12)
Exportation and Importation Act 1804 (c.65)
Exportation and Importation Act 1805 (c.33)
Exportation and Importation Act 1808 (c.27)
Exportation and Importation Act 1811 (c.14)
Exportation and Importation Act 1811 (c.86)
Exportation and Importation Act 1813 (c.67)
Exportation and Importation Act 1815 (c.31)
Exportation and Importation Act 1815 (c.37)
Exportation and Importation (Great Britain) Act 1810 (cc.18, 19)
Exportation and Importation (Ireland) Act 1810 (cc.16, 17)
Exportation, etc. Act 1716 (c.21)
Exportation, etc. Act 1749 (c.14)
Exportation, etc. Act 1758 (c.2)

Exportation, etc. Act 1769 (c.28)
Exportation etc. Act 1771 (c.1)
Exportation, etc. Act 1778 (c.55)
Exportation, etc. Act 1784 (c.50)
Exportation, etc. Act 1801 (c.36)
Exportation, etc. Act 1808 (c.22)
Exportation (Ireland) Act 1807 (c.58)
Exportation (Ireland) Act 1809 (c.76)
Exportation of Arms Act 1900 (c.44)
Exportation of Army Clothing Act 1775 (c.45)
Exportation of Gunpowder Act 1803 (c.52)
Exportation of Horses Act 1914 (c.15)
Exportation of Horses Act 1937 (c.42)
Exportations, etc. Act 1704 (c.7)
Exportations, etc. Act 1780 (c.59)
Exportations, etc. Act 1802 (cc.12, 13)
Exports Act 1786 (c.40)
Exports Act 1787 (c.31)
Extension of Polling Hours Act 1913 (c.6)
Extradition Act 1843 (cc.75, 76)
Extradition Act 1845 (c.120)
Extradition Act 1862 (c.70)
Extradition Act 1866 (c.121)
Extradition Act 1870 (c.52)
Extradition Act 1873 (c.60)
Extradition Act 1895 (c.33)
Extradition Act 1906 (c.15)
Extradition Act 1931 (c.39)
Extradition Act 1932 (c.39)
Extradition Act 1989 (c.33)
Extraordinary Tithe Act 1897 (c.23)
Extraordinary Tithe Redemption Act 1886 (c.54)
Extra-Parochial Places Act 1857 (c.19)
Eyemouth Harbour Act 1797 (c.49)
Eynsham Bridge Act 1767 (c.68)

Fabrics (Misdescription) Act 1913 (c.17)
Factories Act 1802 (c.73)
Factories Act 1937 (c.67)
Factories Act 1844 (c.15)
Factories Act 1847 (c.29)
Factories Act 1850 (c.54)
Factories Act 1853 (c.104)
Factories Act 1856 (c.38)
Factories Act 1948 (c.55)
Factories Act 1959 (c.67)
Factories Act 1961 (c.34)
Factors Act 1842 (c.39)
Factors Act 1889 (c.45)
Factors Acts Amendment 1877 (c.39)
Factors (Scotland) Act 1890 (c.40)
Factory Act 1874 (c.44)
Factory Acts Extension Act 1864 (c.48)
Factory Acts Extension Act 1867 (c.103)
Factory and Workshop Act 1870 (c.62)
Factory and Workshop Act 1871 (c.104)
Factory and Workshop Act 1878 (c.16)
Factory and Workshop Act 1883 (c.53)
Factory and Workshop Act 1891 (c.75)
Factory and Workshop Act 1895 (c.37)
Factory and Workshop Act 1901 (c.22)

Factory and Workshop Act 1907 (c.39)

Factory and Workshop Amendment (Scotland) Act 1888 (c.22)

Factory and Workshop (Cotton Cloth Factories) Act 1911 (c.21)

Factory and Workshop (Cotton Cloth Factories) Act 1929 (c.15)

Failure of Corn Crop Act 1783 (c.53)

Fair Employment (Northern Ireland) Act 1976 (c.25)

Fair Employment (Northern Ireland) Act 1989 (c.32)

Fair Trading Act 1973 (c.41)

Fairs Act 1868 (c.51)

Fairs Act 1871 (c.12)

Fairs Act 1873 (c.37)

Fairs and Market Act 1850 (c.23)

Fairs (Ireland) Act 1868 (c.12)

Falmouth Gaol Act 1865 (c.103)

False Alarms of Fire Act 1895 (c.28)

False Oaths (Scotland) Act 1933 (c.20)

False Personation Act 1874 (c.36)

False Weights and Scales Act 1770 (c.44)

Falsification of Accounts Act 1875 (c.24)

Families of Militiamen Act 1793 (c.8)

Families of Militiamen Act 1795 (c.81)

Families of Militiamen, etc. Act 1794 (c.47)

Families of Militiamen, etc. Act 1796 (c.114)

Family Allowances Act 1944 (c.41)

Family Allowances Act 1965 (c.53)

Family Allowances and National Insurance Act 1952 (c.29)

Family Allowances and National Insurance Act 1956 (c.50)

Family Allowances and National Insurance Act 1959 (c.18)

Family Allowances and National Insurance Act 1961 (c.6)

Family Allowances and National Insurance Act 1963 (c.10)

Family Allowances and National Insurance Act 1967 (c.90)

Family Allowances and National Insurance Act 1968 (c.40)

Family Income Supplements Act 1970 (c.55)

Family Law Act 1986 (c.55)

Family Law Act 1996 (c.27)

Family Law Reform Act 1969 (c.46)

Family Law Reform Act 1987 (c.42)

Family Law (Scotland) Act 1985 (c.37)

Family of Rt. Hon. S. Perceval Act 1812 (c.67)

Family Provision Act 1966 (c.35)

Farm and Garden Chemicals Act 1967 (c.50)

Farm Land and Rural Development Act 1988 (c.16)

Farnborough and Seven Oaks Road Act 1796 (c.128)

Farnborough to Seven Oaks Road Act 1773 (c.92)

Farnhurst, Chichester and Delkey Road Act 1797 (c.148)

Farriers (Registration) Act 1975 (c.35)

Farriers (Registration) (Amendment) Act 1977 (c.31)

Farringdon to Burford Road 1771 (c.84)

Fatal Accidents Act 1846 (c.93)

Fatal Accidents Act 1864 (c.95)

Fatal Accidents Act 1959 (c.65)

Fatal Accidents Act 1976 (c.30)

Fatal Accidents and Sudden Deaths Inquiry (Scotland) Act 1906 (c.35)

Fatal Accidents and Sudden Deaths Inquiry (Scotland) Act 1976 (c.14)

Fatal Accidents (Damages) Act 1908 (c.7)

Fatal Accidents Inquiry (Scotland) Act 1895 (c.36)

Faversham (Improvement) Act 1789 (c.69)

Faversham, Portsmouth, Plymouth Fortifications Act 1786 (c.94)

Federal Council of Australasia Act 1885 (c.60)

Federation of Malaya Independence Act 1957 (c.60)

Fee-Farm Rents (Ireland) Act 1851 (c.20)

Fees, etc., in Public Offices (Ireland) Act 1807 (c.41)

Fees etc., in Public Offices, etc. (Ireland) Act 1811 (c.81)

Fees for Pardons Act 1818 (c.29)

Fees in Public Offices, etc. Act 1809 (c.51)

Fees in Public Offices, etc. (Ireland) Act 1810 (c.81)

Fees in Public Offices, etc. (Ireland) Act 1812 (c.92)

Fees (Increase) Act 1923 (c.4)

Fees of Coroners (Ireland) Act 1810 (c.30)

Fees, Officers of the Exchequer Act 1786 (c.99)

Fees, Port of London, etc. Act 1806 (c.82)

Felony Act 1819 (c.27)

Felony Act 1841 (c.22)

Felony and Piracy Act 1772 (c.20)

Fencibles Act 1793 (c.36)

Fen Drainage Act 1749 (c.18)

Fen Drainage Act 1758 (c.13)

Fen Drainage Act 1774 (c.16)

Fen Drainage Act 1775 (c.65)

Fen Drainage Act 1776 (c.64)

Ferries (Acquisition by Local Authorities) Act 1919 (c.75)

Ferrybridge and Boroughbridge Road Act 1753 (c.77)

Fertilisers and Feeding Stuffs Act 1893 (c.56)

Fertilisers and Feeding Stuffs Act 1906 (c.27)

Fertilisers and Feeding Stuffs Act 1926 (c.45)

Festival of Britain (Additional Loans) Act 1951 (c.47)

Festival of Britain (Sunday Opening) Act 1951 (c.14)

Festival of Britain (Supplementary Provisions) Act (c.102)

Festival Pleasure Gardens 1952 (c.13)

Feudal Casualties (Scotland) Act 1914 (c.48)

Fever (Ireland) Act 1846 (c.6)

Fever (Ireland) Act 1847 (c.22)

Fever (Ireland) Act 1848 (c.131)

Field Monuments Act 1972 (c.43)

Fife (Country) Roads Act 1797 (c.180)
Fife Roads Act 1772 (c.83)
Fife Roads Act 1790 (c.93)
Fife Roads and Bridges Act 1774 (c.31)
Fifield, St. John's and Newbridge Road Act 1763 (c.29)
Fiji Independence Act 1970 (c.50)
Fiji Marriage Act 1878 (c.61)
Film Levy Finance Act 1981 (c.16)
Films Act 1960 (c.57)
Films Act 1964 (c.52)
Films Act 1966 (c.48)
Films Act 1970 (c.26)
Films Act 1979 (c.9)
Films Act 1980 (c.41)
Films Act 1985 (c.21)
Finance Act 1894 (c.30)
Finance Act 1895 (c.16)
Finance Act 1896 (c.28)
Finance Act 1897 (c.24)
Finance Act 1898 (c.10)
Finance Act 1899 (c.9)
Finance Act 1900 (c.7)
Finance Act 1901 (c.7)
Finance Act 1902 (c.7)
Finance Act 1903 (c.8)
Finance Act 1904 (c.7)
Finance Act 1905 (c.4)
Finance Act 1906 (c.8)
Finance Act 1907 (c.13)
Finance Act 1908 (c.16)
Finance (1909–10) Act 1910 (c.8)
Finance Act 1910 (c.35)
Finance Act 1911 (c.48)
Finance Act 1912 (c.8)
Finance Act 1913 (c.30)
Finance Act 1914 (c.10)
Finance Act 1915 (c.62)
Finance Act 1916 (c.24)
Finance Act 1917 (c.31)
Finance Act 1918 (c.15)
Finance Act 1919 (c.32)
Finance Act 1920 (c.18)
Finance Act 1921 (c.32)
Finance Act 1922 (c.17)
Finance Act 1923 (c.14)
Finance Act 1924 (c.21)
Finance Act 1925 (c.36)
Finance Act 1926 (c.22)
Finance Act 1927 (c.10)
Finance Act 1928 (c.17)
Finance Act 1929 (c.21)
Finance Act 1930 (c.28)
Finance Act 1931 (c.25)
Finance Act 1931 (c.28)
Finance Act 1932 (c.25)
Finance Act 1933 (c.19)
Finance Act 1934 (c.32)
Finance Act 1935 (c.24)
Finance Act 1936 (c.34)
Finance Act 1937 (c.54)
Finance Act 1938 (c.46)
Finance Act 1939 (c.41)

Finance Act 1940 (c.29)
Finance Act 1941 (c.30)
Finance Act 1942 (c.21)
Finance Act 1943 (c.28)
Finance Act 1944 (c.23)
Finance Act 1945 (c.24)
Finance Act 1946 (c.64)
Finance Act 1947 (c.35)
Finance Act 1948 (c.49)
Finance Act 1949 (c.47)
Finance Act 1950 (c.15)
Finance Act 1951 (c.43)
Finance Act 1952 (c.33)
Finance Act 1953 (c.34)
Finance Act 1954 (c.44)
Finance Act 1955 (c.15)
Finance Act 1956 (c.54)
Finance Act 1957 (c.49)
Finance Act 1958 (c.56)
Finance Act 1959 (c.58)
Finance Act 1960 (c.44)
Finance Act 1961 (c.36)
Finance Act 1962 (c.44)
Finance Act 1963 (c.25)
Finance Act 1964 (c.49)
Finance Act 1965 (c.25)
Finance Act 1966 (c.18)
Finance Act 1967 (c.54)
Finance Act 1968 (c.44)
Finance Act 1969 (c.32)
Finance Act 1970 (c.24)
Finance Act 1971 (c.68)
Finance Act 1972 (c.41)
Finance Act 1973 (c.51)
Finance Act 1974 (c.30)
Finance Act 1975 (c.7)
Finance Act 1976 (c.40)
Finance Act 1977 (c.36)
Finance Act 1978 (c.42)
Finance Act 1979 (c.25)
Finance Act 1980 (c.48)
Finance Act 1981 (c.35)
Finance Act 1982 (c.39)
Finance Act 1983 (c.28)
Finance Act 1984 (c.43)
Finance Act 1985 (c.54)
Finance Act 1986 (c.41)
Finance Act 1987 (c.16)
Finance Act 1988 (c.39)
Finance Act 1989 (c.26)
Finance Act 1990 (c.29)
Finance Act 1991 (c.31)
Finance Act 1992 (c.20)
Finance Act 1993 (c.34)
Finance Act 1994 (c.9)
Finance Act 1995 (c.4)
Finance Act 1996 (c.8)
Finance Act 1997 (c.16)
Finance (Exchequer Bonds) Amendment Act 1916 (c.36)
Finance (Income Tax Reliefs) Act 1977 (c.53)
Finance (New Duties) Act 1916 (c.11)
Finance (No. 2) Act 1915 (c.89)

Finance (No. 2) Act 1931 (c.49)
Finance (No. 2) Act 1939 (c.109)
Finance (No. 2) Act 1940 (c.48)
Finance (No. 2) Act 1945 (c.13)
Finance (No. 2) Act 1947 (c.9)
Finance (No. 2) Act 1955 (c.17)
Finance (No. 2) Act 1964 (c.92)
Finance (No. 2) Act 1975 (c.45)
Finance (No. 2) Act 1979 (c.47)
Finance (No. 2) Act 1983 (c.49)
Finance (No. 2) Act 1987 (c.51)
Finance (No. 2) Act 1992 (c.48)
Finance (No. 2) Act 1997 (c.58)
Finance (Session 2) Act 1914 (c.7)
Financial Emergency Enactments (Cont.) Act 1931 (c.13)
Financial Powers (U.S.A. Securities) Act 1941 (c.36)
Financial Services Act 1986 (c.60)
Findhorn Harbour Act 1778 (c.70)
Finding of the Longitude at Sea Act 1776 (c.48)
Finding of the Longitude at Sea Act 1780 (c.52)
Finding of the Longitude at Sea Act 1780 (c.61)
Fine Arts Copyright Act 1862 (c.68)
Fine or Imprisonment (Scotland and Ireland) Act 1899 (c.11)
Fines Act 1833 (c.99)
Fines Act (Ireland) 1851 (c.90)
Fines Act (Ireland) 1851, Amendment Act 1874 (c.72)
Fines Act (Ireland) 1874 (c.72)
Fines and Penalties (Ireland) Act 1839 (c.92)
Fines and Recoveries Act 1833 (c.74)
Fines and Recoveries Act 1842 (c.32)
Fines and Recoveries Act 1848 (c.70)
Fines and Recoveries (Ireland) Act 1834 (c.82)
Fines by Justices Act 1801 (c.85)
Fines, etc. (Ireland) Act 1838 (c.99)
Fines, etc. (Ireland) Act 1843 (c.56)
Fines (Ireland) Act 1851 (c.90)
Fines on Stills Act 1810 (c.100)
Finsbury Square Act 1791 (c.90)
Finsbury Square (Paving, Watching, etc.) Act 1795 (c.45)
Fire Brigade Pensions Act 1925 (c.47)
Fire Brigade Pensions Act 1929 (c.35)
Fire Brigades Act 1938 (c.72)
Fire Insurance Duty Act 1782 (c.48)
Fire Precautions Act 1971 (c.40)
Fire Precautions (Loans) Act 1973 (c.11)
Fire Prevention (Metropolis) Act 1774 (c.78)
Fire Safety and Safety of Places of Sport Act 1987 (c.27)
Fire Service College Board (Abolition) Act 1982 (c.13)
Fire Services Act 1947 (c.41)
Fire Services Act 1951 (c.27)
Fire Services Act 1959 (c.44)
Fire Services (Emergency Provisions) Act 1941 (c.22)

Firearms Act 1813 (c.115)
Firearms Act 1815 (c.59)
Firearms Act 1934 (c.16)
Firearms Act 1937 (c.12)
Firearms Act 1965 (c.44)
Firearms Act 1968 (c.27)
Firearms Act 1982 (c.31)
Firearms (Amendment) Act 1936 (c.39)
Firearms (Amendment) Act 1988 (c.45)
Firearms (Amendment) Act 1992 (c.31)
Firearms (Amendment) Act 1994 (c.31)
Firearms (Amendment) Act 1997 (c.5)
Firearms (Amendment) (No. 2) Act 1997 (c.64)
Firearms and Imitation Firearms (Criminal Use) Act 1933 (c.50)
Fires Prevention Act 1785 (c.77)
Fires Prevention Act 1838 (c.75)
Fireworks Act 1951 (c.58)
Fireworks Act 1964 (c.23)
First Meetings of Certain Commissioners Act 1786 (c.95)
First Meetings of Commissioners Act 1808 (c.133)
First Meetings of Commissioners, etc. Act 1776 (c.36)
First Meetings of Commissioners, etc. Act 1779 (c.55)
First Meetings of Commissioners, etc. Act 1782 (c.74)
First Offenders Act 1958 (c.31)
First Offenders (Scotland) Act 1960 (c.23)
First Public Health Supplemental Act 1852 (c.41)
Fish Act 1705 (c.8)
Fish Act 1714 (c.18)
Fish Act 1756 (c.39)
Fish Act 1759 (c.27)
Fish Act 1796 (c.118)
Fish Act 1801 (c.3)
Fish Act 1801 (c.99)
Fish Carriage Act 1762 (c.15)
Fish Market, Westminster Act 1748 (c.49)
Fish, Newfoundland, etc. Act 1801 (c.77)
Fish Teinds (Scotland) Act 1864 (c.33)
Fisheries Act 1780 (c.60)
Fisheries Act 1785 (c.65)
Fisheries Act 1786 (c.41)
Fisheries Act 1786 (c.81)
Fisheries Act 1787 (c.10)
Fisheries Act 1891 (c.37)
Fisheries Act 1955 (c.7)
Fisheries Act 1981 (c.29)
Fisheries Close Season (Ireland) Act 1895 (c.29)
Fisheries, Continuance of Laws Act 1801 (c.97)
Fisheries, Convention with France Act 1839 (c.96)
Fisheries, Convention with France Act 1840 (c.69)
Fisheries, Convention with France Act 1842 (c.63)

Foreign Jurisdiction Act 1913 (c.16)

Foreign Jurisdiction Act Amendment Act 1865 (c.16)

Foreign Jurisdiction Act Amendment Act 1866 (c.87)

Foreign Jurisdiction Act Foreign Law Ascertainment Act 1861 (c.11)

Foreign Law Ascertainment Act 1861 (c.11)

Foreign Limitation Periods Act 1984 (c.16)

Foreign Marriage Act 1891 (c.74)

Foreign Marriage Act 1892 (c.23)

Foreign Marriage Act 1947 (c.33)

Foreign Marriage (Amendment) Act 1988 (c.44)

Foreign Prison-Made Goods Act 1897 (c.63)

Foreign Protestants Naturalization Act 1714 (c.29)

Foreign Service Act 1943 (c.35)

Foreign Service Act 1960 (c.11)

Foreign Ships Act 1797 (c.63)

Foreign Ships, etc. Act 1805 (c.32)

Foreign Tribunals Evidence Act 1856 (c.113)

Forest of Dean Act 1836 (c.3)

Forest of Dean Act 1844 (c.13)

Forest of Dean (Poor Relief) Act 1842 (c.48)

Forestalling, Regrating, etc. Act 1844 (c.24)

Forestry Act 1919 (c.58)

Forestry Act 1921 (c.61)

Forestry Act 1927 (c.6)

Forestry Act 1944 (c.35)

Forestry Act 1947 (c.21)

Forestry Act 1951 (c.61)

Forestry Act 1967 (c.10)

Forestry Act 1979 (c.21)

Forestry Act 1981 (c.39)

Forestry Act 1986 (c.30)

Forestry Act 1991 (c.43)

Forestry (Sale of Land) (Scotland) Act 1963 (c.23)

Forestry (Transfer of Woods) Act 1923 (c.21)

Forfar Roads Act 1789 (c.20)

Forfar Roads Act 1794 (c.100)

Forfeited and Unclaimed Prize Money Act 1811 (c.104)

Forfeited Estates Act 1703 (c.61)

Forfeited Estates—Derwentwater Estate Act 1731 (c.23)

Forfeited Estates, etc. Act 1718 (c.23)

Forfeited Estates—Greenwich Hospital Act 1734 (c.29)

Forfeited Estates (Ireland) Act 1705 (c.11)

Forfeited Estates (Ireland) Act 1703 (c.19)

Forfeited Estates (Ireland) etc. Act 1703 (c.21)

Forfeited Estates (Scotland) Act 1774 (c.65)

Forfeited Estates, Scotland Act 1786 (c.27)

Forfeited Estates (Time for Claims) Act 1716 (c.20)

Forfeiture Act 1870 (c.23)

Forfeiture Act 1982 (c.34)

Forfeiture upon Attainder of Treason Act 1799 (c.93)

Forged Exchequer Bills Act 1842 (c.11)

Forged Exchequer Bills Act 1843 (c.1)

Forged Transfers Act 1891 (c.43)

Forged Transfers Act 1892 (c.36)

Forgeries and Frauds in Bank Transfers Act 1793 (c.30)

Forgery Act 1733 (c.22)

Forgery Act 1778 (c.18)

Forgery Act 1797 (c.122)

Forgery Act 1830 (c.66)

Forgery Act 1837 (c.84)

Forgery Act 1861 (c.98)

Forgery Act 1870 (c.58)

Forgery Act 1913 (c.27)

Forgery and Counterfeiting Act 1981 (c.45)

Forgery of Bank of Ireland Notes, etc. Act 1809 (c.13)

Forgery of Banknotes Act 1801 (c.39)

Forgery of Foreign Bills Act 1803 (c.139)

Form of Deeds Act (Scotland) 1856 (c.89)

Former Enemy Aliens (Disabilities Removal) Act 1925 (c.43)

Forms of Pleading Act 1838 (c.100)

Forms of Pleading in High Court Act 1855 (c.26)

Forsyth's Indemnity Act 1866 (c.20)

Fort Marlborough in India Act 1802 (c.29)

Fort of Senegal Act 1763 (c.20)

Fort William in Bengal Act 1786 (c.25)

Fort William Pulp and Paper Mills Act 1963 (c.15)

Forth and Clyde and Monkland Canal Act 1790 (c.73)

Forth and Clyde Canal (Extinguishment of Rights of Navigation) Act 1962 (c.16)

Forth and Clyde Navigation Act 1768 (c.63)

Forth and Clyde, Navigation Act 1771 (c.62)

Forth and Clyde, Navigation Act 1773 (c.104)

Forth and Clyde: Navigation Act 1784 (c.59)

Forth and Clyde: Navigation Act 1787 (c.20)

Forth and Clyde: Navigation Act 1787 (c.55)

Fortifications Act 1708 (c.26)

Fortifications Act 1709 (c.23)

Fortifications Act 1757 (cc.38, 39)

Fortifications (Expenses) Act 1869 (c.76)

Fortifications for Royal Arsenals, etc. Act 1863 (c.80)

Fortifications for Royal Arsenals, etc. Act 1864 (c.109)

Fortifications - Portsmouth Act 1722 (c.32)

Fortifications - Portsmouth and Dover Act 1806 (c.105)

Fortifications, Portsmouth and Dover Act 1809 (c.39)

Fortifications, Royal Arsenals, etc. Act 1865 (c.61)

Fosdyke Bridge Act 1984 (c.17)

Foss, York: Navigation Act 1793 (c.99)

Foster Children Act 1980 (c.6)

Foster Children (Scotland) Act 1984 (c.56)

Foston Bridge and Witham Common Road Act 1725 (c.16)

Founding Hospital Act 1739 (c.29)

Foundling Hospital, Dublin Act 1801 (c.50)

Four and a Half Per Cent, Duties Repeal Act 1838 (c.92)
Four Courts Library Act 1894 (c.4)
Four Courts Marshalsea Discontinuance Act 1874 (c.21)
Four Courts Marshalsea (Ireland) Act 1842 (c.95)
Foyle College Act 1874 (c.79)
Frame Work Knitters Act 1766 (c.29)
Frampton Mansel Marriage Act 1868 (c.23)
Franchise Prisons Abolition Act 1858 (c.22)
Frauds by Boatmen and Others, etc. Act 1809 (c.122)
Frauds by Boatmen, etc. Act 1813 (c.87)
Frauds by Boatmen in Cinque Ports, etc. Act 1808 (c.130)
Frauds by Journeymen Shoemakers Act 1722 (c.27)
Frauds by Workmen Act 1748 (c.27)
Frauds by Workmen Act 1777 (c.56)
Frauds, etc., in Woollen Manufacturers Act 1774 (c.25)
Frauds in Excise Revenue Act 1791 (c.21)
Frauds in Excise Revenue Act 1792 (c.8)
Frauds in Manufacture of Clocks, etc. Act 1754 (c.7)
Frauds in Manufacture of Sweets Act 1815 (c.177)
Frauds in the Public Revenues, etc. Act 1738 (c.72)
Frauds of Workmen Act 1739 (c.8)
Frauds on Exportation Act 1810 (c.53)
Fraudulent Bankrupts (Scotland) Act 1827 (c.20)
Fraudulent Mediums Act 1951 (c.33)
Free Fishers of Whitstable Act 1793 (c.42)
Free Ports Act 1796 (c.55)
Free Ports Act 1797 (c.77)
Free Ports Act 1800 (c.23)
Free Ports, Jamaica Act 1774 (c.41)
Free Ports, West Indies, etc. Act 1766 (c.49)
Freeman (Admission) Act 1763 (c.15)
Freshwater and Salmon Fisheries (Scotland) Act 1976 (c.22)
Freshwater Fish (Scotland) Act 1902 (c.29)
Freshwater Fisheries Act 1878 (c.39)
Freshwater Fisheries Act 1884 (c.11)
Freshwater Fisheries Act 1886 (c.2)
Friendly and Industrial and Provident Societies Act 1968 (c.55)
Friendly Societies Act 1793 (c.54)
Friendly Societies Act 1795 (c.111)
Friendly Societies Act 1803 (c.111)
Friendly Societies Act 1809 (c.125)
Friendly Societies Act 1840 (c.73)
Friendly Societies Act 1846 (c.27)
Friendly Societies Act 1850 (c.115)
Friendly Societies Act 1852 (c.65)
Friendly Societies Act 1854 (c.101)
Friendly Societies Act 1855 (c.63)
Friendly Societies Act 1858 (c.101)
Friendly Societies Act 1860 (c.13)
Friendly Societies Act 1860 (c.58)

Friendly Societies Act 1875 (c.60)
Friendly Societies Act 1879 (c.9)
Friendly Societies Act 1887 (c.56)
Friendly Societies Act 1888 (c.66)
Friendly Societies Act 1889 (c.22)
Friendly Societies Act 1893 (c.30)
Friendly Societies Act 1895 (c.26)
Friendly Societies Act 1896 (c.25)
Friendly Societies Act 1908 (c.32)
Friendly Societies Act 1916 (c.54)
Friendly Societies Act 1924 (c.11)
Friendly Societies Act 1955 (c.19)
Friendly Societies Act 1971 (c.66)
Friendly Societies Act 1974 (c.46)
Friendly Societies Act 1981 (c.50)
Friendly Societies Act 1984 (c.62)
Friendly Societies Act 1992 (c.40)
Friendly Societies Amendment Act 1876 (c.32)
Friendly Society Amendment Act 1885 (c.27)
Friendly Societies Discharge Act 1854 (c.56)
Friendly Societies (Ireland) Act 1809 (c.58)
Friendly Societies (Quinquennial Returns) Act 1882 (c.35)
Frivolous Arrests Act 1725 (c.29)
Frivolous Arrests Act 1811 (c.124)
Frivolous Suits Act 1772 (c.51)
Frivolous Suits Act 1841 (c.28)
Frogmore House Act 1841 (c.2)
Frome Roads Act 1757 (c.39)
Frome Roads Act 1772 (c.94)
Frome Roads Act 1797 (c.175)
Fuel and Electricity (Control) Act 1973 (c.67)
Fugitive Offenders Act 1881 (c.69)
Fugitive Offenders Act 1967 (c.68)
Fugitive Offenders (Protected States) Act 1915 (c.39)
Fulbourne Church Act 1775 (c.49)
Fulham and Putney Bridge Act 1725 (c.36)
Fulham Bridge Act 1727 (c.18)
Fulham Roads Act 1730 (c.34)
Fulham Roads Act 1749 (c.16)
Fund for Fire Victims in Edinburgh Act 1727 (c.22)
Furnished Houses (Rent Control) Act 1946 (c.34)
Furnished Lettings (Rent Allowances) Act 1973 (c.6)
Further and Higher Education Act 1992 (c.13)
Further and Higher Education (Scotland) Act 1992 (c.37)
Further Education Act 1985 (c.47)

Gainsborough Bridge Act 1787 (c.15)
Gainsborough Church Act 1735 (c.22)
Gainsborough Church Act 1740 (c.15)
Gainsborough: Improvement Act 1769 (c.21)
Gainsborough: Inclosure Act 1796 (c.101)
Gainsborough Inclosure, etc. Act 1795 (c.82)
Galashiels Act 1867 (c.85)
Galashiels and Selkirk Act 1872 (c.47)
Galway Harbour Act 1859 (c.28)

Galway Harbour Act 1867 (c.56)
Gambia Independence Act 1964 (c.93)
Game Act 1706 (c.16)
Game Act 1710 (c.27)
Game Act 1716 (c.11)
Game Act 1721 (c.19)
Game Act 1755 (c.12)
Game Act 1762 (c.19)
Game Act 1766 (c.21)
Game Act 1770 (c.19)
Game Act 1773 (c.80)
Game Act 1796 (c.39)
Game Act 1796 (c.54)
Game Act 1831 (c.32)
Game Act 1970 (c.13)
Game Birds (Ireland) Act 1874 (c.11)
Game Certificates Act 1784 (c.43)
Game Certificates Act 1785 (c.50)
Game Certificates (Ireland) Act 1842 (c.81)
Game (England) Act 1772 (c.55)
Game Laws (Amendment) Act 1960 (c.36)
Game Laws Amendment (Scotland) Act 1877
(c.28)
Game Laws (England); Local Taxes, etc.
(Scotland) Act 1836 (c.65)
Game Licences Act 1860 (c.90)
Game (Scotland) Act 1750 (c.34)
Game (Scotland) Act 1772 (c.54)
Game Trespass (Ireland) Act 1864 (c.67)
Gamekeepers Act 1808 (c.93)
Gaming Act 1710 (c.19)
Gaming Act 1738 (c.28)
Gaming Act 1739 (c.19)
Gaming Act 1744 (c.34)
Gaming Act 1802 (c.119)
Gaming Act 1845 (c.109)
Gaming Act 1892 (c.9)
Gaming Act 1922 (c.19)
Gaming Act 1968 (c.65)
Gaming Act (Northern Ireland) 1845 (c.109)
Gaming (Amendment) Act 1973 (c.12)
Gaming (Amendment) Act 1982 (c.22)
Gaming (Amendment) Act 1980 (c.8)
Gaming (Amendment) Act 1986 (c.11)
Gaming (Amendment) Act 1987 (c.11)
Gaming (Amendment) Act 1990 (c.26)
Gaming (Bingo) Act 1985 (c.35)
Gaming Houses Act 1854 (c.38)
Gaming Machines (Scotland) Act 1917 (c.23)
Gaming Transactions Act 1844 (c.7)
Gaol Fees Abolition Act 1815 (c.50)
Gaol Fees Abolition Act 1845 (c.114)
Gaols Act 1772 (c.58)
Gaols Act 1784 (c.54)
Gaols Act 1789 (c.67)
Gaols Act 1791 (c.46)
Garrotters Act 1863 (c.44)
Gas Act 1948 (c.67)
Gas Act 1960 (c.27)
Gas Act 1965 (c.36)
Gas Act 1972 (c.60)
Gas Act 1980 (c.37)
Gas Act 1986 (c.44)

Gas Act 1995 (c.45)
Gas and Electricity Act 1968 (c.39)
Gas and Electricity (Borrowing Powers) Act
1954 (c.52)
Gas and Steam Vehicles (Excise Duties) Act
1939 (c.6)
Gas and Water Works Facilities Act 1870
(c.70)
Gas and Water Works Facilities Act, 1870,
Amendment 1873 (c.89)
Gas (Borrowing Powers) Act 1965 (c.60)
Gas (Exempt Supplies) Act 1993 (c.1)
Gas Levy Act 1981 (c.3)
Gas (Standard of Calorific Power) Act 1916
(c.25)
Gas Undertakings Act 1929 (c.24)
Gas Undertakings Act 1931 (c.40)
Gas Undertakings Act 1934 (c.28)
Gasworks Clauses Act 1847 (c.15)
Gasworks Clauses Act 1871 (c.41)
General Board of Health Act 1856 (c.85)
General Board of Health Act 1857 (c.38)
General Board of Health Continuance Act
1855 (c.115)
General de Lancey (Crown Claims) Act 1807
(c.69)
General de Lancey (Estates and Crown
Claims) Act 1811 (c.102)
General Dealers (Ireland) Act 1903 (c.44)
General Pardon Act (c.19)
General Pardon Act 1707 (c.22)
General Pardon Act 1720 (c.29)
General Pardon Act 1746 (c.52)
General Pier and Harbour Act 1861 (c.45)
General Pier and Harbour Act, 1861, Amend-
ment Act 1862 (c.19)
General Police and Improvement (Scotland)
Act 1862 (c.101)
General Police and Improvement (Scotland)
Act, 1862, Amendment Act 1877 (c.22)
General Police and Improvement (Scotland)
Act, 1862, Amendment Act 1889 (c.51)
General Police and Improvement (Scotland)
Act 1865 (c.7)
General Police and Improvement (Scotland)
Act 1882 (c.6)
General Police and Improvement (Scotland)
Amendment Act 1878 (c.30)
General Police and Improvement (Scotland)
Supplemental Act 1863
General Police and Improvement (Scotland)
Supplemental Act 1865 (c.7)
General Police and Improvement (Scotland)
Supplemental Act 1866 (c.93)
General Police and Improvement (Scotland)
Supplemental Act 1867 (c.79)
General Prisons (Ireland) Act 1877 (c.49)
General Rate Act 1967 (c.9)
General Rate Act 1970 (c.19)
General Rate Act 1975 (c.5)
General Rate (Public Utilities) Act 1977 (c.11)
General Register House, Edinburgh Act 1847
(c.20)

General Register Office Act 1852 (c.25)
Geneva Convention Act 1911 (c.20)
Geneva Convention Act 1937 (c.15)
Geneva Conventions Act 1957 (c.52)
Geneva Conventions (Amendment) Act 1995 (c.27)
Genocide Act 1969 (c.12)
Geological Survey Act 1845 (c.63)
German Conventions Act 1955 (c.2)
German Reparation (Recovery) Act 1921 (c.5)
Ghana (Consequential Provisions) Act 1960 (c.41)
Ghana Independence Act 1957 (c.6)
Gibraltar Lighthouse, etc. Act 1838 (c.66)
Gifts for Churches Act 1803 (c.108)
Gifts for Churches Act 1811 (c.115)
Glamorgan, Llansamlett–Llangevelach Bridge, River Tawey Act 1778 (c.68)
Glamorgan Roads Act 1764 (c.88)
Glamorgan Roads Act 1771 (c.77)
Glamorgan Roads Act 1779 (c.110)
Glamorgan Roads Act 1785 (c.122)
Glamorgan Roads Act 1793 (c.133)
Glamorganshire Canal Act 1796 (c.69)
Glamorganshire Election Act 1815 (c.72)
Glasgow and Dumbarton Roads Act 1772 (c.106)
Glasgow and Renfrew Road Act 1797 (c.161)
Glasgow and Renfrew Roads Act 1794 (c.140)
Glasgow and Shotts Road Act 1753 (c.81)
Glasgow Beer Duties Act 1715 (c.44)
Glasgow Beer Duties Act 1725 (c.27)
Glasgow Beer Duties Act 1735 (c.31)
Glasgow Beer Duties Act 1755 (c.29)
Glasgow Boundaries Act 1871 (c.68)
Glasgow (Improvement) Act 1768 (c.16)
Glasgow: Improvement Act 1793 (c.124)
Glasgow Parliamentary Divisions Act 1896 (c.17)
Glasgow Roads Act 1753 (c.90)
Glasgow Roads Act 1754 (c.27)
Glasgow Roads Act 1766 (c.82)
Glasgow Roads Act 1774 (c.102)
Glasgow Roads Act 1774 (c.105)
Glasgow Roads Act 1788 (c.92)
Glasgow Roads Act 1792 (c.152)
Glasgow Roads Act 1792 (c.154)
Glasgow Roads Act 1793 (c.160)
Glasgow Roads Act 1793 (c.174)
Glasgow Roads Act 1795 (c.155)
Glass Duties Act 1787 (c.28)
Glass Duties Act 1794 (c.27)
Glass Duties Act 1835 (c.77)
Glass Duties Act 1838 (c.44)
Glass Duties Repeal Act 1845 (c.6)
Glass, etc., Duties Act 1813 (c.70)
Glebe Exchange Act 1815 (c.147)
Glebe Exchange Act 1816 (c.52)
Glebe Houses (Ireland) Act 1803 (c.158)
Glebe (Ireland) Act 1851 (c.73)
Glebe Lands Act 1888 (c.20)

Glebe Lands Leasing Powers (Ireland) Act 1857 (c.47)
Glebe Lands, Representative Church Body, Ireland, Act 1875 (c.42)
Glebe Lands (Scotland) Act 1866 (c.71)
Glebe Loan Act 1870 (c.112)
Glebe Loan Act 1871 (c.100)
Glebe Loan (Ireland) Acts Amendment 1880 (c.2)
Glebe Loan (Ireland) Acts Amendment 1883 (c.8)
Glebe Loan (Ireland) Acts Amendment 1886 (c.6)
Glebe Loan (Ireland) Amendment Act 1875 (c.30)
Glebe Loan (Ireland) Amendment Act 1878 (c.6)
Glebe Loan (Ireland) Amendments Act 1871 (c.100)
Gloucester and Berkeley Canal Act 1793 (c.97)
Gloucester and Berkeley Canal Act 1797 (c.54)
Gloucester and Crickley Hull Road Act 1760 (c.30)
Gloucester and Hereford Roads Act 1746 (c.31)
Gloucester and Hereford Roads Act 1759 (c.34)
Gloucester and Hereford Roads Act 1769 (c.50)
Gloucester and Oxford Road Act 1750 (c.28)
Gloucester and Oxford Roads Act 1768 (c.41)
Gloucester and Oxford Roads Act 1787 (c.77)
Gloucester and Warwick Roads Act 1755 (c.47)
Gloucester and Wiltshire Roads Act 1756 (c.56)
Gloucester and Wiltshire Roads Act 1757 (c.61)
Gloucester and Wiltshire Roads Act 1762 (c.74)
Gloucester and Wiltshire Roads Act 1779 (c.118)
Gloucester and Wiltshire Roads Act 1792 (c.153)
Gloucester and Worcester Roads Act 1764 (c.79)
Gloucester and Worcester Roads Act 1794 (c.135)
Gloucester Gaol Act 1781 (c.74)
Gloucester Gaol Act 1785 (c.10)
Gloucester (Poor Relief, etc.) Act 1764 (c.60)
Gloucester Roads Act 1742 (c.21)
Gloucester Roads Act 1742 (c.22)
Gloucester Roads Act 1745 (c.18)
Gloucester Roads Act 1746 (c.23)
Gloucester Roads Act 1751 (c.13)
Gloucester Roads Act 1756 (c.58)
Gloucester Roads Act 1770 (c.74)
Gloucester Roads Act 1778 (c.102)

Gloucester Roads Act 1779 (c.93)
Gloucester Roads Act 1779 (c.115)
Gloucester Roads Act 1780 (c.70)
Gloucester Roads Act 1780 (c.84)
Gloucester Roads Act 1780 (c.93)
Gloucester Roads Act 1783 (c.104)
Gloucester Roads Act 1787 (c.68)
Gloucester Roads Act 1787 (c.78)
Gloucester Roads Act 1792 (c.146)
Gloucester Roads Act 1795 (c.140)
Gloucester Streets Act 1749 (c.15)
Gloucester to Stroud Road Act 1778 (c.98)
Gloucester Water Supply Act 1740 (c.11)
Gloucestershire Highways Act 1722 (c.31)
Gloucestershire Roads Act 1725 (c.24)
Gloucestershire Roads Act 1741 (c.15)
Gloucestershire Roads Act 1756 (c.51)
Gloucestershire Roads Act 1757 (c.54)
Gloucestershire Roads Act 1757 (c.64)
Gloucestershire Roads Act 1757 (c.65)
Gloucestershire Roads Act 1757 (c.70)
Gloucestershire Roads Act 1769 (c.58)
Gloucestershire Roads Act 1774 (c.111)
Gloucestershire Roads Act 1783 (c.106)
Gloucestershire: Small Debts Act 1792 (c.77)
Glove Duties Act 1785 (c.55)
Godmanchester to Cambridge Road Act 1793 (c.156)
Godstone to Highgate Road Act 1766 (c.58)
Gold and Silver (Export Control, etc.) Act 1920 (c.70)
Gold and Silver Thread Act 1702 (c.11)
Gold and Silver Thread Act 1741 (c.20)
Gold and Silver Thread Act 1788 (c.7)
Gold and Silver Wares Act 1844 (c.22)
Gold and Silver Wares Act 1854 (c.96)
Gold Currency Act 1812 (c.5)
Gold Currency Act 1814 (c.52)
Gold Currency and Bank Notes Act 1811 (c.127)
Gold Currency, etc. Act 1812 (c.50)
Gold Plate (Standard) Act 1798 (c.69)
Gold Standard Act 1925 (c.29)
Gold Standard (Amendment) Act 1931 (c.46)
Golden Square (Rates) Act 1750 (c.27)
Goodman's Fields Act 1778 (c.50)
Goods and Services (Price Control) Act 1941 (c.31)
Goods in Neutral Ships Act 1802 (c.80)
Goods Vehicles (Licensing of Operators) Act 1995 (c.23)
Gordon Memorial College at Khartoum Act 1899 (c.16)
Gosport: Improvement Act 1763 (c.56)
Goswell St., Middlesex Act 1780 (c.48)
Government and Other Stocks (Emergency Provisions) Act 1939 (c.100)
Government Annuities Act 1838 (c.49)
Government Annuities Act 1853 (c.45)
Government Annuities Act 1873 (c.44)
Government Annuities Act 1882 (c.51)
Government Annuities Act 1929 (c.29)
Government Annuities (Investments) Act 1864 (c.46)

Government Contractors Act 1815 (c.195)
Government of Burma Act 1935 (c.3)
Government of Burma (Temporary Provisions) Act 1944 (c.30)
Government of India Act 1800 (c.79)
Government of India Act 1833 (c.85)
Government of India Act 1853 (c.95)
Government of India Act 1854 (c.77)
Government of India Act 1858 (c.106)
Government of India Act 1859 (c.41)
Government of India Act 1865 (c.17)
Government of India Act 1869 (c.97)
Government of India Act 1870 (c.3)
Government of India Act 1912 (c.6)
Government of India Act 1915 (c.61)
Government of India Act 1919 (c.101)
Government of India Act 1935 (c.2)
Government of India Act 1935 (c.42)
Government of India (Aden) Act 1929 (c.2)
Government of India Amendment Act 1911 (c.25)
Government of India Amendment Act 1916 (c.37)
Government of India Amendment Act 1933 (c.23)
Government of India (Amendment) Act 1939 (c.66)
Government of India (Civil Services) Act 1925 (c.83)
Government of India (Indian Navy) Act 1927 (c.8)
Government of India (Leave of Absence) Act 1924 (c.28)
Government of India (Reprinting) Act 1935 (c.1)
Government of India (Statutory Commission) Act 1927 (c.24)
Government of Ireland Act 1914 (c.90)
Government of Ireland Act 1920 (c.67)
Government of New South Wales and Van Diemen's Land Act 1866 (c.74)
Government of New Zealand Act 1846 (c.103)
Government of Newfoundland Act 1847 (c.44)
Government of Northern Ireland (Loan Guarantee) Act 1922 (c.24)
Government of Soudan Loan Act 1919 (c.43)
Government of the Soudan Loan Act 1913 (c.10)
Government of the Soudan Loan Act 1914 (c.9)
Government of the Soudan Loan (Amendment) Act 1922 (c.15)
Government of New Zealand Act 1848 (c.5)
Government Offices Security Act 1810 (c.85)
Government Offices Security Act 1836 (c.28)
Government Offices Security Act 1838 (c.61)
Government Offices (Security) Act 1875 (c.64)
Government Trading Act 1990 (c.30)
Government Trading Funds Act 1973 (c.63)
Government War Obligations Act 1914 (c.11)

Government War Obligations Act 1915 (c.96)

Government War Obligations Act 1916 (c.70)

Government War Obligations Act 1918 (c.28)

Government War Obligations Act 1919 (c.44)

Governors, etc., of West Indies Islands Act 1794 (c.35)

Governors' Pension Act 1956 (c.64)

Governors' Pensions Act 1957 (c.62)

Grain Between Great Britain and Ireland Act 1806 (c.97)

Grammar Schools Act 1840 (c.77)

Grand Canal Branches (Ireland) Act 1844 (c.98)

Grand Canal (Ireland) Act 1813 (c.143)

Grand Junction Canal Act 1793 (c.80)

Grand Junction Canal Act 1794 (c.24)

Grand Junction Canal (No. 1) Act 1795 (c.8)

Grand Junction Canal (No. 2) Act 1795 (c.43)

Grand Junction Canal (No. 3) Act 1795 (c.85)

Grand Junction Canal (No. 4) Act 1795 (c.25)

Grand Juries Act 1856 (c.54)

Grand Juries (Ireland) Act 1843 (c.32)

Grand Juries (Suspension) Act 1917 (c.4)

Grand Jury Cess. Act 1846 (c.60)

Grand Jury Cess. Dublin Act 1838 (c.51)

Grand Jury Cess. (Dublin) Act 1851 (c.65)

Grand Jury Cess. (Ireland) Act 1848 (c.26)

Grand Jury Cess. (Ireland) Act 1849 (c.32)

Grand Jury Cess. (Ireland) Act 1850 (c.82)

Grand Jury Cess. (Ireland) Act 1853 (c.13)

Grand Jury Cess. (Ireland) Act 1857 (c.7)

Grand Jury (Ireland) Act 1816 (c.87)

Grand Jury (Ireland) Act 1836 Amendment 1908 (c.29)

Grand Jury (Ireland) Act 1836 (c.116)

Grand Jury (Ireland) Act 1837 (c.2)

Grand Jury (Ireland) Act 1838 (c.37)

Grand Jury (Ireland) Act 1853 (c.136)

Grand Jury (Ireland) Act 1856 (c.63)

Grand Jury (Ireland) Act 1857 (c.15)

Grand Jury (Ireland) Act 1872 (c.42)

Grand Jury (Ireland) Act 1873 (c.34)

Grand Jury (Ireland) Act 1895 (c.8)

Grand Jury Presentments (Ireland) Act 1842 (c.77)

Grand Jury Presentments (Ireland) Act 1843 (c.71)

Grant of Administration (Bonds) Act 1919 (c.26)

Grant of Feu Duties to John Francis Erskine Act 1815 (c.188)

Grant of Frogmore, etc. Act 1807 (c.45)

Grant of Manor of Corsham to Paul Methuen Act 1770 (c.13)

Grant of Military, etc. Commissions Act 1857 (c.4)

Grant to Duke of Marlborough Act 1704 (c.4)

Grant to J. Palmer, Esq. (Post Office Services) Act 1813 (c.157)

Grant to the House of Orange Act 1803 (c.149)

Grantham Canal Act 1793 (c.94)

Grantham Canal Act 1797 (c.30)

Grantham Town Hall Act 1787 (c.61)

Grants for Glebe Houses (I.) Act 1807 (c.23)

Grants of Life Annuities Act 1776 (c.26)

Grants of Officers Act 1812 (c.40)

Grants of Offices in Reversion, etc. Act 1808 (c.50)

Grants of Pensions Act 1811 (c.21)

Grants to George Keith Act 1760 (c.15)

Graves End: Streets Act 1772 (c.15)

Grease Butter from Ireland Act 1763 (c.20)

Great and Little Botton: Improvement Act 1792 (c.71)

Great Farringdon to Burford Road Act 1792 (c.150)

Great Grimsby (Lincoln) Harbour Act 1796 (c.98)

Great Marlow to Stokenchurch Road Act 1791 (c.135)

Great Seal Act 1851 (c.82)

Great Seal Act 1880 (c.10)

Great Seal Act 1884 (c.30)

Great Seal (Offices) Act 1874 (c.81)

Great Sessions in Wales Act 1768 (c.14)

Great Torrington Roads Act 1765 (c.58)

Great Torrington Roads Act 1786 (c.128)

Great Tower Hill: Improvement, etc. Act 1797 (c.87)

Great Yarmouth Haven Act 1749 (c.6)

Great Yarmouth: Improvement Act 1772 (c.14)

Great Yarmouth: Improvement Act 1785 (c.36)

Great Yarmouth Pier Act (c.10)

Greek Loan Act 1864 (c.40)

Greek Loan Act 1898 (c.4)

Greek Loan Guarantee Act 1836 (c.94)

Greek Marriages Act 1884 (c.20)

Greenland and Whale Fishery Act 1771 (c.38)

Greenland, etc., Fishery Act 1782 (c.19)

Greenland Fishery Act 1723 (c.16)

Greenland Fishery Act 1731 (c.78)

Greenland Fishery Act 1804 (c.23)

Greenland Trade Act 1702 (c.10)

Greenland Whale Fisheries Act 1802 (c.22)

Greenland Whale Fisheries Act 1815 (c.39)

Greenland Whale Fisheries, etc. Act (c.20)

Greenland Whale Fishery Act 1803 (c.32)

Greenland Whale Fishery Act 1805 (c.9)

Greenland Whale Fishery Act 1806 (c.9)

Greenland Whale Fishery Act 1810 (c.11)

Greenock Beer Duties Act 1750 (c.38)

Greenock: Improvement Act 1789 (c.43)

Greenock: Water Supply, etc. Act 1772 (c.28)

Greenwich Hospital Act 1728 (c.7)

Greenwich Hospital Act 1744 (c.31)

Greenwich Hospital Act 1751 (c.42)

Greenwich Hospital Act 1776 (c.24)

Greenwich Hospital Act 1806 (c.100)

Greenwich Hospital Act 1807 (c.52)

Greenwich Hospital Act 1814 (c.110)

Greenwich Hospital Act 1815 (c.56)

Greenwich Hospital Act 1829 (c.25)

Greenwich Hospital Act 1850 (c.24)
Greenwich Hospital Act 1865 (c.89)
Greenwich Hospital Act 1869 (c.44)
Greenwich Hospital Act 1870 (c.100)
Greenwich Hospital Act 1872 (c.67)
Greenwich Hospital Act 1883 (c.32)
Greenwich Hospital Act 1885 (c.42)
Greenwich Hospital Act 1898 (c.24)
Greenwich Hospital Act 1921 (c.41)
Greenwich Hospital Act 1942 (c.35)
Greenwich Hospital Act 1947 (c.5)
Greenwich Hospital Act 1967 (c.74)
Greenwich Hospital Act 1990 (c.13)
Greenwich Hospital (Disused Burial Ground) Act 1925 (c.58)
Greenwich Hospital, etc. Act 1711 (c.27)
Greenwich Hospital (Provision for Widows) Act 1863 (c.67)
Greenwich Markets Act 1849 (c.28)
Greenwich Out-Pensioners Act 1763 (c.16)
Grenada and St. Vincent Traders Act (c.11)
Grenada and St. Vincent Traders Act 1800 (c.27)
Grenada and St. Vincent Traders Act 1803 (c.40)
Grenada and St. Vincent Traders Act 1803 (c.104)
Grenada and St. Vincent Traders Act 1808 (c.135)
Gresham College, etc. Act 1768 (c.32)
Grey Seals Protection Act 1914 (c.3)
Grey Seals Protection Act 1931 (c.23)
Grosvenor Square: Paving, etc. Act 1774 (c.52)
Ground Game Act 1880 (c.47)
Ground Game (Amendment) Act 1906 (c.21)
Groundhurst Roads Act 1768 (c.35)
Growth of Coffee Act 1731 (c.24)
Growth of Coffee Act 1745 (c.23)
Growth of Coffee, etc. Act 1750 (c.35)
Growth of Hemp and Flax Act 1781 (c.58)
Growth of Raw Silk Act 1749 (c.20)
Guarantee by Companies Act 1867 (c.108)
Guard Dogs Act 1975 (c.50)
Guardians (Ireland) Act 1849 (c.4)
Guardianship Act 1973 (c.29)
Guardianship and Maintenance of Infants Act 1951 (c.56)
Guardianship of Infants Act 1886 (c.27)
Guardianship of Infants Act 1925 (c.45)
Guardianship of Minors Act 1971 (c.3)
Guardianship (Refugee Children) Act 1944 (c.8)
Guildford and Arundel Road Act 1757 (c.60)
Guildford and Farnham Road Act 1757 (c.78)
Guildford Hospital Act 1861 (c.32)
Guildford Streets Act 1758 (c.58)
Guildford to Farnham Road Act 1780 (c.96)
Gun Barrel Proof Act 1978 (c.9)
Gun Licence Act 1870 (c.57)
Gunpowder Act 1772 (c.61)
Gunpowder Act Amendment Act 1862 (c.98)
Gunpowder and Fireworks Act 1860 (c.139)

Gunpowder and Fireworks Act 1861 (c.130)
Gunpowder in Mersey Act 1851 (c.67)
Gunpowder Mill, Tonbridge Act 1772 (c.13)
Guyana Independence Act 1966 (c.14)
Guyana Republic Act 1970 (c.18)

Habeas Corpus Act 1679 (c.2)
Habeas Corpus Act 1803 (c.140)
Habeas Corpus Act 1804 (c.102)
Habeas Corpus Act 1816 (c.100)
Habeas Corpus Act 1862 (c.20)
Habeas Corpus (Ireland) Act 1868 (c.7)
Habeas Corpus Suspension Act 1707 (c.67)
Habeas Corpus Suspension Act 1715 (c.30)
Habeas Corpus Suspension Act 1722 (c.1)
Habeas Corpus Suspension Act 1743 (c.6)
Habeas Corpus Suspension Act 1745 (c.1)
Habeas Corpus Suspension Act 1745 (c.17)
Habeas Corpus Suspension Act 1746 (c.1)
Habeas Corpus Suspension Act 1776 (c.9)
Habeas Corpus Suspension Act 1778 (c.1)
Habeas Corpus Suspension Act 1779 (c.1)
Habeas Corpus Suspension Act 1780 (c.2)
Habeas Corpus Suspension Act 1782 (c.1)
Habeas Corpus Suspension Act 1794 (c.54)
Habeas Corpus Suspension Act 1795 (c.3)
Habeas Corpus Suspension Act 1797 (c.36)
Habeas Corpus Suspension Act 1799 (c.15)
Habeas Corpus Suspension Act 1799 (c.44)
Habeas Corpus Suspension Act 1800 (c.20)
Habeas Corpus Suspension Act 1800 (c.32)
Habeas Corpus Suspension Act 1801 (c.26)
Habeas Corpus Suspension, etc. Act 1714 (c.8)
Habeas Corpus Suspension (Ireland) Act 1803 (c.8)
Habeas Corpus Suspension (Ireland) Act 1801 (c.15)
Habeas Corpus Suspension (Ireland) Act 1803 (c.116)
Habeas Corpus Suspension (Ireland) Act 1805 (c.4)
Habeas Corpus Suspension (Ireland) Act 1848 (c.35)
Habeas Corpus Suspension (Ireland) Act 1849 (c.2)
Habeas Corpus Suspension (Ireland) Act 1866 (c.1)
Habeas Corpus Suspension (Ireland) Act 1866 (c.119)
Habeas Corpus Suspension (Ireland) Act 1867 (c.1)
Habeas Corpus Suspension (Ireland) Act 1867 (c.25)
Habitual Criminals Act 1869 (c.99)
Habitual Drunkards Act 1879 (c.19)
Hackney Carriages Act 1815 (c.159)
Hackney Carriages, Metropolis Act 1838 (c.79)
Hackney Chairs Act 1712 (c.15)
Hackney Chairs, etc. Act 1759 (c.25)
Hackney Coach Fares Act 1808 (c.87)

Hackney Coaches Act 1771 (c.24)

Hackney Coaches Act 1772 (c.49)

Hackney Coaches Act 1784 (c.27)

Hackney Coaches Act 1786 (c.72)

Hackney Coaches Act 1792 (c.47)

Hackney Coaches Act 1804 (c.88)

Hackney Coaches Act 1814 (c.147)

Hackney Coaches, etc. Act 1715 (c.57)

Hackney Coaches, etc., London Act 1800 (c.47)

Hackney Coaches, Metropolis Act 1802 (c.78)

Hackney Coachmen Act 1771 (c.28)

Hackney (Poor Relief etc.) Act 1764 (c.43)

Haddington County Roads Act 1749 (c.17)

Haddington Roads Act 1769 (c.74)

Haddington Roads Act 1793 (c.163)

Hagley and Birmingham Road Act 1753 (c.47)

Haileybury College Act 1838 (c.22)

Haileybury College Act 1855 (c.52)

Hainault Forest Act 1851 (c.43)

Hainault Forest (Allotment of Commons) Act 1858 (c.37)

Hair Powder Certificates, etc. Act 1795 (c.112)

Hairdressers' and Barbers' Shops (Sunday Closing) Act 1930 (c.35)

Hairdressers (Registration) Act 1964 (c.89)

Half-Pay and Pensions Act 1807 (c.25)

Half Pay of Officers, etc. 1815 (c.131)

Halifax and Sheffield Road Act 1797 (c.160)

Halifax Church Act 1795 Act (c.71)

Halifax to Manchester Canal Act 1794 (c.78)

Halifax to Sheffield Road Act 1777 (c.106)

Halifax to Sheffield Road Act 1793 (c.142)

Halifax: Water Supply Act 1762 (c.40)

Halifax: (Water Supply, etc.) Act 1768 (c.44)

Hallamshire Cutlers Act 1791 (c.58)

Halliwell and Finsbury Drainage Act 1778 (c.66)

Hallmarking Act 1973 (c.43)

Hall-marking of Foreign Plate Act 1904 (c.6)

Hall-marking of Foreign Plate Act 1939 (c.36)

Hamilton Bridge Act 1770 (c.93)

Hampshire and Berkshire Roads Act 1766 (c.86)

Hampshire and Dorset Roads Act 1762 (c.57)

Hampshire and Dorset Roads Act 1780 (c.92)

Hampshire and Wiltshire Fisheries Act 1797 (c.95)

Hampshire and Wiltshire Roads Act 1774 (c.104)

Hampshire, Kent, Sussex—Fortifications Act 1762 (c.37)

Hampshire, Kent, Sussex—Fortifications Act 1763 (c.35)

Hampshire Roads Act 1741 (c.14)

Hampshire Roads Act 1757 (c.73)

Hampshire Roads Act 1757 (c.74)

Hampshire Roads Act 1765 (c.95)

Hampstead Roads Act 1753 (c.80)

Hampstead: Streets Act 1775 (c.58)

Hampton Court Bridge Act 1749 (c.37)

Hampton to Staines Road Act 1773 (c.105)

Hampton to Staines Road Act 1793 (c.135)

Hanbury Church Act 1793 (c.45)

Hanley Chapel, Stafford Act 1787 (c.62)

Hans Town, Chelsea: Improvement Act 1790 (c.76)

Happing and Tunstead, Norfolk: Poor Relief Act 1785 (c.27)

Harbour Loans Act 1866 (c.30)

Harbour of Colombo Loan Act 1874 (c.24)

Harbour of Galle Loan Act 1869 (c.105)

Harbour of Howth Act 1805 (c.113)

Harbour of Leith Act 1800 (c.57)

Harbour of Leith Act 1805 (c.114)

Harbour Transfer Act 1865 (c.100)

Harbours Act 1745 (c.22)

Harbours Act 1814 (c.159)

Harbours Act 1964 (c.40)

Harbours (Amendment) Act 1970 (c.53)

Harbours and Passing Tolls etc. Act 1861 (c.47)

Harbours Development (Scotland) Act 1972 (c.64)

Harbours, Docks and Piers Clauses Act 1847 (c.27)

Harbours, Docks and Piers (Temporary Increase of Charges) Act 1922 (c.23)

Harbours (Ireland) Act 1805 (c.64)

Harbours (Loans) Act 1972 (c.16)

Harbours, Piers and Ferries (Scotland) Act 1937 (c.28)

Harbours, Piers and Ferries (Scotland) Act 1953 (c.11)

Harbours, Piers and Ferries (Scotland) Act 1972 (c.29)

Harbours (Scotland) Act 1982 (c.17)

Harbours Transfer Act 1862 (c.69)

Hardington and Old Stratford Road Act 1768 (c.52)

Hares Act 1848 (c.29)

Hares Preservation Act 1892 (c.8)

Hares Preservation (Ireland) Act 1879 (c.23)

Hares (Scotland) Act 1848 (c.30)

Harrogate to Ripon Road Act 1794 (c.121)

Hartlepool Pilotage Order Confirmation Act 1864 (c.58)

Hartley's Patent (Fire Prevention) Act 1776 (c.6)

Hartsmere, etc., Suffolk: Poor Relief Act 1779 (c.13)

Harvey's Charity, Folkestone Act 1858 (c.29)

Harwich, etc., Election Act 1842 (c.31)

Harwich Harbour Act 1863 (c.71)

Harwich Harbour Act 1864 (c.102)

Harwich Harbour Act 1865 (c.120)

Hastings: Improvement Act 1789 (c.27)

Hat Duties Act 1803 (c.22)

Hat Duties, etc. Act 1784 (c.51)

Hat Manufacture Act 1731 (c.22)

Hat Manufacture Act 1784 (c.21)

Hatfield Chase Act 1783 (c.13)

Hatfield Chase: Drainage Act 1787 (c.53)

Hawford–Droitwich Canal Act 1768 (c.37)

Hawkers Act 1717 (c.6)

Hawkers Act 1785 (c.78)

Hawkers Act 1810 (c.41)

Hawkers Act 1812 (c.108)

Hawkers Act 1888 (c.33)

Hawkers and Pedlars Act 1795 (c.91)

Hawkers (Scotland) Act 1815 (c.71)

Hay and Straw Act 1796 (c.88)

Hay and Straw Act 1856 (c.114)

Hay Bridge Over Wye Act 1756 (c.73)

Haydon, Chapel, Northumberland Act 1795 (c.47)

Heage to Duffield Road Act 1793 (c.177)

Health and Medicines Act 1988 (c.49)

Health and Safety at Work etc. Act 1974 (c.37)

Health and Social Security Act 1984 (c.48)

Health and Social Services and Social Security Adjudications Act 1983 (c.41)

Health Authorities Act 1995 (c.17)

Health of Prisoners Act 1774 (c.59)

Health Resorts and Watering Places Act 1921 (c.27)

Health Resorts and Watering Places Act 1936 (c.48)

Health Resorts, etc. (Ireland) Act 1909 (c.32)

Health Service Commissioners Act 1993 (c.46)

Health Service Commissioners (Amendment) Act 1996 (c.5)

Health Service Joint Consultative Committees (Access to Information) Act 1986 (c.24)

Health Services Act 1976 (c.83)

Health Services Act 1980 (c.53)

Health Services and Public Health Act 1968 (c.46)

Health Visiting and Social Work (Training) Act 1962 (c.33)

Hearing Aid Council Act 1968 (c.50)

Hearing Aid Council (Amendment) Act 1989 (c.12)

Hearing Aid Council (Extension) Act 1975 (c.39)

Heather Burning (Scotland) Act 1926 (c.30)

Heating Appliances (Fireguards) Act 1952 (c.42)

Heavy Commercial Vehicles (Controls and Regulations) Act 1973 (c.44)

Hedon Haven Act 1774 (c.106)

Heir Apparent's Establishment Act 1795 (c.125)

Hemingbrough to Market Weighton Road Act 1793 (c.159)

Hemlingford Riots Act 1793 (c.39)

Hemp and Flax Act 1770 (c.40)

Hemp and Flax Act 1786 (c.43)

Henley Grammar School Act 1778 (c.41)

Henley Improvement Act 1795 (c.79)

Henley to Oxford Road Act 1781 (c.97)

Henley-upon-Thames Bridge Act 1780 (c.33)

Hereditary Revenues Act 1856 (c.43)

Hereford and Bedford Roads Act 1769 (c.64)

Hereford and Gloucester Roads Act 1764 (c.62)

Hereford and Gloucester Roads Act 1789 (c.104)

Hereford and Salop Roads Act 1758 (c.66)

Hereford and Worcester Roads Act 1782 (c.100)

Hereford Cathedral Act 1792 (c.87)

Hereford (City) Roads Act 1730 (c.18)

Hereford, Radnor and Salop Roads Act 1778 (c.111)

Hereford Roads Act 1748 (c.15)

Hereford Roads Act 1748 (c.18)

Hereford Roads Act 1748 (c.26)

Hereford Roads Act 1751 (c.56)

Hereford Roads Act 1756 (c.65)

Hereford Roads Act 1770 (c.91)

Hereford Roads Act 1773 (c.95)

Hereford Roads Act 1773 (c.96)

Hereford Roads Act 1767 (c.67)

Hereford Roads Act 1769 (c.90)

Hereford Roads Act 1781 (c.105)

Hereford Roads Act 1782 (c.108)

Hereford Roads Act 1782 (c.112)

Hereford Roads Act 1784 (c.69)

Hereford Roads Act 1789 (c.108)

Hereford Roads Act 1791 (c.114)

Hereford Roads Act 1791 (c.130)

Hereford Roads Act 1794 (c.119)

Hereford Roads, etc. Act 1759 (c.58)

Hereford Streets Act 1774 (c.38)

Herefordshire and Gloucestershire Canal Act 1791 (c.89)

Herefordshire Roads Act 1740 (c.13)

Herefordshire Roads Act 1741 (c.17)

Heritable Jurisdictions (Scotland) Act 1746 (c.43)

Heritable Securities (Scotland) Act 1845 (c.31)

Heritable Securities (Scotland) Act 1847 (c.50)

Heritable Securities (Scotland) Act 1854 (c.62)

Heritable Securities (Scotland) Act 1860 (c.80)

Heritable Securities (Scotland) Act 1894 (c.44)

Herring Fisheries (Scotland) Act 1858 (c.69)

Herring Fisheries (Scotland) Act 1860 (c.92)

Herring Fisheries (Scotland) Act 1865 (c.22)

Herring Fisheries (Scotland) Act 1867 (c.52)

Herring Fishery Act 1749 (c.24)

Herring Fishery Act 1753 (c.9)

Herring Fishery Act 1755 (c.14)

Herring Fishery Act 1757 (c.30)

Herring Fishery Act 1765 (c.22)

Herring Fishery Act 1772 (c.58)

Herring Fishery Act 1851 (c.26)

Herring Fishery Barrels Act 1874 (c.25)

Herring Fishery (Scotland) Act 1808 (c.110)

Herring Fishery (Scotland) Act 1815 (c.94)

Herring Fishery (Scotland) Act 1889 (c.23)

Herring Fishery (Scotland) Act Amendment 1890 (c.10)
Herring Fishing (Branding) Act 1913 (c.9)
Herring Industry Act 1935 (c.9)
Herring Industry Act 1938 (c.42)
Herring Industry Act 1944 (c.32)
Hertford and Bedford Roads Act 1757 (c.43)
Hertford and Bedford Roads Act 1769 (c.87)
Hertford and Bedford Roads Act 1790 (c.115)
Hertford and Broadwater Road Act 1757 (c.45)
Hertford and Bucks. Roads Act 1762 (c.63)
Hertford and Cambridge Roads Act 1769 (c.86)
Hertford and Middlesex Roads Act 1791 (c.108)
Hertford and Ware Roads Act 1732 (c.15)
Hertford and Ware Roads Act 1753 (c.56)
Hertford Church Act 1765 (c.94)
Hertford College Act 1874 (c.55)
Hertford Highways Act 1721 (c.9)
Hertford: Improvement Act 1788 (c.75)
Hertford Prison Act 1775 (c.25)
Hertford Roads Act 1762 (c.48)
Hertford Roads Act 1771 (c.57)
Hertford Roads Act 1778 (c.90)
Hertford Roads Act 1778 (c.94)
Hertford Roads Act 1782 (c.91)
Hertford Roads Act 1783 (c.25)
Hertford Shire-House Act 1768 (c.58)
Hertfordshire and Gloucestershire Canal Act 1793 (c.119)
Hertfordshire and Huntingdonshire Highways Act 1713 (c.33)
Hertfordshire and Huntingdonshire Roads Act 1765 (c.77)
Hertfordshire and Huntingdonshire Roads Act 1790 (c.89)
Hertfordshire and Middlesex Roads Act 1770 (c.107)
Hertfordshire Highways Act 1706 (c.14)
Hertfordshire Highways Act 1710 (c.14)
Hertfordshire Highways Act 1719 (c.20)
Hertfordshire Roads Act 1724 (c.11)
Hertfordshire Roads Act 1725 (c.10)
Hertfordshire Roads Act 1726 (c.32)
Hertfordshire Roads Act 1731 (c.10)
Hertfordshire Roads Act 1732 (c.24)
Hertfordshire Roads Act 1742 (c.16)
Hertfordshire Roads Act 1763 (c.26)
Hexham Bridge Act 1778 (c.44)
Hexham: Inclosure Act 1792 (c.110)
Hexham to Alston Road Act 1778 (c.116)
Hides and Skins Act 1769 (c.39)
High Constables Act 1869 (c.47)
High Court and County Court (Judges) Act 1950 (c.4)
High Court of Admiralty Act 1859 (c.6)
High Court of Admiralty (E.) Act 1840 (c.66)
High Court of Justiciary (Scotland) Act 1892 (c.21)
High Highlands Act 1823 (c.79)
High Peak Mining Customs and Mineral Courts Act 1851 (c.94)

Highgate and Chipping Barnet Road Act 1720 (c.18)
Highgate and Chipping Barnet Road Act 1763 (c.37)
Highgate and Hampstead Highways Act 1721 (c.5)
Highgate and Hampstead Roads Act 1734 (c.28)
Highgate and Hampstead Roads Act 1756 (c.88)
Highgate and Hampstead Roads Act 1776 (c.76)
Highgate and Hampstead Roads Act 1780 (c.78)
Highgate: Streets Act 1775 (c.43)
Highland Road and Bridges (Scotland) Act (c.43)
Highland Roads and Bridges Act 1851 (c.66)
Highland Roads and Bridges Act 1862 (c.105)
Highland Schools Act 1838 (c.87)
Highland Schools Act 1873 (c.53)
Highland Services Act 1715 (c.54)
Highlands and Islands Air Services (Scotland) Act 1980 (c.19)
Highlands and Islands Development (Scotland) Act 1965 (c.46)
Highlands and Islands Development (Scotland) Act 1968 (c.51)
Highlands and Islands (Medical Service) Additional Grant Act 1929 (c.13)
Highlands and Islands (Medical Service) Grant Act 1913 (c.26)
Highlands and Islands Shipping Services Act 1960 (c.31)
Highland Roads and Bridges Act 1862 (c.105)
Highland Services Act 1715 (c.54)
Highway Accounts Returns Act 1879 (c.39)
Highway Act 1794 (c.64)
Highway Act 1835 (c.50)
Highway Act 1841 (c.51)
Highway Act 1845 (c.71)
Highway Act 1863 (c.61)
Highway Act 1864 (c.101)
Highway Act Amendment 1885 (c.13)
Highway (Railway Crossing) Act 1839 (c.45)
Highway Rate Assessment and Expenditure Act 1882 (c.27)
Highway Rates Act 1836 (c.63)
Highway Rates Act 1839 (c.81)
Highway Rates Act 1840 (c.98)
Highway Rates Act 1843 (c.59)
Highway Rates Act 1845 (c.59)
Highway Rates Act 1846 (c.49)
Highway Rates Act 1847 (c.93)
Highway Rates Act 1848 (c.66)
Highway Rates Act 1849 (c.54)
Highway Rates Act 1850 (c.58)
Highway Rates Act 1851 (c.30)
Highway Rates Act 1852 (c.19)
Highway Rates Act 1853 (c.66)
Highway Rates Act 1854 (c.52)

Highway Rates Act 1860 (c.67)
Highway (Scotland) Act 1718 (c.30)
Highway (Scotland) Act 1771 (c.53)
Highway (Scotland) Act 1803 (c.80)
Highways Act 1707 (c.56)
Highways Act 1710 (c.23)
Highways Act 1714 (c.11)
Highways Act 1715 (c.52)
Highways Act 1718 (c.12)
Highways Act 1733 (c.9)
Highways Act 1742 (c.29)
Highways Act 1749 (c.28)
Highways Act 1750 (c.43)
Highways Act 1753 (c.28)
Highways Act 1765 (c.38)
Highways Act 1766 (c.42)
Highways Act 1766 (c.43)
Highways Act 1768 (c.5)
Highways Act 1773 (c.78)
Highways Act 1794 (c.74)
Highways Act 1839 (c.40)
Highways Act 1854 (c.69)
Highways Act 1862 (c.61)
Highways Act 1959 (c.25)
Highways Act 1971 (c.41)
Highways Act 1980 (c.66)
Highways (Amendment) Act 1965 (c.30)
Highways (Amendment) Act 1986 (c.13)
Highways and Bridges Act 1891 (c.63)
Highways and Locomotives (Amendment) Act 1878 (c.77)
Highways and Turnpike Roads Act 1753 (c.30)
Highways and Turnpike Roads Act 1755 (c.17)
Highways and Turnpike Roads Act 1757 (cc.27, 28)
Highways (England) Act 1814 (c.109)
Highways, etc. (England) Act 1815 (c.68)
Highways, etc. (Scotland) Act 1845 (c.41)
Highways (Ireland) Act 1805 (c.43)
Highways (Ireland) Act 1805 (c.96)
Highways (Ireland) Act 1806 (c.134)
Highways (Ireland) Act 1809 (c.84)
Highways (Ireland) Act 1810 (c.29)
Highways (Ireland) Act 1811 (c.40)
Highways (Ireland) Act 1811 (c.92)
Highways (Ireland) Act 1813 (c.76)
Highways (Ireland) Act 1813 (c.146)
Highways (Ireland) Act 1814 (c.135)
Highways (Isle of Wight) Act 1881 (c.72)
Highways (Miscellaneous Provisions) Act 1961 (c.63)
Highways, Old Stratford to Dunchurch Act 1757 (c.77)
Highways (Provision of Cattle Grids) Act 1950 (c.24)
Highways Returns Act 1849 (c.35)
Highways, South Wales Act 1851 (c.16)
Highways, South Wales Act 1854 (c.7)
Highworth, Wiltshire (Workhouse and Additional Overseer) Act 1789 (c.29)
Hijacking Act 1971 (c.70)

Hill Farming Act 1946 (c.73)
Hill Farming Act 1954 (c.23)
Hill Farming Act 1956 (c.72)
Hill Farming Act 1985 (c.32)
Hill to Lyde Way Road Act 1782 (c.109)
Hinckley and Coventry Road Act 1756 (c.66)
Hinckley and Coventry Road Act 1762 (c.69)
Hinckley to Melbourne Common Road Act 1774 (c.110)
Hire-Purchase Act 1938 (c.53)
Hire-Purchase Act 1954 (c.51)
Hire-Purchase Act 1964 (c.53)
Hire-Purchase Act 1965 (c.66)
Hire-Purchase (Scotland) Act 1965 (c.67)
Historic Buildings and Ancient Monuments Act 1953 (c.49)
Hockliffe to Stony Stratford Road Act 1786 (c.143)
Holborn: Improvement Act 1766 (c.100)
Holborn: Poor Relief Act 1770 (c.79)
Holborn: Poor Relief Act 1770 (c.80)
Holderness: Drainage Act 1774 (c.107)
Holderness to Beverley Road Act 1782 (c.90)
Holdings of County Courts Act 1732 (c.23)
Holidays Extension Act 1875 (c.13)
Holidays With Pay Act 1938 (c.70)
Holloway Prison Act 1852 (c.70)
Holy Island: Inclosure Act 1791 (c.92)
Holy Trinity Church, Bristol Act 1785 (c.95)
Holyhead Banks (Ireland) Act 1850 (c.111)
Holyhead Harbour Act 1810 (c.93)
Holyhead Harbour Act 1816 (c.84)
Holyhead Harbour Act 1847 (c.76)
Holyhead Harbour Railway Act 1859 (c.60)
Holyhead Harbours Act 1854 (c.44)
Holyhead Old Harbour Road Act 1874 (c.30)
Holyhead Road Act 1861 (c.28)
Holyhead Roads Act 1775 (c.69)
Holyhead Roads Act 1815 (c.152)
Holyhead Roads Act 1840 (c.104)
Home Counties (Music and Dancing) Licensing Act 1926 (c.31)
Home Energy Conservation Act 1995 (c.10)
Home Guard Act 1951 (c.8)
Home Purchase Assistance and Housing Corporation Guarantee Act 1978 (c.27)
Home Safety Act 1961 (c.20)
Homes Insulation Act 1978 (c.48)
Homicide Act 1957 (c.11)
Honiton: Improvement Act 1790 (c.25)
Honorary Freedom of Boroughs Act 1885 (c.29)
Honourable Lady Hylton-Foster's Annuity Act 1965 (c.70)
Hong Kong Act 1985 (c.15)
Hong Kong Economic and Trade Office Act 1996 (c.63)
Hong Kong (Overseas Public Servants) Act 1996 (c.2)
Hong Kong (War Wives and Widows) Act 1996 (c.41)
Hop (Prevention of Frauds) Act 1866 (c.37)
Hop Trade Act 1800 (c.81)

Hop Trade Act 1814 (c.123)

Hops Act 1774 (c.68)

Hops Act 1808 (c.134)

Hops Marketing Act 1982 (c.5)

Horse Breeding Act 1918 (c.13)

Horse Breeding Act 1958 (c.43)

Horse Duty Act 1811 (c.76)

Horse Patrol, Metropolis Act 1836 (c.50)

Horse Racing Act 1840 (c.5)

Horserace Betting Levy Act 1969 (c.14)

Horserace Betting Levy Act 1981 (c.30)

Horserace Totalisator Board Act 1997 (c.1)

Horserace Totalisator and Betting Levy Boards Act 1972 (c.69)

Horses (Protective Headgear for Young Riders) Act 1990 (c.25)

Horsham Roads Act 1792 (c.115)

Horsleytown Parish Act 1732 (c.11)

Horticultural Produce Act 1986 (c.20)

Horticultural Products (Emergency Customs Duties) Act 1931 (c.3)

Horticultural Produce (Sales on Commission) Act 1926 (c.39)

Horticulture Act 1960 (c.22)

Horticulture (Special Payments) Act 1974 (c.5)

Hosiery Act 1845 (c.77)

Hosiery Manufacture (Wages) Act 1874 (c.48)

Hospital Complaints Procedure Act 1985 (c.42)

Hospital Endowments (Scotland) Act 1953 (c.41)

Hospital Endowments (Scotland) Act 1971 (c.8)

Hospitals and Infirmaries (Ireland) Act 1806 (c.95)

Hospitals (Ireland) Act 1807 (c.44)

Hospitals (Ireland) Act 1809 (c.36)

Hospitals (Ireland) Act 1814 (c.112)

Hotel Proprietors Act 1956 (c.62)

Hours of Employment (Conventions) Act 1936 (c.22)

House and Window Duties Act 1766 (c.38)

House Duties Act (c.105)

House Duty Act 1778 (c.26)

House Duty (Ireland) Act 1814 (c.132)

House Letting and Rating (Scotland) Act 1911 (c.53)

House Letting and Rating (Scotland) Act 1920 (c.8)

House Occupiers Disqualification Removal Act 1878 (c.3)

House Occupiers Disqualification Removal (Scotland) Act 1878 (c.5)

House Occupiers in Counties Disqualification Removal (Scotland) Act 1880 (c.6)

House of Commons Act 1800 (c.92)

House of Commons Act 1855 (c.10)

House of Commons Act 1859 (c.5)

House of Commons (Administration) Act 1978 (c.36)

House of Commons (Clergy Disqualification) Act 1801 (c.63)

House of Commons (Commissions in H.M.'s Forces) Act 1914 (c.3)

House of Commons Cost Taxation Act 1847 (c.69)

House of Commons Costs Taxation Act 1879 (c.17)

House of Commons Disqualification Act 1741 (c.22)

House of Commons (Disqualification) Act 1782 (c.45)

House of Commons Disqualification Act 1957 (c.20)

House of Commons Disqualification Act 1975 (c.24)

House of Commons Disqualification (Declaration of Law) Act 1931 (c.13)

House of Commons Disqualification (Declaration of Law) Act 1935 (c.38)

House of Commons Disqualification (Temporary Provisions) Act 1941 (c.8)

House of Commons Disqualifications (Temporary Provisions) Act 1943 (c.10)

House of Commons Disqualification (Temporary Provisions) Act 1944 (c.11)

House of Commons (Disqualifications) Act 1801 (c.52)

House of Commons (Disqualifications) Act 1813 (c.16)

House of Commons (Electors) Act 1786 (c.100)

House of Commons (Indemnification of Certain Members) Act 1949 (c.46)

House of Commons Members' Fund Act 1939 (c.49)

House of Commons Members' Fund Act 1948 (c.36)

House of Commons Members' Fund Act 1957 (c.24)

House of Commons Members' Fund Act 1960 (c.50)

House of Commons Members' Fund Act 1962 (c.53)

House of Commons Members' Fund and Parliamentary Pensions Act 1981 (c.7)

House of Commons Officers Act 1834 (c.70)

House of Commons (Offices) Act 1812 (c.11)

House of Commons Offices Act 1846 (c.77)

House of Commons Offices Act 1849 (c.72)

House of Commons Offices Act 1856 (c.1)

House of Commons Qualification Act 1838 (c.48)

House of Commons (Redistribution of Seats) Act 1944 (c.41)

House of Commons (Redistribution of Seats) Act 1947 (c.10)

House of Commons (Redistribution of Seats) Act 1949 (c.66)

House of Commons (Redistribution of Seats) Act 1958 (c.26)

House of Commons (Redistribution of Seats) Act 1979 (c.15)

House of Commons (Service in His Majesty's Forces) Act 1939 (c.85)

House of Commons (Speaker) Act 1832 (c.105)

House of Correction Act (1852) (c.70)

House of Lords Costs Taxation Act 1849 (c.78)

House of Lords Oath Act 1843 (c.6)

House Purchase and Housing Act 1959 (c.33)

House Purchase Assistance and Housing Corporation Guarantee Act 1978 (c.27)

House Tax Act 1803 (c.161)

House Tax Act 1808 (c.55)

House Tax Act 1851 (c.36)

House Tax Act 1871 (c.103)

House to House Collections Act 1939 (c.44)

Houses of Correction Act 1782 (c.64)

Houses of Correction Act 1784 (c.55)

Houses of Industry, etc. (I.) Act 1841 (c.41)

Houses of Parliament Act 1806 (c.89)

Houses of Parliament Act 1810 (c.119)

Houses of Parliament Act 1837 (c.7)

Houses of Parliament Act 1867 (c.40)

Housing Act 1914 (c.31)

Housing Act 1921 (c.19)

Housing Act 1925 (c.14)

Housing Act 1930 (c.39)

Housing Act 1935 (c.40)

Housing Act 1936 (c.51)

Housing Act 1949 (c.60)

Housing Act 1952 (c.53)

Housing Act 1957 (c.56)

Housing Act 1961 (c.65)

Housing Act 1964 (c.56)

Housing Act 1969 (c.33)

Housing Act 1971 (c.76)

Housing Act 1974 (c.44)

Housing Act 1980 (c.51)

Housing Act 1985 (c.68)

Housing Act 1988 (c.50)

Housing Act 1996 (c.52)

Housing (Agricultural Population) (Scotland) Act 1938 (c.38)

Housing (Agricultural Population) (Scotland) Act 1943 (c.22)

Housing (Amendment) Act 1973 (c.5)

Housing (Amendment) (Scotland) Act 1965 (c.40)

Housing (Amendment) (Scotland) Act 1970 (c.5)

Housing (Amendment) (Scotland) Act 1976 (c.11)

Housing (Amendment) (Scotland) Act 1981 (c.72)

Housing and Building Control Act 1984 (c.29)

Housing and Planning Act 1986 (c.63)

Housing and Town and Development (Scotland) Act 1957 (c.38)

Housing Associations Act 1985 (c.69)

Housing (Consequential Provisions) Act 1985 (c.71)

Housing Defects Act 1984 (c.50)

Housing (Emergency Powers) Act 1939 (c.73)

Housing, etc. Act 1923 (c.24)

Housing Finance Act 1972 (c.47)

Housing Finance (Special Provisions) Act 1975 (c.67)

Housing (Financial and Miscellaneous Provisions) Act 1946 (c.48)

Housing (Financial Provisions) Act 1924 (c.35)

Housing (Financial Provisions) Act 1933 (c.15)

Housing (Financial Provisions) Act 1938 (c.16)

Housing (Financial Provisions) Act 1958 (c.42)

Housing (Financial Provisions) (Scotland) Act 1933 (c.16)

Housing (Financial Provisions) (Scotland) Act 1946 (c.54)

Housing (Financial Provisions) (Scotland) Act 1967 (c.20)

Housing (Financial Provisions) (Scotland) Act 1968 (c.31)

Housing (Financial Provisions) (Scotland) Act 1972 (c.46)

Housing (Financial Provisions) (Scotland) Act 1978 (c.14)

Housing Grants, Construction and Regeneration Act 1996 (c.53)

Housing (Homeless Persons) Act 1977 (c.48)

Housing (Ireland) Act 1919 (c.45)

Housing (No. 2) Act 1914 (c.52)

Housing (No. 2) (Amendment) Act 1914 (c.71)

Housing of the Working Classes Act 1885 (c.72)

Housing of the Working Classes Act 1890 (c.70)

Housing of the Working Classes Act, 1890, Amendment (Scotland) 1892 (c.22)

Housing of the Working Classes Act, 1890, Amendment (Scotland) 1896 (c.31)

Housing of the Working Classes Act 1894 (c.55)

Housing of the Working Classes Act 1900 (c.59)

Housing of the Working Classes Act 1903 (c.39)

Housing of the Working Classes Act 1908 (c.61)

Housing of the Working Classes (Ireland) Act 1893 (c.33)

Housing of the Working Classes (Ireland) Act 1896 (c.11)

Housing of the Working Classes (Ireland) Act 1908 (c.61)

Housing Rents and Subsidies Act 1975 (c.6)

Housing Rents and Subsidies (Scotland) Act 1975 (c.28)

Housing Repairs and Rents Act 1954 (c.53)

Housing (Repairs and Rents) (Scotland) Act 1954 (c.50)

Housing (Revision of Contributions) Act 1929 (c.6)

Housing (Rosyth Dockyard) Act 1915 (c.49)
Housing (Rural Authorities) Act 1931 (c.39)
Housing (Rural Workers) Act 1926 (c.56)
Housing (Rural Workers) Act 1942 (c.32)
Housing (Rural Workers) Amendment Act 1931 (c.22)
Housing (Rural Workers) Amendment Act 1938 (c.35)
Housing (Scotland) Act 1920 (c.71)
Housing (Scotland) Act 1921 (c.33)
Housing (Scotland) Act 1925 (c.15)
Housing (Scotland) Act 1930 (c.40)
Housing (Scotland) Act 1935 (c.41)
Housing (Scotland) Act 1944 (c.39)
Housing (Scotland) Act 1949 (c.61)
Housing (Scotland) Act 1950 (c.34)
Housing (Scotland) Act 1952 (c.63)
Housing (Scotland) Act 1962 (c.28)
Housing (Scotland) Act 1966 (c.49)
Housing (Scotland) Act 1969 (c.34)
Housing (Scotland) Act 1974 (c.45)
Housing (Scotland) Act 1986 (c.65)
Housing (Scotland) Act 1987 (c.26)
Housing (Scotland) Act 1988 (c.43)
Housing (Slum Clearance Compensation) Act 1965 (c.81)
Housing Subsidies Act 1956 (c.33)
Housing Subsidies Act 1967 (c.29)
Housing (Temporary Accommodation) Act 1944 (c.36)
Housing (Temporary Accommodation) Act 1945 (c.39)
Housing (Temporary Accommodation) Act 1947 (c.6)
Housing (Temporary Provisions) Act 1944 (c.33)
Housing, Town Planning etc. Act 1919 (c.35)
Housing, Town Planning, etc. Act 1909 (c.44)
Housing, Town Planning, etc. (Scotland) Act 1919 (c.60)
Housing (Underground Rooms) Act 1959 (c.34)
Hovercraft Act 1968 (c.59)
Howth Harbour Act 1810 (c.72)
Howth Harbour Act 1863 (c.72)
Hubberston and Pill, Pembroke: Docks and Piers Act 1790 (c.55)
Huddersfield Burial Ground Act 1852 (c.41)
Huddersfield Burial Ground Act 1855 (c.89)
Huddersfield Roads Act 1788 (c.103)
Huddersfield to Ashton-under-Lyne Canal Act 1794 (c.53)
Hudson's Bay Company Act 1868 (c.105)
Hue and Cry Act 1734 (c.16)
Hue and Cry Act 1748 (c.24)
Hull: Drainage Act 1792 (c.109)
Hull: Improvement Act 1795 (c.46)
Hull, Poor Relief Act 1741 (c.10)
Hulmes Chapel and Chelpord Road Act 1797 (c.157)
Human Fertilisation and Embryology Act 1990 (c.37)
Human Fertilisation and Embryology (Disclosure of Information) Act 1992 (c.54)

Human Organ Transplants Act 1989 (c.31)
Human Tissue Act 1961 (c.54)
Humber Bridge (Debts) Act 1996 (c.1)
Hundred Foot River and Ouse: Bedford Level Act 1756 (c.22)
Hungerford to Leckford Road Act 1793 (c.168)
Huntingdon Clergy Charity Act 1775 (c.24)
Huntingdon: Drainage Act 1772 (c.39)
Huntingdon: Improvement Act 1785 (c.9)
Huntingdon Roads Act 1755 (c.26)
Huntingdon Roads Act 1765 (c.51)
Huntingdonshire and Cambridgeshire Roads Act 1744 (c.23)
Huntingdonshire and Northamptonshire Roads Act 1750 (c.59)
Huntingdonshire and Northamptonshire Roads Act 1771 (c.80)
Huntingdonshire Roads Act 1727 (c.4)
Huntingdonshire Roads Act 1757 (c.51)
Huntingdonshire Roads Act 1774 (c.118)
Huntingdonshire Roads Act 1779 (c.86)
Huntingdonshire Roads Act 1790 (c.103)
Hyde Park Act 1842 (c.19)
Hyde Park (Underground Parking) Act 1961 (c.26)
Hydrocarbon Oil (Customs and Excise) Act 1971 (c.12)
Hydrocarbon Oil Duties Act 1979 (c.5)
Hydrocarbon Oil Duties (Temporary Increase) Act 1956 (c.2)
Hydro-Electric Development (Scotland) Act 1943 (c.32)
Hydro-Electric Undertaking (Valuation for Rating) (Scotland) Act 1944 (c.34)
Hydro-Electricity Development (Scotland) Act 1952 (c.22)
Hydrogen Cyanide (Fumigation) Act 1937 (c.45)
Hypnotism Act 1952 (c.46)
Hypothec Abolition (Scotland) Act 1880 (c.12)
Hypothec Amendment (Scotland) Act 1867 (c.42)

Idiots Act 1886 (c.25)
Ilfracombe Harbour Act 1730 (c.19)
Illegal Trawling (Scotland) Act 1934 (c.18)
Illegitimate Children (Scotland) Act 1930 (c.33)
Illicit Distillation (Ireland) Act 1813 (c.32)
Illicit Distillation (Ireland) Act 1831 (c.55)
Illicit Distillation (Ireland) Act 1857 (c.40)
Immature Spirits (Restriction) Act 1915 (c.46)
Immigration Act 1971 (c.77)
Immigration Act 1988 (c.14)
Immigration Appeals Act 1969 (c.21)
Immigration (Carriers' Liability) Act 1987 (c.24)
Immoral Traffic (Scotland) Act 1902 (c.11)
Imperial Defence Act 1888 (c.32)
Imperial Institute (Management) Act 1916 (c.8)

Imperial Telegraphs Act 1929 (c.7)
Imperial Telegraphs Act 1938 (c.57)
Imperial War Graves Endowment Fund Act 1926 (c.14)
Imperial War Museum Act 1920 (c.16)
Imperial War Museum Act 1955 (c.14)
Import and Export Control Act 1990 (c.45)
Import and Export Duties Act 1802 (c.117)
Import Duties Act 1931 (c.8)
Import Duties Act 1958 (c.6)
Import Duties (Emergency Provisions) Act 1939 (c.97)
Import Duty Act 1804 (c.85)
Import, Export and Customs Powers (Defence) Act 1939 (c.69)
Import of Live Fish (England and Wales) Act 1980 (c.27)
Import of Live Fish (Scotland) Act 1978 (c.35)
Importation Act 1702 (c.8)
Importation Act 1702 (cc. 21, 22)
Importation Act 1703 (c.15)
Importation Act 1704 (c.9)
Importation Act 1706 (c.19)
Importation Act 1707 (c.60)
Importation Act 1711 (c.36)
Importation Act 1712 (c.9)
Importation Act 1714 (c.15)
Importation Act 1715 (c.40)
Importation Act 1719 (c.14)
Importation Act 1721 (c.12)
Importation Act 1726 (c.5)
Importation Act 1726 (c.25)
Importation Act 1728 (c.9)
Importation Act 1730 (c.12)
Importation Act 1730 (c.15)
Importation Act 1731 (c.9)
Importation Act 1732 (c.7)
Importation Act 1738 (c.36)
Importation Act 1740 (c.36)
Importation Act 1743 (c.36)
Importation Act 1753 (c.8)
Importation Act 1755 (c.21)
Importation Act 1757 (c.3)
Importation Act 1763 (c.6)
Importation Act 1763 (c.28)
Importation Act 1765 (c.1)
Importation Act 1765 (c.3)
Importation Act 1765 (c.10)
Importation Act 1765 (c.48)
Importation Act 1766 (cc.11, 12)
Importation Act 1766 (c.13)
Importation Act 1766 (c.19)
Importation Act 1766 (c.22)
Importation Act 1766 (c.30)
Importation Act 1766 (c.43)
Importation Act 1768 (c.9)
Importation Act 1769 (c.4)
Importation Act 1769 (c.9)
Importation Act 1770 (c.2)
Importation Act 1771 (c.8)
Importation Act 1771 (c.41)
Importation Act 1771 (cc.49, 50)
Importation Act 1772 (c.7)

Importation Act 1772 (cc.32, 33)
Importation Act 1772 (c.67)
Importation Act 1774 (c.9)
Importation Act 1774 (c.74)
Importation Act 1775 (c.1)
Importation Act 1775 (c.7)
Importation Act 1776 (c.8)
Importation Act 1776 (c.35)
Importation Act 1776 (c.41)
Importation Act 1778 (c.56)
Importation Act 1779 (c.28)
Importation Act 1780 (c.6)
Importation Act 1781 (c.62)
Importation Act 1782 (c.7)
Importation Act 1782 (c.30)
Importation Act 1782 (c.38)
Importation Act 1782 (c.72)
Importation Act 1782 (c.78)
Importation Act 1783 (c.1)
Importation Act 1783 (cc.9, 10)
Importation Act 1783 (c.14)
Importation Act 1788 (c.39)
Importation Act 1789 (c.16)
Importation Act 1790 (c.28)
Importation Act 1790 (c.41)
Importation Act 1791 (c.37)
Importation Act 1791 (c.38)
Importation Act 1792 (c.49)
Importation Act 1793 (c.63)
Importation Act 1794 (c.50)
Importation Act 1795 (c.4)
Importation Act 1795 (c.15)
Importation Act 1795 (c.100)
Importation Act 1795 (c.115)
Importation Act 1795 (c.117)
Importation Act 1796 (c.8)
Importation Act 1796 (c.81)
Importation Act 1796 (c.113)
Importation Act 1797 (c.3)
Importation Act 1797 (c.25)
Importation Act 1797 (c.72)
Importation Act 1797 (c.84)
Importation Act 1799 (c.27)
Importation Act 1799 (c.75)
Importation Act 1799 (c.87)
Importation Act 1799 (c.95)
Importation Act 1799 (c.98)
Importation Act 1799 (c.111)
Importation Act 1799 (c.112)
Importation Act 1800 (c.11)
Importation Act 1800 (c.18)
Importation Act 1800 (c.25)
Importation Act 1800 (c.83)
Importation Act 1800 (c.107)
Importation Act 1801 (c.7)
Importation Act 1801 (c.16)
Importation Act 1801 (c.37)
Importation Act 1801 (c.41)
Importation Act 1801 (c.93)
Importation Act 1802 (c.44)
Importation Act 1804 (cc.29, 30)
Importation Act 1806 (c.74)
Importation Act 1806 (c.103)

Importation Act 1806 (c.113)

Importation Act 1806 (c.117)

Importation Act 1806 (c.121)

Importation Act 1807 (c.24)

Importation Act 1807 (cc.25, 26)

Importation Act 1807 (c.27)

Importation Act 1807 (c.67)

Importation Act 1808 (c.11)

Importation Act 1808 (c.19)

Importation Act 1808 (cc.23, 24)

Importation Act 1808 (c.125)

Importation Act 1809 (c.9)

Importation Act 1809 (c.16)

Importation Act 1809 (cc.25, 26)

Importation Act 1809 (c.60)

Importation Act 1809 (c.105)

Importation Act 1810 (c.55)

Importation Act 1810 (c.80)

Importation Act 1811 (c.48)

Importation Act 1811 (c.58)

Importation Act 1811 (c.62)

Importation Act 1812 (c.18)

Importation Act 1812 (c.33)

Importation Act 1812 (c.119)

Importation Act 1813 (c.34)

Importation Act 1813 (c.37)

Importation Act 1813 (c.41)

Importation Act 1814 (c.51)

Importation Act 1814 (c.124)

Importation Act 1814 (c.125)

Importation Act 1815 (c.26)

Importation Act 1815 (c.34)

Importation Act 1815 (c.86)

Importation Act 1816 (c.2)

Importation Act 1816 (cc.25, 26)

Importation Act 1816 (c.36)

Importation Act 1816 (c.37)

Importation Act 1840 (c.32)

Importation Act 1844 (c.100)

Importation Act 1847 (c.2)

Importation Act 1847 (c.86)

Importation and Exportation Act 1766 (cc.1–5)

Importation and Exportation Act 1772 (cc. 1–5)

Importation and Exportation Act 1772 (cc.69, 70)

Importation and Exportation Act 1772 (cc.72, 73)

Importation and Exportation Act 1787 (c.27)

Importation and Exportation Act 1789 (c.58)

Importation and Exportation Act 1790 (c.1)

Importation and Exportation Act 1790 (c.29)

Importation and Exportation Act 1790 (c.42)

Importation and Exportation Act 1791 (c.4)

Importation and Exportation Act 1791 (c.30)

Importation and Exportation Act 1791 (c.47)

Importation and Exportation Act 1792 (c.37)

Importation and Exportation Act 1793 (c.50)

Importation and Exportation Act 1793 (c.65)

Importation and Exportation Act 1797 (c.39)

Importation and Exportation Act 1799 (c.88)

Importation and Exportation Act 1800 (c.58)

Importation and Exportation Act 1804 (c.109)

Importation and Exportation Act 1805 (c.57)

Importation and Exportation Act 1805 (c.86)

Importation and Exportation Act 1807 (c.34)

Importation and Exportation Act 1810 (cc.12, 13)

Importation and Exportation Act 1810 (c.21)

Importation and Exportation Act 1812 (c.8)

Importation and Exportation Act 1812 (c.69)

Importation and Exportation Act 1812 (c.79)

Importation and Exportation Act 1813 (c.55)

Importation and Exportation Act 1814 (c.81)

Importation and Exportation Act 1814 (c.129)

Importation and Exportation Act 1815 (c.117)

Importation and Exportation (Ireland) Act 1807 (c.1)

Importation and Exportation (Ireland) Act 1807 (c.16)

Importation and Exportation (Ireland) Act 1810 (c.97)

Importation, etc. Act 1750 (c.32)

Importation, etc. Act 1766 (c.28)

Importation, etc. Act 1766 (c.36)

Importation, etc. Act 1780 (c.45)

Importation, etc. Act 1801 (c.68)

Importation, etc. Act 1804 (c.35)

Importation, etc. Act 1804 (c.89)

Importation, etc. Act 1806 (c.53)

Importation, etc. Act 1809 (c.18)

Importation, etc. Act 1809 (c.22)

Importation, etc. Act 1812 (c.2)

Importation, etc. Act 1812 (c.20)

Importation, etc. Act 1814 (cc.8, 9)

Importation, etc. Act 1814 (c.111)

Importation, Exportation, etc. Act 1805 (c.26)

Importation in Neutral Vessel, etc. Act 1803 (c.153)

Importation into Isle of Man Act 1813 (c.110)

Importation into Quebec Act 1763 (c.19)

Importation into Quebec Act 1766 (c.42)

Importation into Scotland Act 1740 (c.7)

Importation (Ireland) Act 1807 (c.31)

Importation of Animals Act 1922 (c.5)

Importation of Arms, etc. (Ireland) Act 1841 (c.25)

Importation of Milk Act 1983 (c.37)

Importation of Pedigree Animals Act 1925 (c.30)

Importation of Plumage (Prohibition) Act 1921 (c.16)

Importation of Prize Goods Act 1711 (c.30)

Importation of Silk Act 1779 (c.9)

Imprisonment for Debt (Scotland) Act 1835 (c.70)

Imprisonment for Debts Abroad Act 1801 (c.106)

Imprisonment of Certain Traitors Act 1702 (c.23)

Imprisonment of Certain Traitors Act 1714 (c.7)

Imprisonment of Certain Traitors Act 1727 (c.4)

Imprisonment of Debtors, etc. Act 1786 (c.38)

Imprisonment (Temporary Provisions) Act 1980 (c.57)

Imprisonment with Hard Labour Act 1813 (c.162)

Improvement at Westminster Act 1814 (c.154)

Improvement of Commons Act 1801 (c.20)

Improvement of Land Act 1864 (c.114)

Improvement of Land Act 1899 (c.46)

Improvement of Land Act (1899) Amendment Act 1925 (c.48)

Improvement of Land (Scotland) Act 1893 (c.34)

Improvement of Lands (Ecclesiastical Benefices) Act 1854 (c.67)

Improvement of Live Stock (Licensing of Bulls) Act 1931 (c.43)

Improvements, Metropolis Act 1844 (c.1)

Incapacitated Bishops Act 1843 (c.62)

Incest Act 1567 (c.14)

Incest and Related Offences (Scotland) Act 1986 (c.36)

Incitement to Disaffection Act 1934 (c.56)

Incitement to Mutiny Act 1797 (c.70)

Incitement to Mutiny Act 1814 (c.158)

Inciting to Mutiny, etc. Act 1815 (c.171)

Inclosure Act 1773 (c.81)

Inclosure Act 1801 (c.109)

Inclosure Act 1836 (c.115)

Inclosure Act 1840 (c.31)

Inclosure Act 1845 (c.118)

Inclosure Act 1846 (c.70)

Inclosure Act 1852 (c.79)

Inclosure Act 1854 (c.97)

Inclosure Act 1857 (c.31)

Inclosure Act 1866 (c.94)

Inclosure Act 1867 (c.20)

Inclosure Act 1867 (c.71)

Inclosure, etc., Expenses Act 1868 (c.89)

Inclosures Act 1846 (c.16)

Inclosures Act 1846 (c.117)

Inclosures Act 1847 (c.25)

Income and Corporation Taxes Act 1970 (c.10)

Income and Corporation Taxes Act 1988 (c.1)

Income and Corporation Taxes (No. 2) Act 1970 (c.54)

Income Tax Act 1803 (c.122)

Income Tax Act 1804 (c.37)

Income Tax Act 1804 (c.83)

Income Tax Act 1805 (c.15)

Income Tax Act 1805 (c.49)

Income Tax Act 1805 (c.110)

Income Tax Act 1806 (c.65)

Income Tax Act 1842 (c.35)

Income Tax Act 1844 (c.38)

Income Tax Act 1845 (c.4)

Income Tax Act 1846 (c.81)

Income Tax Act 1871 (c.5)

Income Tax Act 1873 (c.8)

Income Tax Act 1918 (c.40)

Income Tax Act 1944 (c.32)

Income Tax Act 1952 (c.10)

Income Tax Assessment Act 1870 (c.4)

Income Tax (Employments) Act 1943 (c.45)

Income Tax, etc. Act 1810 (c.106)

Income Tax (Foreign Dividends) Act 1842 (c.80)

Income Tax Management Act 1964 (c.37)

Income Tax (Offices and Employment) Act 1944 (c.12)

Income Tax Procedure (Emergency Provisions) Act 1939 (c.99)

Income Tax (Public Offices) Act 1872 (c.82)

Income Tax (Repayment of Post-War Credits) Act 1959 (c.28)

Income Tax Repeal, etc. Act 1802 (c.42)

Increase of Rent and Mortgage Interest (Restrictions) Act 1919 (c.7)

Increase of Rent and Mortgage Interest (Restrictions) Act 1920 (c.17)

Increase of Rent and Mortgage Interest (Restrictions) Act 1935 (c.13)

Increase of Rent and Mortgage Interest (Restrictions) Act 1938 (c.26)

Increase of Rent and Mortgage Interest Restrictions Act 1923 (c.7)

Increase of Rent and Mortgage Interest (War Restrictions) Act 1915 (c.97)

Increase of Rent, etc. (Amendment) Act 1918 (c.7)

Increase of Rent, etc. (Amendment) Act 1919 (c.90)

Increased Assessments Act 1861 (c.27)

Incumbents Act 1868 (c.117)

Incumbents and Benefices Loans Extension Act 1881 (c.25)

Incumbents of Benefices Loans Act 1887 (c.8)

Incumbents of Benefices Loans Extension Act 1886 (c.34)

Incumbents of Benefices Loans Extension Act 1896 (c.13)

Incumbents Resignation Act 1871 (c.44)

Incumbents Resignation Act, 1871, Amendment 1887 (c.23)

Indecent Advertisements (Amendment) Act 1970 (c.47)

Indecent Advertisements Act 1889 (c.18)

Indecent Displays (Control) Act 1981 (c.42)

Indecency with Children Act 1960 (c.33)

Indemnity Act 1715 (c.39)

Indemnity Act 1727 (c.23)

Indemnity Act 1728 (c.31)

Indemnity Act 1730 (c.6)

Indemnity Act 1732 (c.4)

Indemnity Act 1733 (c.10)

Indemnity Act 1734 (c.4)

Indemnity Act 1734 (c.17)

Indemnity Act 1735 (c.6)

Indemnity Act 1736 (c.13)

Indemnity Act 1737 (c.31)

Indemnity Act 1738 (c.6)

Indemnity Act 1739 (c.6)

Indemnity Act 1740 (c.18)

Indemnity Act 1742 (c.30)

India and Burma (Postponement of Elections) Act 1941 (c.44)

India and Burma (Temporary and Miscellaneous Provisions) Act 1942 (c.39)

India (Attachment of States) Act 1944 (c.14)

India (Central Government and Legislature) Act 1946 (c.39)

India (Consequential Provisions) Act 1949 (c.92)

India (Estate Duty) Act 1945 (c.7)

India (Federal Court Judges) Act 1942 (c.7)

India Government, etc. Act 1807 (c.68)

India Home (Appointments) Act 1875 (c.73)

India (Home Charges Arrears) Act 1882 (c.79)

India (Inam Lands) Act 1869 (c.29)

India Independence Act 1947 (c.30)

India Military Funds Act 1866 (c.18)

India (Miscellaneous Provisions) Act 1944 (c.38)

India Office Auditor Act 1881 (c.63)

India Officers' Salaries Act 1837 (c.47)

India Pay (Temporary Abatements) Act 1933 (c.7)

India (Proclamations of Emergency) Act 1946 (c.23)

India Stock Certificate Act 1863 (c.73)

India Stock Dividends Act 1871 (c.29)

India Stock (Powers of Attorney) Act 1880 (c.11)

India Stock Transfer Act 1862 (c.7)

Indian Advance Act 1879 (c.45)

Indian and Colonial Divorce Jurisdiction Act 1926 (c.40)

Indian and Colonial Divorce Jurisdiction Act 1939 (c.35)

Indian Army Pension Deficiency Act 1885 (c.67)

Indian Bishops Act 1842 (c.119)

Indian Bishops Act 1871 (c.62)

Indian Church Act 1927 (c.40)

Indian Civil Service (Temporary Provisions) Act 1915 (c.87)

Indian Councils Act 1869 (c.98)

Indian Councils Act 1871 (c.34)

Indian Councils Act 1874 (c.91)

Indian Councils Act 1892 (c.14)

Indian Councils Act 1904 (c.26)

Indian Councils Act 1909 (c.4)

Indian Divorce Act 1945 (c.5)

Indian Divorces (Validity) Act 1921 (c.18)

Indian Franchise Act 1945 (c.2)

Indian Guaranteed Railways Act 1879 (c.41)

Indian High Courts Act 1911 (c.18)

Indian High Courts Act 1922 (c.20)

Indian Independence Act 1947 (c.30)

Indian Loan Act 1881 (c.54)

Indian Marine Service Act 1884 (c.38)

Indian Pay (Temporary Abatements) Act 1931 (c.7)

Indian Pay (Temporary Abatements) Act 1934 (c.8)

Indian Presidency Towns Act 1815 (c.84)

Indian Prize Money Act 1866 (c.47)

Indian Prize Money Act 1868 (c.38)

Indian Railway Companies Act 1868 (c.26)

Indian Railway Companies Act 1873 (c.43)

Indian Railways Act 1894 (c.12)

Indian Railways Act Amendment 1906 (c.9)

Indian Salaries and Allowances Act 1880 (c.3)

Indian Securities Act 1860 (c.5)

Indictable Offences Act 1848 (c.42)

Indictable Offences Act Amendment 1868 (c.107)

Indictments Act 1915 (c.90)

Indus Basin Development Fund Act 1960 (c.1)

Industrial and Providence Societies Act 1952 (c.17)

Industrial and Providence Societies Act 1961 (c.28)

Industrial and Provident Societies Act 1867 (c.117)

Industrial and Provident Societies Act 1871 (c.80)

Industrial and Provident Societies Act 1876 (c.45)

Industrial and Provident Societies Act 1893 (c.39)

Industrial and Provident Societies Act 1894 (c.8)

Industrial and Provident Societies Act 1965 (c.12)

Industrial and Provident Societies Act 1967 (c.48)

Industrial and Provident Societies Act 1975 (c.41)

Industrial and Provident Societies Act 1978 (c.34)

Industrial and Provident Societies (Amendment) Act 1895 (c.30)

Industrial and Provident Societies (Amendment) Act 1913 (c.31)

Industrial and Provident Societies (Amendment) Act 1928 (c.4)

Industrial and Providence Societies (Amendment) Act 1954 (c.43)

Industrial Assurance Act 1923 (c.8)

Industrial Assurance and Friendly Societies Act 1929 (c.28)

Industrial Assurance and Friendly Societies Act 1948 (c.39)

Industrial Assurance and Friendly Societies Act 1948 (Amendment) Act 1958 (c.27)

Industrial Assurance and Friendly Societies (Emergency Protection from Forfeiture) Act 1940 (c.10)

Industrial Assurance (Juvenile Societies) Act 1926 (c.35)

Industrial Common Ownership Act 1976 (c.78)

Industrial Courts Act 1919 (c.69)

Industrial Development Act 1966 (c.34)

Industrial Development Act 1982 (c.52)

Industrial Development Act 1985 (c.25)

Industrial Development (Ships) Act 1970 (c.2)

Industrial Diseases (Notification) Act 1981 (c.25)

Industrial Expansion Act 1968 (c.32)

Industrial Injuries and Diseases (Northern Ireland Old Cases) Act 1975 (c.17)

Industrial Injuries and Diseases (Old Cases) Act 1967 (c.34)

Industrial Injuries and Diseases (Old Cases) Act 1975 (c.16)

Industrial Organisations and Development Act 1947 (c.40)

Industrial Relations Act 1971 (c.72)

Industrial Reorganisation Corporation Act 1966 (c.50)

Industrial Schools Act 1866 (c.118)

Industrial Schools Act Amendment 1880 (c.15)

Industrial Schools Acts Amendment 1894 (c.33)

Industrial Schools (Ireland) Act 1868 (c.25)

Industrial Schools (Ireland) Act 1885 (c.19)

Industrial Training Act 1954 (c.16)

Industrial Training Act 1964 (c.16)

Industrial Training Act 1982 (c.10)

Industrial Training Act 1986 (c.15)

Industrial Tribunals Act 1996 (c.17)

Industry Act 1971 (c.17)

Industry Act 1972 (c.63)

Industry Act 1975 (c.68)

Industry Act 1979 (c.32)

Industry Act 1980 (c.33)

Industry Act 1981 (c.6)

Industry Act 1982 (c.18)

Industry (Amendment) Act 1976 (c.73)

Inebriates Act 1888 (c.19)

Inebriates Act 1898 (c.60)

Inebriates Act 1899 (c.35)

Inebriates Amendment (Scotland) Act 1900 (c.28)

Infant Felons Act 1840 (c.90)

Infant Life (Preservation) Act 1929 (c.34)

Infant Life Protection Act 1872 (c.38)

Infant Life Protection Act 1897 (c.57)

Infant Suitors in Equity Entitled to Stock Act 1812 (c.32)

Infant Trustees and Mortgages Act 1763 (c.16)

Infanticide Act 1922 (c.18)

Infanticide Act 1938 (c.36)

Infants Property Act 1830 (c.65)

Infants Relief Act 1874 (c.62)

Infants' Settlements Act 1855 (c.43)

Infectious Diseases (Notification) Act 1889 (c.72)

Infectious Diseases (Notification) Extension Act 1899 (c.8)

Infectious Diseases (Prevention) Act 1890 (c.34)

Infeftment Act 1845 (c.35)

Inferior Courts Act 1779 (c.70)

Inferior Courts Act 1844 (c.19)

Inferior Courts Judgments Extension Act 1882 (c.31)

Informal Attestation of Certain Deeds Act 1814 (c.168)

Information in Nature of Quo Warranto Act 1792 (c.58)

Inhabited House Duties Act 1791 (c.2)

Inhabited House, etc., Duties Act 1797 (c.40)

Inheritance (Family Provision) Act 1938 (c.45)

Inheritance (Provision for Family and Dependants) Act 1975 (c.63)

Inheritance Tax (Formerly Capital Transfer Tax) Act 1984 (c.51)

Injured Animals Act 1894 (c.22)

Injured Animals Act 1907 (c.5)

Injuries in War (Compensation) Act 1914 (c.30)

Injuries in War Compensation Act 1914 (Session 2) (c.18)

Injuries in War (Compensation) Act 1915 (c.24)

Inland Excise and Taxes (Ireland) Act 1812 (c.97)

Inland Fisheries (Ireland) Act 1838 (c.76)

Inland Navigation (Ireland) Act 1813 (c.144)

Inland Navigation (Ireland) Act 1815 (c.182)

Inland Revenue Act 1866 (c.64)

Inland Revenue Act 1868 (c.124)

Inland Revenue Act 1880 (c.20)

Inland Revenue Buildings Act 1881 (c.10)

Inland Revenue Regulation Act 1890 (c.21)

Inland Revenue Repeal Act 1870 (c.99)

Inner Urban Areas Act 1978 (c.50)

Innkeepers Act 1878 (c.38)

Inquiries by Board of Trade Act 1872 (c.18)

Inquiry into Certain Frauds and Abuses Act 1802 (c.16)

Inquiry into Fees, Public Offices Act 1785 (c.19)

Inquiry into Fees, Public Offices Act 1786 (c.66)

Inquiry into Fees, Public Offices Act 1787 (c.35)

Inquiry into Military Departments Act 1805 (c.47)

Inquiry into Military Departments Act 1807 (c.33)

Inquiry into Military Departments Act 1808 (c.61)

Inquiry into Military Departments Act 1809 (c.111)

Inquiry into Military Expenditure, etc. Act 1811 (c.19)

Inquiry into Naval Departments Act 1805 (c.46)

Inquiry into Public Expenditure Act 1805 (c.70)

Inquiry into Public Offices (Ireland) Act 1804 (c.106)

Inquiry into Public Offices (Ireland) Act (c.65)

Inquiry into Public Offices (Ireland) Act 1813 (c.130)

Inrolment of Grants of Annuities Act (c.141)
Insane Prisoners Act 1840 (c.54)
Inshore Fishing Industry Act 1945 (c.11)
Inshore Fishing (Scotland) Act 1984 (c.26)
Inshore Fishing (Scotland) Act 1994 (c.27)
Insolvency Act 1976 (c.60)
Insolvency Act 1985 (c.65)
Insolvency Act 1986 (c.45)
Insolvency Act 1994 (c.7)
Insolvency (No. 2) Act 1994 (c.12)
Insolvency Services (Accounting and Invest-
ment) Act 1970 (c.8)
Insolvent Act 1812 (c.163)
Insolvent Debtors Act 1839 (c.39)
Insolvent Debtors Act 1842 (c.116)
Insolvent Debtor's Discharge Act 1794 (c.69)
Insolvent Debtor's Discharge Act 1795 (c.88)
Insolvent Debtors, East Indies Act 1836
(c.47)
Insolvent Debtors (England) Act 1813 (c.23)
Insolvent Debtors (England) Act 1813 (c.102)
Insolvent Debtors (England) Act 1816 (c.102)
Insolvent Debtors (England) Act 1836 (c.44)
Insolvent Debtors, etc., Relief Act 1774 (c.77)
Insolvent Debtors, India Act 1840 (c.80)
Insolvent Debtors, India Act 1846 (c.14)
Insolvent Debtors (Ireland) Act 1810 (c.47)
Insolvent Debtors (Ireland) Act 1813 (c.138)
Insolvent Debtors (Ireland) Act 1814 (c.114)
Insolvent Debtors (Ireland) Act 1816 (c.126)
Insolvent Debtors (Ireland) Act 1836 (c.23)
Insolvent Debtors (Ireland) Act 1840 (c.14)
Insolvent Debtors (Ireland) Act 1840 (c.107)
Insolvent Debtors (Ireland) Act 1841 (c.47)
Insolvent Debtors Relief Act 1702 (c.19)
Insolvent Debtors Relief Act 1703 (c.10)
Insolvent Debtors Relief Act 1711 (c.29)
Insolvent Debtors Relief Act 1724 (c.21)
Insolvent Debtors Relief Act 1728 (c.20)
Insolvent Debtors Relief Act 1730 (c.27)
Insolvent Debtors Relief Act 1737 (c.9)
Insolvent Debtors Relief Act 1755 (c.13)
Insolvent Debtors Relief Act 1765 (c.41)
Insolvent Debtors Relief Act 1769 (c.26)
Insolvent Debtors Relief Act 1776 (c.38)
Insolvent Debtors Relief Act 1781 (c.63)
Insolvent Debtors Relief Act 1801 (c.70)
Insolvent Debtors Relief Act 1804 (c.108)
Insolvent Debtors Relief Act 1805 (c.3)
Insolvent Debtors Relief Act 1806 (c.108)
Insolvent Debtors Relief Act 1809 (c.54)
Insolvent Debtors Relief Act 1809 (c.115)
Insolvent Debtors Relief Act 1812 (c.13)
Insolvent Debtors Relief Act 1812 (c.165)
Insolvent Debtors Relief (England) Act 1811
(c.125)
Insolvent Debtors Relief (England) Act 1812
(c.6)
Insolvent Debtors Relief (England) Act 1813
(c.28)
Insolvent Debtors Relief, etc. Act 1719 (c.22)
Insolvent Debtors Relief, etc. Act 1778 (c.52)
Insolvent Debtors Relief (Ireland) Act 1811
(c.123)

Insurance Brokers (Registration) Act 1977
(c.46)
Insurance Companies Act 1958 (c.72)
Insurance Companies Act 1974 (c.49)
Insurance Companies Act 1980 (c.25)
Insurance Companies Act 1981 (c.31)
Insurance Companies Act 1982 (c.50)
Insurance Companies Amendment Act 1973
(c.58)
Insurance Companies Reserves Act 1995
(c.29)
Insurance Contracts (War Settlement) Act
1952 (c.56)
Insurance (Fees) Act 1985 (c.46)
Insurances on Ships, etc. Act 1785 (c.44)
Insurrection and Disturbances (Ireland) Act
1807 (c.13)
Intelligence Services Act 1994 (c.13)
Interception of Communications Act 1985
(c.56)
Interchange of Grain Between Great Britain
and Ireland Act 1807 (c.7)
Intercourse Between Jamaica and St. Dom-
ingo Act 1812 (c.3)
Intercourse with St. Helena Act 1816 (c.23)
Interest on Damages (Scotland) Act 1958
(c.61)
Interest on Damages (Scotland) Act 1971
(c.31)
Intermediate Education (Ireland) Act 1878
(c.66)
Intermediate Education (Ireland) Act 1882
(c.69)
Intermediate Education (Ireland) Act 1900
(c.43)
Intermediate Education (Ireland) Act 1913
(c.29)
Intermediate Education (Ireland) Act 1914
(c.41)
Interments (Felo de se) Act 1882 (c.19)
International Bank and Monetary Fund Act
1959 (c.17)
International Carriage of Perishable Food-
stuffs Act 1976 (c.58)
International Cocoa Agreement Act 1973
(c.46)
International Copyright Act 1838 (c.59)
International Copyright Act 1844 (c.12)
International Copyright Act 1875 (c.12)
International Copyright Act 1886 (c.33)
International Development Association Act
1960 (c.35)
International Development Association Act
1964 (c.13)
International Finance Corporation Act 1955
(c.5)
International Finance, Trade and Aid Act
1977 (c.6)
International Headquarters and Defence
Organisations Act 1964 (c.5)
International Monetary Arrangements Act
1983 (c.51)
International Monetary Fund Act 1962 (c.20)

International Monetary Fund Act 1968 (c.58)
International Monetary Fund Act 1970 (c.49)
International Monetary Fund Act 1979 (c.29)
International Organisations Act 1968 (c.48)
International Organisations Act 1981 (c.9)
International Organisations (Immunities and Privileges) Act 1950 (c.14)
International Parliamentary Organisations (Registration) Act 1989 (c.19)
International Road Haulage Permits Act 1975 (c.46)
International Sugar Organisation Act 1973 (c.68)
International Transport Conventions Act 1983 (c.14)
Internationally Protected Persons Act 1978 (c.17)
Interpleader (Ireland) Act 1846 (c.64)
Interpretation Act 1889 (c.63)
Interpretation Act 1978 (c.30)
Interpretation of Terms Act 1837 (c.39)
Intestate Husband's Estate (Scotland) Act 1911 (c.10)
Intestate Husband's Estate (Scotland) Act 1919 (c.9)
Intestate Husband's Estate (Scotland) Act 1959 (c.21)
Intestate Moveable Succession (Scotland) Act 1919 (c.61)
Intestates Act 1873 (c.52)
Intestates Act 1875 (c.27)
Intestates' Estates Act 1884 (c.71)
Intestates' Estates Act 1890 (c.29)
Intestates' Estates Act 1952 (c.64)
Intestates' Widows and Children (Scotland) Act 1875 (c.41)
Institute of Management (Customs) Act 1951 (c.51)
Intoxicating Liquor (Sales to Persons Under Eighteen) Act 1923 (c.28)
Intoxicating Liquor (Temporary Restriction) Act 1914 (c.77)
Intoxicating Liquors (Ireland) Act 1906 (c.39)
Intoxicating Liquors (Licences Suspension) Act 1871 (c.88)
Intoxicating Liquors (Sale to Children) Act 1886 (c.56)
Intoxicating Liquors (Sale to Children) Act 1901 (c.27)
Intoxicating Substances (Supply) Act 1985 (c.26)
Inventories (Scotland) Act 1816 (c.107)
Inverness and Elgin County Boundaries Act 1870 (c.16)
Inverness Beer Duties Act 1718 (c.17)
Inverness Beer Duties Act 1737 (c.16)
Inverness Gaol Act 1788 (c.69)
Inverness Roads Act 1793 (c.118)
Investment and Building Grants Act 1971 (c.51)
Investment of Certain Money Act 1808 (c.21)
Investments of Trust Funds Act 1867 (c.132)
Ionian Islands Commissioners Act 1868 (c.128)

Ipswich and Stowmarket Navigation Act 1790 (c.57)
Ipswich and Stowmarket Navigation Act 1793 (c.20)
Ipswich and Yaxley Roads Act 1793 (c.128)
Ipswich: Improvement Act 1793 (c.92)
Ipswich: Improvement, etc. Act 1797 (c.44)
Iran (Temporary Powers) Act 1980 (c.28)
Ireland Act 1949 (c.41)
Ireland (Confirmation of Agreement) Act 1925 (c.77)
Ireland Development Grant Act 1903 (c.23)
Irish and Scotch Paupers Removal Act 1837 (c.10)
Irish Appeals Act 1780 (c.28)
Irish Appeals Act 1783 (c.28)
Irish Bankrupt and Insolvent Act 1857 (c.60)
Irish Charges Act 1801 (c.32)
Irish Church Act 1869 (c.42)
Irish Church Act Amendment Act 1881 (c.71)
Irish Church Act (1869) Amendment Act 1872 (c.90)
Irish Church Amendment Act 1872 (c.13)
Irish Constabulary Act 1874 (c.80)
Irish Education Act 1892 (c.42)
Irish Education Act 1893 (c.41)
Irish Free State (Agreement) Act 1922 (c.4)
Irish Free State (Confirmation of Agreement) Act 1924 (c.41)
Irish Free State (Confirmation of Agreement) Act 1929 (c.4)
Irish Free State (Consequential Provisions) Act 1922 (c.2)
Irish Free State Constitution Act 1922 (c.1)
Irish Free State Land Purchase (Loan Guarantee) Act 1924 (c.3)
Irish Free State (Special Duties) Act 1931 (c.30)
Irish Handloom Weavers Act 1909 (c.21)
Irish Land Act 1903 (c.37)
Irish Land Act 1904 (c.34)
Irish Land Act 1907 (c.38)
Irish Land Act 1909 (c.42)
Irish Land (Provisions for Sailors and Soldiers) Act 1919 (c.82)
Irish Lighthouses Act 1811 (c.66)
Irish Loans Act 1880 (c.44)
Irish Mariners, etc. Act 1802 (c.61)
Irish Militia Act 1805 (c.38)
Irish Militia Act 1806 (c.124)
Irish Militia Act 1807 (c.6)
Irish Police Constables (Naval and Military Service) Act 1914 (c.84)
Irish Police (Naval and Military Service) Act 1915 (c.32)
Irish Presbyterian Church Act 1871 (c.24)
Irish Railways (Confirmation of Agreement) Act 1919 (c.78)
Irish Reformatory Schools Act 1868 (c.59)
Irish Reproductive Loan Fund Act 1883 (c.33)
Irish Reproductive Loan Fund Amendment Act 1882 (c.16)
Irish Sailors and Soldiers Land Trust Act 1952 (c.58)

Irish Sailors and Soldiers Land Trust Act 1967 (c.67)
Irish Sailors and Soldiers Land Trust Act 1987 (c.48)
Irish Tobacco Act 1907 (c.3)
Irish Universities Act 1908 (c.38)
Iron and Steel Act 1949 (c.72)
Iron and Steel Act 1953 (c.15)
Iron and Steel Act 1967 (c.17)
Iron and Steel Act 1969 (c.45)
Iron and Steel Act 1972 (c.12)
Iron and Steel Act 1975 (c.64)
Iron and Steel Act 1981 (c.46)
Iron and Steel Act 1982 (c.25)
Iron and Steel (Amendment) Act 1976 (c.41)
Iron and Steel (Amendment) Act 1978 (c.41)
Iron and Steel (Borrowing Powers) Act 1981 (c.2)
Iron and Steel (Financial Provisions) Act 1960 (c.26)
Irvine Beer Duties Act 1735 (c.27)
Island of Rockall Act 1972 (c.2)
Isle of Axholme: Inclosure, etc. Act 1795 (c.107)
Isle of Ely and Norfolk Roads Act 1767 (c.100)
Isle of Ely: Drainage Act 1757 (c.19)
Isle of Ely: Drainage Act 1772 (c.20)
Isle of Ely: Drainage Act 1791 (c.81)
Isle of Ely: Drainage Act 1792 (c.108)
Isle of Ely: Drainage Act 1795 (c.48)
Isle of Ely: Drainage Act 1797 (c.96)
Isle of Ely, etc.: Drainage Act 1772 (c.19)
Isle of Ely, etc.: Drainage Act 1772 (c.60)
Isle of Ely, etc.: Drainage Act 1775 (c.66)
Isle of Ely: Small Debts Act 1778 (c.36)
Isle of Ely to Ramsey Road Act 1794 (c.127)
Isle of Man Act 1780 (c.42)
Isle of Man 1865 (c.28)
Isle of Man Act 1958 (c.11)
Isle of Man Act 1979 (c.58)
Isle of Man (Church Building and New Parishes) Act 1897 (c.33)
Isle of Man (Customs) Act 1810 (c.42)
Isle of Man (Customs) Act 1887 (c.5)
Isle of Man (Customs) Act 1888 (c.7)
Isle of Man (Customs) Act 1892 (c.28)
Isle of Man (Customs) Act 1895 (c.38)
Isle of Man (Customs) Act 1898 (c.27)
Isle of Man (Customs) Act 1899 (c.39)
Isle of Man (Customs) Act 1900 (c.31)
Isle of Man (Customs) Act 1901 (c.32)
Isle of Man (Customs) Act 1902 (c.23)
Isle of Man (Customs) Act 1903 (c.35)
Isle of Man (Customs) Act 1904 (c.25)
Isle of Man (Customs) Act 1905 (c.16)
Isle of Man (Customs) Act 1906 (c.18)
Isle of Man (Customs) Act 1907 (c.26)
Isle of Man (Customs) Act 1908 (c.9)
Isle of Man (Customs) Act 1909 (c.45)
Isle of Man (Customs) Act 1910 (c.18)
Isle of Man (Customs) Act 1911 (c.14)
Isle of Man (Customs) Act 1912 (c.9)
Isle of Man (Customs) Act 1913 (c.18)

Isle of Man (Customs) Act 1914 (c.19)
Isle of Man (Customs) Act 1915 (c.67)
Isle of Man (Customs) Act 1916 (c.27)
Isle of Man (Customs) Act 1917 (c.35)
Isle of Man (Customs) Act 1918 (c.41)
Isle of Man (Customs) Act 1919 (c.74)
Isle of Man (Customs) Act 1921 (c.40)
Isle of Man (Customs) Act 1922 (c.36)
Isle of Man (Customs) Act 1923 (c.26)
Isle of Man (Customs) Act 1924 (c.24)
Isle of Man (Customs) Act 1925 (c.56)
Isle of Man (Customs) Act 1926 (c.27)
Isle of Man (Customs) Act 1927 (c.20)
Isle of Man (Customs) Act 1928 (c.38)
Isle of Man (Customs) Act 1929 (c.1)
Isle of Man (Customs) Act 1930 (c.42)
Isle of Man (Customs) Act 1931 (c.16)
Isle of Man (Customs) Act 1931 (c.34)
Isle of Man (Customs) Act 1931 (c.41)
Isle of Man (Customs) Act 1933 (c.40)
Isle of Man (Customs) Act 1934 (c.46)
Isle of Man (Customs) Act 1935 (c.34)
Isle of Man (Customs) Act 1936 (c.45)
Isle of Man (Customs) Act 1937 (c.64)
Isle of Man (Customs) Act 1938 (c.68)
Isle of Man (Customs) Act 1939 (c.49)
Isle of Man (Customs) Act 1939 (c.53)
Isle of Man (Customs) Act 1941 (c.32)
Isle of Man (Customs) Act 1942 (c.25)
Isle of Man (Customs) Act 1943 (c.37)
Isle of Man (Customs) Act 1944 (c.27)
Isle of Man (Customs) Act 1945 (c.14)
Isle of Man (Customs) Act 1946 (c.69)
Isle of Man (Customs) Act 1947 (c.50)
Isle of Man (Customs) Act 1948 (c.61)
Isle of Man (Customs) Act 1949 (c.58)
Isle of Man (Customs) Act 1950 (c.19)
Isle of Man (Customs) Act 1952 (c.51)
Isle of Man (Customs) Act 1953 (c.44)
Isle of Man (Customs) Act 1954 (c.54)
Isle of Man (Customs) Act 1955 (c.17)
Isle of Man Customs Duties Act 1867 (c.86)
Isle of Man (Detention) Act 1941 (c.16)
Isle of Man Harbours Act 1771 (c.52)
Isle of Man Harbours Act 1814 (c.143)
Isle of Man Harbours Act 1840 (c.63)
Isle of Man Harbours Act 1872 (c.23)
Isle of Man Harbours Act 1874 (c.8)
Isle of Man Harbours Act 1883 (c.9)
Isle of Man Harbours Act 1884 (c.7)
Isle of Man Harbours Act 1911 (c.33)
Isle of Man (Harbours) Act 1947
Isle of Man Harbours Amendment Act 1864 (c.62)
Isle of Man Loans Act 1880 (c.8)
Isle of Man Loans Act 1931 (c.38)
Isle of Man (Officers) Act 1876 (c.43)
Isle of Man (Officers) Act 1882 (c.46)
Isle of Man Purchase Act 1765 (c.26)
Isle of Man Smuggling Act 1810 (c.62)
Isle of Man Trade Act 1798 (c.63)
Isle of Man Trade Act 1801 (c.54)
Isle of Man Trade Act 1802 (c.98)

Isle of Man Trade Act 1845 (c.94)
Isle of Man (War Legislation) Act 1914 (c.62)
Isle of Man (War Legislation) Act 1939 (c.86)
Isle of Wight, Carriage Rates Act 1783 (c.19)
Isle of Wight Guardians Act 1776 (c.53)
Isle of Wight: Poor Relief Act 1771 (c.43)
Islington: Poor Relief, etc. Act 1776 (c.5)
Islington: Poor Relief, etc. Act 1795 (c.147)
Isolation Hospitals Act 1893 (c.68)
Isolation Hospitals Act 1901 (c.8)
Issue and Payment of Exchequer Bills Act 1808 (c.1)
Issue, etc., of Gold and Silver Tokens Act 1813 (c.19)
Issue, etc., of Gold and Silver Tokens Act 1813 (c.114)
Issue of Bank Notes (Scotland) Act 1797 (c.2)
Issue of Bank Notes (Scotland) Act 1799 (c.10)
Issue of Bank Notes (Scotland) Act 1799 (c.25)
Issue of Bank Notes (Scotland) Act 1799 (c.48)

Jamaica Act 1866 (c.12)
Jamaica and St. Domingo Act 1812 (c.35)
Jamaica Independence Act 1962 (c.40)
Jamaica Loan Act 1854 (c.54)
Jamaica Loan Act 1862 (c.55)
Jamaica Loans Act 1869 (c.69)
James Watt's Fire Engines Patent Act 1775 (c.61)
Japanese Treaty of Peace Act 1951 (c.6)
Jedburgh Beer Duties Act 1720 (c.25)
Jeremy's Ferry Bridge, River Lee Act 1778 (c.10)
Jersey and Guernsey (Financial Provisions) Act 1947 (c.2)
Jews Act 1860 (c.63)
Jews Relief Act 1858 (c.49)
Joanna Stephens' Reward (Cure for Stone) Act 1738 (c.23)
Job Release Act 1977 (c.8)
Jobseekers Act 1995 (c.18)
John F. Kennedy Memorial Act 1964 (c.85)
John Whitehill, Esq Act 1782 (c.69)
John Whitehill, Esq Act 1783 (c.19)
John Wilkinson's Estate Act 1794 (c.67)
John Yeldham's Estate Act 1797 (c.47)
Joint Stock Banking Companies Act 1839 (c.68)
Joint Stock Banking Companies Act 1842 (c.85)
Joint Stock Banking Companies Act 1857 (c.49)
Joint Stock Banks Act 1838 (c.96)
Joint Stock Banks Act 1844 (c.113)
Joint Stock Banks Act 1856 (c.100)
Joint Stock Banks Act 1858 (c.91)
Joint Stock Banks (Scotland) Act 1856 (c.3)
Joint Stock Banks (Scotland) and (Ireland) Act 1846 (c.75)

Joint Stock Companies Act 1840 (c.111)
Joint Stock Companies Act 1844 (cc.110, 111)
Joint Stock Companies Act 1847 (c.78)
Joint Stock Companies Act 1848 (c.45)
Joint Stock Companies Act 1849 (c.108)
Joint Stock Companies Act 1856 (c.47)
Joint Stock Companies Act 1857 (c.14)
Joint Stock Companies Act 1857 (c.80)
Joint Stock Companies Act 1858 (c.60)
Joint Stock Companies Arrangements Act 1870 (c.104)
Joint Stock Companies (Ireland) Act 1845 (c.98)
Joint Stock Companies Winding-up Amendment Act 1857 (c.78)
Journeymen Tailors Act 1720 (c.13)
Journeymen Tailors, London Act 1768 (c.17)
Judges Jurisdiction Act 1870 (c.6)
Judges' Lodgings Act 1839 (c.69)
Judges' Lodgings (Ireland) Act 1801 (c.88)
Judges' Pensions Act 1799 (c.110)
Judges' Pensions Act 1813 (c.153)
Judges' Pensions (India and Burma) Act 1948 (c.4)
Judges' Pensions (Ireland) Act 1814 (c.95)
Judges' Pensions (Scotland) Act 1808 (c.145)
Judges' Remuneration Act 1954 (c.27)
Judges' Remuneration Act 1965 (c.61)
Judges' Salaries Act 1765 (c.47)
Judges' Salaries Act 1872 (c.51)
Judgment Mortgage (Ireland) Act 1850 (c.29)
Judgment Mortgage (Ireland) Act 1858 (c.105)
Judgment of Death Act 1823 (c.48)
Judgments Act 1838 (c.110)
Judgments Act 1839 (c.11)
Judgments Act 1840 (c.82)
Judgments Act 1855 (c.15)
Judgments Act 1864 (c.112)
Judgments Extension Act 1868 (c.54)
Judgments (Ireland) Act 1844 (c.90)
Judgments (Ireland) Act 1849 (c.95)
Judgments Registry Act 1871 (c.72)
Judgments Registry (Ireland) Act 1850 (c.74)
Judgments Registry (Ireland) Act 1871 (c.72)
Judgments, Wales and Counties Palatine Act 1721 (c.25)
Judicature (Northern Ireland) Act 1978 (c.23)
Judicature (Rule Committee) Act 1909 (c.11)
Judicial Committee Act 1833 (c.41)
Judicial Committee Act 1843 (c.38)
Judicial Committee Act 1844 (c.69)
Judicial Committee Act 1845 (c.30)
Judicial Committee Act 1871 (c.91)
Judicial Committee Act 1881 (c.3)
Judicial Committee Act 1915 (c.92)
Judicial Committee Amendment Act 1895 (c.44)
Judicial Factors Act 1849 (c.51)
Judicial Factors (Scotland) Act 1880 (c.4)
Judicial Factors (Scotland) Act 1889 (c.39)

Judicial Offices (Salaries and Pensions) Act 1957 (c.46)
Judicial Officers (Salaries, etc.) Act 1952 (c.12)
Judicial Pensions Act 1959 (c.9)
Judicial Pensions Act 1981 (c.20)
Judicial Pensions and Retirement Act 1993 (c.8)
Judicial Proceedings (Regulation of Reports) Act 1926 (c.61)
Judicial Ratifications (Scotland) Act 1836 (c.43)
Judicial Statistics (Scotland) Act 1869 (c.33)
Judicial Trustees Act 1896 (c.35)
Juries Act 1730 (c.7)
Juries Act 1730 (c.25)
Juries Act 1756 (c.19)
Juries Act 1825 (c.50)
Juries Act 1862 (c.107)
Juries Act 1870 (c.77)
Juries Act 1871 (c.2)
Juries Act 1871 (c.65)
Juries Act 1918 (c.23)
Juries Act 1922 (c.11)
Juries Act 1949 (c.27)
Juries Act 1954 (c.41)
Juries Act 1974 (c.23)
Juries Detention Act 1897 (c.18)
Juries (Disqualification) Act 1984 (c.34)
Juries (Emergency Provisions) Act 1920 (c.78)
Juries (Emergency Provisions) (Renewal) Act 1921 (c.36)
Juries, etc. Act 1750 (c.18)
Juries (Ireland) Act 1839 (c.48)
Juries (Ireland) Act 1845 (c.67)
Juries (Ireland) Act 1868 (c.75)
Juries (Ireland) Act 1871 (c.65)
Juries (Ireland) Act 1872 (c.25)
Juries (Ireland) Act 1873 (c.27)
Juries (Ireland) Act 1874 (c.28)
Juries (Ireland) Act 1875 (c.37)
Juries (Lighthouse Keepers' Exemption) Act 1869 (c.36)
Juries Procedure (Ireland) Act 1876 (c.78)
Juries (Scotland) Act 1826 (c.8)
Jurisdiction in Homicides Act 1862 (c.65)
Jurisdiction in Rating Act 1877 (c.11)
Jurisdiction in Siam Act 1857 (c.75)
Jurors Act 1587 (c.54)
Jurors Affirmation (Scotland) Act 1868 (c.39)
Jurors (Enrolment of Women) (Scotland) Act 1920 (c.53)
Jurors (Ireland) Amendment Act 1894 (c.49)
Jurors Prize Money Act 1868 (c.38)
Jurors Qualification (Ireland) Act 1876 (c.21)
Jurors (Scotland) Act 1745 (c.9)
Jurors (Scotland) Act 1825 (c.22)
Jury Trials Amendment (Scotland) Act 1910 (c.31)
Jury Trials (Scotland) Act 1815 (c.42)
Jury Trials (Scotland) Act 1819 (c.35)
Jury Trials (Scotland) Act 1837 (c.14)

Jury Trials (Scotland) Act 1854 (c.59)
Jury Trials (Scotland) Act 1859 (c.7)
Justice of Assize Act 1809 (c.91)
Justice of Assizes Act 1850 (c.25)
Justice of the Peace Act 1906 (c.16)
Justice of the Peace, Metropolis Act 1811 (c.119)
Justice of the Peace, the Metropolis Act 1792 (c.53)
Justices Act 1753 (c.27)
Justices' Clerks Act 1877 (c.43)
Justices' Clerks' Fees Act 1753 (c.14)
Justices' Clerks' Fees (Middlesex) Act 1754 (c.16)
Justices Commitment Act 1741 (c.24)
Justices Commitment Act 1743 (c.5)
Justices (Ireland) Act 1842 (c.46)
Justices (Ireland) Act 1843 (c.8)
Justices Jurisdiction Act 1742 (c.18)
Justices Jurisdiction Act 1852 (c.38)
Justices of Assize Act 1738 (c.27)
Justices of Assize Act 1839 (c.22)
Justices of the Peace Act 1361 (c.1)
Justices of the Peace Act 1661 (c.38)
Justices of the Peace Act 1788 (c.49)
Justices of the Peace Act 1867 (c.115)
Justices of the Peace Act 1906 (c.16)
Justices of the Peace Act 1949 (c.101)
Justices of the Peace Act 1965 (c.28)
Justices of the Peace Act 1968 (c.69)
Justices of the Peace Act 1979 (c.55)
Justices of the Peace Act 1997 (c.25)
Justices of the Peace in Metropolis Act 1837 (c.37)
Justices of the Peace, Nottingham Act 1803 (c.45)
Justices of the Peace Small Debt (Scotland) Act 1825 (c.48)
Justices of the Peace Small Debt (Scotland) Act 1849 (c.34)
Justices Oaths Act 1766 (c.9)
Justices Proceedings Confirmation (Sussex) Act 1864 (c.100)
Justices Protection Act 1803 (c.141)
Justices Protection Act 1848 (c.44)
Justices Protection (Ireland) Act 1849 (c.16)
Justices Qualification Act 1731 (c.18)
Justices Qualification Act 1744 (c.20)
Justices' Qualification Act 1760 (c.13)
Justices Qualification Act 1871 (c.18)
Justices Qualification Act 1875 (c.54)
Justices Quorum Act 1766 (c.21)
Justices (Scotland) Act 1856 (c.48)
Justices (Supplement List) Act 1941 (c.27)
Justiciary and Circuit Courts (Scotland) Act 1783 (c.45)
Justiciary Court (Scotland) Act 1868 (c.95)
Justiciary Courts (Scotland) Act 1814 (c.67)
Justiciary (Scotland) Act 1848 (c.79)
Juvenile Convict Prison (Ireland) Act 1856 (c.24)
Juvenile Courts (Metropolis) Act 1920 (c.68)
Juvenile Offenders Act 1847 (c.82)

Juvenile Offenders (Ireland) Act 1848 (c.59)

Keeper of Holyrood Park, etc. Act 1843 (c.64)
Keeping, etc., of Gunpowder Act 1748 (c.38)
Keeping, etc., of Gunpowder Act 1771 (c.35)
Keeping of Gunpowder Act 1718 (c.26)
Keeping of Gunpowder Act 1724 (c.23)
Keeping of Gunpowder Act 1741 (c.32)
Keighley to Bradford Road Act 1795 (c.135)
Keighley to Halifax Road Act 1795 (c.151)
Keighley to Kirby Kendal Road Act 1778 (c.113)
Kelso Beer Duties Act 1758 (c.56)
Kelso Beer Duties Act 1780 (c.11)
Kennet and Avon: Canal Act 1796 (c.44)
Kennington Common Act 1852 (c.29)
Kensington, Chelsea and Fulham: Improvements Act 1767 (c.101)
Kensington, Chelsea and Fulham Roads (Toll Continuation) Act 1740 (c.16)
Kensington, Chelsea and Fulham Roads (Tolls) Act 1725 (c.37)
Kensington: Improvement Act 1795 (c.74)
Kensington: Poor Relief Act 1777 (c.64)
Kensington Road Act 1795 (c.142)
Kensington Station and North and South London Junction Railway Act 1872 (c.80)
Kent and Surrey Roads Act 1765 (c.68)
Kent and Surrey Roads Act 1770 (c.62)
Kent and Surrey Roads Act 1781 (c.100)
Kent and Surrey Roads Act 1787 (c.70)
Kent and Surrey Roads Act 1792 (c.151)
Kent and Sussex Roads Act 1740 (c.12)
Kent and Sussex Roads Act 1762 (c.67)
Kent and Sussex Roads Act 1766 (c.56)
Kent and Sussex Roads Act 1767 (c.84)
Kent and Sussex Roads Act 1767 (c.86)
Kent and Sussex Roads Act 1770 (c.108)
Kent and Sussex Roads Act 1772 (c.92)
Kent and Sussex Roads Act 1787 (c.80)
Kent and Sussex Roads Act 1788 (c.85)
Kent and Sussex Roads Act 1789 (c.85)
Kent, Devon Fortifications Act 1794 (c.76)
Kent Fortifications Act 1797 (c.66)
Kent Roads Act 1724 (c.5)
Kent Roads Act 1724 (c.15)
Kent Roads Act 1730 (c.15)
Kent Roads Act 1735 (c.7)
Kent Roads Act 1737 (c.37)
Kent Roads Act 1743 (c.4)
Kent Roads Act 1748 (c.4)
Kent Roads Act 1748 (c.8)
Kent Roads Act 1751 (c.8)
Kent Roads Act 1753 (c.68)
Kent Roads Act 1754 (c.26)
Kent Roads Act 1759 (c.40)
Kent Roads Act 1762 (c.65)
Kent Roads Act 1762 (c.76)
Kent Roads Act 1764 (c.78)
Kent Roads Act 1765 (c.63)
Kent Roads Act 1765 (c.71)
Kent Roads Act 1766 (c.91)

Kent Roads Act 1766 (c.93)
Kent Roads Act 1767 (c.91)
Kent Roads Act 1767 (c.103)
Kent Roads Act 1769 (c.43)
Kent Roads Act 1769 (c.49)
Kent Roads Act 1769 (c.76)
Kent Roads Act 1769 (c.78)
Kent Roads Act 1769 (c.92)
Kent Roads Act 1773 (c.98)
Kent Roads Act 1773 (c.114)
Kent Roads Act 1776 (c.69)
Kent Roads Act 1782 (c.98)
Kent Roads Act 1782 (c.102)
Kent Roads Act 1785 (c.103)
Kent Roads Act 1785 (c.112)
Kent Roads Act 1786 (c.132)
Kent Roads Act 1786 (c.134)
Kent Roads Act 1786 (c.145)
Kent Roads Act 1788 (c.93)
Kent Roads Act 1789 (c.84)
Kent Roads Act 1789 (c.100)
Kent Roads Act 1790 (c.90)
Kent Roads Act 1791 (c.94)
Kent Roads Act 1792 (c.117)
Kent Roads Act 1793 (c.162)
Kent Roads Act 1793 (c.183)
Kent Roads Act 1795 (c.165)
Kent: Small Debts Act 1783 (c.8)
Kent: Small Debts Act 1786 (c.18)
Kent: Small Debts Act 1786 (c.22)
Kent: Small Debts Act 1786 (c.118)
Kent, Sussex Fortifications Act 1780 (c.10)
Kentish Town: Footpath Act 1771 (c.59)
Kenya Divorces (Validity) Act 1922 (c.10)
Kenya Independence Act 1963 (c.54)
Kenya Republic Act 1965 (c.5)
Kettering and Newport Pagnell Road Act 1754 (c.31)
Kettering to Newport Pagnell Roads Act 1773 (c.92)
Kettering to Newport Pagnell Road Act 1781 (c.103)
Kew Bridge (Building and Tolls) Act 1782 (c.42)
Kidderminster Church Act 1785 (c.94)
Kidderminster Roads Act 1777 (c.75)
Kidderminster: Small Debts Act 1772 (c.66)
Kilburn Road Act 1779 (c.120)
Kilmainham Hospital Act 1815 (c. 136)
Kilmainham Hospital Pensions Act 1807 (c.5)
Kilmainham Hospital (Pensions Commutation) Act 1813 (c.154)
Kimbolton Road Act 1755 (c.33)
Kincardine (County) Roads Act 1796 (c.132)
Kinghorn Beer Duties Act 1748 (c.13)
Kinghorn Beer Duties Act 1774 (c.28)
King's Bench Prison Act 1754 (c.17)
King's Bench Prison: Poor Relief Act 1783 (c.23)
King's Lynn: Pilotage Act 1772 (c.30)
King's Lynn: Small Debts Act 1770 (c.20)
Kingsholm District Act 1871 (c.54)
Kingston to Sheetbridge Road Act 1792 (c.119)

Kingston-upon-Hull: Improvement Act 1755 (c.27)

Kingston-upon-Hull: Improvement Act 1762 (c.70)

Kingston-upon-Hull: Improvement Act 1764 (c.74)

Kingston-upon-Hull: Improvement Act 1783 (c.55)

Kingston-upon-Hull Port Act 1774 (c.56)

Kingston-upon-Hull Roads Act 1744 (c.4)

Kingston-upon-Hull Roads Act 1767 (c.70)

Kingston-upon-Hull Roads Act 1788 (c.95)

Kingston-upon-Hull: Small Debts Act 1762 (c.38)

Kingston-upon-Thames: Streets Act 1772 (c.61)

Kingston-upon-Thames to Street Bride Road Act 1768 (c.56)

Kingstown and Dublin Harbours Act 1838 (c.36)

Kingstown Harbour Act 1836 (c.117)

Kingstown Harbour Act 1865 (c.67)

Kingstown Township Act 1898 (c.52)

Kinross and Alloa Road Act 1797 (c.171)

Kirby Kendal and Kirkby Ireleth Road Act 1763 (c.33)

Kirby Kendal to Kirkby Ireleth Road Act 1783 (c.23)

Kirby, Westmorland: Small Debts Act 1764 (c.41)

Kiribati Act 1979 (c.27)

Kirkby Lonsdale and Milnthorpe Road Act 1797 (c.165)

Kirkcaldy Beer Duties Act 1741 (c.8)

Kirkcaldy Beer Duties Act 1757 (c.69)

Kirkcaldy Beer Duties Act 1791 (c.82)

Kirkcudbright Roads Act 1780 (c.24)

Kirkcudbright Roads Act (c.153)

Knackers Act 1786 (c.71)

Knackers Act 1844 (c.87)

Knaresborough and Greenhammerton Road Act 1771 (c.65)

Knaresborough Inclosure Act 1789 (c.76)

Knaresborough: Water Supply Act 1764 (c.93)

Knives Act 1997 (c.21)

L.C.C. (Money) Act 1890 (c.41)

L.C.C. (Money) Act 1891 (c.62)

Labour Bureaux (London) Act 1902 (c.13)

Labour Exchange Act 1909 (c.7)

Labourers' Cottages and Allotments (Ireland) Act 1882 (c.60)

Labourers (Ireland) Act 1883 (c.60)

Labourers (Ireland) Act 1885 (c.77)

Labourers (Ireland) Act 1886 (c.59)

Labourers (Ireland) Act 1891 (c.71)

Labourers (Ireland) Act 1892 (c.7)

Labourers (Ireland) Act 1896 (c.53)

Labourers (Ireland) Act 1906 (c.37)

Labourers (Ireland) Act 1911 (c.19)

Labourers (Ireland) Act 1914 (c.32)

Labourers (Ireland) Act 1918 (c.20)

Labourers (Ireland) Act 1919 (c.55)

Labouring Classes Lodging Houses and Dwellings (Ireland) Act 1866 (c.44)

Lairy Embankment (Plymouth) Act 1802 (c.32)

Lambeth Water Works Act 1785 (c.89)

Lanark and Hamilton Roads Act 1792 (c.122)

Lanark and Renfrew Roads Act 1789 (c.92)

Lanark Prisons Act 1868 (c.50)

Lanark Roads Act 1772 (c.82)

Lanark Roads Act 1792 (c.124)

Lancashire Roads Act 1730 (c.31)

Lancashire Roads Act 1774 (c.99)

Lancashire Roads Act 1784 (c.68)

Lancaster and Westmorland Roads Act 1782 (c.88)

Lancaster Bridge Act 1782 (c.57)

Lancaster Canal Act 1793 (c.107)

Lancaster County Clerk Act 1871 (c.73)

Lancaster: Drainage Act 1779 (c.33)

Lancaster Marsh: Drainage Act 1795 (c.11)

Lancaster Palatine Courts Act 1794 (c.58)

Lancaster Roads Act 1771 (c.91)

Lancaster Roads Act 1785 (c.106)

Lancaster Roads Act 1789 (c.107)

Lancaster Roads Act 1789 (c.110)

Lancaster Roads Act 1792 (c.139)

Lancaster Roads Act 1793 (c.181)

Lancaster Roads Act 1795 (c.144)

Land at Snaith Yorks. Act 1773 (c.85)

Land Charges Act 1900 (c.26)

Land Charges Act 1925 (c.22)

Land Charges Act 1972 (c.61)

Land Charges Registration and Searches Act 1888 (c.51)

Land Clauses Consolidation Act 1845 (c.18)

Land Clauses Consolidation Acts Amendment Act 1860 (c.106)

Land Clauses (Umpire) Act 1883 (c.15)

Land Commisssion Act 1967 (c.1)

Land Commission (Dissolution) Act 1971 (c.18)

Land Commissioners (Ireland) Salaries Act 1892 (c.45)

Land Compensation Act 1961 (c.33)

Land Compensation Act 1967 (c.1)

Land Compensation Act 1973 (c.26)

Land Compensation (Scotland) Act 1963 (c.51)

Land Compensation (Scotland) Act 1973 (c.56)

Land Drainage Act 1845 (c.56)

Land Drainage Act 1914 (c.4)

Land Drainage Act 1918 (c.17)

Land Drainage Act 1926 (c.24)

Land Drainage Act 1929 (c.8)

Land Drainage Act 1930 (c.44)

Land Drainage Act 1961 (c.48)

Land Drainage Act 1976 (c.70)

Land Drainage Act 1991 (c.59)

Land Drainage Act 1994 (c.25)

Land Drainage (Amendment) Act 1976 (c.17)

Land Drainage (Rating) Act 1743 (c.37)
Land Drainage (Scotland) Act 1930 (c.20)
Land Drainage (Scotland) Act 1935 (c.19)
Land Drainage (Scotland) Act 1941 (c.13)
Land Drainage (Scotland) Act 1958 (c.24)
Land Drainage Supplemental (No. 2) Act 1866 (c.80)
Land Drained at Great Carlton, Lincolnshire Act 1792 (c.91)
Land for Ordnance Services Act 1803 (cc. 65, 66)
Land for Prisons (Ireland) Act 1847 (c.26)
Land Law (Ireland) Act 1881 (c.49)
Land Law (Ireland) Act 1887 (c.33)
Land Law (Ireland) Act 1888 (c.13)
Land Law (Ireland) Act, 1888, Amendment 1889 (c.59)
Land Law (Ireland) Act 1896 (c.47)
Land Law (Ireland) Act 1881 (c.49)
Land Law (Ireland) Act 1887 (c.33)
Land Powers (Defence) Act 1958 (c.30)
Land Registers (Scotland) Act 1868 (c.64)
Land Registers (Scotland) Act 1995 (c.14)
Land Registration Act 1925 (c.21)
Land Registration Act 1936 (c.26)
Land Registration Act 1966 (c.39)
Land Registration Act 1986 (c.26)
Land Registration Act 1988 (c.3)
Land Registration Act 1997 (c.2)
Land Registration and Land Charges Act 1971 (c.54)
Land Registration (Scotland) Act 1979 (c.33)
Land Registry Act 1862 (c.53)
Land Registry Act 1886 (c.1)
Land Registry (Middlesex Deeds) Act 1891 (c.64)
Land Registry (New Buildings) Act 1900 (c.19)
Land Revenue of the Crown Act 1815 (c.55)
Land Revenues of the Crown Act 1790 (c.50)
Land Settlement Amendment Act 1921 (c.43)
Land Settlement (Facilities) Act 1919 (c.59)
Land Settlement (Facilities) Amendment Act 1925 (c.85)
Land Settlement (Scotland) Act 1919 (c.97)
Land Settlement (Scotland) Act 1934 (c.35)
Land Tax Act 1702 (c.1)
Land Tax Act 1704 (c.1)
Land Tax Act 1705 (c.1)
Land Tax Act 1707 (c.35)
Land Tax Act 1708 (c.1)
Land Tax Act 1710 (c.1)
Land Tax Act 1711 (c.1)
Land Tax Act 1712 (c.1)
Land Tax Act 1713 (c.1)
Land Tax Act 1714 (c.1)
Land Tax Act 1715 (c.31)
Land Tax Act 1717 (c.1)
Land Tax Act 1718 (c.1)
Land Tax Act 1719 (c.1)
Land Tax Act 1720 (c.4)
Land Tax Act 1721 (c.1)
Land Tax Act 1723 (c.1)

Land Tax Act 1724 (c.1)
Land Tax Act 1725 (c.1)
Land Tax Act 1726 (c.1)
Land Tax Act 1727 (c.5)
Land Tax Act 1728 (c.4)
Land Tax Act 1729 (c.1)
Land Tax Act 1730 (c.4)
Land Tax Act 1732 (c.10)
Land Tax Act 1733 (c.7)
Land Tax Act 1734 (c.23)
Land Tax Act 1735 (c.3)
Land Tax Act 1736 (c.3)
Land Tax Act 1737 (c.14)
Land Tax Act 1746 (c.2)
Land Tax Act 1757 (c.4)
Land Tax Act 1757 (c.7)
Land Tax Act 1771 (c.5)
Land Tax Act 1772 (c.3)
Land Tax Act 1772 (c.8)
Land Tax Act 1774 (c.1)
Land Tax Act 1774 (c.17)
Land Tax Act 1775 (c.3)
Land Tax Act 1775 (c.26)
Land Tax Act 1776 (c.1)
Land Tax Act 1776 (c.4)
Land Tax Act 1776 (c.14)
Land Tax Act 1778 (c.2)
Land Tax Act 1778 (c.23)
Land Tax Act 1780 (c.2)
Land Tax Act 1780 (c.3)
Land Tax Act 1780 (c.23)
Land Tax Act 1782 (c.2)
Land Tax Act 1782 (c.9)
Land Tax Act 1783 (c.3)
Land Tax Act 1783 (c.4)
Land Tax Act 1783 (c.10)
Land Tax Act 1785 (c.4)
Land Tax Act 1785 (c.20)
Land Tax Act 1786 (c.3)
Land Tax Act 1786 (c.54)
Land Tax Act 1786 (c.103)
Land Tax Act 1786 (c.105)
Land Tax Act 1786 (c.121)
Land Tax Act 1787 (c.5)
Land Tax Act 1787 (c.47)
Land Tax Act 1788 (c.2)
Land Tax Act 1789 (c.6)
Land Tax Act 1790 (c.2)
Land Tax Act 1790 (c.13)
Land Tax Act 1791 (c.6)
Land Tax Act 1791 (c.14)
Land Tax Act 1792 (c.5)
Land Tax Act 1792 (c.23)
Land Tax Act 1793 (c.7)
Land Tax Act 1794 (c.8)
Land Tax Act 1795 (c.2)
Land Tax Act 1795 (c.17)
Land Tax Act 1796 (c.2)
Land Tax Act 1796 (c.89)
Land Tax Act 1797 (c.5)
Land Tax Act 1797 (c.26)
Land Tax Act 1797 (c.35)
Land Tax Act 1797 (c.128)

Land Tax Act 1800 (c.68)
Land Tax Act 1805 (c.48)
Land Tax Act 1808 (c.102)
Land Tax Act 1809 (c.55)
Land Tax Act 1809 (c.67)
Land Tax Act 1813 (c.142)
Land Tax Act 1814 (c.190)
Land Tax Act 1842 (c.37)
Land Tax, Assessed Tax, and Income Tax Act 1843 (c.24)
Land Tax Certificates Forgery Act 1812 (c.143)
Land Tax Commissioners Act 1798 (c.48)
Land Tax Commissioners Act 1844 (c.79)
Land Tax Commissioners Act 1867 (c.51)
Land Tax Commissioners Act 1906 (c.52)
Land Tax Commissioners Act 1927 (c.16)
Land Tax Commissioners Act 1937 (c.18)
Land Tax Commissioners (Appointment) Act 1836 (c.80)
Land Tax Commissioners (Appointment) Act 1838 (c.57)
Land Tax Commissioners (Appointment) Act 1866 (c.59)
Land Tax Commissioners (Appointment) Act 1869 (c.64)
Land Tax Commissioners (Appointment) Act 1874 (c.18)
Land Tax Commissioners (Names) Act 1879 (c.52)
Land Tax Commissioners (Names) Act 1881 (c.16)
Land Tax Commissioners Names Act 1886 (c.47)
Land Tax Commissioners Names Act 1893 (c.27)
Land Tax Commissioners Names Act 1899 (c.25)
Land, Tax, etc. Act 1806 (c.107)
Land, Tax, etc. Act 1815 (c.150)
Land Tax, Forfeited Estates, etc. Act 1702 (c.6)
Land Tax Perpetuation Act 1798 (c.60)
Land Tax Redemption Act 1799 (c.10)
Land Tax Redemption Act 1799 (c.21)
Land Tax Redemption Act 1799 (c.40)
Land Tax Redemption Act 1799 (c.43)
Land Tax Redemption Act 1799 (c.108)
Land Tax Redemption Act 1800 (c.28)
Land Tax Redemption Act 1800 (c.30)
Land Tax Redemption Act 1801 (c.72)
Land Tax Redemption Act 1802 (c.116)
Land Tax Redemption Act 1803 (c.51)
Land Tax Redemption Act 1805 (c.77)
Land Tax Redemption Act 1806 (c.133)
Land Tax Redemption Act 1810 (c.58)
Land Tax Redemption Act 1812 (c.80)
Land Tax Redemption Act 1813 (c.123)
Land Tax Redemption Act 1814 (c.173)
Land Tax Redemption Act 1837 (c.17)
Land Tax Redemption Act 1838 (c.58)
Land Tax Redemption, etc. Act 1798 (c.6)
Land Tenure Reform (Scotland) Act 1974 (c.38)

Land Transfer Act 1875 (c.87)
Land Transfer Act 1897 (c.65)
Landed Estates Court (Ireland) Act 1858 (c.72)
Landed Estates Court (Ireland) Act 1866 (c.99)
Landed Property Improvement (Ireland) Act 1847 (c.32)
Landing of Merchandise Act 1796 (c.82)
Landlord and Tenant Act 1709 (c.18(i))
Landlord and Tenant Act 1730 (c.28)
Landlord and Tenant Act 1871 (c.92)
Landlord and Tenant Act 1927 (c.36)
Landlord and Tenant Act 1954 (c.56)
Landlord and Tenant Act 1959 (c.64)
Landlord and Tenant Act 1962 (c.50)
Landlord and Tenant Act 1985 (c.70)
Landlord and Tenant Act 1987 (c.31)
Landlord and Tenant Act 1988 (c.26)
Landlord and Tenant (Covenants) Act 1995 (c.30)
Landlord and Tenant (Ireland) Act 1870 (c.46)
Landlord and Tenant (Ireland) Act 1871 (c.92)
Landlord and Tenant (Ireland) Act 1872 (c.32)
Landlord and Tenant Law Amendment Act Ireland 1860 (c.154)
Landlord and Tenant (Licensed Premises) Act 1990 (c.39)
Landlord and Tenant (Rent Control) Act 1949 (c.40)
Landlord and Tenant (Requisitioned Land) Act 1942 (c.13)
Landlord and Tenant (Requisitioned Land) Act 1944 (c.5)
Landlord and Tenant (Temporary Provisions) Act 1958 (c.68)
Landlord and Tenant (War Damage) Act 1939 (c.72)
Landlord and Tenant (War Damage) (Amendment) Act 1941 (c.41)
Lands at Sheerness and Chatham Act 1816 (c.74)
Lands Clauses Consolidation Act 1845 (c.18)
Lands Clauses Consolidation Act 1869 (c.18)
Lands Clauses Consolidation (Scotland) Act 1845 (c.19)
Lands Clauses (Taxation of Costs) Act 1895 (c.11)
Lands for Ordnance Services, Woolwich Act 1802 (c.89)
Lands for Ordnance Services, Woolwich Act 1803 (c.35)
Lands for the Defence of the Realm Act 1809 (c.112)
Lands of Earl of Pembroke Act 1783 (c.61)
Lands Tribunal Act 1949 (c.42)
Lands Valuation Amendment (Scotland) Act 1982 (c.57)
Lands Valuation (Scotland) Act 1854 (c.91)
Lands Valuation (Scotland) Act 1857 (c.58)

Lands Valuation (Scotland) Amendment Act 1895 (c.41)

Lands Valuation (Scotland) Amendment Act 1902 (c.25)

Lane End Chapel, Stoke upon Trent 1792 (c.88)

Langbaurgh Coroners Act 1873 (c.81)

Lapworth to Kingswood Canal Act 1795 (c.72)

Larceny Act 1808 (c.129)

Larceny Act 1868 (c.116)

Larceny Act 1896 (c.52)

Larceny Act 1901 (c.10)

Larceny Act 1916 (c.50)

Larceny (Advertisements) Act 1870 (c.65)

Late Earl of Seaforth Act 1734 (c.22)

Late Night Refreshment Houses Act 1969 (c.53)

Latent Damage Act 1986 (c.37)

Launceston: Poor Relief Act 1784 (c.17)

Launceston Roads Act 1781 (c.86)

Law Agents and Notaries Public (Scotland) Act 1891 (c.30)

Law Agents Apprenticeship (War Service) (Scotland) Act 1914 (c.20)

Law Agents Apprenticeship (War Service) (Scotland) Act 1919 (c.24)

Law Agents (Scotland) Act 1873 (c.63)

Law Agents (Scotland) Act Amendment 1896 (c.49)

Law and Procedure (Emergency Provisions) (Ireland) Act 1916 (c.46)

Law Commissions Act 1965 (c.22)

Law Costs (Ireland) Act 1823 (c.89)

Law of Commons Amendment Act 1893 (c.57)

Law of Distress Amendment Act 1888 (c.21)

Law of Distress Amendment Act 1895 (c.24)

Law of Distress Amendment Act 1908 (c.53)

Law of Distress and Small Debts (Ireland) Act 1888 (c.47)

Law of Distress and Small Debts (Ireland) Act 1893 (c.36)

Law of Libel Amendment Act 1888 (c.64)

Law of Property Act 1922 (c.16)

Law of Property Act 1925 (c.20)

Law of Property Act 1969 (c.59)

Law of Property Act (Postponement) Act 1924 (c.4)

Law of Property Amendment Act 1859 (c.35)

Law of Property Amendment Act 1860 (c.38)

Law of Property (Amendment) Act 1924 (c.5)

Law of Property (Amendment) Act 1926 (c.11)

Law of Property (Amendment) Act 1926 (c.14)

Law of Property (Amendment) Act 1929 (c.9)

Law of Property (Entailed Interests) Act 1931 (c.27)

Law of Property (Joint Tenants) Act 1964 (c.63)

Law of Property (Miscellaneous Provisions) Act 1989 (c.34)

Law of Property (Miscellaneous Provisions) Act 1994 (c.36)

Law Officers Act 1944 (c.25)

Law Officers Act 1997 (c.60)

Law Officers' Fees Act 1872 (c.70)

Law Reform (Contributory Negligence) Act 1945 (c.28)

Law Reform (Damages and Solatium) (Scotland) Act 1962 (c.42)

Law Reform (Diligence) (Scotland) Act 1973 (c.22)

Law Reform (Enforcement of Contracts) Act 1954 (c.34)

Law Reform (Frustrated Contracts) Act 1943 (c.40)

Law Reform (Husband and Wife) Act 1962 (c.48)

Law Reform (Husband and Wife) (Scotland) Act 1984 (c.15)

Law Reform (Jurisdiction in Delict) (Scotland) Act 1971 (c.55)

Law Reform (Limitation of Actions etc.) Act 1954 (c.36)

Law Reform (Married Women and Tortfeasors) Act 1935 (c.30)

Law Reform (Miscellaneous Provisions) Act 1934 (c.41)

Law Reform (Miscellaneous Provisions) Act 1949 (c.100)

Law Reform (Miscellaneous Provisions) Act 1970 (c.33)

Law Reform (Miscellaneous Provisions) Act 1971 (c.43)

Law Reform (Miscellaneous Provisions) (Scotland) Act 1940 (c.42)

Law Reform (Miscellaneous Provisions) (Scotland) Act 1966 (c.19)

Law Reform (Miscellaneous Provisions) (Scotland) Act 1968 (c.70)

Law Reform (Miscellaneous Provisions) (Scotland) Act 1980 (c.55)

Law Reform (Miscellaneous Provisions) (Scotland) Act 1985 (c.73)

Law Reform (Miscellaneous Provisions) (Scotland) Act 1990 (c.40)

Law Reform (Parent and Child) (Scotland) Act 1986 (c.9)

Law Reform (Personal Injuries) Act 1948 (c.41)

Law Reform (Personal Injuries) Amendment Act 1948 (c.7)

Law Reform (Personal Injuries) Amendment Act 1953 (c.7)

Law Reform (Succession) Act 1995 (c.41)

Law Reform (Year and a Day Rule) Act 1996 (c.19)

Laws Continuation, etc. Act 1739 (c.18)

Laws in Wales Act 1542 (c.39)

Laying of Documents before Parliament (Interpretation) Act 1948 (c.59)

Lazarets Act 1772 (c.57)

Lead Paint (Protection Against Poisoning) Act 1926 (c.37)

Lease of Exeter Castle Act 1710 (c.24)

Leasehold Property Act and Long Leases (Scotland) Act Extension Act 1953 (c.12)

Leasehold Property (Repairs) Act 1938 (c.34)

Leasehold Property (Temporary Provisions) Act 1951 (c.38)

Leasehold Reform Act 1967 (c.88)

Leasehold Reform Act 1979 (c.44)

Leasehold Reform, Housing and Urban Development Act 1993 (c.28)

Leases and Sales of Settled Estates Amendment Act 1874 (c.33)

Leases for Schools (Ireland) Act 1881 (c.65)

Leases (Ireland) Act 1846 (c.112)

Leases of Episcopal Lands (Ireland) Act 1813 (c.92)

Leasing-making, etc. (Scotland) Act 1837 (c.5)

Leasing-making (Scotland) Act 1825 (c.47)

Leasing Powers Amendment Act for Religious Purposes in Ireland Act 1875 (c.11)

Leasing Powers for Religious Worship in Ireland Act 1855 (c.39)

Leatherhead and Guildford Road Act 1757 (c.77)

Lecturers and Parish Clerks Act 1844 (c.59)

Lectures Copyright Act 1835 (c.65)

Ledbury Highways Act 1720 (c.23)

Ledbury Roads Act 1793 (c.132)

Leddon and Clavering, Norfolk: Poor Relief Act 1764 (c.90)

Leeds and Blackburn Roads Act 1781 (c.102)

Leeds and Halifax Roads Act 1740 (c.32)

Leeds and Halifax Roads Act 1751 (c.55)

Leeds and Halifax Roads Act 1783 (c.94)

Leeds and Harrogate Road Act 1796 (c.138)

Leeds and Liverpool Canal Act 1770 (c.114)

Leeds and Liverpool Canal Act 1783 (c.47)

Leeds and Wakefield Road Act 1770 (c.61)

Leeds Bridge Act 1759 (c.54)

Leeds Church Act 1792 (c.89)

Leeds Coal Supply Act 1779 (c.11)

Leeds Coal Supply Act 1793 (c.86)

Leeds Corporation (Consolidation) Act 1905 (c.1)

Leeds: Lighting, etc. Act 1755 (c.41)

Leeds to Liverpool Canal Act 1790 (c.65)

Leeds to Liverpool Canal Act 1794 (c.94)

Leeds to Otley Road Act 1781 (c.98)

Leeds to Sheffield Road Act 1760 (c.33)

Leeds to Wakefield Road Act 1792 (c.131)

Leeds University Act 1904 (c.12)

Leeds: Water Supply Act 1790 (c.68)

Leeward Islands Act 1871 (c.107)

Leeward Islands Act 1956 (c.23)

Legacy Duty Act 1796 (c.52)

Legacy Duty Act 1797 Act (c.135)

Legacy Duty Act 1799 (c.73)

Legacy Duty Act 1805 (c.28)

Legal Advice and Assistance Act 1972 (c.50)

Legal Aid Act 1960 (c.28)

Legal Aid Act 1964 (c.30)

Legal Aid Act 1974 (c.4)

Legal Aid Act 1979 (c.26)

Legal Aid Act 1982 (c.44)

Legal Aid Act 1988 (c.34)

Legal Aid and Advice Act 1949 (c.51)

Legal Aid and Solicitors (Scotland) Act 1949 (c.63)

Legal Aid (Scotland) Act 1967 (c.43)

Legal Aid (Scotland) Act 1986 (c.47)

Legal Practitioners Act 1875 (c.79)

Legal Practitioners Act 1876 (c.66)

Legal Practitioners (Ireland) Act 1876 (c.44)

Legal Proceedings Against Enemies Act 1915 (c.36)

Legal Rate of Interest Act 1774 (c.79)

Legislative Council for Canada Act 1854 (c.118)

Legislative Council of Canada Act 1859 (c.10)

Legislative Council, New Zealand Act 1868 (c.57)

Legitimacy Act 1926 (c.60)

Legitimacy Act 1959 (c.73)

Legitimacy Act 1976 (c.31)

Legitimacy Declaration Act 1858 (c.93)

Legitimacy Declaration Act (Ireland) 1868 (c.20)

Legitimation (Re-registration of Births) Act 1957 (c.39)

Legitimation (Scotland) Act 1968 (c.22)

Leicester and Derby Roads Act 1759 (c.46)

Leicester and Notts. Roads Act 1762 (c.82)

Leicester and Stafford Roads Act 1753 (c.85)

Leicester and Stafford Roads Act 1779 (c.85)

Leicester and Warwick Roads Act 1754 (c.42)

Leicester and Warwick Roads Act 1781 (c.85)

Leicester Navigation Act 1791 (c.65)

Leicester Navigation Act 1797 (c.51)

Leicester Road Act 1725 (c.5)

Leicester Roads Act 1745 (c.10)

Leicester Roads Act 1753 (c.46)

Leicester Roads Act 1757 (c.44)

Leicester Roads Act 1759 (c.41)

Leicester Roads Act 1764 (c.84)

Leicester Roads Act 1769 (c.91)

Leicester Roads Act 1776 (c.81)

Leicester Roads Act 1777 (c.108)

Leicester Roads Act 1779 (c.90)

Leicester Roads Act 1781 (c.89)

Leicester Roads Act 1783 (c.107)

Leicester Roads Act 1785 (c.113)

Leicester Roads Act 1788 (c.100)

Leicester Roads Act 1790 (c.92)

Leicester to Peterborough Road Act 1754 (c.30)

Leicester, Warwick and Coventry Roads Act 1762 (c.80)

Leicestershire and Northamptonshire Union Canal Act 1793 (c.98)

Leicestershire Roads Act 1757 (c.49)

Leicestershire Roads Act 1762 (c.54)

Leicestershire Roads Act 1771 (c.88)
Leigh and Deerhurst Canal Act 1792 (c.83)
Leith and Bruntisland Ferries, etc. Act 1792 (c.93)
Leith Harbour Act 1754 (c.8)
Leith Harbour Act 1788 (c.58)
Leith Harbour and Docks Act 1847 (c.114)
Leith Harbour and Docks Act 1860 (c.48)
Leominster Canal Act 1791 (c.69)
Leominster Canal Act 1796 (c.70)
Leominster Roads Act 1728 (c.13)
Leominster Roads Act 1777 (c.85)
Leominster Roads Act 1797 (c.176)
Lesotho Independence Act 1966 (c.24)
Letter Stealing (Scotland) Act 1836 (c.21)
Letters of Marque Act 1801 (c.76)
Letters Patent for Inventions Act 1835 (c.83)
Levant Trade Act 1753 (c.18)
Level Crossings Act 1983 (c.16)
Lewes and Brighton Road Act 1770 (c.64)
Lewes and Eastbourne Road Act 1758 (c.67)
Lewes: Improvement Act 1791 (c.86)
Lewes to Brighton Road Act 1791 (c.115)
Lewis (Estates and Crown Claims) Act 1806 (c.131)
Lewisham Church Act 1774 (c.93)
Liabilities (War-Time Adjustment) Act 1941 (c.24)
Liabilities (War-Time Adjustment) Act 1944 (c.40)
Liabilities (War-Time Adjustment) (Scotland) Act 1944 (c.29)
Liability for War Damage (Miscellaneous Provisions) Act 1939 (c.102)
Liardet's Cement Patent Act 1776 (c.29)
Libel Act 1792 (c.60)
Libel Act 1843 (c.96)
Libel Act 1845 (c.75)
Libel (Ireland) Act 1868 (c.69)
Liberties Act 1836 (c.87)
Liberties Act 1850 (c.105)
Liberty of Ely Act 1837 (c.53)
Liberty of Religious Worship Act 1855 (c.86)
Libraries Offences Act 1898 (c.53)
Licences for Retailing Beer, etc. Act 1784 (c.30)
Licence to J. Porter etc. to Import Silk Act 1740 (c.4)
Licensed Premises (Exclusion of Certain Persons) Act 1980 (c.32)
Licensed Premises in New Towns 1952 (c.65)
Licensing (Abolition of State Management) Act 1971 (c.65)
Licensing Act 1842 (c.44)
Licensing Act 1872 (c.94)
Licensing Act 1874 (c.49)
Licensing Act 1902 (c.28)
Licensing Act 1904 (c.23)
Licensing Act 1906 (c.42)
Licensing Act 1921 (c.42)
Licensing Act 1949 (c.59)
Licensing Act 1953 (c.46)

Licensing Act 1961 (c.61)
Licensing Act 1964 (c.26)
Licensing Act 1988 (c.17)
Licensing (Airports) Act 1956 (c.37)
Licensing (Alcohol Education and Research) Act 1981 (c.28)
Licensing (Amendment) Act 1967 (c.51)
Licensing (Amendment) Act 1976 (c.18)
Licensing (Amendment) Act 1977 (c.26)
Licensing (Amendment) Act 1980 (c.40)
Licensing (Amendment) Act 1981 (c.40)
Licensing (Amendment) Act 1985 (c.40)
Licensing (Amendment) Act 1989 (c.20)
Licensing Amendment (Scotland) Act 1897 (c.50)
Licensing (Amendment) (Scotland) Act 1992 (c.18)
Licensing (Amendment) (Scotland) Act 1993 (c.20)
Licensing (Amendment) (Scotland) Act 1996 (c.36)
Licensing (Certificates in Suspense) (Scotland) Act 1967 (c.14)
Licensing (Consolidation) Act 1910 (c.24)
Licensing (Evidence) Act 1884 (c.29)
Licensing (Ireland) Act 1836 (c.38)
Licensing (Ireland) Act 1855 (c.62)
Licensing (Ireland) Act 1860 (c.35)
Licensing (Ireland) Act 1874 (c.69)
Licensing (Ireland) Act 1902 (c.18)
Licensing (Ireland) Act 1905 (c.3)
Licensing (Low Alcohol Drinks) Act 1990 (c.21)
Licensing (Occasional Permissions) Act 1983 (c.24)
Licensing of Alehouses Act 1792 (c.59)
Licensing (Permitted Hours) Act 1934 (c.26)
Licensing Planning (Temporary Provisions) Act 1944 (c.15)
Licensing Planning (Temporary Provisions) Act 1946 (c.53)
Licensing (Restaurant Meals) Act 1987 (c.2)
Licensing (Retail Sales) Act 1988 (c.25)
Licensing (Scotland) Act 1903 (c.25)
Licensing (Scotland) Act 1959 (c.51)
Licensing (Scotland) Act 1962 (c.51)
Licensing (Scotland) Act 1969 (c.13)
Licensing (Scotland) Act 1976 (c.66)
Licensing (Seamen's Canteens) Act 1954 (c.11)
Licensing (Sunday Hours) Act 1995 (c.33)
Lichfield Roads Act 1728 (c.5)
Lieutenancies Act 1997 (c.23)
Lieutenancy Clerks Allowances Act 1887 (c.36)
Life Annuities Act 1808 (c.142)
Life Annuities Act 1809 (c.104)
Life Assurance Act 1774 (c.48)
Life Assurance Companies Act 1870 (c.61)
Life Assurance Companies Act 1871 (c.58)
Life Assurance Companies Act 1872 (c.41)
Life Insurance Companies (Payment into Court) Act 1896 (c.8)

Life Insurance (Ireland) Act 1866 (c.42)
Life Peerages Act 1958 (c.21)
Light Locomotives (Ireland) Act 1903 (c.2)
Light Railways Act 1896 (c.48)
Light Railways Act 1912 (c.19)
Light Railways Commissioners (Salaries) Act 1901 (c.36)
Light Railways (Ireland) Act 1889 (c.66)
Light Railways (Ireland) Act 1893 (c.50)
Light Silver Coin Act 1774 (c.42)
Lighthouses Act 1836 (c.79)
Lighthouses (Ireland) Act 1810 (c.95)
Lighting, etc., of Cities (Ireland) Act 1807 (c.42)
Lighting of Towns (Ireland) Act 1857 (c.12)
Lights on Vehicles Act 1907 (c.45)
Limehouse, Stepney Parish Act 1730 (c.17)
Limehouse, Stepney: Streets Act 1782 (c.87)
Limerick Harbour Act 1867 (c.53)
Limitation Act 1939 (c.21)
Limitation Act 1963 (c.47)
Limitation Act 1975 (c.54)
Limitation Act 1980 (c.58)
Limitation Amendment Act 1980 (c.24)
Limitation (Enemies and War Prisoners) Act 1945 (c.16)
Limitation of Action Act 1843 (c.54)
Limitation of Time (Ireland) (Canal Companies) Act 1815 (c.90)
Limitations of Actions and Costs Act 1842 (c.97)
Limited Liability Act 1855 (c.133)
Limited Owners Reservoirs and Water Supply Further Facilities Act 1877 (c.31)
Limited Owners Residence Act 1870 (c.56)
Limited Owners Residences Act (1870) Amendment Act 1871 (c.84)
Limited Partnerships Act 1907 (c.24)
Limited Penalties Act 1864 (c.110)
Lincoln and Northampton Roads Act 1757 (c.68)
Lincoln and Northamptonshire Roads Act 1765 (c.106)
Lincoln and Nottinghamshire Roads Act 1758 (c.57)
Lincoln and Nottinghamshire Roads Act 1766 (c.83)
Lincoln and Nottinghamshire Roads Act 1767 (c.78)
Lincoln and Nottinghamshire Roads Act 1767 (c.79)
Lincoln and Nottinghamshire Roads Act 1780 (c.73)
Lincoln and Nottinghamshire Roads Act 1782 (c.94)
Lincoln and Nottinghamshire Roads Act 1787 (c.71)
Lincoln and Peterborough Roads Act 1756 (c.85)
Lincoln and Rutland Roads Act 1762 (c.73)
Lincoln and Rutland Roads Act 1786 (c.159)
Lincoln (City) Roads Act 1738 (c.10)
Lincoln (City) Roads Act 1797 (c.168)

Lincoln: Drainage Act 1777 (c.70)
Lincoln: Drainage Act 1785 (c.14)
Lincoln: Drainage Act 1787 (c.66)
Lincoln: Drainage Act 1789 (c.32)
Lincoln: Drainage Act 1789 (c.70)
Lincoln: Drainage Act 1793 (c.116)
Lincoln: Drainage Act 1797 (c.67)
Lincoln: Drainage, etc. Act 1794 (c.102)
Lincoln: Improvement Act 1791 (c.80)
Lincoln: Poor Relief Act 1796 (c.102)
Lincoln Roads Act 1738 (c.8)
Lincoln Roads Act 1756 (c.84)
Lincoln Roads Act 1758 (c.44)
Lincoln Roads Act 1764 (c.53)
Lincoln Roads Act 1764 (c.80)
Lincoln Roads Act 1765 (c.73)
Lincoln Roads Act 1765 (c.88)
Lincoln Roads Act 1765 (c.96)
Lincoln Roads Act 1777 (c.109)
Lincoln Roads Act 1778 (c.104)
Lincoln Roads Act 1780 (c.75)
Lincoln Roads Act 1783 (c.34)
Lincoln Roads Act 1785 (c.123)
Lincoln Roads Act 1786 (c.137)
Lincoln Roads Act 1786 (c.138)
Lincoln Roads Act 1786 (c.141)
Lincoln Roads Act 1786 (c.146)
Lincoln Roads Act 1793 (c.150)
Lincoln: Small Debts Act 1778 (c.43)
Lincoln's Inn Fields Rate Act 1734 (c.26)
Lincolnshire Coroners Act 1899 (c.48)
Lincolnshire: Small Debts Act 1777 (c.62)
Lincolnshire: Small Debts Act 1778 (c.34)
Lincolnshire: Small Debts Act 1779 (c.43)
Linen and Hemp Manufacturers Act 1750 (c.31)
Linen and Hempen Manufacturers (Scotland) Act 1726 (c.26)
Linen, etc., Manufacturers (Ireland) Act 1850 (c.48)
Linen, etc., Manufacturers (Ireland) Act 1852 (c.13)
Linen, etc., Manufacturers (Ireland) Act 1853 (c.103)
Linen, etc., Manufacturers (Ireland) Act 1854 (c.46)
Linen, etc., Manufacturers (Ireland) Act 1859 (c.25)
Linen Manufacture (Ireland) Act 1802 (c.75)
Linen Manufacture (Ireland) Act 1804 (c.42)
Linen Manufacture (Ireland) Act 1804 (c.69)
Linen Manufacture, (Scotland) Act (c.23)
Linen Manufacture (Scotland) Act 1753 (c.20)
Linen Manufacturers, etc. (Ireland) Act 1838 (c.52)
Linen Manufacturers (Ireland) Act 1844 (c.47)
Linen (Trade Marks) Act 1743 (c.30)
Linen (Trade Marks) Act 1744 (c.24)
Linens, etc. Act 1794 (c.23)
Linlithgow and Stirling Roads Act 1790 (c.108)

Linlithgow Beer Duties Act 1732 (c.18)
Linlithgow Roads Act 1771 (c.79)
Linlithgow Roads Act 1781 (c.79)
Linlithgow Roads Act 1790 (c.105)
Linlithgow Roads and Bridges Act 1779 (c.12)
Liqueur Act 1848 (c.121)
Liquidation Act 1868 (c.68)
Lis. Pendens Act 1867 (c.47)
Liston, Essex Roads Act 1790 (c.84)
Litchfield Roads Act 1743 (c.24)
Literary and Scientific Institution Act 1854 (c.112)
Literary Copyright Act 1842 (c.45)
Litigants in Person (Costs and Expenses) Act 1975 (c.47)
Litter Act 1958 (c.34)
Litter Act 1983 (c.35)
Little Bowden to Rockingham Road Act 1793 (c.143)
Little Cumbrae Lighthouse Act 1756 (c.20)
Littlehampton Harbour Act 1732 (c.12)
Littlehampton Harbour Act 1793 (c.100)
Liverpool, Admiralty District Registrar Act 1970 (c.45)
Liverpool and Prescot Road Act 1725 (c.21)
Liverpool and Preston Road Act 1771 (c.93)
Liverpool Church Act 1792 (c.76)
Liverpool Churches Act 1767 (c.80)
Liverpool Court of Passage Act 1896 (c.21)
Liverpool Courts of Passage Act 1893 (c.37)
Liverpool Dock Act 1737 (c.32)
Liverpool Docks Act 1709 (c.8)
Liverpool Harbour Act 1762 (c.86)
Liverpool Harbour Act 1785 (c.15)
Liverpool, Improvement Act 1749 (c.24)
Liverpool: Improvement Act 1762 (c.68)
Liverpool: Improvement Act 1786 (c.12)
Liverpool: Improvement Act 1788 (c.13)
Liverpool Note Issue Act 1793 (c.31)
Liverpool Rectory Act 1786 (c.15)
Liverpool Theatre Act 1771 (c.16)
Liverpool to Preston Road Act 1786 (c.126)
Livestock Industry Act 1937 (c.50)
Livestock Rearing Act 1951 (c.18)
Llandilo Rhynws Bridge Act 1784 (c.66)
Llandovery Bridge Act 1773 (c.111)
Llanfyllin Market House Act 1789 (c.24)
Llangollen International Musical Eisteddfod Act 1967 (c.49)
Llanyblodwell to Newtown Canal Act 1794 (c.39)
Lloyd's Signal Stations Act 1888 (c.29)
Loan Act 1901 (c.12)
Loan Act 1902 (c.4)
Loan from Bank of England Act 1815 (c.16)
Loan Societies Act 1840 (c.110)
Loan Societies Act 1841 (c.55)
Loan Societies Act 1842 (c.5)
Loan Societies Act 1843 (c.41)
Loan Societies Act 1844 (c.54)
Loan Societies Act 1845 (c.60)
Loan Societies Act 1846 (c.52)

Loan Societies Act 1848 (c.64)
Loan Societies Act 1849 (c.37)
Loan Societies Act 1850 (c.45)
Loan Societies Act 1851 (c.31)
Loan Societies Act 1852 (c.15)
Loan Societies Act 1853 (c.109)
Loan Societies Act 1857 (c.41)
Loan Societies Act 1858 (c.19)
Loan Societies Act 1863 (c.56)
Loan Societies (Ireland) Act 1836 (c.55)
Loan Societies (Ireland) Act 1838 (c.78)
Loan Societies (Ireland) Act 1843 Amendment Act 1872 (c.17)
Loan to Emperor of Germany Act 1795 (c.93)
Loan to Emperor of Germany Act 1797 (c.59)
Loan to South Australia Act 1841 (c.13)
Loans for Erection of Workhouses Act 1802 (c.74)
Loans for Erection of Workhouses Act 1803 (c.110)
Loans for Parsonages, etc. (Ireland) Act 1803 (c.106)
Loans for Public Works (Ireland) Act 1846 (c.85)
Loans for Public Works (Ireland) Act 1846 (c.108)
Loans for Public Works (Ireland) Act 1851 (c.51)
Loans for Relief of Certain Merchants Act 1799 (c.5)
Loans for Schools, etc. (Ireland) Act 1884 (c.22)
Loans (Incumbents of Benefices) Amendment Act 1918 (c.42)
Loans of Exchequer Bills Act 1771 (c.25)
Loans of Exchequer Bills Act 1792 (cc.15, 16)
Loans of Exchequer Bills Act 1798 (cc.82–84)
Loans of Exchequer Bills Act 1799 (cc.68–71)
Loans or Exchequer Bills Act 1793 (cc.17, 18)
Loans or Exchequer Bills Act 1774 (c.69)
Loans or Exchequer Bills Act 1775 (c.38)
Loans or Exchequer Bills Act 1776 (c.35)
Loans or Exchequer Bills Act 1776 (c.38)
Loans or Exchequer Bills Act 1776 (c.45)
Loans or Exchequer Bills Act 1776 (c.51)
Loans or Exchequer Bills Act 1778 (c.38)
Loans or Exchequer Bills Act 1778 (c.57)
Loans or Exchequer Bills Act 1778 (c.64)
Loans or Exchequer Bills Act 1779 (cc.63, 64)
Loans or Exchequer Bills Act 1779 (c.73)
Loans or Exchequer Bills Act 1780 (cc.41, 42)
Loans or Exchequer Bills Act 1780 (c.43)
Loans or Exchequer Bills Act 1780 (c.53)
Loans or Exchequer Bills Act 1780 (c.57)
Loans or Exchequer Bills Act 1781 (c.59)
Loans or Exchequer Bills Act 1782 (c.36)
Loans or Exchequer Bills Act 1782 (c.76)
Loans or Exchequer Bills Act 1783 (c.12)
Loans or Exchequer Bills Act 1783 (c.72)
Loans or Exchequer Bills Act 1783 (c.84)
Loans or Exchequer Bills Act 1784 (c.33)
Loans or Exchequer Bills Act 1784 (c.52)
Loans or Exchequer Bills Act 1785 (cc.11, 12)

Loans or Exchequer Bills Act 1785 (c.33)

Loans or Exchequer Bills Act 1786 (cc.32, 33)

Loans or Exchequer Bills Act 1787 (c.24)

Loans or Exchequer Bills Act 1788 (cc.18,19)

Loans or Exchequer Bills Act 1789 (cc.34, 35)

Loans or Exchequer Bills Act 1790 (cc.15, 16)

Loans or Exchequer Bills Act 1790 (c.24)

Loans or Exchequer Bills Act 1791 (cc.48–50)

Loans or Exchequer Bills Act 1794 (cc.28, 29)

Loans or Exchequer Bills Act 1794 (c.62)

Loans or Exchequer Bills Act 1795 (cc.21, 22)

Loans or Exchequer Bills Act 1795 (c.37)

Loans or Exchequer Bills Act 1796 (c.31)

Loans or Exchequer Bills Act 1797 (c.8)

Loans or Exchequer Bills Act 1797 (c.20)

Loans or Exchequer Bills Act 1797 (c.114)

Loans or Exchequer Bills Act 1799 (c.4)

Loans or Exchequer Bills Act 1799 (c.18)

Loans or Exchequer Bills Act 1799 (c.33)

Loans or Exchequer Bills Act 1799 (c.41)

Loans or Exchequer Bills Act 1800 (cc.102–104)

Loans or Exchequer Bills Act 1801 (c.9)

Loans or Exchequer Bills Act 1801 (cc.81–83)

Loans or Exchequer Bills Act 1802 (c.5)

Loans or Exchequer Bills Act 1802 (c.17)

Loans or Exchequer Bills Act 1802 (c.21)

Loans or Exchequer Bills Act 1802 (cc.110, 111)

Loans or Exchequer Bills Act 1803 (c.15)

Loans or Exchequer Bills Act 1803 (c.36)

Loans or Exchequer Bills Act 1803 (c.93)

Loans or Exchequer Bills Act 1803 (cc.146, 147)

Loans or Exchequer Bills Act 1804 (c.31)

Loans or Exchequer Bills Act 1804 (cc.45, 46)

Loans or Exchequer Bills Act 1804 (c.81)

Loans or Exchequer Bills Act 1805 (c.7)

Loans or Exchequer Bills Act 1806 (c.6)

Loans or Exchequer Bills Act 1806 (cc.25, 26)

Loans or Exchequer Bills Act 1806 (c.41)

Loans or Exchequer Bills Act 1807 (c.2)

Loans or Exchequer Bills Act 1807 (cc.6, 7)

Loans or Exchequer Bills Act 1807 (c.73)

Loans or Exchequer Bills Act 1812 (c.137)

Loans or Exchequer Bills, etc. Act 1805 (cc.118–120)

Loans to A. Houston and Co., etc. Act 1800 (c.101)

Loans to Grenada and St. Vincent Traders Act 1796 (c.27)

Loans to Grenada and St. Vincent Traders Act 1799 (c.13)

Lobsters (Scotland) Act 1735 (c.33)

Local Acts, Preliminary Inquiries Act 1846 (c.106)

Local Acts, Preliminary Inquiries Act 1848 (c.129)

Local and Personal (Durham University) Act 1861 (c.82)

Local and Personal (Inverness Bridge (Treasury Grant)) Act 1855 (c.113)

Local and Personal (River Suck Drainage) Act 1890 (c.12)

Local Authorities (Admission of the Press to Meetings) Act 1908 (c.43)

Local Authorities (Disqualification Relief) Act 1914 (c.10)

Local Authorities (Emergency Provisions) Act 1923 (c.6)

Local Authorities (Emergency Provisions) Act 1924 (c.29)

Local Authorities (Emergency Provisions) Act 1926 (c.10)

Local Authorities (Emergency Provisions) Act 1928 (c.9)

Local Authorities (Expenditure on Special Purposes) (Scotland) Act 1961 (c.32)

Local Authorities (Expenditure Powers) Act 1983 (c.52)

Local Authorities (Expenses) Act 1887 (c.72)

Local Authorities (Expenses) Act 1956 (c.36)

Local Authorities (Financial Provisions) Act 1921 (c.67)

Local Authorities (Goods and Services) Act 1970 (c.39)

Local Authorities (Historic Buildings) Act 1962 (c.36)

Local Authorities (Ireland) (etc.) Act 1911 (c.35)

Local Authorities (Land) Act 1963 (c.29)

Local Authorities Loans Act 1945 (c.18)

Local Authorities Loans (Scotland) Act 1891 (c.34)

Local Authorities Loans (Scotland) Act, 1891, Amendment 1893 (c.8)

Local Authorities Loans (Scotland) Act 1924 (c.36)

Local Authorities' Mutual Investment Trust Act 1968 (c.25)

Local Authorities (Publicity) Act 1931 (c.17)

Local Authorities (Qualification of Members) Act 1971 (c.7)

Local Authorities (Restoration of Works Powers) Act 1977 (c.47)

Local Authorities (Treasury Powers) Act 1906 (c.33)

Local Authority Social Services Act 1970 (c.42)

Local Bankruptcy (Ireland) Act 1888 (c.44)

Local Commissioners Relief Act 1838 (c.65)

Local Education Authorities (Medical Treatment) Act 1909 (c.13)

Local Elections and Register of Electors (Temporary Provisions) Act 1939 (c.115)

Local Elections and Register of Electors (Temporary Provisions) Act 1940 (c.3)

Local Elections and Register of Electors (Temporary Provisions) Act 1941 (c.3)

Local Elections and Register of Electors (Temporary Provisions) Act 1941 (c.49)

Local Elections and Register of Electors (Temporary Provisions) Act 1942 (c.38)

Local Elections and Register of Electors (Temporary Provisions) Act 1943 (c.2)

Local Elections and Register of Electors (Temporary Provisions) Act 1944 (c.3)

Local Elections (Expenses) Act 1919 (c.13)

Local Elections (Service Abroad) Act 1945 (c.1)

Local Employment Act 1960 (c.18)

Local Employment Act 1963 (c.19)

Local Employment Act 1970 (c.7)

Local Employment Act 1972 (c.5)

Local (Forfeited Estates: Scotland) Act 1789 (c.28)

Local Government Act 1858 (c.98)

Local Government Act 1888 (c.41)

Local Government Act 1894 (c.73)

Local Government Act 1897 (c.1)

Local Government Act 1929 (c.17)

Local Government Act 1933 (c.51)

Local Government Act 1948 (c.26)

Local Government Act 1958 (c.55)

Local Government Act 1966 (c.42)

Local Government Act 1972 (c.70)

Local Government Act 1974 (c.7)

Local Government Act 1978 (c.39)

Local Government Act 1985 (c.51)

Local Government Act 1986 (c.10)

Local Government Act 1987 (c.44)

Local Government Act 1988 (c.9)

Local Government Act 1992 (c.19)

Local Government (Access to Information) Act 1985 (c.43)

Local Government (Adjustments) Act 1913 (c.19)

Local Government (Adjustments) (Scotland) Act 1914 (c.74)

Local Government (Allotments and Land Cultivation) (Ireland) Act 1917 (c.30)

Local Government (Amendment) Act 1863 (c.17)

Local Government (Amendment) Act 1993 (c.27)

Local Government and Housing Act 1989 (c.42)

Local Government and Miscellaneous Financial Provisions (Scotland) Act 1958 (c.64)

Local Government and Other Officers' Superannuation Act 1922 (c.59)

Local Government and Other Officers Superannuation (Temporary Provisions) Act 1933 (c.43)

Local Government and Planning (Amendment) Act 1981 (c.41)

Local Government and Planning (Scotland) Act 1982 (c.43)

Local Government and Rating Act 1997 (c.29)

Local Government Board Act 1871 (c.70)

Local Government Board (Ireland) Act 1872 (c.69)

Local Government Board (Ireland) Amendment Act 1881 (c.28)

Local Government Boundaries Act 1871 (c.70)

Local Government (Boundaries) Act 1887 (c.61)

Local Government (Boundary Commission) Act 1944 (c.38)

Local Government Boundary Commission (Dissolution) Act 1949 (c.83)

Local Government (Clerks) Act 1931 (c.45)

Local Government (Contracts) Act 1997 (c.65)

Local Government (County Boroughs and Adjustments) Act 1926 (c.38)

Local Government (Determination of Differences) Act 1896 (c.9)

Local Government (Development and Finance) (Scotland) Act 1964 (c.67)

Local Government (Elections) Act 1896 (c.1)

Local Government Elections Act 1956 (c.43)

Local Government (Elections) (No. 2) Act 1896 (c.4)

Local Government (Emergency Provisions) Act 1916 (c.12)

Local Government Emergency Provisions (No. 2) Act 1916 (c.55)

Local Government etc. (Scotland) Act 1994 (c.39)

Local Government Finance Act 1982 (c.32)

Local Government Finance Act 1987 (c.6)

Local Government Finance Act 1988 (c.41)

Local Government Finance Act 1992 (c.14)

Local Government Finance and Valuation Act 1991 (c.51)

Local Government Finance (Publicity for Auditors' Reports) Act 1991 (c.15)

Local Government Finance (Supplementary Credit Approvals) Act 1997 (c.63)

Local Government (Financial Provisions) Act 1937 (c.22)

Local Government (Financial Provisions) Act 1941 (c.33)

Local Government (Financial Provisions) Act 1946 (c.24)

Local Government (Financial Provisions) Act 1963 (c.46)

Local Government (Financial Provisions) (Scotland) Act 1937 (c.29)

Local Government (Financial Provisions) (Scotland) Act 1941 (c.45)

Local Government (Financial Provisions) (Scotland) Act 1946 (c.25)

Local Government (Financial Provisions) (Scotland) Act 1954 (c.13)

Local Government (Financial Provisions) (Scotland) Act 1963 (c.12)

Local Government (Financial Provisions etc.) (Scotland) Act 1962 (c.9)

Local Government (Footpath and Open Spaces) (Scotland) Act 1970 (c.28)

Local Government (Gaelic Names) (Scotland) Act 1997 (c.6)

Local Government (General Exchequer Contributions) Act 1933 (c.8)

Local Government Grants (Social Need) Act 1969 (c.2)

Local Government (Hours of Poll) Act 1938 (c.59)

Local Government (Interim Provisions) Act 1984 (c.53)

Local Government (Ireland) Act 1871 (c.109)

Local Government (Ireland) Act 1898 (c.37)

Local Government (Ireland) Act (1898) Amendment 1906 (c.31)

Local Government (Ireland) Act 1900 (c.63)

Local Government (Ireland) Act 1901 (c.28)

Local Government (Ireland) Act 1902 (c.38)

Local Government (Ireland) Act 1919 (c.19)

Local Government (Ireland) (No. 2) Act 1900 (c.41)

Local Government (Joint Committees) Act 1897 (c.40)

Local Government (Members' Travelling Expenses) Act 1937 (c.36)

Local Government (Miscellaneous Provisions) Act 1953 (c.26)

Local Government (Miscellaneous Provisions) Act 1976 (c.57)

Local Government (Miscellaneous Provisions) Act 1982 (c.30)

Local Government (Miscellaneous Provisions) (Scotland) Act 1981 (c.23)

Local Government Act 1898 (c.37)

Local Government (Omnibus Shelters and Queue Barriers) (Scotland) Act 1958 (c.50)

Local Government (Overseas Assistance) Act 1993 (c.25)

Local Government (Pecuniary Interests) Act 1964 (c.77)

Local Government (Pecuniary Interests) (Scotland) Act 1966 (c.7)

Local Government, Planning and Land Act 1980 (c.65)

Local Government (Records) Act 1962 (c.56)

Local Government (Scotland) Act 1889 (c.50)

Local Government (Scotland) Act 1894 (c.58)

Local Government (Scotland) Act, 1894, Amendment 1895 (c.1)

Local Government (Scotland) Act 1908 (c.62)

Local Government (Scotland) Act 1929 (c.25)

Local Government (Scotland) Act 1939 (c.28)

Local Government (Scotland) Act 1947 (c.43)

Local Government (Scotland) Act 1951 (c.15)

Local Government (Scotland) Act 1965 (c.41)

Local Government (Scotland) Act 1966 (c.51)

Local Government (Scotland) Act 1973 (c.65)

Local Government (Scotland) Act 1975 (c.30)

Local Government (Scotland) Act 1978 (c.4)

Local Government (Scotland) Act 1947 (Amendment) Act 1965 (c.41)

Local Government Staffs (War Service) Act 1939 (c.94)

Local Government (Stock Transfer) Act 1895 (c.32)

Local Government (Street Works) (Scotland) (Amendment) Act 1956 (c.40)

Local Government Superannuation Act 1937 (c.68)

Local Government Superannuation Act 1939 (c.18)

Local Government Superannuation Act 1953 (c.25)

Local Government Superannuation (Scotland) Act 1937 (c.69)

Local Government Supplemental Act 1859 (c.31)

Local Government Supplemental Act 1860 (c.44)

Local Government Supplemental Act 1861 (c.39)

Local Government Supplemental Act 1862 (c.25)

Local Government Supplemental Act 1863 (c.32)

Local Government Supplemental Act 1864 (c.26)

Local Government Supplemental Act 1865 (c.24)

Local Government Supplemental Act 1866 (c.24)

Local Government Supplemental Act 1867 (c.21)

Local Government Supplemental (No. 2) Act 1859 (c.11)

Local Government Supplemental (No. 2) Act 1860 (c.118)

Local Government Supplemental (No. 2) Act 1861 (c.128)

Local Government Supplemental (No. 2) Act 1863 (c.64)

Local Government Supplemental (No. 2) Act 1864 (c.83)

Local Government Supplemental (No. 2) Act 1865 (c.25)

Local Government Supplemental (No. 2) Act 1866 (c.79)

Local Government Supplemental (No. 3) Act 1865 (c.41)

Local Government Supplemental (No. 3) Act 1866 (c.106)

Local Government Supplemental (No. 3) Act 1867 (c.49)

Local Government Supplemental (No. 4) Act 1865 (c.110)

Local Government Supplemental (No. 4) Act 1866 (c.107)

Local Government Supplemental (No. 5) Act 1865 (c.108)

Local Government Supplemental (No. 5) Act 1867 (c.83)

Local Government Supplemental (No. 6) Act 1867 (c.123)

Local Government (Termination of Reviews) Act 1967 (c.18)

Local Government (Transfer of Powers) Act 1903 (c.15)

Local Government (Wales) Act 1994 (c.19)

Local Land Charges Act 1975 (c.76)

Local Light Dues Reduction Act 1876 (c.27)

Local Loans Act 1875 (c.83)

Local Loans Sinking Funds Act 1885 (c.30)

Local Militia Ballot Suspension Act 1816 (c.38)

Local Militia (England) Act 1808 (c.111)

Local Militia (England) Act 1809 (c.40)

Local Militia (England) Act 1812 (c.38)
Local Militia (England) Act 1813 (c.28)
Local Militia (Exemption) Act 1812 (c.116)
Local Militia (Great Britain) Act 1809 (c.82)
Local Militia (Great Britain) Act 1813 (c.19)
Local Militia (Great Britain) Act 1815 (c.76)
Local Militia (Ireland) Act 1813 (c.48)
Local Militia Pay (Great Britain) Act 1814 (c.176)
Local Militia Pay (Great Britain) Act 1815 (c.166)
Local Militia Pay (Great Britain) Act 1816 (c.45)
Local Militia (Scotland) Act 1808 (c.150)
Local Militia (Scotland) Act 1809 (c.48)
Local Militia (Scotland) Act 1812 (c.68)
Local Officers Superannuation (Ireland) Act 1869 (c.79)
Local (Redstone Bridge, Severn) Act 1773 (c.113)
Local Registration of Title (Ireland) Act 1891 (c.66)
Local Registration of Title (Ireland) Act 1909 (c.36)
Local Registration of Title (Ireland) Amendment Act 1908 (c.58)
Local (Rutland Roads) Act 1773 (c.108)
Local Stamp Act 1869 (c.49)
Local Tax Act 1731 (c.5)
Local Taxation Account (Scotland) Act 1898 (c.56)
Local Taxation (Customs and Excise) Act 1890 (c.60)
Local Taxation (Ireland) Estate Duty Act 1896 (c.41)
Local Taxation Returns Act 1860 (c.51)
Local Taxation Returns Act 1877 (c.66)
Local Taxation Returns (Scotland) Act 1881 (c.6)
Local (Westminster Streets) Act 1765 (c.13)
Locomotive Act 1861 (c.70)
Locomotive Threshing Engines Act 1894 (c.37)
Locomotives Act 1865 (c.83)
Locomotives Act 1898 (c.29)
Locomotives Amendment (Scotland) Act 1878 (c.58)
Locomotives on Highways Act 1896 (c.36)
Lodgers' Goods Protection Act 1871 (c.79)
Lodgers' Goods Protection Societies Act 1871 (c.80)
Lodging Houses Act 1851 (c.34)
Lodgings of Justices of Assize Act 1799 (c.46)
Loes and Wilford, Suffolk: Poor Relief Act 1791 (c.72)
Lombs's Silk Engines Act 1731 (c.8)
London Act 1532 (c.16)
London and Hertford Hospitals Act 1795 (c.104)
London and Holyhead Road Act 1836 (c.35)
London Assurance Act 1796 (c.27)
London Barbers and Surgeons Act 1744 (c.15)

London Bridge Act 1756 (c.40)
London Bridge Act 1757 (c.20)
London Bridge Act 1762 (c.30)
London Bridge Act 1771 (c.26)
London Bridge Act 1842 (c.64)
London Bridge Approaches Act 1848 (c.124)
London Bridge Approaches Act 1850 (c.103)
London Bridge Approaches Fund Act 1847 (c.115)
London Brokers Relief Act 1870 (c.60)
London Brokers Relief Act 1884 (c.3)
London Cab Act 1896 (c.27)
London Cab Act 1968 (c.7)
London Cab Act 1973 (c.20)
London Cab and Stage Carriage Act 1907 (c.55)
London, City Road Act 1760 (c.26)
London, City Road Act 1783 (c.102)
London Coal and Wine Duties Cont. Act 1863 (c.46)
London Coal and Wine Duties Cont. Act 1868 (c.17)
London Coal Duties Abolition Act 1889 (c.17)
London: Coal Trade Act 1786 (c.14)
London Council (Money) Act 1889 (c.61)
London County Council Electors Qualification Act 1900 (c.29)
London County Council (General Powers) Act 1947 (c.45)
London County Council (Improvements) Act 1962 (c.49)
London Diocese Act 1863 (c.36)
London Docks (Warehousing of Goods) Act (c.100)
London Electric Lighting Areas Act 1904 (c.13)
London Electric Lighting Areas Act 1904 (c.13)
London (Equalization of Rates) Act 1894 (c.53)
London Flour Company Act 1800 (c.97)
London Government Act 1899 (c.14)
London Government Act 1939 (c.40)
London Government Act 1950 (c.22)
London Government Act 1963 (c.33)
London Government Act 1967 (c.5)
London Hackney Carriage Act 1831 (c.22)
London Hackney Carriage Act 1853 (c.33)
London Hackney Carriage (No. 2) Act 1853 (c.127)
London Hackney Carriages Act 1843 (c.86)
London Hackney Carriages Act 1850 (c.7)
London Hospitals Act 1782 (c.77)
London Institution (Transfer) Act 1912 (c.13)
London Militia Act 1795 (c.27)
London Militia Act 1796 (c.91)
London Museum Site Act 1868 (c.8)
London Naval Treaty Act 1930 (c.48)
London Naval Treaty Act 1937 (c.65)
London Park and Works Act 1887 (c.34)
London Passenger Transport Act 1933 (c.14)
London Paving and Lighting Act 1766 (c.26)
London Regional Transport Act 1984 (c.32)

London Regional Transport Act 1996 (c.21)
London Regional Transport (Amendment) Act 1985 (c.10)
London Roads Act 1839 (c.80)
London Street Lighting Act 1743 (c.29)
London Streets Act 1762 (c.21)
London: Streets Act 1771 (c.54)
London: Streets Act 1772 (c.17)
London Streets Act 1772 (c.69)
London: Streets Act 1775 (c.54)
London: Streets Act 1776 (c.22)
London: Streets Act 1776 (c.23)
London: Streets Act 1778 (c.71)
London: Streets Act 1778 (c.73)
London: Streets Act 1782 (c.84)
London (Streets and Sewers) Act 1793 (c.75)
London Streets, City Act 1759 (c.30)
London: Thames Embankment Act 1771 (c.34)
London Traffic Act 1924 (c.34)
London Widening of Passages etc. Act 1766 (c.27)
Londonderry School Act 1808 (c.77)
Long Leases (Scotland) Act 1954 (c.49)
Long Leases (Temporary Provisions) (Scotland) Act 1951 (c.28)
Longitude and Latitude Act 1740 (c.39)
Longitude at Sea Act 1796 (c.107)
Lord Alcester's Grant Act 1883 (c.16)
Lord Blessington's Will Act 1772 (c.17)
Lord Chancellor of Ireland Act 1802 (c.105)
Lord Chancellor (Tenure of Office and Discharge of Ecclesiastical Functions) Act 1974 (c.25)
Lord Chancellor's Augmentation Act 1863 (c.120)
Lord Chancellor's Pension Act 1832 (c.111)
Lord Clerk Register (Scotland) Act 1861 (c.81)
Lord Clerk Register (Scotland) Act 1879 (c.44)
Lord Dundonald's Patent (Tar, Pitch, etc.) Act 1785 (c.42)
Lord High Commission (Church of Scotland) Act 1959 (c.8)
Lord High Commissioner (Church of Scotland) Act 1948 (c.30)
Lord High Commissioner (Church of Scotland) Act 1974 (c.19)
Lord Napier Act 1869 (c.3)
Lord Napier's Salary Act 1869 (c.3)
Lord Nelson, Purchase of Estate for Act 1815 (c.96)
Lord Powerscourt's Mansion Act 1807 (c.78)
Lord Wolseley's Grant Act 1883 (c.17)
Lords Justices Act 1837 (c.72)
Losses During Rebellion in Ireland Act 1805 (c.79)
Losses from Cession of East Florida Act 1786 (c.75)
Losses from Cession of East Florida Act 1788 (c.31)
Lost Property (Scotland) Act 1965 (c.27)

Lotteries Act 1710 (c.6)
Lotteries Act 1721 (c.2)
Lotteries Act 1787 (c.41)
Lotteries Act 1790 (c.30)
Lotteries Act 1802 (c.54)
Lotteries Act 1803 (c.91)
Lotteries Act 1804 (c.93)
Lotteries Act 1805 (c.74)
Lotteries Act 1806 (c.148)
Lotteries Act 1807 (c.9)
Lotteries Act 1808 (c.139)
Lotteries Act 1809 (c.94)
Lotteries Act 1810 (c.94)
Lotteries Act 1811 (c.113)
Lotteries Act 1812 (c.19)
Lotteries Act 1812 (c.125)
Lotteries Act 1813 (c.93)
Lotteries Act 1814 (c.74)
Lotteries Act 1815 (c.73)
Lotteries Act 1816 (c.61)
Lotteries Act 1836 (c.66)
Lotteries Act 1845 (c.74)
Lotteries Act 1975 (c.58)
Lotteries (Amendment) Act 1984 (c.9)
Lotteries and Amusements Act 1976 (c.32)
Lotteries and Gaming Act 1962 (c.55)
Lotteries (Ireland) Act 1780 (c.14)
Lottery Act 1771 (c.47)
Lottery Act 1785 (c.59)
Lottery Act 1786 (c.65)
Lottery Act 1787 (c.1)
Lottery Act 1788 (c.21)
Lottery Act 1789 (c.33)
Lottery Act 1791 (c.53)
Lottery Act 1792 (c.28)
Lottery Act 1793 (c.62)
Lottery Act 1794 (c.40)
Lottery Act 1795 (c.36)
Lottery Act 1796 (c.104)
Lottery Act 1797 (c.113)
Lottery Act 1798 (c.75)
Lottery Act 1799 (c.91)
Lottery Act 1800 (c.52)
Lottery Act 1801 (c.6)
Lottery Act 1801 (c.27)
Lottery Office Keepers Act 1779 (c.21)
Lottery Office Keepers Act 1782 (c.47)
Lottery Regulations Act 1802 (c.104)
Lough Corrib Act 1850 (c.112)
Lough Corrib Navigation Act 1874 (c.71)
Loughborough: Navigation Act 1766 (c.94)
Loughborough Navigation Act 1776 (c.65)
Louth, Lincoln, Roads Act 1770 (c.109)
Louth Roads Act 1780 (c.94)
Lower Canada Government Act 1838 (c.9)
Lower Canada Government Act 1839 (c.53)
Lower Ouse: Navigation Act 1791 (c.76)
Ludlow and Monk's Bridge Road Act 1750 (c.29)
Ludlow Roads Act 1756 (c.59)
Ludlow Roads Act 1779 (c.114)
Ludlow, Salop: Improvement Act 1793 (c.25)
Lunacy Act 1771 (c.20)

Lunacy Act 1842 (c.84)
Lunacy Act 1855 (c.13)
Lunacy Act 1890 (c.5)
Lunacy Act 1891 (c.65)
Lunacy Act 1908 (c.47)
Lunacy Act 1911 (c.40)
Lunacy Act 1922 (c.60)
Lunacy Act Amendment Act 1865 (c.80)
Lunacy Acts Amendment 1885 (c.52)
Lunacy Acts Amendment 1889 (c.41)
Lunacy Acts Amendments Act 1826 (c.111)
Lunacy Acts Amendments Act 1862 (c.111)
Lunacy Board (Scotland) Act 1864 (c.59)
Lunacy Board (Scotland) Salaries and Clerks Act 1900 (c.54)
Lunacy Districts (Scotland) Act 1887 (c.39)
Lunacy (Ireland) Act 1867 (c.118)
Lunacy (Ireland) Act 1901 (c.17)
Lunacy Regulation Act 1853 (c.70)
Lunacy Regulation Act 1855 (c.105)
Lunacy Regulation Act 1862 (c.86)
Lunacy Regulation Act 1871 (c.22)
Lunacy Regulation Amendment Act 1882 (c.82)
Lunacy Regulation (Ireland) Act 1871 (c.22)
Lunacy (Scotland) Act 1857 (c.71)
Lunacy (Scotland) Act 1862 (c.54)
Lunacy (Scotland) Act 1866 (c.51)
Lunacy (Vacating of Seats) Act 1886 (c.16)
Lunatic Asylums Act 1842 (c.87)
Lunatic Asylums Act 1853 (c.97)
Lunatic Asylums Act 1856 (c.87)
Lunatic Asylums, etc. Act 1846 (c.84)
Lunatic Asylums (Ireland) Act 1846 (c.79)
Lunatic Asylums (Ireland) Act 1846 (c.115)
Lunatic Asylums (Ireland) Act 1849 (c.56)
Lunatic Asylums (Ireland) Act 1851 (c.45)
Lunatic Asylums (Ireland) Act 1875 (c.67)
Lunatic Asylums (Ireland) Accounts Audit Act 1868 (c.97)
Lunatic Asylums Loans (Ireland) Act 1878 (c.24)
Lunatic Asylums Repayment of Advances (Ireland) Act 1855 (c.109)
Lunatic Asylums, Superannuations (Ireland) Act 1856 (c.99)
Lunatic Paupers or Criminals Act 1808 (c.96)
Lunatic Paupers, etc. (England) Act 1811 (c.79)
Lunatics Act 1730 (c.10)
Lunatics Act 1838 (c.73)
Lunatics Act 1845 (c.100)
Lunatics Act 1845 (c.126)
Lunatics Removal (India) Act 1851 (c.81)
Lunatics (Scotland) Act 1858 (c.89)
Lunatics (Scotland) Act 1867 (c.55)
Luton and St. Albans Road Act 1726 (c.17)
Luton and St. Albans Road Act 1742 (c.23)
Lying-in Hospitals Act 1773 (c.82)
Lyme Regis Roads Act 1770 (c.59)
Lymington Roads Act 1765 (c.59)
Lymington Roads Act 1786 (c.156)
Lyon King of Arms Act 1867 (c.17)

Macclesfield and Buxton Road Act 1958 (c.41)
Macclesfield to Buxton Road Act 1780 (c.91)
Macclesfield Grammar School Act 1774 (c.51)
Madder Act 1957 (c.12)
Madhouses Act 1774 (c.49)
Madhouses Act 1779 (c.15)
Madhouses Act 1786 (c.91)
Magdalen Hospital, London Act 1769 (c.31)
Magistrates' Courts Act 1952 (c.55)
Magistrates' Courts Act 1957 (c.29)
Magistrates' Courts Act 1980 (c.43)
Magistrates' Courts (Appeals from Binding Over Orders) Act 1956 (c.44)
Maidenhead and Reading, etc. Roads Act 1727 (c.3)
Maidenhead Bridge Act 1772 (c.41)
Maidenhead, Reading etc. Roads Act 1763 (c.46)
Maidenhead Road Act 1743 (c.19)
Maidenhead Roads Act 1779 (c.84)
Maidstone Gaol, Kent (Expenses) Act 1735 (c.12)
Maidstone, Kent: Improvement Act 1791 (c.62)
Maidstone: Poor Relief Act 1780 (c.22)
Maidstone to Ashford Road Act 1973 (c.173)
Maidstone to Cranbrook Road Act 1759 (c.57)
Maidstone to Cranbrook Road Act 1768 (c.43)
Mail to Spain Act 1793 (c.60)
Mail Ships Act 1902 (c.36)
Maintenance Agreements Act 1957 (c.35)
Maintenance Enforcement Act 1991 (c.17)
Maintenance of Church of England Act 1706 (c.8)
Maintenance of Live Stock Act 1915 (c.65)
Maintenance Orders Act 1950 (c.37)
Maintenance Orders Act 1958 (c.39)
Maintenance Orders Act 1968 (c.36)
Maintenance Orders (Facilities for Enforcement) Act 1920 (c.33)
Maintenance Orders (Reciprocal Enforcement) Act 1972 (c.18)
Maintenance Orders (Reciprocal Enforcement) Act 1992 (c.56)
Making of Bread Act 1957 (c.29)
Making of Indigo Act 1755 (c.25)
Making of indigo, etc. 1770 (c.37)
Making of Sail Cloth Act 1741 (c.35)
Malawi Independence 1964 (c.46)
Malaysia Act 1963 (c.35)
Malaysian Act 1963 (c.60)
Malicious Communications Act 1988 (c.27)
Malicious Damage Act 1812 (c.130)
Malicious Damage Act 1861 (c.97)
Malicious Damage Act 1964 (c.76)
Malicious Damage (Scotland) Act 1816 (c.125)
Malicious Injury Act 1769 (c.29)
Mall Approach (Improvement) Act 1914 (c.28)

Malmesbury Roads Act 1778 (c.114)
Malt Duties, etc. Act 1714 (c.2)
Malt Duties, etc. Act 1725 (c.4)
Malt Duties, etc. Act 1759 (c.7)
Malt Duties Act 1762 (c.13)
Malt Duties Act 1762 (c.2)
Malt Duties Act 1766 (c.6)
Malt Duties Act 1768 (c.4)
Malt Duties Act 1769 (c.2)
Malt Duties Act 1770 (c.5)
Malt Duties Act 1772 (c.6)
Malt Duties Act 1772 (c.6)
Malt Duties Act 1774 (c.2)
Malt Duties Act 1775 (c.2)
Malt Duties Act 1776 (c.1)
Malt Duties Act 1776 (c.2)
Malt Duties Act 1778 (c.3)
Malt Duties Act 1779 (c.3)
Malt Duties Act 1780 (c.3)
Malt Duties Act 1780 (c.4)
Malt Duties Act 1782 (c.3)
Malt Duties Act 1782 (c.4)
Malt Duties Act 1783 (c.64)
Malt Duties Act 1783 (c.1)
Malt Duties Act 1785 (c.2)
Malt Duties Act 1786 (c.6)
Malt Duties Act 1788 (c.1)
Malt Duties Act 1789 (c.10)
Malt Duties Act 1790 (c.3)
Malt Duties Act 1791 (c.2)
Malt Duties Act 1791 (c.7)
Malt Duties Act 1791 (c.6)
Malt Duties Act 1791 (c.18)
Malt Duties Act 1793 (c.11)
Malt Duties Act 1794 (c.7)
Malt Duties Act 1837 (c.49)
Malt Duties Act 1971 (c.2)
Malt, etc. Duties Act 1765 (c.2)
Malta Constitution Act 1932 (c.43)
Malta Independence Act 1964 (c.86)
Malta (Letters Patent) Act 1936 (c.29)
Malta (Reconstruction) Act 1947 (c.9)
Malta Republic Act 1975 (c.31)
Malton and Pickering Road Act 1765 (c.108)
Manchester and Oldham Canal Act 1792 (c.84)
Manchester-Oldham Canal Act 1974 (c.26)
Manchester and Salford: Improvement Act 1792 (c.69)
Manchester and Stockport Canal Act 1793 (c.21)
Manchester, Bolton and Bury Canal Act 1791 (c.68)
Manchester Canal Act 1794 (c.37)
Manchester Church Act 1753 (c.45)
Manchester Church Act 1769 (c.60)
Manchester, Church Building 1708 (c.28)
Manchester General Improvement Act 1851 (c.119)
Manchester Improvement Act 1765 (c.81)
Manchester: Poor Relief Act 1790 (c.81)
Manchester Roads Act 1731 (c.10)
Manchester Roads Act 1749 (c.5)

Manchester Roads Act 1771 (c.82)
Manchester Roads Act 1772 (c.88)
Manchester, School Mills Act 1758 (c.61)
Manchester Square: Improvement Act 1789 (c.5)
Manchester: Streets Act 1776 (c.63)
Manchester Theatre Act 1775 (c.47)
Manchester to Buxton Road Act 1793 (c.171)
Manchester to Chester Roads Act 1793 (c.139)
Manchester to Wilmslow Road Act 1793 (c.170)
Mandated and Trust Territories Act 1947 (c.8)
Manning of the Navy, etc. Act 1793 (c.66)
Manning of the Navy Act 1795 (c.5)
Manning of the Navy Act 1795 (c.9)
Manning of the Navy Act 1795 (c.19)
Manning of the Navy Act 1795 (c.29)
Manoeuvres Act 1958 (c.7)
Mansfield and Chesterfield Road Act 1958 (c.37)
Mansfield to Chesterfield Road Act 1780 (c.72)
Manufacture of Cambrics 1763 (c.37)
Manufacture of Hats Act 1776 (c.55)
Manufacture of Leather Act 1784 (c.19)
Manufacture of Ounce Thread Act 1788 (c.17)
Manufacture of Sail Cloth Act 1730 (c.27)
Manufacture of Sail Cloth Act 1735 (c.37)
Manufacture of Serges, etc. Act 1719 (c.13)
Manufacture of Serges, etc. Act 1723 (c.18)
Maplin Development Act 1973 (c.64)
Maplin Development Authority (Dissolution) Act 1976 (c.51)
Mar Peerage Restoration Act 1824 (c.59)
March, Cambridge, Isle of Ely: Drainage Act 1957 (c.36)
Margate Pier Act 1724 (c.3)
Margate Theatre Act 1786 (c.29)
Marine and Aviation Insurance (War Risks) Act 1952 (c.57)
Marine Duty Act 1791 (c.17)
Marine, etc. Broadcasting Offences Act 1967 (c.41)
Marine Insurance Act 1745 (c.37)
Marine Insurance Act 1788 (c.56)
Marine Insurance Act 1906 (c.41)
Marine Insurance (Gambling Policies) Act 1909 (c.12)
Marine Mutiny Act 1755 (c.11)
Marine Mutiny Act 1757 (c.11)
Marine Mutiny Act 1757 (c.6)
Marine Mutiny Act 1757 (c.9)
Marine Mutiny Act 1759 (c.8)
Marine Mutiny Act 1760 (c.8)
Marine Mutiny Act 1761 (c.12)
Marine Mutiny Act 1762 (c.3)
Marine Mutiny Act 1763 (c.8)
Marine Mutiny Act 1765 (c.6)
Marine Mutiny Act 1766 (c.10)
Marine Mutiny Act 1766 (c.13)
Marine Mutiny Act 1768 (c.12)

Marine Mutiny Act 1769 (c.7)
Marine Mutiny Act 1770 (c.7)
Marine Mutiny Act 1771 (c.7)
Marine Mutiny Act 1772 (c.5)
Marine Mutiny Act 1772 (c.11)
Marine Mutiny Act 1774 (c.4)
Marine Mutiny Act 1775 (c.4)
Marine Mutiny Act 1776 (c.7)
Marine Mutiny Act 1776 (c.4)
Marine Mutiny Act 1778 (c.5)
Marine Mutiny Act 1779 (c.8)
Marine Mutiny Act 1780 (c.13)
Marine Mutiny Act 1780 (c.9)
Marine Mutiny Act 1782 (c.5)
Marine Mutiny Act 1782 (c.7)
Marine Mutiny Act 1783 (c.17)
Marine Mutiny Act 1785 (c.3)
Marine Mutiny Act 1786 (c.7)
Marine Mutiny Act 1788 (c.3)
Marine Mutiny Act 1789 (c.3)
Marine Mutiny Act 1790 (c.7)
Marine Mutiny Act 1791 (c.9)
Marine Mutiny Act 1793 (c.6)
Marine Mutiny Act 1794 (c.6)
Marine Mutiny Act 1795 (c.7)
Marine Mutiny Act 1840 (c.8)
Marine Society Act 1772 (c.67)
Marine Works (Ireland) Act 1902 (c.24)
Marines Act 1792 (c.67)
Maritime Conventions Act 1911 (c.57)
Market Harborough and Brampton Road Act 1751 (c.57)
Market Harborough and Brampton Road Act 1754 (c.28)
Market Harborough and Brampton Road Act 1759 (c.38)
Market Harborough to Coventry Road Act 1755 (c.40)
Market Harborough to Coventry Road Act 1779 (c.82)
Market Harborough to Loughborough Road Act 1793 (c.176)
Market Weighton Act 1772 (c.37)
Markets and Fairs Clauses Act 1847 (c.14)
Markets and Fairs (Weighing of Cattle) Act 1887 (c.27)
Markets and Fairs (Weighing of Cattle) Act 1891 (c.70)
Markets and Fairs (Weighing of Cattle) Act 1926 (c.21)
Marriage Act 1939 (c.33)
Marriage Act 1949 (c.76)
Marriage Act 1983 (c.32)
Marriage Act 1949 (Amendment) 1954 (c.47)
Marriage Act 1994 (c.34)
Marriage Acts Amendment Act 1958 (c.29)
Marriage Ceremony (Prescribed Words) Act 1996 (c.34)
Marriage Confirmation Act 1830 (c.18)
Marriage (Enabling) Act 1960 (c.29)
Marriage (Extension of Hours) Act 1934 (c.13)
Marriage Law (Ireland) Amendment Act 1873 (c.16)

Marriage (Members of His Majesty's Forces) Act 1941 (c.47)
Marriage (Naval, Military and Air Force Chapels) Act 1932 (c.31)
Marriage Notice (Scotland) Act 1878 (c.43)
Marriage of British Subjects (Facilities) Act 1915 (c.40)
Marriage of British Subjects (Facilities) Amendment 1916 (c.21)
Marriage of Lunatics Act 1941 (c.30)
Marriage (Prohibited Degrees of Relationship) Act 1931 (c.31)
Marriage (Prohibited Degrees of Relationship) Act 1986 (c.16)
Marriage (Registrar General's Licence Act 1970 (c.34)
Marriage (Registration of Buildings) Act 1990 (c.33)
Marriage (Scotland) Act 1834 (c.28)
Marriage (Scotland) Act 1916 (c.7)
Marriage (Scotland) Act 1939 (c.34)
Marriage (Scotland) Act 1942 (c.20)
Marriage (Scotland) Act 1956 (c.70)
Marriage (Scotland) Act 1977 (c.15)
Marriage (Scotland) Emergency Provisions Act 1940 (c.30)
Marriage (Secretaries of Synagogues) Act 1959 (c.13)
Marriage (Wales) Act 1986 (c.7)
Marriage (Wales and Monmouthshire) Act 1962 (c.32)
Marriage with Foreigners Act 1906 (c.40)
Marriages (Confirmation) Act 1804 (c.77)
Marriages (Confirmation) Act 1808 (c.127)
Marriages (Confirmation) Act 1825 (c.92)
Marriages in Japan (Validity) Act 1912 (c.15)
Marriages (Ireland) Act 1844 (c.81)
Marriages (Ireland) Act 1846 (c.72)
Marriages (Ireland) Act 1918 (c.2)
Marriages Legalisation Act 1901 (c.23)
Marriages Legalisation Act 1903 (c.26)
Marriages (Validity) Act 1939 (c.35)
Marriages Validity (Provisional Orders) Act 1924 (c.20)
Married Women (Maintenance) Act 1920 (c.63)
Married Women (Restraint Upon Anticipation) Act 1949 (c.78)
Married Women's Policies of Assurance Act 1880 (c.26)
Married Women's Policies of Assurance (Scotland) (Amendment) Act 1980 (c.56)
Married Women's Property Act 1882 (c.75)
Married Women's Property Act 1907 (c.18)
Married Women's Property Act 1908 (c.27)
Married Women's Property Act 1964 (c.19)
Married Women's Property (Scotland) Act 1881 (c.21)
Married Women's Property (Scotland) Act 1920 (c.64)
Married Women's Reversionary Interests Act 1857 (c.57)
Marshall Aid Commemoration Act 1953 (c.39)

Marshall Scholarships Act 1959 (c.3)
Marylebone Act 1783 (c.110)
Marylebone: Improvement Act 1768 (c.46)
Marylebone Road Act 1720 (c.26)
Marylebone Road Act 1734 (c.8)
Maryport Harbour Act 1748 (c.6)
Maryport Harbour Act 1756 (c.57)
Maryport Harbour Act 1791 (c.23)
Master and Servant Act 1889 (c.24)
Matches and Mechanical Lighters Duties Act 1979 (c.6)
Maternity and Child Welfare Act 1918 (c.29)
Maternity Services (Scotland) Act 1937 (c.30)
Matrimonial and Family Proceedings Act 1984 (c.42)
Matrimonial Causes Act 1907 (c.12)
Matrimonial Causes Act 1923 (c.19)
Matrimonial Causes Act 1937 (c.57)
Matrimonial Causes Act 1950 (c.25)
Matrimonial Causes Act 1963 (c.45)
Matrimonial Causes Act 1965 (c.72)
Matrimonial Causes Act 1967 (c.56)
Matrimonial Causes Act 1973 (c.18)
Matrimonial Causes and Marriage Law (Ireland) Amendment Act 1871 (c.49)
Matrimonial Causes (Dominions Troops) Act 1919 (c.28)
Matrimonial Causes (Property and Maintenance) Act 1958 (c.35)
Matrimonial Causes (War Marriages) Act (c.43)
Matrimonial Homes Act 1967 (c.75)
Matrimonial Homes Act 1983 (c.19)
Matrimonial Homes and Property Act 1981 (c.24)
Matrimonial Homes (Family Protection) (Scotland) 1981 (c.59)
Matrimonial Proceedings and Property Act 1970 (c.45)
Matrimonial Proceedings (Children) Act 1958 (c.40)
Matrimonial Proceedings (Magistrates' Courts) Act 1960 (c.48)
Matrimonial Proceedings (Polygamous Marriages) Act 1972 (c.38)
Matrimonial Proceedings (Transfers) Act 1988 (c.18)
Mauritius Independence Act 1968 (c.8)
Mauritius Loan (Guarantee) Act 1931 (c.26)
Mauritius Republic Act 1992 (c.45)
Measurement of Coal Wagons, etc. Act 1775 (c.27)
Medical Act 1858 (c.90)
Medical Act 1860 (c.66)
Medical Act 1876 (c.41)
Medical Act 1886 (c.48)
Medical Act 1950 (c.29)
Medical Act 1956 (c.76)
Medical Act 1969 (c.40)
Medical Act 1978 (c.12)
Medical Act 1983 (c.54)
Medical Act (1886) Amendment 1904 (c.14)
Medical Act 1956 (Amendment) Act 1958 (c.58)

Medical Act (Royal College of Surgeons of England) 1875 (c.43)
Medical Act (University of London) 1873 (c.55)
Medical and Dentists Acts Amendment Act 1927 (c.39)
Medical Practitioners and Pharmacists Act 1947 (c.11)
Medical (Professional Performance) Act 1995 (c.51)
Medical Qualifications (Amendment) Act 1991 (c.38)
Medicinal Products: Prescription by Nurses, etc. Act 1992 (c.28)
Medicine Duties Act 1785 (c.79)
Medicines Act 1968 (c.67)
Medicines Act 1971 (c.69)
Mediterranean Passes Act 1730 (c.18)
Medway Fisheries Act 1757 (c.21)
Medway: Navigation Act 1792 (c.105)
Medway Oyster Fishery Act 1728 (c.19)
Melton Mowbray to Grantham Road Act 1780 (c.95)
Members of Local Authorities Relief Act 1900 (c.46)
Memorials of Grants of Annuities Act 1822 (c.92)
Mental Deficiency Act 1913 (c.28)
Mental Deficiency Act 1927 (c.33)
Mental Deficiency Act 1938 (c.43)
Mental Deficiency (Amendment) Act 1925 (c.53)
Mental Deficiency and Lunacy (Amendment) Act 1919 (c.85)
Mental Deficiency (Scotland) Act 1940 (c.8)
Mental Health Act 1959 (c.72)
Mental Health Act 1983 (c.20)
Mental Health (Amendment) Act 1975 (c.29)
Mental Health (Amendment) Act 1982 (c.51)
Mental Health (Amendment) Act 1994 (c.6)
Mental Health (Amendment) (Scotland) Act 1983 (c.39)
Mental Health (Detention) (Scotland) Act 1991 (c.47)
Mental Health (Patients in the Community) Act 1995 (c.52)
Mental Health (Scotland) Act 1960 (c.61)
Mental Health (Scotland) Act 1984 (c.36)
Mental Treatment Act 1930 (c.23)
Mercantile Law Amendment Act 1856 (c.97)
Mercantile Law Amendment (Scotland) Act 1856 (c.60)
Mercers Company, London Act 1751 (c.7)
Mercers Company, London Act 1764 (c.50)
Mercers, London Act 1747 (c.32)
Merchandise Marks Act 1911 (c.31)
Merchandise Marks Act 1926 (c.53)
Merchandise Marks Act 1953 (c.48)
Merchandise Marks (Ireland) Act 1909 (c.24)
Merchant Seamen Act 1728 (c.36)
Merchant Seamen Act 1746 (c.38)
Merchant Seamen Act 1762 (c.31)
Merchant Seamen (Payment of Wages and Rating) Act 1880 (c.16)

Merchant Shipping Act 1786 (c.86)
Merchant Shipping Act 1791 (c.39)
Merchant Shipping Act 1794 (c.68)
Merchant Shipping Act 1872 (c.73)
Merchant Shipping Act 1894 (c.60)
Merchant Shipping Act 1906 (c.48)
Merchant Shipping Act 1907 (c.52)
Merchant Shipping Act 1911 (c.42)
Merchant Shipping Act 1921 (c.28)
Merchant Shipping Act 1937 (c.23)
Merchant Shipping Act 1948 (c.44)
Merchant Shipping Act 1950 (c.9)
Merchant Shipping Act 1952 (c.14)
Merchant Shipping Act 1954 (c.18)
Merchant Shipping Act 1964 (c.47)
Merchant Shipping Act 1965 (c.47)
Merchant Shipping Act 1967 (c.26)
Merchant Shipping Act 1970 (c.36)
Merchant Shipping Act 1974 (c.43)
Merchant Shipping Act 1979 (c.39)
Merchant Shipping Act 1981 (c.11)
Merchant Shipping Act 1983 (c.13)
Merchant Shipping Act 1984 (c.5)
Merchant Shipping Act 1988 (c.12)
Merchant Shipping Act 1995 (c.21)
Merchant Shipping Acts (Amendment) 1923 (c.40)
Merchant Shipping (Amendment) Act 1920 (c.2)
Merchant Shipping and Maritime Security Act 1997 (c.28)
Merchant Shipping (Carriage of Munitions to Spain) Act 1936 (c.1)
Merchant Shipping (Certificates) Act 1914 (c.42)
Merchant Shipping (Convention) Act 1914 (c.50)
Merchant Shipping (Equivalent Provisions) Act 1925 (c.37)
Merchant Shipping (International Labour Convention) Act 1925 (c.42)
Merchant Shipping (Liability of Shipowners and Others) Act 1900 (c.32)
Merchant Shipping (Liability of Shipowners and Others) Act 1958 (c.62)
Merchant Shipping (Line-throwing Appliances) Act 1928 (c.40)
Merchant Shipping (Liner Conferences) Act 1982 (c.37)
Merchant Shipping (Load Lines) Act 1967 (c.27)
Merchant Shipping (Mercantile Marine Fund) Act 1898 (c.44)
Merchant Shipping (Minicoy Lighthouse) 1960 (c.42)
Merchant Shipping (Oil Pollution) Act 1971 (c.59)
Merchant Shipping (Registration, etc.) Act 1993 (c.22)
Merchant Shipping (Safety and Load Line Conventions) Act 1932 (c.9)
Merchant Shipping (Safety Convention) Act 1949 (c.43)

Merchant Shipping (Safety Convention) Act 1977 (c.24)
Merchant Shipping (Salvage and Pollution) Act 1994 (c.28)
Merchant Shipping (Scottish Fishing Boats) Act 1920 (c.39)
Merchant Shipping (Seamen's Allotment) Act 1911 (c.8)
Merchant Shipping (Salvage) Act 1916 (c.41)
Merchant Shipping (Salvage) Act 1940 (c.43)
Merchant Shipping (Spanish Frontiers Observation) Act 1937 (c.19)
Merchant Shipping (Stevedores and Trimmers) Act 1911 (c.41)
Merchant Shipping (Superannuation Contributions) Act 1937 (c.4)
Merchant Shipping (Wireless Telegraphy) Act 1919 (c.38)
Merioneth Roads Act 1777 (c.96)
Merioneth Roads Act 1969 (c.56)
Mersey Canal Act 1775 (c.20)
Methylated Spirits (Sale by Retail) (Scotland) Act 1937 (c.48)
Metropolis Gas Act 1860 (c.125)
Metropolis Gas Act 1861 (c.79)
Metropolis Water Act 1899 (c.41)
Metropolis Water Act 1902 (c.41)
Metropolitan Ambulances Act 1909 (c.17)
Metropolitan Board of Works (Money) Act 1884 (c.50)
Metropolitan Board of Works (Money) Act 1886 (c.44)
Metropolitan Buildings Act 1772 (c.73)
Metropolitan Improvements (Funds) Act 1904 (c.2)
Metropolitan Magistrates' Courts Act 1959 (c.45)
Metropolitan Police Act 1829 (c.44)
Metropolitan Police Act 1838 (c.47)
Metropolitan Police Act 1839 (c.47)
Metropolitan Police Act 1856 (c.2)
Metropolitan Police Act 1860 (c.135)
Metropolitan Police Act 1884 (c.17)
Metropolitan Police Act 1886 (c.22)
Metropolitan Police Act 1912 (c.4)
Metropolitan Police Act 1918 (c.61)
Metropolitan Police Act 1933 (c.33)
Metropolitan Police Act 1958 (c.48)
Metropolitan Police (Borrowing Powers) Act 1935 (c.16)
Metropolitan Police (Borrowing Powers) Act 1952 (c.19)
Metropolitan Police (Commission) Act 1906 (c.6)
Metropolitan Police (Courts) Act 1839 (c.71)
Metropolitan Police (Courts) Act 1897 (c.26)
Metropolitan Police (Employment in Scotland) Act (c.44)
Metropolitan Police (Receiver) Act 1867 (c.39)
Metropolitan Police (Staff Superannuation and Police Fund) Act 1931 (c.12)
Metropolitan Streets Act 1903 (c.17)

Mevagissey Pier, Cornwall Act 1775 (c.62)
Michaelmas Term Act 1750 (c.48)
Middlesex and Essex Roads Act 1785 (c.124)
Middlesex and Hertford Highways Act 1711 (c.3)
Middlesex and Hertford Roads Act 1730 (c.10)
Middlesex and Hertford Roads Act 1743 (c.14)
Middlesex and Hertford Roads Act 1770 (c.71)
Middlesex and Hertford Roads Act 1772 (c.84)
Middlesex and Hertfordshire Roads Act 1748 (c.14)
Middlesex and Surrey Roads Act 1791 (c.134)
Middlesex Deeds Act 1940 (c.34)
Middlesex Gaol Act 1786 (c.55)
Middlesex Highways Act 1711 (c.4)
Middlesex Highways Act 1723 (c.6)
Middlesex Registry Act 1708 (c.20)
Middlesex (Registry of Deeds) Act 1751 (c.4)
Middlesex Road Act 1767 (c.88)
Middlesex Roads Act 1733 (c.26)
Middlesex Roads Act 1741 (c.9)
Middlesex Roads Act 1767 (c.102)
Middlesex Roads Act 1778 (c.84)
Middlesex Roads Act 1789 (c.96)
Middlesex Roads Act 1794 (c.131)
Middlesex Roads Act 1937 (c.6)
Middlesex Sessions Act 1792 (c.48)
Middlesex Sessions House Act 1778 (c.67)
Midwives Act 1902 (c.17)
Midwives Act 1918 (c.43)
Midwives Act 1926 (c.32)
Midwives Act 1936 (c.40)
Midwives Act 1951 (c.53)
Midwives (Amendment) Act 1950 (c.13)
Midwives (Ireland) Act 1918 (c.59)
Midwives (Scotland) Act 1915 (c.91)
Midwives (Scotland) Act 1927 (c.17)
Midwives (Scotland) Act 1951 (c.54)
Milbank New Church Act 1728 (c.15)
Mile End Night Watch Act 1777 (c.66)
Milford Fortifications Act 1758 (c.26)
Milford Haven Conservancy Act 1958 (c.23)
Milford to Portsmouth Road Act 1764 (c.63)
Milford to Portsmouth Road Act 1787 (c.95)
Milk (Special Designations) Act (c.34)
Military Aircraft (Loans) Act 1966 (c.15)
Military and Air Forces (Prolongation of Service) Act 1939 (c.90)
Military Lands Act 1900 (c.56)
Military Lands Act 1903 (c.47)
Military Manoeuvres Act 1911 (c.44)
Military Service Act 1916 (c.104)
Military Service Act 1918 (c.66)
Military Service (No. 2) Act 1918 (c.5)
Military Service (Review of Exceptions) Act 1917 (c.12)
Military Service (Session 2) 1916 (c.15)
Military Training Act 1939 (c.25)

Military Tramways Act 1887 (c.65)
Military Works Act 1901 (c.40)
Military Works Act 1903 (c.29)
Militia Act 1700 (c.8)
Militia Act 1701 (c.17)
Militia Act 1702 (c.15(d))
Militia Act 1703 (c.14(e))
Militia Act 1704 (c.15(l))
Militia Act 1705 (c.10)
Militia Act 1706 (c.28)
Militia Act 1707 (c.63)
Militia Act 1708 (c.23)
Militia Act 1709 (c.22)
Militia Act 1710 (c.31)
Militia Act 1712 (c.8)
Militia Act 1766 (c.15)
Militia Act 1786 (c.107)
Militia Act 1714 (c.14)
Militia Act 1733 (c.23)
Militia Act 1745 (c.2)
Militia Act 1757 (c.25)
Militia Act 1757 (c.26)
Militia Act 1758 (c.20)
Militia Act 1759 (c.2)
Militia Act 1759 (c.2)
Militia Act 1762 (c.20)
Militia Act 1763 (c.17)
Militia Act 1765 (c.36)
Militia Act 1769 (c.40)
Militia Act 1771 (c.32)
Militia Act 1776 (c.3)
Militia Act 1778 (c.14)
Militia Act 1779 (c.76)
Militia Act 1780 (c.8)
Militia Act 1780 (c.44)
Militia Act 1780 (c.7)
Militia Act 1780 (c.18)
Militia Act 1782 (c.6)
Militia Act 1782 (c.62)
Militia Act 1794 (c.81)
Militia Act 1802 (c.90)
Militia Act 1882 (c.49)
Militia and Yeomanry Act 1901 (c.14)
Militia and Yeomanry Act 1902 (c.39)
Militia (City of London) Act 1820 (c.100)
Militia, Derbyshire Act 1795 (c.16)
Militia, etc. Act 1711 (c.33)
Militia, etc. Act 1713 (c.9(c))
Militia, etc. Act 1778 (c.59)
Militia, etc. Act 1779 (c.72)
Militia Pay Act 1757 (c.30)
Militia Pay Act 1758 (c.21)
Militia Pay Act 1759 (c.24)
Militia Pay Act 1760 (c.22)
Militia Pay Act 1762 (c.35)
Militia Pay Act 1762 (c.10)
Militia Pay Act 1763 (c.30)
Militia Pay Act 1765 (c.34)
Militia Pay Act 1768 (c.20)
Militia Pay Act 1770 (c.9)
Militia Pay Act 1772 (c.13)
Militia Pay Act 1772 (c.23)
Militia Pay Act 1774 (c.18)

Militia Pay Act 1775 (c.8)
Militia Pay Act 1776 (c.19)
Militia Pay Act 1776 (c.10)
Militia Pay Act 1779 (c.19)
Militia Pay Act 1780 (c.13)
Militia Pay Act 1780 (c.21)
Militia Pay Act 1782 (c.24)
Militia Pay Act 1783 (c.35)
Militia Pay Act 1785 (c.8)
Militia Pay Act 1786 (c.69)
Militia Pay Act 1788 (c.11)
Militia Pay Act 1789 (c.15)
Militia Pay Act 1790 (c.9)
Militia Pay Act 1791 (c.16)
Militia Pay Act 1791 (c.26)
Militia Pay Act 1793 (c.19)
Militia Pay Act 1794 (c.16)
Militia Pay Act 1794 (c.30)
Militia Pay, etc. Act 1766 (c.30)
Militia Pay, etc. Act 1766 (c.17)
Militia Pay, etc. Act 1783 (c.13)
Militia (Scotland) Act 1802 (c.91)
Militia (Storehouse) Act 1882 (c.12)
Militia, Sussex Act 1793 (c.79)
Milk Act 1934 (c.51)
Milk (Amendment) 1937 (c.66)
Milk and Dairies Act 1914 (c.49)
Milk and Dairies Act Postponement Act 1915 (c.59)
Milk and Dairies (Amendment) 1922 (c.54)
Milk and Dairies (Consolidation) Act 1915 (c.66)
Milk and Dairies (Scotland) Act 1914 (c.46)
Milk (Cessation of Production) Act 1985 (c.4)
Milk (Extension and Amendment) 1938 (c.61)
Milk (Extension of Temporary Provisions) Act 1936 (c.9)
Milk Industry Act 1939 (c.46)
Milk (Special Designations) Act 1949 (c.34)
Mine Adventurers of England Act (c.26(d))
Minehead Harbour Act 1700 (c.9)
Minehead Harbour Act 1711 (c.32)
Minehead Harbour Act 1770 (c.26)
Minehead Harbour Act 1937 (c.8)
Minehead Roads Act 1786 (c.136)
Mineral Exploration and Investment Grants Act 1972 (c.9)
Mineral Workings Act 1951 (c.60)
Mineral Workings Act 1971 (c.71)
Mineral Workings Act 1985 (c.12)
Mineral Workings (Offshore Installations) Act 1971 (c.61)
Miners Welfare Act 1952 (c.23)
Mines Accidents (Rescue and Aid) Act 1910 (c.15)
Mines and Quarries Act 1954 (c.70)
Mines and Quarries Act 1969 (c.10)
Mines and Quarries (Tips) Act 1969 (c.10)
Mines Management Act 1971 (c.20)
Mines (Prohibition of Child Labour Underground) Act 1900 (c.21)
Mines (Working Facilities) Act 1934 (c.27)
Mines (Working Facilities and Support) Act 1923 (c.20)

Mines (Working Facilities and Support) Act 1966 (c.4)
Mines (Working Facilities and Support) Act 1974 (c.36)
Mining Industry Act 1920 (c.50)
Mining Industry Act 1926 (c.28)
Mining Industry (Amendment) Act 1939 (c.45)
Mining Industry (Welfare Fund) Act 1925 (c.80)
Mining Industry (Welfare Fund) Act 1931 (c.23)
Mining Industry (Welfare Fund) Act 1934 (c.9)
Mining Industry (Welfare Fund) Act 1939 (c.9)
Mining Industry (Welfare Fund) Act 1943 (c.3)
Minister of Agriculture and Fisheries Act 1919 (c.91)
Minister of Food (Continuance) Act 1920 (c.47)
Minister of Health Act 1919 (c.21)
Minister of Pensions 1916 (c.65)
Minister of the Crown Act 1964 (c.98)
Minister of Transport Act 1919 (c.50)
Ministerial and Other Pensions and Salaries Act 1991 (c.5)
Ministerial and other Salaries Act 1971 (c.3)
Ministerial and other Salaries Act 1975 (c.27)
Ministerial and other Salaries Act 1997 (c.62)
Ministerial Salaries Act 1946 (c.55)
Ministerial Salaries Act 1957 (c.47)
Ministerial Salaries and Members' Pensions Act 1965 (c.11)
Ministerial Salaries Consolidation 1965 (c.58)
Ministeries of Munitions and Shipping (Cessation) Act 1921 (c.8)
Ministers of the Crown Act 1951 (c.9)
Ministers of the Crown Act 1964 (c.98)
Ministers of the Crown Act 1974 (c.21)
Ministers of the Crown Act 1975 (c.26)
Ministers of the Crown (Parliamentary Secretaries) Act 1960 (c.6)
Ministers of the Crown (Parliamentary Under-Secretaries) Act 1951 (c.9)
Ministers of the Crown (Transfer of Functions) Act 1964 (c.31)
Ministers Widows Fund (Scotland) Act 1779 (c.20)
Ministry of Civil Aviation Act 1945 (c.21)
Ministry of Defence Police Act 1987 (c.4)
Ministry of Food (Financial Powers) Act 1949 (c.15)
Ministry of Fuel and Power Act 1945 (c.19)
Ministry of Materials Act 1951 (c.42)
Ministry of Munitions Act 1915 (c.51)
Ministry of Munitions Act 1918 (c.60)
Ministry of National Insurance Act 1944 (c.46)
Ministry of National Service Act 1917 (c.6)
Ministry of Religion (Removal of Disqualifications) Act 1925 (c.54)
Ministry of Social Security Act 1966 (c.20)
Ministry of Supply Act 1939 (c.38)
Ministry of the Crown Act 1937 (c.38)

Ministry of the Crown and House of Commons Disqualification Act 1942 (c.11)

Ministry of the Crown (Emergency Appointments) Act 1939 (c.77)

Ministry of the Crown (Transfer of Functions) Act 1946 (c.31)

Ministry of the Crown (Treasury Secretaries) Act 1947 (c.5)

Ministry of Town and Country Planning Act 1943 (c.5)

Ministry of Transport Act 1919 (c.50)

Ministry of Works Act 1942 (c.23)

Minority of Heir to the Crown Act 1765 (c.27)

Minority of Successor to Crown Act 1750 (c.24)

Minors' Contracts Act 1987 (c.13)

Mint Prosecutions Expenses Act 1776 (c.46)

Miscellaneous Financial Provisions Act 1946 (c.40)

Miscellaneous Financial Provisions Act 1950 (c.21)

Miscellaneous Financial Provisions Act 1955 (c.6)

Miscellaneous Financial Provisions Act 1968 (c.75)

Miscellaneous Financial Provisions Act 1983 (c.29)

Mischief by Fire 1724 (c.28)

Mischiefs by Fire 1708 (c.17)

Mischiefs from Fire 1707 (c.58)

Misrepresentation Act 1967 (c.7)

Misuse of Drugs Act 1971 (c.38)

Mitford and Launditch, Norfolk: Poor Relief Act 1775 (c.59)

Mobile Homes Act 1975 (c.49)

Mobile Homes Act 1983 (c.34)

Mock Auctions Act 1961 (c.47)

Money Payments (Justices Procedure) Act 1935 (c.46)

Moneylenders Act 1900 (c.51)

Moneylenders Act 1911 (c.38)

Moneylenders Act 1927 (c.21)

Moneylenders (Crown Agents) Act 1975 (c.81)

Monkland, Glasgow: Navigation, etc. Act 1770 (c.105)

Monmouth and Gloucester Roads Act 1757 (c.44)

Monmouth Roads Act 1755 (c.31)

Monmouth Roads Act 1770 (c.106)

Monmouth Roads Act 1777 (c.96)

Monmouth Roads Act 1793 (c.169)

Monmouthshire Canal: Navigation Act 1792 (c.102)

Monopolies and Mergers Act 1965 (c.50)

Monopolies and Restrictive Practices Commission (Inquiry and Control) Act 1948 (c.66)

Monopolies and Restrictive Practices Commission Act 1953 (c.51)

Montgomery: Poor Relief Act 1792 (c.96)

Montgomery, Salop and Denbigh Roads Act 1788 (c.96)

Montrose Beer Duties Act 1719 (c.7)

Montrose Beer Duties Act 1732 (c.5)

Montrose Beer Duties Act 1769 (c.57)

Montrose Bridge Act 1792 (c.38)

Morden College Kent Act 1771 (c.10)

Morpeth and Elsdon Road Act 1751 (c.33)

Morpeth to Elsdon Road Act 1778 (c.107)

Morrison's Haven and Fort, East Lothian (repair) 1708 (c.27)

Mortmain and Charitable Uses Act 1888 (c.42)

Mortgage Act 1733 (c.20)

Mortuaries (Bangor, etc.) Abolition Act 1713 (c.6)

Mortuaries (Chester) Act 1755 (c.6)

Moss Troopers Act 1700 (c.6)

Moss Troopers Act 1712 (c.10)

Motor Car Act 1903 (c.36)

Motor Car (International Circulation) Act 1909 (c.37)

Motor-Cycle Crash-Helmets (Religious Exemption) Act 1976 (c.62)

Motor-Cycle Crash-Helmets (Restriction of Liability) Act 1985 (c.28)

Motor-Cycle Noise Act 1987 (c.34)

Motor Spirit (Regulations) Act 1948 (c.34)

Motor Vehicles (International Circulation) Act 1952 (c.39)

Motor Vehicles (Passenger Insurance) Act 1971 (c.36)

Motor Vehicles (Safety Equipment for Children) Act 1991 (c.14)

Motor Vehicles (Wearing of Rear Seat Belts by Children) Act 1988 (c.23)

Mr Speaker Clifton Brown's Retirement Act 1951 (c.2)

Mr Speaker King's Retirement Act 1970 (c.13)

Mr Speaker Morrison's Retirement Act 1959 (c.1)

Mr Speaker's Retirement Act 1904 (c.5)

Mr Speaker's Retirement Act 1921 (c.10)

Mr Speaker's Retirement Act 1928 (c.16)

Much Wenlock Roads Act 1756 (c.60)

Much Wenlock Roads Act 1778 (c.89)

Multilateral Investment Guarantee Agency Act 1988 (c.8)

Municipal Corporations Act 1882 (c.50)

Municipal Corporations Act 1883 (c.18)

Municipal Corporations Amendment 1906 (c.12)

Municipal Corporations Amendment 1910 (c.19)

Municipal Corporations (Audit) Act 1933 (c.28)

Municipal Corporations (Ireland) Act 1840 (c.108)

Municipal Corporations (Mandamus) Act 1772 (c.21)

Municipal Elections Act 1924 (c.4)

Municipal Elections (Corrupt and Illegal Practices) Act 1884 (c.70)

Municipal Elections (Corrupt and Illegal Practices) Act 1911 (c.7)

Municipal Offices Act 1710 (c.25)
Municipal Rate (Edinburgh) Act 1868 (c.42)
Municipal Savings Banks (War Loan Investment) Act 1916 (c.47)
Munitions (Liability for Explosion) Act 1916 (c.61)
Munitions of War Act 1915 (c.54)
Munitions of War Act 1917 (c.45)
Munitions of War Amendment 1916 (c.99)
Murder (Abolition of Death Penalty) Act 1965 (c.71)
Murder Act 1728 (c.21)
Murder Act 1751 (c.37)
Murders Abroad Act 1817 (c.53)
Murderers of Captain Porteous Act 1735 (c.35)
Museums and Galleries Admission Charges Act 1972 (c.73)
Museums and Gymnasiums Act 1891 (c.22)
Museum of London Act 1965 (c.17)
Museum of London Act 1986 (c.8)
Museums and Galleries Act 1992 (c.44)
Musical Copyright Act 1906 (c.36)
Musical (Summary Proceedings) Copyright Act 1902 (c.15)
Mutford and Lothingland, Suffolk (Poor Relief) Act 1764 (c.89)
Mutiny Act 1701 (c.2)
Mutiny Act 1702 (c.20)
Mutiny Act 1703 (c.17)
Mutiny Act 1704 (c.5)
Mutiny Act 1705 (c.22)
Mutiny Act 1706 (c.18)
Mutiny Act 1707 (c.74)
Mutiny Act 1708 (c.4)
Mutiny Act 1709 (c.6)
Mutiny Act 1710 (c.9)
Mutiny Act 1711 (c.13)
Mutiny Act 1712 (c.13)
Mutiny Act 1713 (c.4)
Mutiny Act 1714 (c.3)
Mutiny Act 1714 (c.9)
Mutiny Act 1715 (c.34)
Mutiny Act 1716 (c.2)
Mutiny Act 1717 (c.4)
Mutiny Act 1718 (c.5)
Mutiny Act 1719 (c.3)
Mutiny Act 1720 (c.6)
Mutiny Act 1721 (c.3)
Mutiny Act 1722 (c.4)
Mutiny Act 1723 (c.3)
Mutiny Act 1724 (c.6)
Mutiny Act 1725 (c.3)
Mutiny Act 1726 (c.2)
Mutiny Act 1727 (c.2)
Mutiny Act 1728 (c.2)
Mutiny Act 1729 (c.2)
Mutiny Act 1730 (c.2)
Mutiny Act 1731 (c.2)
Mutiny Act 1732 (c.3)
Mutiny Act 1733 (c.2)
Mutiny Act 1734 (c.2)
Mutiny Act 1735 (c.2)

Mutiny Act 1736 (c.2)
Mutiny Act 1737 (c.2)
Mutiny Act 1738 (c.2)
Mutiny Act 1739 (c.10)
Mutiny Act 1740 (c.9)
Mutiny Act 1741 (c.4)
Mutiny Act 1742 (c.14)
Mutiny Act 1743 (c.16)
Mutiny Act 1744 (c.7)
Mutiny Act 1745 (c.11)
Mutiny Act 1746 (c.11)
Mutiny Act 1747 (c.6)
Mutiny Act 1747 (c.13)
Mutiny Act 1748 (c.5)
Mutiny Act 1749 (c.4)
Mutiny Act 1750 (c.6)
Mutiny Act 1751 (c.2)
Mutiny Act 1753 (c.5)
Mutiny Act 1754 (c.5)
Mutiny Act 1755 (c.4)
Mutiny Act 1756 (c.3)
Mutiny Act 1757 (c.6)
Mutiny Act 1757 (c.5)
Mutiny Act 1758 (c.5)
Mutiny Act 1759 (c.6)
Mutiny Act 1760 (c.6)
Mutiny Act 1761 (c.11)
Mutiny Act 1762 (c.7)
Mutiny Act 1763 (c.3)
Mutiny Act 1765 (c.7)
Mutiny Act 1766 (c.8)
Mutiny Act 1766 (c.10)
Mutiny Act 1768 (c.7)
Mutiny Act 1769 (c.7)
Mutiny Act 1770 (c.3)
Mutiny Act 1770 (c.15)
Mutiny Act 1771 (c.6)
Mutiny Act 1772 (c.4)
Mutiny Act 1772 (c.10)
Mutiny Act 1774 (c.3)
Mutiny Act 1775 (c.6)
Mutiny Act 1776 (c.2)
Mutiny Act 1776 (c.3)
Mutiny Act 1778 (c.4)
Mutiny Act 1779 (c.16)
Mutiny Act 1780 (c.12)
Mutiny Act 1782 (c.4)
Mutiny Act 1783 (c.17)
Mutiny Act 1783 (c.24)
Mutiny Act 1783 (c.52)
Mutiny Act 1783 (c.11)
Mutiny Act 1785 (c.6)
Mutiny Act 1786 (c.10)
Mutiny Act 1788 (c.12)
Mutiny Act 1789 (c.2)
Mutiny Act 1790 (c.6)
Mutiny Act 1791 (c.13)
Mutiny Act 1791 (c.19)
Mutiny Act 1793 (c.9)
Mutiny Act 1794 (c.13)
Mutiny Act 1795 (c.6)
Mutiny, America Act 1765 (c.33)
Mutiny, America Act 1768 (c.19)

Mutiny, East Indies Act 1754 (c.9)
Mutiny in America Act 1766 (c.18)
Mutiny in America Act 1767 (c.55)
Mutiny in America Act 1769 (c.18)
Mutiny in America Act 1771 (c.11)
Mutiny in America Act 1772 (c.12)
Mutiny in America Act 1773 (c.24)
Mutiny in America Act 1774 (c.6)
Mutiny in America Act 1775 (c.15)
Mutiny in America Act 1776 (c.11)

Namibia Act 1991 (c.4)
Nantwich Canal Act 1777 (c.67)
Nantwich Canal Act 1778 (c.21)
Nantwich to Chester Road Act 1789 (c.91)
Nar: Navigation Act 1750 (c.19)
National Assistance Act 1948 (c.29)
National Assistance Act 1948 (Amendment)
  Act 1962 (c.24)
National Assistance Act 1959 (c.52)
National Assistance (Amendment) Act 1951
  (c.57)
National Assistance (Amendment) Act 1959
  (c.30)
National Audit Act 1983 (c.44)
National Coal Board (Additional Powers) Act
  1966 (c.47)
National Coal Board (Finance) Act 1976 (c.1)
National Debt Act 1714 (c.2)
National Debt Act 1714 (c.12)
National Debt Act 1714 (c.19)
National Debt Act 1714 (c.21)
National Debt Act 1716 (c.7)
National Debt Act 1716 (c.9)
National Debt Act 1717 (c.10)
National Debt Act 1718 (c.3)
National Debt Act 1718 (c.9)
National Debt Act 1718 (c.19)
National Debt Act 1719 (c.4)
National Debt Act 1719 (c.10)
National Debt Act 1720 (c.5)
National Debt Act 1721 (c.1)
National Debt Act 1721 (c.20)
National Debt Act 1721 (c.22)
National Debt Act 1722 (cc.5, 6)
National Debt Act 1722 (c.12)
National Debt Act 1723 (c.5)
National Debt Act 1724 (c.17)
National Debt Act 1726 (c.3)
National Debt Act 1726 (c.21)
National Debt Act 1730 (c.16)
National Debt Act 1730 (c.5)
National Debt Act 1730 (c.9)
National Debt Act 1731 (c.17)
National Debt Act 1732 (c.28)
National Debt Act 1735 (c.34)
National Debt Act 1736 (c.17)
National Debt Act 1737 (c.27)
National Debt Act 1741 (c.19)
National Debt Act 1742 (cc.12, 13)
National Debt Act 1743 (c.18)
National Debt Act 1744 (c.9)

National Debt Act 1745 (c.12)
National Debt Act 1746 (c.3)
National Debt Act 1746 (c.10)
National Debt Act 1747 (c.2)
National Debt Act 1748 (c.23)
National Debt Act 1749 (c.1)
National Debt Act 1749 (c.16)
National Debt Act 1750 (c.2)
National Debt Act 1750 (c.11)
National Debt Act 1751 (c.25)
National Debt Act 1751 (c.27)
National Debt Act 1753 (c.1)
National Debt Act 1753 (c.23)
National Debt Act 1755 (c.15)
National Debt Act 1756 (c.7)
National Debt Act 1757 (c.19)
National Debt Act 1758 (c.22)
National Debt Act 1759 (c.12)
National Debt Act 1760 (c.7)
National Debt Act 1761 (cc.9, 10)
National Debt Act 1762 (c.9)
National Debt Act 1762 (c.12)
National Debt Act 1763 (c.18)
National Debt Act 1763 (c.25)
National Debt Act 1765 (c.16)
National Debt Act 1765 (c.23)
National Debt Act 1765 (c.42)
National Debt Act 1766 (c.21)
National Debt Act 1766 (c.39)
National Debt Act 1766 (cc.24–26)
National Debt Act 1768 (c.29)
National Debt Act 1768 (c.31)
National Debt Act 1770 (c.36)
National Debt Act 1770 (c.46)
National Debt Act 1772 (c.63)
National Debt Act 1774 (c.76)
National Debt Act 1775 (c.41)
National Debt Act 1776 (c.46)
National Debt Act 1778 (c.22)
National Debt Act 1779 (c.18)
National Debt Act 1782 (c.8)
National Debt Act 1782 (c.34)
National Debt Act 1783 (c.35)
National Debt Act 1784 (c.10)
National Debt Act 1784 (c.37)
National Debt Act 1784 (c.39)
National Debt Act 1785 (c.32)
National Debt Act 1785 (c.71)
National Debt Act 1786 (c.34)
National Debt Act 1789 (c.37)
National Debt Act 1793 (c.28)
National Debt Act 1793 (c.32)
National Debt Act 1794 (c.1)
National Debt Act 1794 (c.21)
National Debt Act 1795 (c.14)
National Debt Act 1795 (c.23)
National Debt Act 1795 (c.32)
National Debt Act 1958 (c.6)
National Debt Act 1972 (c.65)
National Debt (Conversion of Stock) Act 1884
  (c.23)
National Debt (No. 2) Act 1749 (c.22)
National Debt Reduction Act 1724 (c.9)

National Debt Reduction Act 1786 (c.31)

National Economy Act 1931 (c.48)

National Film Finance Corporation Act 1981 (c.15)

National Fire Service Regulations (Indemnity) Act 1944 (c.35)

National Galleries of Scotland Act 1906 (c.50)

National Galleries of Scotland Act 1959 (c.61)

National Gallery and St. James's Park Act 1911 (c.23)

National Gallery and Tate Gallery Act 1954 (c.65)

National Gallery Enlargement Act 1866 (c.83)

National Gallery Enlargement Act 1867 (c.41)

National Gallery (Overseas Loans) Act 1935 (c.18)

National Gallery (Purchase of Adjacent Land) Act 1901 (c.16)

National Health (Hospital Boards) Act 1964 (c.32)

National Health Insurance Act 1918 (c.62)

National Health Insurance Act 1919 (c.36)

National Health Insurance Act 1920 (c.10)

National Health Insurance Act 1921 (c.25)

National Health Insurance Act 1922 (c.38)

National Health Insurance Act 1924 (c.38)

National Health Insurance Act 1928 (c.14)

National Health Insurance Act 1936 (c.32)

National Health Insurance (Amendment) Act 1937 (c.24)

National Health Insurance (Amendment) Act 1938 (c.14)

National Health Insurance and Contributory Pensions Act 1932 (c.52)

National Health Insurance and Contributory Pensions Act 1935 (c.44)

National Health Insurance and Contributory Pensions (Emergency Provisions) Act 1939 (c.84)

National Health Insurance, Contributory Pensions and Workmen's Compensation Act 1941 (c.39)

National Health Insurance (Cost of Medical Benefit) Act 1924 (c.10)

National Health Insurance (Juvenile Contributors and Young Persons) Act 1937 (c.3)

National Health Insurance (Prolongation of Insurance) Act 1921 (c.66)

National Health Insurance (Prolongation of Insurance) Act 1931 (c.5)

National Health Insurance (Prolongation of Insurance) Act 1932 (c.6)

National Health Service Act 1946 (c.81)

National Health Service Act 1951 (c.31)

National Health Service Act 1952 (c.25)

National Health Service Act 1961 (c.19)

National Health Service Act 1966 (c.8)

National Health Service Act 1977 (c.49)

National Health Service (Amendment) Act 1949 (c.93)

National Health Service (Amendment) Act 1957 (c.44)

National Health Service (Amendment) Act 1986 (c.66)

National Health Service (Amendment) Act 1995 (c.31)

National Health Service and Community Care Act 1990 (c.19)

National Health Service Contributions Act 1957 (c.34)

National Health Service Contributions Act 1961 (c.13)

National Health Service Contributions Act 1965 (c.54)

National Health Service Contributions Act 1970 (c.16)

National Health Service (Family Planning) Act 1967 (c.39)

National Health Service (Family Planning) Amendment Act 1972 (c.72)

National Health Service (Hospital Boards) Act 1964 (c.32)

National Health Service (Invalid Direction) Act 1980 (c.15)

National Health Service (Primary Care) Act 1997 (c.46)

National Health Service (Private Finance) Act 1997 (c.56)

National Health Service Reorganisation Act 1973 (c.32)

National Health Service (Residual Liabilities) Act 1996 (c.15)

National Health Service (Scotland) Act 1947 (c.27)

National Health Service (Scotland) Act 1972 (c.58)

National Health Service (Scotland) Act 1978 (c.29)

National Health Service (Vocational Training) Act 1976 (c.59)

National Heritage Act 1980 (c.17)

National Heritage Act 1983 (c.47)

National Heritage Act 1997 (c.14)

National Heritage (Scotland) Act 1985 (c.16)

National Insurance Act 1911 (c.55)

National Insurance Act 1913 (c.37)

National Insurance Act 1946 (c.67)

National Insurance Act 1947 (c.37)

National Insurance Act 1949 (c.56)

National Insurance Act 1951 (c.34)

National Insurance Act 1953 (c.29)

National Insurance Act 1955 (c.29)

National Insurance Act 1956 (c.47)

National Insurance Act 1957 (c.26)

National Insurance Act 1959 (c.47)

National Insurance Act 1960 (c.5)

National Insurance Act 1963 (c.7)

National Insurance Act 1965 (c.51)

National Insurance Act 1966 (c.6)

National Insurance Act 1967 (c.73)

National Insurance Act 1969 (c.4)

National Insurance Act 1969 (c.44)

National Insurance Act 1971 (c.50)

National Insurance Act 1972 (c.57)

National Insurance Act 1974 (c.14)

National Insurance &c. Act 1964 (c.96)

National Insurance and Supplementary Benefit Act 1973 (c.42)

National Insurance (Amendment) Act 1972 (c.36)

National Insurance, etc. Act 1969 (c.4)

National Insurance (Industrial Injuries) Act 1953 (c.43)

National Insurance (Industrial Injuries) Act 1946 (c.62)

National Insurance (Industrial Injuries) Act 1948 (c.42)

National Insurance (Industrial Injuries) Act 1965 (c.52)

National Insurance (Industrial Injuries) (Amendment) Act 1967 (c.25)

National Insurance Land Purchase (Winding-up) Act 1935 (c.21)

National Insurance (Miscellaneous Provisions) Act 1928 (c.24)

National Insurance (Miscellaneous Provisions) Act 1932 (c.11)

National Insurance (Miscellaneous Provisions) Act 1945 (c.12)

National Insurance (Navy and Army) Act (c.81)

National Insurance (Navy and Army) (Session 2) Act 1914 (c.15)

National Insurance (No. 2) Act 1957 (c.1)

National Insurance (Old Persons' and Widows' Pensions and Attendance Allowance) Act 1970 (c.51)

National Insurance (Pt. I Amendment) Act 1915 (c.29)

National Insurance (Pt. I Amendment) Act 1917 (c.15)

National Insurance (Pt. II Amendment) Act 1914 (c.57)

National Insurance (Pt. II Amendment) Act 1914 (c.27)

National Insurance (Pt. II) (Munition Workers) Act 1916 (c.20)

National Insurance Regulations (Validation) Act 1972 (c.4)

National Insurance Surcharge Act 1976 (c.85)

National Insurance Surcharge Act 1982 (c.55)

National Insurance (Temporary Employment in Agriculture) Act 1916 (c.53)

National Insurance (Unemployment) Act 1918 (c.63)

National Insurance (Unemployment) Act 1919 (c.77)

National Library of Scotland Act 1925 (c.73)

National Loans Act 1939 (c.117)

National Loans Act 1940 (c.3)

National Loans Act 1941 (c.18)

National Loans Act 1942 (c.14)

National Loans Act 1943 (c.13)

National Loans Act 1944 (c.19)

National Loans Act 1945 (c.23)

National Loans Act 1968 (c.13)

National Loans (No. 2) Act 1940 (c.23)

National Lottery etc. Act 1993 (c.39)

National Maritime Museum Act 1934 (c.43)

National Maritime Museum Act 1989 (c.8)

National Mod (Scotland) Act 1969 (c.41)

National Museum of Antiquities of Scotland Act 1954 (c.14)

National Parks and Access to the Countryside Act 1949 (c.97)

National Portrait Gallery Act 1889 (c.25)

National Registration Act 1915 (c.60)

National Registration Act 1939 (c.91)

National Registration (Amendment) Act 1918 (c.60)

National Savings Bank Act 1971 (c.29)

National Service Act 1941 (c.15)

National Service Act 1942 (c.3)

National Service Act 1947 (c.31)

National Service Act 1948 (c.64)

National Service Act 1950 (c.30)

National Service Act 1955 (c.11)

National Service (Amendment) Act 1948 (c.6)

National Service (Armed Forces) Act 1939 (c.81)

National Service (Armed Forces) Act 1940 (c.22)

National Service (Channel Islands) Act 1940 (c.24)

National Service (Foreign Countries) Act 1942 (c.30)

National Service (No. 2) Act 1941 (c.4)

National Service (Release of Conscientious Objectors) Act 1946 (c.38)

National Theatre Act 1949 (c.16)

National Theatre Act 1969 (c.11)

National Theatre Act 1974 (c.55)

National Theatre and Museum of London Act 1973 (c.2)

Nationalised Industries Loans Act 1958 (c.19)

Natural Heritage (Scotland) Act 1991 (c.28)

Natural-born Children of Aliens Act 1776 (c.52)

Naturalisation Act 1711 (c.9)

Naturalisation Act 1714 (c.4)

Naturalisation Act 1739 (c.7)

Naturalisation Act 1762 (c.25)

Naturalisation Act 1763 (c.4)

Naturalisation Act 1772 (c.25)

Naturalisation Act 1774 (c.84)

Naturalisation of Jews Act 1753 (c.26)

Naturalisation of Jews Act 1754 (c.1)

Nature Conservancy Council Act 1973 (c.54)

Naval Agency and Distribution Act 1864 (c.24)

Naval and Marine Forces (Temporary Release from Service) Act 1941 (c.4)

Naval and Marine Pay and Pensions Act 1865 (c.73)

Naval and Marine Reserves Pay Act 1957 (c.32)

Naval and Military War Pensions, etc. Act 1915 (c.83)

New Office of Excise Act 1770 (c.32)

New Palace Yard, Westminster 1706 (c.15)

New Parishes Act 1843 (c.37)

New Parishes Act 1844 (c.94)

New Parishes Act 1856 (c.104)

New Parishes Acts and Church Building Acts Amendment Act 1869 (c.94)

New Parishes Acts and Church Building Acts Amendment Act 1884 (c.65)

New Roads and Street Works Act 1991 (c.22)

New Sarum: Poor Relief Act 1770 (c.81)

New Shoreham Harbour Act 1759 (c.35)

New Shoreham Harbour Act 1789 (c.21)

New Streets Act 1951 (c.40)

New Streets Act 1951 (Amendment) Act 1957 (c.33)

New Towns Act 1946 (c.68)

New Towns Act 1952 (c.27)

New Towns Act 1953 (c.38)

New Towns Act 1955 (c.4)

New Towns Act 1958 (c.12)

New Towns Act 1959 (c.62)

New Towns Act 1965 (c.59)

New Towns Act 1966 (c.44)

New Towns Act 1969 (c.5)

New Towns Act 1971 (c.81)

New Towns Act 1975 (c.42)

New Towns Act 1977 (c.23)

New Towns Act 1980 (c.36)

New Towns Act 1981 (c.64)

New Towns Act 1982 (c.7)

New Towns (No. 2) Act 1964 (c.68)

New Towns (Amendment) Act 1976 (c.68)

New Towns (Amendment) Act 1994 (c.5)

New Towns and Urban Development Corporations Act 1985 (c.5)

New Towns (Scotland) Act 1968 (c.16)

New Towns (Scotland) Act 1977 (c.16)

New Valuation Lists (Postponement) Act 1952 (c.4)

New Woodstock, Kiddington, etc. Roads Act 1757 (c.48)

New Zealand Constitution (Amendment) 1947 (c.4)

Newbury and Marlborough Roads Act 1744 (c.12)

Newbury to Bath Canal Act 1794 (c.90)

Newbury to Marlborough Road Act 1725 (c.8)

Newcastle and Gateshead Bridge Act 1788 (c.78)

Newcastle and Sunderland: Coals Act 1790 (c.78)

Newcastle: Improvement Act 1763 (c.55)

Newcastle (Sale of Coal by Measured Keel) Act 1791 (c.36)

Newcastle: Streets Act 1786 (c.39)

Newcastle to Buckton Burn Road Act 1794 (c.130)

Newcastle to Carlisle Road Act 1786 (c.160)

Newfoundland Act 1933 (c.2)

Newfoundland (Consequential Provisions) Act 1950 (c.5)

Newfoundland Fisheries Act 1775 (c.31)

Newfoundland Fisheries Act 1786 (c.26)

Newfoundland Fisheries Act 1788 (c.35)

Newgate Gaol Delivery Act 1785 (c.18)

Newgate Gaol and Session House Act 1778 (c.48)

Newhaven Bridge Act 1783 (c.21)

Newhaven Harbour Act 1730 (c.17)

Newmarket and Cambridge Road Act 1763 (c.32)

Newmarket to Cambridge Road Act 1775 (c.68)

Newspaper Duty Act 1772 (c.65)

Newspaper Libel and Registration Act 1881 (c.60)

Newspapers, Printers and Reading Rooms Repeal Act 1869 (c.24)

Newport, Isle of Wight: Improvement Act 1786 (c.119)

Niall Macpherson Indemnity 1954 (c.29)

Nigeria Independence Act 1960 (c.55)

Nigeria (Remission of Payments) Act 1937 (c.63)

Nigeria Republic Act 1963 (c.57)

Night Poaching Act 1828 (c.69)

Night Watch Westminster Act (c.15)

Nisi Prius, Middlesex Act 1725 (c.31)

Nith Fisheries Act 1792 (c.94)

Noise Act 1996 (c.37)

Noise Abatement Act 1960 (c.68)

Noise and Statutory Nuisance Act 1993 (c.40)

Nonconformist Relief Act 1779 (c.44)

Non-Domestic Rating Act 1992 (c.46)

Non-Domestic Rating Act 1993 (c.17)

Non-Domestic Rating Act 1994 (c.3)

Non-Domestic Rating (Information) Act 1996 (c.13)

Non-Ferrous Metal Industry Act 1917 (c.67)

Norfolk and Suffolk Broads Act 1988 (c.4)

Norfolk: Drainage Act 1783 (c,9)

Norfolk Highways Act 1708 (c.8)

Norfolk: Improvement Act 1725 (c.15)

Norfolk Roads Act 1765 (c.83)

Norfolk Roads Act 1765 (c.101)

Norfolk Roads Act 1767 (c.76)

Norfolk Roads Act 1770 (c.54)

Norfolk Roads Act 1770 (c.85)

Norfolk Roads Act 1770 (c.86)

Norfolk Roads Act 1786 (c.127)

Norfolk Roads Act 1790 (c.87)

Norfolk Roads Act 1790 (c.104)

Norfolk Roads Act 1791 (c.100)

Norfolk Roads Act 1791 (c.112)

Norfolk Roads Act 1791 (c.113)

Norfolk Roads Act 1792 (c.148)

Norfolk Roads Act 1792 (c.158)

Norfolk Roads Act 1794 (c.114)

North American Fisheries Act 1819 (c.38)

North Atlantic Shipping Act 1934 (c.10)

North Kyme Drainage Act 1788 (c.14)

North River, Norfolk: Navigation Act 1772 (c.37)

North Shields to Newcastle Road Act 1774 (c.115)

North Shields: Water Supply Act 1786 (c.110)
Northampton and Lincoln Roads Act 1756 (c.76)
Northampton and Lincoln Roads Act 1776 (c.72)
Northampton and Oxford Roads Act 1778 (c.87)
Northampton and Warwick Roads Act 1724 (c.25)
Northampton Highways Act (c.9)
Northampton: Improvement Act 1778 (c.79)
Northampton Roads Act 1748 (c.17)
Northampton Roads Act 1749 (c.8)
Northampton Roads Act 1753 (c.88)
Northampton Roads Act 1754 (c.23)
Northampton Roads Act 1778 (c.112)
Northampton Roads Act 1781 (c.94)
Northampton Roads Act 1783 (c.28)
Northampton Roads Act 1794 (c.126)
Northern Ireland Act 1929 (c.14)
Northern Ireland Act 1947 (c.37)
Northern Ireland Act 1955 (c.8)
Northern Ireland Act 1962 (c.30)
Northern Ireland Act 1972 (c.10)
Northern Ireland Act 1974 (c.28)
Northern Ireland Act 1982 (c.38)
Northern Ireland Arms Decommissioning Act 1997 (c.7)
Northern Ireland Assembly Act 1973 (c.17)
Northern Ireland Assembly Disqualifications Act 1975 (c.25)
Northern Ireland (Border Poll) Act 1972 (c.77)
Northern Ireland Compensation (for Compulsory Purchase) Act 1957 (c.14)
Northern Ireland Constitution Act 1973 (c.36)
Northern Ireland Constitution (Amendment) Act 1973 (c.69)
Northern Ireland (Emergency Provisions) Act 1973 (c.53)
Northern Ireland (Emergency Provisions) Act 1978 (c.5)
Northern Ireland (Emergency Provisions) Act 1987 (c.30)
Northern Ireland (Emergency Provisions) Act 1991 (c.24)
Northern Ireland (Emergency Provisions) Act 1996 (c.22)
Northern Ireland (Emergency Provisions) Amendment Act 1975 (c.62)
Northern Ireland (Emergency Provisions) (Amendment) Act 1977 (c.34)
Northern Ireland (Entry to Negotiations, etc) Act 1996 (c.11)
Northern Ireland (Financial Provisions) Act 1972 (c.76)
Northern Ireland (Foyle Fisheries) Act 1952 (c.11)
Northern Ireland Land Act 1925 (c.34)
Northern Ireland Land Act 1929 (c.14)
Northern Ireland Land Purchase (Winding Up) Act 1935 (c.21)
Northern Ireland (Loans) Act 1975 (c.83)
Northern Ireland (Loans) Act 1985 (c.76)

Northern Ireland (Miscellaneous Provisions) Act 1928 (c.24)
Northern Ireland (Miscellaneous Provisions) Act 1932 (c.11)
Northern Ireland (Miscellaneous Provisions) Act 1945 (c.12)
Northern Ireland (Remission of Sentences) Act 1995 (c.47)
Northern Ireland (Temporary Provisions) Act 1972 (c.22)
Northern Ireland (Young Persons) Act 1974 (c.33)
Northern Roads, London Act 1735 (c.39)
Northumberland Fishery Act 1789 (c.25)
Northumberland and Durham Roads Act 1792 (c.145)
Northumberland Roads Act 1746 (c.9)
Northumberland Roads Act 1748 (c.7)
Northumberland Roads Act 1748 (c.9)
Northumberland Roads Act 1751 (c.18)
Northumberland Roads Act 1751 (c.46)
Northumberland Roads Act 1751 (c.48)
Northumberland Roads Act 1757 (c.52)
Northumberland Roads Act 1776 (c.68)
Northumberland Roads Act 1776 (c.83)
Northumberland Roads Act 1778 (c.83)
Northumberland Roads Act 1778 (c.115)
Northumberland Roads Act 1779 (c.95)
Norton Folley, Middlesex, Lighting etc. Act 1758 (c.49)
Norwich Assizes Act 1746 (c.21)
Norwich and Swaffham Road Act 1770 (c.67)
Norwich and Thetford Road Act 1725 (c.22)
Norwich and Thetford Road Act 1746 (c.16)
Norwich and Watton Road Act 1770 (c.77)
Norwich Mayors, Sheriffs, etc. 1922 (c.9)
Norwich Roads Act 1790 (c.86)
Norwich to Bixley Roads Act 1790 (c.85)
Norwich to New Buckingham Road Act 1772 (c.95)
Norwich to Scole Bridge Road Act 1969 (c.66)
Norwich to Scole Bridge Road Act 1772 (c.76)
Norwich to Thetford Road Act 1792 (c.111)
Norwich to Swaffham Road Act 1792 (c.112)
Norwich to Yarmouth Road Act 1969 (c.68)
Norwich Water Act 1790 (c.21)
Norwich Workhouse Act 1711 (c.15)
Notice of Accidents Act 1906 (c.53)
Notification of Births Act 1907 (c.40)
Notification of Births (Extension) Act 1915 (c.64)
Nottingham Roads Act 1770 (c.92)
Nottingham Roads Act 1774 (c.101)
Nottingham Roads Act 1785 (c.107)
Nottingham and Derby Road Act 1758 (c.38)
Nottingham and Derby Roads Act 1764 (c.83)
Nottingham and Derby Roads Act 1765 (c.90)
Nottingham and Derby Roads Act 1783 (c.24)
Nottingham and Derby Roads Act 1788 (c.87)
Nottingham and Derby Roads Act 1788 (c.99)
Nottingham and Leicester Highways Act 1721 (c.13)
Nottingham and Leicester Roads Act 1737 (c.3)

Nottingham and Leicester Roads Act 1754 (c.22)
Nottingham and Lincoln Roads Act 1765 (c.85)
Nottingham Canal Act 1792 (c.100)
Nottingham, Leicester, Rutland and North-ampton Roads Act 1780 (c.81)
Nottingham: Lighting etc. Act 1762 (c.47)
Nottingham Roads Act 1765 (c.54)
Nottingham Roads Act 1791 (c.131)
Nottingham Roads Act 1791 (c.132)
Nottingham, Shire Hall Act 1769 (c.62)
Nottingham to Mansfield Road Act 1787 (c.76)
Nuclear Industry (Finance) Act 1977 (c.7)
Nuclear Industry (Finance) Act 1981 (c.71)
Nuclear Installations Act 1959 (c.46)
Nuclear Installations Act 1965 (c.57)
Nuclear Installations Act 1969 (c.18)
Nuclear Installations (Amendment) Act 1965 (c.6)
Nuclear Materials (Offences) Act 1983 (c.18)
Nuclear Safeguards and Electricity (Finance) Act 1978 (c.25)
Nuisances Removal (Scotland) Act 1856 (c.103)
Nullity of Marriage Act 1971 (c.44)
Nurseries and Child Minders Regulation Act 1948 (c.53)
Nursery Education and Grant-Maintained Schools Act 1996 (c.50)
Nurses Act 1943 (c.17)
Nurses Act 1945 (c.6)
Nurses Act 1949 (c.73)
Nurses Act 1957 (c.15)
Nurses Act 1964 (c.44)
Nurses Act 1969 (c.47)
Nurses Registration Act 1919 (c.94)
Nurses Registration (Ireland) Act 1919 (c.96)
Nurses Registration (Scotland) Act 1919 (c.95)
Nurses (Scotland) Act 1943 (c.33)
Nurses (Scotland) Act 1949 (c.95)
Nurses (Scotland) Act (c.55)
Nurses Agencies Act 1957 (c.16)
Nurses (Amendment) Act 1961 (c.14)
Nurses, Midwives and Health Visitors Act 1979 (c.36)
Nurses, Midwives and Health Visitors Act 1992 (c.16)
Nurses, Midwives and Health Visitors Act 1997 (c.24)
Nurses (Scotland) Act 1951 (c.55)
Nursing Homes Act 1963 (c.13)
Nursing Homes Act 1975 (c.37)
Nursing Homes Registration Act 1927 (c.38)
Nursing Homes Registration (Scotland) Act 1938 (c.73)

OECD Support Fund Act 1975 (c.80)
Oakham Canal Act 1793 (c.103)
Oakhampton Roads Act 1782 (c.92)

Oaths, etc. Act 1714 (c.3)
Oaths Act 1775 (c.39)
Oaths Act 1838 (c.105)
Oaths Act 1888 (c.46)
Oaths Act 1909 (c.39)
Oaths Act 1961 (c.21)
Oaths Act 1978 (c.19)
Oaths and Evidence (Overseas Authorities) (Land) Act 1963 (c.27)
Oaths at Parliamentary Elections Act 1794 (c.84)
Oaths of Justices of the Peace Act 1745 (c.13)
Obscene Publications Act 1857 (c.83)
Obscene Publications Act 1959 (c.66)
Obscene Publications Act 1964 (c.74)
Observance of Lord's Day by Bakers Act 1794 (c.61)
Obtaining Money by False Pretences, etc. Act 1757 (c.24)
Occasional Licences and Young Persons 1956 (c.42)
Occupiers' Liability Act 1957 (c.31)
Occupiers' Liability Act 1984 (c.3)
Occupiers' Liability (Scotland) Act 1960 (c.30)
Odiham to Farnham Roads Act 1789 (c.89)
Offences Against Customs and Excise Laws Act 1935 (c.35)
Offences Against Customs or Excise Act 1745 (c.34)
Offences Against Excise Laws Act 1758 (c.17)
Offences Against Excise Laws Act 1791 (c.10)
Offences Against the Person Act 1861 (c.100)
Offences Against Persons and Property Act 1936 (c.32)
Offences at Sea Act 1806 (c.54)
Offenders (Conveyance) Act 1753 (c.3)
Offensive Weapons Act 1996 (c.26)
Offices Act 1960 (c.47)
Office and Oath Act 1867 (c.75)
Offices of Court of Chancery Act 1792 (c.42)
Offices, Shops and Railway Premises Act 1963 (c.41)
Officers of Inland Revenue Act (1849) (c.58)
Officer of Late Wine Licences Office Act 1791 (c.28)
Officers of the Royal Naval Reserve Act 1863 (c.69)
Official Secrets Act 1911 (c.28)
Official Secrets Act 1920 (c.75)
Official Secrets Act 1939 (c.121)
Official Secrets Act 1989 (c.6)
Official Solicitor Act 1919 (c.30)
Offshore Petroleum Development (Scotland) Act 1975 (c.8)
Offshore Safety Act 1992 (c.15)
Offshore Safety (Protection against Victimis-ation) Act 1992 (c.24)
Oil and Gas (Enterprise) Act 1982 (c.23)

Oil and Pipelines Act 1985 (c.62)
Oil in Navigable Waters Act 1922 (c.39)
Oil Burners (Standards) Act 1960 (c.53)
Oil in Navigable Waters Act 1963 (c.28)
Oil in Navigable Waters Act 1955 (c.25)
Oil in Navigable Waters Act 1971 (c.21)
Oil in Tobacco Act 1900 (c.35)
Oil Taxation Act 1975 (c.22)
Oil Taxation Act 1983 (c.56)
Okehampton Roads Act 1759 (c.36)
Old Age and Widows Pensions Act 1940 (c.13)
Old Age Pensions Act 1908 (c.40)
Old Age Pensions Act 1911 (c.16)
Old Age Pensions Act 1919 (c.102)
Old Age Pensions Act 1924 (c.33)
Old Age Pensions Act 1936 (c.31)
Old Age and Widows' Pensions Act 1940 (c.13)
Old Brentford Bridge Act 1757 (c.63)
Old Brentford Bridge Act 1757 (c.46)
Old Palace Yard Act 1966 (c.32)
Old Shoreham, Bridge, Sussex Act 1780 (c.35)
Old Stratford to Dunchurch Road Act 1757 (c.57)
Old Stratford to Dunchurch Road Act 1775 (c.73)
Old Street Road Act 1753 (c.87)
Old Street Road Act 1756 (c.44)
Old Street Road Act 1772 (c.99)
Old Street Road Act 1789 (c.82)
Old Swineford: Small Debts Act 1776 (c.19)
Oldham to Alton Road Act 1793 (c.182)
Olympic Symbol etc. (Protection) Act 1995 (c.32)
Opencast Coal Act 1958 (c.69)
Open Spaces Act 1887 (c.32)
Open Spaces Act 1906 (c.25)
Open Space Act 1986 (c.38)
Opticians Act 1958 (c.32)
Opticians Act 1989 (c.44)
Orders, etc. of the Master of the Rolls Act 1730 (c.30)
Ordination of Aliens Act 1783 (c.35)
Ordnance Board Transfer Act 1855 (c.117)
Ordnance Factories and Military Services Act 1984 (c.59)
Ordnance Property Act 1821 (c.69)
Orkney and Shetland Small Piers and Harbours Act 1896 (c.32)
Orphans, London Act 1947 (c.29)
Osborne Estate Act 1902 (c.37)
Osborne Estate Act 1914 (c.36)
Osteopaths Act 1993 (c.21)
Oswestry: Poor Relief Act 1791 (c.24)
Ottawa Agreements Act 1932 (c.53)
Ouse: Navigation Act 1790 (c.52)
Ouse: Navigation Act 1790 (c.83)
Outdoor Relief (Friendly Societies) Act 1904 (c.32)
Outer Space Act 1986 (c.38)
Output of Beer (Restriction) Act 1916 (c.26)

Output of Beer (Restriction) Amendment Act 1916 (c.57)
Ouze Navigation Act 1731 (c.15)
Overseas Aid Act 1966 (c.21)
Overseas Aid Act 1968 (c.57)
Overseas Development and Co-operation Act 1980 (c.63)
Overseas Development and Service Act 1965 (c.38)
Overseas Investment and Export Guarantees Act 1972 (c.40)
Overseas Pensions Act 1973 (c.21)
Overseas Resources Act 1969 (c.36)
Overseas Resources Development Act 1947 (c.15)
Overseas Resources Development Act 1949 (c.65)
Overseas Resources Development Act 1951 (c.20)
Overseas Resources Development Act 1954 (c.71)
Overseas Resources Development Act 1956 (c.71)
Overseas Resources Development Act 1958 (c.15)
Overseas Resources Development Act 1959 (c.23)
Overseas Resources Development Act 1969 (c.36)
Overseas Service Act 1958 (c.14)
Overseas Service Act 1961 (c.10)
Overseas Superannuation Act 1991 (c.16)
Overseas Trade Act 1929 (c.12)
Overseas Trade Act 1930 (c.31)
Overseas Trade Act 1934 (c.12)
Overseas Trade (Credits and Insurance) Act 1920 (c.29)
Overseas Trade (Credits and Insurance) Amendment Act 1921 (c.26)
Overseas Trade Department (Secretary) Act 1918 (c.3)
Overseas Trade Guarantees Act 1939 (c.47)
Oxford and Berkshire Roads Act 1778 (c.81)
Oxford and Buckinghamshire Roads Act 1755 (c.42)
Oxford and Buckinghamshire Roads Act 1781 (c.77)
Oxford and Fifield Road Act 1767 (c.66)
Oxford and Gloucester Roads Act 1743 (c.10)
Oxford and Gloucester Roads Act 1730 (c.23)
Oxford and Gloucester Roads Act 1753 (c.70)
Oxford and Gloucester Roads Act 1765 (c.80)
Oxford and Gloucester Roads Act 1791 (c.111)
Oxford and Leicester Roads Act 1765 (c.105)
Oxford and Northampton Roads Act 1791 (c.128)
Oxford, Gloucester and Nottingham Roads Act 1770 (c.101)

Oxford: Improvement Act 1771 (c.19)
Oxford: Improvements Act 1780 (c.47)
Oxford: Poor Relief Act 1771 (c.14)
Oxford Roads Act 1750 (c.21)
Oxford Roads Act 1768 (c.34)
Oxford Roads Act 1771 (c.73)
Oxford Roads Act 1777 (c.88)
Oxford Roads Act 1778 (c.91)
Oxford Roads Act 1781 (c.87)
Oxford Roads Act 1789 (c.90)
Oxfordshire Roads Act 1739 (c.15)
Oxfordshire Roads Act 1730 (c.21)
Oxfordshire Roads Act 1757 (c.48)
Oxfordshire Roads Act 1762 (c.41)
Oyster and Mussel Fisheries Orders Confirmation Act 1869 (No. 2) (c.31)
Oyster Fisheries Act 1791 (c.51)

Pacific Cable Act 1901 (c.31)
Pacific Cable Act 1911 (c.36)
Pacific Cable Act 1924 (c.19)
Pacific Cable Act 1927 (c.9)
Pacific Cable Amendment Act 1902 (c.26)
Pacific Islands Protection Act 1875 (c.51)
Pacific Islands Regulations (Validation) Act 1916 (c.9)
Packing, etc. of Butter Act 1798 (c.73)
Paddington Churchyard Act 1753 (c.43)
Paddington (Improvement) Act 1763 (c.50)
Paddington Parish Church Act 1788 (c.74)
Paddington Parish Church Act 1793 (c.43)
Paisley Beer Duties Act 1753 (c.96)
Pakistan Act 1973 (c.48)
Pakistan Act 1974 (c.34)
Pakistan Act 1990 (c.14)
Pakistan (Consequential Provisions) Act 1956 (c.31)
Palestine Act 1948 (c.27)
Palestine Loan Act 1934 (c.33)
Pangbourn Bridge Act 1792 (c.97)
Paper Bills of Credit Act 1763 (c.34)
Paper Bills of Credit, American Colonies Act 1951 (c.53)
Paper Currency in America Act 1772 (c.57)
Paper Duties Act 1780 (c.24)
Paper Duties Act 1784 (c.18)
Paper Duties Act 1786 (c.78)
Paper Duties Act 1794 (c.20)
Papists Act 1715 (c.55)
Papists Act 1716 (c.18)
Papists Act 1722 (c.24)
Papists Act 1723 (c.4)
Papists Act 1732 (c.5)
Papists Act 1734 (c.25)
Papists Act 1737 (c.11)
Papists Act 1738 (c.14)
Papists Act 1740 (c.21)
Papists Act 1745 (c.16)
Papists Act 1753 (c.24)
Papists Act 1755 (c.10)
Papists Act 1757 (c.21)
Papists Act 1759 (c.13)

Papists Act 1762 (c.26)
Papists Act 1763 (c.38)
Papists Act 1766 (c.34)
Papists Act 1772 (c.10)
Papists Act 1774 (c.37)
Papists Act 1776 (c.45)
Papists Act 1778 (c.46)
Papists Act 1778 (c.60)
Papists Act 1780 (c.51)
Papists Act 1782 (c.23)
Papists Act 1783 (c.22)
Papists Act 1783 (c.16)
Papists Act 1787 (c.42)
Papists Act 1788 (c.47)
Papists Act 1789 (c.36)
Papists Act 1790 (c.19)
Papua New Guinea, Western Samoa and Nauru (Miscellaneous Provisions) Act 1980 (c.2)
Parish Apprentices Act 1778 (c.47)
Parish Apprentices Act 1792 (c.57)
Parish Church of St. Marylebone Act 1770 (c.112)
Parish Councils Act 1957 (c.42)
Parish Councils and Burial Authorities (Miscellaneous Provisions) Act 1970 (c.29)
Parish of The Trinity, Coventry Act 1779 (c.57)
Parish Officers Act 1793 (c.55)
Parish: Spittlefields, Stepney Act 1727 (c.10)
Park Lane Improvement Act 1958 (c.63)
Parking Act 1989 (c.16)
Parks Regulation Act 1872 (c.15)
Parks Regulation (Amendment) Act 1926 (c.36)
Parks Regulation (Amendment) Act 1974 (c.29)
Parliament Act 1710 (c.5)
Parliament Act 1712 (cc.5,6)
Parliament Act 1712 (c.16)
Parliament Act 1775 (c.36)
Parliament Act 1780 (c.1)
Parliament Act 1780 (c.50)
Parliament Act 1780 (c.43)
Parliament Act 1782 (c.29)
Parliament Act 1782 (c.41)
Parliament Act 1911 (c.13)
Parliament Act 1949 (c.103)
Parliament of Canada Act 1875 (c.38)
Parliament and Local Elections Act 1916 (c.44)
Parliament and Local Elections Act 1917 (c.13)
Parliament and Local Elections Act 1918 (c.22)
Parliament and Local Elections (No.2) Act 1917 (c.50)
Parliament and Registration Act 1916 (c.100)
Parliament (Elections and Meeting) Act 1943 (c.48)
Parliament (Qualification of Women) Act 1918 (c.47)
Parliamentary and Health Service Commissioners Act 1987 (c.39)

Parliamentary and Other Pensions Act 1972 (c.48)

Parliamentary and Other Pensions Act 1987 (c.45)

Parliamentary and Other Pensions and Salaries Act 1976 (c.48)

Parliamentary Commissioner Act 1967 (c.13)

Parliamentary Commissioner Act 1994 (c.14)

Parliamentary Commissioner (Consular Complaints) Act 1981 (c.11)

Parliamentary Constituencies Act 1986 (c.56)

Parliamentary Corporate Bodies Act 1992 (c.27)

Parliamentary Documents Deposit Act 1837 (c.83)

Parliamentary Elections Act 1734 (c.30)

Parliamentary Elections Act 1742 (c.11)

Parliamentary Elections Act 1744 (c.18)

Parliamentary Elections Act 1745 (c.28)

Parliamentary Elections Act 1757 (c.14)

Parliamentary Elections Act 1763 (c.24)

Parliamentary Elections Act 1770 (c.16)

Parliamentary Elections Act 1770 (c.41)

Parliamentary Elections Act 1771 (c.42)

Parliamentary Elections Act 1774 (c.15)

Parliamentary Elections Act 1774 (c.58)

Parliamentary Elections Act 1774 (c.81)

Parliamentary Elections Act 1780 (c.17)

Parliamentary Elections Act 1785 (c.84)

Parliamentary Elections Act 1790 (c.35)

Parliamentary Elections Act 1793 (c.64)

Parliamentary Elections Act 1795 (c.65)

Parliamentary Elections Act 1868 (c.125)

Parliamentary Elections, Cricklade Act 1782 (c.31)

Parliamentary Elections (Fraudulent Conveyances) Act 1739 (c.20)

Parliamentary Elections, New Shoreham Act 1771 (c.55)

Parliamentary Elections, Norwich 1730 (c.8)

Parliamentary Elections (Returning Officers) Act (1875) Amendment Act 1886 (c.57)

Parliamentary Elections Corrupt Practices Act 1879 (c.75)

Parliamentary Elections (Scotland) Act (c.16)

Parliamentary Elections (Soldiers) Act 1919 (c.10)

Parliamentary Electors (War-time Registration) Act 1944 (c.24)

Parliamentary Papers Act 1840 (c.9)

Parliamentary Pensions Act 1978 (c.56)

Parliamentary Pensions etc. Act 1984 (c.52)

Parliamentary Privilege Act 1770 (c.50)

Parliamentary Privilege Act 1937 (c.24)

Parliamentary Witnesses Act 1858 (c.78)

Parliamentary Witnesses Oaths Act 1871 (c.83)

Parochial Libraries Act 1708 (c.14)

Parochial Registers Act 1812 (c.146)

Parsonages Act 1838 (c.23)

Parsonages Act 1911 (c.29)

Participation Agreements Act 1978 (c.1)

Partition Act 1868 (c.40)

Partnership Act 1890 (c.39)

Parton, Cumberland, Harbour Act 1724 (c.16)

Parton Harbour, Cumberland Act 1731 (c.13)

Partridges Act 1799 (c.34)

Party Processions (Ireland) Act 1832 (c.118)

Party Processions (Ireland) Act 1844 (c.63)

Party Wall etc. Act 1996 (c.40)

Passage from Charing Cross Act 1757 (c.36)

Passenger Ships Act 1845 (c.14)

Passenger Vehicles (Experimental Areas) Act 1977 (c.21)

Patent Law Amendment Act 1852 (c.83)

Patents Act 1901 (c.18)

Patents Act 1902 (c.34)

Patents Act 1949 (c.87)

Patents Act 1957 (c.13)

Patents Act 1977 (c.37)

Patents and Designs Act 1907 (c.29)

Patents and Designs Act 1908 (c.4)

Patents and Designs Act 1914 (c.18)

Patents and Designs Act 1919 (c.80)

Patents and Designs Act 1927 (c.3)

Patents and Designs Act 1932 (c.32)

Patents and Designs Act 1942 (c.6)

Patents and Designs Act 1946 (c.44)

Patents and Designs Act 1949 (c.62)

Patents and Designs (Amendment) Act 1907 (c.28)

Patents and Designs (Limits of Time) Act 1939 (c.32)

Patents and Designs (Partial Suspension) Act 1915 (c.85)

Patents and Designs (Renewals, Extensions and Fees) Act 1961 (c.25)

Patents, Designs and Marks Act 1986 (c.39)

Patents, Designs and Trade Marks Act 1883 (c.57)

Patents, Designs and Trade Marks (Temporary Rules) Act 1914 (c.27)

Patents, Designs and Trade Marks (Temporary Rules) Amendment 1914 (c.73)

Patents, Designs, Copyright and Trade Marks (Emergency) Act 1939 (c.107)

Patents etc. (International Conventions) Act 1938 (c.29)

Patriotic Fund Act 1866 (c.120)

Patriotic Fund Reorganisation Act 1903 (c.20)

Pauper Children (Ireland) Act 1902 (c.16)

Paving, etc. of London Act 1768 (c.21)

Pawnbrokers Act 1784 (c.42)

Pawnbrokers Act 1785 (c.48)

Pawnbrokers Act 1787 (c.37)

Pawnbrokers Act 1788 (c.50)

Pawnbrokers Act 1789 (c.57)

Pawnbrokers Act 1791 (c.52)

Pawnbrokers Act 1793 (c.53)

Pawnbrokers Act 1872 (c.93)

Pawnbrokers Act 1922 (c.5)

Pawnbrokers Act 1960 (c.24)

Paymaster General Act 1782 (c.81)

Paymaster General Act 1783 (c.50)
Paymaster General Act 1835 (c.35)
Paymaster General Act 1848 (c.55)
Paymaster General, Balance, etc. Act 1780 (c.48)
Payment of Certain Regiments Act 1705 (c.12)
Payment of Charges of Constables Act 1778 (c.19)
Payment of Creditors (Scotland) Act 1780 (c.41)
Payment of Creditors (Scotland) Act 1783 (c.18)
Payment of Creditors (Scotland) Act 1789 (c.5)
Payment of Creditors (Scotland) Act 1793 (c.74)
Payment of Creditors (Scotland) Act 1804 (c.24)
Payment of Creditors (Scotland) Act 1813 (c.65)
Payment of Lace Makers' Wages Act 1779 (c.49)
Payment of Wages Act 1960 (c.37)
Pedlars Act 1871 (c.96)
Peebles Road Act 1753 (c.93)
Peebles Road Act 1771 (c.85)
Peebles Road Act 1775 (c.71)
Peebles Roads Act 1792 (c.123)
Peerage Act 1963 (c.48)
Pembroke Gaol Act 1779 (c.46)
Pembroke Road Act 1771 (c.96)
Pembroke Roads Act 1788 (c.102)
Pembroke Roads Act 1790 (c.91)
Pembroke Roads Act 1791 (c.102)
Pembroke Roads Act 1791 (c.109)
Pembroke Roads Act 1791 (c.126)
Penal Servitude Act 1891 (c.69)
Penal Servitude Act 1926 (c.58)
Penalties for Drunkenness Act 1962 (c.52)
Penicillin Act 1947 (c.29)
Penicillin (Merchant Ships) 1951 (c.13)
Penitentiary for Convicts Act 1794 (c.84)
Penny Post Act 1794 (c.17)
Pension Duties Act 1720 (c.27)
Pension Duties Act 1725 (c.2)
Pension Duties Act 1757 (c.22)
Pension Duties Act 1758 (c.33)
Pension Schemes Act 1993 (c.48)
Pension Schemes (Northern Ireland) Act 1993 (c.49)
Pensioners and Family Income Supplement Payments Act 1972 (c.75)
Pensioners' Payments Act 1974 (c.54)
Pensioners Payments Act 1977 (c.51)
Pensioners Payments Act 1978 (c.58)
Pensioners' Payments and National Insurance Act 1973 (c.61)
Pensioners' Payments and National Insurance Contributions Act 1972 (c.80)
Pensioners' Payments and Social Security Act 1979 (c.48)
Pensions Act 1839 (c.51)

Pensions Act 1995 (c.26)
Pensions and Determination of Needs Act 1943 (c.27)
Pensions and Yeomanry Pay Act 1884 (c.55)
Pensions Appeal Tribunals Act 1943 (c.39)
Pensions Appeal Tribunals Act 1949 (c.12)
Pensions Commutation Act 1871 (c.36)
Pensions Commutation Act 1882 (c.44)
Pensions Commutation Act 1984 (c.7)
Pensions (Governors of Dominions, etc.) Act 1911 (c.24)
Pensions (Governors of Dominions, etc.) Act 1929 (c.16)
Pensions (Governors of Dominions, etc.) Act 1936 (c.25)
Pensions (Governors of Dominions, etc.) Act 1947 (c.12)
Pensions (Governors of Dominions, etc.) Amendment 1913 (c.26)
Pensions (Increase) Act 1920 (c.36)
Pensions (Increase) Act 1924 (c.32)
Pensions (Increase) Act 1944 (c.21)
Pensions (Increase) Act 1946 (c.7)
Pensions (Increase) Act 1952 (c.45)
Pensions (Increase) Act 1954 (c.25)
Pensions (Increase) Act 1956 (c.39)
Pensions (Increase) Act 1962 (c.2)
Pensions (Increase) Act 1965 (c.78)
Pensions (Increase) Act 1969 (c.7)
Pensions (Increase) Act 1971 (c.56)
Pensions (Increase) Act 1974 (c.9)
Pensions (India, Pakistan and Burma) Act 1955 (c.22)
Pensions (Mercantile Marine) Act 1942 (c.26)
Pensions (Miscellaneous Provisions) Act 1990 (c.7)
Pensions (Navy, Army, Air Force and Mercantile Marine) Act 1939 (c.83)
Pensions to Seamen, etc. Act 1814 (c.1)
Performers' Protection Act 1963 (c.53)
Performers' Protection Act 1972 (c.32)
Performing Animals (Regulation) Act 1925 (c.38)
Perjury Act 1727 (c.25)
Perjury Act 1911 (c.6)
Perpetuation and Amendment of Acts 1904 (c.16)
Perpetuation, etc. of Acts 1708 (c.25)
Perpetuation of Acts, etc. Act 1719 (c.19)
Perpetuation of Testimony Act 1842 (c.69)
Perpetuation of Various Laws Act 1732 (c.37)
Perpetuities and Accumulations Act 1964 (c.55)
Persons Going Armed or Disguised Act 1758 (c.18)
Persons Going Armed and Disguised Act 1754 (c.15)
Personal Injuries (Emergency Provisions) Act 1939 (c.82)
Persuading Soldiers to Desert, etc. Act 1715 (c.47)
Perth: Highways and Bridge Act 1785 (c.13)
Perth Roads Act 1753 (c.91)

Perth Roads Act 1765 (c.89)
Perth Roads Act 1789 (c.17)
Perth Roads Act 1793 (c.158)
Pesticides (Fees and Enforcement) Act 1989 (c.27)
Pests Act 1954 (c.68)
Pet Animals Act 1951 (c.35)
Pet Animals Act 1951 (Amendment) Act 1983 (c.26)
Peterborough: Streets Act 1790 (c.66)
Petersham: Streets Act 1772 (c.42)
Petersfield Highways Act 1710 (c.33(f))
Petersfield to Portsmouth Road Act 1725 (c.19)
Petroleum Act 1879 (c.47)
Petroleum Act 1926 (c.25)
Petroleum Act 1975 (c.74)
Petroleum Act 1987 (c.12)
Petroleum (Amendment) 1928 (c.21)
Petroleum and Submarine Pipelines Act 1975 (c.74)
Petroleum (Consolidation) Act 1928 (c.32)
Petroleum (Production) Act 1918 (c.52)
Petroleum (Production) Act 1934 (c.36)
Petroleum Revenue Tax Act 1980 (c.1)
Petroleum Royalties (Relief) Act 1983 (c.59)
Petroleum Royalties (Relief) and Continental Shelf Act 1989 (c.1)
Petroleum Royalties (Relief) Act 1983 (c.59)
Petroleum (Transfer of Licences) Act 1936 (c.27)
Petty Sessions Act 1849 (c.18)
Petty Sessions Clerks and Fines (Ireland) Act 1878 (c.69)
Petty Sessions (Ireland) Act 1851 (c.93)
Petty Sessions Clerk (Ireland) (Amendment) Act 1901 (c.22)
Pharmacists (Fitness to Practise) Act 1997 (c.19)
Pharmacy Act 1929 (c.31)
Pharmacy Act 1953 (c.19)
Pharmacy Act 1954 (c.61)
Pharmacy and Medicines Act 1941 (c.42)
Pharmacy and Poisons Act 1933 (c.25)
Pharmacy and Poisons (Amendment) Act 1964 (c.35)
Physical Training and Recreation Act 1937 (c.46)
Physical Training and Recreation Act 1958 (c.36)
Piccadilly Act 1844 (c.88)
Piccadilly; Watering Act 1775 (c.57)
Pig Industry Levy Act 1983 (c.4)
Pilchard Fisheries Act 1791 (c.45)
Pilchard Fishery Act 1785 (c.58)
Pilchard Fishery Act 1786 (c.45)
Pilchard Fishery, Cornwall Act 1776 (c.36)
Pillory Abolition Act 1816 (c.138)
Pilotage Act 1716 (c.13)
Pilotage Act 1731 (c.20)
Pilotage Act 1913 (c.31)
Pilotage Act 1983 (c.21)
Pilotage Act 1987 (c.21)

Pilotage Authorities (Limitation of Liability) Act 1936 (c.36)
Pipelines Act 1962 (c.58)
Piracy Act 1717 (c.11)
Piracy Act 1721 (c.24)
Piracy Act 1744 (c.30)
Piracy Act 1837 (c.88)
Pistols Act 1903 (c.18)
Pittenweem Beer Duties Act 1719 (c.9)
Places of Religious Worship Act 1812 (c.155)
Places of Worship (Enfranchisement) Act 1920 (c.56)
Places of Worship Registration Act 1855 (c.81)
Planning and Compensation Act 1991 (c.34)
Planning (Consequential Provisions) Act 1990 (c.11)
Planning (Consequential Provisions) (Scotland) Act 1997 (c.11)
Planning (Hazardous Substances) Act 1990 (c.10)
Planning (Hazardous Substances) (Scotland) Act 1997 (c.10)
Planning Inquiries (Attendance of Public) Act 1982 (c.21)
Planning (Listed Buildings and Conservation Areas) Act 1990 (c.9)
Planning (Listed Buildings and Conservation Areas) (Scotland) Act 1997 (c.9)
Plant Health Act 1967 (c.8)
Plant Varieties Act 1983 (c.17)
Plant Varieties Act 1997 (c.66)
Plant Varieties and Seeds Act 1964 (c.14)
Plantation Trade etc., Act 1741 (c.31)
Plate Act 1696 (c.8)
Plate Assay Act 1700 (c.3)
Plate Assay (Sheffield) Act 1784 (c.20)
Plate Assay (Sheffield and Birmingham) Act 1772 (c.52)
Plate Duties Act 1784 (c.53)
Plate (Duties, Drawbacks) Act 1785 (c.64)
Plate Duty Act 1719 (c.11)
Plate (Duty on Dealer's Licence) Act 1757 (c.24)
Plate (Duty on Dealer's Licence) Act 1757 (c.32)
Plate Glass Manufacture Act 1772 (c.38)
Plate (Offences) Act 1738 (c.26)
Plate (Offences) Act 1772 (c.59)
Plate (Scotland) Act 1836 (c.69)
Plays and Wine Licences 1736 (c.28)
Pleading Act 1711 (c.28)
Pleading in Misdemeanour Act 1819 (c.4)
Pluralities Act 1838 (c.106)
Pluralities Act 1850 (c.98)
Pluralities Act 1887 (c.68)
Pluralities of Living Act 1801 (c.102)
Plymouth and Portsmouth Fortifications Act 1758 (c.30)
Plymouth Dock Act 1766 (c.102)
Plymouth Dock to Torpoint: Ferry Act 1790 (c.61)
Plymouth: Fortifications Act 1774 (c.50)

Plymouth Fortifications Act 1781 (c.61)
Plymouth Fortifications Act 1782 (c.12)
Plymouth Improvement Act 1770 (c.14)
Plymouth Improvement Act 1772 (c.8)
Plymouth: Poor Relief Act 1758 (c.59)
Plymouth: Poor Relief Act 1786 (c.19)
Plymouth: Poor Relief etc, Act 1781 (c.72)
Plymouth, Sheerness, Gravesend, Tilbury-Fortifications Act 1780 (c.38)
Plymouth: Streets Act 1774 (c.8)
Plymouth Water Supply Act 1793 (c.85)
Plymouth Workhouse 1707 (c.46(d))
Pneumoconiosis and Byssinosis Benefit Act 1951 (c.4)
Pneumoconiosis etc. (Workers' Compensation) Act 1979 (c.41)
Poaching Prevention Act 1862 (c.114)
Poisons Act 1972 (c.66)
Poisons and Pharmacy Act 1908 (c.55)
Polehampton Estates Act 1885 (c.40)
Police Act 1909 (c.40)
Police Act 1919 (c.46)
Police Act 1964 (c.48)
Police Act 1969 (c.63)
Police Act 1972 (c.39)
Police Act 1976 (c.46)
Police Act 1996 (c.16)
Police Act 1997 (c.50)
Police and Criminal Evidence Act 1984 (c.60)
Police and Firemen (War Service) Act 1939 (c.103)
Police and Firemen (War Service) Act 1944 (c.22)
Police and Firemen's Pensions Act 1997 (c.52)
Police and Magistrates' Courts Act 1994 (c.29)
Police (Appeals) Act 1927 (c.19)
Police (Appeals) Act 1943 (c.8)
Police Army Act 1946 (c.46)
Police Constables (Naval and Military Service) Act 1914 (c.80)
Police Constables (Naval and Military Service) Act 1917 (c.36)
Police (Emergency Provisions) Act 1915 (c.41)
Police Factories, etc. (Miscellaneous Provisions) Act 1916 (c.31)
Police Federation Act 1959 (c.38)
Police Federations Act 1962 (c.25)
Police Federation Act 1961 (c.51)
Police, Fire and Probation Officers' Remuneration Act 1956 (c.1)
Police (Health and Safety) Act 1997 (c.42)
Police (His Majesty's Inspectors of Constabulary) Act 1945 (c.11)
Police (Insurance of Voluntary Assistants) Act 1997 (c.45)
Police (Liverpool Inquiry) Act 1909 (c.35)
Police Magistrates (Superannuation) Act 1915 (c.74)
Police Magistrates Superannuation Amendment Act 1929 (c.37)

Police Negotiating Board Act 1980 (c.10)
Police Officers (Central Service) Act 1989 (c.11)
Police (Overseas Service) Act 1945 (c.17)
Police (Pensions) Act 1918 (c.51)
Police (Pensions) Act 1921 (c.31)
Police Pensions Act 1926 (c.34)
Police Pensions Act 1948 (c.24)
Police Pensions Act 1961 (c.35)
Police Pensions Act 1976 (c.35)
Police (Property) Act 1897 (c.30)
Police (Property) Act 1997 (c.30)
Police Revenue and Consolidated Fund Charges Act 1854 (c.94)
Police (Scotland) Act 1857 (c.72)
Police (Scotland) Act 1856 (c.26)
Police (Scotland) Act 1890 (c.67)
Police (Scotland) Act 1946 (c.71)
Police (Scotland) Act 1966 (c.52)
Police (Scotland) Act 1967 (c.77)
Police (Scotland) Act (1890) Amendment Act 1910 (c.10)
Police (Scotland) (Limit of Age) Act 1914 (c.69)
Police Reservists Act 1902 (c.10)
Police Reservists (Allowances) Act 1900 (c.9)
Police Reservists (Allowances) Act 1914 (c.34)
Police (Superannuation) Act 1906 (c.7)
Police (Superannuation) Act 1908 (c.5)
Police (Weekly Rest Day) Act 1910 (c.13)
Police (Weekly Rest Day) (Scotland) Act 1914 (c.8)
Policing of Airports Act 1974 (c.41)
Policyholders Protection Act 1975 (c.75)
Policyholders Protection Act 1997 (c.18)
Polish Resettlement Act 1947 (c.19)
Polling Arrangements (Parliamentary Boroughs) Act 1908 (c.14)
Polling Districts (County Councils) Act 1908 (c.13)
Polling Districts and Registration of Voters (Ireland) Act 1908 (c.35)
Ponies Act 1969 (c.28)
Pool Betting Act 1954 (c.33)
Pool Competitions Act 1971 (c.57)
Pool Harbour Act 1756 (c.10)
Poole Roads Act 1756 (c.52)
Poole Roads Act 1757 (c.52)
Poole Roads Act 1757 (c.66)
Poole Roads Act 1777 (c.104)
Poole to Blandford Road Act 1777 (c.86)
Poor Act 1762 (c.22)
Poor Act 1766 (c.39)
Poor Act 1776 (c.40)
Poor Act 1793 (c.35)
Poor Act 1912 (c.18)
Poor Apprentices Act 1780 (c.36)
Poor Law Act 1927 (c.14)
Poor Law Act 1930 (c.17)
Poor Law Act 1934 (c.59)
Poor Law Amendment Act 1844 (c.101)

Poor Law (Amendment) Act 1938 (c.23)

Poor Law Authorities (Transfer of Property) Act 1904 (c.20)

Poor Law (Dissolution of School Districts and Adjustments) Act 1903 (c.19)

Poor Law Emergency Provisions (Scotland) Act 1921 (c.64)

Poor Law Emergency Provisions (Scotland) Act 1927 (c.3)

Poor Law Emergency Provisions Continuance (Scotland) Act 1924 (c.9)

Poor Law Emergency Provisions Continuance (Scotland) Act 1925 (c.35)

Poor Law, Hull Act 1709 (c.24)

Poor Law Officers' Superannuation Act 1896 (c.50)

Poor Law (Scotland) Act 1934 (c.52)

Poor Persons 1495 (c.12)

Poor Prisoners' Defence Act 1903 (c.38)

Poor Prisoners' Defence Act 1930 (c.32)

Poor Prisoners Relief Act 1737 (c.20)

Poor Prisoners (Scotland) Act 1825 (c.62)

Poor Rate Act 1743 (c.3)

Poor Rate Exemption Act 1833 (c.30)

Poor Relief Act 1722 (c.7)

Poor Relief Act 1743 (c.38)

Poor Relief Act 1769 (c.37)

Poor Relief (Deserted Wives and Children) Act 1718 (c.8)

Poor Relief: Gloucester Act 1726 (c.19)

Poor Relief (Ireland) Act 1838 (c.56)

Poor Relief (Ireland) Act 1849 (c.104)

Poor Relief (Ireland) Act 1900 (c.45)

Poor Relief (Ireland) Act 1914 (c.14)

Poor Removal Act 1900 (c.23)

Poor, Staffordshire Act 1791 (c.20)

Population (Statistics) Act 1938 (c.13)

Population (Statistics) Act 1960 (c.32)

Porcelain Patent Act 1775 (c.52)

Port Glasgow Harbour Act 1772 (c.16)

Port of Liverpool Act 1766 (c.61)

Port of London (Financial Assistance) Act 1980 (c.31)

Portman Square: Improvement Act 1782 (c.85)

Ports Act 1991 (c.52)

Ports (Finance) Act 1985 (c.30)

Ports (Financial Assistance) Act 1981 (c.21)

Ports (Reduction of Debt) Act 1983 (c.22)

Portsea Chapel Act 1787 (c.64)

Portsea Common Chapel Act 1753 (c.58)

Portsea: Improvement Act 1792 (c.103)

Portsmouth, Chatham Fortifications Act 1782 (c.80)

Portsmouth, Chatham Fortifications Act 1783 (c.71)

Portsmouth, Faversham Fortifications Act 1783 (c.87)

Portsmouth Improvement Act 1768 (c.62)

Portsmouth, Plymouth Fortifications Act 1784 (c.29)

Portsmouth: Streets Act 1776 (c.59)

Portsmouth Water Supply (Farlington) Act 1740 (c.43)

Possession of Mortgaged Land (Emergency Provisions) Act 1939 (c.108)

Postage Act 1730 (c.33)

Postage Act 1763 (c.24)

Postage Act 1765 (c.25)

Postage Act 1782 (c.70)

Postage Act 1783 (c.69)

Postage Act 1784 (c.8)

Postage Act 1787 (c.9)

Postage Act 1794 (c.18)

Postage Act 1796 (c.18)

Postage Act 1805 (c.11)

Postage Act 1805 (c.21)

Post Fines Act 1758 (c.14)

Post Horse Duties Act 1787 (c.26)

Post Horse Duties Act 1790 (c.23)

Post Horse Duties Act 1793 (c.71)

Post Horse Duties Act 1796 (c.84)

Post Office Act 1748 (c.25)

Post Office Act 1904 (c.14)

Post Office Act 1908 (c.48)

Post Office Act 1913 (c.11)

Post Office Act 1918 (c.10)

Post Office Act 1953 (c.36)

Post Office Act 1961 (c.15)

Post Office Act 1969 (c.48)

Post Office Act 1977 (c.44)

Post Office (Amendment) Act 1935 (c.15)

Post Office and Telegraph Act 1915 (c.82)

Post Office and Telegraph Act 1920 (c.40)

Post Office and Telegraph Act 1940 (c.25)

Post Office and Telegraph (Money) Act 1928 (c.37)

Post Office and Telegraph (Money) Act 1931 (c.20)

Post Office and Telegraph (Money) Act 1935 (c.14)

Post Office and Telegraph (Money) Act 1937 (c.51)

Post Office and Telegraph (Money) Act 1939 (c.42)

Post Office and Telegraph (Money) Act 1942 (c.24)

Post Office and Telegraph (Money) Act 1946 (c.51)

Post Office and Telegraph (Money) Act 1947 (c.16)

Post Office and Telegraph (Money) Act 1950 (c.2)

Post Office and Telegraph (Money) Act 1952 (c.34)

Post Office and Telegraph (Money) Act 1953 (c.4)

Post Office and Telegraph (Money) Act 1955 (c.14)

Post Office and Telegraph (Money) Act 1957 (c.5)

Post Office and Telegraph (Money) Act 1950 (c.2)

Post Office (Banking Services) Act 1976 (c.10)

Post Office (Borrowing Powers) Act 1967 (c.15)

Post Office (Borrowing Powers) Act 1972 (c.79)

Post Office (Data Processing Service) Act 1967 (c.62)

Post Office (Literature for the Blind) Act 1906 (c.22)

Post Office (Money Orders) Act 1903 (c.12)

Post Office (Money Orders) Act 1906 (c.4)

Post Office Offences and Isle of Man Postage Act 1767 (c.50)

Post Office (Parcels) Act 1922 (c.49)

Post Office (Pneumatic Tubes Acquisition) Act 1922 (c.43)

Post Office (Protection) Act 1884 (c.76)

Post Office (Revenues) Act 1710 (c.11(p))

Post Office Savings Bank Act 1908 (c.8)

Post Office Savings Bank Act 1954 (c.62)

Post Office Savings Bank Act 1965 (c.12)

Post Office Savings Bank (Public Trustee) Act 1908 (c.52)

Post Office (Subway) Act 1966 (c.25)

Post Office Works Act 1959 (c.43)

Post Roads in Scotland Act 1951 (c.28)

Post Works Loans Act 1957 (c.4)

Postponement of Enactments (Miscellaneous Provisions) Act 1939 (c.2)

Postponement of Payments Act 1914 (c.11)

Postponement of Polling Day Act 1945 (c.40)

Pot and Pearl Ashes Act 1750 (c.51)

Poultry Act 1911 (c.11)

Powers of Attorney Act 1971 (c.27)

Powers of Criminal Courts Act 1973 (c.62)

Prescription Act 1832 (c.71)

Prescription and Limitation (Scotland) Act 1973 (c.52)

Prescription and Limitation (Scotland) Act 1984 (c.45)

Prescription (Scotland) Act 1987 (c.36)

Presentation of Benefices Act 1713 (c.13)

Preservation of Fish and Conies Act 1965 (c.14)

Preservation of House Doves, etc. Act 1762 (c.29)

Preservation of Roads Act 1740 (c.42)

Preservation of Timber Act 1772 (c.33)

Preservation of Timber Trees Act 1715 (c.48)

Preservation of Timber Trees Act 1766 (c.48)

Preservation of Timber Trees (Scotland) Act 1719 (c.16)

Preservation of Trees, America Act 1710 (c.22)

Preservation of Woods, America Act 1728 (c.35)

President of the Board of Trade 1932 (c.21)

Presteigne Road Act 1756 (c.94)

Preston Bridge Act 1757 (c.55)

Prestonpans Beer Duties Act 1753 (c.79)

Prestonpans Beer Duties Act 1757 (c.52)

Presumption of Death (Scotland) Act 1977 (c.27)

Presumption of Life Limitation (Scotland) Act 1891 (c.29)

Prevention and Treatment of Blindness (Scotland) Act 1938 (c.32)

Prevention of Corruption Act 1906 (c.34)

Prevention of Corruption Act 1916 (c.64)

Prevention of Crimes Act 1871 (c.112)

Prevention of Crime Act 1908 (c.59)

Prevention of Crime Act 1953 (c.14)

Prevention of Cruelty to Children Act 1904 (c.15)

Prevention of Damage by Pests Act 1949 (c.55)

Prevention of Damage by Rabbits 1939 (c.43)

Prevention of Eviction Act 1924 (c.18)

Prevention of Fraud (Investments) Act 1939 (c.16)

Prevention of Fraud (Investments) Act 1958 (c.45)

Prevention of Offences Act 1851 (c.19)

Prevention of Oil Pollution Act 1971 (c.60)

Prevention of Oil Pollution Act 1986 (c.6)

Prevention of Terrorism (Additional Powers) Act 1996 (c.7)

Prevention of Terrorism (Temporary Provisions) Act 1974 (c.55)

Prevention of Terrorism (Temporary Provisions) Act 1976 (c.8)

Prevention of Terrorism (Temporary Provisions Act 1984 (c.8)

Prevention of Terrorism (Temporary Provisions) Act 1989 (c.4)

Prevention of Violence (Temporary Provisions) Act 1939 (c.50)

Previous Conviction Act 1836 (c.111)

Price Commission Act 1977 (c.33)

Price Commission (Amendment) Act 1979 (c.1)

Price Control and Other Orders (Indemnity) Act 1951 (c.59)

Price Control (Regulation of Disposal of Stocks) Act 1943 (c.47)

Price of Coal (Limitation) Act 1915 (c.75)

Prices Act 1974 (c.24)

Prices Act 1975 (c.32)

Prices and Incomes Act 1966 (c.33)

Prices and Incomes Act 1967 (c.53)

Prices and Incomes Act 1968 (c.42)

Prices of Goods Act 1939 (c.118)

Princess Elizabeth's and Duke of Edinburgh's Annuities Act 1947 (c.14)

Printer's Imprint Act 1961 (c.31)

Prison Act 1952 (c.52)

Prison Officers (Pensions) Act (c.9)

Prison Security Act 1992 (c.25)

Prisoners and Criminal Proceedings (Scotland) Act 1993 (c.9)

Prisoners' Earnings Act 1996 (c.33)

Prisoners of War (Escape) Act 1812 (c.156)

Prisoners (Return to Custody) Act 1995 (c.16)

Prisoners (Temporary Discharge for Ill-Health) Act 1913 (c.4)

Prisons (Alcohol Testing) Act 1997 (c.38)

Prisons (Ireland) Act 1819 (c.100)

Prisons (Ireland) Act 1907 (c.19)

Prisons (Scotland) Act 1839 (c.42)
Prisons (Scotland) Act 1844 (c.34)
Prisons (Scotland) Act 1904 (c.35)
Prisons (Scotland) Act 1909 (c.27)
Prisons (Scotland) Act 1926 (c.57)
Prisons (Scotland) Act 1952 (c.61)
Prisons (Scotland) Act 1989 (c.45)
Private International Law (Miscellaneous Provisions) Act 1995 (c.42)
Private Legislation Procedure (Scotland) Act 1933 (c.37)
Private Legislation Procedure (Scotland) Act 1936 (c.52)
Private Place of Entertainment (Licensing) Act 1967 (c.19)
Private Street Works Act 1961 (c.24)
Prize Act 1939 (c.65)
Prize Act 1948 (c.9)
Prize Causes Act 1797 (c.38)
Prize Courts Act 1915 (c.57)
Prize Courts (Procedure) Act 1914 (c.13)
Prize Goods Act 1803 (c.134)
Prize Salvage Act 1943 (c.7)
Prize Salvage Act 1944 (c.7)
Probate and Legacy Duties Act 1808 (c.149)
Probate and Legacy Duties (Ireland) Act 1814 (c.92)
Probate Duty Act 1801 (c.86)
Probate Duty Act 1859 (c.36)
Probate Duty Act 1860 (c.15)
Probate Duty Act 1861 (c.92)
Probate Duty (Ireland) Act 1816 (c.56)
Probates and Letters of Administration Act (Ireland) 1857 (c.79)
Probation of Offenders Act 1907 (c.17)
Probation of Offenders (Scotland) Act 1931 (c.30)
Probation Officers (Superannuation) Act 1947 (c.38)
Probation Service Act 1993 (c.47)
Proceedings Against Estates Act 1970 (c.17)
Proceeds of Crime Act 1995 (c.11)
Proceeds of Crime (Scotland) Act 1995 (c.43)
Professional Cavalry Act 1796 (c.23)
Professions Supplementary to Medicine Act 1960 (c.66)
Profiteering Act 1919 (c.66)
Profiteering Amendment Act 1920 (c.13)
Profiteering (Cont.) Act 1919 (c.87)
Profits Tax Act 1949 (c.64)
Prohibition of Female Circumcision Act 1985 (c.38)
Prolongation of Parliament Act 1940 (c.53)
Prolongation of Parliament Act 1941 (c.48)
Prolongation of Parliament Act 1942 (c.37)
Prolongation of Parliament Act 1943 (c.46)
Prolongation of Parliament Act 1944 (c.45)
Promissory Oaths Act 1868 (c.72)
Promissory Oaths Act 1871 (c.48)
Property Misdescriptions Act 1991 (c.29)
Property Services Agency and Crown Suppliers Act 1990 (c.12)
Prosecution of Offences Act 1879 (c.22)

Prosecution of Offences Act 1884 (c.58)
Prosecution of Offences Act 1908 (c.3)
Prosecution of Offences Act 1979 (c.31)
Prosecution of Offences Act 1985 (c.23)
Protection Against Cruel Tethering Act 1988 (c.31)
Protection from Eviction Act 1964 (c.97)
Protection from Eviction Act 1977 (c.43)
Protection from Harassment Act 1997 (c.40)
Protection of Aircraft Act 1973 (c.47)
Protection of Animals Act 1911 (c.27)
Protection of Animals Act 1934 (c.21)
Protection of Animals Act (1911) Amendment 1921 (c.14)
Protection of Animals (Amendment) 1927 (c.27)
Protection of Animals (Amendment) Act 1954 (c.40)
Protection of Animals (Amendment) Act 1988 (c.29)
Protection of Animals (Anaesthetics) Act 1954 (c.46)
Protection of Animals (Anaesthetics) Act 1964 (c.39)
Protection of Animals (Cruelty to Dogs) Act 1933 (c.17)
Protection of Animals (Cruelty to Dogs) (Scotland) Act 1934 (c.25)
Protection of Animals (Penalties) Act 1987 (c.35)
Protection of Animals (Scotland) Act 1912 (c.14)
Protection of Animals (Scotland) Act, 1912, Amendment Act 1921 (c.22)
Protection of Animals (Scotland) Act 1993 (c.15)
Protection of Birds Act 1925 (c.31)
Protection of Birds Act 1933 (c.52)
Protection of Birds Act 1954 (c.30)
Protection of Birds Act 1967 (c.46)
Protection of Birds Act 1954 (Amendment) Act 1964 (c.59)
Protection of Birds (Amendment) Act 1976 (c.42)
Protection of Children Act 1978 (c.37)
Protection of Children (Tobacco) Act 1986 (c.34)
Protection of Depositors Act 1963 (c.16)
Protection of Lapwings Act 1928 (c.2)
Protection of Military Remains Act 1986 (c.35)
Protection of Trading Interests Act 1980 (c.11)
Protection of Wrecks Act 1973 (c.33)
Provident Nominations and Small Intestacies Act 1883 (c.47)
Provisional Collection of Taxes 1913 (c.3)
Provisional Collection of Taxes Act 1968 (c.2)
Provisional Order Confirmation (Turnpikes) Act 1854 (c.51)
Provisional Order Confirmation (Turnpikes) Act 1855 (c.102)
Provisional Order Confirmation (Turnpikes) Act 1857 (c.9)

Provisional Order Confirmation (Turnpikes) Act 1858 (c.80)

Provisional Order Confirmation (Turnpikes) Act 1859 (c.33)

Provisional Order Confirmation (Turnpikes) Act 1860 (c.70)

Provisional Orders Confirmation (Turnpikes) Act 1862 (c.69)

Provisional Order Confirmation (Turnpikes) Act 1863 (c.98)

Provisional Order Confirmation (Turnpikes) Act 1864 (c.79)

Provisional Order (Marriages) Act 1904 (c.23)

Public Accounts Act 1804 (c.58)

Public Accounts and Charges Act 1891 (c.24)

Public and Other Schools (War Conditions) Act 1941 (c.20)

Public Authorities (Allowances) Act 1961 (c.43)

Public Authorities and Bodies (Loans) Act 1916 (c.69)

Public Bodies (Admission to Meetings) Act 1960 (c.67)

Public Bodies Corrupt Practices Act 1889 (c.69)

Public Buildings Expenses Act 1903 (c.41)

Public Buildings Expenses Act 1913 (c.14)

Public Entertainment Act 1875 (c.21)

Public Entertainments Licences (Drug Misuse) Act 1997 (c.49)

Public Expenditure and Receipts Act 1968 (c.14)

Public Health Act 1875 (c.55)

Public Health Act 1904 (c.16)

Public Health Act 1908 (c.6)

Public Health Act 1925 (c.71)

Public Health Act 1936 (c.49)

Public Health Act (London) Act 1936 (c.50)

Public Health Act 1961 (c.64)

Public Health Acts Amendment Act 1890 (c.59)

Public Health Acts Amendment Act 1907 (c.53)

Public Health (Borrowing Powers) (Ireland) Act (c.35)

Public Health (Cleansing of Shellfish) Act 1932 (c.28)

Public Health (Coal Mine Refuse) Act 1939 (c.58)

Public Health (Coal Mine Refuse) (Scotland) Act 1939 (c.23)

Public Health (Confirmation of Byelaws) Act 1884 (c.12)

Public Health (Control of Disease) Act 1984 (c.22)

Public Health (Drainage of Trade Premises) Act 1937 (c.40)

Public Health (Interments) Act 1879 (c.31)

Public Health (Ireland) Act 1878 (c.52)

Public Health (Ireland) Act 1896 (c.54)

Public Health (Ireland) Act 1900 (c.10)

Public Health (Ireland) Act 1911 (c.12)

Public Health (Laboratory Service) Act 1960 (c.49)

Public Health (Laboratory Service) Act 1979 (c.23)

Public Health (London) Act 1936 (c.50)

Public Health (Medical Treatment, etc.) (Ireland) Act 1919 (c.16)

Public Health (Notification of Births) Act 1965 (c.42)

Public Health (Officers) Act 1921 (c.23)

Public Health Officers (Deputies) Act 1957 (c.19)

Public Health (Prevention and Treatment of Disease) Act 1913 (c.23)

Public Health (Prevention, etc. of Disease) (Ireland) Act 1917 (c.40)

Public Health (Recurring Nuisances) Act 1969 (c.25)

Public Health (Regulations as to Food) Act 1907 (c.32)

Public Health (Scotland) Act 1897 (c.38)

Public Health (Scotland) Amendment Act 1907 (c.30)

Public Health (Scotland) Act (1897) Amendment 1911 (c.30)

Public Health (Scotland) Amendment Act 1925 (c.75)

Public Health (Scotland) Act 1945 (c.15)

Public Health (Smoke Abatement) Act 1926 (c.43)

Public Health (Tuberculosis) Act 1921 (c.12)

Public Health (Water and Sewerage) (Scotland) Act 1935 (c.36)

Public Lavatories (Turnstiles) Act 1963 (c.32)

Public Lending Right Act 1979 (c.10)

Public Libraries Act 1884 (c.37)

Public Libraries Act 1901 (c.19)

Public Libraries Act 1919 (c.93)

Public Libraries and Museums Act 1964 (c.75)

Public Libraries Consolidation (Scotland) Act 1887 (c.42)

Public Libraries (Ireland) Amendment Act 1877 (c.15)

Public Libraries (Ireland) Act 1855 (c.40)

Public Libraries (Ireland) Act 1894 (c.38)

Public Libraries (Ireland) Act 1902 (c.20)

Public Libraries (Ireland) Act 1911 (c.9)

Public Libraries (Ireland) Act 1920 (c.25)

Public Libraries (Scotland) Act 1894 (c.20)

Public Libraries (Scotland) Act 1899 (c.5)

Public Libraries (Scotland) Act 1920 (c.45)

Public Libraries (Scotland) Act 1955 (c.27)

Public Meeting Act 1908 (c.66)

Public Notaries (Articled Clerks) Act 1919 (c.25)

Public Notaries (Ireland) Act 1821 (c.36)

Public Notaries (War Service of Articled Clerks) Act 1946 (c.79)

Public Officers Protection (Ireland) Act 1803 (c.143)

Public Offices Fees Act 1879 (c.58)

Public Offices (Site) Act 1947 (c.45)
Public Order Act 1936 (c.6)
Public Order Act 1963 (c.52)
Public Order Act 1986 (c.64)
Public Order (Amendment) Act 1996 (c.59)
Public Parks (Scotland) Act 1878 (c.8)
Public Passenger Vehicles Act 1981 (c.14)
Public Records Act 1958 (c.51)
Public Records Act 1967 (c.44)
Public Records (Scotland) Act 1937 (c.43)
Public Registers and Records (Scotland) Act 1948 (c.57)
Public Registers and Records (Scotland) Act 1949 (c.11)
Public Roads (Ireland) Act 1911 (c.45)
Public Schools Act 1868 (c.118)
Public Schools (Eton College Property) Act 1873 (c.62)
Public Service Vehicles (Arrest of Offenders) Act 1975 (c.53)
Public Service Vehicles (Travel Concessions) Act 1955 (c.26)
Public Stores Act 1875 (c.25)
Public Trustee Act 1906 (c.55)
Public Trustee and Administration of Funds Act 1986 (c.57)
Public Trustee (Fees) Act 1957 (c.12)
Public Trustee (General Deposit Fund) Act 1939 (c.51)
Public Utilities Street Works Act 1950 (c.39)
Public Utility Companies (Capital Issues) Act 1920 (c.9)
Public Utility Transfers and Water Charges Act 1988 (c.15)
Public Works Facilities Act 1930 (c.50)
Public Works (Festival of Britain) Act 1949 (c.26)
Public Works Loans Act 1900 (c.36)
Public Works Loans Act 1901 (c.35)
Public Works Loans Act 1902 (c.22)
Public Works Loans Act 1903 (c.28)
Public Works Loans Act 1904 (c.22)
Public Works Loans Act 1904 (c.36)
Public Works Loans Act 1906 (c.29)
Public Works Loans Act 1907 (c.36)
Public Works Loans Act 1908 (c.23)
Public Works Loans Act 1909 (c.6)
Public Works Loans Act 1910 (c.21)
Public Works Loans Act 1911 (c.17)
Public Works Loans Act 1912 (c.11)
Public Works Loans Act 1913 (c.22)
Public Works Loans Act 1914 (c.33)
Public Works Loans Act 1915 (c.68)
Public Works Loans Act 1916 (c.28)
Public Works Loans Act 1917 (c.32)
Public Works Loans Act 1918 (c.27)
Public Works Loans Act 1919 (c.52)
Public Works Loans Act 1920 (c.61)
Public Works Loans Act 1921 (c.54)
Public Works Loans Act 1922 (c.33)
Public Works Loans Act 1923 (c.29)
Public Works Loans Act 1924 (c.26)
Public Works Loans Act 1925 (c.62)

Public Works Loans Act 1926 (c.2)
Public Works Loans Act 1927 (c.1)
Public Works Loans Act 1928 (c.5)
Public Works Loans Act 1930 (c.49)
Public Works Loans Act 1931 (c.47)
Public Works Loans Act 1932 (c.42)
Public Works Loans Act 1934 (c.48)
Public Works Loans Act 1935 (c.5)
Public Works Loans Act 1937 (c.11)
Public Works Loans Act 1939 (c.2)
Public Works Loans Act 1941 (c.14)
Public Works Loans Act 1944 (c.16)
Public Works Loans Act 1946 (c.41)
Public Works Loans Act 1947 (c.13)
Public Works Loans Act 1948 (c.48)
Public Works Loans Act 1949 (c.82)
Public Works Loans Act 1950 (c.5)
Public Works Loans Act 1951 (c.5)
Public Works Loans Act 1952 (c.3)
Public Works Loans Act 1953 (c.6)
Public Works Loans Act 1955 (c.11)
Public Works Loans Act 1956 (c.65)
Public Works Loans Act 1964 (c.9)
Public Works Loans Act 1965 (c.63)
Public Works Loans Act 1966 (c.16)
Public Works Loans Act 1967 (c.61)
Public Works Loans (No. 2) Act 1927 (c.28)
Public Works Loans (No. 2) Act 1937 (c.7)
Punishment of Incest Act 1908 (c.45)
Purchase of Land (Ireland) Act 1885 (c.73)
Purchase of Land (Ireland) Act 1891 (c.48)
Purchase of Land (Ireland) Act 1901 (c.3)
Purchase of Land (Ireland) (No. 2) Act 1901 (c.30)
Purchase Tax Act 1963 (c.9)

Quail Protection Act 1937 (c.5)
Quakers and Moravians Act 1833 (c.49)
Quakers and Moravians Act 1838 (c.77)
Qualification of Women (County and Borough Councils) Act 1907 (c.33)
Qualification of Women (County and Town Councils) Act 1907 (c.48)
Quarantine Act 1797 (c.33)
Quarantine Act 1800 (c.80)
Quarantine Act 1805 (c.10)
Quarantine Act 1810 (c.20)
Quarantine Act 1811 (c.46)
Quarantine Act 1825 (c.78)
Quarantine Act (Great Britain) Act 1806 (c.98)
Quarantine, etc., Act 1800 (c.30)
Quarries Act 1894 (c.42)
Quarry (Fencing) Act 1887 (c.19)
Quarter Sessions Act 1814 (c.84)
Quarter Sessions Act 1837 (c.4)
Quarter Sessions Act 1842 (c.38)
Quarter Sessions Act 1849 (c.45)
Quarter Sessions Act 1894 (c.6)
Quarter Sessions (Ireland) Act 1845 (c.80)
Quarter Sessions Jurors (Ireland) Act 1897 (c.20)

Quarter Sessions (London) Act 1896 (c.55)
Quartering of Soldiers Act 1795 (c.64)
Quartering of Soldiers Act 1796 (c.36)
Quartering of Soldiers Act 1797 (c.32)
Quartering of Soldiers Act 1797 (c.41)
Quartering of Soldiers Act 1799 (c.36)
Quartering of Soldiers Act 1800 (c.39)
Quartering of Soldiers Act 1801 (c.35)
Quartering of Soldiers Act 1802 (c.108)
Quartering of Soldiers Act 1803 (c.41)
Quartering of Soldiers Act 1804 (c.38)
Quartering of Soldiers Act 1805 (c.37)
Quartering of Soldiers Act 1806 (c.126)
Quartering of Soldiers Act 1807 (c.54)
Quartering of Soldiers Act 1808 (c.39)
Quartering of Soldiers Act 1809 (c.37)
Quartering of Soldiers Act 1810 (c.28)
Quartering of Soldiers Act 1810 (c.96)
Quartering of Soldiers Act 1811 (c.28)
Quartering of Soldiers Act 1812 (c.43)
Quartering of Soldiers Act 1813 (c.43)
Quartering of Soldiers Act 1814 (c.55)
Quartering of Soldiers Act 1815 (c.154)
Quartering of Soldiers Act 1816 (c.32)
Quartering of Soldiers Act 1817 (c.78)
Quartering of Soldiers Act 1818 (c.22)
Quartering of Soldiers Act 1819 (c.26)
Quartering of Soldiers Act 1820 (c.38)
Quartering of Soldiers Act 1821 (c.25)
Quartering of Soldiers Act 1822 (c.20)
Quartering of Soldiers Act 1823 (c.20)
Quartering of Soldiers Act 1824 (c.31)
Quartering of Soldiers Act 1825 (c.20)
Quartering of Soldiers Act 1826 (c.14)
Quartering of Soldiers Act 1826 (c.24)
Quartering of Soldiers Act 1828 (c.8)
Quartering of Soldiers Act 1828 (c.9)
Quays, etc. Between Tower and London Bridge Act 1832 (c.66)
Quebec Act 1774 (c.88)
Quebec Act 1852 (c.53)
Quebec Civil Government Charges Act 1831 (c.23)
Queen Anne's Bounty Act 1714 (c.10)
Queen Anne's Bounty Act 1803 (c.107)
Queen Anne's Bounty Act 1805 (c.84)
Queen Anne's Bounty Act 1838 (c.20)
Queen Anne's Bounty Act 1840 (c.20)
Queen Anne's Bounty (Superannuation) Act 1870 (c.89)
Queen's Bench (Ireland) Procedure Act 1872 (c.28)
Queen Caroline's Servants' Pension Act 1822 (c.98)
Queen's Colleges (Ireland) Act 1845 (c.66)
Queen's Prison Act 1842 (c.22)
Queen's Prison Act 1848 (c.7)
Queen's Prison Act 1860 (c.60)
Queen's Prison Discontinuance Act 1862 (c.104)
Queen's Remembrance Act 1859 (c.21)
Queensferry, Firth of Forth: Finance Act 1814 (c.138)

Rabies Act 1974 (c.17)
Race Relations Act 1965 (c.73)
Race Relations Act 1968 (c.71)
Race Relations Act 1976 (c.74)
Race Relations (Remedies) Act 1994 (c.10)
Racecourse Betting Act 1928 (c.41)
Racecourse Licensing Act 1879 (c.18)
Radioactive Material (Road Transport) Act 1991 (c.27)
Radioactive Substances Act 1948 (c.37)
Radioactive Substances Act 1960 (c.34)
Radioactive Substances Act 1993 (c.12)
Radiological Protection Act 1970 (c.46)
Rag Flock Act 1911 (c.52)
Rag Flock Act (1911) Amendment Act 1928 (c.39)
Rag Flock and Other Filling Materials Act 1951 (c.63)
Railways Act 1848 (c.3)
Railways Act 1974 (c.48)
Railway and Canal Commission (Abolition) Act 1949 (c.11)
Railway and Canal Commission (Consents) Act 1922 (c.47)
Railway and Canal Traffic Act 1854 (c.31)
Railway and Canal Traffic Act 1888 (c.25)
Railway and Canal Traffic Act 1892 (c.44)
Railway and Canal Traffic Act 1894 (c.54)
Railway and Canal Traffic Act 1913 (c.29)
Railway and Canal Traffic (Provisional Orders) Amendment Act 1891 (c.12)
Railway Assessors (Scotland) Superannuation Act 1897 (c.12)
Railway Clauses Act 1863 (c.92)
Railway Companies Act 1867 (c.127)
Railway Companies Act 1868 (c.79)
Railway Companies Act 1875 (c.31)
Railway Companies (Accounts and Returns) Act 1911 (c.34)
Railway Companies Arbitration Act 1859 (c.59)
Railway Companies (Ireland) Act 1867 (c.138)
Railway Companies (Ireland) Temporary Advances Act 1866 (c.95)
Railway Companies (Ireland) Temporary Advances Act 1868 (c.94)
Railway Companies Meetings Act 1869 (c.6)
Railway Companies Mortgage Trans. (Scotland) Act 1861 (c.50)
Railway Companies' Powers Act 1864 (c.120)
Railway Companies (Scotland) Act 1867 (c.126)
Railway Companies Securities Act 1866 (c.108)
Railway Employment (Prevention of Accidents) Act 1900 (c.27)
Railway Fires Act 1904 (c.11)
Railway Freight Rebates Act 1936 (c.2)
Railway Freight Rebates Act 1943 (c.23)
Railway Heritage Act 1996 (c.42)

Railway Returns (Continuous Brakes) Act 1878 (c.20)
Railways Act 1921 (c.55)
Railways Act 1993 (c.43)
Railways (Agreement) Act 1935 (c.6)
Railways Agreement (Powers) Act 1941 (c.5)
Railways and Canals Act 1860 (c.41)
Railways (Authorisation of Works) Act 1923 (c.30)
Railways Clauses Act 1863 (c.92)
Railways Clauses Consolidation Act 1845 (c.20)
Railways Clauses Consolidation (Scotland) Act 1845 (c.33)
Railways Commission Act 1846 (c.105)
Railway Companies Dissolution 1846 (c.28)
Railways Construction Amendment (Ireland) Act 1880 (c.31)
Railways Construction Facilities Act 1864 (c.121)
Railways (Conveyance of Mails) Act 1838 (c.98)
Railways (Electrical Power) Act 1903 (c.30)
Railways Employment (Prevention of Accidents) Act 1900 (c.27)
Railways (Extension of Time) Act 1868 (c.18)
Railway Fires Act 1905 (c.11)
Railway Fires Act (1905) Amendment Act 1923 (c.27)
Railways (Ireland) Act 1856 (c.72)
Railways (Ireland) Act 1858 (c.34)
Railways (Ireland) Act 1864 (c.71)
Railways (Ireland) Act 1867 (c.104)
Railways (Ireland) Act 1890 (c.52)
Railways (Ireland) Act 1896 (c.34)
Railway Passenger Duty Act 1842 (c.79)
Railway Passenger Duty Act 1847 (c.42)
Railway Passenger Duty Act 1917 (c.3)
Railways (Powers and Construction) Acts, 1864, Amendment Act 1870 (c.19)
Railways (Private Sidings) Act 1904 (c.19)
Railway Regulation Act 1840 (c.97)
Railway Regulation Act 1842 (c.55)
Railway Regulation Act 1844 (c.85)
Railway Regulation Act 1851 (c.64)
Railway Regulation Act 1893 (c.29)
Railway Regulation Act (Returns of Signal Arrangements, Working &c.) Act 1873 (c.76)
Railway Regulation (Gauge) Act 1846 (c.57)
Railway Rolling Stock Protection Act 1872 (c.50)
Railway (Sales and Leases) Act 1845 (c.96)
Railways Act 1921 (c.55)
Railways Act (Ireland) 1851 (c.70)
Railways Act (Ireland) 1860 (c.97)
Railways (Private Sidings) Act 1904 (c.19)
Railways (Settlement of Claims) Act 1921 (c.59)
Railways Traverse Act 1868 (c.70)
Railways (Valuation for Rating) Act 1930 (c.24)
Railways (Valuation for Rating) Act 1946 (c.61)

Ramsey (Huntingdonshire): Drainage, etc. Act 1796 (c.72)
Ramsgate Harbour Act 1797 (c.86)
Ramsgate: Improvement Act 1796 (c.43)
Ranges Act 1891 (c.54)
Rate in Aid of Distressed Unions Act 1849 (c.24)
Rate Rebate Act 1973 (c.28)
Rate of Interest Act 1821 (c.51)
Rate of Interest Act 1822 (c.47)
Rate Support Grants Act 1986 (c.54)
Rate Support Grants Act 1987 (c.5)
Rate Support Grants Act 1988 (c.51)
Rateable Property (Ireland) Act 1846 (c.110)
Rates Act 1984 (c.33)
Rates of Carriage of Goods Act 1827 (c.39)
Rates (Proceedings for Recovery) Act 1914 (c.85)
Rating Act 1874 (c.54)
Rating Act 1966 (c.9)
Rating Act 1971 (c.39)
Rating and Valuation Act 1925 (c.90)
Rating and Valuation Act 1928 (c.8)
Rating and Valuation Act 1932 (c.18)
Rating and Valuation Act 1937 (c.60)
Rating and Valuation Act 1957 (c.17)
Rating and Valuation Act 1959 (c.36)
Rating and Valuation Act 1961 (c.45)
Rating and Valuation (Air-Raid Works) Act 1938 (c.65)
Rating and Valuation (Air-Raid Works) (Scotland) Act 1938 (c.66)
Rating and Valuation (Amendment) (Scotland) Act 1984 (c.31)
Rating and Valuation (Apportionment) Act 1928 (c.44)
Rating and Valuation (Miscellaneous Provisions) Act 1955 (c.9)
Rating and Valuation (No. 2) Act 1932 (c.33)
Rating and Valuation (Postponement of Valuations) Act 1938 (c.19)
Rating and Valuation (Postponement of Valuations) Act 1940 (c.12)
Rating and Valuation (Scotland) Act 1952 (c.47)
Rating (Caravan Sites) Act 1976 (c.15)
Rating (Charity Shops) Act 1976 (c.45)
Rating (Disabled Persons) Act 1978 (c.40)
Rating Exemption (Scotland) Act 1874 (c.20)
Rating (Interim Relief) Act 1964 (c.18)
Rating of Small Tenements Act 1850 (c.99)
Rating of Small Tenements Act 1851 (c.39)
Rating (Revaluation Rebates) (Scotland) Act 1985 (c.33)
Rating (Scotland) Act 1926 (c.47)
Rating (Scotland) Amendment Act 1928 (c.6)
Rating (War Damage Insurance) Act 1941 (c.25)
Rating (War Damages) (Scotland) Act 1941 (c.25)
Ratings (Caravans and Boats) Act 1996 (c.12)
Rats and Mice (Destruction) Act 1919 (c.72)

Reading Charities Act 1861 (c.23)

Ready Money Football Betting Act 1920 (c.52)

Real Estate Charges Act 1854 (c.113)

Real Estate Charges Act 1867 (c.69)

Real Etate Charges Act 1877 (c.34)

Real Property Act 1845 (c.106)

Real Property Limitation Act 1833 (c.27)

Real Property Limitation Act 1837 (c.28)

Real Property Limitation Act 1874 (c.57)

Real Rights Act 1693 (c.22)

Rebuilding of London Bridge Act 1823 (c.50)

Recall of Army and Air Force Pensions Act 1948 (c.8)

Recaptured British-built Ships Act 1809 (c.41)

Receipt and Remittance of Taxes, etc. Act 1831 (c.18)

Receipt Stamps Act 1828 (c.27)

Receiver General of Stamps Act 1806 (c.76)

Receivers of Crown Rents Act 1816 (c.16)

Receivers of Stolen Goods, etc., Act 1822 (c.24)

Recess Elections Act 1784 (c.26)

Recess Elections Act 1975 (c.66)

Reclamation of Lands, etc. Act 1842 (c.105)

Reclamation of Lands, etc. (Ireland) Act 1831 (c.57)

Recognition of Divorces and Legal Separations Act 1971 (c.53)

Recognition of Trusts Act 1987 (c.14)

Recognizances (Ireland) Act 1809 (c.83)

Recognizances (Ireland) Act 1817 (c.56)

Record of Title (Ireland) Act 1865 (c.88)

Recorded Delivery Service Act 1962 (c.27)

Recorders' Courts of Quarter Sessions Act 1837 (c.19)

Recorders, Magistrates and Clerks of the Peace Act 1888 (c.23)

Recorders, Stipendiary Magistrates and Clerks of the Peace Act 1906 (c.46)

Recoveries in Copyhold, etc. Courts Act 1807 (c.8)

Recovery of Advowsons in Ireland Act 1844 (c.27)

Recovery of Alimony (Ireland) Act 1867 (c.11)

Recovery of Possession by Landlords Act 1820 (c.87)

Recovery of Small Tithes Act 1826 (c.15)

Recovery of Tenements, etc. (Ireland) Act 1816 (c.88)

Recovery of Tenements, etc. (Ireland) Act 1818 (c.39)

Recovery of Tenements, etc. (Ireland) Act 1820 (c.41)

Recovery of Tithes (Ireland) Act 1832 (c.41)

Recovery of Wages (Ireland) Act 1814 (c.116)

Recovery of Wages (Ireland) Act 1849 (c.15)

Recreation Grounds Act 1859 (c.27)

Recreational Charities Act 1958 (c.17)

Rectifying of Spirits (Ireland) Act 1807 (c.19)

Rectory of Ewelme Act 1871 (c.23)

Rectory of Ledbury Act 1855 (c.92)

Red Sea and India Telegraph Company Act 1861 (c.4)

Red Sea and India Telegraph Company Act 1862 (c.39)

Redemption of Rent (Ireland) Act 1891 (c.57)

Redemption of Standard Securities (Scotland) Act 1971 (c.45)

Redistribution of Seats Act 1885 (c.23)

Redistribution of Seats (Ireland) Act 1918 (c.65)

Redstone Bridge, Severn Act 1795 (c.108)

Reduction of Annuity Tax Act 1867 (c.107)

Reduction of Duty on Rum Act 1863 (c.102)

Reduction of National Debt 1809 (c.64)

Reduction of National Debt Act 1822 (c.9)

Reduction of National Debt Act 1858 (c.38)

Reduction of National Debt Act 1860 (c.71)

Reductions Ex Capite Lecti Abolished Act 1871 (c.81)

Redundancy Fund Act 1981 (c.5)

Redundancy Payments Act 1965 (c.62)

Redundancy Rebates Act 1969 (c.8)

Redundancy Rebates Act 1977 (c.22)

Redundant Churches and Other Religious Buildings Act 1969 (c.22)

Re-election of Ministers Act 1915 (c.50)

Re-election of Ministers Act 1916 (c.22)

Re-election of Ministers Act 1919 (c.2)

Re-election of Ministers Act (1919) Amendment 1926 (c.19)

Re-election of Ministers (No.2) Act 1916 (c.56)

Referendum Act 1975 (c.33)

Referendums (Scotland and Wales) Act 1997 (c.61)

Refined Sugar Bounties Act 1824 (c.35)

Reformatory and Industrial Schools Act 1891 (c.23)

Reformatory and Industrial Schools Acts Amendment Act 1872 (c.21)

Reformatory and Industrial Schools (Channel Islands Children) Act 1895 (c.17)

Reformatory and Industrial Schools (Manx Children) Act 1884 (c.40)

Reformatory, etc. Schools Act 1856 (c.109)

Reformatory Institutions (Ireland) Act 1881 (c.29)

Reformatory Schools Act 1856 (c.28)

Reformatory Schools Act 1866 (c.117)

Reformatory Schools Act 1893 (c.15)

Reformatory Schools Act 1893 (c.48)

Reformatory Schools Act 1899 (c.12)

Reformatory Schools (England) Act 1854 (c.74)

Reformatory Schools (England) Act 1857 (c.55)

Reformatory Schools (Ireland) Act 1858 (c.103)

Refreshment Houses Act 1860 (c.27)

Refreshment Houses Act 1964 (c.88)

Refreshment Houses Act 1967 (c.38)

Refreshment Houses (Ireland) Act 1860 (c.107)

Refuse Disposal (Amenity) Act 1978 (c.3)
Regency Act 1830 (c.2)
Regency Act 1840 (c.52)
Regency Act 1910 (c.26)
Regency Act 1937 (c.16)
Regency Act 1943 (c.42)
Regency Act 1953 (c.1)
Regency Act Amendment Act 1838 (c.24)
Regent's Park, Regent Street Act 1851 (c.95)
Regent's Park, Regent Street, etc. Act 1817 (c.24)
Regent's Park, Regent Street, etc. Act 1824 (c.100)
Regent's Park, Regent Street, etc. Act 1831 (c.29)
Regent's Park, Regent Street, etc. Act 1832 (c.56)
Regent's Quadrant Colonnade Act 1848 (c.50)
Regent Street, etc. Act 1825 (c.38)
Regent Street Act 1828 (c.64)
Regent Street Act 1829 (c.61)
Regent Street, Caslton Place Act 1826 (c.77)
Regent Street, etc. Act 1828 (c.70)
Regiment of Cornwall and Devon Miners Act 1798 (c.74)
Regimental Accounts Act 1808 (c.128)
Regimental Benefit Societies Act 1849 (c.71)
Regimental Charitable Funds Act 1935 (c.11)
Regimental Debts Act 1863 (c.57)
Regimental Debts Act 1893 (c.5)
Regimental Debts (Deposit of Wills) (Scotland) Act 1919 (c.89)
Regimental Exchange Act 1875 (c.16)
Regional Commissioners Act 1939 (c.76)
Regional Development Grants (Termination) Act 1988 (c.11)
Register of Sasines Act 1828 (c.19)
Register of Sasines (Scotland) Act 1987 (c.23)
Registered Designs Act 1949 (c.88)
Registered Establishments (Scotland) Act 1987 (c.40)
Registered Homes Act 1984 (c.23)
Registered Homes (Amendment) Act 1991 (c.20)
Registering of British Vessels Act 1845 (c.89)
Registering of Vessels Act 1823 (c.41)
Registers of Sasines (Scotland) Act 1848 (c.74)
Registrar General (Scotland) Act 1920 (c.69)
Registration Acceleration Act 1894 (c.32)
Registration Act 1885 (c.15)
Registration Act 1908 (c.21)
Registration Amendment (Ireland) Act 1868 (c.112)
Registration Amendment (Scotland) Act 1885 (c.)
Registration Appeals (Ireland) Act 1885 (c.66)
Registration (Ireland) Act 1898 (c.2)
Registration of Aliens Act 1836 (c.11)
Registration of Assurances (Ireland) Act 1850 (c.72)

Registration of Births and Deaths (Ireland) Act 1863 (c.11)
Registration of Births, Deaths and Marriages (Army) Act 1879 (c.8)
Registration of Births, Deaths and Marriages (Scotland) Act 1854 (c.80)
Registration of Births, Deaths and Marriages (Scotland) Act 1855 (c.29)
Registration of Births, Deaths and Marriages (Scotland) Act 1860 (c.85)
Registration of Births, Deaths and Marriages (Scotland) Act 1965 (c.49)
Registration of Births, Deaths and Marriages (Scotland) Amendment Act 1910 (c.32)
Registration of Births, Deaths and Marriages (Scotland) (Amendment) Act 1934 (c.19)
Registration of Births, Deaths and Marriages (Special Provisions) Act 1957 (c.58)
Registration of Births, etc. Act 1836 (c.1)
Registration of Burials Act 1864 (c.97)
Registration of Business Names Act 1916 (c.58)
Registration of Certain Writs (Scotland) Act 1891 (c.9)
Registration of Clubs (Ireland) Act 1904 (c.9)
Registration of County Electors (Extension of Time) Act 1889 (c.19)
Registration of County Voters (Ireland) Act 1864 (c.22)
Registration of Deeds (Ireland) Act 1864 (c.76)
Registration of Electors 1891 (c.18)
Registration of Leases (Scotland) Act 1857 (c.26)
Registration of Leases (Scotland) Amendment Act 1877 (c.36)
Registration of Marriages (Ireland) Act 1863 (c.90)
Registration of Still-Births (Scotland) Act 1938 (c.55)
Registration of Voters (Ireland) Act 1973 (c.30)
Registration Service Act 1953 (c.37)
Registry Courts (Ireland) Amendment Act 1879 (c.71)
Registry, etc. of Colonial Slaves Act 1819 (c.120)
Registry of Admiralty Court Act 1813 (c.151)
Registry of Boats, etc. Act 1795 (c.58)
Registry of Deeds Act 1822 (c.116)
Registry of Deeds Act 1832 (c.87)
Registry of Deeds Act 1875 (c.5)
Registry of Deeds, etc. (Ireland) Act 1828 (c.57)
Registry of Deeds Office (Ireland) Holidays Act 1883 (c.20)
Registry of Ships Act 1796 (c.112)
Registry of Ships Built in India Act 1815 (c.116)
Registry of Wool Act 1821 (c.81)
Regrating and Ingrossing of Oaken Bark Act 1807 (c.53)
Regular and Elders' Widows' Funds Act 1897 (c.11)

Regulation of Factories Act 1834 (c.1)
Regulation of Railways Act 1868 (c.119)
Regulation of Railways Act 1871 (c.78)
Regulation of Railways Act 1873 (c.48)
Regulation of Railways Acts, 1873 and 1874, Continuance Act 1879 (c.56)
Regulation of Railways Act 1889 (c.57)
Regulation of the Forces Act 1871 (c.86)
Regulation of the Forces Act 1881 (c.57)
Rehabilitation of Offenders Act 1974 (c.53)
Reinstatement in Civil Employment Act 1944 (c.15)
Reinstatement in Civil Employment Act 1950 (c.10)
Reinsurance (Acts of Terrorism) Act 1993 (c.18)
Released Persons (Poor Law Relief) Act 1907 (c.14)
Relief as to Transferable Stocks, etc. Act 1812 (c.158)
Relief of Bankers Act 1824 (c.73)
Relief of Certain Bishops Act 1843 (c.57)
Relief of Certain Curates (England) Act 1803 (c.2)
Relief of Certain Incumbents Act 1824 (c.89)
Relief of Debtors Act 1799 (c.50)
Relief of Debtors in Prison Act 1812 (c.160)
Relief of Discharged Soldiers and Sailors Act 1803 (c.61)
Relief of Distress Act 1849 (c.63)
Relief of Distress (Ireland) Act 1880 (c.4)
Relief of Distress (Ireland) Amendment Act 1880 (c.14)
Relief of Distressed Unions (Ireland) Act 1883 (c.24)
Relief of Families of Militiamen Act 1803 (c.47)
Relief of Families of Militiamen (Scotland) Act 1809 (c.90)
Relief of Families of Militiamen (Ireland) Act 1811 (c.78)
Relief of Families of Militiamen Act 1812 (c.28)
Relief of Insolvent Debtors Act 1797 (c.112)
Relief of Prisoners Act 1797 (c.85)
Relief of Prisoners for Debt Act 1809 (c.6)
Relief of the Poor Act 1795 (c.23)
Relief of the Poor Act 1810 (c.50)
Relief of the Poor Act 1812 (c.73)
Relief of Revenue Prisoners Act 1795 (c.96)
Relief of Rutson & Company Act 1820 (c.30)
Relief of Sailors Abroad Act 1818 (c.38)
Relief of Shipwrecked Mariners, etc. Act 1814 (c.126)
Relief of Stress (Ireland) Act 1849 (c.5)
Relief of Traders for Grenada, etc. Act (c.127)
Relief to Chelsea, etc. Pensioners Act 1825 (c. 27)
Relief to Holders of Certain Securities Act 1818 (c.93)
Religious Congregations, etc. (Scotland) Act 1850 (c.13)
Religious Disabilities Act 1846 (c.59)

Remedies Against the Hundred (England) Act 1827 (c.31)
Remission of Penalties Act 1859 (c.32)
Remission of Penalties Act 1875 (c.80)
Remission of Rates (London) Act 1940 (c.32)
Removal of Goods Act 1812 (c.142)
Removal of Goods for Exportation, etc. Act 1808 (c.126)
Removal of Indictments into King's Bench Act 1835 (c.33)
Removal of Offensive Matter Act 1906 (c.45)
Removal of Prisoners in Custody Act 1854 (c.115)
Removal of Slaves Act 1820 (c.50)
Removal of Wool Act 1814 (c.78)
Removal of Wrecks Act 1877 (c.16)
Removal of Wrecks Act, 1877, Amendment Act 1889 (c.5)
Removal Terms Act 1886 (c.50)
Removal Terms (Burghs) (Scotland) Act 1881 (c.39)
Removal Terms (Scotland) Act, 1886, Amendment Act 1890 (c.36)
Remuneration, Charges and Grants Act 1975 (c.57)
Remuneration of Teachers Act 1963 (c.20)
Remuneration of Teachers Act 1965 (c.3)
Remuneration of Teachers (Scotland) Act 1967 (c.36)
Renewable Leasehold Conversion Act 1849 (c.105)
Renewable Leasehold Conversion (Ireland) Act 1868 (c.62)
Renewal of Leases (Ireland) Act 1838 (c.62)
Rent Act 1957 (c.25)
Rent Act 1965 (c.75)
Rent Act 1968 (c.23)
Rent Act 1974 (c.51)
Rent Act 1977 (c.42)
Rent (Agricultural) Amendment Act 1977 (c.17)
Rent (Agriculture) Act 1976 (c.80)
Rent (Amendment) Act 1985 (c.24)
Rent and Mortgage Interest Restrictions Act 1923 (c.32)
Rent and Mortgage Interest Restriction Act 1939 (c.71)
Rent and Mortgage Interest Restrictions (Amendment) Act 1933 (c.32)
Rent and Mortgage Interest (Restrictions Continuance) Act 1925 (c.32)
Rent (Control of Increases) Act 1969 (c.62)
Rent of Furnished Houses Control (Scotland) Act 1943 (c.44)
Rent Rebate Act 1973 (c.28)
Rent Restrictions (Notices of Increase) Act 1923 (c.13)
Rent (Scotland) Act 1971 (c.28)
Rent (Scotland) Act 1984 (c.58)
Rentcharges Act 1977 (c.30)
Rents of the Rolls Estate, etc. Act 1820 (c.107)
Reorganisation of Offices (Scotland) Act 1928 (c.34)

Reorganisation of Offices (Scotland) Act 1939 (c.20)
Repair of Blenheim Palace Act 1840 (c.43)
Repair of Roads and Bridges (Ireland) Act 1825 (c.101)
Repair of War Damage Act 1941 (c.34)
Repatriation of Prisoners Act 1984 (c.47)
Repayment of Advances (Ireland) Act 1852 (c.16)
Repayment of Certain Loans Act 1802 (c.39)
Repayment of Duty in Certain Cases Act 1810 (c.39)
Repeal of Acts Concerning Importation Act 1822 (cc.41, 42)
Repeal of 39 Eliz. c.17 Act 1812 (c.31)
Repeal of 41 Geo. 3 (Great Britain) 1801 (c.4)
Repeal of Certain Duties Act 1800 (c.69)
Repeal of Certain Duties Act 1824 (c.22)
Repeal, etc. of Certain Duties Act 1802 (c.103)
Repeal of a Certain Tax Act 1801 (c.100)
Repeal of Obsolete Statutes Act 1856 (c.64)
Repeal of Part of 15 Geo.3.c.31 Act 1850 (c.80)
Repeal of Salt Duties Act 1824 (c.65)
Repeal of Sir J. Barnard's Act 1860 (c.28)
Repeal of Nore Tolls Act 1859 (c.29)
Representation of the People Act 1832 (c.45)
Representation of the People Act 1832 (c.88)
Representation of the People Act 1867 (c.102)
Representation of the People Act 1884 (c.3)
Representation of the People Act 1918 (c.64)
Representation of the People Act 1920 (c.15)
Representation of the People Act 1921 (c.34)
Representation of the People Act 1922 (c.12)
Representation of the People Act 1945 (c.5)
Representation of the People Act 1948 (c.65)
Representation of the People Act 1949 (c.68)
Representation of the People Act 1968 (c.15)
Representation of the People Act 1969 (c.15)
Representation of the People Act 1974 (c.10)
Representation of the People Act 1977 (c.9)
Representation of the People Act 1978 (c.32)
Representation of the People Act 1979 (c.40)
Representation of the People Act 1980 (c.3)
Representation of the People Act 1981 (c.34)
Representation of the People Act 1983 (c.2)
Representation of the People Act 1985 (c.50)
Representation of the People Act 1989 (c.28)
Representation of the People Act 1990 (c.32)
Representation of the People Act 1991 (c.11)
Representation of the People Act 1993 (c.29)
Representation of the People (Amendment) Act 1918 (c.50)
Representation of the People Amendment Act 1957 (c.43)
Representation of the People Amendment Act 1958 (c.9)
Representation of the People (Armed Forces) Act 1976 (c.29)
Representation of the People (Equal Franchise) Act 1928 (c.12)

Representation of the People (Ireland) Act 1850 (c.69)
Representation of the People (Ireland) Act 1861 (c.60)
Representation of the People (Ireland) Act 1868 (c.49)
Representation of the People (No. 2) Act 1920 (c.35)
Representation of the People (No. 2) Act 1922 (c.41)
Representation of the People (No. 2) Act 1974 (c.13)
Representation of the People (Reading University) Act 1928 (c.25)
Representation of the People (Returning Officers' Expenses) Act 1919 (c.8)
Representation of the People (Scotland) Act 1832 (c.65)
Representation of the People (Scotland) Act 1868 (c.48)
Representative Peers (Ireland) Act 1857 (c.33)
Representative Peers (Scotland) Act 1847 (c.52)
Representative Peers (Scotland) Act 1851 (c.87)
Representative Peers (Scotland) Act 1852 (c.35)
Reprisals Against Foreign Ships, etc. Act 1808 (c.132)
Reproductive Loan Fund Act 1874 (c.86)
Republic of Gambia Act 1970 (c.37)
Republic of South Africa (Temporary Provisions) Act 1961 (c.23)
Requirements of Writing (Scotland) Act 1995 (c.7)
Requisitioned Houses Act 1960 (c.20)
Requisitioned Houses and Housing (Amendment) Act 1955 (c.24)
Requisitioned Land and War Works Act 1945 (c.43)
Requisitioned Land and War Works Act 1947 (c.17)
Requisitioned Land and War Works Act 1948 (c.17)
Resale Prices Act 1964 (c.58)
Resale Prices Act 1976 (c.53)
Rescue Act 1821 (c.88)
Reserve and Auxiliary Forces Act 1939 (c.24)
Reserve and Auxiliary Forces (Protection of Civil Interests) Act 1951 (c.65)
Reserve and Auxiliary Forces (Training) Act 1951 (c.23)
Reserve Force Act 1859 (c.42)
Reserve Force Act 1867 (c.110)
Reserve Forces Act 1870 (c.67)
Reserve Forces Act 1882 (c.48)
Reserve Forces Act 1890 (c.42)
Reserve Forces Act 1899 (c.40)
Reserve Forces Act 1900 (c.62)
Reserve Forces Act 1906 (c.11)
Reserve Forces Act 1937 (c.17)
Reserve Forces Act 1966 (c.30)

Reserve Forces Act 1980 (c.9)
Reserve Forces Act 1982 (c.14)
Reserve Forces Act 1996 (c.14)
Reserve Forces and Militia Act 1898 (c.9)
Reserve Forces (Safeguard of Employment) Act 1985 (c.17)
Reservoirs Act 1975 (c.23)
Reservoirs (Safety Provisions) Act 1930 (c.51)
Residence in France During the War Act 1798 (c.79)
Residence of Incumbents Act 1869 (c.109)
Residence on Benefices, etc. (England) Act 1814 (c.175)
Residence on Benefices, etc. (England) Act 1816 (c.6)
Residence on Benefices, etc. (England) Act 1816 (c.123)
Residence on Benefices, etc. (England) Act 1817 (c.99)
Resident Magistrates and Police Commissioners Salaries Act 1874 (c.23)
Resident Magistrates (Belfast) Act 1911 (c.58)
Resident Magistrates (Ireland) Act 1920 (c.38)
Resident Magistrates (Ireland) Act 1853 (c.60)
Residential Homes Act 1980 (c.7)
Resignation Bonds Act 1827 (c.25)
Responsibility of Shipowners Act 1813 (c.159)
Restoration of Order in Ireland Act 1920 (c.31)
Restoration of Order In Ireland (Indemnity) Act 1923 (c.12)
Restoration of Pre-War Practices Act 1919 (c.42)
Restoration of Pre-War Trade Practices Act 1942 (c.9)
Restoration of Pre-War Trade Practices Act 1950 (c.9)
Restriction of Advertisement (War Risks Insurance) Act 1939 (c.120)
Restriction of Offensive Weapons Act 1959 (c.37)
Restriction of Ribbon Development (Temporary Development) Act 1943 (c.34)
Restrictions of Ribbon Development Act 1935 (c.47)
Restriction on Cash Payments Act 1797 (c.1)
Restriction on Cash Payments Act 1797 (c.45)
Restriction on Cash Payments Act 1797 (c.91)
Restriction on Cash Payments Act 1802 (c.40)
Restriction on Cash Payments Act 1802 (c.45)
Restriction on Cash Payments Act 1803 (c.1)
Restriction on Cash Payments Act 1803 (c.18)
Restriction on Cash Payments Act 1803 (c.44)

Restriction on Cash Payments Act 1814 (c.99)
Restriction on Cash Payments Act 1814 (c.130)
Restriction on Cash Payments Act 1815 (c.28)
Restriction on Cash Payments Act 1815 (c.41)
Restriction on Cash Payments Act 1816 (c.40)
Restriction on Cash Payments Act 1816 (c.48)
Restriction on Cash Payments Act 1818 (c.37)
Restriction on Cash Payments Act 1818 (c.60)
Restriction on Cash Payments (Ireland) Act 1804 (c.21)
Restrictive Practices Court Act 1976 (c.33)
Restrictive Trade Practices Act 1956 (c.68)
Restrictive Trade Practices Act 1968 (c.66)
Restrictive Trade Practices Act 1976 (c.34)
Restrictive Trade Practices Act 1977 (c.19)
Restrictive Trade Practices (Stock Exchange) Act 1984 (c.2)
Resumption of Cash Payments Act 1819 (c.49)
Resumption of Cash Payments Act 1819 (c.99)
Retail Brewers Act 1828 (c.68)
Retail Meat Dealers' Shops (Sunday Closing) Act 1936 (c.30)
Retailing of Spirits (Scotland) Act 1818 (c.13)
Retail of Sweets, etc. Act 1834 (c.77)
Retired Officers (Civil Employment) Act 1919 (c.40)
Retirement of Officers on Half Pay Act 1811 (c.103)
Retirement of Officers on Half Pay Act 1812 (c.151)
Retirement of Teachers (Scotland) Act 1976 (c.65)
Return of Persons Committed, etc. Act 1815 (c.49)
Returning Officers Act 1854 (c.57)
Returning Officers (Scotland) Act 1886 (c.58)
Returning Officers (Scotland) Act 1891 (c.49)
Returning Officers (Scotland) Act 1977 (c.14)
Returns to Secretary of State Act 1858 (c.67)
Revenue Act 1845 (c.76)
Revenue Act 1862 (c.22)
Revenue Act 1863 (c.33)
Revenue Act 1865 (c.30)
Revenue Act 1866 (c.36)
Revenue Act 1867 (c.114)
Revenue Act 1867 (c.90)
Revenue Act 1868 (c.28)
Revenue Act 1869 (c.14)
Revenue Act 1883 (c.55)
Revenue Act 1884 (c.62)
Revenue Act 1889 (c.42)
Revenue Act 1898 (c.46)
Revenue Act 1903 (c.46)

Revenue Act 1906 (c.20)
Revenue Act 1909 (c.43)
Revenue Act 1911 (c.2)
Revenue Act 1968 (c.11)
Revenue Buildings, Liverpool Act 1832 (c.14)
Revenue Departments Accounts Act 1861 (c.93)
Revenue, Friendly Societies and National Debt Act 1882 (c.72)
Revenue (Ireland) Act 1806 (c.106)
Revenue (Ireland) Act 1821 (c.90)
Revenue Inquiry Act 1824 (c.7)
Revenue (No. 1) Act 1861 (c.21)
Revenue (No. 1) Act 1864 (c.18)
Revenue (No. 2) Act 1861 (c.91)
Revenue (No. 2) Act 1864 (c.56)
Revenue (No. 2) Act 1865 (c.96)
Revenue of Scotland Act 1718 (c.20)
Revenue Officers' Disabilities Act 1868 (c.73)
Revenue Officers' Disabilities Removal Act 1874 (c.22)
Revenue Offices (Scotland) Holidays Act 1880 (c.17)
Revenue Solicitors Act 1828 (c.25)
Revenue (Transfer of Charges) Act 1856 (c.59)
Revenues of Archbishopric of Armagh Act 1864 (c.81)
Reverend J. G. MacManaway's Indemnity Act 1951 (c.29)
Reverter of Sites Act 1987 (c.15)
Review of Justices' Decisions Act 1872 (c.26)
Revising Barristers Act 1866 (c.54)
Revising Barristers Act 1873 (c.70)
Revising Barristers Act 1874 (c.53)
Revising Barristers Act 1885 (c.57)
Revising Barristers Act 1886 (c.42)
Revising Barristers (Ireland) Act 1886 (c.43)
Revision of the Army and Air Force Acts (Transitional Provisions) Act 1955 (c.20)
Revival of Expired Laws, etc. Jamaica Act 1839 (c.26)
Rhodesia and Nyasaland Federation Act 1953 (c.30)
Rhodesia and Nyasaland Act 1963 (c.34)
Richmond Lunatic Asylum Act 1815 (c.107)
Richmond Lunatic Asylum Act 1830 (c.22)
Richmond Lunatic Asylum Act 1831 (c.13)
Richmond Penitentiary, etc. Act 1836 (c.51)
Richmond to Lancaster Road Act 1795 (c.157)
Riding Establishments Act 1939 (c.56)
Riding Establishments Act 1964 (c.70)
Riding Establishments Act 1970 (c.32)
Rifle Volunteer Grounds Act 1860 (c.140)
Rifle Volunteer Grounds Act 1862 (c.41)
Right of Light Act 1959 (c.56)
Rights of Entry (Gas and Electricity Boards) Act 1954 (c.21)
Rights of Way Act 1932 (c.45)
Rights of Way Act 1990 (c.24)
Rights of Way Near Aldershot Camp Act 1856 (c.66)

Riot Act 1714 (c.5)
Riot (Damages) Act 1886 (c.38)
Riotous Assemblies (Scotland) Act 1822 (c.33)
River Boards Act 1948 (c.32)
River Itchin: Navigation Act 1795 (c.86)
River Ivel: Navigation Act 1795 (c.105)
River Liffey, Dublin Act 1833 (c.26)
River Ness Act 1855 (c.113)
River Navigation Improvement (Ireland) Act 1914 (c.55)
River Ouze: Navigation Act 1795 (c.77)
River Poddle Act 1840 (c.58)
River Thames and Isis: Navigation Act 1795 (c.106)
Rivers Pollution Prevention Act 1876 (c.75)
Rivers Pollution Prevention Act 1893 (c.31)
Rivers Pollution Prevention (Border Councils) Act 1898 (c.34)
Rivers (Prevention of Pollution) Act 1951 (c.64)
Rivers (Prevention of Pollution) Act 1961 (c.50)
Rivers (Prevention of Pollution) (Scotland) Act 1951 (c.66)
Rivers (Prevention of Pollution) (Scotland) Act 1965 (c.13)
Road and Rail Traffic Act 1933 (c.53)
Road Haulage Wages Act 1938 (c.44)
Road Safety Act 1967 (c.30)
Road Traffic Act 1930 (c.43)
Road Traffic Act 1934 (c.50)
Road Traffic Act 1937 (c.44)
Road Traffic Act 1956 (c.67)
Road Traffic Act 1959 (c.16)
Road Traffic Act 1960 (c.16)
Road Traffic Act 1962 (c.59)
Road Traffic Act 1964 (c.45)
Road Traffic Act 1967 (c.21)
Road Traffic Act 1972 (c.20)
Road Traffic Act 1974 (c.50)
Road Traffic Act 1988 (c.52)
Road Traffic Act 1991 (c.40)
Road Traffic (Amendment) Act 1931 (c.32)
Road Traffic (Amendment) Act 1960 (c.51)
Road Traffic (Amendment) Act 1967 (c.70)
Road Traffic and Roads Improvement Act 1960 (c.63)
Road Traffic (Consequential Provisions) Act 1988 (c.54)
Road Traffic (Disqualification) Act 1970 (c.23)
Road Traffic (Driving Instruction by Disabled Persons) Act 1993 (c.31)
Road Traffic (Driver Licensing and Information Systems) Act 1989 (c.22)
Road Traffic (Drivers' Ages and Hours of Work) Act 1976 (c.3)
Road Traffic (Driving Instruction) Act 1967 (c.79)
Road Traffic (Driving Instruction) Act 1984 (c.13)
Road Traffic (Driving Licences) Act 1936 (c.23)

Road Traffic (Driving Licences) Act 1946 (c.8)

Road Traffic (Driving Licences) Act 1983 (c.43)

Road Traffic (Driving of Motor Cycles) Act 1960 (c.69)

Road Traffic (Foreign Vehicles) Act 1972 (c.27)

Road Traffic (New Drivers) Act 1995 (c.13)

Road Traffic Offenders Act 1988 (c.53)

Road Traffic (Production of Documents) Act 1985 (c.34)

Road Traffic Reduction Act 1997 (c.54)

Road Traffic Regulation Act 1967 (c.76)

Road Traffic Regulation Act 1984 (c.27)

Road Traffic Regulation (Parking) Act 1986 (c.27)

Road Traffic Regulation (Special Events) Act 1994 (c.11)

Road Traffic (Temporary Restrictions) Act 1991 (c.26)

Road Transport Lighting Act 1927 (c.37)

Road Transport Lighting Act 1953 (c.21)

Road Transport Lighting Act 1957 (c.51)

Road Transport Lighting Act 1967 (c.55)

Road Transport Lighting (No. 2) Act (c.22)

Road Transport Lighting (Amendment) Act 1958 (c.22)

Roads Act 1920 (c.72)

Roads Amendment Act 1880 (c.7)

Roads and Bridges (Scotland) Act 1848 (c.40)

Roads and Bridges (Scotland) Act 1878 (c.51)

Roads and Bridges (Scotland) Amendment Act 1892 (c.12)

Roads and Bridges (Scotland) Act 1878 Amendment Act 1888 (c.9)

Roads and Streets in Police Burghs (Scotland) Act 1891 (c.32)

Roads and Streets in Police Burghs (Scotland) Act 1925 (c.82)

Roads between London and Holyhead Act 1819 (c.48)

Roads, etc. (Ireland) Act 1827 (c.23)

Roads, etc. (Ireland) Act 1829 (c.40)

Roads, etc. (Scotland) Act 1833 (c.33)

Roads (Ireland) Act 1835 (c.31)

Roads Improvement Act 1925 (c.68)

Roads in Lanarkshire, etc. Act 1823 (c.10)

Roads (London to Chirk) Act 1820 (c.70)

Roads (Scotland) Act 1970 (c.20)

Roads (Scotland) Act 1984 (c.54)

Roasted Malt for Colouring Beer Act 1842 (c.30)

Robbery from the Person Act 1837 (c.87)

Rochdale Canal Company Act 1798 (c.49)

Rochdale Road Act 1795 (c.160)

Rochdale and Bury Road Act 1797 (c.145)

Rochdale and Bury and Sudden Roads Act 1797 (c.146)

Rochdale to Bury Road Act 1794 (c.124)

Rochdale Vicarage Act 1866 (c.86)

Rochdale Vicarage Appointment Act 1865 (c.117)

Rock Salt Act 1811 (c.82)

Roe Deer (Close Seasons) Act 1977 (c.4)

Rogue Money Act (Scotland) 1839 (c.65)

Roll of Valuation (1748) (c.29)

Rolls Estate Act 1837 (c.46)

Rolls-Royce (Purchase) Act 1971 (c.9)

Roman Catholic Act 1844 (c.102)

Roman Catholic Charities Act 1831 (c.115)

Roman Catholic Charities Act 1856 (c.76)

Roman Catholic Charities Act 1857 (c.76)

Roman Catholic Charities Act 1858 (c.51)

Roman Catholic Charities Act 1859 (c.50)

Roman Catholic Charities Act 1860 (c.134)

Roman Catholic Relief Act 1791 (c.32)

Roman Catholic Relief Act 1803 (c.30)

Roman Catholic Relief Act 1813 (c.128)

Roman Catholic Relief Act 1829 (c.7)

Roman Catholic Relief Act 1926 (c.55)

Roosevelt Memorial Act 1946 (c.83)

Ropeworks Act 1846 (c.40)

Rothwell Gaol Act 1845 (c.72)

Royal and Parliamentary Titles Act 1927 (c.4)

Royal Arsenals, etc. Act 1862 (c.78)

Royal Assent Act 1967 (c.23)

Royal Burghs (Scotland) Act 1822 (c.91)

Royal Burghs (Scotland) Act 1833 (c.76)

Royal Burghs, etc. (Scotland) Act 1834 (c.87)

Royal Canal Act 1818 (c.35)

Royal Canal Company Act 1813 (c.101)

Royal Exchange Assurance Act 1796 (c.26)

Royal Household, etc., Act 1812 (c.8)

Royal Irish Constabulary Act 1873 (c.74)

Royal Irish Constabulary (Widows' Pensions) Act 1954 (c.17)

Royal (Late Indian) Ordinance Corps Act 1874 (c.61)

Royal Marines Act 1820 (c.91)

Royal Marines Act 1847 (c.63)

Royal Marines Act 1857 (c.1)

Royal Marines Act 1914 (c.16)

Royal Marines Act 1916 (c.23)

Royal Marines Act 1939 (c.88)

Royal Marines Act 1946 (c.4)

Royal Marines Act 1948 (c.25)

Royal Military Asylum, Chelsea Act 1854 (c.61)

Royal Military Asylum Chelsea (Transfer) Act 1884 (c.32)

Royal Military Canal Act 1837 (c.20)

Royal Military Canal Act 1867 (c.140)

Royal Military Canal Act 1872 (c.66)

Royal Naval Asylum Act 181 (c.105)

Royal Naval Asylum, etc. Act 1825 (c.26)

Royal Naval Reserve Act 1902 (c.5)

Royal Naval Reserve Act 1927 (c.18)

Royal Naval Reserve (Volunteer) Act 1859 (c.40)

Royal Naval Reserve Volunteer Act 1896 (c.33)

Royal Naval Volunteer Reserve Act 1917 (c.22)

Royal Naval Volunteer Reserve Act 1942 (c.18)

Royal Niger Company Act 1899 (c.43)

Royal Patriotic Fund Corporation Act 1949 (c.10)

Royal Pavilion, Brighton, etc. Act 1849 (c.102)

Royal Scottish Museum (Extension) Act 1912 (c.16)

Royal Signature by Commission Act 1830 (c.23)

Royal Tithes Act 1876 (c.10)

Royal Titles Act 1901 (c.15)

Royal Titles Act 1952 (c.9)

Royal University of Ireland Act 1881 (c.52)

Rules Publication Act 1893 (c.66)

Rural Water Supplies Act 1934 (c.7)

Rural Water Supplies and Sewerage Act 1944 (c.26)

Rural Water Supplies and Sewerage Act 1951 (c.45)

Rural Water Supplies and Sewerage Act 1955 (c.13)

Rural Water Supplies and Sewerage Act 1961 (c.29)

Rural Water Supplies and Sewerage Act 1965 (c.80)

Rural Water Supplies and Sewerage Act 1971 (c.49)

Rural Water Supplies and Sewerage (No. 2) Act 1955 (c.15)

Rural Water Supplies and Sewerage (Scotland) Act 1969 (c.6)

Russian Dutch Loan Act 1815 (c.115)

Russian Dutch Loan Act 1832 (c.81)

Russian Dutch Loan Act 1891 (c.26)

Russian Goods (Import Prohibition) Act 1933 (c.10)

Russian Government Securities Act 1854 (c.123)

Ruthin Charities Act 1863 (c.59)

Rye Harbour Act 1797 (c.130)

Sacramental Test Act 1828 (c.17)

Sacramental Test (Ireland) Act 1832 (c.7)

Sailcloth Manufacture, etc. Act 1805 (c.68)

Safety at Sea Act 1986 (c.23)

Safety of Sports Grounds Act 1975 (c.52)

Safeguarding of Industries Act 1921 (c.47)

Safeguarding of Industries (Customs Duties) Act 1925 (c.79)

Sailors and Soldiers (Gifts for Land Settlement) Act 1916 (c.60)

Salaries of Bishops, etc. in West Indies Act 1826 (c.4)

Salaries of Chief Baron, etc. Act 1809 (c.127)

Salaries of County Officers (Ireland) Act 1823 (c.43)

Salaries of County Officers (Ireland) Act 1824 (c.93)

Salaries of Judges (Scotland) Act 1806 (c.49)

Salaries of Scotch Judges Act 1800 (c.55)

Salary of Lord Lieutenant Act 1811 (c.89)

Salary of Sir J. Lawrence Act 1864 (c.2)

Salcey Forest Act 1825 (c.132)

Sale and Supply of Goods Act 1994 (c.35)

Sale of Advowsons Act 1856 (c.50)

Sale of Beer Act 1795 (c.113)

Sale of Beer, etc. on Sunday Act 1848 (c.49)

Sale of Beer, etc. Act 1854 (c.79)

Sale of Bread, etc. Act 1800 (c.16)

Sale of Bread Act 1800 (c.71)

Sale of Bread Act 1800 (c.18)

Sale of Bread Act 1801 (c.12)

Sale of Butter Act 1796 (c.86)

Sale of Certain Lands in Worcester Act 1819 (c.137)

Sale of Certain Stock Act 1812 (c.148)

Sale, etc. of Certain Stocks Act 1829 (c.48)

Sale of Church Patronages Belonging to Municipal Corporations Act 1838 (c.31)

Sale of Crown Lands Act 1826 (c.51)

Sale of Crown Rents (Ireland) Act 1806 (c.123)

Sale of Crown Rents, etc. (Ireland) Act 1807 (c.16)

Sale of Exhausted Parish Lands Act 1876 (c.62)

Sale of Farming Stock Act 1816 (c.50)

Sale of Fish Act 1834 (c.20)

Sale of Food and Drugs Act 1875 (c.63)

Sale of Food and Drugs Act 1899 (c.51)

Sale of Food and Drugs Act 1927 (c.5)

Sale of Food and Drugs Amendment Act 1879 (c.30)

Sale of Food (Weights and Measures) Act 1926 c.63)

Sale of Gas Act 1859 (c.66)

Sale of Gas Act 1860 (c.146)

Sale of Gas (Scotland) Act 1864 (c.96)

Sale of Goods Act 1893 (c.71)

Sale of Goods Act 1979 (c.54)

Sale of Goods (Amendment) Act 1994 (c.32)

Sale of Goods (Amendment) Act 1995 (c.28)

Sale of Hares (Ireland) Act 1863 (c.19)

Sale of H. M.'s Bakehouse in Windsor Act 1862 (c.57)

Sale of Horseflesh, etc. Regulation Act 1889 (c.11)

Sale of Land by Auction Act 1867 (c.48)

Sale of Liquors by Retail (Ireland) Act 1807 (c.12)

Sale of Liquors on Sunday Act 1878 (c.72)

Sale of Mill Sites, etc. (Ireland) Act 1863 (c.42)

Sale of Muriate of Potash, etc. Act 1813 (c.97)

Sale of Offices Act 1809 (c.126)

Sale of Post Office Buildings Act 1831 (c.27)

Sale of Prize Ship Constantia Maria Act 1808 (c.147)

Sale of Spirits Act 1862 (c.38)

Sale of Spirits (England) Act 1820 (c.76)

Sale of Spirits, etc. (Ireland) Act 1839 (c.79)

Sale of Spirituous Liquors Act 1805 (c.50)

Sale of Spirituous Liquors, etc. Act 1813 (c.137)

Sale of Tea Act 1922 (c.29)

Sale of Venison (Scotland) Act 1968 (c.38)
Sale of Wine, etc. Act 1801 (c.48)
Sale of Workhouses Act 1821 (c.56)
Sales of Reversions Act 1867 (c.4)
Salmon Act 1696 (c.35)
Salmon Act 1986 (c.62)
Salmon Acts Amendment Act 1863 (c.10)
Salmon Acts Amendment Act 1870 (c.33)
Salmon and Fisheries Act 1965 (c.68)
Salmon and Freshwater Fisheries Act 1886 (c.39)
Salmon and Freshwater Fisheries Act 1892 (c.50)
Salmon and Freshwater Fisheries Act 1907 (c.15)
Salmon and Freshwater Fisheries Act 1921 (c.38)
Salmon and Freshwater Fisheries Act 1923 (c.16)
Salmon and Freshwater Fisheries Act 1923 (Amendment) Act 1964 (c.27)
Salmon and Freshwater Fisheries Act 1935 (c.43)
Salmon and Freshwater Fisheries Act 1972 (c.37)
Salmon and Freshwater Fisheries Act 1975 (c.51)
Salmon and Freshwater Fisheries (Amendment) Act 1929 (c.39)
Salmon and Freshwater Fisheries (Protection) (Scotland) Act 1951 (c.26)
Salmon Fisheries Act 1843 (c.33)
Salmon Fisheries Act 1848 (c.52)
Salmon Fisheries (England) Act 1818 (c.43)
Salmon Fisheries (Scotland) Act 1828 (c.39)
Salmon Fisheries (Scotland) Act 1844 (c.95)
Salmon Fisheries (Scotland) Act 1862 (c.97)
Salmon Fisheries (Scotland) Act 1863 (c.50)
Salmon Fisheries (Scotland) Act 1864 (c.118)
Salmon Fisheries (Scotland) Act 1868 (c.123)
Salmon Fishery Act 1861 (c.109)
Salmon Fishery Act 1865 (c.121)
Salmon Fishery Act 1873 (c.71)
Salmon Fishery Act 1876 (c.19)
Salmon Fishery Commissioners Act 1873 (c.13)
Salmon Fishery (Ireland) Act 1863 (c.114)
Salmon Fishery (Ireland) Act 1869 (c.9)
Salmon Fishery Law Amendment Act 1879 (c.26)
Salop Roads Act 1794 (c.123)
Salop Roads Act 1797 (c.172)
Salop and Hereford Roads Act 1794 (c.122)
Salt Duties Act 1798 (c.89)
Salt Duties Act 1799 (c.77)
Salt Duties Act 1805 (c.14)
Salt Duties Act 1813 (c.22)
Salt Duty Act 1813 (c.124)
Salt Duty Act 1815 (c.179)
Salt Duty Act 1816 (c.94)
Saltcoates Harbour 1797 (c.132)

Saltpetre Act 1800 (c.38)
Sand-Grouse Protection Act 1888 (c.55)
Sandhurst Act 1862 (c.33)
Sanitary Act 1866 (c.90)
Sanitary Act 1868 (c.115)
Sanitary Act 1870 (c.53)
Sanitary Act 1873 (c.78)
Sanitary Act, 1866, Amendment (Ireland) Act 1869 (c.108)
Sanitary Act (Dublin) Amendment Act 1870 (c.106)
Sanitary Inspectors (Change of Designation) Act 1956 (c.66)
Sanitary Law Amendment Act 1874 (c.89)
Sanitary Law (Dublin) Amendment Act 1875 (c.95)
Sanitary Loans Act 1869 (c.100)
Sardinia Loan Act 1855 (c.17)
Sardinian Loan Act 1856 (c.39)
Satisfied Terms Act 1845 (c.112)
Saving Banks Act 1824 (c.62)
Saving Bank Act 1828 (c.92)
Saving Bank Act 1833 (c.14)
Saving Bank Act 1835 (c.57)
Saving Bank Act 1844 (c.83)
Saving Banks Act 1852 (c.60)
Saving Banks Act 1880 (c.36)
Saving Banks Act 1887 (c.40)
Savings Banks Act 1891 (c.21)
Savings Bank Act 1893 (c.69)
Savings Bank Act 1904 (c.8)
Savings Banks Act 1920 (c.12)
Savings Banks Act 1929 (c.27)
Savings Banks Act 1949 (c.13)
Savings Banks and Friendly Societies Act 1854 (c.50)
Savings Banks (Barrister) Act 1876 (c.52)
Savings Bank (Charitable Societies) Act 1859 (c.53)
Savings Bank (England) Act 1817 (c.130)
Savings Bank (England) Act 1818 (c.48)
Savings Bank (England) Act 1820 (c.83)
Savings Bank Investment Act 1863 (c.25)
Savings Bank Investment Act 1866 (c.5)
Savings Bank Investment Act 1869 (c.59)
Savings Bank (Ireland) Act 1817 (c.105)
Savings Bank (Ireland) Act 1848 (c.133)
Savings Bank (Ireland) Act 1850 (c.110)
Savings Banks (Ireland) Act 1859 (c.17)
Savings Banks (Ireland) Cont. Act 1862 (c.75)
Savings Bank (Scotland) Act 1819 (c.62)
School Board Conference Act 1897 (c.32)
School Boards Act 1885 (c.38)
School Boards (Scotland) Act 1988 (c.47)
School Crossing Patrols Act 1953 (c.45)
School Districts Act 1850 (c.11)
School Grants Act 1855 (c.131)
School Inspections Act 1996 (c.57)
School of Physic (Ireland) Amendment Act 1867 (c.9)
School Sites Act 1841 (c.38)
School Sites Act 1844 (c.37)

School Sites Act 1849 (c.49)
School Sites Act 1851 (c.24)
School Sites Act 1852 (c.49)
School Sites (Ireland) Act 1810 (c.32)
School Teachers Pay and Conditions Act 1991 (c.49)
School Teachers (Superannuation) Act 1918 (c.55)
School Teachers (Superannuation) Act 1922 (c.42)
School Teachers (Superannuation) Act 1924 (c.12)
Schools for Science and Art Act 1891 (c.61)
Science and Technology Act 1965 (c.4)
Scientific Societies Act 1843 (c.36)
Scotch and Irish Paupers Act 1840 (c.27)
Scotch and Irish Paupers Removal Act 1844 (c.42)
Scotch Distilleries Act 1797 (c.102)
Scotch Distilleries Act 1798 (c.92)
Scotch Whisky Act 1988 (c.22)
Scotland Act 1978 (c.51)
Scottish Board of Health Act 1919 (c.20)
Scottish Development Agency Act 1975 (c.69)
Scottish Development Agency Act 1987 (c.56)
Scottish Episcopal and other Clergy Act 1840 (c.33)
Scottish Episcopalians Act 1711 (c.10)
Scottish Episcopalians Relief Act 1792 (c.63)
Scottish Fisheries Advisory Council Act 1941 (c.1)
Scottish Land Court Act 1938 (c.31)
Scottish Land Court Act 1993 (c.45)
Scottish Legal Services Ombudsman and Commissioner for Local Administration in Scotland Act 1997 (c.35)
Scottish Universities (Emergency Powers) Act 1915 (c.78)
Scrabster Harbour Act 1841 (c.1)
Scrap Metal Dealers Act 1964 (c.69)
Sculpture Copyright Act 1814 (c.56)
Sea and Coast Fisheries Fund (Ireland) Act 1884 (c.21)
Sea Birds Preservation Act 1869 (c.17)
Sea Fish (Conservation) Act 1967 (c.84)
Sea Fish (Conservation) Act 1992 (c.60)
Sea Fish Industry Act 1938 (c.30)
Sea Fish Industry Act 1951 (c.30)
Sea Fish Industry Act 1959 (c.7)
Sea Fish Industry Act 1962 (c.31)
Sea Fish Industry Act 1970 (c.11)
Sea Fish Industry Act 1973 (c.3)
Sea Fish Industry Act 1980 (c.35)
Sea Fisheries Act 1817 (c.69)
Sea Fisheries Act 1843 (c.79)
Sea Fisheries Act 1868 (c.45)
Sea Fisheries Act 1875 (c.15)
Sea Fisheries Act 1883 (c.22)
Sea Fisheries Act 1884 (c.27)
Sea Fisheries Act 1967 (c.83)
Sea Fisheries Act 1968 (c.77)

Sea Fisheries (Clam and Bait Beds) Act 1881 (c.11)
Sea Fisheries (Compensation) (Scotland) Act 1959 (c.27)
Sea Fisheries (Ireland) Act 1818 (c.94)
Sea Fisheries (Ireland) Act 1883 (c.26)
Sea Fisheries Regulation Act 1888 (c.54)
Sea Fisheries Regulation Act 1966 (c.38)
Sea Fisheries (Regulation) Expenses Act 1930 (c.41)
Sea Fisheries Regulation (Scotland) Act 1895 (c.42)
Sea Fisheries (Scotland) Act 1810 (c.108)
Sea Fisheries (Scotland) Application of Penalties Act 1907 (c.42)
Sea Fisheries (Scotland) Act 1810 (c.108)
Sea Fisheries (Scotland) Amendment Act 1885 (c.70)
Sea Fisheries (Shellfish) Act 1967 (c.83)
Sea Fisheries (Shellfish) Act 1973 (c.30)
Sea Fisheries (Shellfish) (Amendment) Act 1997 (c.3)
Sea Fisheries (Shellfish) Regulation Act 1894 (c.26)
Sea Fisheries (Wildlife Conservation) Act 1992 (c.36)
Sea Fishing Boats (Scotland) Act 1886 (c.53)
Sea Fishing Industry Act 1933 (c.45)
Sea Insurances (Stamping of Policies) Amendment Act 1876 (c.6)
Seal Fisheries (North Pacific) Act 1895 (c.21)
Seal Fisheries (North Pacific) Act 1912 (c.10)
Seal Fishery Act 1875 (c.18)
Seal Fishery (Behring's Sea) Act 1891 (c.19)
Seal Fishery (North Pacific) Act 1893 (c.23)
Seal Office in Courts of Queen's Bench and Common Pleas Act 1845 (c.34)
Seamen Act 1836 (c.15)
Seamen's and Soldiers' False Characters Act 1906 (c.5)
Seamen's Clothing Act 1869 (c.57)
Seamen's Fund Winding-up Act 1851 (c.102)
Seamen's Hospital Society Act 1832 (c.9)
Seamen's Savings Bank Act 1856 (c.41)
Seats for Shop Assistants Act 1899 (c.21)
Second Session (Explanation) Act 1899 (c.3)
Secret Service Money (Repeal) Act 1886 (c.2)
Secretary at War Abolition Act 1863 (c.12)
Secretary for Scotland Act 1885 (c.61)
Secretary for Scotland Act 1887 (c.52)
Secretary for Scotland Act 1889 (c.16)
Secretary for State 1904 (c.27)
Secretaries of State Act 1926 (c.18)
Securities (Validation) Act 1940 (c.55)
Securities (Validation) Act 1942 (c.10)
Security of Public Officers Act 1812 (c.66)
Security of Rents, Durham Act 1830 (c.11)
Security Service Act 1989 (c.5)
Security Service Act 1996 (c.35)
Seditious Meetings Act 1795 (c.8)
Seditious Meetings Act 1817 (c.19)
Seditious Meetings Act 1846 (c.33)

Seditious Meetings, etc. Act 1819 (c.6)

Seditious Meetings Prevention Act 1801 (c.30)

Seed Potatoes and Seed Oats Supply (Ireland) Act 1908 (c.19)

Seed Potatoes Supply (Ireland) Act 1891 (c.1)

Seed Potatoes Supply (Ireland) Act 1891 (c.7)

Seed Potatoes Supply (Ireland) Act 1895 (c.2)

Seed Potatoes Supply (Ireland) Act 1906 (c.3)

Seed Supply and Potato Spraying (Ireland) Act 1898 (c.50)

Seed Supply (Ireland) Act 1880 (c.1)

Seeds Act 1920 (c.54)

Seeds Amendment Act 1925 (c.66)

Sees of St. Asaph and Bangor Act 1842 (c.112)

Seizure of Arms Act 1819 (c.2)

Seizure of Crops (Ireland) Act 1863 (c.62)

Selective Employment Payments Act 1966 (c.32)

Self-Governing Schools etc. (Scotland) Act 1989 (c.39)

Senior Member of Council, India Act 1860 (c.87)

Senior Public Elementary Schools (Liverpool) Act (c.60)

Sentence of Death (Expectant Mothers) Act 1931 (c.24)

Separatists' Affirmations Act 1833 (c.82)

Sequestration Act 1849 (c.67)

Sequestration Act 1871 (c.45)

Sergeants at Law Act 1825 (c.95)

Servants' Characters Act 1792 (c.56)

Servants' Wages (Ireland) Act 1807 (c.43)

Service of Heirs (Scotland) Act 1847 (c.47)

Service of Process (Justices) Act 1933 (c.42)

Service of Process out of the Jurisdiction (England and Ireland) Act 1832 (c.33)

Service of Process out of the Jurisdiction (England and Ireland) Act 1834 (c.82)

Session Court (Scotland) Act 1810 (c.31)

Session of the Peace, Dublin Act 1843 (c.81)

Sessions Houses, Westminster, etc. Act 1804 (c.61)

Sessions of the Peace, Westminster Act 1828 (c.9)

Settled Estates Act 1840 (c.55)

Settled Estates Act 1856 (c.120)

Settled Estates Act 1858 (c.77)

Settled Estates Act 1876 (c.30)

Settled Estates Act 1877 (c.18)

Settled Estates Act Amendment Act 1864 (c.45)

Settled Land Act 1882 (c.38)

Settled Land Act 1884 (c.18)

Settled Land Act 1889 (c.36)

Settled Land Act 1890 (c.69)

Settled Land Act 1925 (c.18)

Settled Land Acts (Amendment) Act 1887 (c.30)

Settled Land and Trustee Acts (Courts General Powers) Act 1943 (c.25)

Settled Land (Ireland) Act 1847 (c.46)

Settlement of Estate on Lord Nelson Act 1813 (c.134)

Settlement of the Poor (England) Act 1819 (c.50)

Settlements on Coast of Africa and Falkland Islands Act 1843 (c.13)

Severn Bridge Tolls Act 1965 (c.24)

Severn Bridge Act 1992 (c.3)

Sewage Utilisation Act 1865 (c.75)

Sewage Utilisation Act 1867 (c.113)

Sewerage (Scotland) Act 1968 (c.47)

Sewers Act 1833 (c.22)

Sewers Act 1841 (c.45)

Sewers Act 1849 (c.50)

Sex Discrimination Act 1975 (c.65)

Sex Discrimination Act 1986 (c.59)

Sex Disqualification (Removal) Act 1919 (c.71)

Sex Offenders Act 1997 (c.51)

Sexual Offences Act 1956 (c.69)

Sexual Offences Act 1967 (c.60)

Sexual Offences Act 1985 (c.44)

Sexual Offences Act 1993 (c.30)

Sexual Offences (Amendment) Act 1976 (c.82)

Sexual Offences (Amendment) Act 1992 (c.34)

Sexual Offences (Conspiracy and Incitement) Act 1996 (c.29)

Sexual Offences (Protected Materials) Act 1997 (c.39)

Sexual Offences (Scotland) Act 1976 (c.67)

Seychelles Act 1976 (c.19)

Shannon Act 1874 (c.60)

Shannon Act 1885 (c.41)

Shannon Navigation Act 1839 (c.61)

Shannon Navigation Act 1847 (c.74)

Sharing of Church Buildings Act 1969 (c.38)

Sheep and Cattle Disease Prevention Act 1850 (c.71)

Sheep, etc. Diseases Act 1851 (c.69)

Sheep, etc. Disorders Prevention Act 1852 (c.11)

Sheep Stealers (Ireland) Act 1849 (c.30)

Sheep Stocks Valuation (Scotland) Act 1937 (c.34)

Sheffield University Act 1914 (c.4)

Sheriff and Sheriff Clerk of Chancery (Scotland) Act 1854 (c.72)

Sheriff Court Houses Act 1860 (c.79)

Sheriff Court Houses (Scotland) Act 1866 (c.53)

Sheriff Court Houses (Scotland) Amendment Act 1884 (c.42)

Sheriff Courts and Legal Officers (Scotland) Act 1927 (c.35)

Sheriff Courts (Civil Jurisdiction and Procedure) (Scotland) Act 1963 (c.22)

Sheriff Courts Consignations (Scotland) Act 1893 (c.44)

Sheriff Courts (Scotland) Act 1825 (c.23)
Sheriff Courts (Scotland) Act 1838 (c.119)
Sheriff Courts (Scotland) Act 1853 (c.80)
Sheriff Courts (Scotland) Act 1870 (c.86)
Sheriff Courts (Scotland) Act 1876 (c.70)
Sheriff Courts (Scotland) Act 1877 (c.50)
Sheriff Courts (Scotland) Act 1907 (c.51)
Sheriff Courts (Scotland) Act 1913 (c.28)
Sheriff Courts (Scotland) Act 1939 (c.98)
Sheriff Courts (Scotland) Act 1971 (c.58)
Sheriff Courts (Scotland) Amendment 1914 (c.5)
Sheriff Courts (Scotland) Extracts Act 1892 (c.17)
Sheriff Deputies, etc. Act 1799 (c.66)
Sheriff of Lanarkshire Act 1887 (c.41)
Sheriff of Selkirkshire Act 1832 (c.101)
Sheriff of Westmoreland Act 1849 (c.42)
Sheriff of Westmoreland Act 1850 (c.30)
Sheriff Substitute (Scotland) Act 1875 (c.81)
Sheriffs Act 1817 (c.68)
Sheriffs Act 1887 (c.55)
Sheriffs Fees Act 1837 (c.55)
Sheriffs (Ireland) Act 1835 (c.55)
Sheriffs (Ireland) Act 1920 (c.26)
Sheriffs of Edinburgh and Lanark Act 1822 (c.49)
Sheriffs' Pension (Scotland) Act 1961 (c.42)
Sheriffs (Scotland) Act 1853 (c.92)
Sheriff's Substitute Act 1864 (c.106)
Sheriff's Tenure of Office (Scotland) Act 1898 (c.8)
Sheriffs, Wales Act 1845 (c.11)
Sherwood Forest Act 1818 (c.100)
Shipbuilding Act 1979 (c.59)
Shipbuilding Act 1982 (c.4)
Shipbuilding Act 1985 (c.14)
Shipbuilding Credit Act 1964 (c.7)
Shipbuilding Industry Act 1967 (c.40)
Shipbuilding Industry Act 1968 (c.6)
Shipbuilding Industry Act 1971 (c.46)
Shipbuilding (Redundancy Payments) Act 1978 (c.11)
Shipowners' Liability for Losses by Fire Act 1836 (c.61)
Shipowners' Negligence (Remedies) Act 1904 (c.10)
Shipping Act 1795 (c.80)
Shipping Act 1799 (c.32)
Shipping Act 1816 (c.114)
Shipping and Trading Interests (Protection) Act 1995 (c.22)
Shipping Casualties Investigations Act 1879 (c.72)
Shipping Dues Exemption Act 1867 (c.15)
Shipping Dues Exemption Act Amendment Act 1869 (c.52)
Shipping Duties Exemption Act 1870 (c.50)
Shipping, etc. Act 1845 (c.88)
Shipping Offences Act 1793 (c.67)
Shipping under Treaties of Commerce Act 1826 (c.5)
Ships and Aircraft (Transfer Restriction) Act 1939 (c.70)

Shoeburyness Artillery Rangers Act 1862 (c.36)
Shooting Hares (Scotland) Act 1808 (c.94)
Shop Clubs Act 1902 (c.21)
Shop Hours Act 1892 (c.62)
Shop Hours Act 1893 (c.67)
Shop Hours Act 1895 (c.5)
Shop Hours Act 1904 (c.31)
Shop Hours Regulation Act 1886 (c.55)
Shops Act 1911 (c.54)
Shops Act 1912 (c.3)
Shops Act 1913 (c.24)
Shops Act 1934 (c.42)
Shops Act 1936 (c.28)
Shops Act 1950 (c.28)
Shops (Airports) Act 1962 (c.35)
Shops (Early Closing) Act 1920 (c.58)
Shops (Early Closing) Act (1920) Amendment Act 1921 (c.60)
Shops (Early Closing Days) Act 1965 (c.35)
Shops (Hours of Closing) Act 1928 (c.33)
Shops (Sunday Trading Restrictions) Act 1936 (c.53)
Shorncliffe Military Canal, etc. Act 1807 (c.70)
Short Titles Act 1892 (c.10)
Short Titles Act 1896 (c.14)
Shrewsbury and Holyhead Road Act 1845 (c.73)
Shrewsbury Improvement Act 1756 (c.78)
Shrewsbury to Bangor Road Act 1835 (c.21)
Shrewsbury to Holyhead Act 1819 (c.30)
Shubenaccasie Canal, Nova Scotia Act 1830 (c.34)
Siam and Straits Settlement Jurisdiction Act 1870 (c.55)
Sierra Leone Act 1853 (c.86)
Sierra Leone Company Act 1807 (c.44)
Sierra Leone Independence Act 1961 (c.16)
Sierra Leone Offences Act 1861 (c.31)
Sierra Leone Republic Act 1972 (c.1)
Sikes' Hydrometer Act 1816 (c.140)
Silk, etc. Bounties Act 1821 (c.91)
Silk Duties Act 1828 (c.23)
Silk Manufacture Act 1811 (c.7)
Silk Manufacture, etc. Act 1821 (c.11)
Silk Manufacture (Ireland) Act 1810 (c.27)
Silk Manufacture (Ireland) Act 1921 (c.20)
Silk Manufactures Act 1809 (c.20)
Silk Manufactures Act 1824 (c.21)
Silk Manufactures Act 1824 (c.66)
Silk Weavers Act 1845 (c.128)
Silver Coin Act 1798 (c.59)
Silver Plate Act 1790 (c.31)
Simony Act 1588 (c.6)
Singapore Act 1966 (c.29)
Sinking Fund Act 1875 (c.45)
Sir H. Pottinger's Annuity Act 1845 (c.49)
Sir J. Soane's Museum Act 1862 (c.9)
Sir John Port's Charity, Repton Act 1867 (c.99)
Sir R. Hitcham's Charity Act 1863 (c.58)
Site for Docks, etc. Dublin Act 1819 (c.82)
Site for Record Office (Ireland) Act 1826 (c.13)

Sites for Schoolrooms Act 1836 (c.70)

Sites of Parish Churches (Ireland) Act 1813 (c.66)

Six Clerks in Chancery (Ireland) Act 1813 (c.129)

Slander of Women Act 1891 (c.51)

Slate Mines (Gunpowder) Act 1882 (c.3)

Slaughter of Animals Act 1914 (c.75)

Slaughter of Animals Act 1933 (c.39)

Slaughter of Animals Act 1958 (c.8)

Slaughter of Animals (Amendment) Act 1951 (c.49)

Slaughter of Animals (Amendment) Act 1954 (c.59)

Slaughter of Animals (Pigs) Act 1953 (c.27)

Slaughter of Animals (Scotland) Act 1928 (c.29)

Slaughter of Animals (Scotland) Act 1949 (c.52)

Slaughter of Animals (Scotland) Act 1980 (c.13)

Slaughter of Poultry Act 1967 (c.24)

Slaughterhouses Act 1954 (c.42)

Slaughterhouses Act 1958 (c.70)

Slaughterhouses Act 1974 (c.3)

Slaughterhouses etc. (Metropolis) Act 1874 (c.67)

Slave Trade Act 1795 (c.90)

Slave Trade Act 1797 (c.104)

Slave Trade Act 1797 (c.118)

Slave Trade Act 1798 (c.88)

Slave Trade Act 1799 (c.80)

Slave Trade Act 1806 (c.52)

Slave Trade Act 1806 (c.119)

Slave Trade Act 1811 (c.23)

Slave Trade Act 1813 (c.112)

Slave Trade Act 1814 (c.59)

Slave Trade Act 1818 (c.36)

Slave Trade Act 1818 (c.49)

Slave Trade Act 1818 (c.85)

Slave Trade Act 1818 (c.98)

Slave Trade Act 1819 (c.97)

Slave Trade Act 1824 (c.17)

Slave Trade Act 1824 (c.113)

Slave Trade Act 1828 (c.84)

Slave Trade Act 1833 (c.72)

Slave Trade Act 1835 (cc.60, 61)

Slave Trade Act 1836 (c.81)

Slave Trade Act 1837 (c.62)

Slave Trade Act 1843 (c.46)

Slave Trade Act 1843 (c.98)

Slave Trade Act 1844 (c.26)

Slave Trade Act 1848 (c.116)

Slave Trade Act 1849 (c.84)

Slave Trade Act 1873 (c.88)

Slave Trade Act 1876 (c.46)

Slave Trade, Brazil Act 1845 (c.122)

Slave Trade Convention with Brazil Act 1827 (c.74)

Slave Trade (East African Courts) Act 1873 (c.59)

Slave Trade (East African Courts) Act 1879 (c.38)

Slave Trade Jurisdiction (Zanzibar) Act 1869 (c.75)

Slave Trade (Muscat) Act 1848 (c.128)

Slave Trade Suppression Act 1838 (c.47)

Slave Trade Suppression Act 1838 (c.102)

Slave Trade Suppression Act 1839 (c.57)

Slave Trade Suppression Act 1839 (c.73)

Slave Trade Suppression Act 1840 (c.64)

Slave Trade Suppression Act 1842 (c.42)

Slave Trade Suppression Act 1842 (c.59)

Slave Trade Suppression Act 1842 (c.91)

Slave Trade Suppression Act 1842 (c.101)

Slave Trade Suppression Act 1842 (c.114)

Slave Trade Suppression, African Treaty Act 1855 (c.85)

Slave Trade Suppression, Netherlands Act 1819 (c.16)

Slave Trade Suppression, Portugal Act 1819 (c.17)

Slave Trade Suppression Treaties with Sohar and New Grenada Act 1853 (cc.16, 17)

Slave Trade Suppression Treaty with Spain Act 1836 (c.6)

Slave Trade Suppression Treaty with Venezuela Act 1840 (c.67)

Slave Trade Treaties Act 1838 (cc.39–41)

Slave Trade Treaties Act 1838 (cc.83, 84)

Slave Trade Treaties Act 1843 (cc.50–53)

Slave Trade Treaties with Bolivia, Texas, Uruguay Act 1843 (cc.14-16)

Slave Trade, Treaty with Sweden Act 1827 (c.54)

Slavery Abolition Act 1833 (c.73)

Sligo and Cashel Disfranchisement Act 1870 (c.38)

Slough Roads Act 1796 (c.140)

Slum Clearance (Compensation) Act 1956 (c.57)

Small Debt Amendment (Scotland) Act 1889 (c.26)

Small Debt (Scotland) Act 1837 (c.41)

Small Debt (Scotland) Act 1924 (c.16)

Small Debt (Scotland) Act 1932 (c.38)

Small Debts Act 1795 (c.123)

Small Debts Act 1845 (c.127)

Small Debts Recovery (Ireland) Act 1837 (c.43)

Small Debts (Scotland) Act 1800 (c.46)

Small Debts (Scotland) Act 1825 (c.24)

Small Debts (Scotland) Act 1829 (c.55)

Small Dwellings Acquisition Act 1899 (c.44)

Small Estates (Representation) Act 1961 (c.37)

Small Holdings Act 1892 (c.31)

Small Holdings Act 1910 (c.34)

Small Holdings and Allotments Act 1907 (c.54)

Small Holdings and Allotments Act 1908 (c.36)

Small Holdings and Allotments Act 1926 (c.52)

Small Holding Colonies Act 1916 (c.38)

Small Holding Colonies (Amendment) Act 1918 (c.26)

Small Landholders and Agricultural Holdings (Scotland) Act 1931 (c.44)

Small Landholders (Scotland) Act 1911 (c.49)

Small Livings Act 1806 (c.60)

Small Lotteries and Gaming Act 1956 (c.45)

Small Lotteries and Gaming Act 1959 (c.35)

Small Penalties Act 1865 (c.127)

Small Penalties (Ireland) Act 1873 (c.82)

Small Tenements Recovery Act 1838 (c.74)

Small Testate Estates (Scotland) Act 1876 (c.24)

Smithfield Market Act 1851 (c.61)

Smoke Abatement, London Act 1853 (c.128)

Smoke Abatement, London Act 1856 (c.107)

Smoke Detectors Act 1991 (c.37)

Smoke Nuisance (Scotland) Act 1857 (c.73)

Smoke Nuisance (Scotland) Act 1865 (c.102)

Smoke of Furnaces (Scotland) Act 1861 (c.17)

Smugglers' Families Act 1830 (c.10)

Smuggling Act 1795 (c.31)

Smuggling Act 1802 (c.82)

Smuggling Act 1803 (c.157)

Smuggling Act 1805 (c.121)

Smuggling Act 1807 (c.66)

Smuggling Act 1819 (c.121)

Smuggling Act 1822 (c.110)

Smuggling Act 1834 (c.13)

Smuggling Customs Regulations etc. Act 1809 (c.62)

Smuggling, etc. Act 1805 (c.99)

Smuggling, etc. Act 1808 (c.84)

Smuggling, etc. Act 1818 (c.76)

Smuggling, etc. Act 1820 (c.43)

Soap Duty Allowances Act 1835 (c.15)

Soap Duties Act 1839 (c.32)

Soap Duties Allowances Act 1842 (c.16)

Soap Duties Allowances Act 1844 (c.51)

Soap Duties Allowances Act 1847 (c.41)

Soap Duties Allowances Act 1849 (c.40)

Soap Duties Allowances Act 1851 (c.59)

Soap Duties Repeal Act 1853 (c.39)

Social Fund (Maternity and Funeral Expenses) Act 1987 (c.7)

Social Security Act 1971 (c.73)

Social Security Act 1973 (c.38)

Social Security Act 1975 (c.14)

Social Security Act 1979 (c.18)

Social Security Act 1980 (c.30)

Social Security Act 1981 (c.33)

Social Security Act 1985 (c.53)

Social Security Act 1986 (c.50)

Social Security Act 1988 (c.7)

Social Security Act 1989 (c.24)

Social Security Act 1990 (c.27)

Social Security Act 1993 (c.3)

Social Security Administration Act 1992 (c.5)

Social Security Administration (Fraud) Act 1997 (c.47)

Social Security Administration (Northern Ireland) Act 1992 (c.8)

Social Security Amendment Act 1974 (c.58)

Social Security and Housing Benefits Act 1982 (c.24)

Social Security and Housing Benefits Act 1983 (c.36)

Social Security Benefits Act 1975 (c.11)

Social Security (Consequential Provisions) Act 1975 (c.18)

Social Security (Consequential Provisions) Act 1992 (c.6)

Social Security (Consequential Provisions) (Northern Ireland) Act 1992 (c.9)

Social Security (Contributions) Act 1981 (c.1)

Social Security (Contributions) Act 1982 (c.2)

Social Security (Contributions) Act 1991 (c.42)

Social Security (Contributions) Act 1994 (c.1)

Social Security Contributions and Benefits Act 1992 (c.4)

Social Security Contributions and Benefits (Northern Ireland) Act 1992 (c.7)

Social Security (Incapacity for Work) Act 1994 (c.18)

Social Security (Miscellaneous Provisions) Act 1977 (c.5)

Social Security (Mortgage Interest Payments) Act 1992 (c.33)

Social Security (Northern Ireland) Act 1975 (c.15)

Social Security (No. 2) Act 1980 (c.39)

Social Security (Overpayments) Act 1996 (c.51)

Social Security Pensions Act 1975 (c.60)

Social Security (Recovery of Benefits) Act 1997 (c.27)

Social Services (Northern Ireland Agreement) Act 1949 (c.23)

Social Work (Scotland) Act 1968 (c.49)

Social Work (Scotland) Act 1972 (c.24)

Societies' Borrowing Powers Act 1898 (c.15)

Societies (Miscellaneous Provisions) Act 1940 (c.19)

Societies (Suspension of Meetings) Act 1917 (c.16)

Sodor and Man Act 1838 (c.30)

Solicitor (Ireland) Act 1822 (c.16)

Solicitors Act 1837 (c.56)

Solicitors Act 1843 (c.73)

Solicitors Act 1860 (c.127)

Solicitors Act 1877 (c.25)

Solicitors Act 1888 (c.65)

Solicitors Act 1894 (c.9)

Solicitors Act 1899 (c.4)

Solicitors Act 1906 (c.24)

Solicitors Act 1919 (c.56)

Solicitors Act 1922 (c.57)

Solicitors Act 1928 (c.22)

Solicitors Act 1932 (c.37)

Solicitors Act 1933 (c.24)

Solicitors Act 1934 (c.45)

Solicitors Act 1936 (c.35)

Solicitors Act 1941 (c.46)

Solicitors Act 1950 (c.6)

Solicitors Act 1957 (c.27)

Solicitors Act 1965 (c.31)
Solicitors Act 1974 (c.47)
Solicitors (Amendment) Act 1956 (c.41)
Solicitors (Amendment) Act 1959 (c.42)
Solicitors (Amendment) Act 1974 (c.26)
Solicitors (Articled Clerks) Act 1918 (c.16)
Solicitors (Articled Clerks) Act 1919 (c.27)
Solicitors (Clerks) Act 1839 (c.33)
Solicitors (Clerks) Act 1844 (c.86)
Solicitors (Disciplinary Committee) Act 1939 (c.110)
Solicitors (Emergency Provisions) Act 1940 (c.15)
Solicitors (Examination) Act 1917 (c.43)
Solicitors (Ireland) Act 1821 (c.48)
Solicitors (Ireland) Act 1849 (c.53)
Solicitors (Ireland) Act 1861 (c.68)
Solicitors (Ireland) Act 1898 (c.17)
Solicitors, Public Notaries, etc. Act 1949 (c.21)
Solicitors Remuneration Act 1881 (c.44)
Solicitors (Scotland) Act 1933 (c.21)
Solicitors (Scotland) Act 1958 (c.28)
Solicitors (Scotland) Act 1965 (c.29)
Solicitors (Scotland) Act 1976 (c.6)
Solicitors (Scotland) Act 1980 (c.46)
Solicitors (Scotland) Act 1988 (c.42)
Solitary Confinement Act 1837 (c.90)
Solomon Islands Act 1978 (c.15)
Solvent Abuse (Scotland) Act 1983 (c.33)
Somerset: Canal Act 1796 (c.48)
Somerset House Act 1853 (c.8)
Somerset House Act 1984 (c.21)
Somerset House (King's College Lease) Act 1873 (c.4)
Somersham Rectory Act 1882 (c.81)
Sound Broadcasting Act 1972 (c.31)
Sound Dues Redemption Act 1857 (c.12)
South Africa Act 1877 (c.47)
South Africa Act 1909 (c.9)
South Africa Act 1962 (c.23)
South Africa Act 1995 (c.3)
South African Loans and War Contribution Act 1903 (c.27)
South African Offences Act 1863 (c.35)
South American Loans Guarantee Act 1852 (c.4)
South Australia Act 1834 (c.95)
South Australia Act 1842 (c.61)
South Australia Government Act 1838 (c.60)
South Indian Railway Purchase Act 1890 (c.6)
South Sea Company Act 1807 (c.23)
South Sea Company Act 1815 (c.57)
South Sea Company Act 1820 (c.2)
South Sea Company's Privileges Act 1815 (c.141)
South Sea Trade Act 1821 (c.60)
South Wales Bridges Act 1881 (c.14)
South Wales Highways Act 1860 (c.68)
South Wales Highway Act Amendment Act 1878 (c.34)
South Wales Turnpike Roads Act 1847 (c.72)

South Wales Turnpike Roads Amendment Act 1882 (c.67)
South Wales Turnpike Trusts Amendment Act 1875 (c.35)
Southampton to New Sarum Canal Act 1795 (c.51)
Southampton, Portsmouth and Sheet Bridge Roads Act 1796 (c.135)
Southern Rhodesia Act 1965 (c.76)
Southern Rhodesia Act 1979 (c.52)
Southern Rhodesia (Constitution) Act 1961 (c.2)
Southern Whale Fisheries Act 1795 (c.92)
Southern Whale Fisheries Act 1797 (c.121)
Southern Whale Fisheries Act 1798 (c.57)
Southern Whale Fisheries Act 1808 (c.124)
Southern Whale Fishery Act 1802 (c.18)
Southern Whale Fishery Act 1802 (c.114)
Southern Whale Fishery Act 1803 (c.90)
Southern Whale Fishery Act 1805 (c.96)
Southern Whale Fishery Act 1811 (c.34)
Southern Whale Fishery Act 1812 (c.103)
Southern Whale Fishery Act 1813 (c.111)
Southern Whale Fishery Act 1815 (c.45)
Southern Whale Fishery Act 1819 (c.113)
Spalding Road Act 1795 (c.166)
Special Acts (Extension of Time) Act 1915 (c.72)
Special Areas (Amendment) Act 1937 (c.31)
Special Areas (Development and Improvement) Act 1935 (c.1)
Special Areas Reconstruction (Agreement) Act 1936 (c.19)
Special Commission Act 1888 (c.35)
Special Commission (Belfast Prison) Act 1918 (c.44)
Special Commission (Dardanelles and Mesopotamia) Act 1916 (c.34)
Special Constables Act 1831 (c.41)
Special Constables Act 1835 (c.43)
Special Constables Act 1838 (c.80)
Special Constables Act 1914 (c.61)
Special Constables Act 1923 (c.11)
Special Constables (Ireland) Act 1832 (c.108)
Special Constables (Ireland) Act 1845 (c.46)
Special Constables (Scotland) Act 1914 (c.53)
Special Constables (Scotland) Act 1915 (c.47)
Special Enactments (Extension of Time) Act 1940 (c.16)
Special Immigration Appeals Commission Act 1997 (c.68)
Special Juries Act 1898 (c.6)
Special Roads Act 1949 (c.32)
Spencer Perceval's Pensions Act 1813 (c.122)
Spirit, etc. Licences (Ireland) Act 1806 (c.70)
Spirit Licences Act 1799 (c.86)
Spirit of Wine Act 1855 (c.38)
Spirit Trade Act 1814 (c.149)
Spirits Act 1805 (c.39)
Spirits Act 1832 (c.74)
Spirits Act 1860 (c.114)

Spirits Act 1880 (c.24)
Spirits (Ireland) Act 1809 (c.99)
Spirits (Ireland) Act 1815 (c.104)
Spirits (Ireland) Act 1844 (c.82)
Spirits (Ireland) Act 1845 (c.64)
Spirits (Ireland) Act 1849 (c.17)
Spirits (Ireland) Act 1854 (c.89)
Spirits (Ireland) Act 1855 (c.103)
Spirits (Scotland): Spirits (Ireland) Act 1832 (c.29)
Spirits (Strength Ascertainment) Act 1818 (c.28)
Spiritual Duties Act 1839 (c.30)
Spitalfields and Shoreditch New Street Act 1853 (c.52)
Spitalfields Improvements Act 1850 (c.109)
Sporting Events (Control of Alcohol etc.) Act 1985 (c.57)
Sporting Events (Control of Alcohol etc.) (Amendment) Act 1992 (c.57)
Sporting Lands Rating (Scotland) Act 1886 (c.15)
Spray Irrigation (Scotland) Act 1964 (c.90)
Spring Assizes Act 1879 (c.1)
Spring Guns Act 1827 (c.18)
Sri Lanka Republic Act 1972 (c.55)
St. Albans Bribery Commission Act 1851 (c.106)
St. Albans Roads Act 1794 (c.113)
St. Briavels Small Debts Court Act 1842 (c.83)
St. Bride's Church, City Act 1796 (c.35)
St. David's College Act 1824 (c.101)
St. Helena Act 1833 (c.85)
St. John's Church, Hackney Act 1795 (c.70)
St. John's, Newfoundland Act 1820 (c.51)
St. John's, Newfoundland, etc. Act 1811 (c.45)
St. Martin Outwich Church, City Act 1796 (c.103)
St. Mary Magdalen Hospital, Bath Act 1856 (c.45)
St. Mary Somerset's Church, London Act 1868 (c.127)
St. Marylebone: Improvement Act 1795 (c.73)
St. Marylebone Rectory, Purchase of Act 1817 (c.98)
St. Michael, Cornhill: Building Act 1716 (c.5)
St. Pancras: Improvements, etc. Act 1797 (c.80)
St. Paul, Covent Garden: Church Rebuilding Act 1796 (c.65)
St. Vincent and Grenada Constitution Act 1876 (c.47)
Stables at Windsor Castle Act 1839 (c.20)
Stafford Election Act 1833 (c.20)
Stafford Election Act 1836 (c.10)
Stafford Roads Act 1770 (c.113)
Staffordshire Potteries Stipendiary Justice Act 1839 (c.15)
Stage Carriages Act 1832 (c.120)
Stage Coach Duties Act 1796 (c.16)

Stage Coaches, etc. Act 1806 (c.136)
Stage Coaches, etc. (Great Britain) Act 1810 (c.48)
Stage Coaches, etc. (Ireland) Act 1810 (c.32)
Stage Coaches (Scotland) Act 1820 (c.4)
Stamford to Greetham Road Act 1795 (c.152)
Stamp Act 1795 (c.30)
Stamp Act 1795 (c.55)
Stamp Act 1795 (c.63)
Stamp Act 1796 (c.19)
Stamp Act 1796 (c.80)
Stamp Act 1797 (c.60)
Stamp Act 1797 (c.90)
Stamp Act 1797 (c.111)
Stamp Act 1797 (c.136)
Stamp Act 1798 (c.56)
Stamp Act 1798 (c.85)
Stamp Act 1799 (c.39)
Stamp Act 1799 (c.92)
Stamp Act 1799 (c.107)
Stamp Act 1804 (c.98)
Stamp Act 1815 (c.184)
Stamp Act 1853 (c.59)
Stamp Act 1854 (c.83)
Stamp Act 1864 (c.90)
Stamp Act 1870 (c.97)
Stamp Act 1891 (c.39)
Stamp Duties Act 1828 (c.49)
Stamp Duties Act 1848 (c.9)
Stamp Duties Act 1850 (c.97)
Stamp Duties Act 1860 (c.111)
Stamp Duties, etc. (Ireland) Act 1812 (c.87)
Stamp Duties (Court of Chancery) (Ireland) Act 1823 (c.78)
Stamp Duties (Ireland) Act 1815 (c.100)
Stamp Duties (Ireland) Act 1826 (c.20)
Stamp Duties in Law Proceedings (Ireland) Act 1821 (c.112)
Stamp Duties (Ireland) Act 1842 (c.82)
Stamp Duties (Ireland) Act 1850 (c.114)
Stamp Duties Management Act 1870 (c.98)
Stamp Duties Management Act 1891 (c.38)
Stamp Duties on Cards and Dice Act 1828 (c.18)
Stamp Duties on Newspapers Act 1836 (c.76)
Stamp Duty Composition (Ireland) Act 1867 (c.89)
Stamp Duty on Certain Leases Act 1870 (c.44)
Stamp Duty (Temporary Provisions) Act 1992 (c.2)
Stamps Act 1800 (c.84)
Stamps Act 1801 (c.58)
Stamps Act 1802 (c.99)
Stamps Act 1803 (c.21)
Stamps Act 1803 (cc.126, 127)
Stamps Act 1810 (c.35)
Stamps Act 1813 (c.108)
Stamps Act 1814 (c.144)
Stamps Act 1815 (c.101)
Stamps Act 1821 (c.55)
Stamps Act 1822 (c.117)

Stamps Act 1824 (c.41)
Stamps Act 1825 (c.41)
Stamps Act 1826 (c.44)
Stamps Act 1832 (c.91)
Stamps Act 1833 (c.23)
Stamps Act 1834 (c.57)
Stamps Act 1838 (c.85)
Stamps Act 1840 (c.79)
Stamps Act 1841 (c.34)
Stamps Act 1843 (c.72)
Stamps Act 1844 (c.21)
Stamps Act 1845 (c.2)
Stamps Act 1849 (c.80)
Stamps Act 1851 (c.18)
Stamps Act 1852 (c.21)
Stamps Act 1856 (c.22)
Stamps Act 1856 (c.81)
Stamps Act 1858 (c.20)
Stamps Act 1858 (c.24)
Stamps Act 1871 (c.4)
Stamps and Excise Act 1836 (c.45)
Stamps and Taxes Act 1835 (c.20)
Stamps, etc. Act 1833 (c.97)
Stamps (Great Britain) Act 1814 (c.133)
Stamps (Ireland) Act 1804 (c.68)
Stamps (Ireland) Act 1805 (c.20)
Stamps (Ireland) Act 1805 (c.51)
Stamps (Ireland) Act 1806 (c.35)
Stamps (Ireland) Act 1806 (c.64)
Stamps (Ireland) Act 1807 (c.50)
Stamps (Ireland) Act 1810 (c.76)
Stamps (Ireland) Act 1812 (c.126)
Stamps (Ireland) Act 1814 (c.118)
Stamps (Ireland) Act 1815 (cc.78, 79)
Stamps (Ireland) Act 1815 (c.80)
Stamps (Ireland) Act 1815 (c.81)
Stamps on Fire Insurances Act 1828 (c.13)
Standards of Weights, Measures and Coinage Act 1866 (c.82)
Stanhope and Wolsingham Rectories Act 1858 (c.58)
Stannaries Act 1836 (c.106)
Stannaries Act 1839 (c.58)
Stannaries Act 1855 (c.32)
Stannaries Act 1869 (c.19)
Stannaries Act 1887 (c.43)
Stannaries Court (Abolition) Act 1896 (c.45)
Stannaries Court of Cornwall Act 1834 (c.42)
Starch and Soap Duties Allowances Act 1822 (c.25)
State Hospitals (Scotland) Act 1994 (c.16)
State Immunity Act 1978 (c.33)
State of Singapore Act 1958 (c.59)
Statement of Rates Act 1919 (c.31)
Statistics of Trade Act 1947 (c.39)
Status of Aliens Act 1914 (c.17)
Statute Duty Act 1804 (c.52)
Statute of Frauds Amendment Act 1828 (c.14)
Statute of Westminster Act 1932 (c.4)
Statute Law (Repeals) Act 1969 (c.52)
Statute Law (Repeals) Act 1971 (c.52)
Statute Law (Repeals) Act 1973 (c.39)

Statute Law (Repeals) Act 1974 (c.22)
Statute Law (Repeals) Act 1975 (c.10)
Statute Law (Repeals) Act 1976 (c.16)
Statute Law (Repeals) Act 1977 (c.18)
Statute Law (Repeals) Act 1978 (c.45)
Statute Law (Repeals) Act 1981 (c.19)
Statute Law (Repeals) Act 1986 (c.12)
Statute Law (Repeals) Act 1989 (c.43)
Statute Law (Repeals) Act 1993 (c.50)
Statute Law (Repeals) Act 1995 (c.44)
Statute Law Revision Act 1861 (c.101)
Statute Law Revision Act 1863 (c.125)
Statute Law Revision Act 1867 (c.59)
Statute Law Revision Act 1870 (c.69)
Statute Law Revision Act 1871 (c.116)
Statute Law Revision Act 1872 (c.63)
Statute Law Revision Act 1873 (c.91)
Statute Law Revision Act 1874 (c.35)
Statute Law Revision Act 1875 (c.66)
Statute Law Revision Act 1878 (c.79)
Statute Law Revision Act 1883 (c.39)
Statute Law Revision Act 1887 (c.59)
Statute Law Revision Act 1888 (c.3)
Statute Law Revision Act 1890 (c.33)
Statute Law Revision Act 1891 (c.67)
Statute Law Revision Act 1892 (c.19)
Statute Law Revision Act 1893 (c.14)
Statute Law Revision Act 1894 (c.56)
Statute Law Revision Act 1898 (c.22)
Statute Law Revision Act 1908 (c.49)
Statute Law Revision Act 1927 (c.42)
Statute Law Revision Act 1948 (c.62)
Statute Law Revision Act 1950 (c.6)
Statute Law Revision Act 1953 (c.5)
Statute Law Revision Act 1958 (c.46)
Statute Law Revision Act 1959 (c.68)
Statute Law Revision Act 1960 (c.56)
Statute Law Revision Act 1963 (c.30)
Statute Law Revision Act 1964 (c.79)
Statute Law Revision Act 1966 (c.5)
Statute Law Revision Act 1969 (c.52)
Statute Law Revision Act 1971 (c.52)
Statute Law Revision and Civil Procedure Act 1881 (c.59)
Statute Law Revision and Civil Procedure Act 1883 (c.49)
Statute Law Revision (Consequential Repeals) Act 1965 (c.55)
Statute Law Revision (Ireland) Act 1872 (c.98)
Statute Law Revision (Ireland) Act 1878 (c.57)
Statute Law Revision (Ireland) Act 1879 (c.24)
Statute Law Revision (Isle of Man) Act 1991 (c.61)
Statute Law Revision (Northern Ireland) Act 1973 (c.55)
Statute Law Revision (Northern Ireland) Act 1976 (c.12)
Statute Law Revision (Northern Ireland) Act 1980 (c.59)
Statute Law Revision (No. 2) Act 1872 (c.97)

Statute Law Revision (No. 2) Act 1874 (c.96)

Statute Law Revision (No. 2) Act 1888 (c.57)

Statute Law Revision (No. 2) Act 1890 (c.51)

Statute Law Revision (No. 2) Act 1893 (c.54)

Statute Law Revision (Scotland) Act 1906 (c.38)

Statute Law Revision (Scotland) Act 1964 (c.80)

Statute Law Revision (Substituted Enactments) Act 1876 (c.20)

Statute of Frauds 1677 (c.3)

Statute of Frauds Amendment Act 1828 (c.14)

Statute of Westminster 1931 (c.4)

Statutes (Definition of Time) Act 1880 (c.9)

Statutory Commissioners Act 1823 (c.35)

Statutory Companies (Redeemable Stock) Act 1915 (c.44)

Statutory Corporations (Financial Provisions) Act 1974 (c.8)

Statutory Corporations (Financial Provisions) Act 1975 (c.55)

Statutory Declarations Act 1835 (c.62)

Statutory Gas Companies (Electricity Supply Powers) Act 1925 (c.44)

Statutory Instruments Act 1946 (c.36)

Statutory Instruments (Production and Sale) Act 1996 (c.54)

Statutory Orders (Special Procedure) Act 1945 (c.18)

Statutory Orders (Special Procedure) Act 1965 (c.43)

Statutory Salaries Act 1937 (c.35)

Statutory Salaries (Restoration) Act 1934 (c.24)

Statutory Sick Pay Act 1991 (c.3)

Statutory Sick Pay Act 1994 (c.2)

Statutory Undertakings (Temporary Increase of Charges) Act 1918 (c.34)

Statutory Water Companies Act 1991 (c.58)

Stealing from Bleaching Grounds (Ireland) Act 1811 (c.39)

Stealing from Gardens Act 1826 (c.69)

Stealing in Shops, etc. Act 1820 (c.117)

Stealing of Linen, etc. Act 1811 (c.41)

Stealing of Records, etc. Act 1824 (c.30)

Stealing Property from Mines Act 1816 (c.73)

Steam Engines Furnaces Act 1821 (c.41)

Steam Navigation Act 1846 (c.100)

Steam Navigation Act 1848 (c.81)

Steam Navigation Act 1851 (c.79)

Steam Trawling (Ireland) Act 1889 (c.74)

Steam Whistles Act 1872 (c.61)

Steeping of Barley Act 1801 (c.31)

Stepney: Improvements, Poor Relief Act 1797 (c.79)

Still-Birth (Definition) Act 1992 (c.29)

Still Licences Act 1846 (c.90)

Stipendiary Curates Act 1813 (c.149)

Stipendiary Magistrate, Manchester Act 1813 (c.72)

Stipendiary Magistrate, Manchester and Salford Act 1854 (c.20)

Stipendiary Magistrate, Staffs Act 1846 (c.65)

Stipendiary Magistrates Act 1858 (c.73)

Stipendiary Magistrates Act 1863 (c.97)

Stipendiary Magistrates Act 1869 (c.34)

Stipendiary Magistrates Jurisdiction (Scotland) Act 1897 (c.48)

Stipendiary Magistrate for Manchester Act 1844 (c.30)

Stirling Roads Act 1794 (c.138)

Stirling, Dumbarton and Perth Roads Act 1794 (c.129)

Stockbridge Roads Act 1797 (c.149)

Stockbrokers (Ireland) Act 1868 (c.31)

Stockbrokers (Ireland) Act 1918 (c.46)

Stock Exchange (Completion of Bargains) Act 1976 (c.47)

Stock Transfer Act 1963 (c.18)

Stock Transfer Act 1982 (c.41)

Stocks, etc. of Lunatics Act 1821 (c.15)

Stoke Poges Hospital Act 1856 (c.111)

Stoke to Newcastle Canal Act 1795 (c.87)

Straits Settlements Act 1866 (c.115)

Straits Settlements and Johore Territorial Waters (Agreement) Act 1928 (c.23)

Straits Settlements (Ecclesiastic) Act 1869 (c.88)

Straits Settlements Offences Act 1874 (c.38)

Straits Settlements (Repeal) Act 1946 (c.37)

Stratified Ironstone Mines (Gunpowder) Act 1881 (c.26)

Stratford and Long Compton Hill Roads Act 1797 (c.152)

Street Betting Act 1906 (c.43)

Street Collections Regulations (Scotland) Act 1915 (c.88)

Street from Coventry Street to Long Acre Act 1841 (c.12)

Street Offences Act 1959 (c.57)

Street Playgrounds Act 1938 (c.37)

Submarine Telegraph Act 1885 (c.49)

Submarine Telegraph Act 1886 (c.3)

Subscriptions to Loan Act 1797 (c.82)

Subscriptions to Loan Act 1847 (c.36)

Substitution of Punishments for Death Act 1841 (c.56)

Succession Duty Act 1853 (c.51)

Succession (Scotland) Act 1964 (c.41)

Succession (Scotland) Act 1973 (c.25)

Succession to the Crown Act 1707 (c.41)

Sudan (Special Payments) Act 1955 (c.11)

Sudbury Bribery Commission Act 1843 (c.97)

Sudbury Disfranchisement Act 1842 (c.52)

Sudbury Disfranchisement Act 1843 (c.11)

Suez Canal (Shares) Act 1876 (c.67)

Suffragan Bishops Act 1898 (c.11)

Suffragans Nomination Act 1888 (c.56)

Sugar Act 1956 (c.48)

Sugar Bounties, etc. Act 1811 (c.13)

Sugar Convention Act 1903 (c.21)

Sugar Duties Act 1828 (c.36)

Sugar Duties Act 1829 (c.39)

Sugar Duties Act 1830 (c.50)

Sugar Duties Act 1831 (c.23)

Sugar Duties Act 1832 (c.22)
Sugar Duties Act 1832 (c.95)
Sugar Duties Act 1834 (c.5)
Sugar Duties Act 1836 (c.26)
Sugar Duties Act 1837 (c.27)
Sugar Duties Act 1838 (c.33)
Sugar Duties Act 1839 (c.21)
Sugar Duties Act 1840 (c.23)
Sugar Duties Act 1840 (c.57)
Sugar Duties Act 1841 (c.29)
Sugar Duties Act 1842 (c.34)
Sugar Duties Act 1843 (c.27)
Sugar Duties Act 1844 (c.28)
Sugar Duties Act 1845 (c.5)
Sugar Duties Act 1846 (c.29)
Sugar Duties Act 1846 (c.41)
Sugar Duties Act 1846 (c.63)
Sugar Duties Act 1848 (c.97)
Sugar Duties Act 1854 (c.30)
Sugar Duties (Ireland) Act 1820 (c.80)
Sugar Duties and Exchequer Bills Act 1835 (c.12)
Sugar, etc. Act 1820 (c.64)
Sugar in Brewing Act 1847 (c.5)
Sugar Industry Act 1942 (c.16)
Sugar Industry (Reorganisation) Act 1936 (c.18)
Suicide Act 1961 (c.60)
Suits Against Spiritual Persons Act 1814 (c.54)
Summary Convictions, etc. Act 1824 (c.18)
Summary Convictions (Ireland) Act 1834 (c.93)
Summary Convictions (Ireland) Act 1849 (c.70)
Summary Jurisdiction Act 1848 (c.43)
Summary Jurisdiction Act 1857 (c.43)
Summary Jurisdiction Act 1863 (c.77)
Summary Jurisdiction Act 1879 (c.49)
Summary Jurisdiction Act 1884 (c.43)
Summary Jurisdiction Act 1899 (c.22)
Summary Jurisdiction (Appeals) Act 1933 (c.38)
Summary Jurisdiction Cinque Ports, etc. Act 1864 (c.80)
Summary Jurisdiction (Ireland) Act 1850 (c.102)
Summary Jurisdiction (Ireland) Act 1851 (c.92)
Summary Jurisdiction (Ireland) Act 1862 (c.50)
Summary Jurisdiction (Ireland) Act 1908 (c.24)
Summary Jurisdiction (Ireland) Act 1918 (c.18)
Summary Jurisdiction (Ireland) Amendment Act 1871 (c.76)
Summary Jurisdiction (Married Women) Act 1895 (c.39)
Summary Jurisdiction over Children (Ireland) Act 1884 (c.19)
Summary Jurisdiction (Process) Act 1881 (c.24)

Summary Jurisdiction (Scotland) Act 1881 (c.33)
Summary Jurisdiction (Scotland) Act 1908 (c.65)
Summary Jurisdiction (Scotland) Act 1909 (c.28)
Summary Jurisdiction (Scotland) Act 1954 (c.48)
Summary Jurisdiction (Separation and Maintenance) Act 1925 (c.51)
Summary Proceedings Act 1822 (c.23)
Summary Procedure (Domestic Proceedings) Act 1937 (c.58)
Summary Procedure on Bills of Exchange Act 1855 (c.67)
Summary Procedure on Bills of Exchange (Ireland) Act 1861 (c.43)
Summary Procedure (Scotland) Act 1864 (c.53)
Summary Prosecutions Appeals (Scotland) Act 1875 (c.62)
Summer Time Act 1916 (c.14)
Summer Time Act 1922 (c.22)
Summer Time Act 1925 (c.64)
Summer Time Act 1947 (c.16)
Summer Time Act 1972 (c.6)
Summons and Process Servers' Fees (Ireland) Act 1919 (c.4)
Sunday and Ragged Schools (Exemption from Rating) Act 1869 (c.40)
Sunday Cinema Act 1972 (c.19)
Sunday Closing (Wales) Act 1881 (c.61)
Sunday Entertainments Act 1932 (c.51)
Sunday Observance Act 1833 (c.31)
Sunday Observation Prosecution Act 1871 (c.87)
Sunday Performances (Temporary Regulation) Act 1931 (c.52)
Sunday Theatre Act 1972 (c.26)
Sunday Trading Act 1994 (c.20)
Sunderland Pilotage Order Confirmation Act 1865 (c.59)
Superannuation Act 1834 (c.24)
Superannuation Act 1859 (c.26)
Superannuation Act 1860 (c.89)
Superannuation Act 1866 (c.68)
Superannuation Act 1872 (c.12)
Superannuation Act 1875 (c.4)
Superannuation Act 1876 (c.53)
Superannuation Act 1881 (c.43)
Superannuation Act 1884 (c.57)
Superannuation Act 1887 (c.67)
Superannuation Act 1892 (c.40)
Superannuation Act 1909 (c.10)
Superannuation Act 1914 (c.86)
Superannuation Act 1935 (c.23)
Superannuation Act 1946 (c.60)
Superannuation Act 1949 (c.44)
Superannuation Act 1950 (c.2)
Superannuation Act 1957 (c.37)
Superannuation Act 1965 (c.74)
Superannuation Act 1972 (c.11)
Superannuation Allowances Act 1824 (c.104)

Superannuation Act Amendment Act 1834 (c.45)

Superannuation Acts Amendment Act 1873 (c.23)

Superannuation Amendment Act 1965 (c.10)

Superannuation and Other Trust Funds (Validation) Act 1927 (c.41)

Superannuation, etc. Act 1828 (c.79)

Superannuation (Diplomatic Service) Act 1929 (c.11)

Superannuation (Ecclesiastical Commissioners and Queen Anne's Bounty) Act 1914 (c.5)

Superannuation (Ecclesiastical Commissioners and Queen Anne's Bounty) Act 1933 (c.47)

Superannuation (Mercantile Marine Fund Officers) Act 1877 (c.44)

Superannuation (Metropolis) Act 1866 (c.31)

Superannuation (Miscellaneous Provisions) Act 1948 (c.33)

Superannuation (Miscellaneous Provisions) Act 1967 (c.28)

Superannuation Post Office and War Office Act 1876 (c.68)

Superannuation (President of Industrial Court) Act 1954 (c.37)

Superannuation (Prison Officers) Act 1919 (c.67)

Superannuation Schemes (War Service) Act 1940 (c.26)

Superannuation (Various Services) Act 1938 (c.13)

Superannuation (War Department) Act 1890 (c.18)

Superintending Magistrates, etc. (Ireland) Act 1814 (c.13)

Superintending Magistrates, etc. (Ireland) Act 1817 (c.22)

Superior Courts (Officers) Act 1837 (c.30)

Supplemental Customs Consolidation Act 1855 (c.96)

Supplemental War Loan Act 1900 (c.61)

Supplemental War Loan (No. 2) Act 1900 (c.1)

Supplementary Benefits Act 1976 (c.71)

Supplementary Benefit (Amendment) Act 1976 (c.56)

Supplementary Militia Act 1797 (c.18)

Supplementary Militia Act 1797 (c.19)

Supplementary Militia Act 1799 (c.14)

Supplies and Services (Defence Purposes) Act 1951 (c.25)

Supplies and Services (Extended Purpose) Act 1947 (c.55)

Supplies and Services (Translation Powers) Act 1945 (c.10)

Supply Act 1820 (c.10)

Supply Act 1821 (c.4)

Supply Act 1821 (c.7)

Supply Act 1823 (c.6)

Supply Act 1823 (c.21)

Supply Act 1824 (c.3)

Supply Act 1824 (c.42)

Supply Act 1825 (c.1)

Supply Act 1825 (c.14)

Supply Act 1826 (c.1)

Supply Act 1827 (c.16)

Supply Act 1827 (c.42)

Supply Act 1828 (c.1)

Supply Act 1828 (c.10)

Supply Act 1828 (c.19)

Supply Act 1828 (c.28)

Supply Act 1828 (c.30)

Supply Act 1829 (c.3)

Supply Act 1830 (c.1)

Supply Act 1830 (c.2)

Supply Act 1830 (c.4)

Supply Act 1830 (c.28)

Supply Act 1831 (cc.9–10)

Supply Act 1831 (c.28)

Supply Act 1832 (c.1)

Supply Act 1832 (c.6)

Supply Act 1832 (c.30)

Supply Act 1832 (c.55)

Supply Act 1833 (c.18)

Supply Act 1834 (c.2)

Supply Act 1834 (c.12)

Supply Act 1835 (c.3)

Supply Act 1835 (c.9)

Supply Act 1836 (c.1)

Supply Act 1836 (c.18)

Supply Act 1837 (c.6)

Supply Act 1837 (c.11)

Supply Act 1838 (c.11)

Supply Act 1838 (c.21)

Supply Act 1839 (c.2)

Supply Act 1839 (c.6)

Supply Act 1840 (c.4)

Supply Act 1840 (c.7)

Supply Act 1841 (c.4)

Supply Act 1842 (c.8)

Supply Act 1843 (c.5)

Supply Act 1843 (c.87)

Supply Act 1844 (c.6)

Supply Act 1845 (c.1)

Supply Act 1846 (c.7)

Supply Act 1846 (c.47)

Supply Act 1847 (c.8)

Supply Act 1848 (c.4)

Supply Act 1848 (c.33)

Supply Act 1849 (c.3)

Supply Act 1849 (c.44)

Supply Act 1850 (c.3)

Supply Act 1851 (c.3)

Supply Act 1852 (c.1)

Supply Act 1853 (c.12)

Supply Act 1853 (c.31)

Supply Act 1854 (c.2)

Supply Act 1854 (c.21)

Supply Act 1855 (cc.5, 6)

Supply Act 1855 (c.37)

Supply Act 1856 (c.4)

Supply Act 1856 (c.7)

Supply Act 1857 (c.4)

Supply Act 1858 (cc.5, 6)

Supply Act 1858 (c.17)
Supply Act 1859 (cc.6, 7)
Supply Act 1859 (c.2)
Supply Act 1860 (cc.2, 3)
Supply Act 1860 (c.12)
Supply Act 1860 (c.25)
Supply Act 1860 (c.103)
Supply Act 1861 (c.2)
Supply Act 1861 (c.6)
Supply Act 1861 (c.19)
Supply Act 1862 (cc.1, 2)
Supply Act 1862 (c.31)
Supply Act 1863 (c.6)
Supply Act 1863 (c.15)
Supply Act 1864 (cc.5, 6)
Supply Act 1864 (c.11)
Supply Act 1864 (c.73)
Supply Act 1865 (c.4)
Supply Act 1865 (c.10)
Supply Act 1866 (c.6)
Supply Act 1866 (c.13)
Supply Act 1867 (c.4)
Supply Act 1867 (c.7)
Supply Act 1867 (c.30)
Supply Act 1867 (c.1)
Supply Act 1868 (c.10)
Supply Act 1868 (c.13)
Supply Act 1868 (c.16)
Supply Act 1869 (c.1)
Supply Act 1869 (c.8)
Supply Act 1870 (c.5)
Supply Act 1870 (c.31)
Supply Act 1871 (cc.6, 7)
Supply Act 1871 (c.20)
Supply Act 1871 (c.51)
Supply Act 1872 (c.1)
Supply Act 1872 (c.11)
Supply Act 1872 (c.37)
Supply Act 1873 (c.26)
Supply Act 1873 (c.3)
Supply Act 1874 (cc.1, 2)
Supply Act 1874 (c.10)
Supply Act 1875 (cc.1, 2)
Supply Act 1875 (c.10)
Supply Act 1876 (c.2)
Supply Act 1876 (c.4)
Supply Act 1876 (c.15)
Supply Act 1877 (c.1)
Supply Act 1877 (c.6)
Supply Act 1877 (c.12)
Supply Act 1877 (c.24)
Supply Act 1878 (c.1)
Supply Act 1878 (c.9)
Supply Act 1878 (c.21)
Supply Act 1878 (c.45)
Supply, etc., Act 1742 (c.25)
Supply of Goods and Services Act 1982 (c.29)
Supply of Goods (Implied Terms) Act 1973 (c.13)
Supply of Seamen Act 1803 (c.64)
Supply of Water in Bulk Act 1934 (c.15)
Supply Powers Act 1975 (c.9)

Support of Captured Slaves Act 1815 (c.172)
Support of Commercial Credit (Ireland) Act 1820 (c.39)
Support of Commercial Credit (Ireland) Act 1822 (c.22)
Support of Commercial Credit (Ireland) Act 1822 (c.118)
Support of Commercial Credit (Ireland) Act 1823 (c.42)
Suppression of Insurrections (Ireland) Act 1822 (c.1)
Suppression of Insurrections (Ireland) Act 1822 (c.80)
Suppression of Insurrection, etc. (Ireland) Act 1810 (c.78)
Suppression of Rebellion Act 1801 (c.14)
Suppression of Rebellion Act 1801 (c.61)
Suppression of Rebellion Act 1801 (c.104)
Suppression of Rebellion, etc. Act 1803 (c.117)
Suppression of Rebellion, etc. (Ireland) Act 1803 (c.9)
Suppression of Rebellion, etc. (Ireland) Act 1803 (c.117)
Suppression of Terrorism Act 1978 (c.26)
Supreme Court Act 1981 (c.54)
Supreme Court Act (Northern Ireland) 1942 (c.2)
Supreme Court (England) Act 1850 (c.16)
Supreme Court (England) Act 1864 (c.15)
Supreme Court (Ireland) Act 1850 (c.18)
Supreme Court (Ireland) Act 1850 (c.19)
Supreme Court (Ireland) (Master of the Rolls) Act 1815 (c.114)
Supreme Court, Madras Act 1830 (c.75)
Supreme Court (Northern Ireland) Act 1942 (c.2)
Supreme Court of Judicature Act 1873 (c.66)
Supreme Court of Judicature Act 1875 (c.77)
Supreme Court of Judicature Act 1877 (c.9)
Supreme Court of Judicature Act 1881 (c.68)
Supreme Court of Judicature Act 1884 (c.61)
Supreme Court of Judicature Act 1890 (c.44)
Supreme Court of Judicature Act 1891 (c.53)
Supreme Court of Judicature Act 1899 (c.6)
Supreme Court of Judicature Act 1902 (c.31)
Supreme Court of Judicature Act 1910 (c.12)
Supreme Court of Judicature (Amendment) Act 1935 (c.2)
Supreme Court of Judicature (Amendment) Act 1938 (c.67)
Supreme Court of Judicature (Amendment) Act 1944 (c.9)
Supreme Court of Judicature (Amendment) Act 1948 (c.20)
Supreme Court of Judicature (Amendment) Act 1959 (c.39)
Supreme Court of Judicature (Circuit Officers) Act 1946 (c.78)
Supreme Court of Judicature (Commencement) Act 1874 (c.83)
Supreme Court of Judicature (Consolidation) Act 1925 (c.49)

Supreme Court of Judicature (Funds, etc.) Act 1883 (c.29)

Supreme Court of Judicature Act (Ireland) Act 1877 (c.57)

Supreme Court of Judicature (Ireland) Act 1882 (c.70)

Supreme Court of Judicature (Ireland) Act 1887 (c.6)

Supreme Court of Judicature (Ireland) Act 1897 (c.17)

Supreme Court of Judicature (Ireland) Act 1907 (c.44)

Supreme Court of Judicature (Ireland) Act 1877, Amendment Act 1878 (c.27)

Supreme Court of Judicature (Ireland) Amendment Act 1888 (c.27)

Supreme Court of Judicature (Ireland) (No. 2) Act 1897 (c.66)

Supreme Court of Judicature of Northern Ireland 1926 (c.44)

Supreme Court of Judicature (London Causes) Act 1891 (c.14)

Supreme Court of Judicature (Officers) Act 1878 (c.35)

Supreme Court of Judicature (Officers) Act 1879 (c.78)

Supreme Court of Judicature (Procedure) Act 1894 (c.16)

Supreme Court Officers (Pensions) Act 1954 (c.38)

Supreme Court Officers (Retirement, Pensions, etc.) Act 1921 (c.56)

Supreme Court Offices Act 1997 (c.69)

Surrey Act 1856 (c.61)

Surrogacy Arrangements Act 1985 (c.49)

Survey Act 1870 (c.13)

Survey, Great Britain Act 1851 (c.22)

Survey (Great Britain) Continuance Act 1875 (c.32)

Suspension of Certain Appointments Act 1837 (c.71)

Suspensory Act 1914 (c.88)

Swansea Harbour Act 1796 (c.93)

Swaziland Independence Act 1968 (c.56)

Sydney Branch Mint Act 1863 (c.74)

Tancred's Charities 1871 (c.117)

Tanganyika Agricultural Corporation Act 1957 (c.54)

Tanganyika and British Honduras Loans Act 1932 (c.17)

Tanganyika Independence Act 1961 (c.1)

Tanganyika Republic Act 1962 (c.1)

Tanners, Curriers, Shoemakers, etc. Act 1808 (c.60)

Tanners' Indemnity, etc. Act 1799 (c.54)

Taking of Hostages Act 1982 (c.28)

Tanzania Act 1969 (c.29)

Tattooing of Minors Act 1969 (c.24)

Tavistock Canal Act 1796 (c.67)

Taxation Act 1797 (c.16)

Taxation Act 1798 (c.81)

Taxation Act 1801 (c.8)

Taxation Act 1801 (c.10)

Taxation Act 1801 (c.33)

Taxation Act 1801 (c.40)

Taxation Act 1801 (c.42)

Taxation Act 1801 (c.44)

Taxation Act 1801 (c.51)

Taxation Act 1801 (c.62)

Taxation Act 1801 (c.69)

Taxation Act 1801 (c.71)

Taxation Act 1801 (c.74)

Taxation Act 1801 (c.75)

Taxation Act 1805 (c.5)

Taxation Act 1806 (c.84)

Taxation of Chargeable Gains Act 1992 (c.12)

Taxation of Colonies Act 1778 (c.12)

Taxes Act 1797 (c.69)

Taxes Act 1803 (c.99)

Taxes Act 1805 (c.71)

Taxes Act 1810 (c.105)

Taxes Act 1821 (c.113)

Taxes Act 1856 (c.80)

Taxes Management Act 1880 (c.19)

Taxes Management Act 1970 (c.9)

Taxes on Carriages, etc., (Ireland) Act 1809 (c.75)

Taxes (Regulation of Remuneration) Act 1891 (c.13)

Taxes (Regulation of Remuneration) Amendment Act 1892 (c.25)

Taxes (Scotland) Act 1803 (c.150)

Taxes (Scotland) Act 1805 (c.95)

Taxes (Scotland) Act 1812 (c.95)

Taxes (Scotland) Act 1815 (c.161)

Taxing Masters (Ireland) Act 1848 (c.132)

Taxing Officer (Ireland) Act 1853 (c.55)

Tea Duties Act 1833 (c.101)

Tea Duties Act 1835 (c.32)

Tea Duties Act 1855 (c.9)

Teachers of Nursing Act 1967 (c.16)

Teachers of Schools (Ireland) Act 1844 (c.8)

Teachers' Pay and Conditions Act 1987 (c.1)

Teachers' (Superannuation) Act 1925 (c.59)

Teachers' (Superannuation) Act 1928 (c.10)

Teachers' (Superannuation) Act 1933 (c.22)

Teachers' (Superannuation) Act 1935 (c.35)

Teachers' (Superannuation) Act 1937 (c.47)

Teachers' (Superannuation) Act 1945 (c.14)

Teachers' Superannuation Act 1965 (c.83)

Teachers' Superannuation Act 1967 (c.12)

Teachers' Superannuation (Scotland) Act 1968 (c.12)

Teachers' Superannuation (War Service) Act 1939 (c.95)

Teaching Council (Scotland) Act 1965 (c.19)

Teaching Council (Scotland) Act 1970 (c.2)

Technical and Industrial Institutions Act 1892 (c.29)

Technical Instruction Act 1889 (c.76)

Technical Instruction Act 1891 (c.4)

Technical Instruction Amendment (Scotland) Act 1892 (c.63)

Technical Schools (Scotland) Act 1887 (c.64)

Teinds Act 1808 (c.138)
Teinds Act 1810 (c.84)
Teinds Act 1824 (c.72)
Telecommunications Act 1984 (c.12)
Telecommunications (Fraud) Act 1997 (c.4)
Telegraph Act 1869 (c.73)
Telegraph Act 1870 (c.88)
Telegraph Act 1873 (c.83)
Telegraph Act 1885 (c.58)
Telegraph Act 1954 (c.28)
Telegraph Act 1863 (c.112)
Telegraph Act 1868 (c.110)
Telegraph Act 1878 (c.76)
Telegraph Act 1892 (c.59)
Telegraph Act 1899 (c.38)
Telegraph Act 1943 (c.26)
Telegraph Act 1949 (c.80)
Telegraph Act 1951 (c.37)
Telegraph Act 1962 (c.14)
Telegraph Act Amendment Act 1866 (c.3)
Telegraph (Arbitration) Act 1909 (c.20)
Telegraph (Construction) Act 1908 (c.33)
Telegraph (Construction) Act 1911 (c.39)
Telegraph (Construction) Act 1916 (c.40)
Telegraph (Isle of Man) Act 1889 (c.34)
Telegraph (Money) Act 1871 (c.75)
Telegraph (Money) Act 1876 (c.5)
Telegraph (Money) Act 1896 (c.40)
Telegraph (Money) Act 1898 (c.33)
Telegraph (Money) Act 1904 (c.3)
Telegraph (Money) Act 1907 (c.6)
Telegraph (Money) Act 1913 (c.24)
Telegraph (Money) Act 1920 (c.37)
Telegraph (Money) Act 1921 (c.57)
Telegraph (Money) Act 1922 (c.45)
Telegraph (Money) Act 1924 (c.25)
Telegraph (Money) Act 1925 (c.65)
Telegraphs (Money) Act 1877 (c.30)
Telephone Act 1951 (c.52)
Telephone Transfer Act 1911 (c.26)
Telephone Transfer Amendment Act 1911 (c.56)
Television Act 1954 (c.55)
Television Act 1963 (c.50)
Television Act 1964 (c.21)
Temperance (Scotland) Act 1913 (c.33)
Temple Balsall Hospital Act 1861 (c.24)
Temple Bar, etc. Act 1795 (c.126)
Temporary Migration of Children (Guardianship) Act 1941 (c.23)
Temporary Removal of Convicts Act 1823 (c.82)
Tenancy of Shops (Scotland) Act 1949 (c.25)
Tenancy of Shops (Scotland) Act 1964 (c.50)
Tenants Compensation 1890 (c.57)
Tenants' Rights, etc. (Scotland) Act 1980 (c.52)
Tenants' Rights, etc. (Scotland) Amendment Act 1980 (c.61)
Tenants' Rights, etc. (Scotland) Amendment Act 1984 (c.18)
Tension's Charity Act 1860 (c.43)
Tenures Abolition Act 1660 (c.24)

Term and Quarter Days (Scotland) Act 1990 (c.22)
Termination of the Present War (Definition) Act 1918 (c.59)
Terms and Conditions of Employment Act 1959 (c.26)
Territorial and Reserve Forces Act 1907 (c.9)
Territorial Army and Militia Act 1921 (c.37)
Territorial Sea Act 1987 (c.49)
Territorial Waters Jurisdiction Act 1878 (c.73)
Test Abolition Act 1867 (c.62)
Textile Manufacturers (Ireland) Act 1840 (c.91)
Textile Manufacturers (Ireland) Act 1842 (c.68)
Textile Manufacturers (Ireland) Act 1867 (c.60)
Thames: Ballastage Act 1795 (c.84)
Thames and Isis, Navigation Act 1771 (c.45)
Thames and Severn Canal Act 1796 (c.34)
Thames Conservancy Act 1864 (c.113)
Thames Embankment Act 1852 (c.71)
Thames Embankment Act 1853 (c.87)
Thames Embankment Act 1862 (c.93)
Thames Embankment Act 1863 (c.75)
Thames Embankment Act 1873 (c.40)
Thames Embankment, etc. (Loans) Act 1864 (c.61)
Thames Embankment, etc. (Loans) Act 1868 (c.43)
Thames Navigation Act 1866 (c.89)
Thames Preservation Act 1885 (c.76)
Thatched House Court and Little St. James's Street, Westminster Act 1843 (c.19)
The Chest at Chatham Act 1803 (c.119)
Theatres Act 1843 (c.68)
Theatres Act 1968 (c.54)
Theatres Trust Act 1976 (c.27)
Theatres Trust (Scotland) Act 1978 (c.24)
Theatrical Employers Act 1928 (c.46)
Theatrical Employers Registration Act 1925 (c.50)
Theatrical Employers Registration (Amendment) Act 1928 (c.46)
Theft Act 1968 (c.60)
Theft Act 1978 (c.31)
Theft (Amendment) Act 1996 (c.62)
Theft of Turnips, etc. Act 1802 (c.67)
Therapeutic Substances Act 1925 (c.60)
Therapeutic Substances Act 1953 (c.32)
Therapeutic Substances Act 1956 (c.25)
Thermal Insulation (Industrial Buildings) Act 1957 (c.40)
Third Parties (Rights against Insurers) Act 1930 (c.25)
Thirlage Act 1799 (c.55)
Thirsk Roads Act 1794 (c.118)
Thomas Macklin's Paintings Act 1797 (c.133)
Thread Lace Manufacture (England) Act 1806 (c.81)
Threatening Letters Act 1825 (c.19)
Threatening Letters, etc. Act 1847 (c.66)
Threshing Machines Act 1878 (c.12)

Threshing Machines, Remedies for Damage Act 1832 (c.72)
Timber (Ireland) Act 1888 (c.37)
Timber Ships Act 1845 (c.45)
Timber Ships, America Act 1842 (c.17)
Timber Ships, British North America Act 1839 (c.44)
Timber Ships, British North America Act 1840 (c.36)
Time (Ireland) Act 1916 (c.45)
Time of Service in the Army Act 1847 (c.37)
Timeshare Act 1992 (c.35)
Tithe Act 1832 (c.100)
Tithe Act 1836 (c.71)
Tithe Act 1837 (c.69)
Tithe Act 1838 (c.64)
Tithe Act 1839 (c.62)
Tithe Act 1840 (c.15)
Tithe Act 1842 (c.54)
Tithe Act 1846 (c.73)
Tithe Act 1847 (c.104)
Tithe Act 1860 (c.93)
Tithe Act 1878 (c.42)
Tithe Act 1891 (c.8)
Tithe Act 1918 (c.54)
Tithe Act 1925 (c.87)
Tithe Act 1936 (c.43)
Tithe Act 1951 (c.62)
Tithe Annuities Apportionment Act 1921 (c.20)
Tithe Arrears Act 1839 (c.3)
Tithe Commutation Acts Amendment Act 1873 (c.42)
Tithe Composition Act 1837 (c.58)
Tithe Compositions (Ireland) Act 1836 (c.95)
Tithe Compositions (Ireland) Act 1841 (c.37)
Tithe Compositions (Ireland) Act 1841 (c.6)
Tithe (Ireland) Act 1840 (c.13)
Tithe Rentcharge (Ireland) Act 1838 (c.109)
Tithe Rentcharge (Ireland) Act 1848 (c.80)
Tithe Rentcharge (Ireland) Act 1900 (c.58)
Tithe Rentcharge (Rates) Act 1899 (c.17)
Tithe Rentcharge Redemption Act 1885 (c.32)
Tithes Act 1841 (c.36)
Tithes Prescription Act 1834 (c.83)
Tithes Rating Act 1851 (c.50)
Title Act 1846 (c.73)
Title Act 1925 (c.87)
Title Act 1936 (c.43)
Title Act 1951 (c.62)
Tin Duties Act 1838 (c.120)
Titles Deprivation Act 1917 (c.47)
Titles to Land Consolidation (Scotland) Act 1868 (c.101)
Titles to Land Consolidation (Scotland) Amendment Act 1869 (c.116)
Titles to Land (Scotland) Act 1858 (c.76)
Titles to Land (Scotland) Act 1860 (c.143)
Tobacco Act 1840 (c.18)
Tobacco Act 1842 (c.93)
Tobacco Cultivation Act 1831 (c.13)
Tobacco Growing (Scotland) Act 1908 (c.10)

Tobacco Products Duty Act 1979 (c.7)
Tokens Act 1812 (c.157)
Tokens Act 1813 (c.4)
Tokens Act 1817 (c.46)
Tokens Act 1817 (c.113)
Tokens Act 1825 (c.98)
Tokyo Convention Act 1967 (c.52)
Tolls for Certain Carriages Act 1813 (c.82)
Tolls (Ireland) Act 1817 (c.108)
Tonga Act 1970 (c.22)
Tonnage Duties Act 1822 (c.48)
Tonnage, etc. of Ships Act 1835 (c.56)
Tonnage Rates (Port of London) Act 1834 (c.32)
Tonnage of Steam Vessels Act 1819 (c.5)
Tortola Trade Act 1802 (c.102)
Tortola Trade, etc. Act 1803 (c.133)
Tortola Trade Act 1806 (c.72)
Torts (Interference with Goods) Act 1977 (c.32)
Tourism (Overseas Promotion) (Scotland) Act 1984 (c.4)
Tourism (Overseas Promotion) (Wales) Act 1992 (c.26)
Towcaser to Hardington Road Act 1795 (c.153)
Tower Burial Ground Act 1811 (c.116)
Tower Hamlets Militia Act 1797 (c.75)
Town and Country Amenities Act 1974 (c.32)
Town and Country Planning Act 1932 (c.48)
Town and Country Planning Act 1943 (c.5)
Town and Country Planning Act 1944 (c.47)
Town and Country Planning Act 1947 (c.51)
Town and Country Planning Act 1953 (c.16)
Town and Country Planning Act 1954 (c.72)
Town and Country Planning Act 1959 (c.53)
Town and Country Planning Act 1962 (c.38)
Town and Country Planning Act 1963 (c.17)
Town and Country Planning Act 1968 (c.72)
Town and Country Planning Act 1969 (c.30)
Town and Country Planning Act 1971 (c.78)
Town and Country Planning Act 1984 (c.10)
Town and Country Planning Act 1990 (c.8)
Town and Country Planning (Amendment) Act 1951 (c.19)
Town and Country Planning (Amendment) Act 1972 (c.42)
Town and Country Planning (Amendment) Act 1977 (c.29)
Town and Country Planning (Amendment) Act 1985 (c.52)
Town and Country Planning (Compensation) Act 1985 (c.19)
Town and Country Planning (Costs of Inquiries etc.) Act 1995 (c.49)
Town and Country Planning (Interim Development) Act 1943 (c.29)
Town and Country Planning (Interim Development) (Scotland) Act 1943 (c.43)
Town and Country Planning (Minerals) Act 1981 (c.36)
Town and Country Planning Regulations (London) (Indemnity) Act 1970 (c.57)

Town and Country Planning (Scotland) Act 1932 (c.49)

Town and Country Planning (Scotland) Act 1945 (c.33)

Town and Country Planning (Scotland) Act 1947 (c.53)

Town and Country Planning (Scotland) Act 1954 (c.73)

Town and Country Planning (Scotland) Act 1959 (c.70)

Town and Country Planning (Scotland) Act 1972 (c.52)

Town and Country Planning (Scotland) Act 1977 (c.10)

Town and Country Planning (Scotland) Act 1997 (c.8)

Town and Country (Scotland) Act 1969 (c.30)

Town Council and Local Bds. Act 1880 (c.17)

Town Councils (Scotland) Act 1900 (c.49)

Town Councils (Scotland) Act 1903 (c.34)

Town Councils (Scotland) Act 1923 (c.41)

Town Development Act 1952 (c.54)

Town Gardens Protection Act 1863 (c.13)

Town Planning Act 1925 (c.16)

Town Planning (Scotland) Act 1925 (c.17)

Town Police Clauses Act 1847 (c.89)

Town Police Clauses Act 1889 (c.14)

Town Tenants (Ireland) Act 1906 (c.54)

Towns Improvements Clauses Act 1847 (c.34)

Towns Improvement (Ireland) Act 1854 (c.103)

Towyn Trewan Common Act 1963 (c.4)

Trade Act 1807 (c.38)

Trade Act 1814 (c.72)

Trade Act 1822 (cc.44,45)

Trade, America, etc. Act 1817 (c.29)

Trade, American Colonies and West Indies Act 1823 (c.2)

Trade Between Bermuda and America Act 1817 (c.28)

Trade Between Great Britain and Ireland Act 1802 (c.14)

Trade Between Great Britain and Ireland Act 1803 (c.78)

Trade Between Europe and British America Act 1809 (c.47)

Trade Between Ireland and East Indies Act 1808 (c.30)

Trade Boards Act 1909 (c.22)

Trade Boards Act 1918 (c.32)

Trade Boards and Road Haulage Wages (Emergency Provisions) Act 1940 (c.7)

Trade Descriptions Act 1968 (c.29)

Trade Descriptions Act 1972 (c.34)

Trade Disputes Act 1906 (c.47)

Trade Disputes Act 1965 (c.48)

Trade Disputes and Trade Unions Act 1927 (c.22)

Trade Disputes and Trade Unions Act 1946 (c.52)

Trade During Hostilities Act 1803 (c.57)

Trade, East Indies and Mediterranean Act 1817 (c.36)

Trade, Europe and American Colonies Act 1811 (c.97)

Trade Facilities Act 1921 (c.65)

Trade Facilities Act 1924 (c.8)

Trade Facilities Act 1925 (c.13)

Trade Facilities Act 1926 (c.3)

Trade Facilities and Loans Guarantee Act 1922 (c.4)

Trade in Grain, etc. Act 1802 (c.35)

Trade in Spirits Act 1815 (c.132)

Trade in Spirits Act 1816 (c.105)

Trade in Spirits Act 1817 (c.72)

Trade in Spirits Act 1818 (c.26)

Trade in Spirits Act 1819 (c.75)

Trade in Spirits Act 1820 (c.77)

Trade Marks Act 1904 (c.15)

Trade Marks Act 1905 (c.15)

Trade Marks Act 1914 (c.16)

Trade Marks Act 1919 (c.79)

Trade Marks Act 1938 (c.22)

Trade Marks Act 1994 (c.26)

Trade Marks (Amendment) Act 1937 (c.49)

Trade Marks (Amendment) Act 1984 (c.19)

Trade Marks Registration Act 1875 (c.91)

Trade Marks Registration Amendment Act 1876 (c.33)

Trade Marks, Registration etc. Act 1877 (c.37)

Trade of British Possessions Act 1845 (c.93)

Trade of Canada Act 1812 (c.55)

Trade of Demerara, etc. Act 1816 (c.91)

Trade of Malta, etc. Act 1814 (c.182)

Trade of Malta, Act 1815 (c.29)

Trade of Nova Scotia, etc. Act 1809 (c.49)

Trade of West Indies Act 1812 (c.100)

Trade of West Indies Act 1814 (c.48)

Trade of West Indies, etc. Act 1814 (c.49)

Trade to the Levant Sea Act 1799 (c.99)

Trade Union Act 1871 (c.31)

Trade Union Act Amendment Act 1876 (c.22)

Trade Union Act 1913 (c.30)

Trade Union Act 1984 (c.49)

Trade Union (Amalgamation) Act 1917 (c.24)

Trade Union (Amalgamations, etc.) Act 1964 (c.24)

Trade Union and Labour Relations Act 1974 (c.52)

Trade Union and Labour Relations (Amendment) Act 1976 (c.7)

Trade Union and Labour Relations (Consolidation) Act 1992 (c.52)

Trade Union Commissions Act 1967 (c.8)

Trade Union Commissions Act Extension 1867 (c.74)

Trade Union (Provident Funds) Act 1893 (c.2)

Trade Union Funds Protection Act 1869 (c.61)

Trade Union Reform and Employment Rights Act 1993 (c.19)

Trade with America Act 1795 (c.26)

Trade with America Act 1796 (c.58)

Trade with America Act 1801 (c.95)

Trade with America Act 1808 (c.85)

Trade with British Possession Act 1831 (c.24)

Trade with French Colonies Act 1815 (c.146)

Trade with India Act 1797 (c.117)

Trade with New South Wales Act 1819 (c.122)

Trade with South America Act 1808 (c.109)

Trade with United States Act 1797 (c.37)

Trade with United States Act 1809 (c.59)

Trade with United States Act 1815 (c.193)

Trade of Tanners and Curriers Act 1816 (c.110)

Trading Partnerships Act 1841 (c.14)

Trading Representations (Disabled Persons) Act 1958 (c.49)

Trading Representations (Disabled Persons) Amendment Act 1972 (c.45)

Trading Schemes Act 1996 (c.32)

Trading Stamps Act 1964 (c.71)

Trading with the Enemy Act 1914 (c.87)

Trading with the Enemy Act 1939 (c.89)

Trading with the Enemy Amendment Act 1914 (c.12)

Trading with the Enemy Amendment Act 1915 (c.79)

Trading with the Enemy Amendment Act 1916 (c.105)

Trading with the Enemy (Amendment) Act 1918 (c.31)

Trading with the Enemy and Export of Prohibited Goods Act 1916 (c.52)

Trading with the Enemy (Copyright) Act 1916 (c.32)

Trading with the Enemy (Extension of Powers) Act 1915 (c.98)

Trafalgar Estates Act 1947 (c.34)

Trafalgar Square Act 1844 (c.60)

Traffic Calming Act 1992 (c.30)

Tralee Navigation and Harbour Act 1844 (c.99)

Tralee Navigation Loan Act 1841 (c.46)

Tramway Act (1865) (c.74)

Tramways Act 1870 (c.78)

Tramways and Public Companies Act 1884 (c.5)

Tramways and Public Companies (Ireland) Act 1883 (c.43)

Tramways and Public Companies (Ireland) Amendment Act 1884 (c.28)

Tramways (Ireland) Act 1860 (c.152)

Tramways (Ireland) Act 1895 (c.20)

Tramways (Ireland) Act 1900 (c.60)

Tramways (Ireland) Amendment Act 1861 (c.102)

Tramways (Ireland) Amendment Act 1871 (c.114)

Tramways (Ireland) Amendment Act 1881 (c.17)

Tramways (Ireland) Amendment Act 1891 (c.42)

Tramways (Scotland) Act 1861 (c.69)

Tramways (Temporary Increase of Charges) Act 1920 (c.14)

Transfer of Aids Act 1853 (c.6)

Transfer of Crofting Estates (Scotland) Act 1997 (c.26)

Transfer of Property Act 1844 (c.76)

Transfer of Railways (Ireland) Act 1891 (c.2)

Transfer of Ulster Canal Act 1865 (c.109)

Transfer of Balance of Fees Act 1830 (c.1)

Transfer of Contracts, etc. Act 1816 (c.31)

Transfer of Public Funds Act 1821 (c.73)

Transfer of Scotch Excise Charity, etc. Act (c.82)

Transfer of Singapore to East India Company, etc., Act 1824 (c.108)

Transfer of Stock Act 1800 (c.36)

Transfer of Stock (Ireland) Act 1820 (c.5)

Transfer of Stock of Hertford College Act 1816 (c.95)

Transfer of Stocks Act 1817 (c.79)

Transfer of Stocks Act 1818 (c.80)

Transfer of Trust Estates Act 1830 (c.60)

Transfer of Trust Estates, etc. (Ireland) Act 1826 (c.43)

Transfer of Works (Ireland) Act 1856 (c.37)

Transfer to Admiralty of Postal Contracts Act 1837 (c.3)

Transferrence of Lands (Scotland) Act 1847 (cc.48, 49)

Transitional Payments Act (Determination of Need) Act 1932 (c.54)

Transitional Payments Prolongation (Unemployed Persons) Act 1932 (c.19)

Transmission of Moveable Property (Scotland) Act 1862 (c.85)

Transport Act 1947 (c.49)

Transport Act 1953 (c.13)

Transport Act 1962 (c.46)

Transport Act 1968 (c.73)

Transport Act 1978 (c.55)

Transport Act 1980 (c.34)

Transport Act 1981 (c.56)

Transport Act 1982 (c.49)

Transport Act 1983 (c.10)

Transport Act 1985 (c.67)

Transport Act 1962 (Amendment) Act 1981 (c.32)

Transport and Works Act 1992 (c.42)

Transport (Borrowing Papers) Act 1954 (c.10)

Transport (Borrowing Papers) Act 1959 (c.16)

Transport Charges, etc. (Miscellaneous Provisions) Act 1954 (c.64)

Transport (Disposal of Road Haulage Property) Act 1956 (c.56)

Transport (Finance) Act 1982 (c.6)

Transport Finances Act 1966 (c.17)

Transport (Financial Provisions) Act 1977 (c.20)

Transport (Grants) Act 1972 (c.15)

Transport Holding Company Act 1968 (c.10)

Transport Holding Company Act 1972 (c.14)

Transport (London) Act 1969 (c.35)

Transport (London) Amendment Act 1969 (c.60)

Transport Police (Jurisdiction) Act 1994 (c.8)
Transport (Railway Finances) Act 1957 (c.9)
Transport (Scotland) Act 1989 (c.23)
Transportation Act 1799 (c.51)
Transportation Act 1802 (c.15)
Transportation Act 1802 (c.28)
Transportation, etc. Act 1806 (c.28)
Transportation Act 1813 (c.39)
Transportation Act 1813 (c.30)
Transportation Act 1815 (c.156)
Transportation Act 1816 (c.27)
Transportation Act 1819 (c.101)
Transportation Act 1821 (c.6)
Transportation Act 1824 (c.84)
Transportation Act 1825 (c.69)
Transportation Act 1830 (c.39)
Transportation Act 1834 (c.67)
Transportation Act 1843 (c.7)
Transportation Act 1846 (c.26)
Transportation Act 1847 (c.67)
Transportation (Ireland) Act 1849 (c.27)
Transvaal Loan (Guarantee) Act 1907 (c.37)
Travel Concessions Act 1964 (c.95)
Travel Concessions (London) Act 1982 (c.12)
Trawling in Prohibited Areas Prevention Act 1909 (c.8)
Treachery Act 1940 (c.21)
Treason Act 1708 (c.21)
Treason Act 1746 (c.30)
Treason Act 1795 (c.7)
Treason Act 1800 (c.93)
Treason Act 1814 (c.146)
Treason Act 1817 (c.6)
Treason Act 1842 (c.51)
Treason Act 1945 (c.44)
Treason Felony Act 1848 (c.12)
Treason (Ireland) Act 1821 (c.24)
Treason (Ireland) Act 1854 (c.26)
Treason in Scotland Act 1714 (c.20)
Treason Outlawries (Scotland) Act 1748 (c.48)
Treasure Act 1996 (c.24)
Treasurer of the Navy Act 1807 (c.56)
Treasurer of the Navy Act 1808 (c.8)
Treasurer of the Navy, etc. Act 1817 (c.121)
Treasurer of the Navy Act 1821 (c.74)
Treasurer of the Navy Act 1830 (c.42)
Treasurers of Counties (Ireland) Act 1855 (c.74)
Treasury Bills Act 1806 (c.32)
Treasury Bills Act 1807 (c.10)
Treasury Bills Act 1877 (c.2)
Treasury Bills Act 1899 (c.2)
Treasury Bills (Ireland) Act 1803 (c.114)
Treasury Bills (Ireland) Act 1804 (c.97)
Treasury Bills (Ireland) Act 1807 (c.72)
Treasury Bills (Ireland) Act 1808 (c.112)
Treasury Bills (Ireland) Act 1809 (c.79)
Treasury Bills (Ireland) Act 1810 (c.98)
Treasury Bills (Ireland) Act 1811 (c.5)
Treasury Bills (Ireland) Act 1811 (c.88)
Treasury Bills (Ireland) Act 1812 (c.90)
Treasury Bills (Ireland) Act 1812 (c.113)

Treasury Bills (Ireland) Act 1813 (c.80)
Treasury Bills (Ireland) Act 1814 (c.75)
Treasury Bills (Ireland) Act 1815 (c.40)
Treasury Bills (Ireland) Act 1816 (cc.41, 42)
Treasury Bills (Ireland) Act 1816 (c.47)
Treasury Bills (Ireland) Act 1817 (c.81)
Treasury Bills (Ireland) Act 1818 (c.87)
Treasury Bills (Ireland) Act 1819 (c.132)
Treasury Bills (Ireland) Act 1820 (c.46)
Treasury Bills (Ireland) Act 1821 (c.80)
Treasury Chest Fund Act 1861 (c.127)
Treasury Chest Fund Act 1873 (c.56)
Treasury Chest Fund Act 1877 (c.45)
Treasury Chest Fund Act 1893 (c.18)
Treasury Instruments (Signature) Act 1849 (c.89)
Treasury of the Ordnance Act 1806 (c.45)
Treasury Solicitor Act 1876 (c.18)
Treasury (Temporary Borrowing) Act 1910 (c.1)
Treaties of Peace (Austria and Bulgaria) Act 1920 (c.6)
Treaties of Peace (Italy, Roumania, Bulgaria, Hungary and Finland) Act 1947 (c.23)
Treaties of Washington Act 1922 (c.21)
Treaty of Commerce, etc. with America Act 1805 (c.35)
Treaty of Commerce, etc. with America Act 1806 (c.16)
Treaty of Commerce, etc. with America Act 1807 (c.2)
Treaty of Commerce, etc. with America Act 1808 (c.6)
Treaty of Peace Act 1919 (c.33)
Treaty of Peace (Hungary) Act 1921 (c.11)
Treaty of Peace (Turkey) Act 1924 (c.7)
Treaty of Washington Act 1872 (c.45)
Treaty with Hayti Act 1842 (c.41)
Treaty with United States 1797 (c.97)
Treaty with United States Act 1819 (c.54)
Trees Act 1970 (c.43)
Trent and Markham Bridges Act 1837 (c.15)
Trespass (Scotland) Act 1865 (c.56)
Trial of Felonies in Certain Boroughs Act 1834 (c.27)
Trial of Lunatics Act 1883 (c.38)
Trial of Offences (Ireland) Act 1833 (c.79)
Trial of Peers (Scotland) Act 1825 (c.66)
Trials for Felony Act 1836 (c.114)
Trials of Murders, etc., in Honduras Act 1819 (c.44)
Tribunals and Inquiries Act 1958 (c.66)
Tribunals and Inquiries Act 1966 (c.43)
Tribunals and Inquiries Act 1971 (c.62)
Tribunals and Inquiries Act 1992 (c.53)
Tribunals of Inquiry (Evidence) Act 1921 (c.7)
Trinidad and Tobago Act 1887 (c.44)
Trinidad and Tobago Independence Act 1962 (c.54)
Trinidad and Tobago Republic Act 1976 (c.54)
Trinity College, Dublin Act 1855 (c.82)
Trout (Scotland) Act 1845 (c.26)

Trout (Scotland) Act 1860 (c.45)
Trout (Scotland) Act 1933 (c.35)
Truck Act 1831 (c.37)
Truck Act 1837 (c.37)
Truck Act 1896 (c.44)
Truck Act 1940 (c.38)
Truck Amendment Act 1887 (c.46)
Truck Commission Act 1870 (c.105)
Trunk Roads Act 1936 (c.5)
Trunk Roads Act 1946 (c.30)
Truro Bishopric and Chapter Acts Amendment Act 1887 (c.12)
Truro Chapter Act 1878 (c.44)
Trust Investment Act 1889 (c.32)
Trust Property, Escheat Act 1834 (c.23)
Trust (Scotland) Amendment Act 1884 (c.63)
Trustee Act 1850 (c.60)
Trustee Act 1852 (c.55)
Trustee Act 1888 (c.59)
Trustee Act 1893 (c.53)
Trustee Act 1925 (c.19)
Trustee Act 1893 Amendment Act 1894 (c.10)
Trustee Appointment Act 1850 (c.28)
Trustee Appointment Act 1869 (c.26)
Trustee Churches (Ireland) Act 1884 (c.10)
Trustee Investments Act 1961 (c.62)
Trustee Savings Banks Act 1863 (c.87)
Trustee Savings Banks Act 1887 (c.47)
Trustee Savings Banks Act 1918 (c.4)
Trustee Savings Banks Act 1946 (c.6)
Trustee Savings Banks Act 1954 (c.63)
Trustee Savings Banks Act 1957 (c.8)
Trustee Savings Banks Act 1969 (c.50)
Trustee Savings Banks Act 1976 (c.4)
Trustee Savings Banks Act 1978 (c.16)
Trustee Savings Banks Act 1981 (c.65)
Trustee Savings Banks Act 1985 (c.58)
Trustee Savings Banks (Pensions) Act 1954 (c.12)
Trustee Savings Banks (Special Investments) Act 1934 (c.37)
Trustee (War Damage Insurance) Act 1941 (c.28)
Trustees Appointment Act 1890 (c.19)
Trustees Relief Act 1847 (c.96)
Trustees Relief Act 1849 (c.74)
Trustees Relief (Ireland) Act 1848 (c.68)
Trustees Savings Banks Act 1968 (c.6)
Trusts of Land and Appointment of Trustees Act 1996 (c.47)
Trusts (Scotland) Act 1861 (c.84)
Trusts (Scotland) Act 1867 (c.97)
Trusts (Scotland) Act 1897 (c.8)
Trusts (Scotland) Act 1898 (c.42)
Trusts (Scotland) Act, 1867, Amendment Act 1887 (c.18)
Trusts (Scotland) Amendment Act 1891 (c.44)
Trustee (Scotland) Act 1910 (c.22)
Trusts (Scotland) Act 1921 (c.58)
Trusts (Scotland) Act 1961 (c.57)
Tuberculosis Prevention (Ireland) Act 1908 (c.56)

Tuberculosis Prevention (Ireland) Act 1913 (c.25)
Tumultuous Petitioning Act 1661 (c.5)
Tumultuous Risings (Ireland) Act 1831 (c.44)
Tunnel Between Devonport and Keyham Act 1854 (c.15)
Turbary (Ireland) Act 1891 (c.45)
Turkish Loan Act 1855 (c.99)
Turks and Caicos Islands Act 1873 (c.6)
Turnpike Acts Act 1843 (c.69)
Turnpike Acts Continuance 1800 (c.26)
Turnpike Acts Continuance Act 1831 (c.6)
Turnpike Acts Continuance Act 1834 (c.10)
Turnpike Acts Continuance Act 1835 (c.49)
Turnpike Acts Continuance Act 1836 (c.62)
Turnpike Acts Continuance Act 1837 (c.18)
Turnpike Acts Continuance Act 1838 (c.68)
Turnpike Acts Continuance Act 1839 (c.31)
Turnpike Acts Continuance Act 1840 (c.45)
Turnpike Acts Continuance Act 1841 (c.9)
Turnpike Acts Continuance Act 1842 (c.60)
Turnpike Acts Continuance Act 1845 (c.53)
Turnpike Acts Continuance Act 1848 (c.96)
Turnpike Acts Continuance Act 1849 (c.87)
Turnpike Acts Continuance Act 1857 (c.24)
Turnpike Acts Continuance Act 1858 (c.63)
Turnpike Acts Continuance Act 1866 (c.105)
Turnpike Acts Continuance (Ireland) Act 1851 (c.44)
Turnpike Acts, Great Britain Act 1844 (c.41)
Turnpike Acts, Great Britain Act 1846 (c.51)
Turnpike Acts, Great Britain Act 1847 (c.105)
Turnpike Acts, Great Britain Act 1852 (c.58)
Turnpike Acts, Great Britain Act 1855 (c.98)
Turnpike Acts, Great Britain Act 1856 (c.49)
Turnpike Acts (Ireland) Act 1838 (c.72)
Turnpike Acts (Ireland) Act 1842 (c.23)
Turnpike Acts (Ireland) Act 1843 (c.21)
Turnpike Acts (Ireland) Act 1844 (c.36)
Turnpike Acts (Ireland) Act 1845 (c.125)
Turnpike Acts (Ireland) Act 1848 (c.73)
Turnpike Acts (Ireland) Act 1849 (c.47)
Turnpike Acts (Ireland) Act 1852 (c.22)
Turnpike Acts (Ireland) Act 1853 (c.76)
Turnpike Acts (Ireland) Act 1854 (c.42)
Turnpike Acts (Ireland) Act 1855 (c.83)
Turnpike Acts, Ireland, Continuance Act 1836 (c.40)
Turnpike Acts, Ireland, Continuance Act 1840 (c.46)
Turnpike Acts, Ireland, Continuance Act 1850 (c.34)
Turnpike Acts, Ireland, Continuance Act 1856 (c.71)
Turnpike Debts Act 1852 (c.33)
Turnpike Roads Act 1815 (c.119)
Turnpike Roads Act 1817 (c.37)
Turnpike Roads Act 1822 (c.126)
Turnpike Roads Act 1823 (c.95)
Turnpike Roads Act 1824 (c.69)
Turnpike Roads Act 1827 (c.24)
Turnpike Roads Act 1828 (c.77)
Turnpike Roads (England) Act 1853 (c.135)

Turnpike Roads (England) Act 1854 (c.58)
Turnpike Roads in Yorkshire Act 1852 (c.45)
Turnpike Roads (Ireland) Act 1834 (c.91)
Turnpike Roads (Ireland) Act 1841 (c.6)
Turnpike Roads (Ireland) Act 1846 (c.89)
Turnpike Roads (Ireland) Act 1847 (c.35)
Turnpike Roads (Scotland) Act 1823 (c.49)
Turnpike Roads (Scotland) Act 1831 (c.43)
Turnpike Roads (Scotland) Act 1849 (c.31)
Turnpike Roads (Tolls on Lime) Act 1823 (c.16)
Turnpike Roads Trusts Act 1820 (c.95)
Turnpike Tolls Act 1835 (c.18)
Turnpike Tolls Act 1839 (c.46)
Turnpike Tolls Act 1840 (c.51)
Turnpike Tolls Act 1841 (c.33)
Turnpike Tolls (Allowance of Wagon Weights) Act 1834 (c.81)
Turnpike Trusts Act 1856 (c.12)
Turnpike Trusts Arrangements Act 1867 (c.66)
Turnpike Trusts Arrangements Act 1868 (c.66)
Turnpike Trusts Arrangements Act 1872 (c.72)
Turnpike Trusts: Making of Provisional Orders Act 1851 (c.38)
Turnpike Trusts Relief Act 1861 (c.46)
Turnpike Trusts Returns Act 1833 (c.80)
Turnpike Trusts, South Wales Act 1845 (c.61)
Turnpikes Abolition (Ireland) Act 1857 (c.16)
Turnpikes Act 1831 (c.25)
Turnpikes Act 1832 (c.124)
Turnpikes Act 1840 (c.39)
Turnpikes Acts Continuation Act 1849 (c.87)
Turnpikes (Provisional Orders Confirmation) Act 1865 (c.91)
Turnpikes (Provisional Orders Confirmation) Act 1866 (c.92)
Turnpikes (Provisional Orders Confirmation) Act 1870 (c.22)
Turnpikes, South Wales Act 1844 (c.91)
Tuvalu Act 1978 (c.20)
Tweed Fisheries Act 1797 (c.48)
Tyne Pilotage Order Confirmation Act 1865 (c.44)
Tyne Pilotage Order Confirmation Act 1867 (c.78)

Uganda Act 1964 (c.20)
Uganda Railway Act 1896 (c.38)
Uganda Railway Act 1900 (c.11)
Uganda Railway Act 1902 (c.40)
Ugandan Independence Act 1962 (c.57)
Ulster Defence Regiment Act 1969 (c.65)
Ulster Defence Regiment Act 1973 (c.34)
Ulster Society 1704 (c.19)
Ulverstone Canal Act 1793 (c.105)
Unclaimed Prize Money, etc. Act 1812 (c.132)

Under Secretaries of State Act 1929 (c.9)
Under Secretary of State Indemnity Act 1864 (c.21)
Underground Works (London) Act 1956 (c.59)
Unemployed Workers' Dependants (Temporary Provisions) Act 1921 (c.62)
Unemployed Workmen Act 1904 (c.18)
Unemployment Act 1934 (c.29)
Unemployment and Family Allowances (Northern Ireland Agreement) Act 1946 (c.3)
Unemployment Assistance (Emergency Powers) Act 1939 (c.93)
Unemployment Assistance (Temporary Provisions) Act 1935 (c.6)
Unemployment Assistance (Temporary Provisions) (Amendment) Act 1937 (c.10)
Unemployment Assistance (Temporary Provisions) (Extension) Act 1936 (c.7)
Unemployment Assistance (Temporary Provisions) (No. 2) Act 1935 (c.22)
Unemployment Insurance Act 1920 (c.30)
Unemployment Insurance Act 1921 (c.1)
Unemployment Insurance Act 1922 (c.7)
Unemployment Insurance Act 1923 (c.2)
Unemployment Insurance Act 1924 (c.1)
Unemployment Insurance Act 1925 (c.69)
Unemployment Insurance Act 1926 (c.12)
Unemployment Insurance Act 1927 (c.30)
Unemployment Insurance Act 1928 (c.1)
Unemployment Insurance Act 1929 (c.3)
Unemployment Insurance Act 1930 (c.16)
Unemployment Insurance Act 1931 (c.8)
Unemployment Insurance Act 1935 (c.8)
Unemployment Insurance Act 1938 (c.8)
Unemployment Insurance Act 1939 (c.29)
Unemployment Insurance Act 1940 (c.44)
Unemployment Insurance (Agriculture) Act 1936 (c.13)
Unemployment Insurance (Crediting of Contributions) Act 1935 (c.33)
Unemployment Insurance (Emergency Powers) Act 1939 (c.92)
Unemployment Insurance (Expiring Enactments) Act 1933 (c.26)
Unemployment Insurance (Eire Volunteers) Act 1946 (c.76)
Unemployment Insurance (Increase of Benefit) Act 1944 (c.42)
Unemployment Insurance (Northern Ireland Agreement) Act 1926 (c.4)
Unemployment Insurance (Northern Ireland Agreement) Act 1929 (c.18)
Unemployment Insurance (No. 2) Act 1921 (c.15)
Unemployment Insurance (No. 2) Act 1922 (c.30)
Unemployment Insurance (No. 2) Act 1924 (c.30)
Unemployment Insurance (No. 2) Act 1930 (c.19)
Unemployment Insurance (No. 2) Act 1931 (c.25)

Unemployment Insurance (No. 3) Act 1924 (c.6)

Unemployment Insurance (No. 3) Act 1930 (c.47)

Unemployment Insurance (No. 3) Act 1931 (c.36)

Unemployment Insurance (No. 4) Act 1931 (c.3)

Unemployment Insurance (Temporary Provisions Amendment) 1920 (c.82)

Unemployment Insurance (Transitional Provisions Amendment) Act 1929 (c.19)

Unemployment (Northern Ireland Agreement) Act 1936 (c.10)

Unemployment Relief Works 1920 (c.57)

Unfair Contract Terms Act 1977 (c.50)

Unfunded Debt Act 1761 (c.7)

Unfunded Debt Act 1765 (c.19)

Unfunded Debt Act 1766 (c.15)

Unfunded Debt Act 1766 (c.16)

Unfunded Debt Act 1768 (c.18)

Unfunded Debt Act 1769 (c.15)

Unfunded Debt Act 1770 (c.11)

Unfunded Debt Act 1772 (c.39)

Unfunded Debt Act 1772 (c.66)

Unfunded Debt Act 1801 (c.4)

Uniform Laws on International Sales Act 1967 (c.45)

Uniformity of Worship Act 1749 (c.28)

Uniforms Act 1894 (c.45)

Union and Parish Property Act 1837 (c.50)

Union Assessment Act 1880 (c.7)

Union Assessment Committee Act 1862 (c.103)

Union Assessment Committee Amendment Act 1864 (c.39)

Union Between England and Scotland Act 1702 (c.8)

Union Chargeability Act 1865 (c.79)

Union Loans Act 1869 (c.45)

Union of Benefices Act 1860 (c.142)

Union of Benefices Act 1898 (c.23)

Union of Benefices Act 1919 (c.98)

Union of Benefices Acts Amendment Act 1871 (c.90)

Union of Benefices, etc. Act 1855 (c.127)

Union of England and Scotland 1704 (c.6)

Union of England and Scotland 1705 (c.15)

Union of Parishes Act 1827 (c.43)

Union of Parishes, etc. (Ireland) Act 1832 (c.67)

Union of Turnpike Trusts Act 1849 (c.46)

Union Officers (Ireland) Act 1872 (c.89)

Union Officers (Ireland) Act 1885 (c.80)

Union Officers Superannuation (Ireland) Act 1865 (c.26)

Union Relief Aid Act 1862 (c.110)

Union Relief Aid Act 1863 (c.91)

Union Relief Aid Continuance Act 1863 (c.4)

Union Relief Aid Continuance Act 1864 (c.10)

Union with Ireland Act 1800 (c.67)

Union with Scotland Act 1706 (c.11)

Union with Scotland (Amendment) Act 1707 (c.40)

United Nations Act 1946 (c.45)

United Nations Personnel Act 1997 (c.13)

United Parishes (Scotland) Act 1868 (c.30)

United Parishes (Scotland) Act 1876 (c.11)

United States of America Veterans' Pensions (Administration) Act 1949 (c.45)

United States of America (Visiting Forces) Act 1942 (c.31)

Universities Act 1825 (c.97)

Universities and College (Emergency Powers) Act 1914 (c.22)

Universities and College (Emergency Provisions) Act 1939 (c.106)

Universities and College Estates Act 1858 (c.44)

Universities and College Estates Act 1898 (c.55)

Universities and College Estates Act 1925 (c.24)

Universities and College Estates Act 1964 (c.51)

Universities and College Estates Act Extension Act 1860 (c.59)

Universities and College Estates Amendment Act 1880 (c.46)

Universities and Colleges (Trust) Act 1943 (c.9)

Universities Election Act 1868 (c.65)

Universities Elections Amendment (Scotland) Act 1881 (c.40)

Universities of Oxford and Cambridge Act 1859 (c.19)

Universities of Oxford and Cambridge Act 1877 (c.48)

Universities of Oxford and Cambridge Act 1880 (c.11)

Universities of Oxford and Cambridge Act 1923 (c.33)

Universities (Scotland) Act 1853 (c.89)

Universities (Scotland) Act 1858 (c.83)

Universities (Scotland) Act 1859 (c.24)

Universities (Scotland) Act 1862 (c.28)

Universities (Scotland) Act 1889 (c.55)

Universities (Scotland) Act 1922 (c.31)

Universities (Scotland) Act 1932 (c.26)

Universities (Scotland) Act 1966 (c.13)

Universities Tests Act 1871 (c.26)

University Education (Ireland) Act 1879 (c.65)

University Elections Act 1861 (c.53)

University of Dublin Registration Act 1842 (c.74)

University of Dublin Tests 1873 (c.21)

University of Durham Act 1908 (c.20)

University of Durham Act 1935 (c.29)

University of Liverpool Act 1904 (c.11)

University of London Act 1898 (c.62)

University of London Act 1899 (c.24)

University of London Act 1926 (c.46)

University of London Medical Graduates Act 1854 (c.114)

University of Oxford Act 1869 (c.20)

University of St. Andrews Act 1746 (c.32)

University of St. Andrews Act 1953 (c.40)
University of Wales Act 1902 (c.14)
University of Wales (Medical Graduates) Act 1911 (c.43)
Universities (Wine Licences) Act 1743 (c.40)
Unlawful Combinations (Ireland) Act 1803 (c.86)
Unlawful Combinations (Ireland) Act 1814 (c.180)
Unlawful Combinations (Ireland) Act 1848 (c.89)
Unlawful Combinations of Workmen Act 1799 (c.81)
Unlawful Combinations of Workmen Act 1800 (c.106)
Unlawful Distillation, etc. (Ireland) Act 1814 (c.12)
Unlawful Drilling Act 1819 (c.1)
Unlawful Games Act 1728 (c.28)
Unlawful Oaths Act 1797 (c.123)
Unlawful Oaths Act 1810 (c.102)
Unlawful Oaths Act 1812 (c.104)
Unlawful Oaths Act 1823 (c.87)
Unlawful Oaths (Ireland) Act 1810 (c.102)
Unlawful Oaths (Ireland) Act 1844 (c.78)
Unlawful Oaths (Ireland) Act 1845 (c.55)
Unlawful Oaths (Ireland) Act 1851 (c.48)
Unlawful Oaths (Ireland) Act 1856 (c.78)
Unlawful Oaths (Ireland) Act 1862 (c.32)
Unlawful Pawning Act 1786 (c.92)
Unlawful Societies Act 1799 (c.79)
Unlawful Societies (Ireland) Act 1839 (c.74)
Unlawful Weights (Ireland) Act 1824 (c.110)
Unreasonable Withholding of Food Supplies Act 1914 (c.51)
Unsolicited Goods and Services Act 1971 (c.30)
Unsolicited Goods and Services (Amendment) Act 1975 (c.13)
Urban Development Corporations (Financial Limits) Act 1987 (c.57)
Use of Clarke's Hydrometer Act 1802 (c.97)
Use of Corn in Distillation of Spirits, etc. Act 1800 (c.3)
Use of Fine Flow Act 1801 (cc.1, 2)
Use of Fire on Steamboats Act 1828 (c.11)
Use of Highland Dress Act 1782 (c.63)
Use of Horsehides etc. Act 1800 (c.66)
Use of Plate Act 1769 (c.11)
Use of Rice in Distillation Act 1856 (c.51)
Use of Salt Duty Free, etc. Act 1800 (c.21)
Use of Sugar in Brewing Act 1800 (c.62)
Use of Sugar in Brewing Act 1812 (c.1)
Use of Sugar in Brewing Act 1812 (c.65)
Use of Wheat in Making Starch Act 1800 (c.25)
Usury Act 1713 (c.15)
Usury Act 1837 (c.80)
Usury Act 1839 (c.37)
Usury Act 1840 (c.83)
Usury Act 1841 (c.54)
Usury Act 1843 (c.45)
Usury Act 1845 (c.102)

Usury Act 1850 (c.56)
Usury Laws Repeal Act 1854 (c.90)
Uttoxeter to Stoke Road Act 1793 (c.131)
Uxbridge: Streets Act 1785 (c.16)

Vacant Ecclesiastical Dignities, etc. Act 1835 (c.30)
Vaccination Act 1840 (c.29)
Vaccination Act 1841 (c.32)
Vaccination Act 1853 (c.100)
Vaccination Act 1867 (c.84)
Vaccination Act 1871 (c.98)
Vaccination Act 1874 (c.75)
Vaccination Act 1898 (c.49)
Vaccination Act 1907 (c.31)
Vaccination Acts Amendment Act 1861 (c.59)
Vaccination Amendment (Ireland) Act 1868 (c.87)
Vaccination Amendment (Ireland) Act 1879 (c.70)
Vaccination (Ireland) Act 1858 (c.64)
Vaccination (Ireland) Act 1863 (c.52)
Vaccination (Scotland) Act 1863 (c.108)
Vaccination (Scotland) Act 1907 (c.49)
Vaccine Damage Payments Act 1979 (c.17)
Vagrance (Ireland) Amendment Act 1865 (c.33)
Vagrancy Act 1824 (c.83)
Vagrancy Act 1838 (c.38)
Vagrancy Act 1898 (c.39)
Vagrancy Act 1935 (c.20)
Vagrancy (England) Act 1822 (c.40)
Vagrancy (Ireland) Act 1847 (c.84)
Vagrant Act Amendment Act 1868 (c.52)
Vagrant Act Amendment Act 1873 (c.38)
Vagrants Act 1706 (c.32)
Vagrants Act 1713 (c.26)
Vagrants Act 1739 (c.24)
Vagrants Act 1821 (c.64)
Vagrants and Criminals Act 1787 (c.11)
Validation of Acts of Hate, Chief Justice of Bombay Act 1858 (c.32)
Validation of Elections Act 1955 (c.10)
Validation of Elections (No. 2) Act 1955 (c.12)
Validation of Elections (No. 3) Act 1955 (c.13)
Validation of Elections (Northern Ireland) Act 1956 (c.35)
Validation of War-time Leases Act 1944 (c.34)
Validity of Certain Contracts Act 1838 (c.10)
Validity of Certain Oaths Act 1812 (c.21)
Validity of Certain Orders in Council, etc. Act 1808 (c.37)
Validity of Certain Proceedings, etc. Act 1854 (c.37)
Validity of Proceedings in the House of Commons Act 1855 (c.33)
Valuation and Rating (Exempted Classes) (Scotland) Act 1976 (c.64)
Valuation and Rating (Scotland) Act 1956 (c.60)
Valuation (Ireland) Act 1834 (c.55)

Valuation (Ireland) Act 1852 (c.63)
Valuation (Ireland) Act 1853 (c.7)
Valuation (Ireland) Act 1854 (c.8)
Valuation (Ireland) Act 1864 (c.52)
Valuation (Ireland) Act 1901 (c.37)
Valuation (Ireland) Amendment Act 1874 (c.70)
Valuation (Metropolis) Act 1869 (c.67)
Valuation Metropolis Amendment Act 1884 (c.5)
Valuation Metropolis Amendment Act 1925 (c.40)
Valuation of Lands (Ireland) Act 1826 (c.62)
Valuation of Lands (Ireland) Act 1831 (c.51)
Valuation of Lands (Ireland) Act 1832 (c.73)
Valuation of Lands (Ireland) Act 1836 (c.84)
Valuation for Rating Act 1953 (c.42)
Valuation for Rating (Scotland) Act 1970 (c.4)
Valuation of Lands (Scotland) Acts Amendment Act 1894 (c.36)
Valuation of Lands (Scotland) Amendment Act 1867 (c.80)
Valuation of Lands (Scotland) Amendment Act 1879 (c.42)
Valuation of Lands (Scotland) Amendment Act 1887 (c.51)
Value Added Tax Act 1983 (c.55)
Value Added Tax Act 1994 (c.23)
Van Diemen's Land Act 1842 (c.3)
Van Diemen's Land Co. Act 1825 (c.39)
Van Diemen's Land Co. Act 1847 (c.57)
Vancouver's Island Act 1849 (c.48)
Variation of Trusts Act 1958 (c.53)
Vehicle and Driving Licences Act 1969 (c.27)
Vehicle Excise and Registration Act 1994 (c.22)
Vehicles (Excise) Act 1949 (c.89)
Vehicles (Excise) Act 1962 (c.13)
Vehicles (Excise) Act 1971 (c.10)
Vendor and Purchaser Act 1874 (c.78)
Venereal Disease Act 1917 (c.21)
Vessels Built at Malta, etc. Act 1820 (c.9)
Vessels Protection Act 1967 (c.85)
Vesting in Crown of Lands at Sandhurst Act 1812 (c.124)
Vestries Act 1818 (c.69)
Vestries Act 1819 (c.85)
Vestries Act 1831 (c.60)
Vestries Act 1850 (c.57)
Vestries Act 1853 (c.65)
Vesty Cess Abolition Act 1864 (c.17)
Veterinary Surgeons Act 1881 (c.62)
Veterinary Surgeons Act 1948 (c.52)
Veterinary Surgeons Act 1966 (c.36)
Veterinary Surgeons Act (1881) Amendment 1920 (c.20)
Veterinary Surgeons Amendment 1900 (c.24)
Veterinary Surgeons (Irish Free State Agreement) Act 1932 (c.10)
Vexatious Actions Act 1896 (c.51)
Vexatious Actions (Scotland) Act 1898 (c.35)
Vexatious Arrests Act 1747 (c.3)

Vexatious Arrests Act 1817 (c.101)
Vexatious Indictments Act 1859 (c.17)
Vice-Admiralty Courts Act 1816 (c.82)
Vice-Admiralty Courts Act 1832 (c.51)
Vice-Admiralty Courts Act 1863 (c.24)
Vice-Admiralty Courts Act Amendment Act 1867 (c.45)
Victoria Constitution Act 1855 (c.55)
Victoria Park Act 1842 (c.20)
Victoria Park Act 1872 (c.53)
Victoria University Act 1888 (c.45)
Victualling Establishment, Plymouth Act 1824 (c.49)
Video Recordings Act 1984 (c.39)
Video Recordings Act 1993 (c.24)
Vinegar Act 1844 (c.25)
Viscount Hardinge's Annuity Act 1846 (c.21)
Visiting Forces Act 1952 (c.67)
Visiting Forces (British Commonwealth) Act 1933 (c.6)
Voluntary Conveyances Act 1893 (c.21)
Voluntary Hospitals (Paying Patients) Act 1936 (c.17)
Voluntary Schools Act 1897 (c.5)
Volunteer Act 1863 (c.65)
Volunteer Act 1869 (c.81)
Volunteer Act 1895 (c.23)
Volunteer Act 1897 (c.47)
Volunteer Act 1900 (c.39)
Volunteer Act 1916 (c.62)
Volunteers Act 1780 (c.37)
Volunteers Act 1782 (c.79)
Volunteers Act 1861 (c.126)
Volunteers and Local Militia Act 1809 (c.113)
Volunteers and Yeomanry (Great Britain) Act 1803 (c.18)
Volunteer Corps Act 1794 (c.31)

Wadeshill and Royston Road Act 1796 (c.129)
Wages Act 1708 (c.16)
Wages Act 1986 (c.48)
Wages and Prize Money, etc. in the Navy Act 1809 (c.108)
Wages Arrestment Act 1845 (c.39)
Wages Arrestment Limitation (Amendment) (Scotland) Act 1960 (c.21)
Wages Arrestment Limitation (Scotland) Act 1870 (c.63)
Wages Attachment Abolition Act 1870 (c.30)
Wages Councils Act 1945 (c.17)
Wages Councils Act 1948 (c.7)
Wages Councils Act 1959 (c.69)
Wages Councils Act 1979 (c.12)
Wages Councils (Northern Ireland) Act 1945 (c.21)
Wages, etc. of Artificers, etc. Act 1813 (c.40)
Wages of Artificers, etc. Act 1820 (c.93)
Wages of Certain Deceased Seamen Act 1819 (c.59)
Wages of Merchant Seamen Act 1819 (c.58)
Wages (Temporary Regulations) Act 1918 (c.61)

Wages (Temporary Regulations) Extension Act 1919 (c.18)
Wakefield Church Act 1791 (c.74)
Wakefield, etc. Roads Act 1740 (c.19)
Wakefield and Halifax Roads Act 1793 (c.129)
Wakefield and Sheffield Road Act 1797 (c.159)
Wakefield (Improvement) Act 1771 (c.44)
Wakefield: Improvement Act 1796 (c.50)
Wakefield Roads Act 1778 (c.85)
Wakefield to Abberford Road Act 1789 (c.86)
Wakefield to Abberford Road Act 1793 (c.179)
Wakefield to Austerlands Road Act 1758 (c.48)
Wakefield to Sheffield Road Act 1778 (c.105)
Walcot, Somerset: Improvement Act 1793 (c.89)
Wales Act 1978 (c.52)
Wales and Berwick Act 1746 (c.42)
Wales, Chester, etc. (Courts) Act 1793 (c.68)
Wallingford: Improvement Act 1795 (c.75)
Walmer Vesting Act 1863 (c.54)
Walmore and Bearce Commons, Forest of Dean Act 1866 (c.70)
Walton - Shepperton Bridge (Building and Tolls) Act 1746 (c.22)
Walton - Shepperton Bridge (Rebuilding and Tolls) Act 1780 (c.32)
Wangford, Suffolk: Poor Relief Act 1764 (c.91)
Wapping, Stepney Act 1728 (c.30)
Wapping, Stepney: Poor Relief Act 1782 (c.35)
Wapping, Stepney: Poor Relief, etc. Act 1783 (c.32)
Wapping, Stepney: Improvement Act 1782 (c.86)
War Charges (Validity) Act 1925 (c.6)
War Charities Act 1916 (c.43)
War Charities Act 1940 (c.31)
War Charities Act (Scotland) 1919 (c.12)
War Crimes Act 1991 (c.13)
War Damage Act 1941 (c.12)
War Damage Act 1943 (c.21)
War Damage Act 1949 (c.36)
War Damage Act 1964 (c.25)
War Damage Act 1965 (c.18)
War Damage (Amendment) Act 1942 (c.28)
War Damages (Amendment) Act 1943 (c.12)
War Damage (Clearance Payments) Act 1960 (c.25)
War Damage (Extension of Risk Period) Act 1941 (c.37)
War Damage (Public Utility Undertakings, etc.) Act 1949 (c.36)
War Damage to Land (Scotland) Act 1939 (c.80)
War Damage to Land (Scotland) Act 1941 (c.40)
War Damage (Valuation Appeals) Act 1945 (c.8)

War Damaged Sites Act 1949 (c.84)
War Department Property Act 1938 (c.49)
War Department Stores Act 1867 (c.128)
War Department Tramway (Devon) Act 1865 (c.74)
War Emergency Laws (Continuance) Act 1920 (c.5)
War Loan Act 1900 (c.2)
War Loan Act 1914 (c.60)
War Loan Act 1915 (c.55)
War Loan Act 1916 (c.67)
War Loan Act 1917 (c.41)
War Loan Act 1918 (c.25)
War Loan Act 1919 (c.37)
War Loan (Redemption) Act 1910 (c.2)
War Loan (Supplemental Provisions) Act 1915 (c.93)
War Memorials (Local Authorities' Powers) Act 1923 (c.18)
War Office Act 1879 (c.17)
War Orphans Act 1942 (c.8)
War Pensions Act 1920 (c.23)
War Pensions Act 1921 (c.49)
War Pensions (Administrative Provisions) Act 1918 (c.57)
War Pensions (Administrative Provisions) Act 1919 (c.53)
War Risks Insurance Act 1939 (c.57)
War Risks (Insurance by Truskes) Act 1916 (c.6)
War Service Canteens (Disposal of Surplus) Act 1922 (c.53)
War Stores (Commission) Act 1904 (c.7)
Warden of Fleet Prison Act 1728 (c.32)
Warden of the Fleet Prison Act 1819 (c.64)
Wareham and Purbeck Roads Act 1786 (c.122)
Wareham: Improvement Act 1763 (c.54)
Warehoused British Spirits Act 1867 (c.27)
Warehoused Goods Act 1809 (c.106)
Warehoused Tobacco, etc. Act 1793 (c.57)
Warehousing of British Compounded Spirits Act 1865 (c.98)
Warehousing of British Spirits Act 1864 (c.12)
Warehousing of Foreign Goods, Manchester Act 1844 (c.31)
Warehousing of Goods Act 1799 (c.59)
Warehousing of Goods Act 1803 (c.132)
Warehousing of Goods Act 1823 (c.24)
Warehousing of Goods Act 1845 (c.91)
Warehousing of Spirits (Ireland) Act 1812 (c.30)
Warehousing of Wines, etc. Act 1795 (c.118)
Warminster Roads Act 1726 (c.16)
Warminster Roads Act 1742 (c.5)
Warminster Roads Act 1765 (c.62)
Warminster Roads Act 1792 (c.141)
Warrants of Attorney Act 1822 (c.39)
Warrants of Attorney Act 1843 (c.66)
Warrick Election Act 1834 (c.17)
Warrington and Wigan Road Act 1726 (c.10)
Warrington and Wigan Road Act 1770 (c.70)
Warrington to Wigan Road Act 1746 (c.8)

Warrington to Wigan Road Act 1793 (c.164)

Warwick and Birmingham Canal Act 1793 (c.38)

Warrington and Birmingham Canal Act 1796 (c.42)

Warwick and Gloucester Roads Act 1773 (c.97)

Warwick and Gloucester Roads Act 1791 (c.116)

Warwick and Napton Canal Act 1794 (c.38)

Warwick and Napton Canal Act 1796 (c.95)

Warwick and Northampton Road Act 1765 (c.107)

Warwick Assizes Act 1854 (c.35)

Warwick, etc. Roads Act 1739 (c.5)

Warwick to Northampton Road Act 1776 (c.80)

Warwick and Northampton Roads Act 1781 (c.106)

Warwick and Northamptonshire Roads Act 1759 (c.44)

Warwick and Oxford Roads Act 1755 (c.46)

Warwick and Oxford Roads Act 1780 (c.69)

Warwick and Worcester Roads Act 1754 (c.36)

Warwick and Worcester Roads Act 1767 (c.81)

Warwick and Worcester Roads Act 1780 (c.71)

Warwick and Worcester Roads Act 1781 (c.88)

Warwick Bridge Act 1788 (c.9)

Warwick Gaol Act 1777 (c.58)

Warwick, Stafford and Worcester Roads Act 1794 (c.117)

Warwick Roads Act 1723 (c.15)

Warwick Roads Act 1730 (c.9)

Warwick Roads Act 1738 (c.18)

Warwick Roads Act 1739 (c.22)

Warwick Roads Act 1742 (c.20)

Warwick Roads Act 1743 (c.12)

Warwick Roads Act 1744 (c.32)

Warwick Roads Act 1753 (c.73)

Warwick Roads Act 1760 (c.36)

Warwick Roads Act 1767 (c.77)

Warwick Roads Act 1770 (c.63)

Warwick Roads Act 1770 (c.69)

Warwick Roads Act 1770 (c.94)

Warwick Roads Act 1772 (c.91)

Warwick Roads Act 1780 (c.80)

Warwick Roads Act 1785 (c.115)

Warwick Roads Act 1788 (c.107)

Warwick Roads Act 1791 (c.98)

Warwick Roads Act 1792 (c.116)

Warwick Roads Act 1794 (c.115)

Warwick Roads Act 1794 (c.116)

Warwick Shire Hall Act 1757 (c.56)

Warwick, Stafford and Worcester Roads Act 1772 (c.110)

Warwick, Worcester and Stafford Roads Act 1787 (c.73)

Warwickshire and Northamptonshire Roads 1736 (c.11)

Warwickshire Roads Act 1744 (c.19)

Washington Treaty (Claims) Act 1875 (c.52)

Waste Lands, Australia Act 1846 (c.104)

Waste Lands, Van Diemen's Land Act 1845 (c.95)

Watch Rates in Boroughs Act 1840 (c.28)

Watching: City of London Act 1736 (c.22)

Watching: Holborn Act 1736 (c.25)

Watching, St. Margaret and St. John, Westminster 1735 (c.17)

Watching, St. Martin's in the Fields Act 1735 (c.8)

Watching, St. Paul (Covent Garden) Act 1735 (c.13)

Watching, Westminster Act 1735 (c.19)

Watchett (Somerset) Harbour Act 1707 (c.69)

Watchett (Somerset) Harbour Act 1720 (c.14)

Watchett Harbour Act 1770 (c.24)

Water Act 1945 (c.42)

Water Act 1948 (c.22)

Water Act 1958 (c.67)

Water Act 1973 (c.37)

Water Act 1981 (c.12)

Water Act 1983 (c.23)

Water Act 1989 (c.15)

Water Charges Act 1976 (c.9)

Water Charges Equalisation Act 1977 (c.41)

Water Companies (Regulation of Powers) Act 1887 (c.21)

Water Consolidation (Consequential Provisions) Act 1991 (c.60)

Water (Fluoridation) Act 1985 (c.63)

Water Industry Act 1991 (c.60)

Water Measure of Fruit 1702 (c.9)

Water Officers Compensation Act 1960 (c.15)

Water Rate Definition Act 1885 (c.34)

Water Resources Act 1963 (c.38)

Water Resources Act 1968 (c.35)

Water Resources Act 1971 (c.34)

Water Resources Act 1991 (c.57)

Water (Scotland) Act 1946 (c.42)

Water (Scotland) Act 1949 (c.31)

Water (Scotland) Act 1967 (c.78)

Water (Scotland) Act 1980 (c.45)

Water Supplies (Exceptional Shortage Orders) Act 1934 (c.20)

Water Supply, London Act 1747 (c.8)

Water Undertakings (Modification of Charges) Act 1921 (c.44)

Waterbeach Level (Cambridge, Isle of Ely): Drainage Act 1797 (c.88)

Waterbeach Level: Drainage Act 1790 (c.74)

Waterbeach Level, Northampton: Drainage Act 1740 (c.24)

Waterford Hospital Act 1839 (c.19)

Waterfront House of Industry Act 1838 (c.13)

Waterloo Subscription Fund Act 1819 (c.34)

Waterworks Clauses Act 1847 (c.17)

Waterworks Clauses Act 1863 (c.93)

Watford Churchyard and Workhouse Act 1772 (c.28)

Wear Coal Trade Act 1792 (c.29)

Wear Navigation Act 1758 (c.64)
Wear Navigation Act 1758 (c.65)
Wearmouth and Tyne Bridge Road Act 1796 (c.136)
Wedding Rings Act 1855 (c.60)
Wednesfield Chapel Act 1746 (c.27)
Weedon Barracks Act 1804 (c.78)
Weeds Act 1959 (c.54)
Weeds and Agricultural Seeds (Ireland) Act 1909 (c.31)
Weights and Measures Act 1795 (c.102)
Weights and Measures Act 1797 (c.143)
Weights and Measures Act 1815 (c.43)
Weights and Measures Act 1824 (c.74)
Weights and Measures Act 1825 (c.12)
Weights and Measures Act 1834 (c.49)
Weights and Measures Act 1855 (c.72)
Weights and Measures Act 1859 (c.56)
Weights and Measures Act 1862 (c.76)
Weights and Measures Act 1878 (c.49)
Weights and Measures Act 1889 (c.21)
Weights and Measures Act 1893 (c.19)
Weights and Measures Act 1904 (c.28)
Weights and Measures Act 1936 (c.38)
Weights and Measures Act 1963 (c.31)
Weights and Measures Act 1979 (c.45)
Weights and Measures Act 1985 (c.72)
Weights and Measures (Amendment) Act 1926 (c.8)
Weights and Measures, Dublin Act 1867 (c.94)
Weights and Measures etc. Act 1976 (c.77)
Weights and Measures (Ireland) Act 1860 (c.119)
Weights and Measures (Leather Measurement) Act 1919 (c.29)
Weights and Measures (Metric System) Act 1897 (c.46)
Weights and Measures (Northern Ireland) Act 1967 (c.6)
Weights and Measures (Purchase) Act 1892 (c.18)
Weights and Measures, Sale of Coal (Scotland) Act 1936 (c.54)
Weights in Sales of Bullion Act 1853 (c.29)
Weights for Coin in the Mint Act 1774 (c.92)
Weights for Coin in the Mint Act 1775 (c.30)
Welfare of Animals at Slaughter Act 1991 (c.30)
Welford and Leicester Road Act 1765 (c.78)
Welford Bridge to Milston Lane Road Act 1786 (c.148)
Wellingborough and Northampton Road Act 1797 (c.167)
Wellington Museum Act 1947 (c.46)
Wells Harbour Act 1769 (c.8)
Wells Roads Act 1753 (c.76)
Wells, Somerset: Improvement Act 1779 (c.31)
Welsh Cathedrals Act 1843 (c.77)
Welsh Church Act 1914 (c.91)
Welsh Church (Amendment) Act 1938 (c.39)
Welsh Church (Burial Grounds) Act 1945 (c.27)

Welsh Church (Temporalities) Act 1919 (c.65)
Welsh Courts Act 1942 (c.40)
Welsh Development Agency Act 1975 (c.70)
Welsh Development Agency Act 1988 (c.5)
Welsh Development Agency Act 1991 (c.69)
Welsh Development Agency Act 1997 (c.37)
Welsh Intermediate Education Act 1889 (c.40)
Welsh Language Act 1967 (c.66)
Welsh Language Act 1993 (c.38)
Welsh National Opera Company 1971 (c.37)
Wendover and Buckingham Road Act 1766 (c.71)
Wern and Bron-y-Garth Road Act 1797 (c.151)
Wesleyan Methodists (Appointments During the War) Act 1917 (c.29)
West Africa Offences Act 1871 (c.8)
West Coast of Africa and Falkland Islands Act 1860 (c.121)
West Coast of Africa Possessions Act 1821 (c.28)
West Cowgate and Alemouth Road Act 1797 (c.163)
West Highland Railway Guarantee Act 1896 (c.58)
West India Island Relief Act 1845 (c.50)
West India Islands Relief Act 1840 (c.40)
West India Loans Act 1848 (c.38)
West India Loans Act 1855 (c.71)
West India Loans Act 1879 (c.16)
West India Relief Commissioners Act 1856 (c.35)
West Indian Bishops, etc. Act 1825 (c.88)
West Indian Court of Appeal Act 1919 (c.47)
West Indian Courts of Appeal Act 1850 (c.15)
West Indian Incumbered Estates Act 1854 (c.117)
West Indian Incumbered Estates Act 1858 (c.96)
West Indian Incumbered Estates Act 1862 (c.45)
West Indian Incumbered Estates Act 1864 (c.108)
West Indian Islands Relief Act 1844 (c.17)
West Indian Islands (Telegraph) Act 1924 (c.14)
West Indian Loans Act 1848 (c.130)
West Indian Mortgages Act 1772 (c.14)
West Indian Prisons Act 1838 (c.67)
West Indies Act 1806 (c.80)
West Indies Act 1962 (c.19)
West Indies Act 1967 (c.4)
West Indies (Encumbered Estates) Act 1872 (c.9)
West Indies (Encumbered Estates) Act 1886 (c.36)
West Indies Relief Act 1843 (c.63)
West Indies (Salaries) Act 1868 (c.120)
West Riding Inclosures Act 1712 (c.4)
West Riding: Small Debts Act 1780 (c.65)
West Riding: Small Debts Act 1793 (c.84)

Westbury, Wilts (Additional Oversees) Act 1786 (c.23)

Western Australia Constitution Act 1890 (c.26)

Western Australia Government Act 1835 (c.14)

Western Australia Government Act 1836 (c.68)

Western Australia Government Act 1838 (c.46)

Western Australia Government Act 1841 (c.43)

Western Australia Government Act 1842 (c.88)

Western Australia Government Act 1844 (c.57)

Western Australia Government Act 1846 (c.35)

Western Highlands and Islands (Transport Services) Act 1928 (c.6)

Western Highlands and Islands (Scotland) Works Act 1891 (c.58)

Westminster Act 1756 (c.25)

Westminster Act 1757 (c.17)

Westminster Act 1861 (c.78)

Westminster Abbey Act 1888 (c.11)

Westminster Bridge Act 1735 (c.29)

Westminster Bridge Act 1736 (c.16)

Westminster Bridge Act 1737 (c.25)

Westminster Bridge Act 1738 (c.33)

Westminster Bridge Act 1739 (c.16)

Westminster Bridge Act 1740 (c.40)

Westminster Bridge Act 1741 (c.26)

Westminster Bridge Act 1743 (c.32)

Westminster Bridge Act 1744 (c.29)

Westminster Bridge Act 1756 (c.38)

Westminster Bridge Act 1757 (c.34)

Westminster Bridge Act 1853 (c.46)

Westminster Bridge Act 1859 (c.58)

Westminster Bridge Act 1864 (c.88)

Westminster Corn and Grain Market Act 1757 (c.25)

Westminster Election Act 1813 (c.152)

Westminster Fish Market Act 1790 (c.54)

Westminster Fish Market Act 1802 (c.19)

Westminster: Improvement Act 1778 (c.72)

Westminster: Improvement Act 1787 (c.54)

Westminster: Improvements Act 1790 (c.53)

Westminster: Improvements Act 1821 (c.45)

Westminster: King's Street Act 1753 (c.101)

Westminster Market Act 1749 (c.14)

Westminster Offices Act 1855 (c.95)

Westminster Offices Act 1859 (c.19)

Westminster Offices Act 1861 (c.33)

Westminster Offices Act 1862 (c.74)

Westminster Offices Act 1864 (c.51)

Westminster Offices Act 1865 (c.31)

Westminster Offices Act 1865 (c.32)

Westminster Parliamentary Elections Act 1811 (c.126)

Westminster Parliamentary Elections Act 1819 (c.2)

Westminster Streets Act 1728 (c.11)

Westminster Streets Act 1763 (c.39)

Westminster Streets Act 1765 (c.50)

Westminster Streets Act 1777 (c.61)

Westminster: Streets Act 1782 (c.44)

Westminster: Streets Act 1783 (c.42)

Westminster: Streets Act 1783 (c.43)

Westminster: Streets Act 1783 (c.89)

Westminster: Streets Act 1783 (c.90)

Westminster: Streets Act 1786 (c.102)

Westminster: Watching Act 1774 (c.90)

Westminster: Watching Act 1786 (c.112)

Westminster (Water Supply) Act 1721 (c.26)

Westmoreland Canals Act 1792 (c.101)

Westmoreland Gaol, etc. Act 1776 (c.54)

Westmoreland Roads Act 1742 (c.3)

Westmoreland Roads Act 1760 (c.43)

Westmoreland Roads Act 1753 (c.67)

Westmoreland Roads Act 1758 (c.69)

Westmoreland Roads Act 1779 (c.106)

Westmoreland Roads Act 1779 (c.108)

Westmoreland Roads Act 1780 (c.88)

Westmoreland Roads Act 1782 (c.111)

Westmoreland and Yorkshire Roads Act 1784 (c.70)

Wetherby to Grassington Road Act 1758 (c.71)

Wetherby to Grassington Road Act 1774 (c.98)

Wetherby to Knaresborough Road Act 1783 (c.103)

Wexford Grand Jury Act 1867 (c.77)

Weyhill and Lyde Way Road Act 1762 (c.60)

Weymouth Harbour Act 1748 (c.22)

Weymouth: Improvement Act 1776 (c.57)

Weymouth: Water Supply Act 1797 (c.129)

Whale Fishery Act 1732 (c.33)

Whale Fishery Act 1748 (c.45)

Whale Fishery Act 1755 (c.20)

Whale Fishery Act 1763 (c.22)

Whale Fishery Act 1768 (c.27)

Whale Fishery, etc. Act 1776 (c.47)

Whale Fisheries Act 1789 (c.53)

Whale Fisheries (Scotland) Act 1907 (c.41)

Whale Fisheries (Scotland) Act Amendment 1922 (c.34)

Whales Fisheries (Ireland) Act 1908 (c.31)

Whaling Industry (Regulation) Act 1934 (c.49)

Wharves Between London Bridge and Temple Act 1821 (c.89)

Wheat Act 1932 (c.24)

Wheat (Amendment) Act 1939 (c.37)

Whichwood Disafforesting Act 1853 (c.36)

Whichwood Disafforesting Act 1856 (c.32)

Whipping Act 1820 (c.57)

Whipping Act 1862 (c.18)

Whipping of Female Offenders, Abolition Act 1817 (c.75)

Whitby Harbour Act 1734 (c.10)

Whitby Harbour Act 1749 (c.39)

Whitby Harbour Act 1766 (c.81)

Whitby Harbour Act 1780 (c.12)

Whitby Harbour Act 1796 (c.121)

Whitby: Improvement Act 1764 (c.73)
Whitby: Improvement Act 1789 (c.12)
Whitby Piers 1702 (c.13)
Whitby Piers Act 1708 (c.7)
Whitby Roads Act 1785 (c.111)
Whitchurch, Salop: Poor Relief Act 1792 (c.85)
White Cross and Beverley Roads Act 1760 (c.42)
White Fish and Herring Industries Act 1948 (c.51)
White Fish and Herring Industries Act 1953 (c.17)
White Fish and Herring Industries Act 1957 (c.22)
White Fish and Herring Industries Act 1961 (c.18)
White Herring Fisheries Act 1771 (c.31)
White Herring Fishery Act 1779 (c.26)
White Herring Fishery (Scotland) Act 1821 (c.79)
White Herring Fishery (Scotland) Act 1861 (c.72)
White Phosphorus Matches Prohibition Act 1908 (c.42)
Whitechapel Highways Act 1721 (c.30)
Whitechapel: Improvement Act 1778 (c.37)
Whitechapel: Improvement Act 1778 (c.80)
Whitechapel (Poor Relief) Act 1763 (c.53)
Whitechapel: Poor Relief Act 1766 (c.74)
Whitechapel Roads Act 1736 (c.36)
Whitechapel, Stepney: Improvement Act 1793 (c.82)
Whitechapel: Streets Act 1783 (c.91)
Whitechapel to Aldermaston Road Act 1770 (c.88)
Whitehaven Harbour Act 1708 (c.9)
Whitehaven Harbour Act 1710 (c.17)
Whitehaven Harbour Improvement Act 1739 (c.14)
Whitehaven Harbour Impovement Act 1760 (c.44)
Whitehaven Harbour Improvement Act 1762 (c.87)
Whitehaven: Improvement Act 1788 (c.61)
Whitgift, Yorks (Drainage) Act 1793 (c.108)
Whitney Bridge, Hereford Act 1797 (c.56)
Whitney Bridge, Wye Act 1780 (c.27)
Whittlesey Drainage Act 1797 (c.68)
Whittlewood Disafforesting Act 1853 (c.42)
Whittlewood Forest Act 1824 (c.99)
Wicklow Harbour Act 1897 (c.55)
Wide Streets and Coal Trade, Dublin Act 1809 (c.72)
Wide Streets, Dublin Act 1811 (c.10)
Widows', Orphans' and Old Age Contributory Pensions Act 1925 (c.70)
Widows', Orphans' and Old Age Contributory Pensions Act 1929 (c.10)
Widows', Orphans' and Old Age Contributory Pensions Act 1931 (c.19)
Widows', Orphans' and Old Age Contributory Pensions Act 1936 (c.33)

Widows', Orphans' and Old Age Contributory Pensions (Voluntary Contributors) Act 1937 (c.39)
Wigan to Preston Road Act 1726 (c.9)
Wigan to Preston Road Act 1779 (c.92)
Wigan to Preston Road Act 1795 (c.145)
Wigan: Water Supply Act 1764 (c.75)
Wiggenhall Drainage Act 1757 (c.32)
Wigtown Roads Act 1778 (c.7)
Wild Animals in Captivity Protection Act 1900 (c.33)
Wild Animals in Captivity Protection (Scotland) Act 1909 (c.33)
Wild Birds (Duck and Geese) Protection Act 1939 (c.19)
Wild Birds Protection Act 1880 (c.35)
Wild Birds Protection Act 1881 (c.51)
Wild Birds Protection Act 1894 (c.24)
Wild Birds (Protection) Act 1896 (c.56)
Wild Birds Protection Act 1902 (c.6)
Wild Birds Protection Act 1904 (c.4)
Wild Birds Protection Act 1908 (c.11)
Wild Birds Protection (St. Kilda) Act 1904 (c.10)
Wild Creatures and Forest Laws Act 1971 (c.47)
Wild Mammals (Protection) Act 1996 (c.3)
Wilden Ferry Bridge Act 1757 (c.59)
Wildlife and Countryside Act 1981 (c.69)
Wildlife and Countryside (Amendment) Act 1985 (c.31)
Wildlife and Countryside (Amendment) Act 1991 (c.39)
Wildlife and Countryside (Service of Notices) Act 1985 (c.59)
Will of Sir Joseph Jekyll Act 1746 (c.34)
Willian Preston Indemnity Act 1925 (c.7)
Wills Act 1703 (c.5)
Wills Act 1751 (c.6)
Wills Act 1837 (c.26)
Wills Act 1861 (c.114)
Wills Act 1963 (c.44)
Wills Act 1968 (c.28)
Wills Act Amendment Act 1852 (c.24)
Wills, etc. of Seamen, etc. Act 1815 (c.60)
Wills (Soldiers and Sailors) Act 1918 (c.58)
Wiltshire Highways 1706 (c.26)
Wiltshire Highways Act 1707 (c.76)
Wiltshire Highways Act 1713 (c.17)
Wiltshire Highways Act 1728 (c.12)
Wiltshire Roads Act 1724 (c.27)
Wiltshire Roads Act 1725 (c.7)
Wiltshire Roads Act 1725 (c.11)
Wiltshire Roads Act 1736 (c.6)
Wiltshire Roads Act 1740 (c.29)
Wiltshire Roads Act 1742 (c.10)
Wiltshire Roads Act 1743 (c.23)
Wiltshire Roads Act 1743 (c.27)
Wiltshire Roads Act 1744 (c.14)
Wiltshire Roads Act 1750 (c.9)
Wiltshire Roads Act 1751 (c.5)
Wiltshire Roads Act 1751 (c.12)
Wiltshire Roads Act 1753 (c.42)

Wiltshire Roads Act 1755 (c.44)
Wiltshire Roads Act 1756 (c.67)
Wiltshire Roads Act 1757 (c.41)
Wiltshire Roads Act 1757 (c.68)
Wiltshire Roads Act 1758 (c.63)
Wiltshire Roads Act 1760 (c.37)
Wiltshire Roads Act 1762 (c.49)
Wiltshire Roads Act 1762 (c.51)
Wiltshire Roads Act 1762 (c.59)
Wiltshire Roads Act 1762 (c.66)
Wiltshire Roads Act 1766 (c.57)
Wiltshire Roads Act 1768 (c.49)
Wiltshire Roads Act 1769 (c.48)
Wiltshire Roads Act 1769 (c.73)
Wiltshire Roads Act 1771 (c.81)
Wiltshire Roads Act 1772 (c.74)
Wiltshire Roads Act 1772 (c.85)
Wiltshire Roads Act 1773 (c.101)
Wiltshire Roads Act 1777 (c.72)
Wiltshire Roads Act 1777 (c.98)
Wiltshire Roads Act 1779 (c.111)
Wiltshire Roads Act 1780 (c.82)
Wiltshire Roads Act 1780 (c.98)
Wiltshire Roads Act 1783 (c.30)
Wiltshire Roads Act 1783 (c.111)
Wiltshire Roads Act 1788 (c.86)
Wiltshire Roads Act 1790 (c.96)
Wiltshire Roads Act 1790 (c.98)
Wiltshire Roads Act 1791 (c.121)
Wiltshire Roads Act 1792 (c.114)
Wiltshire Roads Act 1795 (c.136)
Wiltshire and Berkshire Roads Act 1757 (c.66)
Wiltshire, Dorset and Somerset Roads Act 1753 (c.60)
Wiltshire, Dorset and Somerset Roads Act 1756 (c.92)
Wiltshire, Dorset and Somerset Roads Act 1756 (c.54)
Wiltshire and Dorset Roads Act 1777 (c.83)
Wiltshire, Dorset and Somerset Roads Act 1779 (c.94)
Wiltshire and Gloucester Roads Act 1751 (c.59)
Wiltshire and Gloucester Roads 1778 (c.103)
Wiltshire and Hampshire Roads 1764 (c.47)
Wiltshire and Somerset Roads Act 1751 (c.17)
Wiltshire and Somerset Roads Act 1751 (c.52)
Wiltshire and Somerset Roads Act 1751 (c.24)
Wiltshire and Somerset Roads Act 1757 (c.46)
Wiltshire and Somerset Roads Act 1768 (c.49)
Wiltshire and Somerset Roads Act 1777 (c.93)
Wiltshire and Somerset Roads Act 1777 (c.99)
Wiltshire and Somerset Roads Act 1792 (c.137)
Wiltshire and Somerset Roads Act 1793 (c.155)

Wiltshire and Southampton Roads Act 1753 (c.66)
Wiltshire and Southampton Roads Act 1756 (c.45)
Wiltshire and Southampton Roads Act 1782 (c.110)
Wincanton Roads 1756 (c.49)
Winchester: Improvement Act 1771 (c.9)
Window Duties Act 1747 (c.10)
Window Duties Act 1753 (c.17)
Window Duties Act 1761 (c.8)
Window Duties (Scotland) Act 1817 (c.128)
Window Duty (Ireland) Act 1810 (c.75)
Windows Duties Act 1796 (c.117)
Windsor Bridge Act 1735 (c.15)
Windsor Castle Act 1848 (c.53)
Windsor Forest Act 1806 (c.143)
Windsor Forest Act 1813 (c.158)
Windsor Forest Act 1815 (c.122)
Windsor Forest Act 1816 (c.132)
Windsor Forest Boundary Commission Act 1807 (c.46)
Windsor Forest Road Act 1758 (c.46)
Windsor Lands Act 1702 (c.27)
Windward Islands Appeal Court Act 1889 (c.33)
Wine and Beerhouse Act 1869 (c.27)
Wine and Beerhouse Amendment Act 1870 (c.29)
Wine, etc. Duties Act 1825 (c.13)
Wine Licences Act 1758 (c.19)
Winfrith Heath Act 1957 (c.61)
Winter Assizes Act 1876 (c.57)
Winter Assizes Act 1877 (c.46)
Winterbourne Parish Act 1841 (c.42)
Wireless Telegraph (Blind Person' Facilities) Act 1926 (c.54)
Wireless Telegraphy Act 1904 (c.24)
Wireless Telegraphy Act 1906 (c.13)
Wireless Telegraphy Act 1949 (c.54)
Wireless Telegraphy Act 1955 (c.10)
Wireless Telegraphy Act 1967 (c.72)
Wireless Telegraphy (Explanation) Act 1925 (c.67)
Wireless Telegraphy (Validation of Charges) Act 1954 (c.2)
Wisbech Canal Act 1794 (c.92)
Wisbech Roads Act 1786 (c.133)
Witchcraft Act 1735 (c.5)
Witchcraft, etc. (Ireland) Act 1821 (c.18)
Witford, etc. Suffolk: Poor Relief Act 1765 (c.97)
Witham Drainage Act 1762 (c.32)
Witnesses Act 1806 (c.37)
Witnesses' Indemnity, Penryn Act 1828 (c.13)
Witnesses on Petitions Act 1801 (c.105)
Witnesses on Trial for Treason 1702 (c.9)
Witnesses (Public Inquiries) Protection Act 1892 (c.64)
Witney to Chanfield Road Act 1793 (c.137)
Wiveliscombe Roads Act 1786 (c.135)
Wolverhampton Church Act 1755 (c.34)

181

Wolverhampton: Improvements Act 1776 (c.25)
Wolverhampton Parish Act 1848 (c.95)
Wolverhampton Roads Act 1772 (c.101)
Wolverhampton Roads 1747 (c.25)
Wolverhampton Roads Act 1793 (c.147)
Wolverhampton Roads Act 1794 (c.133)
Wolverhampton Roads Act 1796 (c.146)
Women and Young Persons (Employment in Lead Processes) Act 1920 (c.62)
Woods and Forest Act 1803 (c.31)
Woods and Forests Act 1806 (c.142)
Woodstock, Oxford, Roads Act 1784 (c.61)
Wool Act 1738 (c.21)
Wool Act 1780 (c.55)
Wool Duties, etc. Act 1824 (c.47)
Woolcombers Act 1795 (c.124)
Woollen Cloths Act 1707 (c.43)
Woollen Cloths Act 1708 (c.13)
Woollen, etc. Manufacturers Act 1710 (c.32)
Woollen, etc. Manufacturers 1735 (c.4)
Woollen, etc. Manufactures Act 1720 (c.7)
Woollen, etc. Manufactures, Bedfordshire Act 1785 (c.40)
Woollen, etc. Manufactures, Norfolk Act 1791 (c.56)
Woollen Manufacturers Act 1702 (c.22)
Woollen Manufacture Act 1711 (c.26)
Woollen Manufacture Act 1714 (c.15)
Woollen Manufacture Act 1715 (c.41)
Woollen Manufactures Act 1725 (c.34)
Woollen Manufactures Act 1726 (c.23)
Woollen Manufactures Act 1731 (c.21)
Woollen Manufacture Act 1756 (c.33)
Woollen Manufactures Act 1757 (c.12)
Woollen Manufactures Act 1803 (c.136)
Woollen Manufacture Act 1804 (c.64)
Woollen Manufacture Act 1805 (c.83)
Woollen Manufacture Act 1806 (c.18)
Woollen Manufacture Act 1807 (c.43)
Woollen Manufacture Act 1808 (c.131)
Woollen Manufacture Act 1809 (c.109)
Woollen Manufacture Act 1810 (c.83)
Woollen Manufactures, Suffolk Act 1784 (c.3)
Woollen Trade Act 1833 (c.28)
Woolmer Forest Act 1812 (c.71)
Woolmer Forest Act 1855 (c.46)
Woolwich Church Act 1738 (c.9)
Woolwich Dockyard Act 1833 (c.65)
Woolwich Fortifications Act 1780 (c.46)
Worcester Roads Act 1725 (c.14)
Worcester Roads Act 1736 (c.5)
Worcester Roads act 1743 (c.13)
Worcester Roads Act 1753 (c.50)
Worcester Roads Act 1759 (c.50)
Worcester Roads Act 1767 (c.65)
Worcester Roads Act 1782 (c.95)
Worcester Roads Act 1783 (c.98)
Worcester Roads Act 1788 (c.88)
Worcester Roads Act 1789 (c.102)
Worcester Roads Act 1793 (c.175)
Worcester Roads Act 1795 (c.133)
Worcester and Birmingham Canal Act 1791 (c.59)

Worcester Bridge Act 1769 (c.84)
Worcester Bridge Act 1779 (c.42)
Worcester to Droitwich Road Act 1725 (c.20)
Worcester: Improvement Act 1770 (c.22)
Worcester: Poor Relief, Burial Ground and Hopmarket 1703 (c.8)
Worcester: Poor Relief, Burial Ground and Hopmarket Act 1730 (c.23)
Worcester: Poor Relief, Burial Ground and Hopmarket Act 1730 (c.25)
Worcester: Poor Relief, Burial Ground and Hopmarket Act 1792 (c.99)
Worcester and Salop Roads Act 1762 (c.78)
Worcester and Salop Roads Act 1763 (c.51)
Worcester, Salop and Stafford Roads Act 1790 (c.102)
Worcester: Streets Act 1780 (c.21)
Worcester and Warwick Roads Act 1767 (c.68)
Worcester and Warwick Roads Act 1771 (c.92)
Worcester and Warwick Roads Act 1773 (c.106)
Worcester and Warwick Roads Act 1773 (c.107)
Worcester and Warwick Roads Act 1788 (c.115)
Worcester and Warwick Roads Act 1789 (c.106)
Worcester and Warwick Roads Act 1792 (c.140)
Worcester and Warwick Roads Act 1794 (c.136)
Worcester, Warwick and Gloucester Roads Act 1757 (c.64)
Worcester: Water Supply, etc., Act 1771 (c.13)
Worcestershire Highways Act 1713 (c.27)
Worcestershire Roads Act 1748 (c.43)
Worcestershire Roads Act 1751 (c.60)
Worcestershire Roads Act 1755 (c.48)
Worcestershire Roads Act 17776 (c.78)
Worcestershire Roads Act 1779 (c.89)
Worcestershire, Staffordshire, Shropshire Roads Act 1781 (c.93)
Workhouses Act 1790 (c.49)
Workhouse Act 1816 (c.129)
Workhouses (Ireland) Act 1849 (c.86)
Workhouse Sites Act 1857 (c.13)
Workhouse, Westminster Act 1772 (c.34)
Working Classes Dwellings Act 1890 (c.16)
Working Men's Dwellings Act 1874 (c.59)
Working of Jews on Sunday Act 1871 (c.19)
Workmen's Compensation Act 1897 (c.37)
Workmen's Compensation Act 1900 (c.22)
Workmen's Compensation Act 1906 (c.58)
Workmen's Compensation Act 1909 (c.16)
Workmen's Compensation Act 1923 (c.42)
Workmen's Compensation Act 1925 (c.84)
Workmen's Compensation Act 1926 (c.42)
Workmen's Compensation Act 1931 (c.18)
Workmen's Compensation Act 1943 (c.6)
Workmen's Compensation (Amendment) Act 1938 (c.27)

Workmen's Compensation and Benefit (Amendment) Act 1965 (c.79)
Workmen's Compensation and Benefit (Byssinosis) Act 1940 (c.56)
Workmen's Compensation and Benefit (Supplementation) Act 1956 (c.51)
Workmen's Compensation (Coal Mines) Act 1934 (c.23)
Workmen's Compensation (Illegal Employment) Act 1918 (c.8)
Workmen's Compensation (Pneumoconiosis) Act 1945 (c.16)
Workmen's Compensation (Silicosis) Act 1918 (c.14)
Workmen's Compensation (Silicosis) Act 1924 (c.40)
Workmen's Compensation (Silicosis and Asbestosis) Act 1930 (c.29)
Workmen's Compensation (Supplementary Allowances) Act 1940 (c.47)
Workmen's Compensation (Supplementation) Act 1951 (c.22)
Workmen's Compensation (Temporary Increase) Act 1943 (c.49)
Workmen's Compensation (Transfer of Funds) Act 1927 (c.15)
Workmen's Compensation (War Addition) Act 1917 (c.42)
Workmen's Compensation (War Addition) Amendment Act 1919 (c.83)
Works and Public Buildings Act 1874 (c.84)
Works of Utility, etc. Indemnity Act 1858 (c.102)
Workshop Regulation Act 1867 (c.146)
Worksop and Attercliffe Road Act 1764 (c.52)
Worksop and Attercliffe Road Act 1786 (c.125)
Worsley Brook: Navigation Act 1736 (c.9)
Worstead Act 1776 (c.11)
Wreak and Eye: Navigation Act 1791 (c.77)
Wreck and Salvage Act 1846 (c.99)
Wrecking (Ireland) Act 1803 (c.79)
Wrexham to Barnhill Road Act 1782 (c.105)
Writ of Subpoena Act 1805 (c.92)
Writs Execution (Scotland) Act 1877 (c.40)
Writs of Assistance Act 1814 (c.46)
Writs of Error Act 1718 (c.13)
Writs of Error Act 1825 (c.96)
Writs of Execution Act 1833 (c.67)
Writs of Mandamus Act 1843 (c.67)
Writs Registration (Scotland) Act 1868 (c.34)

Yarmouth Coal Import Duties 1706 (c.10)
Yarmouth Coal Import Duties (Privileges of Freemen, etc.) 1782 (c.22)
Yarmouth Haven Act 1746 (c.40)
Yarmouth Haven and Pier Repairs 1702 (c.7)
Yarmouth Naval Hospital Act 1931 (c.15)
Yarmouth Naval Hospital Transfer Act 1957 (c.3)
Yarmouth: Small Debts Act 1757 (c.24)
Yarmouth to Gorleston Road Act 1775 (c.67)

Yarmouth to Gorleston Road Act 1795 (c.132)
Yaxley: Drainage Act 1772 (c.46)
Yeomanry Act 1804 (c.54)
Yeomanry Act 1817 (c.44)
Yeomanry Act 1826 (c.58)
Yeomanry (Accounts) Act 1804 (c.94)
Yeomanry Cavalry Act 1798 (c.51)
Yeomanry (Ireland) Act 1802 (c.68)
Yeomanry (Training) Act 1816 (c.39)
Yeomanry and Volunteers Act 1802 (c.66)
Yeomanry and Volunteers Act 1803 (c.121)
Yeomanry Corps, etc. (Ireland) Act 1814 (c.178)
Yeomanry Corps (Ireland) Act 1816 (c.72)
Yeomanry Corps (Ireland) Act 1818 (c.40)
Yeomanry Corps (Ireland) Act 1820 (c.48)
Yeomanry Corps (Ireland) Act 1823 (c.15)
Yeomanry Corps (Ireland) Act 1828 (c.30)
Yeomanry, etc. Act 1806 (c.125)
York and Boroughbridge Road Act 1749 (c.38)
York and Boroughbridge Road Act 1771 (c.66)
York and Boroughbridge Road Act 1797 (c.149)
York and Durham Roads Act 1753 (c.95)
York Buildings Company, Sale of Scottish Estates Act 1776 (c.24)
York Buildings: Rates Act 1756 (c.90)
York Butter Trade Supervision Act 1721 (c.27)
York House and Victoria Park Act 1841 (c.27)
York: Lighting and Watching Act 1763 (c.48)
York Roads Act 1765 (c.99)
York Roads Act 1792 (c.155)
Yorkshire Registries Act 1884 (c.54)
Yorkshire Registries Amendment Act 1884 (c.4)
Yorkshire Registries Amendment Act 1885 (c.26)
Yorkshire Roads Act 1740 (c.23)
Yorkshire Roads Act 1742 (c.7)
Yorkshire Roads Act 1743 (c.22)
Yorkshire Roads Act 1743 (c.25)
Yorkshire Roads Act 1744 (c.6)
Yorkshire Roads Act 1744 (c.16)
Yorkshire Roads Act 1748 (c.39)
Yorkshire Roads Act 1751 (c.47)
Yorkshire Roads Act 1751 (c.53)
Yorkshire Roads Act 1751 (c.58)
Yorkshire Roads Act 1755 (c.50)
Yorkshire Roads Act 1756 (c.71)
Yorkshire Roads Act 1756 (c.83)
Yorkshire Roads Act 1757 (c.54)
Yorkshire Roads Act 1758 (c.70)
Yorkshire Roads Act 1759 (c.55)
Yorkshire Roads Act 1760 (c.35)
Yorkshire Roads Act 1762 (c.71)
Yorkshire Roads Act 1764 (c.66)
Yorkshire Roads Act 1764 (c.69)
Yorkshire Roads Act 1765 (c.72)
Yorkshire Roads Act 1766 (c.59)

Yorkshire Roads Act 1766 (c.62)
Yorkshire Roads Act 1767 (c.71)
Yorkshire Roads Act 1768 (c.54)
Yorkshire Roads Act 1769 (c.54)
Yorkshire Roads Act 1769 (c.75)
Yorkshire Roads Act 1769 (c.79)
Yorkshire Roads Act 1771 (c.63)
Yorkshire Roads Act 1771 (c.68)
Yorkshire Roads Act 1771 (c.71)
Yorkshire Roads Act 1774 (c.117)
Yorkshire Roads Act 1777 (c.73)
Yorkshire Roads Act 1777 (c.77)
Yorkshire Roads Act 1777 (c.78)
Yorkshire Roads Act 1777 (c.80)
Yorkshire Roads Act 1777 (c.102)
Yorkshire Roads Act 1778 (c.96)
Yorkshire Roads Act 1780 (c.86)
Yorkshire Roads Act 1780 (c.89)
Yorkshire Roads Act 1781 (c.96)
Yorkshire Roads Act 1782 (c.97)
Yorkshire Roads Act 1783 (c.29)
Yorkshire Roads Act 1783 (c.95)
Yorkshire Roads Act 1786 (c.142)
Yorkshire Roads Act 1786 (c.144)
Yorkshire Roads Act 1787 (c.86)
Yorkshire Roads Act 1788 (c.106)
Yorkshire Roads Act 1788 (c.108)
Yorkshire Roads Act 1788 (c.110)
Yorkshire Roads Act 1789 (c.109)
Yorkshire Roads Act 1790 (c.99)
Yorkshire Roads Act 1792 (c.132)
Yorkshire Roads Act 1792 (c.133)
Yorkshire Roads Act 1792 (c.136)
Yorkshire Roads Act 1793 (c.157)
Yorkshire Roads Act 1794 (c.134)
Yorkshire and Chester Roads Act 1767 (c.94)
Yorkshire and Derby Roads Act 1757 (c.62)
Yorkshire and Derby Roads Act 1768 (c.47)
Yorkshire and Derby Roads Act 1771 (c.76)
Yorkshire and Derby Roads Act 1779 (c.96)
Yorkshire and Derby Roads Act 1795 (c.164)
Yorkshire, Derby and Chester Roads Act 1793 (c.140)
Yorkshire and Derbyshire Roads Act 1793 (c.184)
Yorkshire and Durham Roads Act 1746 (c.28)
Yorkshire and Durham Roads Act 1748 (c.32)
Yorkshire and Durham Roads Act 1755 (c.51)
Yorkshire and Durham Roads Act 1756 (c.80)
Yorkshire and Durham Roads Act 1760 (c.41)

Yorkshire and Durham Roads Act 1779 (c.80)
Yorkshire and Durham Roads Act 1782 (c.93)
Yorkshire and Durham Roads Act 1792 (c.118)
Yorkshire and Durham Roads Act 1792 (c.135)
Yorkshire and Lancaster Roads Act 1755 (c.59)
Yorkshire and Lancaster Roads Act 1755 (c.60)
Yorkshire and Lancaster Roads Act 1756 (c.91)
Yorkshire and Lancaster Roads Act 1759 (c.48)
Yorkshire and Lancaster Roads Act 1777 (c.90)
Yorkshire and Nottinghamshire Roads Act 1766 (c.67)
Yorkshire and Westmorland Roads Act 1753 (c.86)
Yorkshire and Westmorland Roads Act 1791 (c.122)
Yorkshire Coroners Act 1897 (c.39)
Yorkshire: Drainage Act 1789 (c.78)
Yorkshire (East Riding) Land Registry Act 1707 (c.62)
Yorkshire (North Riding) Land Registry Act 1734 (c.6)
Yorkshire: Small Debts Act 1776 (c.15)
Yorkshire (West Riding) Land Registry Act 1703 (c.4)
Yorkshire (West Riding) Land Registry 1706 (c.20)
Youghal Rectory Act 1827 (c.26)
Young Persons (Employment) Act 1938 (c.69)
Young Persons (Employment) Act 1964 (c.66)
Youthful Offenders Act 1855 (c.87)
Youthful Offenders Act 1901 (c.20)
Youthful Offenders, Great Britain Act 1854 (c.86)
Yule Vacance Act 1711 (c.22)
Yule Vacance Act 1714 (c.28)

Zambia Independence Act 1964 (c.65)
Zanzibar Act 1963 (c.55)
Zanzibar Indemnity Act 1894 (c.31)
Zimbabwe Act 1979 (c.60)
Zoo Licensing Act 1981 (c.37)

INDEX

This is the third part of the Current Law Statutes Index 1997 and is up to date to February 13, 1998. References, *e.g.* 58/21, are to the Statutes of 1997, Chapter 58, section 21.

ACQUISITION OF LAND,
  Scots Planning Law, *see* PLANNING LAW (SCOTS LAW)
ACTION IN RESPECT OF PROPERTY,
  authorisations,
    appeals,
      by authorising officers, **50**/104–105
      by complainants, **50**/106
    authorising officer: meaning, **50**/93(5)
    effect of, **50**/92
    form and duration, **50**/95
    given in absence of authorising officer, **50**/94
    notification of, **50**/96
    quashing of, **50**/103
    requiring approval, **50**/97
      confidential journalistic material, **50**/97(2)(b)(iii), 100
      confidential personal information, **50**/97(2)(b)(ii), 99
      matters subject to legal privilege, **50**/97(2)(b)(i), 98
    when applicable, **50**/93
  code of practice, **50**/101
  Commissioners,
    appointment, **50**/91
    functions, **50**/107
    removal from office, **50**/91(7)
  complaints, **50**/102, Sched. 7
  interpretation, **50**/108
ADMINISTRATION OF ESTATES,
  distributions of untaxed income,
    in and after 1999–00, **58**/34 Sched. 4
    on and after July 2, 1997, **58**/21
ADVERTISEMENTS,
  Scots Planning Law, *see* PLANNING LAW (SCOTS LAW)
AGRICULTURE,
  blight notices and agricultural units, *see* PLANNING LAW (SCOTS LAW)
  disposal of crofting property, *see* CROFTING PROPERTY, DISPOSAL OF
AIR PASSENGER DUTY, **16**/9
ALCOHOL,
  confiscation, **33**/1
    Scots Law, **48**/61
  liquor duties, *see* EXCISE DUTIES
  in possession of young person in public place, **33**/1
  testing prisoners for, **38**/1
    Scots Law, **48**/42
ALCOHOLIC LIQUOR DUTY, *see* EXCISE DUTIES

ANCIENT MONUMENTS,
  exemption from listed building legislation (Scotland), **9**/5
ANIMALS,
  dogs,
    destruction orders,
      contingent, **53**/2
      exemptions from, **53**/1
      otherwise than on a conviction, **53**/3
      orders under S.I. 1991/1744, **53**/4
    humane killing, **5**/3
    vermin shooting, **5**/4
    weapons and ammunition for treating, **5**/8
Appropriation Act 1997 (c.31)
Appropriation (No. 2) Act 1997 (c.57)
ARCHITECTS,
  "architect" as title, **22**/20–21
  Architects Registration Board, **22**/1, Sched. 1
    committees, **22**/1, Sched. 1, Pts. II, III, IV
  discipline,
    code of practice, **22**/13
    disciplinary orders, **22**/15
      erasure orders, **22**/18
      penalty orders, **22**/16
      suspension orders, **22**/17
    EEA architects, **22**/19
    professional misconduct and incompetence, **22**/14
  European Economic Area (EEA) architects,
    disciplinary proceedings and, **22**/19
    disqualification in EEA States, **22**/10
    list of, **22**/12
    qualifications, **22**/5
    use of title "architect," **22**/20(5)
  Professional Conduct Committee, **22**/1, Sched. 1, Pt. II
  registration,
    appeals, **22**/22
    EEA qualifications, **22**/5
    entitlement to, **22**/4
    list of visiting EEA architects, **22**/12
    obtaining by false pretences, **22**/7
    procedure, **22**/6
    Register, **22**/3
    Registrar of Architects, **22**/2
    removal from Register,
      competence to practise, **22**/9
      disqualification in EEA State, **22**/10
      failure to notify change of address, **22**/11
      retention of name in Register, **22**/8
    rules, **22**/23

INDEX

[2]

INDEX

[3]

INDEX

INDEX

INDEX

INDEX

INDEX

INDEX

INDEX

INDEX

[16]

INDEX

INDEX

INDEX

[23]

INDEX

INDEX

INDEX